Lecture Notes in Computer Science   1713

Edited by G. Goos, J. Hartmanis and J. van Leeuwen

Springer
Berlin
Heidelberg
New York
Barcelona
Hong Kong
London
Milan
Paris
Singapore
Tokyo

Joxan Jaffar (Ed.)

Principles and Practice of Constraint Programming – CP'99

5th International Conference, CP'99
Alexandria, VA, USA, October 11-14, 1999
Proceedings

Springer

Series Editors

Gerhard Goos, Karlsruhe University, Germany
Juris Hartmanis, Cornell University, NY, USA
Jan van Leeuwen, Utrecht University, The Netherlands

Volume Editor

Joxan Jaffar
School of Computing, National University of Singapore
3 Science Drive 2, Singapore, Republic of Singapore 117543
E-mail: joxan@comp.nus.edu.sg

Cataloging-in-Publication data applied for

Die Deutsche Bibliothek - CIP-Einheitsaufnahme

Principles and practice of constraint programming : 5th international conference
; proceedings / CP '99, Alexandria, VA, USA, October 11 - 14, 1999 / Joxan
Jaffar (ed.). - Berlin ; Heidelberg ; New York ; Barcelona ; Hong Kong ; London
; Milan ; Paris ; Singapore ; Tokyo : Springer, 1999
(Lecture notes in computer science ; Vol. 1713)
ISBN 3-540-66626-5

CR Subject Classification (1998): D.1, D.3.2-3, I.2.3-4, F.3.2, F.4.1, I.2.8

ISSN 0302-9743
ISBN 3-540-66626-5 Springer-Verlag Berlin Heidelberg New York

Typesetting: Camera-ready by author
SPIN: 10705084   06/3142 – 5 4 3 2 1 0   Printed on acid-free paper

Preface

This is the conference record for the Fifth International Conference on Principles and Practice of Constraint Programming (CP'99), held in Alexandria, Virginia, USA, on October 11–14, 1999. The series of CP conferences deal with original papers on most aspects of constraint programming. After a few annual workshops, CP'95 took place in Cassis, France, CP'96 in Cambridge, USA, CP'97 in Schloss Hagenberg, Austria, and CP'98 in Pisa, Italy.

This year a total of 97 papers were submitted, and 30 were accepted as regular papers. In addition, there were three invited papers, by Krzysztof Apt, Christian Bessièrre and Benjamin Wah, and eight poster papers, included to showcase yet more interesting directions. The posters appear as short papers in this volume. In the conference, there was an invited tutorial, and following the conference, there were five workshops. All papers were reviewed by an excellent program committee and their designated referees. Detailed email discussions preceded the actual program committee meeting, which was held near the conference location in mid-July, 1999.

The CP conferences have had two major directions: constraint satisfaction problems and programming with constraints. This year, the submission/acceptance breakdown was subjectively estimated at 56/19 and 33/8, respectively, with the remaining ratio of 8/3 for application papers. The regional distribution of (first) authors for all submissions was 21 for France, 15 for Germany, 12 for USA, 7 for UK, 6 for Japan, 5 for Spain, 4 for Australia and Singapore, 3 each for Italy, Portugal, Sweden, and Switzerland, 2 for Canada and Belgium, and finally, one each for Greece, Finland, Hong Kong, Indonesia, Ireland, Korea, and the Netherlands.

Last, but certainly not least of all, much is owed to the organizational skills of the CP'99 General Chairman Alex Brodsky. We are also indebted to Sean Wang, the Publicity Chair, and Jimmy Lee, the Workshops and Tutorials Chair. Finally, I would like to say a special thank you to Zhang Yuanlin who was instrumental in setting up and running the web-based review system, and to Răzvan Voicu for editorial help.

August 1999

Joxan Jaffar
Program Chair
CP'99

Organization

Conference Chair:	Alex Brodsky, George Mason University, USA
Program Chair:	Joxan Jaffar, National University of Singapore, Singapore
Publicity Chair:	X. Sean Wang, George Mason University, USA
Workshop Chair:	Jimmy Lee, Chinese University of Hong Kong, Hong Kong

Program Committee

Alexander Bockmayr, Universite Henri Poincare, Nancy 1, France
Roberto Bayardo, IBM Almaden Research Center, USA
Rina Dechter, University of California, Irvine, USA
François Fages, Ecole Normal Supierieure, France
Boi Faltings, Federal Institute of Technology, Lausanne, Switzerland
Thom Frühwirth, Ludwig Maximilians University, Germany
Vineet Gupta, NASA Ames Research Center, USA
Nevin Heintze, Lucent Bell Laboratories, USA
Joxan Jaffar (Chair), National University of Singapore, Singapore
Claude Kirchner, LORIA & INRIA, France
Jimmy Lee, Chinese University of Hong Kong, Hong Kong
Claude Le Pape, Bouygues Telecom - R&D, France
Thomas Schiex, INRA Toulouse, France
Bart Selman, Cornell University, USA
Helmut Simonis, Cosytec, France
Edward Tsang, University of Essex, UK
Kazunori Ueda, Waseda University, Japan
Peter Van Beek, University of Alberta, Canada
Mark Wallace, Imperial College, UK
Toby Walsh, University of Strathclyde, Scotland

Referees

Slim Abdennadher
Farid Ajili
Rolf Backofen
Roberto Bayardo
N. Beldiceanu
Frederic Benhamouand
Christian Bessière
Alexander Bockmayr
Patrice Boizumault
James Borrett
E. Bourreau
Alex Brodsky
Bjorn Carlson
Carlos Castro
Emmanuel Chailloux
François Charpillet
Hoong Chuin Lau
Angelo Ciarlini
Horaţiu Cîrstea
Andrew Davenport
Romuald Debruyne
Rina Dechter
Didier Dubois
H. El Sakkout
Andrew Eremin
François Fages
Boi Faltings
Miguel Filgueiras
Dominique Fortin
Jeremy Frank
Dan Frost
Thom Frühwirth

C. Gaspin
Tim Geisler
Frederic Goualard
Vineet Gupta
Nevin Heintze
Miki Hermann
Christian Holzbaur
Yeh Hong-ming
Joxan Jaffar
Kalev Kask
Thomas Kasper
Claude Kirchner
Alvin Kwan
François Laburthe
Javier Larrosa
Tung-Leng Lau
Claude Le Pape
Jimmy Lee
Philip Leong
Allen Leung
Ho-fung Leung
Bing Liu
C. Lottaz
David McAllester
P. Meseguer
S. Novello
Stefano Novello
Patrick Prosser
Alessandra Raffaeta
Rafael Ramirez
A. Rauzy
Peter Revesz

Irina Rish
Gianfranco Rossi
Benoit Rottembourg
Fabrice Rouillier
Vincent Schachter
Thomas Schiex
J. Schimpf
Eddie Schwalb
Luc Segoufin
Bart Selman
Kish Shen
Helmut Simonis
Barbara Smith
Georgios Stephanopoulos
Kostas Stergiou
Paul Strooper
Shin Takahashi
Vincent Tam
Kazunori Ueda
Peter Van Beek
G. Verfaillie
Răzvan Voicu
Benjamin Wah
Mark Wallace
Toby Walsh
Armin Wolf
Limsoon Wong
Quanshi Xia
Roland Yap
Yuanlin Zhang
Jianyang Zhou

CP Organizing Committee

Alan Borning, University of Washington, USA
Jacques Cohen, Brandeis University, USA
Alain Colmerauer, University of Marseille, France
Eugene Freuder, Chair, University of New Hampshire, USA
Hervé Gallaire, Xerox, France
Jean-Pierre Jouannaud, University of Paris-Sud, France
Jean-Louis Lassez, New Mexico Institute of Technology, USA
Michael Maher, Griffith University, Australia
Ugo Montanari, University of Pisa, Italy
Anil Nerode, Cornell University, USA
Jean-François Puget, ILOG, France
Francesca Rossi, University of Padova, Italy
Vijay Saraswat, AT&T Research, USA
Gert Smolka, DFKI and University of the Saarland, Germany
Ralph Wachter, Office of Naval Research, USA

Sponsors

Support from following institutions is gratefully acknowledged.

George Mason University, USA
Center for Secure Information Systems (GMU), USA
IC-Parc (ECliPSe project), UK
NASA Ames Research Center, USA
Office of Naval Research, USA
Prologia, France

Table of Contents

Invited Papers

Regular Papers

Poster Papers

The Rough Guide to Constraint Propagation

Krzysztof R. Apt[1,2]

[1] CWI
P.O. Box 94079, 1090 GB Amsterdam, the Netherlands
K.R.Apt@cwi.nl
[2] University of Amsterdam, the Netherlands

Abstract. We provide here a simple, yet very general framework that allows us to explain several constraint propagation algorithms in a systematic way. In particular, using the notions commutativity and semi-commutativity, we show how the well-known AC-3, PC-2, DAC and DPC algorithms are instances of a single generic algorithm. The work reported here extends and simplifies that of Apt [1].

1 Introduction

Constraint programming in a nutshell consists of formulating and solving so-called constraint satisfaction problems. One of the most important techniques developed in this area is constraint propagation that aims at reducing the search space while maintaining equivalence.

We call the corresponding algorithms constraint propagation algorithms but several other names have also been used in the literature: consistency, local consistency, consistency enforcing, Waltz, filtering or narrowing algorithms. These algorithms usually aim at reaching some form of "local consistency", a notion that in a loose sense approximates the notion of "global consistency".

Over the last twenty few years several constraint propagation algorithms were proposed and many of them are built into the existing constraint programming systems. In Apt [1] we introduced a simple framework that allows us to explain many of these algorithms in a uniform way. In this framework the notion of chaotic iterations, so fair iterations of functions, on Cartesian products of specific partial orderings played a crucial role. In Monfroy and Réty [13] this framework was modified to study distributed chaotic iterations. This resulted in a general framework for distributed constraint propagation algorithms.

We stated in Apt [1] that "the attempts of finding general principles behind the constraint propagation algorithms repeatedly reoccur in the literature on constraint satisfaction problems spanning the last twenty years" and devoted three pages to survey this work. Two references that are perhaps closest to our work are Benhamou [2] and Telerman and Ushakov [16].

These developments led to an identification of a number of mathematical properties that are of relevance for the considered functions, namely monotonicity, inflationarity and idempotence (see, e.g., Saraswat, Rinard and Panangaden [15] and Benhamou and

Older [3]). Here we show that also the notions of commutativity and so-called semi-commutativity are important.

As in Apt [1], to explain the constraint propagation algorithms, we proceed here in two steps. First, we introduce a generic iteration algorithm on partial orderings and prove its correctness in an abstract setting. Then we instantiate this algorithm with specific partial orderings and functions. The partial orderings will be related to the considered variable domains and the assumed constraints, while the functions will be the ones that characterize considered notions of local consistency in terms of fixpoints.

This presentation allows us to clarify which properties of the considered functions are responsible for specific properties of the corresponding algorithms. The resulting analysis is simpler than that of Apt [1] because we concentrate here on constraint propagation algorithms that always terminate. This allows us to dispense with the notion of fairness. On the other hand, we can now prove stronger results by taking into account the commutativity and semi-commutativity information.

This article is organized as follows. First, in Section 2, drawing on the approach of Monfroy and Réty [13], we introduce a generic algorithm for the case when the partial ordering is not further analyzed. Next, in Section 3, we refine it for the case when the partial ordering is a Cartesian product of component partial orderings and in Section 4 explain how the introduced notions should be related to the constraint satisfaction problems.

In the next four sections we instantiate the algorithm of Section 2 or some of its refinements to obtain specific constraint propagation algorithms. In particular, in Section 5 we derive algorithms for arc consistency and hyper-arc consistency. These algorithms can be improved by taking into account information on commutativity. This is done in Section 6 and yields the well-known AC-3 algorithm. Next, in Section 7 we derive an algorithm for path consistency and in Section 8 we improve it, again by using information on commutativity. This yields the PC-2 algorithm.

In Section 9 we clarify under what assumptions the generic algorithm of Section 2 can be simplified to a simple **for** loop statement. Then we instantiate this simplified algorithm to derive in Section 10 the DAC algorithm for directional arc consistency and in Section 11 the DPC algorithm for directional path consistency. Finally, in Section 12 we briefly discuss possible future work.

So we deal here only with the classical algorithms that establish (directional) arc consistency and (directional) path consistency and that are more than twenty, respectively ten, years old. However, several more "modern" constraint propagation algorithms can also be explained in this framework. In particular, in Apt [1, page 203] we derived from a generic algorithm a simple algorithm that achieves the notion of relational consistency of Dechter and van Beek [7]. In turn, we can use the framework of Section 9 to derive the adaptive consistency algorithm of Dechter and Pearl [6]. Now, Dechter [5] showed that this algorithm can be formulated in a very general framework of bucket elimination that in turn can be used to explain such well-known algorithms as directional resolution, Fourier-Motzkin elimination, Gaussian elimination, and also various algorithms that deal with belief networks.

Due to lack of space we do not define here formally the considered local consistency notions and refer the interested reader instead to the original papers or to Tsang [17].

2 Generic Iteration Algorithms

Our presentation is completely general. Consequently, we delay the discussion of constraint satisfaction problems till Section 4. In what follows we shall rely on the following concepts.

Definition 1. *Consider a partial ordering $(D, \sqsubseteq)$ with the least element $\bot$ and a finite set of functions $F := \{f_1, \ldots, f_k\}$ on D.*

- *By an* iteration *of F we mean an infinite sequence of values $d_0, d_1, \ldots$ defined inductively by*

$$d_0 := \bot,$$

$$d_j := f_{i_j}(d_{j-1}),$$

where each i_j is an element of $[1..k]$.
- *We say that an increasing sequence $d_0 \sqsubseteq d_1 \sqsubseteq d_2 \ldots$ of elements from D* eventually stabilizes *at d if for some $j \geq 0$ we have $d_i = d$ for $i \geq j$.* □

In what follows we shall consider iterations of functions that satisfy some specific properties.

Definition 2. *Consider a partial ordering $(D, \sqsubseteq)$ and a function f on D.*

- *f is called* inflationary *if $x \sqsubseteq f(x)$ for all x.*
- *f is called* monotonic *if $x \sqsubseteq y$ implies $f(x) \sqsubseteq f(y)$ for all x, y.* □

The following simple observation clarifies the role of monotonicity. The subsequent result will clarify the role of inflationarity.

Lemma 1 (Stabilization). *Consider a partial ordering $(D, \sqsubseteq)$ with the least element $\bot$ and a finite set of monotonic functions F on D.*
Suppose that an iteration of F eventually stabilizes at a common fixpoint d of the functions from F. Then d is the least common fixed point of the functions from F.

Proof. Consider a common fixpoint e of the functions from F. We prove that $d \sqsubseteq e$. Let $d_0, d_1, \ldots$ be the iteration in question. For some $j \geq 0$ we have $d_i = d$ for $i \geq j$.

It suffices to prove by induction on i that $d_i \sqsubseteq e$. The claim obviously holds for $i = 0$ since $d_0 = \bot$. Suppose it holds for some $i \geq 0$. We have $d_{i+1} = f_j(d_i)$ for some $j \in [1..k]$.

By the monotonicity of f_j and the induction hypothesis we get $f_j(d_i) \sqsubseteq f_j(e)$, so $d_{i+1} \sqsubseteq e$ since e is a fixpoint of f_j. □

We fix now a partial ordering $(D, \sqsubseteq)$ with the least element $\bot$ and a set of functions $F := \{f_1, \ldots, f_k\}$ on D. We are interested in computing the least common fixpoint of the functions from F. To this end we study the following algorithm that is inspired by a similar algorithm of Monfroy and Réty [13].

GENERIC ITERATION ALGORITHM (GI)

$d := \bot;$
$G := F;$
while $G \neq \emptyset$ **do**
    choose $g \in G;$
    $G := G - \{g\};$
    $G := G \cup update(G, g, d);$
    $d := g(d)$
od

where for all G, g, d the set of functions $update(G, g, d)$ from F is such that

A. $\{f \in F - G \mid f(d) = d \wedge f(g(d)) \neq g(d)\} \subseteq update(G, g, d),$
B. $g(d) = d$ implies that $update(G, g, d) = \emptyset.$

Intuitively, assumption **A** states that $update(G, g, d)$ at least contains all the functions from $F - G$ for which d is a fixpoint but $g(d)$ is not. The idea is that such functions are repeatedly added to the set G. In turn, assumption **B** states that no functions are added to G in case the value of d did not change.

An obvious example of an *update* function that satisfies assumptions **A** and **B** is

$$update(G, g, d) := \{f \in F - G \mid f(d) = d \wedge f(g(d)) \neq g(d)\}.$$

However, this choice of the *update* function is computationally expensive because for each function f in $F - G$ we would have to compute the values $f(g(d))$ and $f(d)$. In practice, we are interested in some approximations of the above *update* function. We shall deal with this matter in the next section.

We now prove correctness of this algorithm in the following sense.

Theorem 1 (GI).
  (i) *Every terminating execution of the* GI *algorithm computes in d a common fixpoint of the functions from F.*
 (ii) *Suppose that all functions in F are monotonic. Then every terminating execution of the* GI *algorithm computes in d the least common fixpoint of the functions from F.*
(iii) *Suppose that all functions in F are inflationary and that* $(D, \sqsubseteq)$ *is finite. Then every execution of the* GI *algorithm terminates.*

Proof.

(i) Consider the predicate I defined by:

$$I := \forall f \in F - G \; f(d) = d.$$

Note that I is established by the assignment $G := F$. Moreover, it is easy to check that I is preserved by each **while** loop iteration. Thus I is an invariant of the **while** loop of the algorithm. Hence upon its termination

$$(G = \emptyset) \wedge I$$

5

holds, that is

$$\forall f \in F \; f(d) = d.$$

(ii) This is a direct consequence of (i) and the Stabilization Lemma 1.

(iii) Consider the lexicographic ordering of the partial orderings $(D, \sqsupseteq)$ and $(\mathcal{N}, \leq)$, defined on the elements of $D \times \mathcal{N}$ by

$$(d_1, n_1) \leq_{lex} (d_2, n_2) \text{ iff } d_1 \sqsupset d_2 \text{ or } (d_1 = d_2 \text{ and } n_1 \leq n_2).$$

We use here the inverse ordering $\sqsupset$ defined by: $d_1 \sqsupset d_2$ iff $d_2 \sqsubseteq d_1$ and $d_2 \neq d_1$.

Given a finite set G we denote by $card\,G$ the number of its elements. By assumption all functions in F are inflationary so, by virtue of assumption **B**, with each **while** loop iteration of the modified algorithm the pair

$$(d, card\,G)$$

strictly decreases in this ordering $\leq_{lex}$. But by assumption $(D, \sqsubseteq)$ is finite, so $(D, \sqsupseteq)$ is well-founded and consequently so is $(D \times \mathcal{N}, \leq_{lex})$. This implies termination. $\quad\square$

In particular, we obtain the following conclusion.

Corollary 1 (GI) . *Suppose that $(D, \sqsubseteq)$ is a finite partial ordering with the least element $\perp$. Let F be a finite set of monotonic and inflationary functions on D. Then every execution of the GI algorithm terminates and computes in d the least common fixpoint of the functions from F.* $\quad\square$

In practice, we are not only interested that the *update* function is easy to compute but also that it generates small sets of functions. Therefore we show how the function *update* can be made smaller when some additional information about the functions in F is available. This will yield specialized versions of the GI algorithm. First we need the following simple concepts.

Definition 3. *Consider two functions f, g on a set D.*

- *We say that f and g commute if $f(g(x)) = g(f(x))$ for all x.*
- *We call f idempotent if $f(f(x)) = f(x)$ for all x.* $\quad\square$

The following result holds.

Theorem 2 (Update).

(i) *If $update(G, g, d)$ satisfies assumptions **A** and **B**, then so does the function*

$$update(G, g, d) - \{g \mid g \text{ is idempotent}\}.$$

(ii) *Suppose that for each $g \in F$ the set of functions $Comm(g)$ from F is such that*
- *$g \notin Comm(g)$,*
- *each element of $Comm(g)$ commutes with g.*

*If update(G, g, d) satisfies assumptions **A** and **B**, then so does the function*

$$update(G, g, d) - Comm(g).$$

Proof. It suffices to establish in each case assumption **A**.

(i) Suppose that g is idempotent. Then any function f such that $f(g(d)) \neq g(d)$ differs from g.

(ii) Consider a function f from $F - G$ such that $f(d) = d$ and $f(g(d)) \neq g(d)$. Suppose that $f \in Comm(g)$. Then $f(g(d)) = g(f(d)) = g(d)$ which is a contradiction. So $f \notin Comm(g)$. Consequently, $f \in update(G, g, d) - Comm(g)$ by virtue of assumption **A** for $update(G, g, d)$. □

We conclude that given an instance of the GI algorithm that employs a specific *update* function, we can obtain other instances of it by using *update* functions modified as above. Note that both modifications are independent of each other and therefore can be applied together. In particular, when each function is idempotent and the function *Comm* satisfied the assumptions of (ii), then if $update(G, g, d)$ satisfies assumptions **A** and **B**, then so does the function $update(G, g, d) - (Comm(g) \cup \{g\})$.

3 Compound Domains

In the applications we study the iterations are carried out on a partial ordering that is a Cartesian product of the partial orderings. So assume now that the partial ordering $(D, \sqsubseteq)$ is the Cartesian product of some partial orderings $(D_i, \sqsubseteq_i)$, for $i \in [1..n]$, each with the least element $\perp_i$. So $D = D_1 \times \cdots \times D_n$.

Further, we assume that each function from F depends from and affects only certain components of D. To be more precise we introduce a simple notation and terminology.

Definition 4. *Consider a sequence of partial orderings $(D_1, \sqsubseteq_1), \ldots, (D_n, \sqsubseteq_n)$.*

- *By a* scheme *(on n) we mean a growing sequence of different elements from $[1..n]$.*
- *Given a scheme $s := i_1, \ldots, i_l$ on n we denote by $(D_s, \sqsubseteq_s)$ the Cartesian product of the partial orderings $(D_{i_j}, \sqsubseteq_{i_j})$, for $j \in [1..l]$.*
- *Given a function f on D_s we say that f is* with scheme s *and say that f* depends on i *if i is an element of s.*
- *Given an n-tuple $d := d_1, \ldots, d_n$ from D and a scheme $s := i_1, \ldots, i_l$ on n we denote by $d[s]$ the tuple $d_{i_1}, \ldots, d_{i_l}$. In particular, for $j \in [1..n]$ $d[j]$ is the j-th element of d.* □

Consider now a function f with scheme s. We extend it to a function f^+ from D to D as follows. Take $d \in D$. We set

$$f^+(d) := e$$

where $e[s] = f(d[s])$ and $e[n - s] = d[n - s]$, and where $n - s$ is the scheme obtained by removing from $1, \ldots, n$ the elements of s. We call f^+ the *canonic extension* of f to the domain D.

So $f^+(d_1,\ldots,d_n) = (e_1,\ldots,e_n)$ implies $d_i = e_i$ for any i not in the scheme s of f. Informally, we can summarize it by saying that f^+ does not change the components on which it does not depend. This is what we meant above by stating that each considered function affects only certain components of D.

We now say that two functions, f with scheme s and g with scheme t *commute* if the functions f^+ and g^+ commute.

Instead of defining iterations for the case of the functions with schemes, we rather reduce the situation to the one studied in the previous section and consider, equivalently, the iterations of the canonic extensions of these functions to the common domain D. However, because of this specific form of the considered functions, we can use now a simple definition of the *update* function. More precisely, we have the following observation.

Note 1 (Update). Suppose that each function in F is of the form f^+. Then the following function *update* satisfies assumptions **A** and **B**:

$$update(G, g^+, d) :=$$
$$\{f^+ \in F - G \mid f \text{ depends on some } i \text{ in } s \text{ such that } d[i] \neq g^+(d)[i]\},$$

where g is with scheme s.

Proof. To deal with assumption **A** take a function $f^+ \in F - G$ such that $f^+(d) = d$. Then $f(e) = e$ for any e that coincides with d on all components that are in the scheme of f.

Suppose now additionally that $f^+(g^+(d)) \neq g^+(d)$. By the above $g^+(d)$ differs from d on some component i in the scheme of f. In other words, f depends on some i such that $d[i] \neq g^+(d)[i]$. This i is then in the scheme of g.

The proof for assumption **B** is immediate. $\qquad\qquad\square$

This, together with the GI algorithm, yields the following algorithm in which we introduced a variable d' to hold the value of $g^+(d)$, and used $F_0 := \{f \mid f^+ \in F\}$ and the functions with schemes instead of their canonic extensions to D.

GENERIC ITERATION ALGORITHM FOR COMPOUND DOMAINS (CD)

$d := (\perp_1,\ldots,\perp_n);$
$d' := d;$
$G := F_0;$
while $G \neq \emptyset$ **do**
    choose $g \in G$; suppose g is with scheme s;
    $G := G - \{g\};$
    $d'[s] := g(d[s]);$
    $G := G \cup \{f \in F_0 - G \mid f \text{ depends on some } i \text{ in } s \text{ such that } d[i] \neq d'[i]\};$
    $d[s] := d'[s]$
od

The following corollary to the GI Theorem 1 and the Update Note 1 summarizes the correctness of this algorithm.

Corollary 2 (CD) . *Suppose that* $(D, \sqsubseteq)$ *is a finite partial ordering that is a Cartesian product of n partial orderings, each with the least element* $\perp_i$ *with* $i \in [1..n]$. *Let F be a finite set of functions on D, each of the form* f^+.

Suppose that all functions in F are monotonic and inflationary. Then every execution of the CD *algorithm terminates and computes in d the least common fixpoint of the functions from F.* □

In the subsequent presentation we shall deal with the following two modifications of the CD algorithm:

- CDI *algorithm.* This is the version of the CD algorithm in which all the functions are idempotent and the function *update* defined in the Update Theorem 2(i) is used.
- CDC *algorithm.* This is the version of the CD algorithm in which all the functions are idempotent and the combined effect of the functions *update* defined in the Update Theorem 2 is used for some function *Comm*.

For both algorithms the counterparts of the CD Corollary 2 hold.

4 From Partial Orderings to Constraint Satisfaction Problems

We have been so far completely general in our discussion. Recall that our aim is to derive various constraint propagation algorithms. To be able to apply the results of the previous section we need to relate various abstract notions that we used there to constraint satisfaction problems.

This is perhaps the right place to recall the definition and to fix the notation. Consider a finite sequence of variables $X := x_1, \ldots, x_n$, where $n \geq 0$, with respective domains $\mathcal{D} := D_1, \ldots, D_n$ associated with them. So each variable x_i ranges over the domain D_i. By a *constraint* C on X we mean a subset of $D_1 \times \ldots \times D_n$.

By a *constraint satisfaction problem*, in short CSP, we mean a finite sequence of variables X with respective domains $\mathcal{D}$, together with a finite set $\mathcal{C}$ of constraints, each on a subsequence of X. We write it as $\langle \mathcal{C} \; ; \; x_1 \in D_1, \ldots, x_n \in D_n \rangle$, where $X := x_1, \ldots, x_n$ and $\mathcal{D} := D_1, \ldots, D_n$.

Consider now an element $d := d_1, \ldots, d_n$ of $D_1 \times \ldots \times D_n$ and a subsequence $Y := x_{i_1}, \ldots, x_{i_\ell}$ of X. Then we denote by $d[Y]$ the sequence $d_{i_1}, \ldots, d_{i_\ell}$.

By a *solution* to $\langle \mathcal{C} \; ; \; x_1 \in D_1, \ldots, x_n \in D_n \rangle$ we mean an element $d \in D_1 \times \ldots \times D_n$ such that for each constraint $C \in \mathcal{C}$ on a sequence of variables Y we have $d[Y] \in C$. We call a CSP *consistent* if it has a solution. Two CSP's $\mathcal{P}_1$ and $\mathcal{P}_2$ with the same sequence of variables are called *equivalent* if they have the same set of solutions. This definition extends in an obvious way to the case of two CSP's with the same *sets* of variables.

Let us return now to the framework of the previous section. It involved:

(i) Partial orderings with the least elements;
    These will correspond to partial orderings on the CSP's. In each of them the original CSP will be the least element and the partial ordering will be determined by the local consistency notion we wish to achieve.

(ii) Monotonic and inflationary functions with schemes;
   These will correspond to the functions that transform the variable domains or the constraints. Each function will be associated with one or more constraints.

(iii) Common fixpoints;
   These will correspond to the CSP's that satisfy the considered notion of local consistency.

In what follows we shall discuss two specific partial orderings on the CSP's. In each of them the considered CSP's will be defined on the same sequences of variables.

We begin by fixing for each set D a collection $\mathcal{F}(D)$ of the subsets of D that includes D itself. So $\mathcal{F}$ is a function that given a set D yields a set of its subsets to which D belongs.

When dealing with the hyper-arc consistency $\mathcal{F}(D)$ will be simply the set $\mathcal{P}(D)$ of all subsets of D but for specific domains only specific subsets of D will be chosen. For example, to deal with the the constraint propagation for the linear constraints on integer interval domains we need to choose for $\mathcal{F}(D)$ the set of all subintervals of the original interval D.

When dealing with the path consistency, for a constraint C the collection $\mathcal{F}(C)$ will be also the set $\mathcal{P}(C)$ of all subsets of C. However, in general other choices may be needed. For example, to deal with the cutting planes method, we need to limit our attention to the sets of integer solutions to finite sets of linear inequalities with integer coefficients (see Apt [1, pages 193-194]).

Next, given two CSP's, $\phi := \langle \mathcal{C} \ ; \ x_1 \in D_1, \ldots, x_n \in D_n \rangle$ and $\psi := \langle \mathcal{C}' \ ; \ x_1 \in D'_1, \ldots, x_n \in D'_n \rangle$, we write $\phi \sqsubseteq_d \psi$ iff

- $D'_i \in \mathcal{F}(D_i)$ (and hence $D'_i \subseteq D_i$) for $i \in [1..n]$,
- the constraints in $\mathcal{C}'$ are the restrictions of the constraints in $\mathcal{C}$ to the domains $D'_1, \ldots, D'_n$.

So $\phi \sqsubseteq_d \psi$ if ψ can be obtained from ϕ by a domain reduction rule and the domains of ψ belong to the appropriate collections of sets $\mathcal{F}(D)$.

Next, given two CSP's, $\phi := \langle C_1, \ldots, C_k \ ; \ \mathcal{DE} \rangle$ and $\psi := \langle C'_1, \ldots, C'_k \ ; \ \mathcal{DE} \rangle$, we write $\phi \sqsubseteq_c \psi$ iff

- $C'_i \in \mathcal{F}(C_i)$ (and hence $C'_i \subseteq C_i$) for $i \in [1..k]$.

In what follows we call $\sqsubseteq_d$ the *domain reduction ordering* and $\sqsubseteq_c$ the *constraint reduction ordering*. To deal with the arc consistency, hyper-arc consistency and directional arc consistency notions we shall use the domain reduction ordering, and to deal with path consistency and directional path consistency notions we shall use the constraint reduction ordering.

We consider each ordering with some fixed initial CSP $\mathcal{P}$ as the least element. In other words, each domain reduction ordering is of the form

$$(\{\mathcal{P}' \mid \mathcal{P} \sqsubseteq_d \mathcal{P}'\}, \sqsubseteq_d)$$

and each constraint reduction ordering is of the form

$$(\{\mathcal{P}' \mid \mathcal{P} \sqsubseteq_c \mathcal{P}'\}, \sqsubseteq_c).$$

Note that $\langle \mathcal{C} \ ; \ x_1 \in D_1', \ldots, x_n \in D_n' \rangle \sqsubseteq_d \langle \mathcal{C}' \ ; \ x_1 \in D_1'', \ldots, x_n \in D_n'' \rangle$ iff $D_i' \supseteq D_i''$ for $i \in [1..n]$.

This means that for $\mathcal{P} = \langle \mathcal{C} \ ; \ x_1 \in D_1, \ldots, x_n \in D_n \rangle$ we can identify the domain reduction ordering $(\{\mathcal{P}' \mid \mathcal{P} \sqsubseteq_d \mathcal{P}'\}, \sqsubseteq_d)$ with the Cartesian product of the partial orderings $(\mathcal{F}(D_i), \supseteq)$, where $i \in [1..n]$. Additionally, each CSP in this domain reduction ordering is uniquely determined by its domains and by the initial $\mathcal{P}$.

Similarly,

$$\langle C_1', \ldots, C_k' \ ; \ \mathcal{DE} \rangle \sqsubseteq_c \langle C_1'', \ldots, C_k'' \ ; \ \mathcal{DE} \rangle \text{ iff } C_i' \supseteq C_i'' \text{ for } i \in [1..k].$$

This allows us for $\mathcal{P} = \langle C_1, \ldots, C_k \ ; \ \mathcal{DE} \rangle$ to identify the constraint reduction ordering $(\{\mathcal{P}' \mid \mathcal{P} \sqsubseteq_c \mathcal{P}'\}, \sqsubseteq_c)$ with the Cartesian product of the partial orderings $(\mathcal{F}(C_i), \supseteq)$, where $i \in [1..k]$. Also, each CSP in this constraint reduction ordering is uniquely determined by its constraints and by the initial $\mathcal{P}$.

In what follows instead of the domain reduction ordering and the constraint reduction ordering we shall use the corresponding Cartesian products of the partial orderings. So in these compound orderings the sequences of the domains (respectively, of the constraints) are ordered componentwise by the reversed subset ordering $\supseteq$. Further, in each component ordering $(\mathcal{F}(D), \supseteq)$ the set D is the least element.

Consider now a function f on some Cartesian product $\mathcal{F}(E_1) \times \ldots \times \mathcal{F}(E_m)$. Note that f is inflationary w.r.t. the componentwise ordering $\supseteq$ if for all $(X_1, \ldots, X_m) \in \mathcal{F}(E_1) \times \ldots \times \mathcal{F}(E_m)$ we have $Y_i \subseteq X_i$ for all $i \in [1..m]$, where $f(X_1, \ldots, X_m) = (Y_1, \ldots, Y_m)$.

Also, f is monotonic w.r.t. the componentwise ordering $\supseteq$ if for all $(X_1, \ldots, X_m)$, $(X_1', \ldots, X_m') \in \mathcal{F}(E_1) \times \ldots \times \mathcal{F}(E_m)$ such that $X_i \subseteq X_i'$ for all $i \in [1..m]$, the following holds: if

$$f(X_1, \ldots, X_m) = (Y_1, \ldots, Y_m) \text{ and } f(X_1', \ldots, X_m') = (Y_1', \ldots, Y_m'),$$

then $Y_i \subseteq Y_i'$ for all $i \in [1..m]$.

In other words, f is monotonic w.r.t. $\supseteq$ iff it is monotonic w.r.t. $\subseteq$. This reversal of the set inclusion of course does not hold for the inflationarity notion.

5 A Hyper-arc Consistency Algorithm

We begin by considering the notion of hyper-arc consistency of Mohr and Masini [12] (we use here the terminology of Marriott and Stuckey [10]). The more known notion of arc consistency of Mackworth [9] is obtained by restricting one's attention to binary constraints.

To employ the CDI algorithm of Section 3 we now make specific choices involving the items (i), (ii) and (iii) of the previous section.

Re: (i) Partial orderings with the least elements.

As already mentioned in the previous section, for the function $\mathcal{F}$ we choose the powerset function $\mathcal{P}$, so for each domain D we put $\mathcal{F}(D) := \mathcal{P}(D)$.

Given a CSP $\mathcal{P}$ with the sequence $D_1, \ldots, D_n$ of the domains we take the domain reduction ordering with $\mathcal{P}$ as its least element. As already noted we can identify this ordering with the Cartesian product of the partial orderings $(\mathcal{P}(D_i), \supseteq)$, where $i \in [1..n]$. The elements of this compound ordering are thus sequences $(X_1, \ldots, X_n)$ of respective subsets of the domains $D_1, \ldots, D_n$ ordered componentwise by the reversed subset ordering $\supseteq$.

Re: (ii) Monotonic and inflationary functions with schemes.

Given a constraint C on the variables $y_1, \ldots, y_k$ with respective domains $E_1, \ldots, E_k$, we abbreviate for each $j \in [1..k]$ the set $\{d[j] \mid d \in C\}$ to $\Pi_j(C)$. Thus $\Pi_j(C)$ consists of all j-th coordinates of the elements of C. Consequently, $\Pi_j(C)$ is a subset of the domain E_j of the variable y_j.

We now introduce for each $i \in [1..k]$ the following function π_i on $\mathcal{P}(E_1) \times \cdots \times \mathcal{P}(E_k)$:

$$\pi_i(X_1, \ldots, X_k) := (X_1, \ldots, X_{i-1}, X_i', X_{i+1}, \ldots, X_k)$$

where

$$X_i' := \Pi_i(C \cap (X_1 \times \cdots \times X_k)).$$

That is, $X_i' = \{d[i] \mid d \in X_1 \times \cdots \times X_k \text{ and } d \in C\}$. Each function π_i is associated with a specific constraint C. Note that $X_i' \subseteq X_i$, so each function π_i boils down to a projection on the i-th component.

Re: (iii) Common fixpoints.

Their use is clarified by the following lemma that also lists the relevant properties of the functions π_i.

Lemma 2 (Hyper-arc Consistency).

(i) *A CSP $\langle \mathcal{C} ; x_1 \in D_1, \ldots, x_n \in D_n \rangle$ is hyper-arc consistent iff $(D_1, \ldots, D_n)$ is a common fixpoint of all functions π_i^+ associated with the constraints from $\mathcal{C}$.*

(ii) *Each projection function π_i associated with a constraint C is*
   - *inflationary w.r.t. the componentwise ordering $\supseteq$,*
   - *monotonic w.r.t. the componentwise ordering $\supseteq$,*
   - *idempotent.* □

By taking into account only the binary constraints we obtain an analogous characterization of arc consistency. The functions π_1 and π_2 can then be defined more directly as follows:

$$\pi_1(X, Y) := (X', Y),$$

where $X' := \{a \in X \mid \exists b \in Y \ (a, b) \in C\}$, and

$$\pi_2(X, Y) := (X, Y'),$$

where $Y' := \{b \in Y \mid \exists a \in X \ (a, b) \in C\}$.

Fix now a CSP $\mathcal{P}$. By instantiating the CDI algorithm with

$$F_0 := \{f \mid f \text{ is a } \pi_i \text{ function associated with a constraint of } \mathcal{P}\}$$

and with each $\perp_i$ equal to D_i we get the HYPER-ARC algorithm that enjoys following properties.

Theorem 3 (HYPER-ARC **Algorithm**). *Consider a CSP $\mathcal{P} := \langle \mathcal{C} \; ; \; x_1 \in D_1, \ldots, x_n \in D_n \rangle$ where each D_i is finite.*

The HYPER-ARC *algorithm always terminates. Let $\mathcal{P}'$ be the CSP determined by $\mathcal{P}$ and the sequence of the domains $D'_1, \ldots, D'_n$ computed in d. Then*

(i) $\mathcal{P}'$ is the $\sqsubseteq_d$-least CSP that is hyper-arc consistent,
(ii) $\mathcal{P}'$ is equivalent to $\mathcal{P}$. □

Due to the definition of the $\sqsubseteq_d$ ordering the item (i) can be rephrased as follows. Consider all hyper-arc consistent CSP's that are of the form $\langle \mathcal{C}' \; ; \; x_1 \in D'_1, \ldots, x_n \in D'_n \rangle$ where $D'_i \subseteq D_i$ for $i \in [1..n]$ and the constraints in $\mathcal{C}'$ are the restrictions of the constraints in $\mathcal{C}$ to the domains $D'_1, \ldots, D'_n$. Then among these CSP's $\mathcal{P}'$ has the largest domains.

6 An Improvement: the AC-3 Algorithm

In this section we show how we can exploit an information about the commutativity of the π_i functions. Recall that in Section 3 we modified the notion of commutativity for the case of functions with schemes. We now need the following lemma.

Lemma 3 (Commutativity). *Consider a CSP and two constraints of it, C on the variables $y_1, \ldots, y_k$ and E on the variables $z_1, \ldots, z_\ell$.*

(i) For $i,j \in [1..k]$ the functions π_i and π_j of the constraint C commute.
(ii) If the variables y_i and z_j are identical then the functions π_i of C and π_j of E commute. □

Fix now a CSP. We derive a modification of the HYPER-ARC algorithm by instantiating this time the CDC algorithm. As before we use the set of functions $F_0 := \{ f \mid f \text{ is a } \pi_i \text{ function associated with a constraint of } \mathcal{P} \}$ and each $\perp_i$ equal to D_i. Additionally we employ the following function *Comm*, where π_i is associated with a constraint C:

$Comm(\pi_i) := \{ \pi_j \mid i \neq j \text{ and } \pi_j \text{ is associated with the constraint } C \}$
$\qquad \cup \; \{ \pi_j \mid \pi_j \text{ is associated with a constraint } E \text{ and }$
$\qquad\qquad \text{the } i\text{-th variable of } C \text{ and the } j\text{-th variable of } E \text{ coincide} \}$.

By virtue of the Commutativity Lemma 3 each set $Comm(g)$ satisfies the assumptions of the Update Theorem $2(ii)$.

By limiting oneself to the set of functions π_1 and π_2 associated with the binary constraints, we obtain an analogous modification of the corresponding arc consistency algorithm.

Using now the counterpart of the CD Corollary 2 for the CDC algorithm we conclude that the above algorithm enjoys the same properties as the HYPER-ARC algorithm, that is the counterpart of the HYPER-ARC Algorithm Theorem 3 holds.

Let us clarify now the difference between this algorithm and the HYPER-ARC algorithm when both of them are limited to the binary constraints.

Assume that the considered CSP is of the form $\langle C \; ; \; \mathcal{DE} \rangle$. We reformulate the above algorithm as follows. Given a binary relation R, we put

$$R^T := \{(b,a) \mid (a,b) \in R\}.$$

For F_0 we now choose the set of the π_1 functions of the constraints or relations from the set

$S_0 := \{C \mid C$ is a binary constraint from $C\}$
$\cup \; \{C^T \mid C$ is a binary constraint from $C\}$.

Finally, for each π_1 function of some $C \in S_0$ on x, y we define

$Comm(\pi_1) := \{f \mid f$ is the π_1 function of $C^T\}$
$\cup \; \{f \mid f$ is the π_1 function of some $E \in S_0$ on x, z where $z \not\equiv y\}$.

Assume now that

for each pair of variables x, y at most one constraint exists on x, y. (1)

Consider now the corresponding instance of the CDC algorithm. By incorporating into it the effect of the functions π_1 on the corresponding domains, we obtain the following algorithm known as the AC-3 algorithm of Mackworth [9].
We assume here that $\mathcal{DE} := x_1 \in D_1, \ldots, x_n \in D_n$.

AC-3 ALGORITHM

$S_0 := \{C \mid C$ is a binary constraint from $C\}$
$\cup \; \{C^T \mid C$ is a binary constraint from $C\}$;
$S := S_0$;
while $S \neq \emptyset$ **do**
    choose $C \in S$; suppose C is on x_i, x_j;
    $D_i := \{a \in D_i \mid \exists\, b \in D_j \; (a,b) \in C\}$;
    if D_i changed **then**
        $S := S \cup \{C' \in S_0 \mid C'$ is on the variables y, x_i where $y \not\equiv x_j\}$
    fi;
    $S := S - \{C\}$
od

It is useful to mention that the corresponding reformulation of the HYPER-ARC algorithm differs in the second assignment to S which is then

$$S := S \cup \{C' \in S_0 \mid C' \text{ is on the variables } y, z \text{ where } y \text{ is } x_i \text{ or } z \text{ is } x_i\}.$$

So we "capitalized" here on the commutativity of the corresponding projection functions π_1 as follows. First, no constraint or relation on x_i, z for some z is added to S. Here we exploited part (ii) of the Commutativity Lemma 3.
Second, no constraint or relation on x_j, x_i is added to S. Here we exploited part (i) of the Commutativity Lemma 3, because by assumption (1) C^T is the only constraint or relation on x_j, x_i and its π_1 function coincides with the π_2 function of C.

In case the assumption (1) about the considered CSP is dropped, the resulting algorithm is somewhat less readable. However, once we use the following modified definition of $Comm(\pi_1)$:

$$Comm(\pi_1) := \{f \mid f \text{ is the } \pi_1 \text{ function of some } E \in S_0 \text{ on } x, z \text{ where } z \not\equiv y\}$$

we get an instance of the CDC algorithm which differs from the AC-3 algorithm in that the qualification "where $y \not\equiv x_j$" is removed from the definition of the second assignment to the set S.

7 A Path Consistency Algorithm

The notion of path consistency was introduced in Montanari [14]. It is defined for special type of CSP's. For simplicity we ignore here unary constraints that are usually present when studying path consistency.

Definition 5. *We call a CSP* normalized *if it has only binary constraints and for each pair x, y of its variables exactly one constraint on them exists. We denote this constraint by $C_{x,y}$.* $\square$

Every CSP with only unary and binary constraints is trivially equivalent to a normalized CSP. Consider now a normalized CSP $\mathcal{P}$. Suppose that $\mathcal{P} = \langle C_1, \ldots, C_k ; \mathcal{DE}\rangle$.

We proceed now as in the case of hyper-arc consistency. First, we choose for the function $\mathcal{F}$ the powerset function. For the partial ordering we choose the constraint reduction ordering of Section 4, or rather its counterpart which is the Cartesian product of the partial orderings $(\mathcal{P}(C_i), \supseteq)$, where $i \in [1..k]$.

Second, we introduce appropriate monotonic and inflationary functions with schemes. To this end, given two binary relations R and S we define their composition $\cdot$ by

$$R \cdot S := \{(a, b) \mid \exists c\, ((a, c) \in R, (c, b) \in S)\}.$$

Note that if R is a constraint on the variables x, y and S a constraint on the variables y, z, then $R \cdot S$ is a constraint on the variables x, z.

Given a subsequence x, y, z of the variables of $\mathcal{P}$ we now introduce three functions on $\mathcal{P}(C_{x,y}) \times \mathcal{P}(C_{x,z}) \times \mathcal{P}(C_{y,z})$:

$$f^z_{x,y}(P, Q, R) := (P', Q, R),$$

where $P' := P \cap Q \cdot R^T$,

$$f^y_{x,z}(P, Q, R) := (P, Q', R),$$

where $Q' := Q \cap P \cdot R$, and

$$f^x_{y,z}(P, Q, R) := (P, Q, R'),$$

where $R' := R \cap P^T \cdot Q$.

Finally, we introduce common fixpoints of the above defined functions. To this end we need the following counterpart of the Hyper-arc Consistency Lemma 2.

Lemma 4 (Path Consistency).

(i) *A normalized CSP $\langle C_1, \ldots, C_k \,;\, \mathcal{DE}\rangle$ is path consistent iff $(C_1, \ldots, C_k)$ is a common fixpoint of all functions $(f_{x,y}^z)^+$, $(f_{x,z}^y)^+$ and $(f_{y,z}^x)^+$ associated with the subsequences x, y, z of its variables.*

(ii) *The functions $f_{x,y}^z$, $f_{x,z}^y$ and $f_{y,z}^x$ are*
- *inflationary w.r.t. the componentwise ordering $\supseteq$,*
- *monotonic w.r.t. the componentwise ordering $\supseteq$,*
- *idempotent.* □

We now instantiate the CDI algorithm with the set of functions

$$F_0 := \{f \mid x, y, z \text{ is a subsequence of the variables of } \mathcal{P} \text{ and } f \in \{f_{x,y}^z, f_{x,z}^y, f_{y,z}^x\}\},$$

$n := k$ and each $\bot_i$ equal to C_i.

Call the resulting algorithm the PATH algorithm. It enjoys the following properties.

Theorem 4 (PATH Algorithm). *Consider a normalized CSP $\mathcal{P} := \langle C_1, \ldots, C_k \,;\, \mathcal{DE}\rangle$. Assume that each constraint C_i is finite.*

The PATH algorithm always terminates. Let $\mathcal{P}' := \langle C_1', \ldots, C_k' \,;\, \mathcal{DE}\rangle$, where the sequence of the constraints $C_1', \ldots, C_k'$ is computed in d. Then

(i) *$\mathcal{P}'$ is the $\sqsubseteq_c$-least CSP that is path consistent,*

(ii) *$\mathcal{P}'$ is equivalent to $\mathcal{P}$.* □

As in the case of the HYPER-ARC Algorithm Theorem 3 the item (i) can be rephrased as follows. Consider all path consistent CSP's that are of the form $\langle C_1', \ldots, C_k' \,;\, \mathcal{DE}\rangle$ where $C_i' \subseteq C_i$ for $i \in [1..k]$. Then among them $\mathcal{P}'$ has the largest constraints.

8 An Improvement: the PC-2 Algorithm

As in the case of the hyper-arc consistency we can improve the PATH algorithm by taking into account the commutativity information.

Fix a normalized CSP $\mathcal{P}$. We abbreviate the statement "x, y is a subsequence of the variables of $\mathcal{P}$" to $x \prec y$. We now have the following lemma.

Lemma 5 (Commutativity). *Suppose that $x \prec y$ and let z, u be some variables of $\mathcal{P}$ such that $\{u, z\} \cap \{x, y\} = \emptyset$. Then the functions $f_{x,y}^z$ and $f_{x,y}^u$ commute.* □

In other words, two functions with the same pair of variables as a subscript commute.

We now instantiate the CDC algorithm with the same set of functions F_0 as in Section 7. Additionally, we use the function $Comm$ defined as follows, where $x \prec y$ and where $z \notin \{x, y\}$:

$$Comm(f_{x,y}^z) = \{f_{x,y}^u \mid u \notin \{x, y, z\}\}.$$

Thus for each function g the set $Comm(g)$ contains precisely $m - 3$ elements, where m is the number of variables of the considered CSP. This quantifies the maximal "gain" obtained by using the commutativity information: at each "update" stage of the corresponding instance of the CDC algorithm we add up to $m - 3$ less elements than in the case of the corresponding instance of the CDI algorithm considered in the previous section.

By virtue of the Commutativity Lemma 5 each set $Comm(g)$ satisfies the assumptions of the Update Theorem $2(ii)$. We conclude that the above instance of the CDC algorithm enjoys the same properties as the original PATH algorithm, that is the counterpart of the PATH Algorithm Theorem 4 holds. To make this modification of the PATH algorithm easier to understand we proceed as follows.

Each function of the form $f_{x,y}^u$ where $x \prec y$ and $u \notin \{x,y\}$ can be identified with the sequence x, u, y of the variables. (Note that the "relative" position of u w.r.t. x and y is not fixed, so x, u, y does not have to be a subsequence of the variables of $\mathcal{P}$.) This allows us to identify the set of functions F_0 with the set

$$V_0 := \{(x, u, y) \mid x \prec y, u \notin \{x, y\}\}.$$

Next, assuming that $x \prec y$, we introduce the following set of triples of different variables of $\mathcal{P}$:

$$V_{x,y} := \{(x, y, u) \mid x \prec u\} \cup \{(y, x, u) \mid y \prec u\}$$
$$\cup \{(u, x, y) \mid u \prec y\} \cup \{(u, y, x) \mid u \prec x\}.$$

Informally, $V_{x,y}$ is the subset of V_0 that consists of the triples that begin or end with either x, y or y, x. This corresponds to the set of functions in one of the following forms: $f_{x,u}^y, f_{y,u}^x, f_{u,y}^x$ and $f_{u,x}^y$.

The above instance of the CDC algorithm then becomes the following PC-2 algorithm of Mackworth [9]. Here initially $E_{x,y} = C_{x,y}$.

PC-2 ALGORITHM

$V_0 := \{(x, u, y) \mid x \prec y, u \notin \{x, y\}\};$
$V := V_0;$
while $V \neq \emptyset$ **do**
    choose $p \in V$; suppose $p = (x, u, y);$
    apply $f_{x,y}^u$ to its current domains;
    if $E_{x,y}$ changed **then**
        $V := V \cup V_{x,y};$
    fi;
    $V := V - \{p\}$
od

Here the phrase "apply $f_{x,y}^u$ to its current domains" can be made more precise if the "relative" position of u w.r.t. x and y is known. Suppose for instance that u is "before" x and y. Then $f_{x,y}^u$ is defined on $\mathcal{P}(C_{u,x}) \times \mathcal{P}(C_{u,y}) \times \mathcal{P}(C_{x,y})$ by

$$f_{x,y}^u(E_{u,x}, E_{u,y}, E_{x,y}) := (E_{u,x}, E_{u,y}, E_{x,y} \cap E_{u,x}^T \cdot E_{u,y}),$$

so the above phrase "apply $f^u_{x,y}$ to its current domains" can be replaced by the assignment

$$E_{x,y} := E_{x,y} \cap E^T_{u,x} \cdot E_{u,y}.$$

Analogously for the other two possibilities.

The difference between the PC-2 algorithm and the corresponding representation of the PATH algorithm lies in the way the modification of the set V is carried out. In the case of the PATH algorithm the second assignment to V is

$$V := V \cup V_{x,y} \cup \{(x,u,y) \mid u \notin \{x,y\}\}.$$

9 Simple Iteration Algorithms

Let us return now to the framework of Section 2. We analyze here when the **while** loop of the GENERIC ITERATION ALGORITHM GI can be replaced by a **for** loop. First, we weaken the notion of commutativity as follows.

Definition 6. *Consider a partial ordering $(D, \sqsubseteq)$ and functions f and g on D. We say that f semi-commutes with g (w.r.t. $\sqsubseteq$) if $f(g(x)) \sqsubseteq g(f(x))$ for all x.* □

The following lemma provides an answer to the question just posed. Here and elsewhere we omit brackets when writing repeated applications of functions to an argument.

Lemma 6 (Simple Iteration). *Consider a partial ordering $(D, \sqsubseteq)$ with the least element $\bot$. Let $F := f_1, \ldots, f_k$ be a finite sequence of monotonic, inflationary and idempotent functions on D. Suppose that f_i semi-commutes with f_j for $i > j$, that is,*

$$f_i(f_j(x)) \sqsubseteq f_j(f_i(x)) \text{ for all } x. \tag{2}$$

Then $f_1 f_2 \ldots f_k(\bot)$ is the least common fixpoint of the functions from F. □

Proof. We prove first that for $i \in [1..k]$ we have

$$f_i f_1 f_2 \ldots f_k(\bot) \sqsubseteq f_1 f_2 \ldots f_k(\bot).$$

Indeed, by the assumption (2) we have the following string of inclusions, where the last one is due to the idempotence of the considered functions:

$$f_i f_1 f_2 \ldots f_k(\bot) \sqsubseteq f_1 f_i f_2 \ldots f_k(\bot) \sqsubseteq \ldots \sqsubseteq f_1 f_2 \ldots f_i f_i \ldots f_k(\bot) \sqsubseteq f_1 f_2 \ldots f_k(\bot).$$

Additionally, by the inflationarity of the considered functions, we also have for $i \in [1..k]$

$$f_1 f_2 \ldots f_k(\bot) \sqsubseteq f_i f_1 f_2 \ldots f_k(\bot).$$

So $f_1 f_2 \ldots f_k(\bot)$ is a common fixpoint of the functions from F. This means that the iteration of F that starts with $\bot$, $f_k(\bot)$, $f_{k-1} f_k(\bot), \ldots, f_1 f_2 \ldots f_k(\bot)$ eventually stabilizes at $f_1 f_2 \ldots f_k(\bot)$. By the Stabilization Lemma 1 we get the desired conclusion. □

The above lemma provides us with a simple way of computing the least common fixpoint of a set of finite functions that satisfy the assumptions of this lemma, in particular condition (2). Namely, it suffices to order these functions in an appropriate way and then to apply each of them just once, starting with the argument $\perp$.

To this end we maintain the considered functions not in a set but in a list. Given a non-empty list L we denote its head by $\mathbf{head}(L)$ and its tail by $\mathbf{tail}(L)$. Next, given a sequence of elements $a_1, \ldots, a_n$ with $n \geq 0$, we denote by $[a_1, \ldots, a_n]$ the list formed by them. If $n = 0$, then this list is empty and is denoted by $[\,]$ and if $n > 0$, then $\mathbf{head}([a_1, \ldots, a_n]) = a_1$ and $\mathbf{tail}([a_1, \ldots, a_n]) = [a_2, \ldots a_n]$.

The following algorithm is a counterpart of the GI algorithm. We assume in it that condition (2) holds for the functions $f_1, \ldots, f_k$.

SIMPLE ITERATION ALGORITHM (SI)

```
d := ⊥;
L := [f_k, f_{k-1}, ..., f_1];
for i := 1 to k do
    g := head(L);
    L := tail(L);
    d := g(d)
od
```

The following immediate consequence of the Simple Iteration Lemma 6 is a counterpart of the GI Corollary 1.

Corollary 3 (SI) . *Suppose that* $(D, \sqsubseteq)$ *is a partial ordering with the least element* $\perp$. *Let* $F := f_1, \ldots, f_k$ *be a finite sequence of monotonic, inflationary and idempotent functions on* D *such that (2) holds. Then the* SI *algorithm terminates and computes in* d *the least common fixpoint of the functions from* F. □

Note that in contrast to the GI Corollary 1 we do not require here that the partial ordering is finite. Because at each iteration of the **for** loop exactly one element is removed from the list L, at the end of this loop the list L is empty. Consequently, this algorithm is a reformulation of the one in which the line

$$\mathbf{for}\ i := 1\ \mathbf{to}\ k\ \mathbf{do}$$

is replaced by

$$\mathbf{while}\ L \neq [\,]\ \mathbf{do}.$$

So we can view the SI algorithm as a specialization of the GI algorithm of Section 2 in which the elements of the set of functions G (here represented by the list L) are selected in a specific way and in which the *update* function always yields the empty set.

In Section 3 we refined the GI algorithm for the case of compound domains. An analogous refinement of the SI algorithm is straightforward and omitted. In the next two sections we show how we can use this refinement of the SI algorithm to derive two well-known constraint propagation algorithms.

10 DAC: a Directional Arc Consistency Algorithm

We consider here the notion of directional arc consistency of Dechter and Pearl [6]. To derive an algorithm that achieves this local consistency notion we first characterize it in terms of fixpoints. To this end, given a $\mathcal{P}$ and a linear ordering $\prec$ on its variables, we rather reason in terms of the equivalent CSP $\mathcal{P}_\prec$ obtained from $\mathcal{P}$ by reordering its variables along $\prec$ so that each constraint in $\mathcal{P}_\prec$ is on a sequence of variables $x_1, \ldots, x_k$ such that $x_1 \prec x_2 \prec \ldots \prec x_k$.

The following characterization holds.

Lemma 7 (Directional Arc Consistency). *Consider a CSP $\mathcal{P}$ with a linear ordering $\prec$ on its variables. Let $\mathcal{P}_\prec := \langle \mathcal{C} ; x_1 \in D_1, \ldots, x_n \in D_n \rangle$. Then $\mathcal{P}$ is directionally arc consistent w.r.t. $\prec$ iff $(D_1, \ldots, D_n)$ is a common fixpoint of the functions π_1^+ associated with the binary constraints from $\mathcal{P}_\prec$.* □

We now instantiate in an appropriate way the SI algorithm for compound domains with all the π_1 functions associated with the binary constraints from $\mathcal{P}_\prec$. In this way we obtain an algorithm that achieves for $\mathcal{P}$ directional arc consistency w.r.t. $\prec$. First, we adjust the definition of semi-commutativity to functions with different schemes. To this end consider a sequence of partial orderings $(D_1, \sqsubseteq_1), \ldots, (D_n, \sqsubseteq_n)$ and their Cartesian product $(D, \sqsubseteq)$. Take two functions, f with scheme s and g with scheme t. We say that f *semi-commutes with* g (*w.r.t.* $\sqsubseteq$) if f^+ semi-commutes with g^+ w.r.t. $\sqsubseteq$, that is if

$$f^+(g^+(Q)) \sqsubseteq g^+(f^+(Q)).$$

for all $Q \in D$.

The following lemma is crucial.

Lemma 8 (Semi-commutativity). *Consider a CSP and two binary constraints of it, C_1 on u, z and C_2 on x, y, where $y \prec z$.*

Then the π_1 function of C_1 semi-commutes with the π_1 function of C_2 w.r.t. the componentwise ordering $\supseteq$. □

Consider now a CSP $\mathcal{P}$ with a linear ordering $\prec$ on its variables and the corresponding CSP $\mathcal{P}_\prec$. To be able to apply the above lemma we order the π_1 functions of the binary constraints of $\mathcal{P}_\prec$ in an appropriate way. Namely, given two π_1 functions, f associated with a constraint on u, z and g associated with a constraint on x, y, we put f before g if $y \prec z$.

More precisely, let $x_1, \ldots, x_n$ be the sequence of the variables of $\mathcal{P}_\prec$. So $x_1 \prec x_2 \prec \ldots \prec x_n$. Let for $m \in [1..n]$ the list L_m consist of the π_1 functions of those binary constraints of $\mathcal{P}_\prec$ that are on x_j, x_m for some x_j. We order each list L_m arbitrarily. Consider now the list L resulting from appending $L_n, L_{n-1}, \ldots, L_1$, in that order, so with the elements of L_n in front. Then by virtue of the Semi-commutativity Lemma 8 if the function f precedes the function g in the list L, then f semi-commutes with g w.r.t. the componentwise ordering $\supseteq$.

We instantiate now the refinement of the SI algorithm for the compound domains by the above-defined list L and each $\perp_i$ equal to the domain D_i of the variable x_i. We assume that L has k elements. We obtain then the following algorithm.

DIRECTIONAL ARC CONSISTENCY ALGORITHM (DARC)

$d := (\perp_1, \ldots, \perp_n);$
for $i := 1$ **to** k **do**
    $g := \textbf{head}(L);$ suppose g is with scheme s;
    $L := \textbf{tail}(L);$
    $d[s] := g(d[s])$
od

This algorithm enjoys the following properties.

Theorem 5 (DARC **Algorithm**). *Consider a CSP $\mathcal{P}$ with a linear ordering $\prec$ on its variables. Let $\mathcal{P}_\prec := \langle \mathcal{C} \; ; \; x_1 \in D_1, \ldots, x_n \in D_n \rangle$.*

    The DARC algorithm always terminates. Let $\mathcal{P}'$ be the CSP determined by $\mathcal{P}_\prec$ and the sequence of the domains $D'_1, \ldots, D'_n$ computed in d. Then

  (i) $\mathcal{P}'$ is the $\sqsubseteq_d$-least CSP in $\{\mathcal{P}_1 \mid \mathcal{P}_\prec \sqsubseteq_d \mathcal{P}_1\}$ that is directionally arc consistent w.r.t. $\prec$,

  (ii) $\mathcal{P}'$ is equivalent to $\mathcal{P}$. $\qquad\qquad\qquad\qquad\qquad\qquad\qquad\qquad$ $\square$

Note that in contrast to the HYPER-ARC Algorithm Theorem 3 we do not need to assume here that each domain is finite.

Assume now that for each pair of variables x, y of the original CSP $\mathcal{P}$ there exists precisely one constraint on x, y. The same holds then for $\mathcal{P}_\prec$. Suppose that $\mathcal{P}_\prec := \langle \mathcal{C} \; ; \; x_1 \in D_1, \ldots, x_n \in D_n \rangle$. Denote the unique constraint of $\mathcal{P}_\prec$ on x_i, x_j by $C_{i,j}$. The above DARC algorithm can then be rewritten as the following algorithm known as the DAC algorithm of Dechter and Pearl [6]:

for $j := n$ **to** 2 **by** -1 **do**
    for $i := 1$ **to** $j - 1$ **do**
        $D_i := \{a \in D_i \mid \exists b \in D_j \; (a, b) \in C_{i,j}\}$
    od
od

11 DPC: a Directional Path Consistency Algorithm

In this section we deal with the notion of directional path consistency defined in Dechter and Pearl [6]. As before we first characterize this local consistency notion in terms of fixpoints. To this end, as in the previous section, given a normalized CSP $\mathcal{P}$ we rather consider the equivalent CSP $\mathcal{P}_\prec$. The variables of $\mathcal{P}_\prec$ are ordered according to $\prec$ and on each pair of its variables there exists a unique constraint.

    The following is a counterpart of the Directional Arc Consistency Lemma 7.

Lemma 9 (Directional Path Consistency). *Consider a normalized CSP $\mathcal{P}$ with a linear ordering $\prec$ on its variables. Let $\mathcal{P}_\prec := \langle C_1, \ldots, C_k \; ; \; \mathcal{DE} \rangle$. Then $\mathcal{P}$ is directionally path consistent w.r.t. $\prec$ iff $(C_1, \ldots, C_k)$ is a common fixpoint of all functions $(f^z_{x,y})^+$ associated with the subsequences x, y, z of the variables of $\mathcal{P}_\prec$.* $\qquad\qquad$ $\square$

To obtain an algorithm that achieves directional path consistency we now instantiate in an appropriate way the SI algorithm. To this end we need the following lemma.

Lemma 10 (Semi-commutativity). *Consider a normalized CSP and two subsequences of its variables, x_1, y_1, z and x_2, y_2, u. Suppose that $u \prec z$.*

Then the function $f^z_{x_1, y_1}$ semi-commutes with the function $f^u_{x_2, y_2}$ w.r.t. the componentwise ordering $\supseteq$. □

Consider now a normalized CSP $\mathcal{P}$ with a linear ordering $\prec$ on its variables and the corresponding CSP $\mathcal{P}_\prec$. To be able to apply the above lemma we order in an appropriate way the $f^t_{r,s}$ functions, where the variables r, s, t are such that $r \prec s \prec t$. Namely, we put $f^z_{x_1, y_1}$ before $f^u_{x_2, y_2}$ if $u \prec z$.

More precisely, let $x_1, \ldots, x_n$ be the sequence of the variables of $\mathcal{P}_\prec$, that is $x_1 \prec x_2 \prec \ldots \prec x_n$. Let for $m \in [1..n]$ the list L_m consist of the functions $f^{x_m}_{x_i, x_j}$ for some x_i and x_j. We order each list L_m arbitrarily and consider the list L resulting from appending $L_n, L_{n-1}, \ldots, L_1$, in that order. Then by virtue of the Semi-commutativity Lemma 9 if the function f precedes the function g in the list L, then f semi-commutes with g w.r.t. the componentwise ordering $\supseteq$.

We instantiate now the refinement of the SI algorithm for the compound domains by the above-defined list L and each $\perp_i$ equal to the constraint C_i. We assume that L has k elements. This yields the DIRECTIONAL PATH CONSISTENCY ALGORITHM (DPATH) that, apart from of the different choice of the constituent partial orderings, is identical to the DIRECTIONAL ARC CONSISTENCY ALGORITHM DARC of the previous section. Consequently, the DPATH algorithm enjoys analogous properties as the DARC algorithm. They are summarized in the following theorem.

Theorem 6 (DPATH Algorithm). *Consider a CSP $\mathcal{P}$ with a linear ordering $\prec$ on its variables. Let $\mathcal{P}_\prec := \langle C_1, \ldots, C_k \,;\, \mathcal{DE} \rangle$.*

The DPATH algorithm always terminates. Let $\mathcal{P}' := \langle C'_1, \ldots, C'_k \,;\, \mathcal{DE} \rangle$, where the sequence of the constraints $C'_1, \ldots, C'_k$ is computed in d. Then

(i) $\mathcal{P}'$ is the $\sqsubseteq_c$-least CSP in $\{\mathcal{P}_1 \mid \mathcal{P}_\prec \sqsubseteq_d \mathcal{P}_1\}$ that is directionally path consistent w.r.t. $\prec$,

(ii) $\mathcal{P}'$ is equivalent to $\mathcal{P}$. □

As in the case of the DARC Algorithm Theorem 5 we do not need to assume here that each domain is finite.

Assume now that that $x_1, \ldots, x_n$ is the sequence of the variables of $\mathcal{P}_\prec$. Denote the unique constraint of $\mathcal{P}_\prec$ on x_i, x_j by $C_{i,j}$.

The above DPATH algorithm can then be rewritten as the following algorithm known as the DPC algorithm of Dechter and Pearl [6]:

```
for m := n to 3 by −1 do
    for j := 1 to m − 1 do
        for i := 1 to j − 1 do
            C_{i,j} := C_{i,m} · C^T_{j,m}
        od
    od
od
```

12 Conclusions

In this article we introduced a general framework for constraint propagation. It allowed us to present and explain various constraint propagation algorithms in a uniform way. Using such a single framework we can easier verify, compare, modify, parallelize or combine these algorithms. The last point has already been made to large extent in Benhamou [2]. Additionally, we clarified the role played by the notions of commutativity and semi-commutativity.

The line of research presented here could be extended in a number of ways. First, it would be interesting to find examples of existing constraint propagation algorithms that could be improved by using the notions of commutativity and semi-commutativity.

Second, as already stated in Apt [1], it would be useful to explain in a similar way other constraint propagation algorithms such as the AC-4 algorithm of Mohr and Henderson [11], the PC-4 algorithm of Han and Lee [8], or the GAC-4 algorithm of Mohr and Masini [12]. The complication is that these algorithms operate on some extension of the original CSP.

Finally, it would be useful to apply the approach of this paper to derive constraint propagation algorithms for the semiring-based constraint satisfaction framework of Bistarelli, Montanari and Rossi [4] that provides a unified model for several classes of "nonstandard" constraints satisfaction problems.

References

1. K. R. Apt. The essence of constraint propagation. *Theoretical Computer Science*, 221(1–2):179–210, 1999. Available via http://xxx.lanl.gov/archive/cs/.
2. F. Benhamou. Heterogeneous constraint solving. In M. Hanus and M. Rodriguez-Artalejo, editors, *Proceeding of the Fifth International Conference on Algebraic and Logic Programming (ALP 96)*, Lecture Notes in Computer Science 1139, pages 62–76, Berlin, 1996. Springer-Verlag.
3. F. Benhamou and W. Older. Applying interval arithmetic to real, integer and Boolean constraints. *Journal of Logic Programming*, 32(1):1–24, 1997.
4. S. Bistarelli, U. Montanari, and F. Rossi. Semiring-based constraint satisfaction and optimization. *Journal of the ACM*, 44(2):201–236, March 1997.
5. R. Dechter. Bucket elimination: A unifying framework for structure-driven inference. *Artificial Intelligence*, 1999. To appear.
6. R. Dechter and J. Pearl. Network-based heuristics for constraint-satisfaction problems. *Artificial Intelligence*, 34(1):1–38, January 1988.
7. R. Dechter and P. van Beek. Local and global relational consistency. *Theoretical Computer Science*, 173(1):283–308, 20 February 1997.
8. C. Han and C. Lee. Comments on Mohr and Henderson's path consistency algorithm. *Artificial Intelligence*, 36:125–130, 1988.
9. A. Mackworth. Consistency in networks of relations. *Artificial Intelligence*, 8(1):99–118, 1977.
10. K. Marriott and P. Stuckey. *Programming with Constraints*. The MIT Press, Cambridge, Massachusetts, 1998.
11. R. Mohr and T.C. Henderson. Arc-consistency and path-consistency revisited. *Artificial Intelligence*, 28:225–233, 1986.

12. R. Mohr and G. Masini. Good old discrete relaxation. In Y. Kodratoff, editor, *Proceedings of the 8th European Conference on Artificial Intelligence (ECAI)*, pages 651–656. Pitman Publishers, 1988.

13. E. Monfroy and J.-H. Réty. Chaotic iteration for distributed constraint propagation. In J. Carroll, H. Haddad, D. Oppenheim, B. Bryant, and G. Lamont, editors, *Proceedings of The 1999 ACM Symposium on Applied Computing, SAC'99*, pages 19–24, San Antonio, Texas, USA, March 1999. ACM Press.

14. U. Montanari. Networks of constraints: Fundamental properties and applications to picture processing. *Information Science*, 7(2):95–132, 1974. Also Technical Report, Carnegie Mellon University, 1971.

15. V.A. Saraswat, M. Rinard, and P. Panangaden. Semantic foundations of concurrent constraint programming. In *Proceedings of the Eighteenth Annual ACM Symposium on Principles of Programming Languages (POPL'91)*, pages 333–352, 1991.

16. V. Telerman and D. Ushakov. Data types in subdefinite models. In J. A. Campbell J. Calmet and J. Pfalzgraf, editors, *Artificial Intelligence and Symbolic Mathematical Computations*, Lecture Notes in Computer Science 1138, pages 305–319, Berlin, 1996. Springer-Verlag.

17. E. Tsang. *Foundations of Constraint Satisfaction*. Academic Press, 1993.

Non-Binary Constraints

Christian Bessière

LIRMM-CNRS, 161 rue Ada, 34392 Montpellier, France
bessiere@lirmm.fr

Abstract

Since the origins of the constraint satisfaction paradigm, its restriction to binary constraints has concentrated a significant part of the work. This is understandable because new ideas/techniques are usually much simpler to present/ elaborate by first restricting them to the binary case. (See for example the arc consistency algorithms, such as AC-3 or AC-4, which have been presented first in their binary version [10, 12], before being extended to non-binary constraints [11, 13].) But this inclination has highly increased in the early nineties. Authors indeed justified this restriction by the fact that any non-binary constraint network can polyniomally be converted into an equivalent binary one [6, 8, 5, 19]. And, in most cases, they never extended their work to non-binary constraints.

Up to now, constraint reasoning has generated robust formal definitions (local consistencies, etc.), original resolution methods (filtering, look-back schemes, decomposition techniques, heuristics, etc.), and theoretical results on tractable classes. They were proved useful on many academic problems, and are probably at the origin of the success of this area. But now, constraint reasoning is going towards its maturity, and should then be able to propose efficient resolution techniques for real-world problems, for which the binary conversion is sometimes/often impracticable. This observation, stressed by van Beek in its CP'96 invocation, has started having its effect since papers especially devoted to non-binary constraints or to their binary conversion begin to appear in this end of decade [4, 1, 22, 2].

Dealing with non-binary constraints for real-world problems raises questions that do not appear as crucial on binary constraints. Applying filtering techniques during search is central in the efficiency of constraint satisfaction algorithms. But applying filtering on non-binary constraints is much more expensive than on binary ones. The weaknesses of the algorithms appear more accurately. Does this mean that we must circumscribe filtering to its weakest form, as in the classical extension to non-binary constraints of the forward checking algorithm? The answer is no. This algorithm is much more subject to thrashing than on binary networks [1]. Local consistencies, which are one of the strengths of constraint reasoning, must also be applied in the non-binary case. But they have perhaps to be seen in a new way.

Perhaps we should accept the idea that the constraint solving tool of the next years will apply different levels of local consistency on different constraints at each node of the search tree, and more, a different algorithm for the same level of consistency depending on the constraint on which it applies. In the first case, the differences can come from the position of the constraint w.r.t. the current node,[1] or from the constraint type itself.[2] In the second case, specific constraint semantics can make efficient adapted algorithms applicable.[3]

Because of this already mentioned high complexity of applying local consistencies on non-binary constraints, the theoretically wide expressive power of constraint reasoning is perhaps not as wide as that in practice. If applying local consistency on a given constraint is extremely expensive even for low levels (arc consistency is usually the standard level), it is as if this constraint was not allowed by the model. This leads us to the modelling aspects of constraint reasoning. Modelling a problem as a constraint network requires finding the "best" representation of the original knowledge. The criterion under which to decide which representation is better than the others is the efficiency of the available resolution technique to solve it [16, 21]. If no acceptable representation is found, this can be because for some of the original constraints, neither their decomposition in simple sub-constraints nor their direct integration were satisfactory. The former reason is usually due to a loss of globality in the decomposition. (Reasoning locally on the sub-constraints of the decomposition cannot detect inconsistencies.) The latter comes from the fact that no efficient filtering algorithm dedicated to this constraint exists while generic filtering algorithms are very time-consuming when applied to it. If we want to solve the original problem, an alternative is to write a dedicated filtering algorithm efficient enough to be incorporated in the solving engine. This has the clear advantage of saving the semantics of the constraint, and thus the potential ability to deal globally with it. We know indeed that the more globally we deal with locality, the more we are able to detect inconsistencies. This approach has been initiated with success on the very common *alldiff* constraint [17] for which the decomposition in a clique of binary "$\neq$" constraints was almost unaffected by arc consistency processing. Even in paradigms such as SAT, where the simplicity and genericity of the model is claimed as its strength, recent works have shown the advantage of making global inferences specific to the problem type before losing all the structure in the SAT encoding [9]. After a few years, that approach will of course have to deal with the issue of the size of the constraint solving engine. The number of different constraints added with their associated filtering algorithm will probably

---

[1] This is already done in the search algorithm *forward checking* [7], which does not apply arc consistency on all the constraints, as opposed to algorithms such as *really full look ahead* [15] or *MAC* [20].

[2] In [18], a filtering algorithm is proposed for a particular type of constraint. It achieves something which is stronger than arc consistency but not equivalent to any level of local consistency already known.

[3] For the binary case, this approach has already been addressed in extensions of AC-4 [14], in AC-5 [23], and in AC-Inference [3].

increase with the needs of modelling. The risk could then be the impossibility of having a complete and competitive solver outside a commercial product (as what appeared in operation research for the simplex). From an academic point of view, a trade-off will perhaps have to be found between the systematic integration of any new type of constraint, and their systematic representation in "basic" sub-constraints. Ideally, this trade-off would lead to the emergence of a sufficiently powerful stabilized model. Then, the other sub-areas of constraint reasoning could take back the lead and continue enriching the whole area...

This abstract is no more than a snapshot of a subjective[4] view of a topic that arrives at a crucial phase of its evolution. The direction in which it will finally go is not evident yet. I have emphasized the filtering aspects, which are among the main originalities of constraint reasoning, but other parameters will influence the future of the area, such as its reaction to the closer and closer vicinity of operation research.

References

1. F. Bacchus and P. van Beek. On the conversion between non-binary and binary constraint satisfaction problems. In *Proceedings AAAI'98*, pages 311–318, Madison WI, 1998.
2. C. Bessière, P. Meseguer, E.C. Freuder, and J. Larrosa. On forward checking for non-binary constraint satisfaction. In *Proceedings CP'99*, Alexandria VA, 1999.
3. C. Bessière, E.C. Freuder, and J.C. Régin. Using constraint metaknowledge to reduce arc consistency computation. *Artificial Intelligence*, 107:125–148, 1999.
4. C. Bessière and J.C. Régin. Arc consistency for general constraint networks: preliminary results. In *Proceedings IJCAI'97*, pages 398–404, Nagoya, Japan, 1997.
5. R. Dechter. On the expressiveness of networks with hidden variables. In *Proceedings AAAI'90*, pages 556–562, Boston MA, 1990.
6. R. Dechter and J. Pearl. Tree clustering for constraint networks. *Artificial Intelligence*, 38:353–366, 1989.
7. R.M. Haralick and G.L. Elliot. Increasing tree seach efficiency for constraint satisfaction problems. *Artificial Intelligence*, 14:263–313, 1980.
8. P. Janssen, P. Jégou, B. Nouguier, and M. C. Vilarem. A filtering process for general constraint-satisfaction problems: Achieving pairewise-consistency using an associated binary representation. In *Proceedings of the IEEE Workshop on Tools for Artificial Intelligence*, pages 420–427, Fairfax VA, 1989.
9. H. Kautz and B. Selman. Unifying sat-based and graph-based planning. In *Proceedings IJCAI'99*, pages 318–325, Stockholm, Sweden, 1999.
10. A.K. Mackworth. Consistency in networks of relations. *Artificial Intelligence*, 8:99–118, 1977.
11. A.K. Mackworth. On reading sketch maps. In *Proceedings IJCAI'77*, pages 598–606, Cambridge MA, 1977.
12. R. Mohr and T.C. Henderson. Arc and path consistency revisited. *Artificial Intelligence*, 28:225–233, 1986.

---

[4] "Subjective" but not only personal, since this view has been greatly influenced by discussions with E.C. Freuder, J.C. Régin, U. Junker, and others.

13. R. Mohr and G. Masini. Good old discrete relaxation. In *Proceedings ECAI'88*, pages 651–656, Munchen, FRG, 1988.
14. R. Mohr and G. Masini. Running efficiently arc consistency. In G. Ferraté et al., editor, *Syntactic and Structural Pattern Recognition*, pages 217–231. Springer-Verlag, Berlin, 1988.
15. B.A. Nadel. Tree search and arc consistency in constraint satisfaction algorithms. In L.Kanal and V.Kumar, editors, *Search in Artificial Intelligence*, pages 287–342. Springer-Verlag, 1988.
16. J.C. Régin. Minimization of the number of breaks in sports scheduling problems using constraint programming. In *Proceedings DIMACS workshop on Constraint Programming and Large Scale Discrete Optimization*, pages P7:1–23, 1998.
17. J.C. Régin. A filtering algorithm for constraints of difference in CSPs. In *Proceedings AAAI'94*, pages 362–367, Seattle WA, 1994.
18. J.C. Régin. The symmetric alldiff constraint. In *Proceedings IJCAI'99*, pages 420–425, Stockholm, Sweden, 1999.
19. F. Rossi, C. Petrie, and V. Dhar. On the equivalence of constraint satisfaction problems. In *Proceedings ECAI'90*, pages 550–556, Stockholm, Sweden, 1990.
20. D. Sabin and E.C. Freuder. Contradicting conventional wisdom in constraint satisfaction. In *Proceedings PPCP'94*, Seattle WA, 1994.
21. B. Smith, K. Stergiou, and T. Walsh. Modelling the golomb ruler problem. In J.C. Régin and W. Nuijten, editors, *Proceedings IJCAI'99 workshop on non-binary constraints*, Stockholm, Sweden, 1999.
22. K. Stergiou and T. Walsh. Encodings of non-binary constraint satisfaction problems. In *Proceedings AAAI'99*, Orlando, FL, 1999.
23. P. Van Hentenryck, Y. Deville, and C.M. Teng. A generic arc-consistency algorithm and its specializations. *Artificial Intelligence*, 57:291–321, 1992.

The Theory of Discrete Lagrange Multipliers for Nonlinear Discrete Optimization*

Benjamin W. Wah and Zhe Wu

Department of Electrical and Computer Engineering
and the Coordinated Science Laboratory
University of Illinois, Urbana-Champaign
Urbana, IL 61801, USA
{wah, zhewu}@manip.crhc.uiuc.edu
http://www.manip.crhc.uiuc.edu

Abstract. In this paper we present a Lagrange-multiplier formulation of discrete constrained optimization problems, the associated discrete-space first-order necessary and sufficient conditions for saddle points, and an efficient first-order search procedure that looks for saddle points in discrete space. Our new theory provides a strong mathematical foundation for solving general nonlinear discrete optimization problems. Specifically, we propose a new vector-based definition of descent directions in discrete space and show that the new definition does not obey the rules of calculus in continuous space. Starting from the concept of saddle points and using only vector calculus, we then prove the discrete-space first-order necessary and sufficient conditions for saddle points. Using well-defined transformations on the constraint functions, we further prove that the set of discrete-space saddle points is the same as the set of constrained local minima, leading to the first-order necessary and sufficient conditions for constrained local minima. Based on the first-order conditions, we propose a local-search method to look for saddle points that satisfy the first-order conditions.

1 Introduction

Many applications in engineering, decision science and operations research can be formulated as nonlinear discrete optimization problems, whose variables are restricted to discrete values and whose objective and constraint functions are nonlinear. The general formulation of a *nonlinear, nonconvex, discrete constrained minimization problem* is as follows:

$$\text{minimize} \quad f(x)$$
$$\text{subject to} \quad g(x) \le 0 \qquad x = (x_1, x_2, \ldots, x_n) \text{ is a vector} \qquad (1)$$
$$h(x) = 0 \qquad \qquad \text{of discrete variables}$$

where $f(x)$ is the objective function, $g(x) = [g_1(x), \ldots, g_k(x)]^T$ is a k-component vector of inequality constraints, and $h(x) = [h_1(x), \ldots, h_m(x)]^T$ is an m-component vector of equality constraints, $f(x)$, $g(x)$, and $h(x)$ can be either

---
* Research supported by National Science Foundation Grant NSF MIP 96-32316.

convex or non-convex, linear or nonlinear, continuous or discontinuous, and analytic (in closed-form formulae) or procedural.

The possible solutions to (1) are local minima that satisfy all the constraints. To formally characterize the solutions to be found, we introduce the concepts of neighborhoods and constrained local minima in discrete space.

Definition 1. $\mathcal{N}(x)$, the *neighborhood* of point x in space X, is a user-defined set of points $\{x' \in X\}$ such that $x \notin \mathcal{N}(x)$ and that $x' \in \mathcal{N}(x) \Longleftrightarrow x \in \mathcal{N}(x')$. Neighborhoods must be defined such that any point in the finite search space is reachable from any other point through traversals of neighboring points.

For example, in $\{0,1\}^n$ space, y (the neighborhood of x) can be points whose Hamming distance between x and y is less than 2. In modulo-integer space in which a variable is an integer element in $\{0, 1, \ldots, q-1\}$, y can be the set of points in which $\mathrm{mod}(y_1 - x_1, k) + \ldots + \mathrm{mod}(y_n - x_n, k)$ is less than 2.

Definition 2. A point x is a *discrete constrained local minimum* if it satisfies the following two properties:

- x is a feasible point, implying that x satisfies all the constraints;
- For all $x' \in \mathcal{N}(x)$ such that x' is feasible, $f(x') \geq f(x)$ holds true.

Note that when all neighboring points of x are infeasible and that x is the only feasible point surrounded by infeasible points, x is still a constrained local minimum. Further, note that point x may be a local minimum to one definition of $\mathcal{N}(x)$ but may not be for another definition of $\mathcal{N}'(x)$.

In general, the choice of neighborhoods is application-dependent. The choice, however, does not affect the validity of a search as long as one definition of neighborhood is used consistently throughout. Normally, one may choose $\mathcal{N}(x)$ to include the nearest discrete points to x so that neighborhood still carries its original meaning. However one can also choose the neighborhood to contain points that are "far away." Intuitively, neighboring points close to x can provide guidance for doing local descents, while neighboring points far away allow the search to explore larger regions in the search space.

Example 1. Consider the following one-dimensional nonlinear discrete constrained minimization problem whose constraints are satisfied at integer points between -2 and 3.

$$\text{minimize } f(x) = 2 - 0.4x - 2.0x^2 + 0.75x^3 + 0.4x^4 - 0.15x^5 + \sin(5x)$$
$$\text{subject to } h(x) = 0 \tag{2}$$
$$\text{where } \quad h(x) = \begin{cases} \sin(\pi x) & \text{if } -2 \leq x \leq 3 \\ 1 & \text{otherwise} \end{cases}$$

and x is an integer variable. Figure 1 plots the curve of the objective function.

Applying the first two definitions on the example, the neighborhood of x can be defined as $\{x - 1, x + 1\}$. Given that $x = -3$ and $x = 4$ are infeasible,

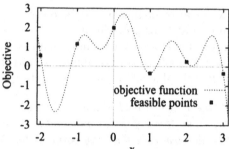

Fig. 1. The objective function and feasible points defined in (2)

$f(-1) > f(-2)$, $f(0) > f(1)$, $f(2) > f(1)$, and $f(2) > f(3)$, $x = -2, 1, 3$ are all the constrained local minima in (2), Out of the six points in the feasible region, the global minimum is at $x = 1$ where $f(1) = -0.359$. ■

Our goal in this paper is to show the equivalence between the set of discrete saddle points and the set of constrained local minima in the discrete Lagrangian space of a discrete nonlinear constrained optimization problem. That is, the condition for a saddle point is necessary and sufficient for a point to be a discrete constrained local minimum. The condition, therefore, provides a formal basis for the development of efficient algorithms for solving problems in this class. Our work here extends substantially our previous results in this area [23] that only proved the condition to be sufficient.

It is worth emphasizing that the theories and methods proposed here address discrete constrained *non-convex* optimization problems. We do not require the objective or constraint functions to be convex, as some of the existing continuous optimization methods do, because convexity is too restricted in general applications. Further, the original concept of convexity [20] is only applicable to continuous space, although some recent research [19] tries to extend the theory of convex analysis using matroids [5] to integer-valued functions.

The paper is organized as follows. Section 2 surveys existing work on discrete nonlinear constrained optimization and the basic concepts, theories and methods of continuous Lagrange multipliers. In Section 3, we prove the discrete-space first-order necessary and sufficient conditions, after introducing the concept of direction of maximum potential drop. These conditions form the mathematical foundation that leads to the discrete space first-order local-search method proposed in Section 4. Finally, Section 5 concludes the paper.

2 Existing Work

We summarize in this section related work in the area of discrete optimization and that in Lagrange multipliers for continuous optimization.

2.1 Transformation-Based Methods for Solving Discrete Problems

In the past, there has been extensive work on efficient techniques to solve (1). One major approach is to rewrite a discrete optimization problem as a constrained nonlinear 0-1 programming problem before solving it. Existing nonlinear 0-1 integer programming algorithms can be classified into four categories [12]. First, a nonlinear problem can be linearized by replacing each distinct product of variables by a new 0-1 variable and by adding some new constraints [30, 10]. This method only works for simple nonlinear problems. Second, algebraic methods [21] express the objective function as a polynomial function of the variables and their complements. These only work for the case in which all the constraints can be removed. Third, enumerative methods [29] utilize branch-and-bound algorithms to find lower bounds using linearized constraints. Lower bounds found this way are inaccurate when constraints are highly nonlinear. For a similar reason, branch-and-bound methods do not work well on general nonlinear integer programming problems. Last, cutting-plane methods [11] reduce a constrained nonlinear 0-1 problem into a generalized covering problem. However, they are limited because not all nonlinear 0-1 problems can be transformed this way.

A second approach to solving (1) is to transform it into an unconstrained problem before solving it using incomplete methods that may find a feasible solution in finite time if one exists but are not able to prove infeasibility. In this approach, an unconstrained problem is generally formulated as a weighted sum of the objective and the constraints. Examples of methods in this class include simulated annealing (SA) [16], genetic algorithms (GA) [13], tabu search [9], gradient descent [1], Hopfield networks [14], and penalty methods. These methods generally have difficulties in finding feasible solutions when their weights are not chosen properly. A class of penalty methods adjust the penalties (or weights) dynamically according to the amount of constraint violation in order to force all the constraints into satisfaction; examples of which include heuristic repair methods [4] and break-out strategies [18]. Although they work well in practice, there is no theoretical foundation on why they work well and under what conditions they will converge.

2.2 Lagrangian Methods for Solving Continuous Problems

Traditionally, Lagrangian methods were developed for solving continuous optimization problems. In this section, we present briefly their basic definitions and concepts, and examine the relationships among their solution spaces. These relationships are important because they show that some constrained local minima may not be found by existing continuous Lagrangian methods. This issue can be overcome in Lagrangian methods that work in discrete space (see Section 3).

Basic Definitions. A general *continuous equality-constrained minimization problem* is formulated as follows:

$$
\begin{array}{lll}
\text{minimize} & f(x) & x = (x_1, x_2, \ldots, x_n) \text{ is a vector} \\
\text{subject to} & h(x) = 0 & \text{of continuous variables}
\end{array}
\tag{3}
$$

where $h(x) = [h_1(x), \ldots, h_m(x)]^T$ is an m-component vector. Both $f(x)$ and $h(x)$ may be linear or nonlinear continuous functions.

In continuous space, the solutions to (3) are also called constrained local minima. However, their definition is slightly different from that in discrete space defined in Definition 2.

Definition 3. *A point x in continuous space is a* <u>constrained local minimum</u> *[17] iff there exists a small $\varepsilon > 0$ such that for all x' that satisfy $|x' - x| < \varepsilon$ and that x' is also a feasible point, $f(x') \geq f(x)$ holds true.*

The following two definitions define the Lagrangian function as a weighted sum of the objective and the constraints, and the saddle point as a point in the Lagrangian space where the Lagrange multipliers are at their local maxima and the objective function is at its local minimum.

Definition 4. *The <u>Lagrangian function</u> of (3) is $L(x, \lambda) = f(x) + \lambda^T h(x)$, where λ is a vector of Lagrange multipliers.*

Definition 5. *A saddle point (x^*, λ^*) of function L is defined as one that satisfies $L(x^*, \lambda) \leq L(x^*, \lambda^*) \leq L(x, \lambda^*)$ for all (x^*, λ) and all (x, λ^*) sufficiently close to (x^*, λ^*).*

In general, there is no efficient method to find saddle points in continuous space.

First-Order Necessary Conditions for Continuous Problems. There are various continuous Lagrangian methods that can be used to locate constrained local minima. They are all based on two first-order necessary conditions.

Theorem 1. *First-order necessary conditions for continuous problems [17]].* *Let x be a local extremum point of $f(x)$ subject to $h(x) = 0$. Further, assume that $x = (x_1, \ldots, x_n)$ is a regular point (see [17]) of these constraints. Then there exists $\lambda \in E^m$ such that $\nabla_x f(x) + \lambda^T \nabla_x h(x) = 0$. Based on the definition of Lagrangian function, the necessary conditions can be expressed as:*

$$\nabla_x L(x, \lambda) = 0; \qquad \nabla_\lambda L(x, \lambda) = 0. \tag{4}$$

First-Order Methods for Solving Continuous Problems. Based on the first-order necessary conditions in continuous space, there are a number of methods for solving constrained minimization problems. These include the first-order method, Newton's method, modified Newton's methods, quasi-Newton methods [17], and sequential quadratic programming [15]. Among these methods, a popular one is the first-order method represented as an iterative process:

$$x^{k+1} = x^k - \alpha_k \nabla L_x(x^k, \lambda^k)^T \tag{5}$$
$$\lambda^{k+1} = \lambda^k + \alpha_k h(x^k) \tag{6}$$

where α_k is a step-size parameter to be determined.

Intuitively, these two equations represent two counter-acting forces to resolve constraints and find high-quality solutions. When any of the constraints is violated, its degree of violation is used in (6) to increase the corresponding Lagrange multiplier in order to increase the penalty on the unsatisfied constraint and to force it into satisfaction. When the constraint is satisfied, its Lagrange multiplier stops to grow. Hence, (6) performs ascents in the Lagrange-multiplier space until each Lagrange multiplier is at its maximum. In contrast, (5) performs descents in the objective space when all the constraints are satisfied and stops at an extremum in that space. By using a combination of simultaneous ascents and descents, an equilibrium is eventually reached in which all the constraints are satisfied and the objective is at a local extremum.

To guarantee that the equilibrium point is a local minimum, there are second-order sufficient conditions to make the solution a strict constrained local minimum. They are omitted since they are irrelevant to solving discrete problems.

Relationships among solution spaces in continuous problems. We present without proof [32] three lemmas and one theorem to show the relationships among the three solution spaces: the set of constrained local minima (**A**), the set of solutions satisfying the first-order necessary and second-order sufficient conditions (**B**), and the set of saddle points (**C**).

Lemma 1. *The set of saddle points is a proper subset of the set of constrained local minima; i.e., $x \in \mathbf{C} \Rightarrow x \in \mathbf{A}$, and $x \in \mathbf{A} \not\Rightarrow x \in \mathbf{C}$.*

Lemma 2. *The set of solutions satisfying the first-order necessary and second-order sufficient conditions is a proper subset of the set of constrained local minima; i.e., $x \in \mathbf{B} \Rightarrow x \in \mathbf{A}$, and $x \in \mathbf{A} \not\Rightarrow x \in \mathbf{B}$.*

Lemma 3. *The set of solutions (x^*, λ^*) to the first-order necessary and second-order sufficient conditions may not be equal to the set of saddle points; i.e., $x \in \mathbf{B} \not\Rightarrow x \in \mathbf{C}$, and $x \in \mathbf{C} \not\Rightarrow x \in \mathbf{B}$.*

Theorem 2. *The relationships among the solutions sets $\mathbf{A}$, $\mathbf{B}$, and $\mathbf{C}$ is as follows: (a) $\mathbf{B} \subseteq \mathbf{A}$, (b) $\mathbf{C} \subseteq \mathbf{A}$, and $\mathbf{B} \neq \mathbf{C}$. Figure 2 depicts their relationships.*

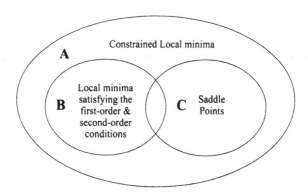

Fig. 2. Relationship among solution sets of Lagrangian methods for solving continuous problems.

2.3 Lagrangian Relaxation

There is a class of algorithms called *Lagrangian relaxation* [7, 8, 6, 24, 3] proposed in the literature that should not be confused with the Lagrange-multiplier methods proposed in this paper. Lagrangian relaxation reformulates a *linear* integer minimization problem:

$$z = \text{minimize}_x \ Cx$$

$$\text{subject to } Gx \leq b \quad \text{where } x \text{ is an integer vector of variables} \quad (7)$$

$$x \geq 0 \quad \text{and } C \text{ and } G \text{ are constant matrices}$$

into the following form:

$$L(\lambda) = \text{minimize}_x \ (Cx + \lambda(b - Gx))$$

$$\text{subject to } \quad x \geq 0. \quad (8)$$

Obviously, the new relaxed problem is simple and can be solved efficiently for any given vector λ. The method is based on Lagrangian Duality theory [25] upon which a general relationship between the solution to the original minimization problem and the solution to the relaxed problem can be deduced. There was some research [2] addressing nonlinear optimization problems. However, as pointed out in [25], Lagrangian relaxation aims to find an optimal primal solution given an optimal dual solution, or vice versa. This approach is simple in the case of linear functions but not for nonlinear functions. It has been proved [7] that $L(\lambda)$ can be used as an upper bound on z in (7), although better bounds can be computed in some special cases [6]. The bounds computed can be applied in a branch-and-bound search to solve linear integer programming problems.

In contrast, our Lagrange-multiplier formulation addresses *nonlinear* discrete constrained minimization problems defined in (1) that cannot be solved by Lagrangian relaxation. The mathematical foundation of our proposed formulation is based on two new discrete-space first-order necessary and sufficient conditions that define the necessary and sufficient conditions when the search finds a constrained local minimum.

3 Discrete Space Lagrangian Formulations/Methods

In this section we derive a new theory of Lagrange multipliers to work in discrete space.

3.1 Basic Definitions

We first consider a special case of (1) with equality constraints, and will defer till Section 3.3 to discuss ways to handle inequality constraints.

$$\text{minimize} \ f(x) \quad x = (x_1, x_2, \ldots, x_n) \text{ is a vector} \quad (9)$$

$$\text{subject to } h(x) = 0 \quad \text{of discrete variables}$$

Similar to the continuous case [17], the *discrete Lagrangian function* [23] of (9) is defined to be:

$$L_d(x, \lambda) = f(x) + \lambda^T H(h(x)). \tag{10}$$

where H is a continuous transformation function that satisfies $H(x) = 0 \Leftrightarrow x = 0$. There are various transformation functions that can be used. Note that function H was not used in our previous paper [23] and is introduced here to prove the necessary and sufficient condition. Its exact form is discussed in the next subsection.

We cannot use L_d to derive first-order necessary conditions similar to those in continuous space [17] because there are no gradients or differentiation in discrete space. Without these concepts, none of the calculus in continuous space is applicable in discrete space.

An understanding of gradients in continuous space shows that they define directions in a small neighborhood in which function values decrease. To this end, we define in discrete space a *direction of maximum potential drop* (DMPD) for $L_d(x, \lambda)$ at point x for fixed λ as a vector[1] that points from x to a neighbor of $x \in \mathcal{N}(x)$ with the minimum L_d:

$$\Delta_x L_d(x, \lambda) = \nu_x = y \ominus x = (y_1 - x_1, \ldots, y_n - x_n) \tag{11}$$
$$\text{where} \quad y \in \mathcal{N}(x) \cup \{x\} \text{ and } L_d(y, \lambda) = \min_{\substack{x' \in \mathcal{N}(x) \\ \cup \{x\}}} L_d(x', \lambda).$$

Here, $\ominus$ is the vector-subtraction operator for changing x in discrete space to one of its "user-defined" neighborhood points $\mathcal{N}(x)$. Intuitively, ν_x is a vector pointing from x to y, the point with the minimum L_d value among all neighboring points of x, including x itself. That is, if x itself has the minimum L_d, then $\nu_x = \mathbf{0}$. It is important to emphasize that, with this definition of discrete descent directions, DMPDs cannot be added/subtracted in discrete space [32]. Consequently, the proof procedure of first-order conditions in continuous space is not applicable here. This is shown in the following lemma.

Lemma 4. *There is no addition operation for* DMPD *defined in (11).*

Proof. In general, *DMPD* of $[f_1(x) + f_2(x)]$ is not the same as the summation of *DMPDs* of $f_1(x)$ and of $f_2(x)$. The following example illustrates the point.

$$f_1(0,0) = 0, f_1(0,1) = -3, f_1(1,0) = 0, \quad f_1(-1,0) = -2, f_1(0,-1) = 0,$$
$$f_2(0,0) = 0, f_2(0,1) = 0, \quad f_2(1,0) = -3, f_2(-1,0) = -2, f_2(0,-1) = 0.$$

From the definition of *DMPD*, we know that $\Delta_x f_1(0,0) = (0,1)$, $\Delta_x f_2(0,0) = (1,0)$ and $\Delta_x (f_1 + f_2)(0,0) = (-1,0)$. Hence, $\Delta_x (f_1 + f_2)(0,0) \neq \Delta_x f_1(0,0) \oplus \Delta_x f_2(0,0)$. ∎

---

[1] To simplify our symbols, we represent points in x space without the explicit vector notation.

The result of this lemma implies that the addition of two *DMPD*s cannot be carried out, rendering it impossible to prove the first-order conditions similar to those proved in Theorem 1 for continuous problems.

Based on DMPD, we define the concept of discrete saddle points [23,32] in discrete space similar to those in continuous space [17].

Definition 6. *A point* (x^*, λ^*) *is a* <u>*discrete saddle point*</u> *when:*

$$L_d(x^*, \lambda) \le L_d(x^*, \lambda^*) \le L_d(x, \lambda^*), \tag{12}$$

for all $x \in \mathcal{N}(x^*)$ *and all possible* λ.

Note that the first inequality in (12) only holds when all the constraints are satisfied, which implies that it must be true for all λ.

3.2 Characteristics of Discrete Saddle Points

The concept of saddle points is of great importance to discrete problems because, starting from saddle points, we can derive first-order necessary and sufficient conditions for discrete problems and develop efficient first-order procedures for finding constrained local minima. Although these conditions are similar to those for continuous problems, they were derived from the concept of saddle points rather than from regular points [17].

Similar to the continuous case, we denote **A** to be the set of all constrained local minima, **B** to be the set of all solutions that satisfy the discrete-space first-order necessary and sufficient conditions (13) and (14), and **C** to be the set of all discrete saddle points satisfying (12).

Lemma 5. *First-order necessary and sufficient conditions for discrete saddle points. In discrete space, the set of all saddle points is equal to the set of all solutions that satisfy the following two equations:*

$$\Delta_x L_d(x, \lambda) = \Delta_x [f(x) + \lambda^T H(h(x))] = 0 \tag{13}$$
$$h(x) = 0 \tag{14}$$

Note that the Δ *operator in (13) is for discrete space.*

Proof. The proof is done in two parts:

"⇒" part: Given a saddle point (x^*, λ^*), we like to prove it to be a solution to (13) and (14). Eq. (13) is true because L_d cannot be improved among $\mathcal{N}(x^*)$ from the definition of saddle points. Hence, $\Delta_x L_d(x^*, \lambda^*) = 0$ must be true from the definition of *DMPD*. Eq. (14) is true because $h(x) = 0$ must be satisfied at any solution point.

"⇐" part: Given a solution (x^*, λ^*) to (13) and (14), we like to prove it to be a discrete saddle point. The first condition $L_d(x^*, \lambda^*) \le L_d(x, \lambda^*)$ holds for all $x \in \mathcal{N}(x^*)$ because $\Delta_x L_d(x^*, \lambda^*) = 0$. Hence, no improvement of L_d can be found in the neighborhood of x^*. The second condition $L_d(x^*, \lambda) \le L_d(x^*, \lambda^*)$ is true for all λ because $h(x^*) = 0$ according to (14). Thus, (x^*, λ^*) is a saddle point in discrete space. ∎

For the discrete Lagrangian definition in (10), we found that, if $H\left(h(x)\right)$ is always non-negative (or non-positive), then the set of constrained local minima is the same as the set of saddle points. Examples of transformation H are the absolute function and the square function.

Lemma 6. *Sufficient conditions for constrained local minimum to be a saddle point. In the discrete Lagrangian function defined in (10), if $H(x)$ is a continuous function satisfying $H(x) = 0 \Leftrightarrow x = 0$ and is non-negative (or non-positive), then* $\mathbf{A} = \mathbf{C}$ *holds.*

Proof. We only prove the case when $H(x)$ is non-negative, and the other case can be proved similarly. To prove this lemma, we construct λ^* for every constrained local minimum x^* in order to make (x^*, λ^*) a saddle point. This λ^* must be bounded and be found in finite time in order for the procedure to be useful.

(a): *Constructing λ^**. Given x^*, consider $x \in \mathcal{N}(x^*)$. Let $h(x) = (h_1(x), \dots , h_m(x))$ be an m-element vector, and the initial $\lambda^* = (\lambda_1^*, \dots , \lambda_m^*) = (0, \dots , 0)$. For every x such that $H(h(x)) > 0$, there is at least one constraint that is not satisfied, say $H(h_i(x)) > 0$. For this constraint, we set:

$$\lambda_i^* \to \max \left(\lambda_i^*, \frac{f(x^*) - f(x)}{H(h_i(x))} \right) \tag{15}$$

The update defined in (15) is repeated for every unsatisfied constraint of x and every $x \in \mathcal{N}(x^*)$ until no further update is possible. Since $\mathcal{N}(x^*)$ has finite number of elements in discrete space, (15) will terminate in finite time and result in finite λ^* values.

(b) *Proving that (x^*, λ^*) is a saddle point.* To prove that (x^*, λ^*) is a saddle point, we need to prove that, for all $x \in \mathcal{N}(x^*)$, $L_d(x^*, \lambda) \le L_d(x^*, \lambda^*) \le L_d(x, \lambda^*)$. The first inequality is trivial because $L_d(x^*, \lambda) = f(x^*) = L_d(x^*, \lambda^*)$. In the second inequality, for all $x \in \mathcal{N}(x^*)$ such that $h(x) = 0$, it is obvious that $L_d(x^*, \lambda^*) = f(x^*) \le f(x) = L_d(x, \lambda^*)$ since x^* is a constrained local minimum. For all $x \in \mathcal{N}(x^*)$ such that $h(x) \neq 0$, there must be at least one constraint that is not satisfied, say $H(h_i(x)) > 0$. Moreover, from the construction method, we know that $\lambda_i^* \ge \frac{f(x^*)-f(x)}{H(h_i(x))}$. Therefore, $L_d(x^*, \lambda^*) = f(x^*) \le f(x) + \lambda_i^* H(h_i(x))$ holds. Further, since $\sum_{j=1, j\neq i}^{m} \lambda_j^* H(h_j(x))$ is non-negative (assuming all constraints are transformed by H into non-negative functions), it is obvious true that

$$L_d(x^*, \lambda^*) = f(x^*) \le f(x) + \sum_{j=1}^{m} \lambda_j^* H(h_j(x)) = L_d(x, \lambda^*).$$

Hence, (x^*, λ^*) is a saddle point. ∎

The above lemma shows that transformation function H should be non-negative or non-positive, but not both. We illustrate in the following example that, given the discrete Lagrangian function $L_d(x, \lambda) = f(x) + \lambda^T h(x)$, a constrained local minimum x^* may not be a saddle point when $h(x)$ can have both positive and negative values. We construct a counter example to demonstrate that it is not always possible to find λ^* to make (x^*, λ^*) a saddle point even when x^* is a constrained local minimum in discrete space.

Consider a two-dimensional discrete equality-constrained problem with objective $f(x)$ and constraint $h(x) = 0$, where

$$f(0,0) = 0, \ f(0,1) = 1, \ f(0,-1) = 0, \ f(1,0) = 0, \ f(-1,0) = -1,$$
$$h(0,0) = 0, \ h(0,1) = 0, \ h(0,-1) = 1, \ h(1,0) = 0, \ h(-1,0) = -1.$$

Obviously, $(x^*, y^*) = (0, 0)$ is a constrained local minimum. Furthermore, from the definition of Lagrangian function, we know that $L_d((0,0), \lambda) = 0$ holds true for any λ because $h(0,0) = f(0,0) = 0$.

To draw a contradiction, assume that $(0,0)$ is a saddle point. Hence, there exists λ^* such that $L_d((0,0), \lambda^*) \leq L_d((-1,0), \lambda^*)$, and $L_d((0,0), \lambda^*) \leq L_d((0,-1), \lambda^*)$. After substitution, we get the following equations:

$$0 \leq f(-1,0) + \lambda^* \times h(-1,0) = -1 + \lambda^* \times (-1), \tag{16}$$
$$0 \leq f(0,-1) + \lambda^* \times h(0,-1) = 0 + \lambda^* \times 1.$$

Since there is no solution for λ^* in (16), the example shows that $(0,0)$ is a constrained local minimum but not a saddle point.

Finally, we show that finding any $\lambda \geq \lambda^*$ suffices to find a saddle point.

Corollary 1. *Given λ^* defined in Lemma 6, (x^*, λ') is a saddle point for any $\lambda' \geq \lambda^*$, where $\lambda' \geq \lambda^*$ means that every element of λ' is not less than the corresponding element of λ^*.*

Proof. The proof of the corollary is similar to that of Lemma 6 and will not be shown here. The corollary is important because, in practice, a search algorithm may only be able to find $\lambda \geq \lambda^*$ but not exactly λ^*. ∎

3.3 Handling Inequality Constraints

The results discussed so far apply only to discrete optimization problems with equality constraints. To handle (1) with inequality constraints, we need to transform them into equality constraints.

One general method of transforming inequality constraint $g_j(x) \leq 0$ is to apply a maximum function to convert the constraint into $\max(g_j(x), 0) = 0$. Obviously, the new constraint is satisfied iff $g_j(x) \leq 0$. The discrete Lagrangian function using the maximum transformation for inequality constraints is:

$$L_d(x, \lambda, \mu) = f(x) + \lambda^T H(h(x)) + \sum_{i=1}^{k} \mu_i H(\max(0, g_i(x))) \tag{17}$$

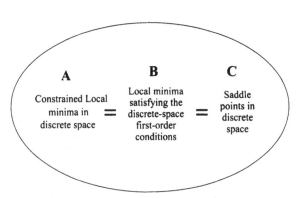

Fig. 3. Relationship among solution sets of Lagrangian methods for solving discrete problems when H satisfies the conditions in Theorem 3.

3.4 Discrete Space First-Order Necessary & Sufficient Conditions

This section summarizes the main theorem on discrete Lagrange multipliers.

Theorem 3. *First-order necessary and sufficient conditions for discrete constrained local minima. In discrete space, if $H(x)$ in the discrete Lagrangian definition in (10) is a continuous function satisfying $H(x) = 0 \Leftrightarrow x = 0$ and is non-negative (or non-positive), then the three solutions sets are equal, namely,* $\mathbf{A} = \mathbf{B} = \mathbf{C}$.

Proof. The proof follows from Lemmas 5 and 6. Figure 3 illustrates the relationships proved by this theorem. ∎

Theorem 3 is of great importance in the following sense:

- Any search strategy aiming to find saddle points is sufficient because it is equivalent to searching for constrained local minima.
- A global optimization strategy looking for the saddle point with the minimum objective value will result in the constrained global minimum because the set of global minima is a subset of the set of saddle points.

In contrast, a continuous-space global-minimization method based on continuous first-order necessary and second-order sufficient conditions is not guaranteed to find the global minimum because the global solution may be outside the set of solutions that satisfy the first-order and second-order conditions. This fact is illustrated in Figure 2.

4 Discrete Space First-Order Local-Search Methods

The first-order necessary and sufficient conditions provide a basis for an efficient local-search method. In a way similar to that in continuous space, we propose an iterative *discrete first-order method* that looks for discrete saddle points.

$$x^{k+1} = x^k \oplus \Delta_x L_d(x^k, \lambda^k) \tag{18}$$
$$\lambda^{k+1} = \lambda^k + c_1 H(h(x^k)) \tag{19}$$

where $\oplus$ is the vector-addition operator $(x \oplus y = (x_1 + y_1, \ldots x_n + y_n))$, and c_1 is a positive step-wise real number controlling how fast the Lagrange multipliers change. This method is more general than the one used earlier [23] because it is not restricted to a special neighborhood function of Hamming distance one and arithmetic additions.

It should be obvious that the necessary condition for (18) and (19) to converge is when $h(x) = 0$, implying that x is a feasible solution to the original problem. If any of the constraints in $h(x)$ is not satisfied, then λ will continue to evolve to suppress the unsatisfied constraints. Further, as in continuous Lagrangian methods, the time for (18) and (19) to find a saddle point may be unbounded and can only be determined empirically, even when there exist feasible solutions.

The first-order search method in (18) and (19) has been applied to design multiplierless filter banks [26, 28], solve satisfiability problems [23, 22, 31], and evaluate nonlinear discrete optimization benchmarks [32].

The following theorem guarantees that (18) and (19) can be used to locate saddle points [23].

Theorem 4. *Fixed-point theorem for discrete problems. A saddle point (x^*, λ^*) of (10) is reached iff (18) and (19) terminates [23].*

Proof. The proof consists of two parts.

"$\Rightarrow$" part: We prove that at a saddle point (18) and (19) will stop. This means that if (x^*, λ^*) is a saddle point, then it is also a fixed point of the iterative process. Given a saddle point (x^*, λ^*), we know from its definition that $L_d(x^*, \lambda^*) \leq L_d(x, \lambda^*)$ holds true for all $x \in \mathcal{N}(x^*)$. Thus, from the definition of *DMPD*, we conclude that $x_{k+1} = x_k$. In addition, since x^* is feasible, we conclude that $H(h(x_k)) = 0 = h(x_k)$. Since $x_{k+1} = x_k$ and $\lambda_{k+1} = \lambda_k$, (18) and (19) will stop at (x^*, λ^*).

"$\Leftarrow$" part: We prove the point that (18) and (19) stop at must be a saddle point of $L_d(x, \lambda) = f(x) + \lambda^T H(h(x))$. This also means that the method will not stop at points other than saddle points. Since the method stops at (x_k, λ_k), it implies that $x_{k+1} = x_k$ and $\lambda_{k+1} = \lambda_k$. These conditions imply that $\Delta_x L_d(x_k, \lambda_k) = 0$, meaning that $L_d(x_k, \lambda_k) \leq L_d(x'_k, \lambda_k)$ for any $x'_k \in \mathcal{N}(x_k)$. Moreover, $h(x_k) = 0$ is true because $\lambda_{k+1} = \lambda_k$. Hence, x_k is a feasible point, and (x_k, λ_k) is a saddle point. ∎

5　Conclusions

In this paper, we have extended the theory of Lagrange multipliers to discrete optimization problems and have shown two important results that form the mathematical foundation in this area:

- For general discrete constrained optimization problems, we have shown the first-order necessary and sufficient conditions for saddle points in the solution space.
- After transforming general constraints into non-negative or non-positive functions, we have further shown the equivalence between the set of saddle points and the set of constrained local minima. Hence, the same first-order necessary and sufficient conditions derived for saddle points become the necessary and sufficient conditions for constrained local minima.

The last result is particularly significant because it implies that finding the saddle point with the best solution value amounts to global optimization of a discrete constrained optimization problem. A global optimization procedure with asymptotic convergence is presented in another paper [27].

References

1. K. J. Arrow and L. Hurwicz. Gradient method for concave programming, I: Local results. In K. J. Arrow, L. Hurwica, and H. Uzawa, editors, *Studies in Linear and Nonlinear Programming*. Stanford University Press, Stanford, CA, 1958.
2. E. Balas. *Minimax and Duality for Linear and Nonlinear Mixed-Integer Programming*. North-Holland, Amsterdam, Netherlands, 1970.
3. M. S. Bazaraa and J. J. Goode. A survey of various tactics for generating Lagrangian multipliers in the context of Lagrangian duality. *European Journal of Operational Research*, 3:322–338, 1979.
4. K. F. M. Choi, J. H. M. Lee, and P. J. Stuckey. A Lagrangian reconstruction of a class of local search methods. In *Proc. 10th Int'l Conf. on Artificial Intelligence Tools*. IEEE Computer Society, 1998.
5. A. Frank. An algorithm for submodular functions on graphs. *Ann. Discrete Math.*, 16:97–120, 1982.
6. B. Gavish. On obtaining the 'best' multilpliers for a lagrangean relaxation for integer programming. *Comput. & Ops. Res.*, 5:55–71, 1978.
7. A. M. Geoffrion. Lagrangean relaxation for integer programming. *Mathematical Programming Study*, 2:82–114, 1974.
8. F. R. Giles and W. R. Pulleyblank. *Total Dual Integrality and Integer Polyhedra*, volume 25. Elsevier North Holland, Inc., 1979.
9. F. Glover. Tabu search — Part I. *ORSA J. Computing*, 1(3):190–206, 1989.
10. F. Glover and E. Woolsey. Converting the 0-1 polynomial programming problem to a 0-1 linear program. *Operations Research*, 22:180–182, 1975.
11. D. Granot, F. Granot, and W. Vaessen. An accelerated covering relaxation algorithm for solving positive 0-1 polynomial programs. *Mathematical Programming*, 22:350–357, 1982.
12. P. Hansen, B. Jaumard, and V. Mathon. Constrained nonlinear 0-1 programming. *ORSA Journal on Computing*, 5(2):97–119, 1993.
13. J. H. Holland. *Adaption in Natural and Adaptive Systems*. University of Michigan Press, Ann Arbor, 1975.
14. J. J. Hopfield and D. W. Tank. Neural computation by concentrating information in time. In *Proc. National Academy of Sciences*, volume 84, pages 1896–1900, Washington, D.C., 1987. National Academy of Sciences.

15. M. E. Hribar. Large scale constrained optimization. *Ph.D. Disertation, Northeasten University*, 1996.
16. S. Kirkpatrick, C. D. Gelatt, Jr., and M. P. Vecchi. Optimization by simulated annealing. *Science*, 220(4598):671–680, May 1983.
17. D. G. Luenberger. *Linear and Nonlinear Programming*. Addison-Wesley Publishing Company, 1984.
18. P. Morris. The breakout method for escaping from local minima. In *Proc. of the 11th National Conf. on Artificial Intelligence*, pages 40–45, Washington, DC, 1993.
19. K. Murota. Discrete convex analysis. *Mathematical Programming*, 83(3):313 – 371, 1998.
20. R. T. Rockafellar. *Convex Analysis*. Princeton University Press, Princeton, NJ, 1970.
21. I. Rosenberg. Minimization of pseudo-boolean functions by binary development. *Discrete Mathematics*, 7:151–165, 1974.
22. Y. Shang and B. W. Wah. Discrete Lagrangian-based search for solving MAX-SAT problems. In *Proc. Int'l Joint Conf. on Artificial Intelligence*, pages 378–383. IJCAI, August 1997.
23. Y. Shang and B. W. Wah. A discrete Lagrangian based global search method for solving satisfiability problems. *J. Global Optimization*, 12(1):61–99, January 1998.
24. J. F. Shapiro. Generalized Lagrange multipliers in integer programming. *Operations Research*, 19:68–76, 1971.
25. J. Tind and L. A. Wolsey. An elementary survey of general duality theory in mathematical programming. *Mathematical Programming*, pages 241–261, 1981.
26. B. W. Wah, Y. Shang, and Z. Wu. Discrete Lagrangian method for optimizing the design of multiplierless QMF filter banks. *IEEE Transactions on Circuits and Systems, Part II*, (accepted to appear) 1999.
27. B. W. Wah and T. Wang. Simulated annealing with asymptotic convergence for nonlinear constrained global optimization. *Principles and Practice of Constraint Programming*, (accepted to appear) October 1999.
28. B. W. Wah and Z. Wu. Discrete Lagrangian method for designing multiplierless two-channel PR-LP filter banks. *VLSI Signal Processing*, 21(2):131–150, June 1999.
29. X. D. Wang. An algorithm for nonlinear 0-1 programming and its application in structural optimization. *Journal of Numerical Method and Computational Applications*, 1(9):22–31, 1988.
30. L. J. Watters. Reduction of integer polynomial programming to zero-one linear programming problems. *Operations Research*, 15:1171–1174, 1967.
31. Z. Wu and B. W. Wah. Solving hard satisfiability problems using the discrete Lagrange-multiplier method. In *Proc. 1999 National Conference on Artificial Intelligence*, pages 673–678. AAAI, July 1999.
32. Zhe Wu. *Discrete Lagrangian Methods for Solving Nonlinear Discrete Constrained Optimization Problems*. M.Sc. Thesis, Dept. of Computer Science, Univ. of Illinois, Urbana, IL, May 1998.

Operational Equivalence of CHR Programs and Constraints

Slim Abdennadher and Thom Frühwirth

Computer Science Department, University of Munich
Oettingenstr. 67, D-80538 Munich, Germany
{Slim.Abdennadher, Thom.Fruehwirth}@informatik.uni-muenchen.de

Abstract. A fundamental question in programming language semantics is when two programs should be considered equivalent. In this paper we introduce a notion of operational equivalence for CHR programs and user-defined constraints. Constraint Handling Rules (CHR) is a high-level language for writing constraint solvers either from scratch or by modifying existing solvers.

We give a decidable, sufficient and necessary syntactic condition for operational equivalence of terminating and confluent CHR programs.

For practical reasons, we also investigate a notion of operational equivalence for user-defined constraints that are defined in different programs. We give a sufficient syntactic condition for constraints defined in terminating and confluent CHR programs. For a subclass of programs which have only one user-defined constraint in common, we are able to give a sufficient and necessary syntactic condition.

1   Introduction

Constraint Handling Rules (CHR) [Frü98] is essentially a committed-choice language consisting of multi-headed guarded rules that transform constraints into simpler ones until they are solved. CHR defines both *simplification* of and *propagation* over user-defined constraints. Simplification replaces constraints by simpler constraints while preserving logical equivalence, e.g. $X \geq Y \wedge Y \geq X \Leftrightarrow X=Y$. Propagation adds new constraints, which are logically redundant but may cause further simplification, e.g. $X \geq Y \wedge Y \geq Z \Rightarrow X \geq Z$.

As a special-purpose language for writing constraint solvers, CHR aims to fulfill the promise of user-defined constraints as stated in [ACM96]: "For the theoretician meta-theorems can be proved and analysis techniques invented once and for all; for the implementor different constructs (backward and forward chaining, suspension, compiler optimization, debugging) can be implemented once and for all; for the user only one set of ideas need to be understood, though with rich (albeit disciplined) variations (constraint systems)."

A fundamental and hard question in programming language semantics is when two programs should be considered equivalent. For example correctness of program transformation can be studied only with respect to a notion of equivalence.

Also, if modules or libraries with similar functionality are used together, one may be interested in finding out if program parts in different modules or libraries are equivalent. In the context of CHR, this case arises frequently when constraint solvers written in CHR are combined. Typically, a constraint is only partially defined in a constraint solver. We want to make sure that the operational semantics of the common constraints of two programs do not differ, and we are interested in finding out if they are equivalent.

The literature on equivalence of programs in logic-based languages is sparse. In most papers that touch the subject, a suitable notion of program equivalence serves as a correctness criterion for transformations between programs, e.g. in partial evaluation and deduction. Our concern is the problem of program equivalence in its generality, where the programs to be compared are independent from each other.

[Mah86] provides a systematic comparison of the relative strengths of various formulations of equivalence of logic programs. These formulations arise naturally from several formal semantics of logic programs. Maher does not study how to test for equivalence. The results may be extensible to constraint logic programs, but committed-choice languages like CHR have different semantics that induce different notions of equivalence. In particular, in CHR the distinction between successful, failed or deadlocked goals is secondary, but the distinction between a goal and its instances is vital. For similar reasons, [GLM95] among other things extends Maher's work by considering relationships between equivalences derived from semantics that are based e.g. on computed answer substitutions. Gabbrielli et. al. are not concerned with tests for equivalence, either.

Like [GLM95] we are concerned with equivalences of the observable behavior of programs. Observables are then a suitable abstraction of execution traces. In case of equivalence based on operational semantics expressed by a transition system, it is common to define as observables the results of finite computations, where one abstracts away local variables, see e.g. [EGM98].

We have already shown in previous work [Abd97] that analysis techniques are available for an important property of any constraint solver, namely confluence: The result of a computation should be independent from the order in which constraints arrive and in which rules are applied to the constraints. For confluence of terminating CHR programs we were able to give a decidable, sufficient and necessary condition [Abd97,AFM99]. A completion algorithm that makes programs confluent if it terminates, was presented in [AF98].

It is tempting to think that a suitable modification of the concept of confluence can be used to express equivalence of programs. In this paper we show that a straightforward application of our confluence test is too weak to capture the operational equivalence of CHR programs.

In practice, one is often interested in comparing implementations of constraints instead of whole programs. Hence we investigate a notion of operational equivalence for user-defined constraints that are defined in different programs. We give a sufficient syntactic condition for constraints defined in terminating and confluent CHR programs. For a subclass of programs which have only one user-defined constraint in common, we are able to give a sufficient and necessary syntactic condition.

Based on these results, we are finally able to give a decidable, sufficient and necessary syntactic condition for operational equivalence of terminating and confluent CHR programs.

This paper is organized as follows: In Section 2 we define the CHR language and summarize previous confluence results. Section 3 presents our notion of operational equivalence for CHR and the results about this notion. Finally, we conclude with a summary and directions for future work.

2 Preliminaries

In this section we give an overview of syntax and semantics as well as confluence results for constraint handling rules. More detailed presentations can be found in [AFM96,Abd97,AFM99].

2.1 Syntax of CHR

We use two disjoint kinds of predicate symbols for two different classes of constraints: *built-in constraint symbols* and *user-defined constraint symbols (CHR symbols)*. We call an atomic formula with a constraint symbol a *constraint*. Built-in constraints are handled by a predefined, given constraint solver that already exists as a certified black-box solver. user-defined constraints are defined in a CHR program.

A *CHR program* is a finite set of rules. There are two kinds of rules:
A *simplification rule* is of the form

$$H \Leftrightarrow C \mid B.$$

A *propagation rule* is of the form

$$H \Rightarrow C \mid B,$$

where the *head* H is a non-empty conjunction of user-defined constraints, the *guard* C is a conjunction of built-in constraints, and the *body* B is a goal. A *goal* is a conjunction of built-in and user-defined constraints. A guard *"true"* is usually omitted together with the commit symbol |. A CHR symbol is *defined* in a CHR program if it occurs in the head of a rule in the program.

2.2 Declarative Semantics of CHR

The logical meaning of a simplification rule is a logical equivalence provided the guard holds. $\forall F$ denotes the universal closure of a formula F.

$$\forall (C \to (H \leftrightarrow \exists \bar{y} \, B)),$$

where $\bar{y}$ are the variables that appear only in the body B.

The logical meaning of a propagation rule is an implication provided the guard holds

$$\forall(C \rightarrow (H \rightarrow \exists \bar{y}\ B)).$$

The logical meaning $\mathcal{P}$ of a CHR program P is the conjunction of the logical meanings of its rules united with a consistent *constraint theory* CT that defines the built-in constraint symbols. We require CT to define the constraint symbol $=$ as syntactic equality.

2.3 Operational Semantics of CHR

The operational semantics of CHR is given by a transition system.

A state $G_\mathcal{V}$ is a goal G together with a sequence of variables, $\mathcal{V}$. Where it is clear from the context, we will drop the annotation $\mathcal{V}$.

We require that states are normalized so that they can be compared syntactically in a meaningful way. Basically, we require that the built-in constraints are in a (unique) normal form, where all syntactic equalities are made explicit and are propagated to the user-defined constraints. Furthermore, we require that the normalization projects out strictly local variables, i.e. variables appearing in the built-in constraints only. A precise definition of the normalization function $\mathcal{N}$ can be found in [Abd97,AFM99].

Given a CHR program P we define the transition relation $\mapsto_P$ by introducing two kinds of computation steps (Figure 1). $\mapsto_P^+$ denotes the transitive closure, $\mapsto_P^*$ denotes the reflexive and transitive closure of $\mapsto_P$.

An *initial state* for a goal G is the state $\mathcal{N}(G_\mathcal{V})$, where $\mathcal{N}$ is a function that normalizes a state as defined below and $\mathcal{V}$ is a sequence of all variables appearing in G. A *final state* is one where either no computation step is possible anymore or where the built-in constraints are inconsistent.

A *computation* of a goal G in a program P is a sequence $S_0, S_1, \ldots$ of states with $S_i \mapsto_P S_{i+1}$ beginning with the initial state for G and ending in a final state or diverging. Where it is clear from the context, we will drop the reference to the program P.

In Figure 1, the notation G_{built} denotes the built-in constraints in a goal G. We will also use the notation G_{user} to denote the user-defined constraints in a goal G. An equation $c(t_1, \ldots, t_n) = d(s_1, \ldots, s_n)$ of two constraints stands for $t_1 = s_1 \wedge \ldots \wedge t_n = s_n$ if c and d are the same CHR symbols and for *false* otherwise. An equation $(p_1 \wedge \ldots \wedge p_n) = (q_1 \wedge \ldots \wedge q_m)$ stands for $p_1 = q_1 \wedge \ldots \wedge p_n = q_n$ if $n = m$ and for *false* otherwise. Conjuncts can be permuted since conjunction is associative and commutative.

To **Simplify** user-defined constraints H' means to remove them from the state $H' \wedge G$ and to add the body B of a fresh variant of a simplification rule $(H \Leftrightarrow C \mid B)$ and the equation $H = H'$ and the guard C to the resulting state G, provided H' matches the head H and the guard C is implied by the built-in constraints appearing in G, and finally to normalize the resulting state. In this case we say

Simplify

If $(H \Leftrightarrow C \mid B)$ is a fresh variant of a rule with variables $\bar{x}$

and $CT \models \forall\, (G_{built} \rightarrow \exists \bar{x}(H{=}H' \wedge C))$

then $(H' \wedge G)_\nu \mapsto_P \mathcal{N}((H{=}H' \wedge B \wedge C \wedge G)_\nu)$

Propagate

If $(H \Rightarrow C \mid B)$ is a fresh variant of a rule with variables $\bar{x}$

and $CT \models \forall\, (G_{built} \rightarrow \exists \bar{x}(H{=}H' \wedge C))$

then $(H' \wedge G)_\nu \mapsto_P \mathcal{N}((H{=}H' \wedge B \wedge C \wedge H' \wedge G)_\nu)$

Fig. 1. Computation Steps of Constraint Handling Rules

that the rule R is *applicable to H'*. A "variant" of a formula is obtained by renaming its variables. "Matching" means that H' is an instance of H, i.e. it is only allowed to instantiate (bind) variables of H but not variables of H'. In the logical notation this is achieved by existentially quantifying only over the fresh variables $\bar{x}$ of the rule to be applied in the condition.

The **Propagate** transition is like the **Simplify** transition, except that it keeps the constraints H' in the state. Trivial nontermination caused by applying the same propagation rule again and again is avoided by applying a propagation rule at most once to the same constraints. A more complex operational semantics that addresses this issue can be found in [Abd97].

Example 1. Let $\leq$ and $<$ be built-in constraint symbols. We define a CHR symbol `max`, where `max(X,Y,Z)` means that Z is the maximum of X and Y:

```
max(X,Y,Z) ⇔ X≤Y | Z=Y.
max(X,Y,Z) ⇔ Y≤X | Z=X.
max(X,Y,Z) ⇒ X≤Z ∧ Y≤Z.
```

The first rule states that `max(X,Y,Z)` can be simplified into Z=Y in any goal where it holds that X≤Y. Analogously for the second rule. The third rule propagates constraints. It states that `max(X,Y,Z)` unconditionally implies X≤Z ∧ Y≤Z. Operationally, we add these logical consequences as redundant constraints, the `max` constraint is kept.

To the goal `max(1,2,M)` the first rule is applicable: `max(1,2,M)` ↦ M=2.

To the goal `max(A,B,M)` ∧ A<B the first rule is applicable:

`max(A,B,M)` ∧ A<B ↦ M=B ∧ A<B.

To the goal `max(A,A,M)` both simplification rules are applicable, and in both cases: `max(A,A,M)` ↦ M=A.

Redundancy from the propagation rule is useful, as the goal `max(A,3,3)` shows: To this goal only the propagation rule is applicable, and then the first rule:

`max(A,3,3)` ↦ `max(A,3,3)` ∧ A≤3 ↦ A≤3.

Note, that the constraint 3=3 is simplified to true by the built-in constraint solver; according to our assumption about the built-in constraint symbol =.

2.4 Confluence

The confluence property of a program guarantees that any computation starting from an arbitrary initial state, i.e. any possible order of rule applications, results in the same final state. Due to space limitations, we can just give an overview on confluence results for CHR programs, for details see [AFM99,Abd97].

Definition 1. A CHR program is called *confluent* if for all states S, S_1, S_2: If $S \mapsto^* S_1$ and $S \mapsto^* S_2$ then S_1 and S_2 are joinable. Two states S_1 and S_2 are called *joinable* if there exist states T_1 and T_2 such that $S_1 \mapsto^* T_1$ and $S_2 \mapsto^* T_2$ and T_1, T_2 are variants of each other.

To analyze confluence of a given CHR program we cannot check joinability starting from any given ancestor state S, because in general there are infinitely many such states. However one can restrict the joinability test to a finite number of "minimal" states based on the following observations: First, adding constraints to a state cannot inhibit the application of a rule as long as the built-in constraints remain consistent (monotonicity property, cf. Lemma 2 in Section 3.2). Hence we can restrict ourselves to ancestor states that consist of the head and guards of two rules. Second, joinability can only be destroyed if one rule inhibits the application of another rule. Only the removal of constraints can affect the applicability of another rule, in case the removed constraint is needed by the other rule. Hence at least one rule must be a simplification rule and the two rules must *overlap*, i.e. have at least one head atom in common in the ancestor state. This is achieved by equating head atoms in the state.

Definition 2. Given a simplification rule R_1 and an arbitrary (not necessarily different) rule R_2, whose variables have been renamed apart. Let $H_i \wedge A_i$ be the head and C_i be the guard of rule R_i ($i = 1, 2$). Then a *critical ancestor state of R_1 and R_2* is

$$(H_1 \wedge A_1 \wedge H_2 \wedge (A_1 = A_2) \wedge C_1 \wedge C_2)\nu,$$

provided A_1 and A_2 are non-empty conjunctions and $CT \models \exists((A_1 = A_2) \wedge C_1 \wedge C_2)$.

The application of R_1 and R_2, respectively, to a critical ancestor state of R_1 and R_2 leads to two states that form the so-called *critical pair*.

Definition 3. Let S be a critical ancestor state of R_1 and R_2. If $S \mapsto S_1$ using rule R_1 and $S \mapsto S_2$ using rule R_2 then the tuple (S_1, S_2) is the *critical pair* of R_1 and R_2. A critical pair (S_1, S_2) is *joinable*, if S_1 and S_2 are joinable.

Definition 4. A CHR program is called *terminating*, if there are no infinite computations.

The following theorem from [AFM96,Abd97,AFM99] gives a decidable, sufficient and necessary condition for confluence of a terminating CHR program:

Theorem 1. A terminating CHR program is confluent iff all its critical pairs are joinable.

Example 2. Consider the program for **max** of Example 1. The following critical pair stems from the critical ancestor state[1] $(\text{max}(X,Y,Z) \wedge X \leq Y)_{[X,Y,Z]}$ of the first rule and the third one:

$$(S_1, S_2) := (Z=Y \wedge X \leq Y \quad , \quad \text{max}(X,Y,Z) \wedge X \leq Y \wedge X \leq Z \wedge Y \leq Z)$$

(S_1, S_2) is joinable since S_1 is a final state and the application of the first rule to S_2 results in S_1.

3 Operational Equivalence

In this section we give sufficient and necessary conditions for equivalence of terminating programs. The following definition states that two programs are operationally equivalent if for each goal, the final state in one program is the same as the final state in the other program.

Definition 5. Let P_1 and P_2 be CHR programs. A state S is P_1, P_2-*joinable*, iff there are two computations $S \mapsto^{*}_{P_1} S_1$ and $S \mapsto^{*}_{P_2} S_2$, where S_1 and S_2 are final states, and S_1 and S_2 are variants of each other.
Let P_1 and P_2 be CHR programs. P_1 and P_2 are *operationally equivalent* if all states are P_1, P_2-joinable.

We will see in Section 3.1 that an adaptation of our confluence test - that we call compatibility - does not yield a test for operational equivalence. In Section 3.3, we will be able to give a decidable, sufficient and necessary syntactic condition for operational equivalence of terminating and confluent programs based on results in Section 3.2.

In practice, we want to combine CHR programs which define different CHR symbols, but also have some CHR symbols in common. A typical scenario is that of modules or libraries implementing similar functionality. In the context of CHR, this case arises frequently when constraint solvers written in CHR are combined. Typically, a CHR symbol is only partially defined in a constraint solver.

A closer look at Definition 5 reveals that for these practical scenarios, it is much too strict: States that involve CHR symbols that are defined in one program only, are rarely P_1, P_2-joinable. Therefore, in Section 3.2, we investigate operational equivalence of user-defined constraints that are implemented in different programs.

3.1 Compatibility of Programs

We can use our confluence test to ensure that the different, confluent programs are "compatible": The union of the programs is confluent.

---

[1] For readability, variables from different rules have been identified to have an overlap.

Definition 6. Let P_1 and P_2 be two confluent and terminating CHR programs and let the union of the two programs, $P_1 \cup P_2$, be terminating. P_1 and P_2 are *compatible* if $P_1 \cup P_2$ is confluent.

Testing the compatibility of P_1 and P_2 means to test the joinability of the critical pairs of $P_1 \cup P_2$, i.e. the critical pairs of P_1 united with the critical pairs of P_2 united with critical pairs coming from one rule in P_1 and one rule in P_2. Note that critical pairs from rules of different programs can only exist, if the heads of the rules have at least one constraint in common.

If the confluence test fails, we can locate the rules responsible for the problem. If the test succeeds, we can just take the union of the rules in the two programs. This means that a common CHR symbol can even be partially defined in the programs which are combined.

Example 3. P_1 contains the following CHR rules defining `max`:

```
max(X,Y,Z) ⇔ X<Y | Z=Y.
max(X,Y,Z) ⇔ X≥Y | Z=X.
```

whereas P_2 has the following definition of `max`:

```
max(X,Y,Z) ⇔ X≤Y | Z=Y.
max(X,Y,Z) ⇔ X>Y | Z=X.
```

We want to know whether the definitions of `max` are compatible. There are three critical ancestor states coming from one rule in P_1 and one rule in P_2:

- `max(X,Y,Z)` $\wedge$ `X<Y` $\wedge$ `X≤Y` stems from the first rule of P_1 and the first rule of P_2.
- `max(X,Y,Z)` $\wedge$ `X≥Y` $\wedge$ `X≤Y` stems from the second rule of P_1 and the first rule of P_2.
- `max(X,Y,Z)` $\wedge$ `X≥Y` $\wedge$ `X>Y` stems from the second rule of P_1 and the second rule of P_2.

Since the critical pairs coming from the critical ancestor states described above are joinable, the two definitions of `max` are compatible. Hence we can just take the union of the rules and define `max` by all four rules.

Note that the compatibility test does not ensure that the constraints are operationally equivalent. In P_1 the goal `max(X,Y,Z)` $\wedge$ `X≥Y` has the following computation:

$$\texttt{max(X,Y,Z)} \wedge \texttt{X}{\geq}\texttt{Y} \quad \mapsto_{P_1} \quad \texttt{Z=X} \wedge \texttt{X}{\geq}\texttt{Y}$$

In P_2 the initial state `max(X,Y,Z)` $\wedge$ `X≥Y` is also final state, i.e. no computation step is possible. On the other hand, in P_2 the goal `max(X,Y,Z)` $\wedge$ `X≤Y` has a non-trivial computation, while the goal is a final state in P_1.

The constraint `max` is "operationally stronger" in $P_1 \cup P_2$ than in each program alone, in the sense that more computation steps are possible.

3.2   Equivalence of Constraints

We now introduce a test to ensure that the definitions of the same CHR symbol in different programs are not only compatible, but indeed are operationally equivalent. We first restrict our attention to states that consist of one CHR symbol (only) being common to both programs.

Definition 7. Let c be a CHR symbol. A *c-state* is a state where all user-defined constraints have the same CHR symbol c.

Definition 8. Let c be a CHR symbol defined in two CHR programs P_1 and P_2. P_1 and P_2 are *operationally c-equivalent* if all c-states are P_1, P_2-joinable.

We give now a sufficient syntactic condition for operational c-equivalence of terminating CHR programs. As with confluence, we will try to find a finite subset of states, such that the P_1, P_2-joinability of the subset implies P_1, P_2-joinability of all c-states. As we will see, the similarities with confluence will not go much beyond that, mainly because in operational c-equivalence two different programs are involved.

The following example illustrates that, first of all, the critical pairs known from confluence (and compatibility) are not the right subset of states to ensure operational equivalence.

Example 4. Let P_1 be the following CHR program:

```
p(a) ⇔ s.
p(b) ⇔ r.
s∧r ⇔ true.
```

and let P_2 consist only of the first two rules.

It is not sufficient for operational equivalence to consider the critical pairs coming from the critical ancestor states p(a) and p(b): In P_1 the conjunction p(a) ∧ p(b) leads to true, but in P_2 the goal s∧r is a final state.

The example indicates that we not only have to consider c-states, but also those states that can be reached from c-states. Because even if these states can be reached in different programs due to confluence and even if they are final states, there may be contexts (extensions of the states by more constraints) in which the computation can be continued, and it can be continued in different ways in the different programs. The idea is to avoid this by making sure that also the user-defined constraints that occur in these states are operationally equivalent. For a given CHR symbol c one can safely approximate the set of all CHR symbols that appear in successor states to a c-state by looking at the bodies of rules with c in the head. Based on this idea we introduce the notion of dependency between CHR symbols.

Definition 9. A CHR symbol c *depends directly* on a CHR symbol c', if there is a rule in whose head c appears and in whose body c' appears. A CHR symbol c

depends on a CHR symbol c', if c depends directly on c', or if c depends directly on a CHR symbol d and d depends on c'.

The *dependency set* of a CHR symbol c is the the set of all CHR symbols that c depends on. Let C_{P_1}, C_{P_2} be the dependency sets of c with respect to P_1 and P_2, respectively. Each CHR symbol from $(C_{P_1} \cap C_{P_2}) \cup \{c\}$ is called a *c-dependent CHR symbol*.

Definition 10. Let P_1 and P_2 be CHR programs. The set of *c-critical states* is defined as follows:

$$\{H \wedge C \mid (H \odot C \mid B) \in P_1 \cup P_2, \text{ where } \odot \in \{ \Leftrightarrow, \Rightarrow \} \text{ and}$$
$$H \text{ contains only } c\text{-dependent CHR symbols}\}$$

The set of c-critical states is formed by taking the head and guards of all rules in whose heads c-dependent CHR symbols appear.

In the following we will show that P_1, P_2-joinability of these minimal states is sufficient for P_1, P_2-joinability of arbitrary c-states. Before we can state and prove the theorem, we need several lemmata.

The first lemma states that normalization has no influence on applicability of rules. We therefore can assume in the following that states are normalized except where otherwise noted.

Lemma 1. Let S and S' be states.

$$S \mapsto S' \text{ holds iff } \mathcal{N}(S) \mapsto S'.$$

Proof. Can be found in [AFM99].

The following lemma shows that a computation can be repeated in any context, i.e. with states in which constraints have been added.

Definition 11. The pair of constraints (G_1, G_2) is called *connected via* $\mathcal{V}$ iff all variables that appear both in G_1 and in G_2 also appear in $\mathcal{V}$.

Lemma 2. *[Monotonicity]* If (G, H) is connected via $\mathcal{V}'$ and $G_{\mathcal{V}} \mapsto^* G'_{\mathcal{V}}$, and $\mathcal{V} \subseteq \mathcal{V}'$, then

$$(G \wedge H)_{\mathcal{V}'} \mapsto^* \mathcal{N}((G' \wedge H)_{\mathcal{V}'}).$$

Proof. Can be found in [AFM99].

Next we show that a computation can be repeated in a state where variables have been instantiated according to some equations.

Definition 12. Let C be a conjunction of built-in constraints. Let H and H' be conjunctions of user-defined constraints with disjoint variables. $C[H{=}H']$ is obtained from C by replacing all variables x by the corresponding term t, where $CT \models H{=}H' \rightarrow (x{=}t)$ and x appears in H and t appears in H'.

Lemma 3. Let P be a CHR program and let R be a rule from P with head H and guard C. Let H' be a conjunction of user-defined constraints. Let $(H \wedge H{=}H' \wedge C)_V$ and $(H' \wedge C[H{=}H'])_{V'}$ be intial states, where H and H' have disjoint variables. If $CT \models \exists \bar{x}(H = H' \wedge C)$, where $\bar{x}$ are the variables appearing in H, and $(H \wedge H = H' \wedge C)_V \mapsto_P^* G_V$, then $(H' \wedge C[H{=}H'])_{V'} \mapsto_P^* G_{V'}$.

Proof. The claim holds due to the equality propagation property of the normalization function $\mathcal{N}$ and according to Lemma 1. A detailed proof can be found in [AF99]. □

Next we show that a computation can be repeated in a state where redundant built-in constraints have been removed.

Lemma 4. Let C be a conjunction of built-in constraints. If $H \wedge C \wedge G \mapsto^* S$ and $CT \models \forall (G_{built} \rightarrow C)$ then $H \wedge G \mapsto^* S$.

Proof. This is a consequence of the following claim: If $H \wedge C \wedge G \mapsto S$ and $CT \models \forall (G_{built} \rightarrow C)$ then $H \wedge G \mapsto S$. This claim can be proven by analyzing each kind of computation step [AF99]. □

Finally, the last Lemma refers to joinability of c-critical states.

Definition 13. Let $C = \bigwedge_{i=1}^{n} C_i$ be a conjunction of constraints, π a permutation on $[1, \ldots, n]$, where $0 \leq m \leq n$, then $\bigwedge_{i=1}^{m} C_{\pi_i}$ is a *subconjunction* of C.

Lemma 5. Let P_1 and P_2 be terminating CHR programs defining a CHR symbol c and let G be a goal. If all c-critical states are P_1, P_2-joinable and there is a rule in P_1 that is applicable to G_{user} then there is a rule in P_2 that is applicable to a subconjunction of G_{user}.

Proof. Can be found in [AF99]. □

We are now ready to state and prove the main theorem of the paper, that gives a sufficient condition for operational c-equivalence.

Theorem 2. Let c be a CHR symbol defined in two confluent and terminating CHR programs P_1 and P_2. Then the following holds: P_1 and P_2 are operationally c-equivalent if all c-critical states are P_1, P_2-joinable.

The proof can be found in [AF99].

We now give an example of two operationally equivalent user-defined constraints.

Example 5. The constraint sum(List,Sum) holds if Sum is the sum of elements of a given list List. The CHR symbol sum can be implemented in different ways. Let P_1 be the following CHR program:

```
sum([],Sum) ⟺ Sum=0.
sum([X|Xs],Sum) ⟺ sum(Xs,Sum1) ∧ Sum = Sum1 + X.
```

Let P_2 be a CHR program defining sum using an auxiliary CHR symbol sum1:

```
sum([],Sum) ⇔ Sum = 0.
sum([X|Xs],Sum) ⇔ sum1(X,Xs,Sum).
sum1(X,[],Sum) ⇔ Sum = X.
sum1(X,Xs,Sum) ⇔ sum(Xs,Sum1) ∧ Sum = Sum1 + X.
```

sum([],Sum) and sum([X|Xs],Sum) are the sum-critical states coming from P_1 and P_2. The sum-critical states are P_1, P_2-joinable:
For the sum-critical state sum([],Sum) the final state is Sum = 0 in both P_1 and P_2.
A computation of the sum-critical state sum([X|Xs],Sum) in P_1 proceeds as follows:
sum([X|Xs],Sum) $\mapsto_{P_1}$ sum(Xs,Sum1) ∧ Sum = Sum1 + X
A computation of the same initial state in P_2 results in the same final state:
sum([X|Xs],Sum) $\mapsto_{P_2}$ sum1(X,Xs,Sum) $\mapsto_{P_2}$ sum(Xs,Sum1) ∧ Sum = Sum1 + X
Since all sum-critical states are P_1, P_2-joinable, P_1 and P_2 are operationally sum-equivalent.

The next example shows why our joinability test for critical states is a sufficient, but not necessary condition for operational equivalence.

Example 6. Let P_1 be the following CHR program

```
p(X) ⇔ X>0 | q(X).
q(X) ⇔ X<0 | true.
```

and let P_2 be the following one

```
p(X) ⇔ X>0 | q(X).
q(X) ⇔ X<0 | false.
```

P_1 and P_2 are operationally p-equivalent, but the p-critical state $q(X) \land X < 0$ is not P_1, P_2-joinable.

The reason that we can only give a sufficient, but not necessary condition for operational c-equivalence in the general class of CHR programs is that the dependency relation between user-defined constraints only approximates the actual set of user-defined constraints that occur in states that can be reached from a c-state.

A sufficient and necessary condition: In practice, one is often interested to compare constraint solvers which have only one CHR symbol in common. In this case we can give a decidable, sufficient and necessary condition.

Theorem 3. Let c be the only CHR symbol defined in two confluent and terminating CHR programs P_1 and P_2. P_1 and P_2. Then the following holds: P_1 and P_2 are operationally c-equivalent iff all c-critical states are P_1, P_2-joinable.

Proof. "$\Longrightarrow$" direction: Let P_1 and P_2 be operationally c-equivalent. We prove by contradiction that all c-critical states are P_1, P_2-joinable: Assume that $H \wedge C$ is a c-critical state that is not P_1, P_2-joinable, where H is the head of a rule from $P_1 \cup P_2$ and C its guard.

Since P_1 and P_2 have only c in common, the constraint symbol c is the only c-dependent CHR symbol, i.e. $(C_{P_1} \cap C_{P_2}) \cup \{c\} = \{c\}$. Therefore $H \wedge C$ is a c-state. This contradicts the prerequisite that P_1 and P_2 are operationally c-equivalent.

"$\Longleftarrow$" direction: This is a special case of Theorem 2.

Theorem 3 gives a decidable characterization of the c-equivalent subset of terminating and confluent CHR programs: P_1, P_2-joinability of a given c-critical state is decidable for a terminating CHR program and there are only finitely many c-critical states.

Example 7. The user-defined constraint `range(X,Min,Max)` holds if `X` is between `Min` and `Max`.

Let P_1 be a CHR program defining `range` using the CHR symbol `max`:

```
max(X,Y,Z) ⇔ X<Y | Z=Y.
max(X,Y,Z) ⇔ X≥Y | Z=X.

range(X,Min,Max) ⇔ max(X,Min,X) ∧ max(X,Max,Max).
```

Let P_2 be a program defining `range` using the built-in constraint symbols $<, \leq$:

```
range(X,Min,Max) ⇔ Max<Min | false.
range(X,Min,Max) ⇔ Min≤Max | Min≤X ∧ X≤Max.
```

P_1 and P_2 are not operationally **range**-equivalent, since the **range**-critical state `range(X, Min, Max)` coming from P_1 is not P_1, P_2-joinable: `range(X, Min, Max)` can be reduced to `max(X,Min,X) ∧ max(X,Max,Max)` in P_1. In P_2 the answer for the state `range(X, Min, Max)` is the state itself, because no rule is applicable.

P_1 is "operationally stronger" than P_2, since the computation step in P_1 does not require that the values of `Max` and `Min` are known. This can be exemplified by the goal `range(5,6,Max)`. The inconsistency of the goal can be detected in P_1. In P_2, `range(5,6,Max)` is a final state.

3.3 Equivalence of Programs

Based on the condition presented above for the operational equivalence of constraints we can also give a decidable, sufficient and necessary condition for operational equivalence of terminating and confluent programs.

However, it is not enough to consider the union of all c-critical states for all common CHR symbols c, as the following example illustrates.

Example 8. Let P_1 be

```
p ⇔ s.
s∧q ⇔ true.
```

and let P_2 be

```
p ⇔ s.
s∧q ⇔ false.
```

P_1 and P_2 have three common CHR symbols, p, s and q. s and p are the p-dependent constraint symbols. There are no s-dependent CHR symbols except s itself. Analogously for q.

p is the only p-critical state. It is P_1, P_2-joinable. There is no s-critical state, since q is not a s-dependent CHR symbol. Analogously for q.

Hence all p-, s and q-critical states are P_1, P_2-joinable, but the programs are not operationally equivalent. s∧q leads in P_1 to true and with P_2 to false.

Still we can prove the operational equivalence of two programs by adapting the definition of c-critical states:

Definition 14. Let P_1 and P_2 be CHR programs. The *set of critical states of P_1 and P_2* is defined as follows:

$$\{H \wedge C \mid (H \odot C \mid B) \in P_1 \cup P_2, \text{ where } \odot \in \{\Leftrightarrow, \Rightarrow\}\}$$

Theorem 4. Let P_1 and P_2 be terminating and confluent programs. P_1 and P_2 are operationally equivalent iff all critical states of P_1 and P_2 are P_1, P_2-joinable.

Proof. Follows the proof of Theorem 3.

Relationships. Operational equivalence of two confluent and terminating CHR programs implies their compatibility, since operational equivalence of P_1 and P_2 implies the confluence of $P_1 \cup P_2$. The converse does not hold, as the programs of Example 3 show. Furthermore operational equivalence of two CHR programs implies the operational c-equivalence of all common constraints, since the set of critical states is a superset of the union of all sets of the c-critical states. The converse does not hold, as the programs of Example 8 show.

4 Conclusion

We introduced the notion of operational equivalence of CHR programs. We gave a decidable, sufficient and necessary syntactic condition for operational equivalence of terminating and confluent CHR programs. A decidable, sufficient and necessary condition for confluence of a terminating CHR programs was given in earlier work [AFM96,Abd97,AFM99]. We have also shown that an extension of the confluence notion to two programs, called compatibility, is not sufficient.

For practical reasons, we also investigated a notion of operational equivalence for user-defined constraints that are defined in different programs. We gave a sufficient syntactic condition for constraints defined in terminating and confluent CHR programs. For programs which have only one user-defined constraint in common, we were able to give a sufficient and necessary syntactic condition.

Future work aims to enlarge the class of CHR programs for which we can give a sufficient and necessary syntactic condition for operational equivalence. We also plan to investigate the relationship between operational equivalence and logical equivalence of CHR programs. The complication is that different programs have different signatures and are therefore hard to compare logically. Roughly, operational equivalence seems to imply logical equivalence (but not the other way round, see e.g. Example 3). Furthermore, operational equivalence together with completion [AF98] provide a good starting point for investigating partial evaluation, and program transformation in general, of constraint solvers.

Acknowledgements. We would like to thank Norbert Eisinger and Holger Meuss for useful comments on a preliminary version of this paper.

References

[Abd97] S. Abdennadher. Operational semantics and confluence of constraint propagation rules. In *Third International Conference on Principles and Practice of Constraint Programming, CP97*, LNCS 1330. Springer-Verlag, November 1997.

[ACM96] ACM. The constraint programming working group. Technical report, ACM-MIT SDRC Workshop, Report Outline, 1996.

[AF98] S. Abdennadher and T. Frühwirth. On completion of constraint handling rules. In *4th International Conference on Principles and Practice of Constraint Programming, CP98*, LNCS 1520. Springer-Verlag, 1998.

[AF99] S. Abdennadher and T. Frühwirth. Operational equivalence of constraint handling rules. Research report PMS-FB-1999-4, Computer Science Department, University of Munich, 1999.

[AFM96] S. Abdennadher, T. Frühwirth, and H. Meuss. On confluence of constraint handling rules. In *2nd International Conference on Principles and Practice of Constraint Programming, CP96*, LNCS 1118. Springer-Verlag, August 1996.

[AFM99] S. Abdennadher, T. Frühwirth, and H. Meuss. Confluence and semantics of constraint simplification rules. *Constraints Journal, Special Issue on the Second International Conference on Principles and Practice of Constraint Programming*, 4(2), May 1999.

[EGM98] S. Etalle, M. Gabrielli, and M. Meo. Unfold/fold transformations of CCP programs. In *9th International Conference on Concurrency Theory*, 1998. Corrected version.

[Frü98] T. Frühwirth. Theory and practice of constraint handling rules, special issue on constraint logic programming. *Journal of Logic Programming*, pages 95–138, October 1998.

[GLM95] M. Gabbrielli, G. Levi, and M. Chiara Meo. Observable behaviors and equivalences of logic programs. *Information and Computation*, 122(1):1–29, October 1995.

[Mah86] M. J. Maher. Equivalences of logic programs. In *Proceedings of Third International Conference on Logic Programming*, Berlin, 1986. Springer.

Automatic Generation of Constraint Propagation Algorithms for Small Finite Domains

Krzysztof R. Apt[1,2] and Eric Monfroy[1]

[1] CWI
P.O. Box 94079, 1090 GB Amsterdam, the Netherlands
{K.R.Apt,Eric.Monfroy}@cwi.nl
[2] University of Amsterdam, the Netherlands

Abstract. We study here constraint satisfaction problems that are based on pre-defined, explicitly given finite constraints. To solve them we propose a notion of *rule consistency* that can be expressed in terms of rules derived from the explicit representation of the initial constraints.

This notion of local consistency is weaker than arc consistency for constraints of arbitrary arity but coincides with it when all domains are unary or binary. For Boolean constraints rule consistency coincides with the closure under the well-known propagation rules for Boolean constraints.

By generalizing the format of the rules we obtain a characterization of arc consistency in terms of so-called inclusion rules. The advantage of rule consistency and this rule based characterization of the arc consistency is that the algorithms that enforce both notions can be automatically generated, as CHR rules. So these algorithms could be integrated into constraint logic programming systems such as ECL^{i}PS^e.

We illustrate the usefulness of this approach to constraint propagation by discussing the implementations of both algorithms and their use on various examples, including Boolean constraints, three valued logic of Kleene, constraints dealing with Waltz's language for describing polyhedreal scenes, and Allen's qualitative approach to temporal logic.

1 Introduction

In constraint programming the programming process is limited to a generation of constraints and a solution of the so obtained constraint satisfaction problems (CSP's) by general or domain dependent methods.

On the theoretical side several notions of local consistency, notably arc consistency for constraints of arbitrary arity, have been defined and various search methods have been proposed. On the practical side several constraint programming systems were designed and implemented that provide a substantial support for constraint programming. This support is usually provided in the form of specific built-in constructs that support search and constraint propagation. For example, the arc consistency is built in the ILOG Solver and is present in a library of the most recent version of ECL^{i}PS^e.

In this paper we study CSP's that are built out of predefined, explicitly given finite constraints. Such CSP's often arise in practice. Examples include Boolean constraints,

constraints dealing with Waltz's language for describing polyhedreal scenes, Allen's temporal logic, and constraints in any multi-valued logic.

In such situations it is natural to explore the structure of these explicitly given constraints first and to use this information to reduce the considered CSP to a simpler yet equivalent one. This information can be expressed in terms of rules. This leads to a local consistency notion called *rule consistency* that turns out to be weaker than arc consistency for constraints of arbitrary arity.

When the original domains are all unary or binary, rule consistency coincides with arc consistency. When additionally the predefined constraints are the truth tables of the Boolean connectives, these rules coincide with the well-known rules for Boolean constraints, sometimes called unit propagation rules (see, e.g. [3]). As a side effect, this shows that the unit propagation rules characterize arc consistency. Rule consistency is thus a generalization of the unit propagation to non-binary domains.

Next, we show that by generalizing the notion of rules to so-called inclusion rules, we obtain a notion of local consistency that coincides with arc consistency for constraints of arbitrary arity.

The advantage of the rule consistency and this rule based characterization of the arc consistency is that the algorithms that enforce them can be automatically generated and provided on the constraint programming language level. For example, the rules in question can be generated automatically and represented as rules of the CHR language of [6] that is part of the ECL^{i}PS^e system. (For a more recent and more complete overview of CHR see [5].)

Consequently, the implementations of the algorithms that achieve rule consistency and arc consistency for the considered CSP's are simply these automatically generated CHR programs. When combined with a labeling procedure such CHR programs constitute automatically derived decision procedures for these CSP's.

The availability of the algorithms that enforce rule consistency and arc consistency on the constraint programming language level further contributes to the automatization of the programming process within the constraint programming framework. In fact, in the case of such CSP's built out of predefined, explicitly given finite constraints the user does not need to write one's own CHR rules for the considered constraints and can simply adopt all or some of the rules that are automatically generated. In the final example of the paper we also show how using the rules and the inclusion rules, we can implement more powerful notions of local consistency.

Alternatively, the generated rules and inclusion rules could be fed into any of the generic *Chaotic Iteration* algorithms of [2] and made available in such systems as the ILOG solver. This would yield rule consistency and an alternative implementation of arc consistency.

The algorithms that for an explicitly given finite constraint generate the appropriate rules that characterize rule consistency and arc consistency have (unavoidably) a running time that is exponential in the number of constraint variables and consequently are in general impractical.

To test the usefulness of these algorithms for small finite domains we implemented them in ECL^{i}PS^e and successfully used them on several examples including the ones mentioned above. The fact that we could handle these examples shows that this approach is of practical value and can be used to automatically derive practical decision procedures for constraint satisfaction problems defined over small finite domains. Also it shows the usefulness of the CHR language for an automatic generation of constraint solvers and of decision procedures.

The rest of the paper is organized as follows. In the next section we formalize the concept that a CSP is built out of predefined constraints. Next, in Section 3 we introduce the notion of a rule, define the notion of rule consistency and discuss an algorithm that can be used to generate the minimal set of rules that characterize this notion of local consistency. Then, in Section 4 we compare rule consistency to arc consistency. In Section 5 we generalize the notion of rules to so-called inclusion rules and discuss an algorithm analogous to the one of Section 3. This entails a notion of local consistency that turns out to be equivalent to arc consistency. Finally, in Section 6 we discuss the implementation of both algorithms. They generate from an explicit representation of a finite constraint a set of CHR rules that characterize respectively rule consistency and arc consistency. We also illustrate the usefulness of these implementations by means of several examples. Due to lack of space all proofs are omitted.

2 CSP's Built out of Predefined Constraints

Consider a finite sequence of variables $X := x_1, \ldots, x_n$ where $n \geq 0$, with respective domains $\mathcal{D} := D_1, \ldots, D_n$ associated with them. So each variable x_i ranges over the domain D_i. By a *constraint* C on X we mean a subset of $D_1 \times \ldots \times D_n$. In this paper we consider only finite domains.

By a *constraint satisfaction problem*, in short CSP, we mean a finite sequence of variables X with respective domains $\mathcal{D}$, together with a finite set $\mathcal{C}$ of constraints, each on a subsequence of X. We write it as $\langle \mathcal{C} ; x_1 \in D_1, \ldots, x_n \in D_n \rangle$, where $X := x_1, \ldots, x_n$ and $\mathcal{D} := D_1, \ldots, D_n$.

Consider now an element $d := d_1, \ldots, d_n$ of $D_1 \times \ldots \times D_n$ and a subsequence $Y := x_{i_1}, \ldots, x_{i_\ell}$ of X. Then we denote by $d[Y]$ the sequence $d_{i_1}, \ldots, d_{i_\ell}$.

By a *solution* to $\langle \mathcal{C} ; x_1 \in D_1, \ldots, x_n \in D_n \rangle$ we mean an element $d \in D_1 \times \ldots \times D_n$ such that for each constraint $C \in \mathcal{C}$ on a sequence of variables X we have $d[X] \in C$. We call a CSP *consistent* if it has a solution.

Consider now a constraint C on a sequence of variables X. Given a subsequence Y of X by the *domain of* Y we mean the set of all tuples from $D_1 \times \ldots \times D_k$, where $D_1, \ldots, D_k$ are the respective domains of the variables from Y.

In the introduction we informally referred to the notion of a CSP "being built out of predefined, explicitly given finite constraints." Let us make now this concept formal. We need two auxiliary notions first, where in preparation for the next definition we already consider constraints together with the domains over which they are defined.

Definition 1.

- *Given a constraint* $C \subseteq D_1 \times \ldots \times D_n$ *and a permutation* π *of* $[1..n]$ *we denote by* C^π *the relation defined by*

$$(a_1, \ldots, a_n) \in C^\pi \text{ iff } (a_{\pi(1)}, \ldots, a_{\pi(n)}) \in C.$$

– *Given two constraints $C \subseteq D_1 \times \ldots \times D_n$ and $E \subseteq D'_1 \times \ldots \times D'_n$ we say that C is based on E if*
  - $D_i \subseteq D'_i$ *for* $i \in [1..n]$,
  - $C = E \cap (D_1 \times \ldots \times D_n)$. □

So the notion of "being based on" involves the domains of both constraints. If C is based on E, then C is the restriction of E to the domains over which C is defined.

Definition 2. *We assume that the "predefined constraints" are presented as a given in advance CSP $\mathcal{BASE}$ and the considered CSP $\mathcal{P}$ is related to $\mathcal{BASE}$ as follows:*

– *There is a mapping f that relates each constraint C of $\mathcal{P}$ to a constraint $f(C)$ of $\mathcal{BASE}$.*
– *Each constraint C of $\mathcal{P}$ is based on $f(C)^\pi$, where π is a permutation of $[1..n]$ and n the arity of C.*

We say then that $\mathcal{P}$ is based on $\mathcal{BASE}$. □

In the above definition the "permuted" relations R^π allow us to abstract from the variable ordering used in $\mathcal{BASE}$. The following example illustrates this notion.

Example 1. Consider the well-known full adder circuit. It is defined by the following formula:

$$add(i_1, i_2, i_3, o_1, o_2) \equiv$$
$$xor(i_1, i_2, x_1), and(i_1, i_2, a_1), xor(x_1, i_3, o_2), and(i_3, x_1, a_2), or(a_1, a_2, o_1),$$

where *and, xor* and *or* are defined in the expected way. We can view the original constraints as the following CSP:

$$\mathcal{BOOL} := \langle and(x, y, z), xor(x, y, z), or(x, y, z) \, ; \, x \in \{0, 1\}, y \in \{0, 1\}, z \in \{0, 1\} \rangle.$$

$\mathcal{BOOL}$ should be viewed just as an "inventory" of the predefined constraints and not as a CSP to be solved. Now, any query concerning the full adder can be viewed as a CSP based on $\mathcal{BOOL}$. For example, in Section 6 we shall consider the query $add(1, x, y, z, 0)$. It corresponds to the following CSP based on $\mathcal{BOOL}$:

$$\langle \, xor(i_1, i_2, x_1), \, and(i_1, i_2, a_1), \, xor(x_1, i_3, o_2), \, and(i_3, x_1, a_2), \, or(a_1, a_2, o_1) \, ;$$
$$i_1 \in \{1\}, i_2 \in \{0, 1\}, i_3 \in \{0, 1\}, o_1 \in \{0, 1\}, o_2 \in \{0\}, a_1 \in \{0, 1\}, a_2 \in \{0, 1\},$$
$$x_1 \in \{0, 1\} \, \rangle.$$

□

3 Rule Consistency

Our considerations crucially rely on the following notion of a rule.

Definition 3. *Consider a constraint C on a sequence of variables VAR, a subsequence X of VAR and a variable y of VAR not in X, a tuple s of elements from the domain of X and an element a from the domain of y. We call $X = s \to y \neq a$ a rule (for C).*

- *We say that $X = s \to y \neq a$ is valid (for C) if for every tuple $d \in C$ the equality $d[X] = s$ implies $d[y] \neq a$.*
- *We say that $X = s \to y \neq a$ is feasible (for C) if for some tuple $d \in C$ the equality $d[X] = s$ holds.*
- *Suppose that $X := x_1, \ldots, x_k$ and $s := s_1, \ldots, s_k$. We say that C is closed under the rule $X = s \to y \neq a$ if the fact that the domain of each variable x_j equals $\{s_j\}$ implies that a is not an element of the domain of the variable y.*

Further, given a sequence of variables Z that extends X and a tuple of elements u from the domain of Z that extends s, we say that the rule $Z = u \to y \neq a$ extends $X = s \to y \neq a$. We call a rule minimal if it is feasible and it does not properly extend a valid rule. □

Note that rules that are not feasible are trivially valid. To illustrate the introduced notions consider the following example.

Example 2. Take as a constraint the ternary relation that represents the conjunction $and(x, y, z)$. It can be viewed as the following relation:

$$\{(0,0,0), (0,1,0), (1,0,0), (1,1,1)\}.$$

In other words, we assume that each of the variables x, y, z has the domain $\{0,1\}$ and view $and(x, y, z)$ as the constraint on x, y, z that consists of the above four triples.

It is easy to see that the rule $x = 0 \to z \neq 1$ is valid for $and(x, y, z)$. Further, the rule $x = 0, y = 1 \to z \neq 1$ extends the rule $x = 0 \to z \neq 1$ and is also valid for $and(x, y, z)$. However, out of these two rules only $x = 0 \to z \neq 1$ is minimal.

Finally, both rules are feasible while the rules $x = 0, z = 1 \to y \neq 0$ and $x = 0, z = 1 \to y \neq 1$ are not feasible. □

Note that a rule that extends a valid rule is valid, as well. So validity extends "upwards".

Next, we introduce a notion of local consistency that is expressed in terms of rules.

Definition 4. *Consider a CSP P is based on a CSP $BASE$. Let C be a constraint of P on the variables $x_1, \ldots, x_n$ with respective non-empty domains $D_1, \ldots, D_n$. For some constraint $f(C)$ of $BASE$ and a permutation π we have $C = f(C)^\pi \cap (D_1 \times \ldots \times D_n)$.*

- *We call the constraint C rule consistent (w.r.t. $BASE$) if it is closed under all rules that are valid for $f(C)^\pi$.*
- *We call a CSP rule consistent (w.r.t. $BASE$) if all its constraints are rule consistent.*

□

In what follows we drop the reference to $BASE$ if it is clear from the context.

Example 3. Take as the base CSP

$$BASE := \langle and(x, y, z) \,;\, x \in \{0,1\}, y \in \{0,1\}, z \in \{0,1\}\rangle$$

and consider the following four CSP's based on it:

1. $\langle and(x, y, z) \; ; \; x \in \{0\}, y \in D_y, z \in \{0\}\rangle$,
2. $\langle and(x, y, z) \; ; \; x \in \{1\}, y \in D_y, z \in \{0, 1\}\rangle$,
3. $\langle and(x, y, z) \; ; \; x \in \{0, 1\}, y \in D_y, z \in \{1\}\rangle$,
4. $\langle and(x, y, z) \; ; \; x \in \{0\}, y \in D_y, z \in \{0, 1\}\rangle$,

where D_y is a subset of $\{0, 1\}$. We noted in Example 2 that the rule $x = 0 \rightarrow z \neq 1$ is valid for $and(x, y, z)$. In the first three CSP's its only constraint is closed under this rule, while in the fourth one not since 1 is present in the domain of z whereas the domain of x equals $\{0\}$. So the fourth CSP is not rule consistent. One can show that the first two CSP's are rule consistent, while the third one is not since it is not closed under the valid rule $z = 1 \rightarrow x \neq 0$.

The following observation is useful.

Note 1. Consider two constraints C and E such that $C \subseteq E$. Then C is closed under all valid rules for E iff it is closed under all minimal valid rules for E.

This allows us to confine our attention to minimal valid rules. We now introduce an algorithm that given a constraint generates the set of all minimal valid rules for it. We collect the generated rules in a list. We denote below the empty list by **empty** and the result of insertion of an element r into a list L by **insert**(r, L).

By an *assignment* to a sequence of variables X we mean here an element s from the domain of X such that for some $d \in C$ we have $d[X] = s$. Intuitively, if we represent the constraint C as a table with rows corresponding to the elements (tuples) of C and the columns corresponding to the variables of C, then an assignment to X is a tuple of elements that appears in some row in the columns that correspond to the variables of X. This algorithm has the following form where we assume that the considered constraint C is defined on a sequence of variables *VAR* of cardinality n.

RULES GENERATION algorithm

```
L := empty;
FOR i:= 0 TO n-1 DO
    FOR each subset X of VAR of cardinality i DO
        FOR each assignment s to X DO
            FOR each y in VAR-X DO
                FOR each element d from the domain of y DO
                    r := X = s → y ≠ d;
                    IF r is valid for C
                        and it does not extend an element of L
                    THEN insert (r, L)
```

The following result establishes correctness of this algorithm.

Theorem 1. *Given a constraint C the* RULES GENERATION *algorithm produces in L the set of all minimal valid rules for C.*

Note that because of the minimality property no rule in L extends another.

4 Relating Rule Consistency to Arc Consistency

To clarify the status of rule consistency we compare it now to the notion of arc consistency. This notion was introduced in [8] for binary relations and was extended to arbitrary relations in [9]. Let us recall the definition.

Definition 5.

- We call a constraint C on a sequence of variables X arc consistent *if for every variable x in X and an element a in its domain there exists $d \in C$ such that $a = d[x]$. That is, each element in each domain participates in a solution to C.*
- We call a CSP arc consistent *if all its constraints are arc consistent.* □

The following result relates for constraints of arbitrary arity arc consistency to rule consistency.

Theorem 2. *Consider a CSP $\mathcal{P}$ based on a CSP $\mathcal{BASE}$. If $\mathcal{P}$ is arc consistent then it is rule consistent w.r.t. $\mathcal{BASE}$.*

The converse implication does not hold in general as the following example shows.

Example 4. Take as the base the following CSP

$$\mathcal{BASE} := \langle C \; ; \; x \in \{0,1,2\}, y \in \{0,1,2\}\rangle$$

where the constraint C on x, y that equals the set $\{(0,1),(1,0),(2,2)\}$. So C can be viewed as the following relation:

$$\{(0,1),(1,0),(2,2)\}.$$

Next, take for D_1 the set $\{0,1\}$ and D_2 the set $\{0,1,2\}$. Then the CSP $\langle C \cap (D_1 \times D_2) \; ; \; x \in D_1, y \in D_2\rangle$, so $\langle\{(0,1),(1,0)\} \; ; \; x \in \{0,1\}, y \in \{0,1,2\}\rangle$ is based on $\mathcal{BASE}$ but is not arc consistent since the value 2 in the domain of y does not participate in any solution. Yet, it is easy to show that the only constraint of this CSP is closed under all rules that are valid for C. □

However, if each domain has at most two elements, then the notions of arc consistency and rule consistency coincide. More precisely, the following result holds.

Theorem 3. *Let $\mathcal{BASE}$ be a CSP each domain of which is unary or binary. Consider a CSP $\mathcal{P}$ based on $\mathcal{BASE}$. Then $\mathcal{P}$ is arc consistent iff it is rule consistent w.r.t. $\mathcal{BASE}$.*

5 Inclusion Rule Consistency

We saw in the previous section that the notion of rule consistency is weaker than that of arc consistency for constraints of arbitrary arity. We now show how by modifying the format of the rules we can achieve arc consistency. To this end we introduce the following notions.

Definition 6. *Consider a constraint C over a sequence variables VAR, a subsequence $X := x_1, \ldots, x_k$ of VAR and a variable y of VAR not in X, a tuple $S := S_1, \ldots, S_k$ of respective subsets of the domains of the variables from X and an element a from the domain of y.*

We call $X \subseteq S \to y \neq a$ an inclusion rule (for C). We say that $X \subseteq S \to y \neq a$ is valid (for C) if for every tuple $d \in C$ the fact that $d[x_i] \in S_i$ for $i \in [1..k]$ implies that $d[y] \neq a$ and that $X \subseteq S \to y \neq a$ is feasible (for C) if for some tuple $d \in C$ we have $d[x_i] \in S_i$ for $i \in [1..k]$.

Further, we say that a constraint C is closed under the inclusion rule $X \subseteq S \to y \neq a$ *if the fact that the domain of each variable x_j is included in S_j implies that a is not an element of the domain of the variable y.* □

By choosing in the above definition singleton sets $S_1, \ldots, S_k$ we see that the inclusion rules generalize the rules of Section 3. Note that inclusion rules that are not feasible are trivially valid.

In analogy to Definition 4 we now introduce the following notion.

Definition 7. *Consider a CSP $\mathcal{P}$ is based on a CSP $\mathcal{BASE}$. Let C be a constraint of $\mathcal{P}$ on the variables $x_1, \ldots, x_n$ with respective non-empty domains $D_1, \ldots, D_n$. For some constraint $f(C)$ of $\mathcal{BASE}$ and a permutation π we have $C = f(C)^\pi \cap (D_1 \times \ldots \times D_n)$.*

- *We call the constraint C* inclusion rule consistent *(w.r.t. $\mathcal{BASE}$) if it is closed under all inclusion rules that are valid for $f(C)^\pi$.*
- *We call a CSP* inclusion rule consistent *(w.r.t. $\mathcal{BASE}$) if all its constraints are inclusion rule consistent.* □

We now have the following result.

Theorem 4. *Consider a CSP $\mathcal{P}$ based on a CSP $\mathcal{BASE}$. Then $\mathcal{P}$ is arc consistent iff it is inclusion rule consistent w.r.t. $\mathcal{BASE}$.*

Example 4 shows that the notions of rule consistency and inclusion rule consistency do not coincide.

In Section 3 we introduced an algorithm that given a constraint C generated the set of all minimal rules valid for C. We now modify it to deal with the inclusion rules. First we need to adjust the notions of an extension and of minimality.

Definition 8. *Consider a constraint C on a sequence of variables VAR. Let $X := x_1, \ldots, x_k$ and $Z := z_1, \ldots, z_\ell$ be two subsequences of VAR such that Z extends X and y a variable of VAR not in Z. Further, let $S := S_1, \ldots, S_k$ be the sequence of respective subsets of the domains of the variables from X, $U := U_1, \ldots, U_\ell$ the sequence of respective subsets of the domains of the variables from Z, and a an element from the domain of y.*

We say that the inclusion rule $r_1 := Z \subseteq U \to y \neq a$ extends $r_2 := X \subseteq S \to y \neq a$ *if for each common variable of X and Z the corresponding element of U is a subset of the corresponding element of S. We call an inclusion rule* minimal *if it is feasible and it does not properly extend a valid inclusion rule.* □

To clarify these notions consider the following example.

Example 5. Consider a constraint on variables x, y, z, each with the domain $\{+, -, l, r\}$, that is defined by the following relation:

$$\{(+, +, +), (-, -, -), (l, r, -), (-, l, r), (r, -, l)\}$$

This constraint is the so-called *fork* junction in the language of [10] for describing polyhedreal scenes. Note that the following three inclusion rules

$$r_1 := x \subseteq \{+, -\} \to z \neq l,$$

$$r_2 := x \subseteq \{+\} \to z \neq l,$$

and

$$r_3 := x \subseteq \{-\}, y \subseteq \{l\} \to z \neq l$$

are all valid. Then the inclusion rules r_2 and r_3 extend r_1 while the inclusion rule r_1 extends neither r_2 nor r_1. Further, the inclusion rules r_2 and r_3 are incomparable in the sense that none extends the other. $\qquad\square$

The following counterpart of Note 1 holds.

Note 2. Consider two constraints C and E such that $C \subseteq E$. Then C is closed under all valid inclusion rules for E iff it is closed under all minimal valid inclusion rules for E.

As in Section 3 we now provide an algorithm that given a constraint generates the set of all minimal valid inclusion rules. We assume here that the considered constraint C is defined on a sequence of variables *VAR* of cardinality n.

Instead of assignments that are used in the RULES GENERATION algorithm we now need a slightly different notion. To define it for each variable x from *VAR* we denote the set $\{d[x] \mid d \in C\}$ by $C[x]$. By a *weak assignment* to a sequence of variables $X := x_1, \ldots, x_k$ we mean here a sequence $S_1, \ldots, S_k$ of subsets of, respectively, $C[x_1], \ldots, C[x_k]$ such that some $d \in C$ exists such that $d[x_i] \in S_i$ for each $i \in [1..k]$.

Intuitively, if we represent the constraint C as a table with rows corresponding to the elements of C and the columns corresponding to the variables of C and we view each column as a set of elements, then a weak assignment to X is a tuple of subsets of the columns that correspond to the variables of X that "shares" an assignment.

In the algorithm below the weak assignments to a fixed sequence of variables are considered in decreasing order in the sense that if the weak assignments $S_1, \ldots, S_k$ and $U_1, \ldots, U_k$ are such that for $i \in [1..k]$ we have $U_i \subseteq S_i$, then $S_1, \ldots, S_k$ is considered first.

INCLUSION RULES GENERATION algorithm

```
L := empty;
FOR i:= 0 TO n-1 DO
    FOR each subset X of VAR of cardinality i DO
        FOR each weak assignment S to X in decreasing order DO
            FOR each y in VAR-X DO
                FOR each element d from the domain of y DO
```

```
r := X ⊆ S → y ≠ d;
IF r is valid for C
      and it does not extend an element of L
   THEN insert(r, L)
```

The following result establishes correctness of this algorithm.

Theorem 5. *Given a constraint C the* INCLUSION RULES GENERATION *algorithm produces in L the set of all minimal valid inclusion rules for C.*

6 Applications

In this section we discuss the implemention of the RULES GENERATION and INCLUSION RULES GENERATION algorithms and discuss their use on selected domains.

6.1 Constraint Handling Rules (CHR)

In order to validate our approach we have realized in the Prolog platform ECL^{i}PS^e a prototype implementation of both the RULES GENERATION algorithm and the INCLUSION RULES GENERATION algorithm. These implementations generate CHR rules that deal with finite domain variables using an ECL^{i}PS^e library.

Constraint Handling Rules (CHR) of [6] is a declarative language that allows one to write guarded rules for rewriting constraints. These rules are repeatedly applied until a fixpoint is reached. The rule applications have a precedence over the usual resolution step of logic programming.

CHR provides two types of rules: simplification rules that replace a constraint by a simpler one, and propagation rules that add new constraints.

Our rules and inclusion rules can be modelled by means of propagation rules. To illustrate this point consider some constraint *cons* on three variables, A, B, C, each with the domain $\{0, 1, 2\}$.

The RULES GENERATION algorithm generates rules such as $(A, C) = (0, 1) \to B \neq 2$. This rule is translated into a CHR rule of the form: `cons(0,B,1) ==> B##2`. Now, when a constraint in the program query matches `cons(0,B,1)`, this rule is fired and the value 2 is removed from the domain of the variable B.

In turn, the INCLUSION RULES GENERATION algorithm generates rules such as $(A, C) \subseteq (\{0\}, \{1, 2\}) \to B \neq 2$. This rule is translated into the CHR rule

```
cons(0,B,C) ==>in(C,[1,2]) | B##2
```

where the in predicate is defined by

```
in(X,L):- dom(X,D), subset(D,L).
```

So `in(X,L)` holds if the current domain of the variable X (yielded by the built-in dom of ECL^{i}PS^e) is included in the list L.

Now, when a constraint matches `cons(0,B,C)` *and* the current domain of the variable C is included in [1,2], the value 2 is removed from the domain of B. So for both types of rules we achieve the desired effect.

In the examples below we combine the rules with the same premise into one rule in an obvious way and present these rules in the CHR syntax.

6.2 Generating the rules

We begin by discussing the generation of rules and inclusion rules for some selected domains. The times given refer to an implementation ran on a Silicon Graphics O2 with 64 Mbytes of memory and a 180 MHZ processor.

Boolean constraints As the first example consider the Boolean constraints, for example the conjunction constraint and(X,Y,Z) of Example 2. The RULES GENERATION algorithm generated in 0.02 seconds the following six rules:

```
and(1,1,X)  ==>  X##0.
and(X,0,Y)  ==>  Y##1.
and(0,X,Y)  ==>  Y##1.
and(X,Y,1)  ==>  X##0,Y##0.
and(1,X,0)  ==>  X##1.
and(X,1,0)  ==>  X##1.
```

Because the domains are here binary we can replace the conclusions of the form U ## 0 by U = 1 and U ## 1 by U = 0. These become then the well-known rules that can be found in [5, page 113].

In this case, by virtue of Theorem 3, the notions of rule and arc consistency coincide, so the above six rules characterize the arc consistency of the and constraint. Our implementations of the RULES GENERATION and the INCLUSION RULES GENERATION algorithms yield here the same rules.

Three valued logics Next, consider the three valued logic of [7, page 334] that consists of three values, t (true), f (false) and u (unknown). We only consider here the crucial equivalence relation ≡ defined by the truth table

≡	t f u
t	t f u
f	f t u
u	u u u

that determines a ternary constraint with nine triples. We obtain for it 20 rules and 26 inclusion rules. Typical examples are

```
equiv(X,Y,f)  ==>  X##u,Y##u.
```
and
```
equiv(t,X,Y)  ==>  in(Y,[f, u])  |  X##t.
```

Waltz' language for describing polyhedreal scenes Waltz' language consists of four constraints. One of them, the fork junction was already mentioned in Example 5. The RULES GENERATION algorithm generated for it 12 rules and the INCLUSION RULES GENERATION algorithm 24 inclusion rules.

Another constraint, the so-called T junction, is defined by the following relation:

$$\{(r,l,+),(r,l,-),(r,l,r),(r,l,l)\}.$$

In this case the RULES GENERATION algorithm and the INCLUSION RULES GENERATION algorithm both generate the same output that consists of just one rule:

```
t(X,Y,Z) ==> X##'l',X##'-',X##'+',Y##'r',Y##'-',Y##'+'.
```

So this rule characterizes both rule consistency and arc consistency for the CSP's based on the T junction.

For the other two constraints, the L junction and the arrow junction, the generation of the rules and inclusion rules is equally straightforward.

6.3 Using the rules

Next, we show by means of some examples how the generated rules can be used to reduce or to solve specific queries. Also, we show how using compound constraints we can achieve local consistency notions that are stronger than arc consistency for constraints of arbitrary arity.

Waltz' language for describing polyhedreal scenes The following predicate describes the impossible object given in Figure 12.18 of [11, page 262]:

```
imp(AF,AI,AB,IJ,IH,JH,GH,GC,GE,EF,ED,CD,CB):-
    S1=[AF,AI,AB,IJ,IH,JH,GH,GC,GE,EF,ED,CD,CB],
    S2=[FA,IA,BA,JI,HI,HJ,HG,CG,EG,FE,DE,DC,BC],
    append(S1,S2,S), S :: [+,-,l,r],

    arrow(AF,AB,AI), l(BC,BA), arrow(CB,CD,CG),
    l(DE,DC), arrow(ED,EG,EF), l(FA,FE), fork(GH,GC,GE),
    arrow(HG,HI,HJ), fork(IA,IJ,IH), l(JH,JI),

    line(AF,FA), line(AB,BA), line(AI,IA), line(IJ,JI),
    line(IH,HI), line(JH,HJ), line(GH,HG), line(FE,EF),
    line(GE,EG), line(GC,CG), line(DC,CD), line(ED,DE),
    line(BC,CB).
```

where the supplementary constraint `line` is defined by the following relation:

$$\{(+,+),(-,-),(l,r),(r,l)\}$$

When using the rules obtained by the RULES GENERATION algorithm and associated with the `fork`, `arrow`, `t`, `l`, and `line` constraints, the query

```
imp(AF,AI,AB,IJ,IH,JH,GH,GC,GE,EF,ED,CD,CB)
```

reduces in 0.009 seconds the variable domains to $AF \in [+,-,\ 1], AI \in [+,-],$
$AB \in [+,-,r], IJ \in [+,-,l,r], IH \in [+,-,l,r], JH \in [+,-,l,r],$
$GH \in [+,-,l,r], GC \in [+,-,l,r], GE \in [+,-,l,r], EF \in [+,-],$
$ED \in [+,-,l], CD \in [+,-,r],$ and $CB \in [+,-,l].$

But some constraints remain unsolved, so we need to add a labeling mechanism to prove the inconsistency of the problem. On the other hand, when using the inclusion rules, the inconsistency is detected without any labeling in 0.06 seconds.

In the well-known example of the cube given in Figure 12.15 of [11, page 260] the inclusion rules are also more powerful than the rules and both sets of rules reduce the problem but in both cases labeling is needed to produce all four solutions.

Temporal reasoning In [1] approach to temporal reasoning the entities are intervals and the relations are temporal binary relations between them. [1] found that there are 13 possible temporal relations between a pair of events, namely before, during, overlaps, meets, starts, finishes, the symmetric relations of these six relations and equal. We denote these 13 relations respectively by b, d, o, m, s, f, b-, d-, o-, m-, s-, f-, e and their set by TEMP.

Consider now three events, A, B and C and suppose that we know the temporal relations between the pairs A and B, and B and C. The question is what is the temporal relation between A and C. To answer it [1] provided a 13 × 13 table. This table determines a ternary constraint between a triple of events, A, B and C that we denote by tr. For example,

$$(\texttt{overlaps}, \texttt{before}, \texttt{before}) \in \texttt{tr}$$

since A overlaps B and B is before C implies that A is before C.

Using this table, the RULE GENERATION algorithm produced for the constraint tr 498 rules in 31.16 seconds.

We tried this set of rules to solve the following problem from [1]: "John was not in the room when I touched the switch to turn on the light.". We have here three events: S, the time of touching the switch; L, the time the light was on; and J, the time that John was in the room. Further, we have two relations: R1 between L and S, and R2 between S and J. This problem is translated into the CSP ⟨tr ; R1 ∈ [o-,m-], R2 ∈ [b,m,b-,m-], R3 ∈ TEMP⟩, where tr is the above constraint on the variables R1, R2, R3.

To infer the relation R3 between L and J we can use the following query[1]:

```
R1::[o-,m-], R2::[b,m,b-,m-],
R3::[b,d,o,m,s,f,b-,d-,o-,m-,s-,f-,e],
tr(R1,R2,R3), labeling([R1,R2,R3]).
```

We then obtain the following solutions in 0.06 seconds: (R1,R2,R3) ∈ { (m-,b,b), (m-,b,d-), (m-,b,f-), (m-,b,m), (m-,b,o), (m-,b-,b-), (m-,m,e), (m-,m,s), (m-,m,s-), (m-,m-,b-), (o-,b,b), (o-,b,d-), (o-,b,f-), (o-,b,m), (o-,b,o), (o-,b-,b-), (o-,m,d-), (o-,m,f-), (o-,m,o), (o-,m-,b-)}.

To carry on (as in [1]), we now complete the problem with: "But John was in the room later while the light went out.". This is translated into: "L overlaps, starts, or is during J", i.e., R3 ∈ [o,s,d].

We now run the following query:

```
R1::[o-,m-], R2::[b,m,b-,m-], R3::[o,s,d],
tr(R1,R2,R3), labeling([R1,R2,R3]).
```

and obtain four solutions in 0.04 seconds:
(R1,R2,R3) ∈ { (m-,b,o), (m-,m,s), (o-,b,o), (o-,m,o)}.

---

[1] Since no variable is instantiated, we need to perform labeling to effectively apply the rules.

Full adder This final example illustrates how we can use the rules and the inclusion rules to implement more powerful notions of local consistency. The already discussed in Example 1 full adder circuit can be defined by the following constraint logic program (see, e.g., [5]) that uses the Boolean constraints and, xor and or:

```
add(I1,I2,I3,O1,O2):-
        [I1,I2,I3,O1,O2,A1,A2,X1]:: 0..1,
        xor(I1,I2,X1), and(I1,I2,A1), xor(X1,I3,O2),
        and(I3,X1,A2), or(A1,A2,O1).
```

The query add(I1,I2,I3,O1,O2) followed by a labeling mechanism generates the explicit definition (truth table) of the full_adder constraint with eight entries such as full_adder(1,0,1,1,0).

We can now generate rules and inclusion rules for the compound constraint (here the full_adder constraint) that is defined by means of some basic constraints (here the and, or and xor constraints). These rules refer to the compound constraint and allow us to reason about it directly instead of by using the rules that deal with the basic constraints.

In the case of the full_adder constraint the RULES GENERATION algorithm generated 52 rules in 0.27 seconds. The constraint propagation carried out by means of these rules is more powerful than the one carried out by means of the rules generated for the and, or and xor constraints.

For example, the query [X,Y,Z]::[0,1], full_adder(1,X,Y,Z,0) reduces Z to 1 whereas the query [X,Y,Z]::[0,1], add(1,X,Y,Z,0) does not reduce Z at all.

This shows that the rule consistency for a compound constraint defined by means of the basic constraints is in general stronger than the rule consistency for the basic constraints treated separately. In fact, in the above case the rules for the full_adder constraint yield the relational (1,5)-consistency notion of [4], whereas by virtue of Theorem 3, the rules for the and, or and xor constraints yield a weaker notion of arc consistency.

7 Conclusions

The aim of this paper was to show that constraint satisfaction problems built out of explicitly given constraints defined over small finite domains can be often solved by means of automatically generated constraint propagation algorithms.

We argued that such CSP's often arise in practice and consequently the methods here developed can be of practical use. Currently we are investigating how the approach of this paper can be applied to a study of various decision problems concerning specific multi-valued logics and how this in turn could be used for an analysis of digital circuits. Other applications we are now studying involve non-linear constraints over small finite domains and the analysis of polyhedreal scenes in presence of shadows (see [10]).

The introduced notion of rule consistency is weaker than arc consistency and can be in some circumstances the more appropriate one to use. For example, for the case of temporal reasoning considered in the last section we easily generated all 498 rules that enforce rule consistency whereas 24 hours turned out not be enough to generate the inclusion rules that enforce arc consistency.

Finally, the notions of rule consistency and inclusion rule consistency could be parametrized by the desired maximal number of variables used in the rule premises. Such parametrized versions of these notions could be useful when dealing with constraints involving a large number of variables. Both the RULES GENERATION algorithm and the INCLUSION RULES GENERATION algorithm and their implementations can be trivially adapted to such parametrized notions.

The approach proposed in this paper could be easily integrated into constraint logic programming systems such as ECL^{i}PS^e. This could be done by providing an automatic constraint propagation by means of the rules or the inclusion rules for flagged predicates that are defined by a list of ground facts, much in the same way as now constraint propagation for linear constraints over finite systems is automatically provided.

Acknowledgements

We would like to thank Thom Frühwirth, Andrea Schaerf and the anonymous referees for useful suggestions concerning this paper.

References

1. J.F. Allen. Maintaining knowledge about temporal intervals. *Communications of ACM*, 26(11):832–843, 1983.
2. K. R. Apt. The essence of constraint propagation. *Theoretical Computer Science*, 221(1–2):179–210, 1999. Available via http://xxx.lanl.gov/archive/cs/.
3. M. Dalal. Efficient Propositional Constraint Propagation. In *Proceedings of the 10th National Conference on Artificial Intelligence, AAAI'92*, pages 409–414, 1992. San Jose, California.
4. R. Dechter and P. van Beek. Local and global relational consistency. *Theoretical Computer Science*, 173(1):283–308, 20 February 1997.
5. T. Frühwirth. Theory and practice of constraint handling rules. *Journal of Logic Programming*, 37(1–3):95–138, October 1998. Special Issue on Constraint Logic Programming (P. Stuckey and K. Marriot, Eds.).
6. Thom Frühwirth. Constraint Handling Rules. In Andreas Podelski, editor, *Constraint Programming: Basics and Trends*, LNCS 910, pages 90–107. Springer-Verlag, 1995. (Châtillon-sur-Seine Spring School, France, May 1994).
7. S. C. Kleene. *Introduction to Metamathematics*. van Nostrand, New York, 1952.
8. A. Mackworth. Consistency in networks of relations. *Artificial Intelligence*, 8(1):99–118, 1977.
9. R. Mohr and G. Masini. Good old discrete relaxation. In Y. Kodratoff, editor, *Proceedings of the 8th European Conference on Artificial Intelligence (ECAI)*, pages 651–656. Pitman Publishers, 1988.
10. D. L. Waltz. Generating semantic descriptions from drawings of scenes with shadows. In P. H. Winston, editor, *The Psychology of Computer Vision*. McGraw Hill, 1975.
11. P.H. Winston. *Artificial Intelligence*. Addison-Wesley, Reading, Massachusetts, third edition, 1992.

Excluding Symmetries in Constraint-Based Search

Rolf Backofen and Sebastian Will

Institut für Informatik, LMU München
Oettingenstraße 67, D-80538 München

Abstract. We introduce a new method for excluding symmetries in constraint based search. To our knowledge, it is the first declarative method that can be applied to *arbitrary* symmetries. Our method is based on the notion of symmetric constraints, which are used in our modification of a general constraint based search algorithm. The method does not influence the search strategy. Furthermore, it can be used with either the full set of symmetries, or with an subset of all symmetries.

We proof correctness, completeness and symmetry exclusion properties of our method. We then show how to apply the method in the special case of geometric symmetries (rotations and reflections) and permutation symmetries. Furthermore, we give results from practical applications.

1 Introduction

In many search problems, one is faced with the existence of symmetries. Symmetries give rise to many different solutions found by the search procedure, which are all considered to be "similar". Often, one is not interested in also getting all the symmetric solutions to every found solution. Without exclusion of symmetries, whenever a solution is found or proven to be inconsistent with the search problem, the search algorithm still considers all symmetric solutions. Those symmetries will then give rise to an (often exponential) amplification of the search space. Hence, symmetry exclusion promises to efficiently prune the search tree.

E.g., consider constraint problems, where finite domain variables have a geometric interpretation such as in the N-queens problem or the square-tiling problem (where set of squares of given sizes must fit exactly into a fixed square). A more complex, real-world problem is the lattice protein structure prediction problem. In [2], it is shown how to find solutions for this problem using constraint programming techniques. In this case, different solutions are symmetric if they can be generated using reflections or rotations. In other problems, symmetric solutions can be generated by performing permutations on variables valuations (like in the map coloring (or graph coloring) problem).

In the following, we consider search problems that stems from constraint satisfaction problems (CSP). A common approach is to transform (problem specifically) a CSP C_1 into a CSP C_2 that excludes at least some of the symmetries of the original problem C_1.

Unfortunately, symmetry exclusion was often not straightforward to implement. Even then, it had to be redesigned for every special problem or enumeration strategy. This leaded to an inflexibility in the program structure once it was introduced. Thus, the widespread usage of symmetry exclusion was strongly hindered by its complexity. Often symmetry exclusion was not done at all or only for a small set of symmetries. In other cases, where symmetry exclusion was implemented it distracted the programmers attention from more important tasks.

In this paper, we will present a new approach for symmetry exclusion, which works by modifying the search algorithm. The technique of modifying the search algorithm to exclude symmetries was already used in the literature. In contrast to the known approaches, our approach is (to our knowledge) the first declarative method that can be applied to *arbitrary* symmetries that can be defined declaratively. Furthermore, it does not restrict the search strategy (i.e., the symmetry exclusion can be done independently of the search strategy). This is important since in many constraint problems, major part of the knowledge of the problem is encoded in the search strategy.

We have implemented our method in the concurrent constraint programming language Oz [10] using the programmable search engine described in [9]. But the method can be implemented in any system that handles implication (via entailment), and allows to modify the search procedure such that additional constraints are added in one branch of a branching step.

Related Work Previous work on symmetry exclusion by modifying the search algorithm handled only restricted forms of symmetries. In [7], the notion of interchangeable values is introduced. Two values a and b are interchangeable for a variable V iff for every solution that maps V to a, the corresponding valuation that maps V to b is also a solution.

The method in [3] handles only permutations of domain values in the case of binary constraints (thus, e.g., the all-distinct constraint has to be translated into binary inequalities, which implies that efficient propagation methods for all-distinct cannot be applied). Furthermore, it works by introducing a symmetry excluding form of constraint propagation, which is a modified form of domain propagation (thus, the method cannot make use of interval propagation).

[1] and [4] consider only propositional calculus. The symmetries there are permutations of Boolean variables. These methods do not apply to general constraint satisfaction problems.

The symmetry exclusion algorithm presented in [8] is essentially an implementation and application of our method to solve practical problems, which will be compared in greater detail in Section 3.

An example of a symmetry exclusion method that works by a (not problem specific) transformation of the constraint satisfaction problem is [5]. They introduce symmetry breaking predicates, which are true only for the smallest solution within an equivalence class (where the ordering is fixed in advance). Thus, if the search strategy encounters a non-minimal (according to the pre-fixed ordering) solution first, then it will be excluded by the symmetry breaking predicates. This implies that not every search strategy is possible given the pre-fixed ordering.

In contrast, there is no prefixed ordering in which symmetrical solutions will be excluded by our method. This implies that we respect used-defined search strategies as much as possible.[1]

Overview of the paper We start with an introductory example explaining the basic ideas of our method. After some preliminaries, we present the formal definition as wells as completeness and correctness proofs in Section 3. Additionally, we show that our method guarantees to exclude all specified symmetries. The proofs indicate that a subset of all symmetries can be enough to exclude the complete symmetry group. In Section 4, we treat geometric symmetries. We show how to define symmetric constraints and present the results of applying the problem to a complex problem. In Section 5, we consider symmetries which are generated by permuting the values of the variables. E.g., such symmetries occur in the graph coloring problem. We proof, that in this case, it is sufficient to exclude the subset of transposition in order to exclude all permutations. Furthermore, we present the results of applying the method to random instances of graph coloring.

Introductory Example We start with a simple example to explain the main concepts. Consider the N-queens problem, where we have an array $Q[1..N]$, whose elements can take values from $1..N$. $Q[i] = j$ states that there is a queen at position (i, j). Now consider the symmetry corresponding to the reflection at the axis $y = \frac{N}{2}$, which is parallel to the x-axis (in the sequel denoted by Rx). Clearly, for every solution of the N-queens, the the Rx-symmetric version is also a solution of N-queens. Hence, we want to exclude these symmetric solutions.

To use our method, we have first to introduce symmetric versions of the constraints which are inserted by the search procedure. One kind of constraint is $Q[i] = j$. If we have any distribution of queens on the board satisfying $Q[i] = j$, then the Rx-symmetric distribution will satisfy $Q[i] = N - j$. Hence, the constraint $Q[i] = N - j$ is the Rx-symmetric version of the constraint $Q[i] = j$. Similarly, we get that the Rx-symmetric constraint of $Q[i] \leq j$ is $Q[i] \geq N - j$. In the following, we write $S^{Rx}(c)$ to denote the Rx-symmetric constraint to c.

Our method works by adding additional constraints at the right branches of the search tree, which exclude the symmetric solutions that are encountered in the right branch. Consider the following search tree for the 10-queens problem, where we indicate the constraints added by symmetry exclusion via frames:

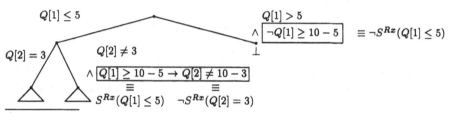

---

[1] Clearly, if the search strategy depends on the constraint store, then any method of symmetry exclusion that prunes the search tree must influence the way solutions are encountered (since the constraint store is changed by the symmetry exclusion).

This can be interpreted intuitively as follows. In the topmost branch, if we search for a solution in the right branch satisfying $Q[1] > 5$, then the Rx-symmetric solution will satisfy $Q[1] < 5$. Hence, the symmetric solution was already encountered earlier in the left branch (under $Q[1] \leq 5$), which is the reason that we can close the topmost right branch. For the second right branch labeled $Q[2] \neq 3$, we want again to exclude the Rx-symmetric solutions found in the right branch. Hence, we would like to add the constraint $\neg S^{Rx}(Q[2] = 3)$ to the right branch. But this would exclude too many solutions. The prerequisite of the Rx-symmetric solution to be found in the right branch is that both the solution and its Rx-symmetric version satisfies $Q[1] \leq 5$. Now the only solutions that satisfying this conditions are solutions that satisfy $Q[1] = 5$. Hence, we can add $\neg S^{Rx}(Q[2] = 3)$ *under the condition* that $Q[1] = 5$. But this is exactly the effect that we achieve by adding $(Q[1] \geq 10 - 5) \rightarrow (Q[2] \neq 10 - 3)$ at the second right branch (since the constraint store contains already $Q[1] \leq 5$).

2 Preliminaries

We fix a first-order signature Σ including the equality $\doteq$ with a set of variables $\mathcal{V}$. Constraints are literals, and constraint formulae are quantifier-free formulae over Σ. We identify $t \doteq t'$ with $t' \doteq t$. $\mathcal{C}$ denotes the set of all constraints. A set of constraints $C \subseteq \mathcal{C}$ is interpreted as the conjunction of the constraints contained in C, and we will freely mix set notation and conjunction. The set of free variables of C is denoted by $\mathcal{V}(C)$.

We fix a standard interpretation $\mathcal{A}$ with domain $\mathcal{D}^{\mathcal{A}}$, which describes our constraint theory. In the following, we assume a fixed constraint set C_{Pr} describing the problem to be solved. An *assignment* α in $\mathcal{A}$ is a partial function $\alpha : \mathcal{V} \to \mathcal{D}^{\mathcal{A}}$. We say that an (possible partial) assignment α *satisfies* ϕ (short $\alpha \models \phi$) if there is a total assignment $\alpha' \supseteq \alpha$ with $\mathcal{A}, \alpha' \models \phi$. We write $\phi \models \psi$ if for every α we have $\alpha \models \phi \to \psi$. A constraint set C *(syntactically) determines* a set of variables $\mathcal{X}$ to an assignment α iff for all $x \in \mathcal{X}$ exists a t such that $x \doteq t \in C$ and $\alpha(x) = \alpha(t)$.

In many problems, one is interested in only a subset of all variables, whose valuations uniquely determine the valuation of the other (auxiliary) variables. This is captured by the definition of solution variables.

Definition 1 (Solution Variables). *Let $\mathcal{X} \subseteq \mathcal{V}$ be a set of variables. $\mathcal{X}$ is a solution variables set for C if*

$$\forall \alpha \left[(\mathrm{dom}(\alpha) = \mathcal{X} \wedge \alpha \models C) \Rightarrow (\exists! \alpha' (\alpha \subseteq \alpha' \wedge \mathrm{dom}(\alpha') = \mathcal{V}(C) \wedge \alpha' \models C)) \right],$$

where $\exists! \alpha \phi(\alpha)$ ('exists a unique α satisfying $\phi(\alpha)$') is short for $\exists \alpha (\phi(\alpha) \wedge \forall \alpha' : \phi(\alpha') \Rightarrow \alpha = \alpha')$. For a solution variables set $\mathcal{X}$, we say that α is a $\mathcal{X}$-solution for C if $\mathrm{dom}(\alpha) = \mathcal{X}$ and $\alpha \models C$. With $\|C\|^{\mathcal{X}}$ we denote the set of $\mathcal{X}$-solutions of C.

In the following, we fix $\mathcal{X}$. Hence, we use the term 'solution' as short for '$\mathcal{X}$-solution for C', and we write $\|C\|$ as short for $\|C\|^{\mathcal{X}}$.

Definition 2 (Symmetry). *A symmetry s for C_{Pr} is a bijective function*

$$s : \|C_{\mathrm{Pr}}\| \rightarrow \|C_{\mathrm{Pr}}\|.$$

A symmetry set S for C_{Pr} is a set of symmetries operating on $\|C_{\mathrm{Pr}}\|$. A symmetry group S is a symmetry set for C_{Pr} which is a group.

Note that for every symmetry s for C_{Pr}, also s^{-1} is a symmetry for C_{Pr}. We denote the identity function on $\|C_{\mathrm{Pr}}\|$ with $\mathrm{id}_{C_{\mathrm{Pr}}}$ (which is a symmetry by definition). Clearly, the set of all symmetries for C_{Pr} is a group. But many cases, we do not want to consider all symmetries, since either there are too many of them, or some of them do not have an intuitive characterization. In this case, we consider only a subset of all symmetries, which may not be a group.

3 Symmetry Excluding Search Trees

Now we have to define the notion of a search tree as we need it for the symmetry exclusion. We describe the effects of applying a constraint solver to a constraint set C by a function $P(C)$, which returns the closure of C under constraint propagation. Clearly, we have $P(C) \models C$.

Usually, a search tree is a labeled tree, where the nodes are labeled with the constraints in the constraint store, and the edges are labled by constraints or negated constraints. A single node v is of the form

$$C_{\mathrm{store}}$$
$$\overset{c}{\diagup} \quad \overset{\neg c}{\diagdown}$$
$$P(C_{\mathrm{store}} \wedge c) \qquad P(C_{\mathrm{store}} \wedge \neg c)\ .$$

The root node is labeled with $P(C_{\mathrm{Pr}})$. Additionally, we need for the symmetry exclusion to store at a node v the positive and negative constraints that have been used along the path from the root to v to generate the node v.

Definition 3 (Search Tree). *Let t be a finite, binary, rooted and ordered tree, whose egdes are labeled by literals, and whose nodes are labeled by triples of constraint sets. The tree t is a search tree for C_{Pr} if the following conditions are satisfied:*

1. *The root node has the label $(\emptyset, \emptyset, P(C_{\mathrm{Pr}}))$,*
2. *every binary node has the form*

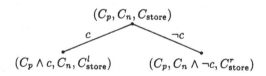

with $C_{\mathrm{store}}^{l} \models C_{\mathrm{store}} \wedge c$ and $C_{\mathrm{store}}^{r} \models C_{\mathrm{store}} \wedge \neg c$.

Intuitively, the reason for distinguishing between positive and negative constraints is just that C_n describes the previously found solutions, i.e.

$$\forall v' \prec_t v \forall \alpha \in \|C_{\text{store}}(v')\| : (\alpha \models \neg C_n).$$

Here, we denote with $\prec_t$ the partial ordering of nodes induced by t.

Note that we do not force C_{store}^l (resp. C_{store}^r) to be equivalent to $C_{\text{store}} \wedge c$ (resp. $C_{\text{store}} \wedge \neg c$). The reason is that we do have to add some additional constraints during search for excluding symmetries. Since C_{store} describes all constraints valid at some node v, we set $\|v\| = \|C_{\text{store}}\|$ for a node v in t with label $(C_p, C_n, C_{\text{store}})$.

We now state general properties of search tree in the presence of symmetries.

Definition 4 (Expanded, C_{Pr}-Complete and S-Reduced Trees).
The search tree t is completely expanded *if every unary node $v = (C_p, C_n, C_{\text{store}})$, either $\perp \in C_{\text{store}}$, or $\|v\| = \{\alpha\}$ and C_{store} determines $\mathcal{X}$ to α. A search tree t is C_{Pr}-complete if for every $\alpha \in \|C_{\text{Pr}}\|$ there is a leaf v in t with $\{\alpha\} = \|v\|$. Let S be a symmetry set for C_{Pr}. A search tree is C_{Pr}-complete w.r.t. S if for every $\alpha \in \|C_{\text{Pr}}\|$ there is a leaf v for such that*

$$\|v\| = \{\alpha\} \vee \exists s \in S \backslash \{\text{id}_{C_{\text{Pr}}}\} : \|v\| = \{s(\alpha)\}.$$

A search tree is S-reduced if for every leaf v with $\|v\| = \{\alpha\}$ we have

$$\forall s \in S \; \forall \text{leafs } v' \text{ with } v' \prec_t v : (\|v'\| = \{\alpha'\} \Rightarrow s(\alpha') \neq \alpha), \qquad (1)$$

Note that (1) is equivalent to $\forall s \in S \; \forall v' \neq v : (\|v'\| = \{\alpha'\} \Rightarrow s(\alpha') \neq \alpha)$, if S is closed under inversion.

Before we can show how to produce a S-reduced search tree that is C_{Pr}-complete w.r.t S, we first have to define how symmetries operate on constraints. In the following, we will assume that for every constraint c and every s, there is a constraint c' such that $s^*(\|c\|) = \|c'\|$, where we define s^* on sets of C_{Pr}-solutions by $s^*(A) = \{s(\alpha) \mid \alpha \in A\}$. For every c, there are usually different constraints c' with $s^*(\|c\|) = \|c'\|$. Hence, fix a function s_{con} on constraints such that

$$s^*(\|c\|) = \|s_{\text{con}}(c)\|.$$

In the next sections, we give examples of how to construct this function.

Proposition 1. *Let s_{con} be defined as before. Then s_{con} distributes over the Boolean operators, i.e., $s^*(\|c \wedge c'\|) = \|s_{\text{con}}(c) \wedge s_{\text{con}}(c')\|$, $s^*(\|c \vee c'\|) = \|s_{\text{con}}(c) \vee s_{\text{con}}(c')\|$ and $s^*(\|\neg c\|) = \|s_{\text{con}}(\neg c)\|$.*

Hence, we identify s_{con} with its homomorphic extension to constraint sets and arbitrary formulae. Now we can state a general mechanism for generating a search tree that is S-reduced.

Definition 5 (S-excluding). *Let S be a symmetry set. A search tree for C_{Pr} is S-excluding if every binary node v has the form*

$$(C_p, C_n, C_{\mathrm{store}})$$

$$c \qquad\qquad \neg c$$

$$(C_p \wedge c, C_n, C^l_{\mathrm{store}}) \qquad\qquad (C_p, C_n \wedge \neg c, C^r_{\mathrm{store}})$$

with $C^l_{\mathrm{store}} = P(C_{\mathrm{store}} \wedge c)$ and
$$C^r_{\mathrm{store}} = P(C_{\mathrm{store}} \wedge \neg c \wedge E^v(\neg c)), \text{ where } E^v(\neg c) = \bigwedge_{s \in S} s_{\mathrm{con}}(C_p) \to \neg s_{\mathrm{con}}(c).$$

Before we prove S-reducedness and C_{Pr}-completeness w.r.t S of S-excluding search trees, we state a proposition to precise the effect of adding the implications in definition 5 to C^r_{store}. For convenience, we write C^v_p, C^v_n and C^v_{store} to access C_p, C_n and C_{store} in the label $(C_p, C_n, C_{\mathrm{store}})$ of v. For a binary node v we refer to its left child as v_l and to its right child as v_r.

Proposition 2. *Let S be a symmetry set and t a S-excluding search tree. For every symmetry $s \in S$ and for every node v of t we have $C^v_{\mathrm{store}} \models s_{\mathrm{con}}(C^v_p) \to s_{\mathrm{con}}(C^v_n)$.*

For notational convenience we introduce the notation $C_{path}(v) = C^v_p \wedge C^v_n \wedge C_{\mathrm{Pr}}$. A good intuition is to think of $C_{path}(v)$ describing the constraint store of v in a simple not symmetry excluding search tree.

Reducedness and completeness will be essentially corollaries to the following proposition.

Lemma 1. *Let S be a symmetry set. Every S-excluding search tree t for C_{Pr} satisfies for every node v*

$$\|v\| = \|C_{path}(v)\| - A^v_S, \tag{2}$$
$$\text{where } A^v_S = \{s(\alpha) \mid s \in S \wedge \exists v' \prec_t v : \alpha \in \|C_{path}(v')\|\}.$$

Proof. We proof this by tree induction. For the root this is valid, since $A^v_S = \emptyset$ and $\|v\| = \|C_{\mathrm{Pr}}\| = \|C_{path}(v)\|$. Assume that we have proven the claim for a binary node v:

$$(C_p, C_n, C_{\mathrm{store}})$$

$$c \qquad\qquad \neg c$$

$$(C_p \wedge c, C_n, C^l_{\mathrm{store}}) \qquad\qquad (C_p, C_n \wedge \neg c, C^r_{\mathrm{store}})$$

For the left child v_l the claim follows immediately from the induction hypotheses, since $A^{v_l}_S = A^v_S$.

For v_r, we have to show $\|v_r\| = \|C_{path}(v_r)\| - A^{v_r}_S$. Note that $A^{v_r}_S = \{s(\alpha) \mid s \in S \wedge \exists v' \prec_t v_r : (\alpha \in \|C_{path}(v')\|)\}$ subdivides into its two subsets A^v_S and

$\{s(\alpha) \mid s \in \mathcal{S} \wedge \exists v'(v' \not\prec_t v \wedge v' \prec_t v_r \wedge \alpha \in \|C_{path}(v')\|)\}$. Further according to our definitions $C_{path}(v_r)$ is equivalent to $C_{path}(v) \wedge \neg c$.

To show that $\|v_r\| \subseteq \|C_{path}(v) \wedge \neg c\| - A_{\mathcal{S}}^{v_r}$, fix a symmetry $s \in \mathcal{S}$, then we have to show for every $v' \prec_t v$ that

$$\forall \alpha \in \|C_{path}(v')\| : s(\alpha) \notin \|v_r\|.$$

The first case is $v' \prec_t v$. Let $\alpha \in \|C_{path}(v')\|$. Then $s(\alpha) \notin \|v\|$ by induction hypotheses. Since $\|v_r\| \subseteq \|v\|$, this immediately implies $s(\alpha) \notin \|v_r\|$.

The second case is $(v' \not\prec_t v)$ and $v' \prec_t v_r$, i.e., v' is a subnode of v_l. Let $\alpha \in \|v_l\|$ and assume $s(\alpha) \in \|v_r\|$. From $\alpha \in \|v_l\|$ we have $\alpha \models C_p \wedge c$ and $s(\alpha) \models s_{con}(C_p \wedge c)$. That's a contradiction, because from definition of $\mathcal{S}$-excluding search tree $s(\alpha) \models s_{con}(C_p) \rightarrow \neg s_{con}(c)$, since $(s_{con}(C_p) \rightarrow \neg s_{con}(c)) \in E^v(\neg c)$.

It remains to be shown that $\|v_r\| \supseteq \|C_{path}(v_r)\| - A_{\mathcal{S}}^{v_r}$ Let $\alpha \notin \|v_r\|$. We have to show

$$\alpha \notin \|C_{path}(v_r)\| - A_{\mathcal{S}}^{v_r} \tag{3}$$

We have the following cases:
1. $\alpha \notin \|C_{path}(v_r)\|$. Then (3) follows immediately.
2. $\alpha \in \|C_{path}(v_r)\|$ and $\alpha \notin \|v\|$. We have to show $\alpha \in A_{\mathcal{S}}^{v_r}$.

Now $\alpha \in \|C_{path}(v_r)\|$ implies $\alpha \in \|C_{path}(v)\|$ and henceforth $\alpha \in A_{\mathcal{S}}^v \subseteq A_{\mathcal{S}}^{v_r}$ by induction hypotheses.
3. $\alpha \in \|C_{path}(v_r)\|$ and $\alpha \in \|v\|$. We will show that

$$\alpha \in A_{\mathcal{S}}^{v_r} - A_{\mathcal{S}}^v = \{s(\beta) \mid s \in \mathcal{S} \wedge \exists v' : (v' \prec_t v_r \wedge v' \not\prec_t v \wedge \beta \in \|C_{path}(v')\|\}$$
$$= \{s(\beta) \mid s \in \mathcal{S} \wedge \beta \in \|C_{path}(v_l)\|\} \tag{4}$$

Since $\alpha \models C_{store} \wedge \neg c$, but $\alpha \not\models C_{store}^r$, there is at least one $s \in \mathcal{S}$ with $\alpha \not\models s_{con}(C_p) \rightarrow \neg s_{con}(c)$ by the definition of an $\mathcal{S}$-excluding tree. Fix one of these symmetries s. Then $\alpha \models s_{con}(C_p) \wedge s_{con}(c)$. Since $C_{store} \models s_{con}(C_p) \rightarrow s_{con}(C_n)$ by Proposition 2, we get

$$\alpha \models s_{con}(C_p) \wedge s_{con}(c) \wedge s_{con}(C_n).$$

Hence, $s^{-1}(\alpha)$, which exists by definition of symmetries, satisfies $s^{-1}(\alpha) \models C_{path}(v) \wedge c$ (recall that $C_{path}(v) = C_p \wedge C_n$). I.e., $s^{-1}(\alpha) \in \|C_{path}(v_l)\|$. Hence, with $\beta = s^{-1}(\alpha)$ we have a valuation such that $\beta \in \|C_{path}(v_l)\|$ and $\alpha = s(\beta)$, which shows that α is in the set defined by (4).

Theorem 1. *Let S be a symmetry set. Every $\mathcal{S}$-excluding search tree t for C_{Pr} is $\mathcal{S}$-reduced.*

Proof. Fix a symmetry $s \in \mathcal{S}$, let v be a leaf of t with $\|v\| = \{\alpha\}$. We have to show for every node v' of t with $v' \prec_t v$ that $\|v'\| = \{\alpha'\} \rightarrow s(\alpha') \neq \alpha$. Assume v' to be a node of t with $v' \prec_t v$ and $\|v'\| = \{\alpha'\}$ and $s(\alpha') = \alpha$. It follows $\alpha \in \{s(\alpha) \mid s \in \mathcal{S} \wedge \exists v' \prec_t v : \alpha \in \|C_{path}(v')\|\}$, and from this the contradiction $\alpha \notin \|v\|$ by Lemma 1.

By now we understand that an S-excluding search tree may exclude more symmetries than actually declared by S directly. Hence, we have to investigate the completeness property of S-excluding search trees.

Theorem 2. *Let S be a symmetry set. Every S-excluding search tree t for C_{Pr} is C_{Pr}-complete w.r.t S', where S' is the closure of S under composition and inversion.*

Proof. We have to show that t is C_{Pr}-complete w.r.t. to S', where S' is the closure under composition of S, i.e. for every $\alpha \in \|C_{Pr}\|$ there is a leaf v with

$$\|v\| = \{\alpha\} \ \lor \ \exists s \in S' : \|v\| = \{s(\alpha)\}. \tag{5}$$

Hence fix an $\alpha \in \|C_{Pr}\|$. Then there exists a leaf v' in t with $\alpha \in \|C_{path}(v')\|$ from definition 5. There are two cases.

1. $\alpha \in \|v'\|$. This yields immediately $\|v'\| = \{\alpha\}$ and (5) is proven.
2. $\alpha \notin \|v'\|$. By Lemma 1 follows $\alpha \in A_S^v$, i.e., there is a $s_1 \in S$ and a $v'' \prec_t v'$ such that $\alpha = s_1(\alpha')$, where $\alpha' \in \|C_{path}(v'')\|$. By induction we get a sequence of symmetries $s_1, \ldots, s_n \in S$, where

$$\alpha = s_1 \circ \cdots \circ s_n(\alpha^{(n)}) \ \text{ and } \ \{\alpha^{(n)}\} = \|v^{(n+1)}\|$$

for a leaf $v^{(n+1)}$ of t. Since S' is the closure of S, claim (5) follows.

We will given an example for symmetry excluding search trees in Secion 5, where the symmetrie group of permutation are excluded by the subset of all transpositions (as indicated by the above theorem).

Now we are able to give a more detailed comparison with [8]. The SBDS-method therein is essential our symmetry exclusion restricted to the case where the search tree branches over constraints of the form $Var = Val$. In this case, the constraint collected in C_p is of the form $Var_1 = Val_1 \land \ldots \land Var_n = Val_n$, i.e., C_p is a partial assignment A. For the restricted SBDS-method, consider the case that a symmetry S_σ is defined by a permutation σ first. Then $S_\sigma(Var = Val)$ is $Var = \sigma(Val)$. Now let C_p be $Var_1 = Val_1 \land \ldots Var_n = Val_n$ at some node v of the search tree, which branches over $Var = Val$. Then the constraint added by our method for excluding the symmetry S_σ is $S_\sigma(Var_1 = Val_1 \land \ldots \land Var_n = Val_n) \implies \neg S_\sigma(Var = Val)$, which is by the definition of S_σ the same as

$$Var_1 = S_\sigma(Val_1) \land \ldots \land Var_n = S_\sigma(Val_n) \to Var \neq S_\sigma(Val).$$

Now the antecedence is nothing else than a test whether S_σ leaves C_p (i.e., the partial assignment at the node v) unchanged. Thus, the entailment will be evaluated and removed directly at the right subnode of v. The restricted SBDS-method essentially replaces the entailment test by the test whether the symmetry leaves the assignment unchanged. Only those symmetries are excluded, where the test can be decided at the node the corresponding implication would be integrated by our method (even if the corresponding implication would delay this test to a later point).

Note on implementation For the symmetry exclusion we have to add implications of the form $s_{con}(C_p^v) \to s_{con}(c)$ during the search procedure. Hence, one has to change the search procedure for implementing the symmetry exclusion. The antecedents of these implications can be computed during the search efficiently, using the observation that the antecedences of the added implications of ancestor nodes are prefixes of the ones added in their offspring. To be more precise, let v be a node, which branches over the constraint c, and let v^l (resp. v^r) its left (resp. right) daughter. Now

$$s_{con}(C_p^{v^l}) = s_{con}(C_p^v \wedge c) = s_{con}(C_p^v) \wedge s_{con}(c).$$

For v_r, $s_{con}(C_p^{v_r})$ equals $s_{con}(C_p^v)$. Therefore the computation of the condition $s_{con}(C_p)$ can be done incrementally. We maintain Boolean variables for this reason in our implementation. We need one variable for each symmetry s, containing the values for $s_{con}(C_p)$.

4 Geometric Symmetries

We will give now a concrete example for symmetries, namely geometry symmetries. We will treat the special case where we have points in $\mathbb{Z}^d$, although our method is not restricted to this case. We will exemplify the symmetry constructions in two dimensions, and give an example for the exclusion of additional symmetries as indicated by Theorem 2.

Definition of Geometric Symmetries There are many problems where one encodes the two-dimensional position of an object i using finite domain integer variables X_i, Y_i. Examples are the N-queens and the tiling problem. A more complex and realistic example (in three dimensions) is the lattice protein structure prediction problem [2].

The symmetries for $\mathbb{Z}^2$ have exactly the same structure as for the general case $\mathbb{Z}^d$. They are defined by affine mappings $S : \mathbb{Z}^d \to \mathbb{Z}^d$ with $S(x) = A_S x + v_S$ that map $\mathbb{Z}^d$ onto $\mathbb{Z}^d$. I.e., the matrix A_S is an orthogonal matrix with the property that the set of columns $\{v_1, \ldots, v_d\}$ of A_S equals $\{\pm e \mid e$ is a unit-vector of $\mathbb{Z}^d\}$. E.g., for $\mathbb{Z}^2$, the matrix $\begin{pmatrix} 0 & -1 \\ 1 & 0 \end{pmatrix}$ denotes the rotation by 90°. For $\mathbb{Z}^2$, we have 8 symmetries consisting of the identity, the 4 reflections (at x- and y-axis, and the two diagonals) and the 3 rotations by 90°, 180° and 270°. For $\mathbb{Z}^3$, we have 48 symmetries including the identity.

By now, the vector v_S is not yet fixed. There are two different approaches for fixing the symmetry. We will consider $\mathbb{Z}^2$ as an example. The methods work for all other dimensions as well.

The first case is that every possible solution lies within a fixed square (in the general case, within a hypercube).[2] This is equivalent to the proposition that there are integers $x_{min}, x_{max}, y_{min}, y_{max}$ such that for all $\alpha \in \|C_{Pr}\|$ we have

$$\min\{\alpha(X_i)\} = x_{min} \qquad \max\{\alpha(X_i)\} = x_{max}$$
$$\min\{\alpha(Y_i)\} = y_{min} \qquad \max\{\alpha(Y_i)\} = y_{max}.$$

---

[2] The technique can be extended to the case that the hypercube is not fixed in advance.

Thus, the minimal square around the position of all objects is defined by the points (x_{min}, y_{min}) and (x_{max}, y_{max}) in every solution. We call this the *frame* of the problem C_{Pr}. In the N-queens problem, this is just the board.

Now knowing the frame of a problem C_{Pr}, we can fix the vector $\boldsymbol{v}_S$ for all symmetries. Consider as an example a problem whose frame is defined by $(0,0)$ and $(3,2)$. Furthermore, consider the three symmetries reflection at the y-axis, rotation by $90°$ and rotation by $180°$, which we will name S_1, S_2 and S_3 in the following. The corresponding mappings are defined by $S_i(\boldsymbol{x}) = A_{S_i}(\boldsymbol{x}) + \boldsymbol{v}_{S_i}$, where the matrices A_{S_1}, A_{S_2} and A_{S_3} are defined by

$$A_{S_1} = \begin{pmatrix} -1 & 0 \\ 0 & 1 \end{pmatrix} \quad A_{S_2} = \begin{pmatrix} 0 & -1 \\ 1 & 0 \end{pmatrix} \quad A_{S_3} = \begin{pmatrix} -1 & 0 \\ 0 & -1 \end{pmatrix}.$$

The corresponding mappings of the frame are

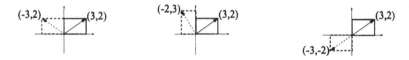

A symmetry S is compatible with the above defined frame if the frame is mapped to itself, i.e., if $\{\boldsymbol{v} \mid (0,0) \leq \boldsymbol{v} \leq (3,2)\} = \{S(\boldsymbol{v}) \mid (0,0) \leq \boldsymbol{v} \leq (3,2)\}$. For a given matrix A_S, there exists a $\boldsymbol{v}_S$ such that $S(\boldsymbol{x}) = A_S\boldsymbol{x} + \boldsymbol{v}_S$ satisfies this condition if and only if A_S satisfies

$$A_S(3,2) = (\pm 3, \pm 2) \tag{6}$$

For the matrices A_{S_1}, A_{S_2} and A_{S_3}, we get $(-3,2)$, $(-2,3)$ and $(-3,-2)$, which excludes the symmetry characterized by A_{S_2}. We finally get

$$\boldsymbol{v}_{S_1} = (3,0) \quad \text{and} \quad \boldsymbol{v}_{S_3} = (3,2).$$

The second case is that we know a point $\boldsymbol{p} = (p_x, p_y)$ which should remain unchanged under the symmetries. In that case, we know that the symmetries are defined by $S_i(\boldsymbol{x}) = A_{S_i}(\boldsymbol{x} - \boldsymbol{p}) + \boldsymbol{p} = A_{S_i}(\boldsymbol{x}) - A_{S_i}(\boldsymbol{p}) + \boldsymbol{p}$. Hence, $\boldsymbol{v}_{S_i} = \boldsymbol{p} - A_{S_i}(\boldsymbol{p})$.

The remaining part is to define symmetric constraints. We use a specific example where we leave the point $(5,5)$ fix. Consider the two symmetries reflection at the y-axis and rotation by $90°$. By what we have said above, the corresponding mappings are

$$S^{Ry}(\boldsymbol{x}) = \begin{pmatrix} -1 & 0 \\ 0 & 1 \end{pmatrix} \boldsymbol{x} + \begin{pmatrix} 10 \\ 0 \end{pmatrix} \quad \text{and} \quad S^{90°}(\boldsymbol{x}) = \begin{pmatrix} 0 & -1 \\ 1 & 0 \end{pmatrix} \boldsymbol{x} + \begin{pmatrix} 10 \\ 0 \end{pmatrix}$$

Now suppose that we have modeled points $p_1, \ldots, p_n$ using variables $X_1, \ldots, X_n$ and $Y_1, \ldots, Y_n$, and we want to define S_{con}^{Ry} and $S_{con}^{90°}$ for the constraints of the form $X_i = c$ (for other kind of constraints c, the definition $S_{con}(c)$ is analogous). Now the symmetric constraints $S_{con}^{Ry}(X_i = c)$ (resp. $S_{con}^{90°}(X_i = c)$) must express the constraint valid for $S^{Ry}(\alpha)$ (resp. $S^{90°}(\alpha)$) for every possible α with

$\alpha \models X_i = c$. Then

$$\alpha \models X_i = c \Leftrightarrow p_i = (c, \alpha(Y_i))$$
$$\Leftrightarrow S^{\mathrm{Ry}}(p_i) = (10 - c, \alpha(Y_i))$$
$$\Leftrightarrow S^{\mathrm{Ry}}(\alpha) \models X_i = 10 - c$$

$$\alpha \models X_i = c \Leftrightarrow p_i = (c, \alpha(Y_i))$$
$$\Leftrightarrow S^{90°}(p_i) = (10 - \alpha(Y_i), c)$$
$$\Leftrightarrow S^{90°}(\alpha) \models Y_i = c$$

Since $X_i = c$ does not restrict the valuation of $\alpha(Y_i)$, we know that $S^{\mathrm{Ry}}_{con}(X_i = c)$ is $X_i = 10 - c$, and $S^{90°}_{con}(X_i = c)$ is $Y_i = c$. Analagously, we get that $S^{\mathrm{Ry}}_{con}(Y_i = c)$ is $Y_i = c$, and that $S^{90°}_{con}(Y_i = c)$ is $X_i = 10 - c$. Note that $S^{\mathrm{Ry}}(c)$ has the same type as c (i.e., both have the same variable). This does not hold for c and $S^{90°}(c)$.

We will now turn to an example where we exclude only one symmetry, but the exclusion method excludes compositions of this symmetry. This shows that there are cases where the symmetry exclusion method excludes more than the symmetries contained in the symmetry set S (as indicated by Theorem 2). We will use an artificial example to show the existence of such a case.

Example 1. Let C_{Pr} be a geometric constraint problem over the variables X, Y, where X and Y have the domain $[0..10]$ associated. Furthermore, suppose that C_{Pr} has $(6, 6)$ as a solution that we can apply the rotational symmetries with fix point $(5, 5)$. This implies, that $(4, 4)$, $(4, 6)$ and $(6, 4)$ are also solutions of C_{Pr}.

Now consider the following S-excluding search tree for $S = \{S^{90°}\}$ (where the constraints added by the symmetry exclusion are in a framed box):

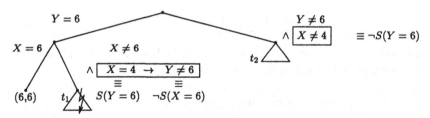

Then the solution $(4, 6)$ (which is $(6, 6)$ rotated by 90°) is excluded by the symmetry exclusion in t_1. But furthermore, the solution $(4, 4)$ is excluded in t_2 by our symmetry exclusion method. This is $(6, 6)$ rotated by 180°. Hence, although S contains only $S^{90°}$, the symmetry $S^{180°}$ (which is just $S^{90°} \circ S^{90°}$) is also excluded by our method. Note that $(6, 4)$ (which is $(6, 6)$ rotated by 270°) is not excluded and may be found in t_2.

Clearly, in the case of geometric symmetries, the full symmetry group is usually small enough that we can include all symmetries. But we wanted to show the effects of excluding only a subset of the full symmetry group using the above simple example. In the next section on permutation, we will give an example where the exclusion of transpositions allows to exclude all permutations.

Results We have applied the method to the lattice protein structure prediction [2], which is a hard combinatorical problem. The following table shows the number of solutions, search steps and runtimes for finding all minimal energy structures for 4 sequences, in the first case without symmetry exclusions, and with symmetry exclusion in the second part:

seq.	length	without sym. excl.			with sym. excl.			ratio		
		$\#_{noex}$	n_{noex}	t_{noex}	$\#_{ex}$	n_{ex}	t_{ex}	$\frac{\#_{noex}}{\#_{ex}}$	$\frac{n_{noex}}{n_{ex}}$	$\frac{t_{noex}}{t_{ex}}$
S1	27	4,752	45,924	15.1 min	297	2,998	69 sec	16	15.32	13.17
S2	27	408,864	2,465,728	6.2 h	25,554	155,693	26.3 min	16	15.84	14.18
S3	31	53,472	351,101	3.4 h	1,114	11,036	7.4 min	48	31.81	27.43
S4	36	56,448	732,952	3.7 h	3,528	55,086	19.9 min	16	13.31	11.24

We have added simple exclusion methods in both cases, which is the reason that we have only 16 (instead of 48) symmetries left in $S1, S2$ and S_6. As one can see from the table, we have a nearly linear speedup in number of search steps, and a close to linear speedup in runtime. In $S3$, the simple exclusion does not apply, which gives rise to 48 symmetries. Furthermore, the optimal conformations and the symmetric ones are very similar, which implies that we have less speedup (since detecting the symmetric solution is harder).

5 Permutation symmetries

In the following, we consider finite domain integer problems, where the variables have the domain $D \subseteq \mathbb{N}$ associated. In the following, we denote with $\text{Perm}(D)$ the set of all permutations of D, and with $\text{Trans}(D)$ the set of all transpositions of D (i.e., those permutations, which exchange just two elements of D). With $S^{\mathcal{X}}_{\text{Perm}(D)}$, we denote the set of all symmetries that permute the values of the variables in $\mathcal{X}$.

Definition 6. *Let $\mathcal{X}$ be the set of solution variables. The set of all value permutations of $\mathcal{X}$ is defined as the symmetry set*

$$S^{\mathcal{X}}_{\text{Perm}(D)} = \{S \mid \exists \pi \in \text{Perm}(D) \forall \alpha : S(\alpha)(X) = \pi(\alpha(X))\}$$

The subset of all transposition symmetries $S^{\mathcal{X}}_{\text{Trans}(D)}$ is defined analogously.

Now we consider search trees that branch over constraints having one single free variable (e.g., constraints of the forms $X = c$, $X < c$, $Even(X)$ and so on). The interesting part is that if a search tree branches over constraints that have one single free variable, then every $S^{\mathcal{X}}_{\text{Trans}(D)}$-excluding tree is even $S^{\mathcal{X}}_{\text{Perm}(D)}$-reduced. Thus, we need to exclude only the quadratically many transpositions to exclude the exponentially many permutations in this case.

Theorem 3. *Let C_{Pr} be a problem which has $S^{\mathcal{X}}_{\text{Perm}(D)}$ as a symmetry group. Let t be a $S^{\mathcal{X}}_{\text{Trans}(D)}$-excluding search tree such that for every branch v, the constraint c used at this branch has one free variable out of $\mathcal{X}$. Then t is $S^{\mathcal{X}}_{\text{Perm}(D)}$-reduced.*

Proof (sketch). Consider a permutation σ and the corresponding symmetry S_σ. Now consider any node

Since $\alpha \models c(x)$ and $S_\sigma(\alpha) \models \neg c(x)$, we know that $\sigma(\alpha(x))$ must be different from $\alpha(x)$. Now let τ be the transposition such that $\tau(\alpha(x)) = \sigma(\alpha(x))$, and let S_τ be the corresponding symmetry. Then the exclusion of all transposition would exclude the solution β if we can show that in the node considered above, we have that $S_\tau{}^{-1} \circ S_\sigma(\beta) \in \|v_l\|$. But this can be shown under the assumption that the search tree uses only constraints that have one free variable. $\qquad\square$

Graph Coloring As noted above the graph coloring is an example for a problem with value permutations as symmetries. The graph coloring problem is as follows. Given a graph $G = (V, E)$ and a set of colors. An admissible coloring c of G, is a mapping of the vertices V to the set of colors, satisfying the constraint that for all $(v_1, v_2) \in E$: $c(v_1) \neq c(v_2)$. What is the minimal set of colors, where we still can find an admissible coloring.

In this problem colorings are considered to be symmetric, if they are just permuted in colors to each other.

We compare two implementations of a solver for this problem. The first one is a naive implementation that uses a simple first fail heuristic. This implementation does not have symmetry exclusion. The second implementation with full exclusion of symmetries is just a simple extension of the first one, where we added our symmetry exclusion mechanism. Note that, due to the above theorem, it suffices to handle only the set of transpositions instead of handling the group of all permutations to get the full symmetry exclusion.

We give the results for some randomly generated problem instances of different problem sizes.

problem size			with symmetry excl.			without symmetry excl.			ratio	
verts	edges	colors	cloned	failed	time	cloned	failed	time	cloned	time
20	114	6	24	16	50	162	154	90	6.8	1.8
18	101	7	35	22	70	887	874	450	25.3	6.4
25	185	8	61	47	170	52,733	52,719	29,710	864.5	487.0
50	506	8	434	406	2,280	1,440,549	1,440,521	1,588,340	3,319.2	696.6
30	292	9	97	81	230	551,022	551,006	385,100	5,680.6	1674.3
35	339	9	168	150	370	3,428,853	3,428,835	2,569,200	20,409.8	6943.8

6 Conclusion and Future Work

We have introduced the first method that can exclude *arbitrary* symmetries in constraint-based search. In contrast to many other methods that can be found in the literature, the method does not restrict the search strategy.

The method is based on a declarative description of the symmetries in the form of symmetric constraints, which usually can be obtained easily. We have

87

given completeness and correctness proofs as well as the proof, that the method exclude all considered symmetries. In the case that the full symmetry group is too large, our method can handle arbitrary subsets of the full symmetry group. We have shown for the case of permutation symmetries that it is sufficient to exclude the (quadratically many) transposition to exclude all (exponentially many) permutations.

The method can be implemented in any (constraint-based) search machinery that handles implications and allows to introduce additional, user-defined constraints during search. This holds for the most modern constraint programming systems. Since the method is very general, we plan to investigate in which other (logic-based) search methods our symmetry exclusion can be used. Furthermore, we intend to investigate more general conditions under which a subset of the full symmetry group allows to exclude all symmetries (as it is the case for the permutations).

References

1. Alfonso San Miguel Aguirre. How to use symmetries in boolean constraint solving. In Frdric Benhamou and Alain Colmerauer, editors, *Constraint Logic Programming, Selected Research*, chapter 16, pages 287–306. The MIT Press, 1993.
2. Rolf Backofen. Constraint techniques for solving the protein structure prediction problem. In *Proceedings of 4th International Conference on Principle and Practive of Constraint Programming (CP'98)*, 1998.
3. Belaid Benhamou. Study of symmetry in constraint satisfaction problems. In Alan Borning, editor, *Principles and Practice of Constraint Programming, Second International Workshop, PPCP'94,*, volume 874 of *Lecture Notes in Computer Science*. Springer, 1994.
4. Belaid Benhamou and Lakhdar Sais. Tractability through symmetries in propositional calculus. *Journal of Automated Reasoning*, 12:89–102, 1994.
5. James M. Crawford, Matthew Ginsberg, Eugene Luks, and Amitabha Roy. Symmetry breaking predicates for search problems. In *Proc. of the 5th International Conference on Principles of Knowledge Representation and Reasoning (KR'96)*, pages 149–159, 1996.
6. Thierry Boy de la Tour. Minimizing the number of clauses by renaming. In M. E. Stickel, editor, *Proc. of the 10th Int. Conf. on Automated Deduction (CADE90)*, number 449 in LNAI, pages 558–572. Springer, 1990.
7. Eugene Freuder. Eliminating interchangeable values in constraint satisfaction problems. In *Proc. of AAAI'91*, pages 227–233, 1991.
8. Ian P. Gent and Barbara Smith. Symmetry breaking during search in constraint programming. Report 99.02, University of Leeds, January 1999.
9. Christian Schulte, Gert Smolka, and Jörg Würtz. Encapsulated search and constraint programming in Oz. In A.H. Borning, editor, *Second Workshop on Principles and Practice of Constraint Programming*, Lecture Notes in Computer Science, vol. 874, pages 134–150, Orcas Island, Washington, USA, May 1994. Springer-Verlag.
10. Gert Smolka. The Oz programming model. In Jan van Leeuwen, editor, *Computer Science Today*, Lecture Notes in Computer Science, vol. 1000, pages 324–343. Springer-Verlag, Berlin, 1995.

On Forward Checking for Non-binary
Constraint Satisfaction *

Christian Bessière[1], Pedro Meseguer[2], Eugene C. Freuder[3], and Javier Larrosa[4]

[1] LIRMM-CNRS, 161 rue Ada, 34392 Montpellier, France
bessiere@lirmm.fr,
[2] IIIA-CSIC, Campus UAB, 08193 Bellaterra, Spain
pedro@iiia.csic.es,
[3] University of New Hampshire, Durham, NH 03824, USA
ecf@cs.unh.edu,
[4] Dep. LSI, UPC, Jordi Girona Salgado, 1-3, 08034 Barcelona, Spain
larrosa@lsi.upc.es

Abstract. Solving non-binary constraint satisfaction problems, a crucial challenge for the next years, can be tackled in two different ways: translating the non-binary problem into an equivalent binary one, or extending binary search algorithms to solve directly the original problem. The latter option raises some issues when we want to extend definitions written for the binary case. This paper focuses on the well-known forward checking algorithm, and shows that it can be generalized to several non-binary versions, all fitting its binary definition. The classical version, proposed by Van Hentenryck, is only one of these generalizations.

1 Introduction

Up to now, most of the research done in constraint satisfaction assumes that constraint problems can be exclusively formulated in terms of binary constraints. While many academic problems (n-queens, zebra, etc.) fit this condition, many real problems include non-binary constraints. It is well known the equivalence between binary and non-binary formulations [8]. Theoretically, this equivalence solves the issue of algorithms for non-binary problems. In practice, however, it presents serious drawbacks concerning spatial and temporal requirements, which often make it inapplicable. The translation process generates new variables, which may have very large domains, causing extra memory requirements for algorithms. In some cases, solving the binary formulation can be very inefficient [1]. In any case, this forced binarization generates unnatural formulations, which cause extra difficulties for constraint solver interfaces with human users.

An alternative approach consists in extending binary algorithms to non-binary versions, able to solve non-binary problems in their original formulations.

---

* P. Meseguer and J. Larrosa were supported by an Integrated Action financed by the Generalitat de Catalunya, and by the Spanish CICYT project TIC96-0721-C02-02, C. Bessière was supported by an "action CNRS/NSF" under Grant no. 0690, and E.C. Freuder by the National Science Foundation under Grant No. IRI-9504316.

This approach eliminates the translation process and its drawbacks, but it raises other issues, among which how a binary algorithm is generalized is a central one. For some algorithms, like backtracking or MAC, this extension presents no conceptual difficulties: their binary definitions allow only one possible non-binary generalization. For other algorithms, like forward checking (FC), several generalizations are possible.

In this paper, we study how the popular FC algorithm can be extended to consider non-binary constraints. We present different generalizations, all collapsing to the standard version in the binary case. Our intention is mainly conceptual, trying to draw a clear picture of the different options for non-binary FC. We also provide some experimental results to initially assess the performance of the proposed algorithms with respect to other non-binary FC algorithms previously presented.

This paper is organized as follows. In Section 2, we present basic concepts used in the rest of the paper. In Section 3, we show the different ways in which binary FC can be generalized into non-binary versions. In Section 4, we provide properties and analysis of these generalizations, relating them to the algorithm FC+ [1]. In Section 5, we provide experimental results of the proposed algorithms on random ternary problems. Finally, Section 6 contains some conclusions and directions for further research.

2 Preliminaries

A finite *constraint network* $\mathcal{CN}$ is defined as a set of n *variables* $\mathcal{X} = \{x_1, \ldots, x_n\}$, a current *domain* $D(x_i)$ of possible values for each variable x_i, and a set $\mathcal{C}$ of *constraints* among variables. A constraint c_j on the ordered set of variables $var(c_j) = (x_{j_1}, \ldots, x_{j_{r(j)}})$ specifies the relation $rel(c_j)$ of the *allowed* combinations of values for the variables in $var(c_j)$. $rel(c_j)$ is a subset of $D_0(x_{j_1}) \times \cdots \times D_0(x_{j_{r(j)}})$, where $D_0(x_i)$ is the initial domain of x_i. (The definition of a constraint does not depend on the current domains.) An element of $D_0(x_{j_1}) \times \cdots \times D_0(x_{j_{r(j)}})$ is called a *tuple on* $var(c_j)$. An element of $D(x_{j_1}) \times \cdots \times D(x_{j_{r(j)}})$ is called a *valid* tuple on $var(c_j)$. We introduce the notions of *initial* and *current* domains to explicitly differentiate the initial network, $\mathcal{CN}_0$, from a network $\mathcal{CN}$, obtained at a given node of a tree search after some operations (instantiations and/or filtering). The tuple I_P on the ordered set of *past* variables P represents the sequence of instantiations performed to reach a given node. The set $\mathcal{X} \setminus P$ of the *future* variables is denoted by F. The tuple I_P on P is said to be *consistent* iff for all c such that $var(c) \subseteq P$, I_P satisfies c.

A value a for variable x is *consistent with* a constraint c iff $x \notin var(c)$, or there exists a valid tuple in $rel(c)$ with value a for x. A variable x is *consistent with* a constraint c iff $D(x)$ is not empty and all its values are consistent with c. A constraint c is *arc consistent* iff for all $x \in var(c)$, x is consistent with c. A set of constraints C is *arc consistent* iff all its constraints are arc consistent [6, 7].

Let $C = \{c_1, \ldots, c_k\}$ be a set of constraints. We will denote by $AC(C)$ the procedure which enforces arc consistency on the set C.[1] Given an arbitrary ordering of constraints $c_1, \ldots, c_k$, we say that AC is applied on each constraint *in one pass* (denoted by $AC(\{c_1\}), \ldots, AC(\{c_k\})$) when AC is executed once on each individual constraint following the constraint ordering. We will denote by $\Pi_{x \in S} D(x)$ the Cartesian product of the domains of the variables in S. Let σ be a tuple on the set of variables S. The *projection* of σ on a subset S' of S, denoted by $\sigma[S']$, is the restriction of σ to the variables of S'. The projection $c[S']$ of the constraint c on the subset S' of $var(c)$ is a constraint defined by $var(c[S']) = S'$, and $rel(c[S']) = \{t[S']/t \in rel(c)\}$. The *join* of σ and a relation $rel(c)$ on $var(c)$, denoted by $\sigma \bowtie rel(c)$, is the set $\{t/t$ is a tuple on $S \cup var(c)$, and $t[var(c)] \in rel(c)$, and $t[S] = \sigma\}$.

3 From Binary to Non-binary FC

FC (from now on, bFC) was defined in [4] for binary constraint networks. They described bFC as an algorithm pursuing this condition at each node,

> there is no future unit having any of its labels inconsistent with any past unit-label pairs

where unit stands for variable, and label for value. Values in future domains are removed to achieve this condition, and if a future domain becomes empty, bFC backtracks. This condition is equivalent to require that the set $C_{p,f}^b$, composed of constraints connecting one past and one future variable, is arc consistent. To do this, it is enough performing arc consistency on the set $C_{c,f}^b$ of constraints involving the current and a future variable, each time a new current variable is assigned (Proposition 2, Section 4.1). In addition, arc consistency on this set can be achieved by computing arc consistency on each constraint in one single pass (Corollary 1, Section 4.1). With this strategy, after assigning the current variable we have,

$$AC(C_{p,f}^b) = AC(C_{c,f}^b) = AC(\{c_1\}), \ldots, AC(\{c_q\}) \quad (\alpha)$$

where $c_i \in C_{c,f}^b$ and $|C_{c,f}^b| = q$. So, bFC works as follows,

bFC: After assigning the current variable, apply arc consistency on each constraint of $C_{c,f}^b$ in one pass. If success (i.e., no empty domain detected), continue with a new variable, otherwise backtrack.

How can the FC strategy be extended for non-binary constraints? It seems reasonable to achieve arc consistency (the same level of consistency as bFC)

---

[1] Abusing notation, we will also denote by $AC(C)$ the set of values removed by the procedure $AC(C)$.

on a set of constraints involving past and future variables. In the binary case, there is only one option for such a set: constraints connecting *one* past variable (the current variable) and *one* future variable. In the non-binary case, there are different alternatives. We analyze the following ones,

1. Constraints involving *at least one* past variable and *at least one* future variable;
2. Constraints or constraint projections involving *at least one* past variable and *exactly one* future variable;
3. Constraints involving *at least one* past variable and *exactly one* future variable.

Considering option (1), we define the set $C_{p,f}^n$ of the constraints involving *at least* one past variable and *at least* one future variable, and the set $C_{c,f}^n$ composed of constraints involving the current variable and *at least* one future variable. The big difference with the binary case is that, in these sets, we have to deal with partially instantiated constraints, with more than one uninstantiated variable. In this situation, the equivalences of (α) no longer hold for the non-binary case, that is,

$$AC(C_{p,f}^n) \neq AC(C_{c,f}^n) \neq AC(\{c_1\}), \ldots, AC(\{c_q\}) \quad (\beta)$$

where $c_i \in C_{c,f}^n$ and $|C_{c,f}^n| = q$. Then, we have different alternatives, depending on the set of constraints considered ($C_{p,f}^n$ or $C_{c,f}^n$) and whether arc consistency is achieved on the whole set, or applied on each constraint one by one. They are the following,

nFC5: After assigning the current variable, make the set $C_{p,f}^n$ arc consistent. If success, continue with a new variable, otherwise backtrack.
nFC4: After assigning the current variable, apply arc consistency on each constraint of $C_{p,f}^n$ in one pass. If success, continue with a new variable, otherwise backtrack.
nFC3: After assigning the current variable, make the set $C_{c,f}^n$ arc consistent. If success, continue with a new variable, otherwise backtrack.
nFC2: After assigning the current variable, apply arc consistency on each constraint of $C_{c,f}^n$ in one pass. If success, continue with a new variable, otherwise backtrack.

Regarding options (2) and (3), we define the set $C_{p,1}^n$ of the constraints involving at least one past variable and exactly one future variable, and the set $C_{c,1}^n$ of the constraints involving the current variable and exactly one future variable. Analogously, we define the set $CP_{p,1}^n$ of the constraint projections[2] involving at least one past variable and exactly one future variable, and the set $CP_{c,1}^n$ of the constraint projections involving the current variable and exactly one future variable. Both cases are concerned with the following generalization of (α) (proved in Section 4.1), stating that after assigning the current variable we have,

$$AC(C_{p,1}^n) = AC(C_{c,1}^n) = AC(\{c_1\}), \ldots, AC(\{c_q\}) \quad (\gamma)$$

---

[2] A constraint projection is computed from the constraint definition which involves initial domains.

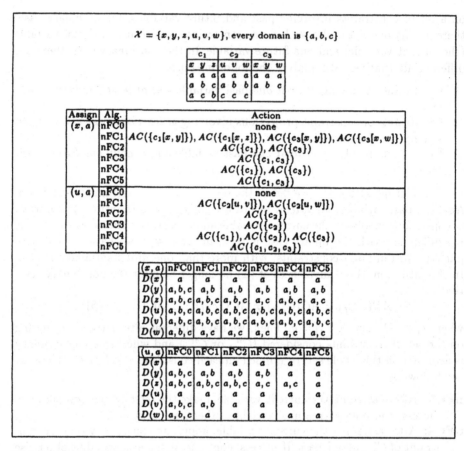

Fig. 1. A simple problem and the filtering caused by the six algorithms, after the assignments (x, a) and (u, a).

where $c_i \in C_{c,1}^n$ and $|C_{c,1}^n| = q$. As a result, only one alternative exists for each of the options (2) and (3), and they are the following,

nFC1: ([5]) After assigning the current variable, apply arc consistency on each constraint of $C_{c,1}^n \cup CP_{c,1}^n$ in one pass. If success, continue with a new variable, otherwise backtrack.

nFC0: ([10]) After assigning the current variable, apply arc consistency on each constraint of $C_{c,1}^n$ in one pass. If success, continue with a new variable, otherwise backtrack.

To illustrate the differences between the six proposed algorithms, a simple example is presented in Figure 1. It is composed of 6 variables $\{x, y, z, u, v, w\}$, sharing the same domain $\{a, b, c\}$, and subject to three ternary constraints, $c_1(x, y, z)$, $c_2(u, v, w)$ and $c_3(x, y, w)$. After the assignment (x, a), none of the constraints have two instantiated variables. Therefore, nFC0 does no filtering.

nFC1 applies arc consistency on the constraint projections of c_1 and c_3 on the subsets $\{x, y\}$, $\{x, z\}$ and $\{x, w\}$, removing c from $D(y)$ and b from $D(w)$. nFC2 applies arc consistency on c_1 and later on c_3, pruning the same values as nFC1. Notice that if we consider these constraints in a different order, the filtering will be different. nFC3 achieves arc consistency on the subset $\{c_1, c_3\}$, which causes the filtering of nFC2 plus the removal of b from $D(z)$. Given that x is the first instantiated variable, nFC4 applies arc consistency on the same constraints as nFC2, and it causes the same filtering. For the same reason, nFC5 performs the same filtering as nFC3.

After the assignment (u, a), none of the constraints have two instantiated variables. So, nFC0 does no filtering. nFC1 applies arc consistency on the constraint projections of c_1 on the subsets $\{u, v\}$ and $\{u, w\}$, removing c from $D(v)$ and c from $D(w)$. nFC2 applies arc consistency on c_2, and it removes b and c from $D(v)$ and c from $D(w)$. nFC3 achieves arc consistency on the subset $\{c_2\}$, thus causing the same filtering as nFC2 (differences in $D(z)$ come from the previous assignment). nFC4 applies arc consistency on the constraints c_1, c_2 and c_3, removing b from $D(y)$ and $D(z)$, b and c from $D(v)$ and c from $D(w)$. nFC5 achieves arc consistency on the whole constraint set. It removes b from $D(y)$, c from $D(z)$, b and c from $D(v)$ and c from $D(w)$.

4 Formal Results on nFC

4.1 Properties

In the next results, we prove the equivalences of (γ) used in Section 3.

Proposition 1 *Let c be a constraint such that all its variables but one are instantiated. If c is made arc consistent, it remains arc consistent after achieving arc consistency on any other problem constraint.*

Proof. Let $\tilde{c}$ be another constraint sharing an uninstantiated variable x_j with c. If $\tilde{c}$ is made arc consistent after c, this may cause further filtering in $D(x_j)$ but c will remain arc consistent since all remaining values in $D(x_j)$ are already consistent with c. $\square$

Corollary 1 *Let C be a set of constraints such that all their variables but one are instantiated. Achieving arc consistency on C is equivalent to make each of its constraints arc consistent in one pass.*

Proposition 2 *Let P be the ordered set of past variables. Let $C_{p,1}$ be the set of constraints involving at least one past variable and exactly one future variable. If each time a variable of P was assigned, the set $C_{c,1}$ of constraints involving that variable and one future variable was made arc consistent, the set $C_{p,1}$ is arc consistent.*

Proof. Let us assume that $C_{c,1}$ has been made arc consistent after assigning each variable in P. If $C_{p,1}$ is not arc consistent, this means that there is at least one of its constraints c which is not arc consistent. Let x_k be the last assigned variable in $var(c)$. Because of Proposition 1 this is in contradiction with the assumption that it was made arc consistent after assigning x_k. Therefore, $C_{p,1}$ is arc consistent. $\square$

Regarding the correctness of the proposed algorithms, we have to show that they are sound (they find only solutions), complete (find all solutions) and terminate. All algorithms follow a depth-first strategy with chronological backtracking, so it is clear that all terminate. Then, we have to show soundness and completeness.

Proposition 3 *Any nFCi (i:$\{0,\ldots,5\}$) is correct.*

Proof. *Soundness.* We prove that, after achieving the corresponding arc consistency condition, the tuple I_P of past variables reached by any algorithm is consistent. When this tuple includes all variables, we have a solution. The sets of constraints to be made arc consistent by the proposed algorithms all include the set $C_{p,1}$ of nFC0. By Proposition 1, we know that once those constraints are made arc consistent, they remain arc consistent after processing any other constraint. So, proving this result for nFC0 makes it valid for any nFCi algorithm ($i:\{0,\ldots,5\}$). If I_P of nFC0 is inconsistent then at least one constraint c involving only variables in P is inconsistent. Let x_i and x_j be the two last assigned variables in $var(c)$, in this order. After assigning x_i, c was in $C_{p,1}$ which was made arc consistent. Assigning x_j a value inconsistent with c is in contradiction with the assumption that $C_{p,1}$ was made arc consistent. So, I_P is consistent.

Completeness. We show completeness for nFC5, proofs for other algorithms are similar. Given a variable ordering, it is clear that nFC5 visits all successors of nodes compatible with such ordering where the set $C_{p,f}^n$ can be made arc consistent. Let us suppose that there is a node solution, I_P, where all variables are past. If x_n is the last variable to be instantiated, the parent node $I_{P\setminus\{x_n\}}$ is a node where $C_{p,f}^n$ can be made arc consistent. By induction, nFC5 visits the node solution I_P. $\square$

At a given node k, we define the *filtering* caused by an algorithm nFCi, $\Phi(nFCi,k)$, as the set of pairs (x,a) where a is a value removed from the future domain $D(x)$ by the corresponding arc consistency condition.

Proposition 4 *At any node k these relations hold,*

1. $\Phi(nFC0,k) \subseteq \Phi(nFC1,k) \subseteq \Phi(nFC2,k)$
2. $\Phi(nFC2,k) \subseteq \Phi(nFC3,k) \subseteq \Phi(nFC5,k)$
3. $\Phi(nFC2,k) \subseteq \Phi(nFC4,k) \subseteq \Phi(nFC5,k)$

Proof. Regarding nFC0 and nFC1, the relation is a direct consequence of $C_{c,1}^n \subseteq C_{c,1}^n \cup CP_{c,1}^n$. Regarding nFC1 and nFC2, constraint projections are semantically included in $C_{c,f}^n$. Regarding nFC2 and nFC3, applying arc consistency on each constraint of $C_{c,f}^n$ in one pass is part of the process of achieving arc consistency on the set $C_{c,f}^n$. Regarding nFC3 and nFC5, $C_{c,f}^n \subseteq C_{p,f}^n$. Regarding nFC2 and nFC4, $C_{c,f}^n \subseteq C_{p,f}^n$. Regarding nFC4 and nFC5, applying arc consistency on each constraint of $C_{p,f}^n$ in one pass is part of the process of achieving arc consistency on the set $C_{p,f}^n$. $\Box$

Regarding nFC3 and nFC4, their filterings are incomparable as can be seen in example of Figure 1. (After assigning (x, a), nFC3 filtering is stronger than nFC4 filtering; the opposite occurs after assigning (u, a).) A direct consequence of this result involves the set of nodes visited by each algorithm. Defining $nodes(nFCi)$ as the set of nodes visited by nFCi until finding a solution,

Corollary 2 *Given a constraint network with a fixed variable and value ordering, the following relations hold,*

1. $nodes(nFC2) \subseteq nodes(nFC1) \subseteq nodes(nFC0)$
2. $nodes(nFC5) \subseteq nodes(nFC3) \subseteq nodes(nFC2)$
3. $nodes(nFC5) \subseteq nodes(nFC4) \subseteq nodes(nFC2)$

4.2 Complexity Analysis

In this subsection, we give upper bounds to the number of constraint checks the different nFC algorithms perform at one node. First, let us give an upper bound to the number of checks needed to make a variable x_j consistent with a given constraint c. For each value b in $D(x_j)$, we have to find a subtuple σ in $\Pi_{x \in var(c) \setminus \{x_j\}} D(x)$ such that σ extended to (x_j, b) is allowed by c. So, the number of checks needed to make x_j consistent with c is in $O(d \cdot |V|)$, where $V = \Pi_{x \in var(c) \setminus \{x_j\}} D(x)$, and d denotes the maximal size of a domain.

In nFC0, a constraint c is made arc consistent at a given node iff $var(c)$ contains only one future variable. Thus, enforcing arc consistency on c is in $O(d)$ since $|V| = 1$. (Domains of past variables are singletons.) Therefore, the number of checks performed by nFC0 at one node is in $O(|C_{c,1}^n| \cdot d)$. For the same reason the number of checks performed by nFC1 at one node is in $O(|C_{c,1}^n \cup CP_{c,1}^n| \cdot d)$, assuming that the constraint projections have been built in a preprocessing phase.

In nFC2 and nFC4, $|V|$ is bounded above by $d^{|var(c) \cap F| - 1}$ for a given constraint c, and a given future variable x_j in $var(c)$. Thus, making x_j consistent with c is bounded above by $d \cdot d^{|var(c) \cap F| - 1}$, and enforcing arc consistency on c is in $O(|var(c) \cap F| \cdot d^{|var(c) \cap F|})$ since there are $|var(c) \cap F|$ variables to make arc consistent with c. So, the number of checks performed at one node is in $O(|C_{c,f}^n| \cdot |var(c) \cap F| \cdot d^{|var(c) \cap F|})$ for nFC2, and in $O(|C_{p,f}^n| \cdot |var(c) \cap F| \cdot d^{|var(c) \cap F|})$ for nFC4.

At a given node in the search, nFC3 (resp. nFC5) deals with the same set of constraints as nFC2 (resp. nFC4). The difference comes from the propagations nFC3 (resp. nFC5) performs in order to reach an arc consistent state on $C_{c,f}^n$ (resp. $C_{p,f}^n$), whereas nFC2 (resp. nFC4) performs "one pass" arc consistency on them. Thus, if we suppose that arc consistency is achieved by an optimal algorithm, such as GAC4 [7] or GAC-schema [2], the upper bound in the number of constraint checks performed by nFC3 (resp. nFC5) at a given node is the same as nFC2 (resp. nFC4) bound. (With an AC3-like algorithm [6], nFC3 and nFC5 have a greater upper bound.)

4.3   FC+ and nFC1

The hidden variable representation is a general method for converting a non-binary constraint network into an equivalent binary one [3, 8]. In this representation, the problem has two sets of variables: the set of the *ordinary* variables, those of the original non-binary network, with their original domain of values, plus a set of *hidden* variables, or h-variables. There is a h-variable h_c for each constraint c of the original network, with $rel(c)$ as initial domain (i.e., the tuples allowed by c become the values in $D_0(h_c)$). A h-variable h_c is involved in a binary constraint with each of the ordinary variables x in $var(c)$. Such a constraint allows the set of pairs $\{(a, t)/a \in D_0(x), t \in D_0(h_c), t[x] = a\}$.

FC+ is an algorithm designed to run on the hidden representation [1]. It operates like bFC except that when the domain of a h-variable is pruned, FC+ removes from adjacent ordinary variables those values whose support has been lost. Besides, FC+ never instantiates h-variables. When all its neighboring (ordinary) variables are instantiated, the domain of a h-variable is already reduced to one value. Its assignment is, in a way, implicit. Therefore, there is a direct correspondence between the search space of FC+ and any nFC. The following proposition shows that FC+ is equivalent to nFC1.

Proposition 5 *Given any non-binary constraint network, nFC1 visits exactly the same nodes as FC+ applied to the hidden representation, provided that both algorithms use the same variable and value orderings.*

Proof. Because of the algorithmic description of FC+, we know that h-variables may only have their domain pruned by the bFC look ahead. An arbitrary h-domain, $D(h_c)$, may only be pruned if $P \cap var(c) \neq \emptyset$, and $D(h_c) = \{(I_P \bowtie rel(c))[var(c)]\}$. Domains of ordinary variables may only be pruned by the extra look ahead of FC+. At a given node, value b for a future variable x_j belongs to $D(x_j)$ iff it still has support from all its adjacent h-variables that may have been pruned. That is, $\forall x_j \in F$, $b \in D(x_j)$ iff $\forall c$ s.t. $var(c) \cap P \neq \emptyset$ and $x_j \in var(c)$, $b \in D(h_c)[x_j] = ((I_P \bowtie rel(c))[var(c)])[x_j] = (I_P \bowtie rel(c))[x_j]$. Now, because of its definition, we know that at a given node nFC1 ensures that value b for a future variable x_j belongs to $D(x_j)$ iff it is consistent with the projections $rel(c)[var(c) \cap P \cup \{x_j\}]$ for all the constraints c such that $var(c) \cap P \neq \emptyset$ and $x_j \in var(c)$. That is, $\forall x_j \in F$, $b \in D(x_j)$ iff $\forall c$ s.t. $var(c) \cap P \neq \emptyset$ and $x_j \in var(c)$, $b \in (I_P \bowtie (rel(c)[var(c) \cap P \cup \{x_j\}]))[x_j] = (I_P \bowtie rel(c))[var(c) \cap P \cup \{x_j\}][x_j] = (I_P \bowtie rel(c))[x_j]$, which is exactly what we found for FC+. Since FC+ and nFC1 prune exactly the same values on the ordinary variables at a given node, we have the proof. □

5 Experimental Results

We have performed some experiments to preliminary assess the potential of the proposed algorithms. In our experiments we have used random problems extending the well known four-parameter binary model [9] to ternary problems as follows. A ternary random problem is defined by four parameters $\langle n, m, p_1, p_2 \rangle$ where n is the number of variables, m is the cardinality of their domains, p_1 is the problem connectivity as the ratio between existing constraints and the maximum number of possible constraints (the problem has exactly $p_1 n(n-1)(n-2)/6$ constraints), and p_2 is the constraint tightness as the proportion of forbidden value triplets between three constrained variables (the number of forbidden value triplets is exactly $T = p_2 m^3$). The constrained variables and their nogoods are randomly selected following a uniform distribution.

We performed experiments on the following classes of problems:

(a) $\langle 10, 10, 100/120, p_2 \rangle$,

(b) $\langle 30, 6, 75/4060, p_2 \rangle$,

(c) $\langle 75, 5, 120/67525, p_2 \rangle$.

Regarding connectivity, (a) is a dense class while (b) and (c) are sparse classes. The complexity peak location appears in (a) at low tightness, in (b) at medium tightness, and in (c) at high tightness.

We solved 50 instances for each set of parameters, using nFC0, nFC1, FC+, nFC2, nFC3, nFC4, and nFC5,[3] with the heuristic $minimum \ \frac{domain \ size}{degree}$ for variable selection and lexicographic value selection. Figure 2 shows the mean number of visited nodes to solve each problem class. Only the complexity peak region is shown. With no surprise, it is in agreement with Corollary 2, which establishes that nFC0 is the algorithm visiting the most nodes while nFC5 is the one that visits the least nodes. Because of Proposition 5, nFC1 and FC+ visit the same nodes. The new information is about the relation between nFC3 and nFC4, algorithms unordered by Corollary 2. Consistently in the three problem classes, nFC4 visits less nodes than nFC3, which implies that nFC4 performs more pruning than nFC3.

Figures 3 and 4 show the average computational effort[4] (as mean number of consistency checks and mean CPU time) required. We observe that, for easy problems (with peak at low tightness) the winner is nFC0, the algorithm that performs the simplest lookahead. For this class of problems, sophisticated forms of lookahead do not pay-off: the proposed algorithms nFC1 to nFC5 are 1.8 to 4.8 times slower than nFC0 at the peak. FC+ on the hidden representation is orders of magnitude slower. For problems with the peak at medium tightness, no single algorithm clearly outperforms the others. nFC0, nFC1, nFC2, and nFC5 are very close. nFC3 and nFC4 are slightly worse. The bad behavior of FC+ is confirmed. For difficult problems with the peak located at high tightness, the proposed

---

[3] In nFC3 and nFC5, the technique used to achieve arc consistency on a set of constraints is a brute force non optimal GAC3-based algorithm.

[4] This effort includes the preprocessing phase for nFC1 and the conversion into the hidden representation for FC+.

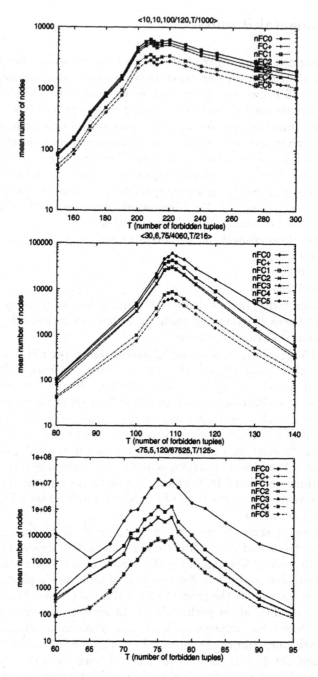

Fig. 2. Average number of visited nodes for three classes of ternary random problems.

99

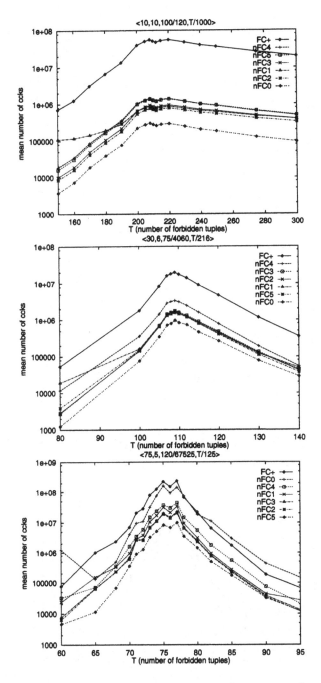

Fig. 3. Average number of checks for three classes of ternary random problems.

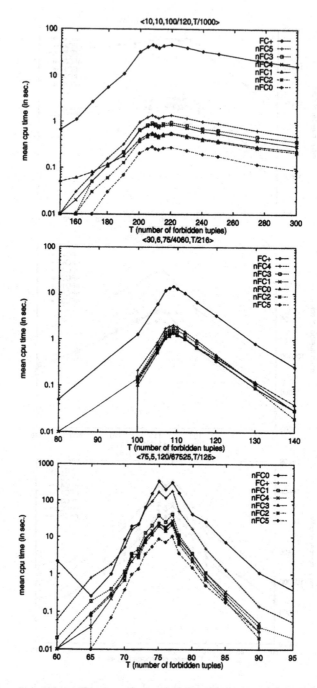

Fig. 4. Average cpu time for three classes of ternary random problems.

algorithms nFC1 to nFC5 clearly outperform nFC0. Even FC+ performs better than nFC0. The winner is nFC5, the algorithm which performs the greatest effort per node, and causes the highest filtering. It is 32 times faster than nFC0 at the peak. The good behaviour of nFC4 in number of visited nodes has no translation in performance. However, nFC2 visiting more nodes than nFC4 is the second best algorithm in performance in the three problem classes. Considering FC+, it has the worst performance for loose and medium constraints, and it is the second worst (after nFC0) for tight constraints. Any of the proposed algorithms outperforms FC+ in the three problem classes.

We can also point out some other noteworthy phenomena that are not visible in the figures reported here. First, on the problem classes presented there, nFC0 is the only algorithm that encountered an exceptionally hard problem, located in the satisfiable region of the $\langle 75, 5, 120/67525, p_2 \rangle$ class. Second, when the heuristic *minimum domain size* for variable selection is used instead of *minimum* $\frac{domain\ size}{degree}$, nFC0 becomes more frequently subject to thrashing, even on problem sizes remaining very easy for the algorithms nFC1 to nFC5.

6 Summary and Conclusion

We presented several possible generalizations of the FC algorithm to non-binary constraint networks. We studied their properties, and analyzed their complexities. We also compared these non-binary algorithms to the binary FC+ algorithm, which runs on the hidden conversion of non-binary networks.

We provided initial empirical results on the performance of these algorithms. From them, we conclude that the proposed algorithms outperform existing approaches on sparse problems with tight constraints. On easier problems, the benefits caused by their early lookahead do not outweigh the propagation effort. This unsurprising conclusion fits the already known trade-off between benefits and costs in constraint satisfaction. Nevertheless, more empirical studies are needed to substantiate which of these algorithms are promising, and on which constraints they perform better. An ultimate goal could be to exhibit a criterion under which to decide when a constraint should be processed by the nFC0 principle, and when it should be propagated with a more pruningful mechanism. The result would be a mixed algorithm, taking the best of both techniques.

References

1. F. Bacchus and P. van Beek. On the conversion between non-binary and binary constraint satisfaction problems. In *Proceedings AAAI'98*, pages 311–318, Madison WI, 1998.
2. C. Bessire and J.C. Rgin. Arc consistency for general constraint networks: preliminary results. In *Proceedings IJCAI'97*, pages 398–404, Nagoya, Japan, 1997.
3. R. Dechter. On the expressiveness of networks with hidden variables. In *Proceedings AAAI'90*, pages 556–562, Boston MA, 1990.
4. R.M. Haralick and G.L. Elliot. Increasing tree seach efficiency for constraint satisfaction problems. *Artificial Intelligence*, 14:263–313, 1980.

5. J. Larrosa and P. Meseguer. Adding constraint projections in n-ary csp. In J.C. Rgin and W. Nuijtens, editors, *Proceedings of the ECAI'98 workshop on non-binary constraints*, pages 41–48, Brighton, UK, 1998.

6. A.K. Mackworth. On reading sketch maps. In *Proceedings IJCAI'77*, pages 598–606, Cambridge MA, 1977.

7. R. Mohr and G. Masini. Good old discrete relaxation. In *Proceedings ECAI'88*, pages 651–656, Munchen, FRG, 1988.

8. F. Rossi, C. Petrie, and V. Dhar. On the equivalence of constraint satisfaction problems. In *Proceedings ECAI'90*, pages 550–556, Stockholm, Sweden, 1990.

9. B. Smith. Phase transition and the mushy region in constraint satisfaction problems. In *Proceedings ECAI'94*, pages 100–104, Amsterdam, The Netherlands, 1994.

10. Pascal Van Hentenryck. *Constraint Satisfaction in Logic Programming*. MIT Press, Cambridge, MA, 1989.

Enforcing Arc Consistency on Global Constraints by Solving Subproblems on the Fly*

Christian Bessière[1] and Jean-Charles Régin[2]

[1] LIRMM-CNRS
161, rue Ada
34292 Montpellier, France
e-mail: bessiere@lirmm.fr
[2] ILOG
1681, route des Dolines
06560 Valbonne, France
e-mail: regin@ilog.fr

Abstract. Constraint networks are used more and more to solve combinatorial problems in real-life applications. As pointed out in [1], this success requires dealing with non-binary constraints, which are widely needed in real world constraint solvers. Since arc consistency is a fundamental piece of reasoning that seems to be of great help during search for solutions, it is important to have efficient arc consistency algorithms for non-binary constraints. In this paper, we propose a new instantiation of GAC-Schema [1] that achieves arc consistency on global constraints (sets of original constraints taken globally). This algorithm, which searches for supports on these global constraints by solving the corresponding subproblem on the fly, outperforms the previous available techniques, such as GAC-Schema and its instantiation to predicates. It can simultaneously take into account the multidirectionality of the global constraint, and take advantage of the knowledge of the constraints of the subproblem. Furthermore, we show on several experiments the interest of our approach for problem modelling.

1 Introduction

In constraint programming, to solve a problem, we begin by designing a model of it using predefined constraints, such as sum, alldiff. Next, we define other constraints specific to the problem. Then we call a procedure to search for a solution.

Often when we are solving a real problem, say problem $\mathcal{P}$, the various simple models that we come up with cannot be solved within a reasonable period of time. In such a case, we may consider a subproblem of the original problem, say subproblem $\mathcal{R}$. We then try to improve the resolution of $\mathcal{R}$ with the hope of thus eventually solving $\mathcal{P}$.

* This work has been partially financed by ILOG S.A. under research contract ILOG/LIRMM no. 980330.

More precisely, for each possible relevant subproblem of $\mathcal{P}$, we construct a *global* constraint that is the conjunction of the constraints involved in the subproblem. We then apply arc consistency to these new constraints. Suppose that this improves the resolution of $\mathcal{P}$ (i.e., the number of backtracks markedly decreases). In this case, we know that it is worthwhile to write another algorithm dedicated to solving the subproblem $\mathcal{R}$ under consideration. In contrast, if the number of backtracks decreases only slightly, then we know that the resolution of $\mathcal{R}$ has only modest effect on the resolution of $\mathcal{P}$. By proceeding in this way, we can improve the resolution of $\mathcal{P}$ much faster.

Let us consider a simple example. This is a problem used in cryptography. It consists of a square with r rows and r columns, each row i (resp. each column j) being associated with an integer $rsum(i)$ (resp. $csum(j)$). The goal is to find a key, i.e., to put the integers 1 to r^2 in the cells of the square in such a way that the sum of the values affected to row i is equal to $rsum(i)$, and the sum of the values affected to column j is equal to $csum(j)$, $\forall i, j \in [1..r]$. (We deal only with satisfiable instances.)

This problem can be modelled as follows. The associated constraint network involves a set $\{V_{ij} | i, j \in [1..r]\}$ of r^2 variables representing the r^2 cells. Each variable takes its values in the domain $\{1..r^2\}$. In order to guarantee that the sums are respected, there is a constraint $C_{Sr} = (\Sigma_{j \in [1..r]} V_{ij} = rsum(i))$ on each row i, and a constraint $C_{Sc} = (\Sigma_{i \in [1..r]} V_{ij} = csum(j))$ on each column j. An *alldiff* constraint is defined on all the variables.

With this modelization it is difficult to solve some instances of the problem when r is greater than 6. Thus we have to improve this model, but how can we do it? At present, we are not able to give a general answer to this question. There are few studies on this topic [5, 4]. In fact, it may not be easy to identify the parts of the problem that lend themselves to relevant subproblems. For instance, we would like to know if it is interesting to be able to achieve arc consistency for the constraint "sum of n all different variables". That is, if it would be of interest to replace each constraint C_S constraining the sum of a row or a column, by a global constraint $C_{S\neq}$, which is the conjunction of C_S and of an *alldiff* constraint $C_{\neq}$ involving the same variables as C_S.

The interest of achieving arc consistency for one constraint is the amount of deletions of values that can follow. Then, the other constraints can use these deletions to perform further domain reductions, and so on.

Unfortunately, there is no specific arc consistency algorithm available for $C_{S\neq}$ constraints, and it is not obvious to find one. Writing such a new algorithm will be time-consuming and subtle in itself. Furthermore, we do not know whether it is interesting to introduce such a constraint inside our model or not. Hence, developing such a specific algorithm can lead to a loss of human time.

When dealing with global constraints, the arc consistency mechanism can be seen as the deletion of the values that do not belong to any solution (or allowed tuple) of the subproblem (or constraint). Therefore, arc consistency can be achieved by checking for each value a of each variable x involved in the subproblem whether the subproblem has a solution when x is instantiated with *a.* Thus, if we are able to compute a solution for a subproblem, we can achieve arc consistency for its associated global constraint.

Several possibilities can be considered:

(1) All the possible solutions of the subproblem, called allowed tuples, are computed once and for all. They are saved in a database (that can sometimes fit in memory) and the existence of a solution is obtained by searching in the database;

(2) Only the combinations of values that are not solutions are saved. These combinations are called forbidden tuples. Most of the time, this way is chosen when almost all the combinations are solutions;

(3) Finally, solutions can be computed on the fly when the consistency of a value with the global constraint has to be checked.

Bessière and Régin have proposed a general framework, GAC-Schema, in which one can incorporate any specific algorithm to calculate arc consistency on any given kind of constraint [1]. They also provided three instantiations of the schema to efficiently handle constraints defined by a list of allowed tuples (GAC-Schema+allowed), by a list of forbidden tuples (GAC-Schema+forbidden), and by any predicate (GAC-Schema+predicate).

The possibilities (1) and (2) above can be handled by GAC-Schema+allowed and GAC-Schema+forbidden. Their time and space complexity depends on the number of involved tuples. For the example we considered above, these numbers prevent us from using these possibilities. Only the third possibility is acceptable. Therefore, we could use directly GAC-Schema+predicate by representing the subproblem as a predicate. (A tuple would satisfy the predicate iff it is a solution of the subproblem.) However, such an instantiation of GAC-Schema is incapable of using specific knowledge (if available) that underlies the constraint it handles. It will not use the basic constraints composing the subproblem. In other words, the solutions will be computed by a kind of generate-and-test algorithm. This is not acceptable.

In this paper we propose to instantiate GAC-Schema with an algorithm that calls a solver to compute allowed tuples/solutions on the fly. The advantage of this approach is that the knowledge available for the subproblem can be used. Thus, some combinations of values that are forbidden by constraints of the subproblem will be avoided, and then time efficiency improves.

The rest of the paper is organized as follows. In Section 2 we give background on constraint networks and GAC-schema, and recall the property of multidirectionality. In Section 3 we present a simple technique to achieve arc consistency on global constraints by solving the associated subproblem on the fly. This first technique does not take completely multidirectionality into account, whereas it is usually the case in GAC-schema instantiations. In Section 4 we show how to consider multidirectionality as a particular constraint with its own propagation algorithm. Adding it to the subproblem permits to solve it while taking completely multidirectionality into account. Finally, in Section 5, we propose several experiments that show the interest of our approach to efficiently solve some problems, and to identify where are located some difficult parts of a problem. We also study the behavior of the presented algorithm with the classical instantiations of GAC-Schema.

2 Background

2.1 Preliminary definitions

Constraint network. A finite *constraint network* $\mathcal{N} = (X, \mathcal{D}, \mathcal{C})$ is defined as a set of n *variables* $X = \{x_1, \ldots, x_n\}$, a set of *domains* $\mathcal{D} = \{D(x_1), \ldots, D(x_n)\}$ where $D(x_i)$ is the finite set of possible *values* for variable x_i, and a set $\mathcal{C}$ of *constraints* between variables. A total ordering $<_d$ can be defined on $D(x_i), \forall x_i \in X$, without loss of generality. $highest(D(x_i))$ denotes the highest value in $D(x_i)$ w.r.t. $<_d$.

Constraint. A constraint C on the ordered set of variables $X(C) = (x_{i_1}, \ldots, x_{i_r})$ is a subset of the Cartesian product $D(x_{i_1}) \times \cdots \times D(x_{i_r})$ that specifies the *allowed* combinations of values for the variables $x_{i_1}, \ldots, x_{i_r}$. An instantiation of the variables in $X(C)$ is called a *tuple on* $X(C)$. Two tuples τ and τ' on $X(C)$ can be ordered by the natural lexicographic order $\prec_{lo}$ in which $\tau \prec_{lo} \tau'$ iff $\exists k / \tau[1..k-1] = \tau'[1..k-1]$ and $\tau[k] <_d \tau'[k]$ ($\tau[1..k]$ being the prefix of size k of τ, and $\tau[k]$ the kth value of τ). The tuples on $X(C)$ not allowed by C are called the *forbidden* tuples of C. $|X(C)|$ is the *arity* of C.

Global constraint. A *global constraint* (also called *subproblem* by misuse of language) $C_\Pi = c_1 \wedge \cdots \wedge c_q$ is represented indifferently by its set of (*underlying*) constraints $\{c_1, \ldots, c_q\}$ or by the subnetwork $\Pi = (X(C_\Pi) = \cup_{c \in C_\Pi} X(c), \mathcal{D}_{X(C_\Pi)}, \{c_1, \ldots, c_q\})$. The set of tuples allowed by C_Π is equal to the set of solutions of Π.

Notation. A value a for a variable x is often denoted by (x, a). $var(C, i)$ represents the ith variable of $X(C)$, while $index(C, x)$ is the position of variable x in $X(C)$.

Arc consistency. Let $\mathcal{N} = (X, \mathcal{D}, \mathcal{C})$ be a constraint network, C a constraint in $\mathcal{C}$. A tuple τ on $X(C)$ is *valid* iff $\forall x \in X(C), \tau[index(C, x)] \in D(x)$; otherwise, it is *rejected*. A value $a \in D(x)$ is *consistent with* C iff $x \notin X(C)$, or $\exists \tau$ allowed by C, such that $a = \tau[index(C, x)]$ and τ is valid. (τ is then called a *support* for (x, a) on C.) C is *arc consistent* iff $\forall x \in X(C), D(x) \neq \varnothing$ and $\forall a \in D(x)$, a is consistent with C. We achieve arc consistency on C by removing every value not consistent with C. Note that a value is consistent with a global constraint C_Π iff it belongs to a solution of the subnetwork Π.

2.2 The GAC-Schema

Let us review the GAC-Schema presented in [1] since the algorithms we will propose in the following sections are instantiations of that schema. GAC-Schema has been built to take into account the *multidirectionality* inherent in any constraint when achieving arc consistency.

PROPAGATION(C: constraint; x: variable; a: value, $deletionSet$: list): Bool
for each $\tau \in S_C(x,a)$ do
 for each $(z,c) \in \tau$ do remove τ from $S_C(z,c)$
 for each $(y,b) \in S(\tau)$ do
  remove (y,b) from $S(\tau)$
  if $b \in D(y)$ then
1    $\sigma \leftarrow$ SEEKINFERABLESUPPORT(C,y,b)
2   if $\sigma \neq nil$ then add (y,b) to $S(\sigma)$
   else
    $\sigma \leftarrow$ SEEKNEXTSUPPORT$(C,y,b,last_C(y,b))$
    if $\sigma \neq nil$ then
     add (y,b) to $S(\sigma)$
     $last_C(y,b) \leftarrow \sigma$
     for $k = 1$ to $|X(C)|$ do add σ to $S_C(var(C,k),\sigma[k])$
    else
     remove b from $D(y)$
     if $D(y) = \varnothing$ then return False
     add (y,b) to $deletionSet$

return True

Algorithm 1: function PROPAGATION

Definition 1 (multidirectionality) *Let C be a constraint on $X(C)$. If σ is a support for a value (x,a) on C, then it is a support on C for all the values $(y, \sigma[index(C,y)])_{y \in X(C)}$ composing it.*

We say that GAC-Schema takes multidirectionality into account because:

(1) it never looks for a support for a value on a constraint C when a tuple supporting this value has already been checked, and
(2) it never checks whether a tuple is a support for a value when it has already been unsuccessfully checked for another value.

The function PROPAGATION of GAC-Schema is given in Algorithm 1. The program including it must create and initialize the data structures (S_C, S, and $last_C$), and call $Propagation(C, x, a, deletionSet)$ for each constraint C involving x, each time a value a is removed from $D(x)$, in order to propagate the consequences of this deletion. $deletionSet$ is updated to contain the deleted values not yet propagated. S_C, S, and $last_C$ must be initialized in a way such that:

- $S_C(x,a)$ contains all the allowed tuples τ that are the current support for some value, and such that $\tau[index(C,x)] = a$.
- $S(\tau)$ contains all values for which τ is the current support.
- $last_C(y,b)$ is the last tuple returned by SEEKNEXTSUPPORT as a support for (y,b) if $seekNextSupport(C,y,b,-)$ has already been called; nil otherwise. There is an ordering on the tuples, which is proper to SEEKNEXTSUPPORT, and $last_C(y,b)$ gives the point where SEEKNEXTSUPPORT will have to restart the search for a support for (y,b) on C at the next call.

Line 1 of PROPAGATION "infers" an already checked allowed tuple as support for (y, b) if possible, in order to ensure that the point (1) above is satisfied. The search for support (function SEEK NEXT SUPPORT —see line 2 of PROPAGATION) is instantiated differently depending on the type of the constraint involved. The point (2) above must be taken into account by SEEK NEXT SUPPORT.

SEEK INFERABLE SUPPORT(C: constraint; y: variable, b: value): tuple
while $S_C(y, b) \neq \varnothing$ **do**
$\quad \sigma \leftarrow first(S_C(y, b))$
$\quad$ **if** σ *is valid* **then** return σ $\quad$ /* σ is a support */
$\quad$ **else** remove σ from $S_C(y, b)$
return nil

Algorithm 2: function SEEK INFERABLE SUPPORT

3 A first algorithm

In this section, we propose a first instantiation of the GAC-schema that deals with global constraints but that does not take into account the point (2) of multidirectionality (see Section 2).

As stated in the introduction, a global constraint is a subproblem that is considered globally as a constraint for which the allowed tuples are the solutions of the subproblem. Let us denote by C_Π such a constraint if $\Pi = (X(C_\Pi), \mathcal{D}_{X(C_\Pi)}, C_\Pi)$ is the subproblem. Achieving arc consistency on C_Π is done by looking for supports for the values of the variables in $X(C_\Pi)$. A support for a value (y, b) on C_Π can be seeked by any search procedure since a support for (y, b) is a solution of the subnetwork $(X(C_\Pi), \mathcal{D}_{X(C_\Pi)}, C_\Pi \cup \{y = b\})$.

SEEK NEXT SUPPORT(C_Π: constraint; y: variable, b: value, τ: tuple): tuple
$\Pi_2 \leftarrow (X(C_\Pi), \mathcal{D}_{X(C_\Pi)}, \{y = b\} \cup C_\Pi)$
$\sigma \leftarrow$ SEARCH FOR SOLUTION(Π_2, τ)
return σ

Algorithm 3: function seekNextSupport

The new function SEEK NEXT SUPPORT is given by Algorithm 3. First it defines $\Pi_2 = (X(C_\Pi), \mathcal{D}_{X(C_\Pi)}, \{y = b\} \cup C_\Pi)$ a new CSP and then function SEARCH FOR SOLUTION is called. The specification of SEARCH FOR SOLUTION(Π_2, τ) is that it must return a solution to the subnetwork Π_2, knowing that τ was the previous solution returned; or *nil* if there is no solution. Starting a search algorithm with an instantiation for which we know there is no solution before it has already been studied in [2]. However, SEARCH FOR SOLUTION can also be implemented as a classical search procedure, without using the previous solution found.

4 Dealing with multidirectionality

4.1 Properties

In Section 3, we have proposed a simple instantiation of GAC-schema to global constraints, which does not guarantee the point (2) of multidirectionality. In this section, we give an algorithm that completely takes into account multidirectionality. From now, a global constraint will be denoted C or C_Π indifferently.

Definition 2 *Given a constraint C on $X(C)$, a valid tuple on $X(C)$ that has never been checked against C is called a* candidate tuple. *A partial instantiation of $X(C)$ that can be extended to $X(C)$ as a candidate tuple is called a* candidate.

In order to ensure the point (2) of multidirectionality, it is necessary to define an ordering on the tuples that will be followed when looking for a support for a value on a constraint C. The lexicographic ordering $\prec_{lo}$ defined previously is used to visit the tuples on $X(C)$. The function $seekNextSupport(C, y, b, \tau)$ must return the *smallest* support for (y, b) on C greater than τ w.r.t. $\prec_{lo}$. To deal completely with multidirectionality requires checking only candidate tuples. This is done by means of the following property.

Property 1 *Let σ be a valid tuple on $X(C)$. σ is a candidate tuple iff $\not\exists x \in X(C)$ such that $\sigma \prec_{lo} last_C(x, \sigma[index(C, x)])$.*

This property can be implemented in different ways. For instance, GAC-Schema+predicate is a possible implementation. Nevertheless, this implementation is a specific algorithm that cannot use the constraints composing a subproblem Π. It, indeed, only checks the satisfiability of the associated global constraint C_Π, i.e., complete instantiations of $X(C_\Pi)$. Thus, GAC-schema+predicate is a generic algorithm for dealing with multidirectionality, but it is not able to efficiently handle global constraints and their underlying constraints.

In fact, satisfying property 1 can be seen as a particular constraint that guarantees that multidirectionality is used completely during the search for support in the constraint C_Π. However, because of its formulation, property 1 cannot be used by SEEKNEXTSUPPORT to perform look ahead on the domains of the variables of $X(C_\Pi)$ during a search for support. Indeed, property 1 states what a non candidate tuple is, but does not state what an "impossible" value (i.e., a value that cannot belong to any candidate tuple) is, because in chronological backtracking, a value has to be added to a partial instantiation to be detected as "impossible" by property 1. In the following section, we give a reformulation of property 1 that gives a condition under which a value cannot belong to any candidate, and thus does not need to be considered by SEEKNEXTSUPPORT. Then, we present an original and efficient way for taking completely into account multidirectionality and for taking advantage of the knowledge of all the underlying constraints in a global constraint.

4.2 Implementation of multidirectionality as a constraint

The idea is thus to define, for each global constraint C, a new constraint, denoted by M_C, whose filtering algorithm removes the values that do not belong to any candidate during a search for support in C. In this way, the PROPAGATION algorithm associated with this constraint will guarantee the point (2) of multidirectionality without any restriction on the search algorithm used in SEEKNEXTSUPPORT, and thus the constraint C will be efficiently handled.

SEEKNEXTSUPPORT2(C: constraint; y: variable, b: value, τ: tuple):tuple
$\Pi \leftarrow (X(C), \mathcal{D}(X(C)), \{y = b\} \cup C \cup \{M_C\})$
$\sigma \leftarrow$ SEARCHFORSOLUTION(Π, τ)
return σ

Algorithm 4: function SEEKNEXTSUPPORT2

Function SEEKNEXTSUPPORT is modified in order to take into account this new constraint. The specification of SEEKNEXTSUPPORT2(C, y, b, τ), the new version of SEEKNEXTSUPPORT, is the same as for SEEKNEXTSUPPORT, except that the set of constraints of the subnetwork to solve is $\{y = b\} \cup C \cup \{M_C\}$ instead of $\{y = b\} \cup C$.

In order to avoid confusion, let us denote $D^{in}(x)$, the domain of x during the current search for support, as opposed to $D(x)$ the domain of x when that search for support began. In other words, $\mathcal{D}^{in}_{X(C)}$ is the set of domains inside the call of function SEARCHFORSOLUTION.

Definition 3 (breakpoint) *Let $y \in X(C)$, and $b \in D^{in}(y)$.*
The value k such that $\forall i \in [1..k-1]$, $highest(D^{in}(var(C,i))) = last_C(y,b)[i]$ and $highest(D^{in}(var(C,k))) \neq last_C(y,b)[k]$ is called the breakpoint of (y,b) on C w.r.t. $\mathcal{D}^{in}_{X(C)}$, and is denoted by $breakpoint_C(y,b)$.

The following corollary is a reformulation of property 1.

Corollary 1 *Let $X(C) = (x_{i_1}, \ldots, x_{i_r})$, $y \in X(C)$, $b \in D^{in}(y)$, and $k = breakpoint_C(y,b)$. If $highest(D^{in}(var(C,k))) <_d last_C(y,b)[k]$ then (y,b) cannot belong to any candidate on C in $\mathcal{D}^{in}_{X(C)}$ w.r.t. $\prec_{lo}$.*

Proof. Suppose (y,b) belongs to a candidate partial instantiation σ. By hypothesis (see Definition 3), for any extension τ of σ, $\tau \in D^{in}(x_{i_1}) \times \cdots \times D^{in}(x_{i_r})$ implies that $\tau \prec_{lo} last_C(y,b)$, which is impossible for a candidate tuple.

The following corollary is a particular case of the previous one.

Corollary 2 *Let $x, y \in X(C)$. If $D^{in}(x) = \{a\}$ then,*
$index(C,y) \leq breakpoint_C(x,a)$ and $b <_d last_C(x,a)[index(C,y)]$
$\Rightarrow (y,b)$ cannot belong to any candidate on C in $\mathcal{D}^{in}_{X(C)}$ w.r.t. $\prec_{lo}$.

With these corollaries, we can predict that a value (x_{i_k}, v_{i_k}) cannot belong to any candidate in $D^{in}(x_{i_1}) \times \cdots \times D^{in}(x_{i_r})$ without instantiating all the variables from x_{i_1} to x_{i_k}.

We can first define a simple filtering algorithm that only deals with instantiated variables. Due to corollary 2, when a variable x is instantiated with a value a, all the variables that precede $breakpoint_C(x, a)$ in $X(C)$ can be instantiated to the maximal value of their domain. Furthermore, the values less than $last_C(x, a)$ of the variable $var(C, breakpoint_C(x, a))$ can be deleted. Function INSTANTIATEDVAR is a possible implementation of this filtering algorithm and is called each time a variable is instantiated. Parameter k of this function represents the breakpoint value of the invoked instantiated variable.

INSTANTIATEDVAR(C: constraint; y: variable; b: value; k: integer)
for $i \in [1..k]$ *while* $i \le |X(C)|$ do
| for $a = first(D^{in}(var(C, k)))$ to $last_C(y, b)[k] - 1$ do
| | remove a from $D^{in}(var(C, k))$
| | add $(var(C, k), a)$ to *deletionSet*

Algorithm 5: function INSTANTIATEDVAR

A better filtering algorithm can be obtained by the exact application of corollary 1. However, the problem is to determine which values can be deleted by applying this corollary. It is not practicable to recompute the breakpoint value of all the values when a modification arises. In fact, we show that it is not necessary. Consider a value b of a variable y, then $breakpoint_C(y, b)$ can change only in one of the two following cases:

1. $last_C(y, b)$ is changed,
2. the highest value of a domain is removed.

The first case is easy to deal with. For the second, it is necessary to introduce a new data structure in order to determine when some breakpoint values could have changed. When a highest value (x, a) is removed from $D^{in}(x)$, the values (y, b) such that $last_C(y, b)$ contains (x, a) must be reachable. Therefore, we introduce the following list:

$$L_C(x, a) = \{(y, b) \text{ s.t. } last_C(y, b) \text{ contains } (x, a)\}$$

The filtering algorithm can be defined by implementing the different operations:

- When (x, a) is added to $last_C(y, b)$ then (y, b) is added to $L_C(x, a)$. And, when (x, a) is no longer in $last_C(y, b)$ then (y, b) is removed from $L_C(x, a)$.
- When a variable is instantiated then INSTANTIATEDVAR is called.
- When the $last_C$ of an element is changed, the breakpoint value of this element is recomputed.

PROPAGATION(M_C: constraint; x: variable; a: value; *deletionSet*: list)

3 **if** $a > highest(D^{in}(x))$ **then**

    for $(y,b) \in L_C(x,a)$ **do**

      if $b \in D^{in}(y)$ **and** $breakpoint_C(y,b) \geq index(C,x)$ **then**

        remove b from $D^{in}(y)$

        add (y,b) to *deletionSet*

    for $(y,b) \in L_C(x,highest(D^{in}(x)))$ **do**

      if $b \in D^{in}(y)$ **and** $breakpoint_C(y,b) = index(C,x)$ **then**

        $k \leftarrow$ COMPUTEBREAKPOINT(y,b)

        if $k \leq |X(C)|$ **and** $highest(D^{in}(var(C,k))) <_d last_C(y,b)[k]$ **then**

          remove b from $D^{in}(y)$

          add (y,b) to *deletionSet*

      else

        $breakpoint_C(y,b) \leftarrow k$

Algorithm 6: function PROPAGATION

– When a value a is removed from $D^{in}(x)$, we check whether it was the highest value of $D^{in}(x)$ or not (line 3 of PROPAGATION). Then, we check whether corollary 1 is satisfied for each value of $L_C(x,a)$. Then, the breakpoint of each value (y,b) of $L_C(x,highest(D^{in}(x)))$ satisfying $breakpoint_C(y,b) = index(C,x)$ is recomputed and corollary 1 is checked. [1]

This last point is implemented by function PROPAGATION which is called when the highest value of a variable x has been reduced. (Function COMPUTE-BREAKPOINT(y,b) recomputes the breakpoint value of (y,b).)

4.3 Analysis

First, let us report the worst-case space complexity of the algorithms we proposed to achieve arc consistency on C a global constraint. In the case of SEEKNEXTSUP-PORT, the only data structures used are those of GAC-Schema. The worst-case space complexity is then in $O(|X(C)|^2 \cdot d)$, where d is the size of the largest domain (see [1]). When we use SEEKNEXTSUPPORT2, some additional data structures are used to implement the propagation procedure of the multidirectionality constraint M_C. But their size is less than $|X(C)|^2 \cdot d$, so the space complexity remains in $O(|X(C)|^2 \cdot d)$. The worst-case time complexity is bounded above by the complexity of the search procedure, SEARCHFORSOLUTION, used to search for supports.

The ordering of the variables that is used in SEEKNEXTSUPPORT2 must be a static variable ordering (SVO). This SVO is required to deal with the constraint

---

[1] In some solvers, such as ILOG Solver, the values higher than the highest of a domain that have been deleted since the last propagation are provided by the solver. Thus, they can be dealt with together in one turn, improving our algorithm.

of multidirectionality. With the possibility of using look ahead search algorithms such as FC or MAC to search for supports on $X(C)$, it can seem a strong limitation to use them with a SVO. But we have to keep in mind that this restriction holds only for the subnetwork defined on $X(C)$ by the constraints in C. Nevertheless, in cases where a SVO in the search for support would be a too strong limitation, we can relax the constraint of using complete multidirectionality and use SEEKNEXTSUPPORT with a search algorithm with dynamic variable ordering (DVO). The counterpart is that only one side of multidirectionality is used, the one performed in SEEKINFERABLESUPPORT (i.e., never seeking a support for a value when a tuple supporting it has already been checked). We cannot guarantee that we never check whether a tuple is a support for a value when it has already been unsuccessfully checked for another value.

5   Experimental results

In this section we will present three kinds of experiments. Here is an overall presentation of them:

1. The first one aims at showing that computing arc consistency of a subproblem can greatly improve the resolution of the whole problem. It also shows that computing the solutions of the subproblem on the fly can be sufficient in itself to improve the resolution of the whole problem, even without developing a specific algorithm;
2. The second kind of experiments stresses on the interest of our approach for exhibiting the difficult parts of a problem;
3. The last experiments compare our approach to GAC-Schema+allowed on instances favorable for this algorithm. This proves that even for such problems our algorithm behaves well.

Furthermore, they all show that GAC-Schema+predicate can always be replaced by the algorithm we presented.

5.1   Improvement of the resolution

First, we report a small sample of the results we obtained for the problem defined in the introduction of this paper.

The results presented in the following are obtained with a MAC search procedure with the "minimum domain" variable ordering heuristic. The procedure used to search for supports inside the arc consistency process of a constraint representing a subproblem is also a MAC procedure. It uses a lexicographic variable ordering. These MAC procedures are those of ILOG Solver [3] without any special features except those presented in this paper.

Let us compare three possible representations of the problem. The first one, denoted by stand, corresponds to the standard representation. It does not involve any constraint "sum of n all different variables" (denoted by $C_{S\neq}$). The second one, denoted by pred, represents each constraint $C_{S\neq}$ as a predicate and uses

GAC-Schema+predicate to handle it. In the third one, denoted by conj, each global constraint $C_{S\neq}$ is handled by the new algorithm we have proposed in this paper.

For 5×5 square:

	# backtracks			cpu time (sec.)		
	stand	pred	conj	stand	pred	conj
easiest	4	0	0	0	8.5	0.5
average	2373	127	127	0.3	18	1.7
hardest	9985	591	591	1.36	51	7.2

The search space is reduced by introducing the $C_{S\neq}$ constraints. The results show that a dedicated constraint should be written, because the overall time performance is not improved, but the number of backtracks is dramatically reduced. However, we have to check if this behavior is true when the size of the square increases.

For 6×6 square:

	# backtracks			cpu time (sec.)		
	stand	pred	conj	stand	pred	conj
easiest	3	0	0	0.03	too long	2.5
average	75,548	281	281	26.2	too long	6.7
hardest	1,623,557	2,598	2,598	520	too long	42.0

In this case it is not possible to use GAC-Schema+predicate because it needs too much time. The new technique becomes really interesting. For the 5×5 square, in average, the number of backtracks is reduced by a factor of 18 compared to the standard modelling. For the 6×6 square the factor becomes 269. Further experiments have shown that this factor increases when the size of the square increases. Thus, there is no doubt about the interest of the $C_{S\neq}$ constraints.

On the other hand, the algorithm we proposed is the best existing way to solve this problem. This means that for the 6×6 square, the best way is to solve subproblems on the fly. This kind of result is not always observed but it is interesting to mention it. In some cases, there is no need to develop a specific algorithm, our approach is in itself sufficient to improve the resolution of a hard problem.

5.2 Identification of the difficulty

Let us consider another problem: the Golomb Ruler Problem. This problem is problem prob006 of the CSPLib benchmark library. Here is its specification taken from this library: " A Golomb ruler may be defined as a set of n integers $0 = x_1 < x_2 < ... < x_n$, such that the $n(n-1)/2$ differences $x_j - x_i$, $1 \leq i < j \leq n$, are distinct. Such a ruler is said to contain n marks and is of length x_n. The objective is to find optimal (minimum length) or near optimal rulers."

This problem is hard to solve with constraint programming. It is difficult to obtain solutions for $n > 13$. We study three possible modelizations of the problem.

The first one is classical: each integer and each difference between integer is represented by a variable, an alldiff constraint involving all the differences is defined.

Since this problem is hard to solve, we need to try to identify some difficult parts, and parts that could be improved.

The second model introduces a $C_{S\neq}$ constraint involving variables $x_i - x_{i-1}$. Arc consistency for this constraint is achieved by using the algorithm we propose in the paper, because even for small n it is impossible to use GAC-Schema+predicate.

The third model proposes to focus on a particular subpart of the Golomb Ruler Problem. In the previous models, the alldiff constraint involves $O(n^2)$ variables. We propose to study a subproblem which involves only $O(n)$ variables. This subproblem is defined by the following constraints:

- a sum constraint: $\sum_{i=2}^{n}(x_i - x_{i-1}) = x_n$
- an alldiff constraint defined on $\{x_i, i = 1..n\} \cup \{(x_i - x_{i-1}), i = 2..n\} \cup \{(x_i - x_{i-2}), i = 3..n\}$

For all the experiment we fix the value of x_n and search for a solution. Here are some results (time is given in seconds):

	$n = 8$				$n = 9$				$n = 10$			
	$x_n = 34$		$x_n = 33$		$x_n = 44$		$x_n = 43$		$x_n = 55$		$x_n = 54$	
	#bk	time	#bk	time	#bk	time	#bk	time	#bk	time	#bk	time
model 1	22	0.3	297	0.4	213	0.4	1298	2.7	844	2.2	5326	19
model 2	3	0.3	122	2.8	48	2.4	343	18.2	183	16.6	1967	161
model 3	0	1.4	5	1.5	4	10.5	25	18.1	16	120	96	226

The comparison of model 1 and model 2 shows that the introduction of the $C_{S\neq}$ constraint reduces the number of backtracks by a factor around 4, which is less than with the previous experiments. The time needed by model 2 is greater than the time needed by model 1. Thus, for this experiment it is necessary to develop a specific algorithm for this constraint if we want to improve in time the resolution of the problem.

With model 3 the number of backtracks is dramatically reduced, but the time needed to achieve arc consistency for the subproblem we consider is large. Thus, this model can be used only if a specific filtering algorithm is written. From this result we also learn that it seems that if we are able to solve quickly the subproblem we will be able to solve the Golomb Ruler Problem efficiently. This is particularly interesting because this subproblem involves only $O(n)$ variables, whereas the Golomb Ruler Problem involves $O(n^2)$ variables.

In conclusion, for this experiment the algorithm we proposed is not able to improve in time the resolution of the problem. However, with it we have identified a subproblem for which the design of a specific algorithm would improve the resolution of the whole problem. We have understood where a part of the difficulty of the problem is.

5.3 Comparison with GAC-Schema+allowed

Finally, we propose to study a configuration problem. The general formulation is this: given a supply of components and bins of given types, determine all assignments of components to bins satisfying specified assignment constraints subject to an optimization criterion.

In the example we will consider that there are 5 types of components: {glass, plastic, steel, wood, copper}. There are three types of bins: {red, blue, green} whose capacity constraints are: red has capacity 5, blue has capacity 5, green has capacity 6.

The containment constraints are:
- red can contain glass, copper, wood
- blue can contain glass, steel, copper
- green can contain plastic, copper, wood

The requirement constraints are (for all bin types): wood requires plastic.

Certain component types cannot coexist: glass exclusive copper

Certain bin types have capacity constraint for certain components:
- red contains at most 1 of wood
- green contains at most 2 of wood

- for all the bins there is either no plastic or at least 2 plastic.

Given an initial supply of: 12 of glass, 10 of plastic, 8 of steel, 12 of wood, and 8 of copper; what is the minimum total number of bins required to contain the components?

A description of a possible implementation of a similar problem is given in [3]. We will call it "standard model".

Almost all the constraints between types of bins and components are local. The filtering algorithm associated with them leads to few domain reductions. Therefore, we propose to group them inside a single global constraint. Then we can test GAC-Schema+allowed against the algorithm we proposed. It is possible to use GAC-Schema+allowed because the number of allowed tuples is small: 79. They can be computed and stored in a preprocessing phase. However, in real-world applications the number of components can largely grow and this method will no longer be possible.

Here are the results:

	# Backtracks	time (s)
standard model	1,361,709	430
allowed	12,659	9.7
new algorithm	12,659	11

Once again it is quite interesting to represent a part of a problem by a constraint. Moreover, we observe that our algorithm does not loose too much time compared to GAC-Schema+allowed, while this problem was an ideal case for GAC-Schema+allowed.

6 Conclusion

Following the intuition that "the more globally you filter, the more able you are to tackle combinatorial explosion", we proposed a new instantiation of GAC-Schema which achieves arc consistency on global constraints by solving subproblems on the fly. We proved that the knowledge of a subproblem and multidirectionality can be taken into account in a generic way by adding to the considered subproblem a special constraint representing multidirectionality. This instantiation clearly outperforms the technique in which the subproblem is considered as a predicate without the possibility of using underlying knowledge (GAC-Schema+predicate).

The experiments we presented, show that as soon as a problem is difficult enough, the cost of solving subproblems on the fly can be outweighed by the reduction of the search space it implies.

In addition, beyond efficiency concerns, we pointed out that in constraint programming, when a problem is hard to solve, the new instantiation of GAC-Schema we proposed can be very helpful in the modelling phase to isolate parts of the problem on which writing a dedicated filtering algorithm will have chances to pay off.

References

1. C. Bessière and J-C. Régin. Arc consistency for general constraint networks: preliminary results. In *Proceedings of IJCAI'97*, pages 398–404, Nagoya, 1997.
2. P. Van Hentenryck. Incremental constraint satisfaction in logic programming. In *proceedings ICLP'90*, pages 189–202, Jerusalem, Israel, 1990.
3. ILOG. *ILOG Solver 4.4 User's manual*. ILOG S.A., 1999.
4. J-C. Régin. Minimization of the number of breaks in sports scheduling problems using constraint programming. In *proceedings DIMACS Workshop on Constraint Programming and Large Scale Discrete Optimization*, pages P7:1–23, 1998.
5. B.M. Smith. Succeed-first or fail-first: A case study in variable and value ordering. In *proceedings ILOG Solver and ILOG Scheduler Second International Users' Conference*, Paris, France, 1996.

Exploiting Bipartiteness to Identify
Yet Another Tractable Subclass of CSP

Marcus Bjäreland*
Peter Jonsson**

Dept. of Comp. and Info. Sci.
Linköpings universitet
S-581 83 Linköping, Sweden
{marbj, petej}@ida.liu.se

Abstract. The class of constraint satisfaction problems (CSPs) over finite domains has been shown to be NP-complete, but many tractable subclasses have been identified in the literature. In this paper we are interested in restrictions on the types of constraint relations in CSP instances. By a result of Jeavons *et al.* we know that a key to the complexity of classes arising from such restrictions is the closure properties of the sets of relations. It has been shown that sets of relations that are closed under constant, majority, affine, or associative, commutative, and idempotent (ACI) functions yield tractable subclasses of CSP. However, it has been unknown whether other closure properties may generate tractable subclasses.

In this paper we introduce a class of tractable (in fact, *SL*-complete) CSPs based on bipartite graphs. We show that there are members of this class that are not closed under constant, majority, affine, or ACI functions, and that it, therefore, is incomparable with previously identified classes.

1 Introduction

In general, the class of *constraint satisfaction problems* (CSPs) over finite domains is NP-complete. However, much more is known about the complexity of CSP and its variants. For example, Schaefer [14] provided a complete complexity classification of subproblems of CSP with domains of size 2. Other examples of complexity analyses of CSPs can be found in [12, 4, 5], and in more recent work, such as [1, 10, 3].

By looking at subclasses of CSP restricted by the types of constraint relations allowed, Jeavons *et al.* [8] showed that the complexity of such subclasses can be characterized by the functions under which the respective sets of relations

---
* This research has been supported in parts by *Swedish Research Council for the Engineering Sciences* (TFR) and the Knut and Alice Wallenberg Foundation

** This research has been supported by the *Swedish Research Council for the Engineering Sciences* (TFR) under grant 97-301.

are closed. In particular, sets of relations closed under constant, majority, affine, or associative, commutative, and idempotent (ACI) functions are shown to be tractable. It has been unknown whether any tractable CSP subclass exists that is not closed under any of those four types of functions. In this paper we introduce such a class, which is based on a strong result in graph theory by Hell and Nešetřil [6] stating that the H-coloring problem (that is, the problem of finding homomorphisms from graphs to a fixed graph H) is tractable if H is bipartite, and NP-complete otherwise (discussed in Sect. 2). This result is relevant since a solution to a CSP can be seen as a homomorphism from the structure of variables in a CSP instance to the constraint relations [9]. Thus, for CSPs with only one binary relation we have tractability if the relation defines a bipartite graph, and NP-completeness otherwise. In fact, this result does by itself yield a new class of tractable CSPs. We show that the bipartite graph C_6, that is, the cycle of length 6, is a counterexample to each of the four closure functions (Sect. 4.1). However, for CSPs with more than one constraint relation bipartiteness alone does not provide tractability. We identify (in Sect. 4) three global properties on the sets of relations (seen as graphs) in a CSP, namely that every relation is in itself bipartite (local bipartiteness), that all relations have the same partitions (partition equivalence), and that all relations have at least one edge in common (non-disjoint). The class of all sets of relations with these three properties is denoted **lpn**. We show (in Theorem 15) that the problem CSP(Γ) for $\Gamma \in$ **lpn** is tractable. In Corollary 16 we strengthen this by showing that this problem in fact is complete for the complexity class SL (Symmetric Logspace).

In Sect. 5 we show that any attempt to remove any of the three restrictions results in NP-completeness, and here we again rely on Hell and Nešetřil's theorem.

As a result of the work presented in this paper we have identified a number of open questions, which we state in Sect. 6.

2 Preliminaries

In this section we define the concepts that will be used in this paper.

Definition 1. Let $\Gamma = \{R_1, \ldots, R_n\}$ be a set of relations over a domain D, such that R_i has arity k_i. An *instance* of the constraint satisfaction problem over Γ, $\mathcal{P}$, is a tuple,

$$\mathcal{P} = \langle V, D, R_1(S_1), \ldots, R_n(S_n) \rangle$$

where

- V is a finite set of *variables*;
- D is the finite domain;
- Each pair $R_i(S_i)$ is a *constraint*, where $R_i \in \Gamma$, and S_i is an ordered list of k_i variables.

Definition 2 (Solution). A *solution* to $\mathcal{P} = \langle V, D, R_1(S_1), \ldots, R_n(S_n) \rangle$ is a function $h : V \to D$ such that $h(S_i) \in R_i$ for all i, where $h(S_i)$ denotes the coordinate-wise application of h to the variables in S_i (i.e. if $S_i = \langle v_1, \ldots, v_{k_i} \rangle$, then $h(S_i) = \langle h(v_1), \ldots, h(v_{k_i}) \rangle$). The set of solutions to an instance $\mathcal{P}$ is denoted $Sol(\mathcal{P})$.

Given a finite set of relations Γ, we define the computational problem $\mathrm{CSP}(\Gamma)$ as follows: given a CSP instance over Γ, does it have a solution?

Following the work on constraints and universal algebra in [9] we can equivalently define a solution to an instance as a homomorphism between two algebraic structures.

Definition 3 (CSP Homomorphism). Let $\mathcal{P} = \langle V, D, R_1(S_1), \ldots, R_n(S_n) \rangle$ be a CSP where each relation R_i has arity k_i. Then construct $\Sigma = \langle V, \{S_1\}, \ldots, \{S_n\} \rangle$ and $\Sigma' = \langle D, R_1, \ldots, R_n \rangle$. A CSP *homomorphism* is a function $g : V \to D$ such that for all $i = 1, \ldots, n$,

$$\langle v_1, \ldots, v_{k_i} \rangle \in \{S_i\} \Rightarrow \langle g(v_1), \ldots, g(v_{k_i}) \rangle \in R_i.$$

The set of all homomorphisms for $\mathcal{P}$ is denoted $Hom(\mathcal{P})$.

We establish the relation between the solutions to a CSP instance and CSP homomorphism.

Proposition 4 ([9]).

$$Sol(\mathcal{P}) = Hom(\mathcal{P}),$$

for an instance $\mathcal{P}$.

As we will rely heavily on viewing binary relations as graphs, we define the necessary concepts here.

Definition 5. A *graph*, G, is a tuple, $G = \langle V, E \rangle$ where V is a (non-empty) set of *vertices*, and E a set of *edges*, $\langle v_i, v_j \rangle$, such that $v_i, v_j \in V$. Two vertices $v_i, v_j \in V$ are *adjacent* if $\langle v_i, v_j \rangle \in E$ or $\langle v_j, v_i \rangle \in E$. A *cycle* in a graph is a sequence of vertices, $v_{i_1}, v_{i_2}, \ldots, v_{i_m}$ such that $\langle v_{i_j}, v_{i_{j+1}} \rangle \in E$ for $j = 1, \ldots, n-1$, and $\langle v_{i_n}, v_{i_1} \rangle \in E$. The natural number m is the *length* of the cycle. A graph is *undirected* if, whenever $\langle v_i, v_j \rangle \in E$, then $\langle v_j, v_i \rangle \in E$. A graph is *bipartite* if it is possible to partition V into two disjoint sets X and Y, such that every edge with the left vertex in one of the partitions has the right vertex in the other partition, and no edges contain vertices from the same partition. Equivalently, a bipartite graph is a graph without cycles of odd length.

Unless otherwise stated, we will assume that graphs are irreflexive, that is, that for any $v \in V$, $\langle v, v \rangle \notin E$. Moreover, all isolated vertices (that is, vertices that does not belong to any edge) are assumed to belong to one partition.

Definition 6 (Graph Homomorphism). Let $G = \langle V, E \rangle$ and $G' = \langle V', E' \rangle$ be two graphs. A graph *homomorphism* from G to G' is a function $f : V \to V'$ such that, if v_i and v_j are adjacent vertices in G, then $f(v_i)$ and $f(v_j)$ are adjacent vertices in G'.

For graphs, the k-coloring problem, for natural numbers k, is defined as the problem of finding a function $f : V \to \{0, 1, \ldots, k-1\}$ such that adjacent vertices in the graph are not mapped to the same number. We will use the fact that 2-coloring is a tractable problem.

A more general problem, for a fixed graph H, is the problem of deciding whether there exists a graph homomorphism from a graph G to H. This problem is called is called $H - coloring$. For H-coloring we have the following strong complexity result, proven in [6]. Note that for a non-irreflexive graph H, H-coloring is trivial.

Theorem 7 ([6]). *Let H be a fixed undirected graph. If H is bipartite then the H-coloring problem is in P. If H is not bipartite then the H-coloring problem is NP-complete.*

We can now prove

Proposition 8. *For a symmetric binary relation, R, $CSP(\{R\})$ is tractable if the graph $\langle D, R \rangle$, where D is the domain of R, is bipartite, and NP-complete otherwise.*

Proof. Follows immediately from Proposition 4 and Theorem 7.

For instances with more than one constraint, it does not suffice that every relation is bipartite for tractability. As we will show in Sect. 5, it is necessary to impose global restrictions on the set of relations.

Since we only consider binary constraint relations in this paper, we will use the words "graph" and "relation" interchangeably.

3 Closure and complexity

We will be interested in closure properties of sets of binary relations, which motivates the following definition.

Definition 9. Given a binary relation R, and a function $\phi : D^n \to D$, we say that R is closed under ϕ, if for all sets of tuples

$$\langle d_1^1, d_2^1 \rangle \in R$$

$$\vdots$$

$$\langle d_1^n, d_2^n \rangle \in R$$

the tuple

$$\langle \phi(d_1^1, \ldots, d_1^n), \phi(d_2^1, \ldots, d_2^n) \rangle$$

also belongs to R.

Below we will assume that Γ is a set of relations over a finite set D with at least two elements. The set of all functions $\phi : D^n \to D$, any n, under which every member of Γ is closed, will be denoted $Fun(\Gamma)$.

If we define $\phi(R)$ to be the binary relation

$$\{\phi(d_1, d_2) \mid \langle d_1, d_2 \rangle \in R\},$$

we can equivalently define R to be closed under ϕ iff $\phi(R) \subseteq R$. From this definition it is easy to prove

Theorem 10 ([8]). *For any set of finite relations Γ, and any $\phi \in Fun(\Gamma)$, there is a polynomial reduction from $CSP(\Gamma)$ to $CSP(\phi(\Gamma))$, with $\phi(\Gamma) = \{\phi(R) \mid R \in \Gamma\}$. That is, under the polynomial reduction $CSP(\Gamma)$ is satisfiable iff $CSP(\phi(\Gamma))$ is satisfiable.*

From Theorem 10 it follows that if $Fun(\Gamma)$ contains a non-injective unary function, then $CSP(\Gamma)$ can be reduced to a problem with smaller domain. We say that Γ is *reduced* if $Fun(\Gamma)$ does not contain any non-injective unary functions.

Theorem 11 ([8]). *For any reduced set of relations Γ over a finite set D the set $Fun(\Gamma)$ must contain at least one of the following six types of functions:*

1. *A constant function;*
2. *A binary idempotent function, that is, a function ϕ such that $\phi(d, d) = d$ for all $d \in D$;*
3. *A ternary majority function, that is, a function ϕ such that $\phi(d, d, d') = \phi(d, d', d) = \phi(d', d, d) = d$ for all $d, d' \in D$;*
4. *A ternary affine function, that is, a function ϕ such that $\phi(d_1, d_2, d_3) = d_1 - d_2 + d_3$ for all $d_1, d_2, d_3 \in D$, where $\langle D, + \rangle$ is an abelian group;*
5. *A semiprojection, ϕ, that is, for $n \geq 3$, there exists $i \in \{1, \ldots, n\}$ such that for all $d_1, \ldots, d_n \in D$ with $|\{d_1, \ldots, d_n\}| < n$, we have $\phi(d_1, \ldots, d_n) = d_i$;*
6. *An essentially unary function, that is, a function ϕ of arity n such that $\phi(d_1, \ldots, d_n) = f(d_i)$ for some i and some non-constant unary function f, for all $d_1, \ldots, d_n \in D$.*

The complexity and closure function results in [8] can be summarized as follows:

- If $Fun(\Gamma)$ contains a constant function, then $CSP(\Gamma)$ is tractable.
- If $Fun(\Gamma)$ contains a binary function that is associative, commutative, and idempotent (ACI), then $CSP(\Gamma)$ is tractable.
- If $Fun(\Gamma)$ contains a majority function, then $CSP(\Gamma)$ is tractable.
- If $Fun(\Gamma)$ contains an affine function, then $CSP(\Gamma)$ is tractable.
- If $Fun(\Gamma)$ contains only semiprojections, then $CSP(\Gamma)$ is NP-complete.
- If $Fun(\Gamma)$ contains only essentially unary functions, then $CSP(\Gamma)$ is NP-complete.

Classes of problems that are tractable due to the closure properties have been extensively studied in the literature. For instance, the class of max-closed constraints [10] are closed under an ACI function [8], and the class of CRC constraints [2] are closed under a majority function [7].

In [8] Jeavons *et al.* state that

It is currently unknown whether there are tractable sets of relations closed under some combination of semiprojections, unary operations, and binary operations which are not included in any of the tractable classes above.

Below, we will introduce a class that is not closed under constant, ACI, majority, or affine functions.

4 A new tractable subclass

We saw in Proposition 8 that for a single binary and bipartite constraint relation CSP was tractable. However, if we introduce more relations it is easy to see that bipartiteness alone on the union of the relations does not yield tractability.

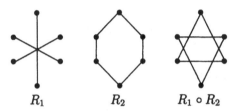

$$R_1 \qquad\qquad R_2 \qquad\qquad R_1 \circ R_2$$

Fig. 1. Composition of the two bipartite relations R_1 and R_2 yielding a non-bipartite relation $R_1 \circ R_2$.

Definition 12. *Intersection* and *union* of relation is defined as set theoretic intersection and union. *Composition* of binary relations R_1 and R_2 is defined as $R_1 \circ R_2 = \{\langle x, z\rangle \mid \exists y. \langle x, y\rangle \in R_2 \wedge \langle y, z\rangle \in R_1\}$. We often write R^2 instead of $R \circ R$.

Note that if CSP$(\{R_1 \circ R_2\})$ is NP-complete, then CSP$(\{R_1, R_2\})$ is too, since we can go back and forth from $\{R_1 \circ R_2\}$ to $\{R_1, R_2\}$ in polynomial time. This also holds for intersection.

Example 13. In Fig. 1 two bipartite relations, R_1 and R_2, are depicted. By composing them we get a relation $R_1 \circ R_2$ that contains cycles of odd length, which means that the composition is not bipartite. Thus, by Theorem 8, CSP$(\{R_1, R_2\})$ is NP-complete.

Definition 14 (lpn). Let $\Gamma = \{R_1, \dots, R_n\}$ be a set of binary symmetric relations over a finite domain D, and construct the graphs $G_1 = \langle D, R_1\rangle, \dots, G_n = \langle D, R_n\rangle$. Γ is said to be *locally bipartite* if G_i is bipartite, for all i. If Γ is locally bipartite, with partitions X_i, Y_i for G_i we say that Γ is *partition equivalent* if $X_1 = X_2 = \dots = X_n$ and $Y_1 = Y_2 = \dots = Y_n$. Furthermore, Γ is said to be *non-disjoint* if $R_1 \cap \dots \cap R_n \neq \emptyset$.

We will refer to the class of locally bipartite, partition equivalent, non-disjoint sets of relations as **lpn**.

Henceforth, when we write CSP(Γ), we assume that $\Gamma \in$ **lpn**.

Theorem 15. CSP(Γ) *is tractable.*

Proof. Given $\mathcal{P} = \langle V, D, R_1(x_1, x_1'), \dots, R_n(x_n, x_n') \rangle \in$ CSP(Γ) we show that there exists a solution to $\mathcal{P}$ iff the graph $G_V = \langle V, \{\langle x_1, x_1' \rangle, \dots, \langle x_n, x_n' \rangle\} \rangle$ is 2-colorable.

$\Leftarrow$). Assume that G_V is 2-colorable, and choose $\langle d, d' \rangle \in \bigcap_{i=1}^n R_i$ (which exists since the set of relations is non-disjoint). Color G_V with d and d'. Clearly, this coloring is a solution to $\mathcal{P}$.

$\Rightarrow$). Let $h : V \to D$ be a solution to $\mathcal{P}$. Since the set of relations is bipartite and partition equivalent we name the partitions X and Y and construct a function $f : V \to \{0, 1\}$, as follows:

$$f(v) = \begin{cases} 0 & \text{if } h(v) \in X, \\ 1 & \text{if } h(v) \in Y. \end{cases}$$

Clearly, f is a 2-coloring of G_V.

It is known that 2-coloring is $co - SL$-complete [11], that is, it is complete for the complement of the class of symmetric logspace problems. Moreover, Nisan and Ta-Schma have shown that $SL = co - SL$ [13], which gives us the following:

Corollary 16. CSP(Γ) *is SL-complete.*

Proof. In the proof of Theorem 15, CSP(Γ) is trivially reduced to 2-colorability (and *vice versa*). Thus we can immediately apply Reif's result [11] followed by Nisan and Ta-Schma's result [13].

4.1 Non-closure properties of lpn

In this section we will show that some sets of relations in **lpn** are not closed under constant, majority, ACI, or affine functions. Consider the graph C_6 in Fig. 2 representing a bipartite relation R. Since the graph is irreflexive, we can immediately see that $\{R\}$ is not closed under a constant function.

For the existence of a majority function d we can note that

$$d(a, a, b) = a$$
$$d(b, a, b) = b$$
$$d(b, c, c) = c$$
$$d(i, j, k) = x,$$

with $x \in \{a, b, c, i, j, k\}$. We will show that x cannot be chosen such that C_6 is closed under a majority function. Consider the following three edges of C_6:

Fig. 2. The graph C_6, with partitions $\{a, b, c\}$ and $\{i, j, k\}$.

$\langle a, i \rangle, \langle a, j \rangle, \langle b, k \rangle$ we can see that if we apply d to the edges component-wise, we get that $x \in \{i, j\}$ for C_6 to be closed under any majority function. For the following three edges: $\langle b, i \rangle, \langle a, j \rangle, \langle b, k \rangle$, we get $x \in \{i, k\}$. Finally, for $\langle b, i \rangle, \langle c, j \rangle, \langle c, k \rangle$ we get $x \in \{j, k\}$. Thus, there is no choice of x that satisfies the three triplets simultaneously, and therefore there cannot exist a majority function under which C_6 is closed.

Next, we turn our attention to ACI functions. We can easily see that undirected and irreflexive graphs are not closed under any *commutative* function, that is, if d is commutative then $d(x, y) = d(y, x)$, for all $x, y \in D$. If the graph is undirected there exists a pair of edges, $\langle x, x' \rangle$ and $\langle x', x \rangle$, and if we apply d component-wise to the edges we get $\langle d(x, x'), d(x', x) \rangle = \langle y, y \rangle$, for some $y \in D$. Since the graph was irreflexive, it cannot be closed under an ACI function.

Finally, we prove that C_6 is not closed under affine functions. Consider the three edges of C_6: $\langle a, i \rangle, \langle a, j \rangle, \langle c, j \rangle$. Choose $+$ so that $\langle D, + \rangle$ is an abelian group, and let $-x$ denote the inverse of the element $x \in D$. Next, we consider $\langle a + (-a) + c, i + (-j) + j \rangle$ which is the component-wise application of any affine function on the three edges. Since $\langle D, + \rangle$ is associative and that there exists a neutral group element, we have

$$\langle a + (-a) + c, i + (-j) + j \rangle = \langle (a + (-a)) + c, i + ((-j) + j) \rangle = \langle c, i \rangle,$$

which is not an edge in C_6. Thus, we have showed the following

Proposition 17. *Members in* **lpn** *are not in general closed under constant, majority, ACI, or affine functions.*

We have shown that members of **lpn** do not have closure properties that are known to yield tractable CSP instances. However, in similar spirit as the proof of Theorem 15, we can construct a unary non-injective function under which members of **lpn** are closed.

Let $\Gamma = \{R_1, \dots, R_n\} \in$ **lpn**, X and Y be the two partitions, and $\langle d_X, d_Y \rangle \in \bigcap_{i=1}^n R_i$, such that $d_X \in X$ and $d_Y \in Y$. Then, construct the unary function $f : D \to D$

$$f(d) = \begin{cases} d_X & \text{if } d \in X, \\ d_Y & \text{if } d \in Y. \end{cases}$$

Since every edge in any relation has one vertex in X, and the other in Y, Γ is closed under f. Whenever the domain of Γ is larger than 2, f is non-injective. If we then look at $f(\Gamma)$ we can see that the remaining domain only contains 2 elements, namely d_X and d_Y, and that there are no non-injective unary functions under which this new relation is closed. The relation $\{\langle d_X, d_Y\rangle, \langle d_Y, d_X\rangle\}$ is thus reduced, and it is a trivial exercise to find a majority function under which it is closed.

5 The restrictions on lpn cannot be removed

The tractability proof of CSP(Γ) (Theorem 15) relies on the locally bipartite, partition equivalent, and non-disjoint properties of the sets of relations of the instances. We will now show that we cannot remove any of the three properties and still maintain tractability. The arguments will be similar to that in Example 13, that is, we start with some graphs, put them together somehow and end up with a non-bipartite result on which we can apply Hell and Nešetřil's theorem (Theorem 7). Clearly, if we remove the local bipartiteness property, we have an NP-complete problem, so we direct the attention to the other two cases.

5.1 Disjoint relations

In Example 13 we saw an example of two bipartite and partition equivalent relations, without any common edge (that is, disjoint relations). By composition we constructed a non-bipartite relation, which by Proposition 8 gives us NP-completeness.

5.2 Non-partition equivalent relations

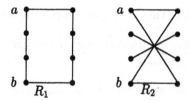

Fig. 3. Two relations R_1 and R_2 that are bipartite and non-disjoint, but does not have the same partitions.

In Fig. 3 we can see two relations that are locally bipartite and non-disjoint, but that does not have the same partitions (the two vertices a and b cannot belong to the same partition of both relations). In Fig. 4 we see that by composing R_1 with itself, we get a reflexive relation (remember that the corresponding

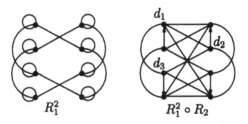

Fig. 4. R_1 composed with itself, and the result of $R_1^2 \circ R_2$, which is not bipartite due to the odd cycle between d_1, d_2, and d_3.

CSP then is trivially tractable), but when R_1^2 is composed with R_2 we get an odd cycle between the vertices d_1, d_2, and d_3. Note that the second graph in Fig. 4 is directed. We can, however, easily restore the undirectedness by intersecting the graph with its complement. NP-completeness then follows from Proposition 8.

6 Conclusion and open problems

In this paper we have exploited the notion of bipartite graphs to identify a new class of tractable CSPs. For a deeper understanding of the results presented in this paper a number of open problems need to solved. Here, we state some of the more interesting of them.

How do we extend CSP(Γ) to a *maximal* tractable class?
It is easy to see that CSP(Γ) is not a maximal tractable class, since we, for example, can add non-irreflexive relations to the sets of relations and still have tractability. However, Hell and Nešetřil's theorem hints that we are quite "close" to a maximal tractable class, but it remains to be investigated how close we really are.

Can the results be generalized to relations with higher arity?
In our tractability proof we rely on 2-coloring. However, for hypergraphs (that is, relations with arity > 2) it is known that 2-coloring is NP-complete. Thus, a generalization would have to rely on some other concept.

7 Acknowledgment

The authors would like to thank Pete Jeavons for insightful comments that improved the clarity and precision of this paper.

References

1. M. Cooper, D. Cohen, and P. Jeavons. Characterizing tractable constraints. *Artificial Intelligence*, 65:347 – 361, 1994.
2. Y. Deville, O. Barette, and P. Van Hentenryck. Constraint satisfaction over connected row convex constraints. In M.E. Pollack, editor, *Proceedings of the Fifteenth International Joint Conference on Artificial Intelligence*, Nagoya, Japan, August 1997. Morgan Kaufmann.
3. T. Feder and M.Y. Vardi. The computational structure of monotone monadic snp and constraint satisfaction: a study through Datalog and group theory. *SIAM Journal of Computing*, 28(1):57 – 104, 1998.
4. E.C. Freuder. Synthesizing constraint expressions. *Communications of the ACM*, 21:958 – 966, 1978.
5. E.C. Freuder. A sufficient condition for backtrack-free search. *Journal of the ACM*, 29(1):24 –32, 1982.
6. P. Hell and Nešetřil. On the complexity of H-coloring. *Journal of Combinatorial Theory, ser. B*, 48:92–110, 1990.
7. P. Jeavons, D. Cohen, and M. Cooper. Constraints, consistency, and closure. *Artificial Intelligence*, 101(1-2):251 – 265, 1998.
8. P. Jeavons, D. Cohen, and M. Gyssens. Closure properties of constraints. *Journal of the ACM*, 44:527–548, 1997.
9. P. Jeavons, D. Cohen, and J. Pearson. Constraints and universal algebra. *Annals of Mathematics and Artificial Intelligence*, 1999. To Appear.
10. P. Jeavons and M. Cooper. Tractable constraints in ordered domains. *Artificial Intelligence*, 79:327 – 339, 1996.
11. Reif. J.H. Symmetric complementation. In *Proceedings of the 14th ACM Symposium on Theory of Computing*, pages 210 – 214, 1982.
12. U. Montanari. Networks of constraints: fundamental properties and applications to picture processing. *Information Sciences*, 7:95 – 132, 1974.
13. N. Nisan and A. Ta-Schma. Symmetric logspace is closed under complement. In *Proceedings of the 27th ACM Symposium on Theory of Computing (STOC'95)*, 1995.
14. T.J. Schaefer. The complexity of satisfiability problems. In *Proceedings of the Tenth ACM Symposium on Theory of Computing*, pages 216 – 226, 1978.

Towards a Complete Classification of Tractability in Point Algebras for Nonlinear Time

Mathias Broxvall * and Peter Jonsson **

Department of Computer and Information Science
Linköpings Universitet
S-581 83 Linköping, Sweden
{matbr,petej}@ida.liu.se

Abstract. Efficient reasoning about temporal constraints over nonlinear time models is vital in numerous application areas, such as planning, distributed systems and cooperating agents. We identify all tractable subclasses of the point algebra for partially-ordered time and examine one large, nontrivial tractable subclass of the point algebra for branching time.

1 Introduction

Reasoning about temporal knowledge is a common task in computer science and elsewhere. In most applications, knowledge of temporal constraints is expressed in terms of collections of relations between time intervals or time points. Typical reasoning tasks include determining the satisfiability of such collections and deducing new relations from those that are known.

Research on automated reasoning about temporal constraints has largely concentrated on simple, linear models of time. However, it has been observed over and over again that more complex time models are needed in the analysis of concurrent and distributed systems, where simultaneous actions and their interactions must be represented and the order relationships between events are recorded by unsynchronized clocks. Typical problems in distributed system development include the traditional difficulties of synchronization and communication problems, network and bus protocol correctness and decision making in the absence of a global clock. Nonlinear time models are also needed in a number of other applications such as certain planning domains, robot motion problems and cooperating agents, to mention only a few.

For analyzing such systems, a number of time models have been proposed. Examples include temporal logics corresponding to *branching* time [6, 4] and *partially-ordered* time [1, 9]. The branching time model has been especially successful in its application to planning problems [5, 10]. Since most of the previous

---

* This research has been supported by the ECSEL graduate student program.
** This research has been supported by the Swedish Research Council for the Engineering Sciences (TFR) under grant 97-301.

research on nonlinear time have concentrated on modelling properties and theoretical foundations, computational aspects have received relatively little attention. There are a few papers that address such questions, though. Clarke *et al.* [4] have provided an apparently efficient algorithm than can check the correctness of certain circuits and algorithms. The method builds on a propositional branching-time logic based on CTL (Computation Tree Logic). Anger *et al.* [2] have studied whether standard constraint-based approaches can be applied to reasoning about nonlinear time; their results show that this is possible in certain restricted cases.

The main result of this paper is a total classification of the point algebra over partially-ordered time (by partially-ordered time, we mean a time structure where the time points are ordered by some partial order). We show that there exists exactly three maximal tractable classes and our proof does not rely on computer-assisted case analyses which has been the standard method in solving similar problems (*cf.* [11, 8]). We also examine the point algebra for branching time and identify a large, nontrivial tractable subclass (by *branching time*, we mean a partially-ordered time structure where no two incomparable time points have an upper bound. Intuitively, this condition prohibits joining of different branches of time).

The paper is structured as follows: Section 2 contains basic definitions and some auxiliary results. Section 3 and Sect. 4 contains the results on partially-ordered and branching time, respectively. Some concluding remarks are given in Section 5. For a technical report containing somewhat more exhaustive proofs as well as examples see Broxvall [3].

2   Preliminaries

The point algebra is based on the notion of *relations* between pairs of variables interpreted over a partially-ordered set. In this paper we consider four *basic relations* which we denote by $<, >, =$ and $\|$. If x, y are points in a partial order $\langle T, \leq \rangle$ then we define these relations in terms of the partial ordering $\leq$ as follows:

1. $x < y$ iff $x \leq y$ and not $y \leq x$
2. $x > y$ iff $y \leq x$ and not $x \leq y$
3. $x = y$ iff $x \leq y$ and $y \leq x$
4. $x \| y$ iff neither $x \leq y$ nor $y \leq x$

The relations we consider are always disjunctions of basic relations and they are represented as sets of basic relations. Since we have 4 different basic relations we get $2^4 = 16$ possible disjunctive relations. The set of basic relations is denoted $\mathcal{B}$ and the set of all 16 relations is denoted by $\mathcal{PA}$. Sometimes we use a short-hand notation for certain relations, for example, $\{<, =\}$ is sometimes written as $\leq$ and $\{=, \|\}$ as $\|$. The empty relations is denoted by $\perp$ and it is always unsatisfied.

The basic computational problem of the point algebra is the satisfiability problem where we have a set of variables and a set of constraints over the variables and the question is whether there exists a mapping from the variables to a specific domain such that all constraints are satisfied. Here we choose to consider a problem instance to be a graph where the nodes represents the variables and the labelled edges represents the constraints.

Definition 1. *Let $\Re \subseteq \mathcal{PA}$ be a set of point relations and P a class of partial orders. A problem instance of $PSAT_P(\Re)$ is a directed multigraph $\Pi = \langle V, E \rangle$ where the nodes in V are point variables and $E \subseteq V \times \Re \times V$ denotes the constraints imposed on the variables. A tuple $\langle f, \langle T, \leq \rangle \rangle$ where $f : V \to T$ is a total function and $\langle T, \leq \rangle \in P$ is called an interpretation of Π.*

A problem instance Π is satisfiable iff there exists an interpretation $M = \langle f, \langle T, \leq \rangle \rangle$ such that $f(u)\ R\ f(v)$ holds for every $\langle u, R, v \rangle \in E$. M is called a model of Π. Given a model $M = \langle f, \langle T, \Re \rangle \rangle$, we sometimes write $M(x)$ to denote $f(x)$.

The size of a problem instance $\langle V, E \rangle$ is $|V| + |E|$.

Given an instance Π of $PSAT_p(\Re)$ and two variables x, y we write $x \leq^+ y$ to say that there exists zero or more variables $z_1, \ldots, z_n$ such that

$$x \leq z_1 \wedge z_1 \leq z_2 \wedge \cdots \wedge z_{n-1} \leq z_n \wedge z_n \leq y$$

and we write $x \leq^* y$ to say $x \leq^+ y$ or $x = y$. An R-subgraph Π' of Π is defined as $\langle V, E \cap (V \times \{R\} \times V) \rangle$. A node n is R-*minimal* of the graph Π iff n is minimal in the R-subgraph of Π. The R-*components* of a graph Π are the components of the R-subgraph of Π. A graph Π is $(\leq)$-*acyclic* iff the $(\leq)$-subgraph of Π is acyclic.

We will consider two classes of partial orders: *po* which is the class of all partial orders and $br \subset po$ which is the class of all partial orders satisfying the *branching condition*:

$$\forall x, y, z : \text{IF } x \| y \text{ AND } y < z \text{ THEN } x \| z.$$

Note that in a partial order of class br two incomparable points cannot have an upper bound.

Next, we define two operations on point relations. The *intersection* operator takes two point relations R_1, R_2 to their intersection $R_3 = R_1 \cap R_2$ such that: $\forall x, y : x\ R_3\ y \leftrightarrow x\ R_1\ y \wedge x\ R_2\ y$. The *composition* operator takes two point relations R_1, R_2 to their composition $R_3 = R_1 \circ R_2$ such that: $\forall x, y : x\ R_3\ y \leftrightarrow \exists z : x\ R_1\ z \wedge z\ R_2\ y$. The composition of R_1, R_2 evaluates to the union of the composition of each pair of basic relations $r_1 \in R_1, r_2 \in R_2$. Composition tables for *po* and *br* can be found in Table 1.

We will now introduce the concept of gadgets which play an imporant role since they allow us to concentrate on smaller sets of relations while proving tractability for a larger set which can be implemented in terms of the smaller set.

Definition 2. *Let Θ be an instance of $PSAT_p(\Re)$ containing the variables $x, y, z_1, \cdots, z_n$. Assume that the following holds: In every model of Θ, $x\ R\ y$ holds for some $R \in \mathcal{PA}$. Then we say that $\Re$ implements the relation R and we say that Θ is a gadget that implements R.*

Table 1. Composition of basic relations in partially-ordered time (left figure) and branching time (right figure).

	<	>	=	‖
<	{<}	B	{<}	{‖ <}
>	B	{>}	{>}	{> ‖}
=	{<}	{>}	{=}	{‖}
‖	{‖ <}	{> ‖}	{‖}	B

	<	>	=	‖
<	{<}	{<=>}	{<}	{‖ <}
>	B	{>}	{>}	{‖}
=	{<}	{>}	{=}	{‖}
‖	{‖}	{> ‖}	{‖}	B

The intersection and composition operators are frequently used to verify that a given gadget implements a certain relation.

Example 1. The following gadget implements $\{<>\}$ for the branching point algebra since $\{<=\} \circ \{>=\}$ is $\{<=>\}$ and $\{<=>\} \cap \{< \parallel >\}$ is $\{<>\}$.

Gadgets and implementations play an important role in proving tractability and NP-completeness results and the main vehicle is the following simple lemma.

Lemma 1. *If $\Re$ implements $R_1, \ldots, R_k$ and $PSAT_p(\Re)$ is tractable, then $PSAT_p(\Re \cup \{R_1, \ldots, R_k\})$ is tractable. If $\Re$ implements $R_1, \ldots, R_k$ and $PSAT_p(\{R_1, \ldots, R_k\})$ is NP-hard, then $PSAT_p(\Re)$ is NP-hard.*

Proof. Assume $PSAT_p(\Re)$ to be solvable in polynomial time. We replace each edge marked with R in a problem instance $\Pi = \langle V, E \rangle$ one by one with the edges and nodes in a gadget implementing R until no more such edges exists. Let $\langle a, R, b \rangle \in E$ be an arbitrary edge marked with R and let $\Theta = \langle \{a, b, v_1, \cdots, v_n\}, E' \rangle$ be a gadget that implements $a \, R \, b$. Construct

$$\Pi' = \langle V \cup \{v_1, \cdots, v_n\}, E \cup E' - \langle a, R, b \rangle \rangle$$

Clearly Π' is satisfiable iff Π is satisfiable. Repeat until no more edges marked with R exists. Clearly all reductions can be performed in polynomial time. Hence, $PSAT_p(\Re)$ is solvable in polynomial time. $\square$

If f is a function which is undefined for n, then $(f|n \longmapsto c)$ is defined as the function $f \cup \{\langle n, c \rangle\}$. Let n_1, n_2 be nodes in a graph Π and let,

$$\Pi' = \langle V - \{n_2\}, E \cup \{\langle n_1, x \rangle | \langle n_2, x \rangle \in E\}$$
$$\cup \{\langle x, n_1 \rangle | \langle x, n_2 \rangle \in E\}$$
$$- \{\langle x, n_2 \rangle, \langle n_2, x \rangle | x \in V\} \rangle$$

We say that Π' is obtained by *contracting* n_1, n_2. That is, we identify the nodes n_1, n_2 by n_1. Note that there may be edges from n_1 to n_1.

Finally, we give a simple result which is needed several times to prove correctness of different algorithms.

133

Table 2. The classes $\mathcal{A}_{14}$, $\mathcal{A}_{13}$, $\mathcal{A}_9$, and $\mathcal{A}_{10}$

	$\mathcal{A}_{14}$	$\mathcal{A}_{13}$	$\mathcal{A}_9$	$\mathcal{A}_{10}$
$\perp$	•	•	•	•
$\{<\}$	•	•		•
$\{>\}$	•	•		•
$\{<>\}$		•		•
$\{\|\|\}$	•	•		
$\{\|\| <\}$	•	•		
$\{> \|\|\}$	•	•		
$\{< \|\| >\}$	•	•		•
$\{=\}$	•	•	•	•
$\{<=\}$	•	•	•	•
$\{>=\}$	•	•	•	•
$\{<=>\}$		•	•	•
$\{= \|\|\}$	•		•	
$\{<= \|\|\}$	•		•	
$\{>= \|\|\}$	•		•	
$\mathcal{B}$	•	•	•	•

Lemma 2. *Let Π be an instance of $PSAT_{\mathrm{p}}(\Re)$ such that for every model M of Π holds that $M(n_1) = M(n_2)$ and Π' be the graph resulting from contracting the nodes n_1, n_2 in Π. Then, Π is satisfiable iff Π' is satisfiable.*

Proof. Assume Π has a model M. Clearly M is also a model of Π'. Assume Π' has model $M' = \langle f, \langle T, \Re \rangle \rangle$, the following is a model of Π:

$$M = \langle (f|n_2 \longmapsto f(n_1)), \langle T, \Re \rangle \rangle$$

$\square$

3 Partially-Ordered Time

When examining the point algebra for partially-ordered time we begin by examining three classes $\mathcal{A}_{14}$, $\mathcal{A}_{10}$ and $\mathcal{A}_9$ and show that they are tractable. These results are collected in Subsection 3.1. We continue by showing that these classes are maximal[1] and that there exists no other maximal tractable classes in Subsection 3.2. The classes are defined in Table 2.

3.1 Tractable subclasses

To prove the tractability of $\mathcal{A}_{14}$ and $\mathcal{A}_{10}$ we present an algorithm PO in Fig. 3.1 and claim that it correctly solves the problems $PSAT_{\mathrm{po}}(\mathcal{C})$ (where $\mathcal{C} = \{\leq, \|, \neq\}$)

---

[1] We say that a set of relations C is a *maximal tractable* subclass of $\mathcal{PA}$ iff $PSAT_{\mathrm{p}}(C)$ is tractable and there exist no proper superclass of C that is tractable.

```
1   algorithm PO
2   Input: An instance Π of PSAT_po(C) or PSAT_po(D)
3   repeat
4       Π' ← Π
5       for each pair of nodes n₁, n₂ ∈ Π do
6           if n₁‖n₂ and n₁ ≤* n₂ then
7               if n₁ ≠ n₂ then return false
8               else Π' ← contract(Π, n₁, n₂)
9           elsif n₁ ≤* n₂ and n₂ ≤* n₁ then
10              if n₁ ≠ n₂ ∈ Π then return false
11              else Π' ← contract(Π, n₁, n₂)
12          end if
13      end for
14  until Π' = Π
15  return true
```

Fig. 1. Algorithm PO

and $\text{PSAT}_{po}(\mathcal{D})$ (where $\mathcal{D} = \{\leq, \{<=>\}, \neq\}$). By proving that $\mathcal{C}$ implements $\mathcal{A}_{14}$ and $\mathcal{D}$ implements $\mathcal{A}_{10}$, we are done. Note that algorithm PO runs in polynomial time since every loop removes at least one element from the given instance Π, so at most $|\Pi|$ loops can be made. Algorithm PO return boolean values where the answer "true" means the algorithm accepts the given problem instance (it is satisfiable) and the answer "false" denotes a rejection of the problem instance (it is not satisfiable). One auxiliary function of the form $\text{contract}(G, n_1, n_2)$ is used which gives the graph resulting from contracting the nodes n_1, n_2 in the graph G.

Theorem 1. $PSAT_{po}(\mathcal{A}_{14})$ *is tractable.*

Proof. We begin by showing that algorithm PO solves $\text{PSAT}_{po}(\mathcal{C})$ correctly.

If the algorithm contracts two nodes n_1, n_2 in a graph Π, then Π is satisfiable iff the contracted graph is satisfiable by Lemma 2 since either $n_1 \leq^* n_2, n_2 \leq^* n_1$ or $n_1\|n_2, n_2 \leq^* n_1$ which both lead to $M(n_1) = M(n_2)$ in every model M of Π. Thus, it is easy to see that if the algorithm rejects the graph Π after n iterations, the original instance cannot have a model.

Assume to the contrary that the algorithm accepts an instance. Consider the graph Π after the last iteration and recall that the original graph is satisfiable iff Π is satisfiable. The $(\leq)$-subgraph of Π is acyclic and there exist no n_1, n_2 such that $n_1\|n_2$ and $n_1 \leq^* n_2$. Let,

$$M = \langle f, \langle T, \Re \rangle \rangle = \langle \{\langle n_i, p_i \rangle | n_i \in \Pi\}, \langle \{p_i | n_i \in \Pi\}, \{\langle p_i, p_j \rangle | n_i \leq^* n_j\} \rangle \rangle$$

and note that $\langle T, \Re \rangle$ is a partial order. Arbitrarily choose $\langle x, R, y \rangle$ in Π and assume without loss of generality that x, y are distinct nodes. If R is $\neq$ the relation holds since every node n_i is mapped to a unique point p_i, if R is $\|$ the relation holds since neither $x \leq^* y$ nor $y \leq^* x$ in Π. The last case when R is $\leq$ trivially holds. Consequently M is a model of Π and the original problem instance is satisfiable. The algorithm trivially runs in polynomial time since every loop of the algorithm removes at least one node from the graph.

Finally, we note that $\mathcal{C}$ implements $\mathcal{A}_{14}$ by the following gadgets and the tractability of $\text{PSAT}_{\text{po}}(\mathcal{A}_{14})$ follows from Lemma 1.

$$x \overset{\leq}{\underset{\neq}{\rightleftarrows}} y \;\Rightarrow x\{<\}y \qquad x \overset{\|}{\underset{\neq}{\rightleftarrows}} y \;\Rightarrow x\{\|\}y$$

$$x \xrightarrow{\leq} z \xleftarrow{\|} y \;\Rightarrow x\{<= \|\}y \qquad x \overset{\neq}{\underset{\leq}{\rightleftarrows}} z \overset{}{\underset{\|}{\rightleftarrows}} y \;\Rightarrow x\{\| <\}y$$

$$x \overset{\leq}{\underset{\leq}{\rightleftarrows}} y \;\Rightarrow x\{=\}y$$

$\square$

An alternative algorithm for $\text{PSAT}_{\text{po}}(\mathcal{A}_{14})$ is given in Anger *et al.* [2]

Theorem 2. *$PSAT_{po}(\mathcal{A}_{10})$ is tractable.*

Proof. We begin by showing that Algorithm PO correctly solves the $\text{PSAT}_{\text{po}}(\mathcal{D})$ problem. First note that lines 7–8 of the algorithm is never executed since $\| \notin \mathcal{D}$. If the algorithm contracts two nodes n_1, n_2 in a graph Π, then Π is satisfiable iff the contracted graph is satsfiable by Lemma 2 since there exists a cycle $n_1 \leq^* n_2 \leq^* n_1$ which leads to $M(n_1) = M(n_2)$ in every model M of Π. After having made this observation, it is trival to show that if the algorithm rejects a graph Π, then it does not have a model.

Assume to the contrary that the algorithm accepts the graph Π and let Π' denote the graph after the last iteration of the algorithm. We can construct a model for Π' by induction over the number of nodes in Π'. If Π' is empty then $M = \langle \emptyset, \langle \emptyset, \emptyset \rangle \rangle$ is a model of Π'. Assume we can construct a model for every graph with k or fewer nodes. Let Π' be an arbitrary graph containing $k+1$ nodes. Note that the ($\leq$)-subgraph of Π' is acyclic and thus contains at least one minimal node x. By the induction hypothesis there exists a model $M' = \langle f, \langle T, \Re \rangle \rangle$ of $\Pi' - \{x\}$. Let,

$$M = \langle (f|n \longmapsto c), \langle T \cup \{c\}, \Re \cup \{\langle c, x \rangle | x \in T\} \rangle \rangle$$

where c is a fresh point. Clearly M is a model of Π' and thus Π is satisfiable.

To conclude the theorem, $\mathcal{D}$ implements $\mathcal{A}_{10}$ by the following gadgets and the tractability of $\text{PSAT}_{\text{po}}(\mathcal{A}_{10})$ follows by Lemma 1. Note that the gadgets for $\{>\}, \{>=\}$ have been omitted since they can easily be expressed with $\{<\}, \{<=\}$, respectively.

$$x \underset{\{<\|>\}}{\overset{\{<=\}}{\rightleftharpoons}} y \;\Rightarrow\; x\{<\}y \qquad x \underset{\{<=\}}{\overset{\{<=\}}{\rightleftharpoons}} y \;\Rightarrow\; x = y$$

$$x \underset{\{<\|>\}}{\overset{\{<=>\}}{\rightleftharpoons}} y \;\Rightarrow\; x\{<>\}y$$

$\square$

Finally, $\text{PSAT}_{\text{po}}(\mathcal{A}_9)$ is easily seen to be a tractable problem. Given an arbitrary instance, note that if two variables are related by the empty relation $\perp$, then the instance is not satisfiable. Otherwise, it has the trivial model which maps every node onto the same point.

3.2 The classification

The proof of the claim that there exists no other maximal tractable subclasses of $\text{PSAT}_{\text{po}}(\mathcal{PA})$ than those presented in the previous subsection is given in Theorem 3. Before that, we need a number of auxiliary results, though.

We begin by noting that $\text{PSAT}_{\text{po}}(\mathcal{PA})$ is in NP. This follows immediately since we can nondeterministically guess a model M and verify it in polynomial time; it is sufficient to check the following: (1) M is a partial order; and (2) each constraint $x \; R \; y$ holds under the interpretation.

Our hardness results rely on the fact that $\text{PSAT}_{\text{po}}(\mathcal{A}_2)$ is NP-complete where $\mathcal{A}_2 = \{\{<>\}, \{\|\}\}$. We know that $\text{PSAT}_{\text{po}}(\mathcal{A}_2)$ is in NP and we show hardness for NP by a polynomial-time reduction from the BETWEENNESS problem which is defined as follows:.

INSTANCE: A pair $\langle A, T \rangle$ consisting of a finite set A and a collection T of ordered triples $\langle a, b, c \rangle$ of distinct elements from A.
QUESTION: Is there a one-to-one mapping $f : A \to \{1, 2, \ldots, |A|\}$ such that for each $\langle a, b, c \rangle \in T$ we have either $f(a) < f(b) < f(c)$ or $f(c) < f(b) < f(a)$.

The BETWEENNESS problem is known to be NP-complete [7, page 279].

Given an arbitrary instance $\langle A, T \rangle$ of BETWEENNESS where $A = \{a_1, \ldots, a_k\}$, construct an instance Π of $\text{PSAT}_{\text{po}}(\mathcal{A}_2)$ as follows:

1. for each $a_i \in A$, introduce a fresh variable a_i';
2. for each pair of distinct $a_i, a_j \in A$, add the constraint $a_i\{<>\}a_j$;
3. for each triple $t_m = \langle a_i, a_j, a_k \rangle \in T$, introduce two fresh variables x_m', y_m' and add the following constraints:

$$x_m'\{\|\}a_i', \; x_m'\{\|\}a_j', \; x_m'\{<>\}a_k'$$

$$y_m'\{<>\}a_i', \; y_m'\{\|\}a_j', \; y_m'\{\|\}a_k'$$

Fig. 2. The problem instance Π and its model M. To clarify the picture, dotted arrows have been used to mark the relation $\{\|\}$ and filled arrows for the relation $\{<>\}$.

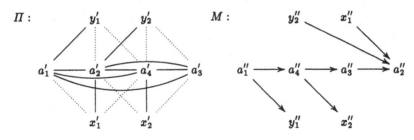

We show that Π is satisfiable iff $\langle A, T \rangle$ has a solution. For the if-direction, assume $g : A \rightarrow \{1, \ldots, k\}$ is a solution to $\langle A, T \rangle$. Let $M = \langle f, \langle T, \Re \rangle \rangle$ where,

$$f = \{\langle a_i', a_i'' \rangle | a_i' \in \Pi\}$$
$$T = \{a_i'' | a_i' \in \Pi\}$$
$$\Re = \{\langle a_i'', a_j'' \rangle | a_i, a_j \in A, g(a_i) < g(a_j)\} \qquad (1)$$
$$\cup \{\langle x_m'', a_k'' \rangle, \langle a_i'', y_m'' \rangle | t_m = \langle a_i, a_j, a_k \rangle \in T, g(a_i) < g(a_j)\} \quad (2)$$
$$\cup \{\langle a_k'', x_m'' \rangle, \langle y_m'', a_i'' \rangle | t_m = \langle a_i, a_j, a_k \rangle \in T, g(a_i) > g(a_j)\} \quad (3)$$
$$\cup \{\langle x, y \rangle | \exists z : \langle x, z \rangle, \langle z, y \rangle \in \Re\} \qquad (4)$$

M is a model of Π since (1) satisfies all the constraints $a_i\{<>\}a_j$ introduced by step 2 above and (2), (3) satisfies the constraints introduced by step 3 above. (4) ensures that the transitive closure of $\Re$ is preserved.

To clarify the steps of the model construction above we provide a small example. The BETWEENNESS problem instance

$$\langle \{a_1, a_2, a_3, a_4\}, \{\langle a_1, a_4, a_2 \rangle, \langle a_2, a_3, a_4 \rangle\} \rangle$$

gives the point algebra problem instance Π in figure 2 and has a solution $g = \{\langle a_1, 1 \rangle, \langle a_2, 4 \rangle, \langle a_3, 3 \rangle, \langle a_4, 2 \rangle\}$. From the solution of the BETWEENNESS problem we can construct a model M of Π depicted in the same figure. Transitive edges are omitted.

We continue by showing the only-if direction. Assume Π has a model M. Note that the variables $a_1', a_2', \ldots$ in Π corresponding to variables $a_1, a_2, \ldots$ in A are totally ordered, i.e., for arbitrary distinct a_i', a_j', either $M(a_i') < M(a_j')$ or $M(a_j') < M(a_i')$. Choose indices $m_1, \ldots, m_k$ such that $a_{m_1}' < \cdots < a_{m_k}'$. Define a solution $f : A \rightarrow \{1, \ldots, k\}$ of $\langle A, T \rangle$ as follows: $f(a_i) = m_i$. Clearly, this function is a one-to-one mapping from A to $\{1, \ldots, k\}$

Arbitrarily choose a triple $\langle a_i, a_j, a_k \rangle \in T$. We show that $f(a_i) < f(a_j) < f(a_k)$ or $f(a_k) < f(a_j) < f(a_i)$. Assume to the contrary that $f(a_j) < f(a_i) < f(a_k)$. Then, the model M implies that $M(a_j') < M(a_i') < M(a_k')$ under the partial order of M. By the construction of Π we know that there exists a variable

y'_m such that $M(y'_m)$ $\{<>\}$ $M(a'_i)$, $M(y'_m)$ $\{\|\}$ $M(a'_j)$ and $M(y'_m)$ $\{\|\}$ $M(a'_k)$. Assume first that $M(y'_m)$ $\{<\}$ $M(a'_i)$, then $M(y'_m)$ $\{<\}$ $M(a'_k)$ which contradicts the fact that $M(y'_m)$ $\{\|\}$ $M(a'_k)$. Similary, if $M(y'_m)$ $\{>\}$ $M(a'_i)$ then $M(a'_j)$ $\{<\}$ $M(y'_m)$ and we have a contradiction since $M(y'_m)$ $\{\|\}$ $M(a'_j)$. The remaining three cases can be proven analogously.

Thus, we have proven the following lemma.

Lemma 3. $PSAT_{po}(A_2)$ *is NP-complete.*

We also need an auxiliary result that proves NP-completeness of all classes containing $\{<>\}$ and a relation not present in A_{10}.

Lemma 4. *If C is a set of relations containing $\{<>\}$ and one of $\{\| <\}, \{= \|\}$ or $\{<= \|\}$, then $PSAT_{po}(C)$ is NP-complete.*

Proof. Assume $\{\| <\}$ or $\{= \|\}$ is in C. Then, the following gadgets show that C implements $\{\|\}$ and NP-completeness follows by Lemma 1 and Lemma 3.

$$x \overset{\{\| <\}}{\underset{\{\| <\}}{\rightleftharpoons}} y \qquad x \overset{\{= \|\}}{\underset{\{<>\}}{\leftrightarrows}} z \underset{\{= \|\}}{\rightarrow} y$$

If C contains $\{<= \|\}$, then it is easy to show that C implements $\{= \|\}$ and NP-completeness follows from the previous case. $\qquad\qquad\square$

We can now give the complete classification of the point algebra for partially-ordered time.

Theorem 3. *The classes A_{14}, A_{10} and A_9 are the only maximal tractable subclasses of $PSAT_{po}(\mathcal{PA})$.*

Proof. Assume there exists a maximal tractable subclass C of $\mathcal{PA}$ which is not A_{14}, A_{10} nor A_9. Then C must contain (not neccessarily distinct) elements which are not present in either one of those classes. That is,

$$\exists x, y, z \in C : x \in A_{14}^{-1}, y \in A_{10}^{-1}, z \in A_9^{-1}$$

where

$$A_{14}^{-1} = \{\{<>\}, \{<=>\}\}$$
$$A_{10}^{-1} \equiv \{\{\|\}, \{\| <\}, \{= \|\}, \{<= \|\}\}$$
$$A_9^{-1} \equiv \{\{<\}, \{<>\}, \{\|\}, \{\| <\}, \{< \| >\}\}$$

Note that the relations $\{>\}, \{> \|\}$ and $\{>= \|\}$ have been omitted since they can trivially be expressed with $\{<\}, \{\| <\}$ and $\{<= \|\}$, respectively.

Assume that $\{<>\} \in C$. By Lemma 3 and Lemma 4, C is NP-complete, since one element in A_{10}^{-1} must be in C. Contradiction, and it follows that $\{<=>\} \in C$.

We know that C contains $\{<=>\}$, one element from $\{\{<\}, \{\|\}, \{\| <\}, \{< \| >\}\}$ and one element from $\{\{\|\}, \{\| <\}, \{= \|\}, \{<= \|\}\}$. First we consider two cases that eliminates the relations $\{\|\}, \{< \| >\}$ and $\{\| <\}$.

(1) If $\{\|\} \in C$ or $\{< \| >\} \in C$ then the following gadgets implement $\{<>\}$ which contradicts our previously made assumptions.

$$x \xrightarrow[\{<=>\}]{\{<=>\}} z \xrightarrow[\{\|\}]{} y \qquad x \underset{\{<=>\}}{\overset{\{<\|>\}}{\rightleftarrows}} y$$

(2) If $\{\| <\} \in C$ then it is trivial to implement $\{\|\}$ which leads to a contradiction by (1).

Now we know that $\{<=>\}, \{<\} \in C$ and that either $\{= \|\}$ or $\{<= \|\}$ is in C. We show that the last two cases also leads to a contradiction which prove the theorem.

(3) If $\{<\} \in C$ and $\{= \|\} \in C$, then the following gadget implements $\{\|\}$ which leads to a contradiction by (1).

$$x \xrightarrow[\{<\}]{\{=\|\}} z \xrightarrow[\{=\|\}]{} y$$

(4) If $\{<\} \in C$ and $\{<= \|\} \in C$, then it is trivial to implement $\{= \|\}$ which lead to a contradiction by (3). □

4 Branching Time

When examining the case of branching time, we begin by studying a small set $\mathcal{E}$ containing the three relations $\leq, \|, \neq$. We will show that $\text{PSAT}_{br}(\mathcal{E})$ is tractable and that $\mathcal{E}$ implements the relations in the set $\mathcal{A}_{13}$. Consequently, $\text{PSAT}_{br}(\mathcal{A}_{13})$ is tractable. It should be noted that $\mathcal{A}_{13}$ is a nontrivial subclass which, for instance, contains all basic relations.

A node n is said to be *superminimal* in a problem instance Π iff n is a $(\leq)$-minimal node of Π and there exists no x such that $n\|x$. A *semipath* between two nodes n_1, n_2 in a graph Π is a set of nodes $a_1, \ldots, a_k, b_1, \ldots, b_k$ such that:

$$n_1 \leq^* a_1 \geq^* b_1 \leq^* \ldots \leq^* a_k \geq^* b_k \leq^* n_2$$

It should be noted that iff two nodes n_1, n_2 are part of the same $(\leq)$-component in a graph Π then there exists a semipath between n_1, n_2.

Before we can prove the main result of this section, we need several lemmata.

Lemma 5. *If $a \leq^* b$ and $b(<=>)c$, then $a(<=>)c$.*

Proof. Immediate consequence of the composition table for branching time □

In the point algebra of branching time we have an important propery which helps us prove correctness of the algorithm BR. Only superminimal nodes in a problem instance Π may be mapped to a minimal point in any model of Π, which the following lemma proves.

Lemma 6. *Assume that Π is a problem instance containing nodes n_1, n_2 such that $n_1 \| n_2$ and there exists a semipath between n_1, n_2, the image of n_1 cannot be a minimal node in any model of Π.*

Proof. Assume M is a model of Π such that $M(n_1)$ is a minimal node. Since there exists a semipath between n_1, n_2 there exists $a_1, \ldots, a_k, b_1, \ldots, b_k$ such that:

$$n_1 \leq^* a_1 \geq^* b_1 \leq^* \ldots \leq^* a_k \geq^* b_k \leq^* n_2$$

Lemma 5 gives $n_1(<=>)b_1$, $M(n_1)$ minimal gives $n_1 \leq b_1$. Note that $n_1 \leq b_1 \leq^* a_2$ and $b_2 \leq^* a_2$, Lemma 5 gives $n_1(<=>)b_2$ thus $n_1 \leq b_2$. Repeat for each b in $b_2, \cdots, b_k$ and we have $n_1 \leq b_k \leq^* n_2$. Hence $n_1 \leq^* n_2$ and $n_1 \| n_2$, contradiction. Thus there exists no model M such that $M(n_1)$ is a minimal node. □

A model $M = \langle f, \langle T, \Re \rangle \rangle$ of Π is said to be *non-redundant* iff f is surjective, ie. every point in M is the image of some node in Π. Let Π be a problem instance of $\mathrm{PSAT_p}(\Re)$. If Π is satisfiable then there exists a non-redundant model of Π. Assume Π is satisfiable, then there exists a model $M = \langle f, \langle T, \Re \rangle \rangle$. Let T' be the points in T that are the image of some node in Π and let

$$M' = \langle f, \langle T', \Re \cap (T' \times T') \rangle \rangle$$

Clearly M' is a model of Π and M' is non-redundant.

Lemma 7. *Let Π be a problem instance of $\mathrm{PSAT_{br}}(\mathcal{E})$ such that Π is $(\leq)$-acyclic and $M = \langle f, \langle T, \leq \rangle \rangle$ is a non-redundant model of Π. Then there exists at least one minimal point p in $\langle T, \leq \rangle$ which is the image of a $(\leq)$-minimal node in Π.*

Proof. Since $\langle T, \leq \rangle$ is a finite partial order, it contains a minimal point p. Let $N = n_1, \cdots, n_k$ be the nodes in Π that are mapped to p by f. We know that M is nonredundant so $N \neq \emptyset$. Assume now that no member of N is $(\leq)$-minimal. Π is acylic so there exists a $(\leq)$-minimal node n' such that $n' \leq^* n_1 \in N$. The $(\leq)$-minimality of n' implies that $n' \notin N$ and $f(n') \neq p$. This leads immediatly to a contradiction since $f(n') < f(n_1) = p$ and p is minimal in $\langle T, \leq \rangle$. Consequently, there exists a $(\leq)$-minimal node in N that is mapped to p. □

Now, we can prove that algorithm BR correctly solves $\mathrm{PSAT_{br}}(\mathcal{E})$.

Lemma 8. *The algorithm in Fig. 3 correctly solve the $\mathrm{PSAT_{br}}(\mathcal{E})$ problem.*

Proof. We prove correctness of the algorithm by induction over the number of nodes in the instance. The algorithm accepts all instances Π containing zero nodes since $M = \langle \{\emptyset\}, \langle \emptyset, \{\emptyset\} \rangle \rangle$ is a model of every such instance.

Assume the algorithm correctly solves the problem for every graph containing k nodes. Let Π be an arbitrary graph of $k + 1$ nodes. We consider four cases:

1. (lines 5-7) There exists two nodes n_1, n_2 such that $n_1 \leq^* n_2, n_2 \leq^* n_1$. If $n_1 \neq n_2$ in Π, then there can be no model of Π and the algorithm rejects. Otherwise, by Lemma 2 Π is satisfiable iff $\text{contract}(\Pi, n_1, n_2)$ is satisfiable and the algorithm is correct by the induction hypothesis.

2. (lines 10-11) There exists at least two ($\leq$)-components $C_1, \cdots, C_n$ of Π. If the algorithm rejects some C_i then C_i cannot have a model by the induction hypothesis. Since C_i is a subgraph of Π, there exist no model of Π.

   We show that if C_i is satisfiable for every i then Π is satisfiable. For each $i \leq n$, let $M_i = \langle f_i, \langle T_i, \Re_i \rangle \rangle$ denote a model for C_i and let

   $$M = \langle f_1 \cup f_2 \cup \cdots \cup f_n, \langle T_1 \cup T_2 \cup \cdots \cup T_n, \Re_1 \cup \Re_2 \cup \cdots \Re_n \rangle \rangle$$

   Clearly M in an interpretation of Π since every M_i is an interpretation of C_i. The only constraint between two distinct nodes $n_i \in C_i, n_j \in C_j$ can be $\neq$ or $\parallel$ which trivially holds so M is a model of Π.

3. (lines 12-13) There exists only one ($\leq$)-component of Π which has a super-minimal node n. If the algorithm rejects then $\Pi - \{n\}$ is unsatisfiable by the induction hypothesis and Π cannot have a model.

   If $\Pi - \{n\}$ is satisfiable, then Π is satisfiable: let $M' = \langle f, \langle T, \Re \rangle \rangle$ denote a model of $\Pi - \{n\}$ and let

   $$M = \langle (f|n \longmapsto c), \langle T \cup \{c\}, \Re \cup \{\langle c, x \rangle | x \in T\} \rangle \rangle$$

   where c is a fresh point. Clearly M is an interpretation of Π since the only point c added to M' is a minimal point. Assume $\langle n, R, v \rangle \in \Pi$. If R is $\neq$, then the relation holds since $f(n)$ is a fresh point. Otherwise R is $\leq$ since the superminimality of n prohibits R from being either $\parallel$ or $\geq$. Hence, the relation holds since $f(n)$ is a minimal point and M is a model of Π.

4. (line 15) There exists only one ($\leq$)-component of Π and Π contains no super-minimal node. Assume Π is satisfiable. Then, there exists a non-redundant model M of Π. By Lemma 7, M has a minimal point p which is the image of some ($\leq$)-minimal node n. Since n is a minimal node but not a supermin-imal node there exists an x such that $n\|x$. Since Π only has one component there exists a ($\leq$)-semipath between n and x. By Lemma 6 the image p of n cannot be a minimal node which is a contradiction. Hence, there cannot exist a model of Π.

   $\square$

Lemma 9. $PSAT_{br}(\mathcal{E})$ is tractable.

Proof. The correctness of algorithm BR for the $PSAT_{br}(\mathcal{E})$ problem follows from Lemma 8. To show that BR runs in polynomial time, let $p(n)$ be a polynomial that is an upper bound for the time complexity of which steps 5 and 9 can be performed. The time complexity of the algorithm is bounded from above by the solution to the following recursive equation:

```
1  Algorithm BR
2  Input  Graph Π
3  if Π is empty then
4     return true
5  elsif ∃n₁, n₂ : n₁ ≤* n₂, n₂ ≤* n₁  then
6     if n₁ ≠ n₂ then return false
7     else return BR(contract(Π,n₁,n₂))
8  else
9     Identify the (≤)-components C₁,···,Cₖ of Π.
10    if k > 1 then
11       return BR(C₁) ∧ BR(C₂) ∧···∧ BR(Cₖ)
12    elsif ∃n : superminimal(n) then
13       return BR(Π − {n})
14    else
15       return false
16    end if
17 end if
```

Fig. 3. The algorithm for solving $\text{PSAT}_{\text{br}}(\mathcal{E})$

$$f(1) = 1$$
$$f(n) = \max \begin{cases} p(n) + f(n-1) \\ p(n) + \sum_{i=1}^{k} f(c_i) : k \geq 2, c_i > 0, \sum_{i=1}^{k} c_i = n \end{cases}$$

The case $f(n) = p(n) + f(n-1)$ occurs when the algorithm recurse at line 13 and the case $f(n) = \sum f(c_i)$ occurs when the algorithm recurse at line 11 (where c_i denotes the size of component C_i). It can be shown that $f(n) \leq n^2 p(n)$ by a straightforward induction over n. □

Theorem 4. *$PSAT_{br}(\mathcal{A}_{13})$ is tractable.*

Proof. The following gadgets prove that $\mathcal{E}$ implements $\mathcal{A}_{13}$, by the previous lemma $\text{PSAT}_{\text{br}}(\mathcal{E})$ is tractable. Hence, $\text{PSAT}_{\text{br}}(\mathcal{A}_{13})$ is tractable.

$$x \overset{\leq}{\underset{\neq}{\rightleftarrows}} y \Rightarrow x\{<\}y \qquad x \overset{\neq}{\underset{\leq}{\rightarrow}} z \overset{}{\underset{\leq}{\leftarrow}} y \Rightarrow x\{<>\}y$$

$$x \overset{\leq}{\rightarrow} z \overset{\leq}{\leftarrow} y \Rightarrow x\{<=>\}y \qquad x \overset{\leq}{\underset{\leq}{\rightleftarrows}} y \Rightarrow x\{=\}y$$

$$x \overset{\|}{\rightarrow} z \overset{\leq}{\rightarrow} y \Rightarrow x\{\| <\}y$$

□

5 Concluding Remarks

We have identified all tractable subclasses of the point algebra for partially-ordered time and studied one large tractable subclass of the point algebra for branching time. In the case of branching time, there is one major question left open by this paper: is $\mathcal{A}_{13}$ a maximal tractable subclass of $\mathrm{PSAT_{br}}(\mathcal{PA})$? Or is $\mathrm{PSAT_{br}}(\mathcal{PA})$ itself tractable? In the case of partially-ordered time, several minor questions are still to be answered. One quite interesting question is whether path-consistency is enough to decide satisfiability of the tractable classes.

References

1. F. Anger. On Lamport's interprocessor communication model. *ACM Transactions on Programming Languages Systems*, 11(3):404–417, 1989.
2. F. Anger, D. Mitra, and R. Rodriguez. Temporal constraint networks in nonliear time. Technical report, ECAI Workshop on Temporal and Spatial Reasoning, 1998.
3. M. Broxvall. Computational complexity of point algebras for nonlinear time. Master Thesis Report LiTH-IDA-Ex-99/48, Department of Computer Science, Linköping, Sweden, June 1999.
4. E. Clarke, E. Emerson, and A. Sistla. Automatic verification of finite-state concurrent systems using temporal logic specifications. *ACM Transactions on Programming Languages Systems*, 8(2):244–263, 1986.
5. T. Dean and M. Boddy. Reasoning about partially ordered events. *Artificial Intelligence*, 36:375–399, 1988.
6. A. E. Emerson and J. Y. Halpern. "Sometimes" and "not never" revisited: On branching versus linear temporal logic. *Journal of the ACM*, 33(1):151–178, Jan. 1986.
7. M. Garey and D. Johnson. *Computers and Intractability: A Guide to the Theory of NP-Completeness.* Freeman, New York, 1979.
8. P. Jonsson and T. Drakengren. A complete classification of tractability in RCC-5. *Journal of Artificial Intelligence Research*, 6:211–221, 1997.
9. L. Lamport. The mutual exclusion problem: Part I—a theory of interprocess communication. *Journal of the ACM*, 33(2):313–326, 1986.
10. D. McDermott. A temporal logic for reasoning about processes and plans. *Cognitive Science*, 6:101–155, 1982.
11. B. Nebel and H.-J. Bürckert. Reasoning about temporal relations: A maximal tractable subclass of Allen's interval algebra. *Journal of the ACM*, 42(1):43–66, 1995.

A Meta-Heuristic Factory for Vehicle Routing Problems
Meta-Programming for Meta-Heuristics

Yves Caseau[1], François Laburthe[1], Glenn Silverstein[2]

[1] BOUYGUES D.T.N., 1 av. E. Freyssinet, 78061 St. Quentin en Yvelines cedex, FRANCE
ycs;flaburth@challenger.bouygues.fr
[2] Telcordia Technologies, 445 South Street, Morristown, NJ, 07960, USA
silverst@research.telcordia.com

Abstract. This paper presents a generic technique for improving constraint-based heuristics through the discovery of meta-heuristics. The idea is to represent a family of "push/pull" algorithms, based on inserting and removing tasks in a current solution, with an algebra and let a learning algorithm search for the best possible algebraic term (which represents a hybrid algorithm), for a given set of problems and an optimization criterion. This paper describes an application of this idea using vehicle routing with time windows (VRPTW) as the domain example, although this approach can be applied to many other problems which can be seen as the assignment of tasks to resources (generalized assignments). We suppose that a domain-dependent (constraint-based) algorithm has been built, which is able to insert and remove tasks and handle the domain-specific constraints. Our goal is to improve such an algorithm with techniques like LDS (Limited Discrepancy Search), LNS (Large Neighborhood Search), ejection trees or chains, which can be described in a generic manner using the insertion and deletion operations. We show that the automatic tuning of the best hybrid combination of such techniques yields a better solution than hand-tuning, with considerably less effort. The contribution of the paper is thus twofold: we demonstrate a combination of meta-heuristics that yields new best-known results on the Solomon benchmarks, and we provide with a method to automatically adjust this combination to handle problems with different sizes, complexity and optimization objectives.

1. Introduction

Hybrid Algorithms are combinatorial optimization algorithms that incorporate different types of techniques to produce higher quality solutions. The recent years have seen the rise of hybrid algorithms in most fields (scheduling, routing, etc.) as well as of generic techniques that seem to prove useful in many different domains. Limited Discrepancy Search (LDS) [7] and Large Neighborhood Search (LNS) [16] are such examples. Hybrid algorithms are not a panacea yet, since they imply a very large amount of tuning, and they are often not robust enough: the combination that works wonders for a given data set does poorly on another one. Hybrid algorithms also cause software engineering problems because of their very nature, and the application to the "real world" of an algorithm that works well on academic benchmarks is often a challenging task.

The field of Vehicle Routing is an interesting example, since real-world applications mostly rely on insertion algorithms, which are known to be poor heuristics but have two major advantages: they are incremental by nature and they easily support the addition of domain-dependent side constraints. The use of constraint programming makes these heuristics even more attractive since the constraint solver can handle the side constraints and produces a high-quality insertion [3]. Real problems have lots of side-constraints, and the software engineering issues become rapidly overwhelming. The problem that we address is twofold:

- how can we build a library of meta-methods that is totally problem-independent, so that any insertion algorithm based on a constraint solver can be plugged ?
- how can we achieve the necessary tuning to produce at a low cost a robust solution for each different configuration ?

The first question is motivated by the fact that the generic (meta) aspect is the part of the software that is most difficult to maintain when new constraints are added. There is a tremendous value in confining the domain-dependent part to where constraint-programming techniques can be used. The second question is drawn from our practical experience: the speed of the hardware, the runtime constraints, the objective functions (total travel, number of routes, priority respect, ...) all have a strong influence when designing a hybrid algorithm. For instance, it is actually a difficult problem to re-tune a hybrid algorithm when faster hardware is installed.

This paper presents a preliminary contribution towards these two goals, which already yields impressive and encouraging results. We built on the ideas expressed in the SALSA language [4], and propose an algebra of hybrid algorithms for VRPTW. This algebra is generated by a set of operators corresponding to various meta-heuristics proposed in the literature, which are combined into terms. The base heuristic to which the meta- components apply is an insertion heuristic where a new task is inserted into the current solution using a constraint solver (the one-route sub-problem is a TSP, i.e. a traveling salesman problem). Thus, the link with the routing domain is ensured only at the heuristic level and the same algebra can be used for crew scheduling, where the TSP solver is replaced by a task scheduler (another CP module). The algebra can be used to test various combinations and we identify some interesting hybrid approaches. However, the real value comes from applying learning techniques to either automatically tune an existing combination or discover a brand new one, following an approach similar to MULTI-TAC [10]. Although we have only implemented a very preliminary learning algorithm, we report positive results that demonstrate the value of this approach. Hence, instead of simply providing yet-another-hybrid algorithm for the Solomon benchmarks, we propose a framework that can be used for a large range of problems and configurations.

This paper is organized as follows. Section 2 reviews techniques for VRPTW. A simple insertion heuristic based on constraint propagation is presented with some variations using incremental local optimization. We then demonstrate how efficient meta-heuristics can be built on top of this algorithm, such as LDS [7], LNS [16] and ejection chains [3]. Section 3 applies the concepts of the SALSA approach [4] to VRPTW and presents an algebra of hybrid algorithms based on the above techniques. We show that this algebra is very useful to build and compare various combinations of methods. Section 4 reports some preliminary results towards the automatic discovery of hybrid algorithms. A simple learning algorithm is applied to different optimization goals (on-line optimization, truck vs. distance optimization).

2. Routing Techniques

2.1. Insertion Algorithms and Constraint Solvers

A vehicle routing problem is defined by a set of tasks (or nodes) i and a distance matrix ($d[i,j]$). Each task may be given a duration (in which case the matrix d denotes travel times) and a weight (for the load to be picked up). The goal is to find a set of routes that start from a given node (called the depot) and return to it, so that each task is visited only once and so that each route obeys some constraints about its maximal length or the maximum load (the sum of the weights of the visited tasks). A VRP is an optimization problem, where the objective is to minimize the sum of the lengths of the routes and/or the number of routes [9].

We report experiments with the Solomon benchmarks [15], which are both relatively small (100 customers) and simple (truck capacity and time-windows). Real-world routing problems include a lot of side constraints (not every truck can go everywhere at anytime, drivers have breaks and meals, some tasks have higher priorities, etc.). Because of this additional complexity, the most commonly used algorithm is an insertion algorithm, one of the simplest algorithm for solving a VRP. The tasks to be visited are placed in a stack, that may be sorted statically (once) or dynamically, and a set of empty routes is created. For each task, a set of candidate routes is selected and the feasibility of the insertion is evaluated. The task is inserted into the route for which the increase in length due to the insertion is minimal. This loop is run until all tasks have been inserted.

The key component is the node insertion procedure, since it must check all side constraints. The use of constraint programming techniques is quite natural: they can be used to supplement a simple insertion heuristic by doing all the side-constraint checking, or through the full resolution of the one-vehicle problem (a small TSP with side-constraints). In a previous paper [2], we have shown that CP is the technology of choice for solving small TSPs with side constraints. In order to insert a node n into a route r, we simply solve a TSP on the set of nodes spanned by r, augmented with n.

We have shown in [3] that using a CP solver for the node insertion increases the quality of the global algorithm, whether this global algorithm is a simple greedy insertion algorithm or a more complex tree search algorithm.

In this paper, we want to demonstrate a technique that can improve the quality level of a "bland" insertion algorithm so we use a simpler approach to node insertion. Instead of solving the small TSP to optimality, we simply try all possible sequential insertions (between two consecutive nodes of the existing routes) and we perform all 2- and 3-opt local optimization moves that do not violate local constraints. The CP engine is used purely for propagating the constraints during the local moves as explained in [5]. The consequence is that our results should be easily reproducible and the ability to boost the performance of a really simple node insertion algorithm based purely on constraint propagation is better demonstrated in this paper.

2.2 Incremental Local Optimization

The first hybridization that we had proposed in an earlier paper [3] is the introduction of incremental local optimization. This is a very powerful technique, since we have shown that it is much more efficient than applying local optimization as a post-treatment, and that it scales very well to large problems (many thousands of nodes).

The interest of incremental local optimization (ILO) is that it is defined with primitive operations for which the constraint propagation can be easily implemented. Thus, it does not violate the principle of separating the domain-dependent part of the problem from the optimization heuristics.

Instead of applying the local moves once the first solution is built, the principle of ILO is to apply them after each insertion and only for those moves that involve the new node that got inserted. The use of ILO within an insertion algorithm has already brought good results in [6], [13] and [8].

Our algorithm uses three moves, which are all 2- or 3- edge exchanges. The first three are used once the insertion is performed. These moves are performed in the neighborhood of the inserted node, to see if some chains from another route would be better if moved into the same route. They include a 2-edge *exchange* for crossing routes (see Figure 2), a 3-edge exchange for *transferring* a chain from one route to another and a simpler *node transfer* move (a limited version of the chain transfer).

Fig. 1. edge exchange moves used for ILO

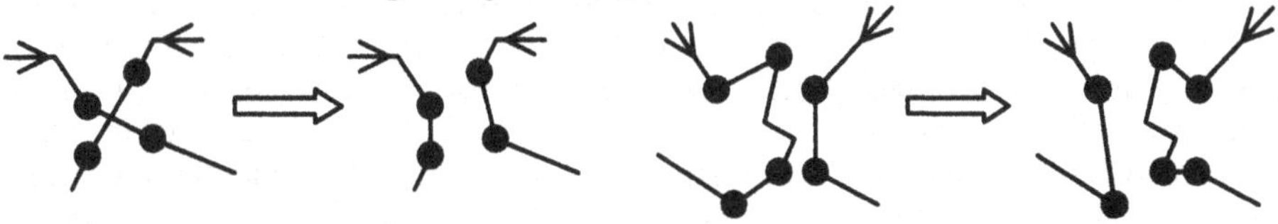

exchange (2opt / 2routes)   transfer (3opt / 2routes)

We will call INSERT(i) the insertion heuristic obtained by applying greedily the node insertion procedure and a given level of ILO depending on the value i:
- $i = 0$ ⇔ basic greedy insertion, without ILO
- $i = 1$ ⇔ performs only 2-opt moves (*exchange*)
- $i = 2$ ⇔ performs 2 and 3-opt moves (*exchange* and *transfer*)
- $i = 3$ ⇔ performs 2 and 3-opt moves, and applies node-transfer moves before selecting the best 2- or 3-opt exchange.
- $i = 4$ ⇔ similar, but in addition, when the insertion seems infeasible, tries to reconstruct the route by inserting the new node first.

We have already shown in [3] that INSERT(4) is a powerful technique, which scales well and yields almost-state-of-the-art results (the number of routes is very close to the best tabu approach of [17], with a much shorter running time). Our initial goal was to improve these results by introducing other techniques. Our first attempt was the introduction of LDS, followed by the use of ejection chains to reduce the number of routes. The algorithm quickly grew into a complex piece of software that was hard to maintain. The approach presented in the remainder of this paper is an attempt to escape from this hybrid software engineering nightmare.

2.3 Meta-Heuristics for insertion algorithms

In the rest of this section we present a set of well-known meta-heuristics that have in common the property that they only rely on inserting and removing nodes from routes. Thus, if we can use a node insertion procedure that checks all domain-dependent side-constraints, we can apply these meta-heuristics freely. It might be argued that the actual implementation or the parameter adjustment of these heuristics could be improved by taking the domain-specific aspects into account. However, the gain is rather small for a big loss since we can no longer reuse the library of meta-heuristics for different domains.

It is important to note that not all meta-heuristics have this property (e.g., splitting and recombining routes does not), but the ones that do amount to a large subset and we will show that these heuristics, together with ILO, yield powerful hybrid combinations. We have implemented a parameterized library of "push/pull" meta-heuristics in CLAIRE [1] where node insertion and removal (which can also trigger constraints) procedures are seen as functional parameters.

2.3.1. Limited Discrepancy Search

Limited Discrepancy Search is an efficient technique that has been used for many different problems. In this paper, we use the term LDS loosely to describe the following idea: transform a greedy heuristic into a search algorithm by branching only in a few (i.e., limited number) cases when the heuristic is not "sure" about the best insertion. A classical complete search (i.e., trying recursively all insertions for all nodes) is impossible because of the size of the problem and a truncated search (i.e., limited number of backtracks) yields poor improvements. The beauty of LDS is to focus the "power of branching" to those nodes for which the heuristic decision is the least compelling. Here the choice heuristic is to pick the feasible route for which the increase in travel is minimal. Applying the idea of LDS, we branch when two routes have very similar "insertion costs" and pick the obvious choice when one route clearly dominates the others. There are two parameters in our LDS scheme: the maximum number of branching points along a path in the search tree and the threshold for branching. A low threshold will provoke a lot of branching in the earlier part of the search process, whereas a high threshold will move the branching points further down. These two parameters control the shape of the search tree and have, needless to say, a definite impact on the quality of the solutions.

In [3], we have experimented with more complex schemes of LDS, using a more complex branching scheme (using swap moves) and more complex branching criteria. Here, we follow our goal of simplicity and limit ourselves to binary branching.

2.3.2 Ejection Chains and Trees

The search for ejection chains is a technique that was proposed a few years ago for tabu search approaches [11]. An ejection link is an edge between a and b that represents the fact that a can be inserted in the route that contains b if b is removed. An ejection chain is a chain of ejection edges where the last node is free, which means that it can be inserted freely in a route that does not intersect the ejection chain, without removing any other node. Each time an ejection chain is found, we can compute its cost, which is the difference in total length once all the substitutions have been performed (which also implies the insertion of the root node).

The search for ejection chains can be used in two cases:

- *To insert a node x that cannot be inserted otherwise*. In this case, any chain is acceptable but we prefer to use the chain with minimal cost. The lowest cost chain is found by a breadth-first search algorithm iterating all chains starting from root x.
- *As an optimization technique*: we remove one node n and try to find the ejection chain with root n with minimal cost. We first remove the nodes with the higher insertion cost (the difference in length for the route with and without the node).

The search for ejection chains was found to be an efficient technique in [3] to minimize the number of routes by calling it each time no feasible insertion was found during the greedy insertion. However, it is problem-dependent since it only works well when nodes are of similar importance (as in the Solomon benchmarks). When nodes have different characteristics, one must move to ejection trees.

An ejection tree is similar to an ejection chain but we allow multiple edges from one node a to $b_1, .. , b_n$ to represent the fact that the "forced insertion" of a into a route r causes the ejection of $b_1, ..$ and b_n. For one node a and a route r, there are usually many such sets $\{b_1, .., b_n\}$ so we use a heuristic to find sets as small as possible. An ejection tree is then a tree of root a such that all leaves are free nodes that can be inserted into different routes that all have an empty intersection with the tree.

There are many more ejection trees than there are chains, and the search for ejection trees with lowest possible cost must be controlled with topological parameters (maximum depth, maximum width, etc.). We put an upper bound on the depth of the tree and on the branching factor. We select no more than k routes for the forced insertion, by filtering the k best routes once all possible routes have been tried. Furthermore, we use a LDS scheme: each time we use a route that was not the best route found (the valuation is simply the weight of the ejected set), we count one discrepancy and cut all trees that would require more than D (a fixed parameter) discrepancies.

The search for ejection trees is a complex process but it is effective for real-world application for many reasons:

- It scales well and can be applied to very large problems, where "blind" local optimization would fail.
- It is generic and has already been used for bin-packing and dispatching problems.
- It is well suited to reactive scheduling: if we introduce the notion of node priority, this algorithm is quite good for re-arranging a schedule when new tasks come in.
- It is possible to have a precise control on the topology of the search space and to guarantee a real-time behavior.

2.3.3. Large Neighborhood Search

The principle of Large Neighborhood Search (LNS) [16] is to forget (remove) a fragment of the current solution and to rebuild it using limited search algorithm. In his paper, Shaw introduced a heuristic randomized criterion for computing the "forgotten" set and proposed to use LDS to re-build the solution. Since he obtained excellent results with this approach, we have implemented the same heuristic to select the set of n (an integer parameter) nodes that are removed from the current solution. His procedure is based on a relatedness criteria and a pseudo-random selection of successive "neighbors". A parameter is used to vary the heuristic from deterministic to totally random. We have extended this heuristic so that nodes that are already without a route are picked first (when they exist).

The implementation of LNS is then straightforward: select a set of k nodes to be removed from the current solution. These nodes are then re-inserted using a LDS insertion algorithm. There are thus four parameters in this algorithm: two for LDS (number of discrepancies and threshold), a randomness parameter and the number of nodes to be reinserted. As we shall later see, the procedure for re-constructing the solution could be anything, which opens many possible combinations.

3. An Algebra for Hybrid Algorithms

3.1. An Algebra for Combining Algorithms

To experiment, automatically tune and create new hybrid algorithms, we need an abstract and concise representation, We could have used the SALSA language [4], but we found that the expressive power of SALSA was more than we needed and would yield some unnecessary complexity. We decided instead to "project" SALSA onto our own domain, that is to create an algebra whose terms represent a hybrid algorithm for routing using the previously defined techniques.

There are two kinds of terms in the grammar: *<Build>* terms represent algorithms that create a solution and *<Optimize>* terms for algorithms that improve a solution.

Fig. 2. A grammar for hybrid algorithms

<Build>::	*INSERT(i)*	*<Optimize> ::*	*CHAIN(n,m)*
	<LDS>		*TREE(n,m,k)*
	DO(<Build>,<Optimize>)		*LNS(n,h,<Build>)*
	FORALL(<LDS>, <Optimize>)		*LOOP(n,<Optimize>)*
			THEN(<Optimize>, ...,
<LDS> ::	*LDS(i,n,l)*		*<Optimize>)*

The definition of the elementary operators is straightforward:

- INSERT(*i*) builds a solution by applying a greedy insertion approach and a varying level of ILO according to the parameter *i* (from 0 to 4, cf. Section 2.2),
- LDS(*i,n,l*) builds a solution by applying a limited discrepancy search on top of the INSERT(*i*) greedy heuristic. *l* represents the threshold and *n* the maximum number of discrepancies (number of branching points for one solution).
- FORALL(*t1, t2*) produces all the solutions (not only the best one) that can be built with *t1* which is necessarily a *<LDS>* and applies the post-optimization step *t2* to each of them. The result is the best solution found.
- CHAIN(*n,m*) is a post-optimization step that select *n* nodes using the heuristic represented by *m* and successively removes them (one at a time) and tries to re-insert them using an ejection chain.
- TREE(*n,m,k*) is similar with an ejection tree strategy for post-optimization; *k* represents the number of discrepancies for the LDS search (of the ejection tree).
- LNS(*n,h,t*) applies Large Neighborhood Search as a post-optimization step; *n* is the number of removed nodes and *h* is the randomness parameter [16]. We rebuild the solution using the algorithm represented by *t*, which must be a *<Build>*. Notice that we do not restrict ourselves to a simple *<LDS>* term.
- DO(*t1,t2*) simply applies *t1* to build a solution and *t2* to post-optimize it
- THEN(*t1,...,tk*) is the sequential composition of optimization algorithms *t1 ... tk*
- LOOP(*n,t*) repeats *n* times the optimization algorithm *t*

Here are some examples of algebraic terms.

- *LDS(3,3,100)* represents a LDS search using the 3rd level of ILO (every move is tried) yielding 2^3 solutions (at most 3 choice points when the difference between the two best routes is less than 100) and returning the best one.

- *DO(INSERT(2),CHAIN(80,2))* is an algorithm obtained by combining a regular greedy heuristic with the 2nd level of ILO with a post-optimization phase of 80 removal/re-insertion through an ejection chain.
- *FORALL(LDS(0,4,100),LOOP(3,TREE(5,2)))* is an algorithm that performs a LDS search with no ILO and 2^4 branching points and then applies 3 times an ejection tree post-optimization step for each intermediate solution.

3.2. Implementation

The grammar is embedded into a CLAIRE class hierarchy: each operator is represented by a class and each term A(...) is an instance of the class A. The use of constructors and pretty-printing makes the algebra an extension of the programming language, making it very easy to manipulate terms (they can be interpreted at the top-level, written in a file, cut-and-pasted, etc.). Therefore, it is possible to introduce new (higher order) operators. For instance, a common approach is to try an optimization strategy, that takes a parameter n which represents the size of the set of nodes that are being displaced, and applies it with successively increasing values of n. Here is how we can define this strategy for LNS:

```
LNS*(n:integer,h:integer,t:Build)
  -> let lt = LNS(n,h,t) in
     (if (n <= 3) lt else THEN(LNS*(n - 1,h,t), lt)
```

To evaluate the algorithms represented by the terms, we have defined a small interpreter (only the control represented by the algebraic term is interpreted, everything else is compiled [1]). The *run* method is defined on each operator class and applies the algorithm represented by the operator (a <Build> or an <Optimize>) to the current problem (and to the current solution for an <Optimize>).

The metric for complexity that we use is the number of calls to the insertion procedure. The advantage of this approach is that it is machine independent and is easier to predict based on the structure of the term (cf. Section 4.1). The CPU time is roughly linear in the number of insertions, and it is convenient as well to use a metric that is independent from the CP insertion procedure, which we would like to see as an external functional parameter to the whole system.

To evaluate the quality of a term, we run it on a set of test files and average the results. The generic objective function is defined as the sum of the total lengths plus a penalty for the excess in the number of routes over a pre-defined objective. By changing the value of this objective, we can optimize either the number of trucks or the total length. In the rest of the paper, we report the number of insertions and the average value of the objective function. When it is relevant (in order to compare with other approaches) we will translate them into CPU (s) and (number of routes, travel).

3.3. Results

3.3.1. Impact of ILO

We first used the algebra to make a series of tests to evaluate the contribution of ILO. In a previous paper we had demonstrated that applying 2- and 3-opt moves (with a hill-climbing strategy) as a post-processing step was both much slower and less effective than ILO. Here we tried a different set of post-optimization techniques that are illustrated in the table below. We used the total travel length as the optimization criterion and the result is the average for the 12 R1* Solomon benchmarks.

Table 1. Impact of ILO

Term (algorithm)	objective	Complexity (insertions)
INSERT(3)	**22703**	**1000 i**
INSERT(0)	25293	1000 i
LDS(0,5,100)	24462	30 ki
DO(INSERT(0), CHAIN(80,2))	23326	129 ki
DO(INSERT(0), TREE(80,2,4))	24052	146 ki
DO(INSERT(0), LOOP(3,CHAIN(80,2)))	23064	194 ki
LNS1 = DO(INSERT(3), **THEN(LOOP(50,LNS(10,10,LDS(3,4,100)),** **LOOP(50,LNS(20,3,LDS(3,4,100)))))**	**21927**	**180 ki**
LNS2 = DO(INSERT(3), THEN(LOOP(50,LNS(10,10,LDS(0,4,100)), LOOP(50,LNS(20,3,LDS(0,4,100)))))	24344	190 ki
LNS3 = DO(INSERT(3), THEN(LOOP(100,LNS(5,10,LDS(0,4,100)), LOOP(100,LNS(10,10,LDS(0,4,100)), LOOP(100,LNS(20,3,LDS(0,4,100))))	23881	980 ki

In table 1, the first solution that is built with ILO (first row) is significantly better than the one without it (second row), and it takes very aggressive optimization algorithms to compensate for the difference (rows 3 to 6). The next rows evaluate several LNS algorithms. The strategy in [16] can be described as a sequence of *LOOP(200,LNS(i,10,LDS(0,5,100))* for increasing values of i, which need to be run for a much longer time than ILO. We with experimented faster variations: LNS1 uses the basic ILO algorithm (INSERT(3)), LNS2 does not use any ILO, and LNS3 compensates for the fact that not using ILO is faster and performs more thorough application of LNS. These experiments demonstrate the benefits from ILO: both rows using ILO (in bold) achieve much better results than similar algorithms without it.

3.3.2. Ejection chains and trees

We have also used the algebra to evaluate the relative strength of the various optimization techniques. Since we are using a Solomon benchmark as the test set (the R1* set), we have mostly investigated terms that are using a few 100 000 insertions, corresponding to run times of a few seconds. As a matter of fact, as we explained in [3], most real-time problems have much larger data sets (including those from our own industrial experiments) and it is difficult to apply techniques that use an hour of CPU time for the Solomon problems. Our experience is that a few seconds on Solomon's benchmarks translate into a few minutes for our real-size problems (1000 to 5000 customers), which is acceptable.

Table 2 shows a set of terms that we produced manually to best represent each meta-heuristic. Complexities are adjusted so that they all have the same order of magnitude. The objective is either to minimize the total travel (objective T) or the number of routes and then, total travel (objective R). The last algorithm, succLNS, applies successive LNS loops removing increasingly large fragments of the solution.

Table 2. Various Meta-heursitics

Term (algorithm)	Obj. R	Perf.	Obj. T	Perf.
LDS(3,8,50)	53190	161Ki	22314	182Ki
DO(LDS(4,3,100),CHAIN(80,2))	59113	203Ki	22041	187Ki
DO(LDS(3,3,100), LOOP(30,LNS(10,4,LDS(4,4,1000))))	43813	155Ki	21981	300Ki
FORALL(LDS(3,2,100),CHAIN(20,2))	59732	190Ki	22179	142Ki
DO(INSERT(3),CHAIN(90,2))	70857	169Ki	22165	154Ki
DO(LDS(3,2,100),LOOP(2,TREE(40,2)))	47038	278Ki	22383	120Ki
DO(LDS(3,2,100),LOOP(6,CHAIN(25,2)))	61003	271Ki	22127	235Ki

SuccLNS = DO(LDS(3,0,100),
THEN(LOOP(30,LNS(4,4,LDS(3,3,1000))),
    LOOP(25,LNS(6,4,LDS(3,3,1000))),
    LOOP(20,LNS(8,4,LDS(3,3,1000))),
    LOOP(10,LNS(10,4,LDS(3,3,1000))),
    LOOP(8,LNS(12,4,LDS(3,3,1000)))))
	38095	**271Ki**	**21970**	**307Ki**

In these experiments, LNS dominates as the technique of choice (coupled with LDS). However, these are preliminary results and we have found that ejection tree optimization works well on larger problems. The experiments in Section 4 will also show that the combination of these techniques can also work better than LNS.

3.3.3. LNS and complex strategies
Last, we have used the algebra to compare more complex strategies that produce better quality solutions with run times that are comparable to what is found in the literature for the Solomon benchmarks.

We compare three strategies: LNS4 applies two passes of LNS after an LDS construction phase. LNS5 applies LNS at each solution produced by an LDS construction. LNS6 makes several passes of LNS* for fragments of increasing size (removing 10 to 30 of the 100 customers). The run-time per experiment varies from 5 to 30 minutes of CPU time on a Pentium II 366 MHz laptop. We have added comparative results from [17] and [16], since they provide average results for various running-time, making the comparison difficult because of the different hardware but still meaningful.

Table 3. Various LNS terms on R1 Solomon benchmarks

Term (algorithm)	Objective R	Perf.	Avg # of trucks	Avg travel
LNS4	22080	15Mi	12.23	1210.0
LNS5	22150	15Mi	12.28	1208.0

LNS6 = DO(LDS(4,5,200),
THEN(LNS*(10,3,LDS(4,5,200)),
    LNS*(20,3,LDS(4,5,200)),
    LNS*(30,3,LDS(4,5,200))))
	22030	45Mi	12.19	1207.8

[17] with CPU < 40 mns		~ 15Mi	12.64	1233.8
[17] with CPU < 2h		~ 50 Mi	12.39	1230.8
[16] with CPU < 15mns		~15 Mi	12.45	1198.8
[16] with CPU < 1h		~ 60 Mi	12.33	1201.7

These preliminary results are impressive, for such a limited amount of CPU time. If we limit ourselves to 5 minutes of CPU time on our machine (10 minutes for [16] or 30 minutes for [17]), we get an average number of route of 12.23 on R1 and 12.0 on RC1, whereas [17] and [16] respectively get 12.64 & 12.08 and 12.45 & 12.05. If we raise the available CPU time limit by a factor of 3, we get the same results for RC1 (12.0) and still a little better for R1 (12.19 vs. 12.39 and 12.33). The increase in CPU time has a smaller effect and we cannot obtain results as good as those of the best hybrid combination of tabu and genetic algorithms if a longer run-time is acceptable. More generally, it can be said that the approach presented here is a significant contribution for solving the Solomon benchmarks with a limited amount of time, but there are many other interesting approaches when longer execution times are considered [5] (which also relies on a set of optimization operators coupled with the use of constraint programming and report 12.08 routes on R1* and 11.63 routes on RC1*, for 3 hours of CPU).

The fact that we obtain state-of-the-art results is even more interesting if we consider that the CP node insertion procedure is not state-of-the-art and that the code for the meta-heuristics is less than 100 lines long, However, it is also clear that the term that we used is in no way optimal, but there are too many alternate approaches that should be tested. This leads naturally to the idea of automatic tuning and automatic discovery of algebraic terms that we shall now develop.

4. Learning New Terms

4.1 Invention and Mutation

The first step to discover new terms is to create them randomly. We have implemented an invention method that is defined by structural induction from the grammar definition. The choice among the different subclasses (e.g. what to pick when we need an <Optimize>) is done by using a random number generator and a pre-determined distribution. The result is that we can create terms with an arbitrary complexity (there are no boundaries on the level of recursion, but the invention algorithm terminates with probability 1).

A key concept to guide the invention is the expected complexity for a term. It is easy to define a complexity oracle (prediction) by structural induction. There is no point in generating terms that are obviously too complex, so we guide the invention by giving a target complexity.

The second step is to be able to mutate terms, i.e., to modify them partially. Mutation is also defined by structural induction according to two parameters. The first parameter tells if we want a shallow modification, an average modification or a deep modification. In the first case, the structure of the term does not change and the mutation only changes the leaf constants that are involved in the term (integers). Moreover, only small changes for these parameters are supported. In the second case, the type (class) does not change, but large changes in the parameters are allowed and, with a given probability, some sub-terms can be replaced by terms of other classes. In the last case, a complete substitution with a different term is allowed (with a given probability). The second parameter gives the actual performance of the term, as measured in the experiment. The mutation algorithm tries to adjust the term in such a way that the (real) complexity of the new term is as close as possible to the global objective. This compensates the biases of the complexity oracle quite effectively.

4.2. Learning new terms

The learning process works with a pool of terms (ie. algorithms). At each iteration, the terms are evaluated, the best ones are selected and mutated in different ways. The next generation of terms consists in these new ones together with the very best ones from the previous generation.

The next step in developing a better learning algorithm will include raising the size of the pool and the number of iterations, as well as introducing some crossing between terms. In addition, we will explore the use of abstract patterns such as the relational cliché approach described in [14] to expand the search space around the most promising terms and to abstract commonalties from terms that have been successful in the past. Although our initial experiments have shown that changing even the performance objective for a problem can lead to the discovery of different terms, it makes good intuitive sense that the ways in which the meta-heuristics themselves can be effectively combined are more structured. The abstract patterns uncovered by an "cliché learner" could very well capture the implicit knowledge of how to combine the strategies employed by these meta-heuristics.

The keys here are to form the appropriate generalization language to describe the pattern abstractions and to learn patterns that are restrictive enough to effectively guide the search yet general enough to uncover any natural patterns that may exist.

4.3. Experiments

4.3.1. Travel optimization
The first experiment applies our learning algorithm to the discovery of an algorithm for minimizing the total travel time within a relatively strict computation time (the complexity goal is set at 50Ki). We first report the scores of different terms : the first four were built manually to solve this problem, the last term is the result of the learning algorithm.

Table 4. A first learning experiment

Term	objective	Run-time (i)
LDS(3,5,0)	22385	27Ki
DO(LDS(3,3,100), LOOP(8,LNS(10,4,LDS(4,4,1000))))	22147	99Ki
DO(LDS(3,2,100),TREE(20,2))	22439	23Ki
FORALL(LDS(3,2,100),CHAIN(8,2))	22310	59Ki
FORALL(LDS+(0,2,2936,CHAIN(1,1)), LOOP(48,LOOP(4, LNS(3,16,LDS(3,1,287))))))	21946 (invented !)	57ki

This is quite an astonishing results, since the term "found" by the algorithm is significantly better than those that we had thought about initially[1].

From an academic perspective, it will be more interesting to report the result of letting the learning algorithm run with a high complexity objective and see if the previous results on Solomon's benchmark (Section 2.3.3) can be improved. However,

---

[1] Obviously, once we see the results, we get new ideas for "hand-picked" terms ...

we did not have enough time when writing this paper (training the algorithm for these small terms takes a few hours and it would take many weeks of CPU time for a complexity goal of 15Mi). Besides, the tuning of algorithms with a realistic boundary on execution time (cf. Section 2.3.2) is quite interesting from an industrial point of view.

4.3.2. Truck optimization

The second experiment is similar but we changed the objective function since our goal now is to minimize the number of trucks. A simple LDS algorithm (LDS(3,5,0)) yields a result of 53471 for a complexity of 24 ki. The previously invented term yields 39730 (within 57 ki). The learning algorithm produces a new term, DO(LDS(2,5,145), THEN(CHAIN(5,2), TREE(9,2,2))) yielding 36531 in 56 ki.

Thus, the learning algorithm found a combination of techniques that is different from the one used in the previous experiment and which works significantly better (this is an average of 12 problems). It is interesting to note that the new term found for this problem does poorly (22430) for the previous test.

4.3.3. Impact of running time

The third experiment is similar to the first with a different complexity goal. Here, we are trying to simulate what happens when a new piece of hardware is introduced. The hybrid algorithm needs to be re-tuned and it is not always easy to find out how the parameters need to be adjusted to best take advantage of the increased computing power. We compare several algorithms

- A Standard LDS scheme LDS(3,8,50) yields 53190 (in 161 ki.)
- Adaptation of the term that was invented in section 3.3.1 (best for 50Ki) DO(LDS(4,5,145), THEN(CHAIN(10,2), TREE(20,2,2))) gets 33298 (in 245 ki.) and DO(LDS(2,5,145), LOOP(4,THEN(CHAIN(15,2),
                                    TREE(9,2,2)))) gets 31071 (in 120 ki.)
- the term that is invented for this new performance goal, FORALL(LDS(3,4,191), LOOP(97,LNS(4,8,LDS(3,4,357)))) yields 30726 (in 126ki.)

Here again, we see that automatic discovery makes sense since the term that was discovered is better than the result of hand-tuning the previous best solution.

4.3.4. Smaller trucks

In the last experiment, we now suppose that we have a new kind of trucks (their load capacity is reduced by half). We compare several algorithms:

- A standard LDS scheme LDS(3,5,0) yields 25400 (in 34 ki.),
- The term that was invented (see table 5) obtains 24718 (in 74 ki.)
- The new term invented, yields 24703 (in 47 ki.):
        FORALL(FORALL(1,1,7456,CHAIN(3,3)),LOOP(65,LNS(6,24,LDS(3,2,187))))

This last experiment is a good illustration of our initial remark that hybrid algorithms require non-trivial tuning as part of their maintenance. The change in truck capacity causes an important change in the performances of the various algorithm. The new term that is invented is not only slightly better in quality, it is also much closer to the original complexity goal.

5. Future directions

There are still many directions that need to be investigated. These research directions have a very interesting potential, and the complete exploration of the paradigm proposed in this paper is beyond the scope of a single paper. We intend to explore the following topics in the future :

- Experimenting further on routing problems: in particular, we intend to apply the optimization framework to harder problems with tighter time windows and to larger problems.
- Using an exact TSP solver: the insertion heuristic which inserts a node between two consecutive nodes and re-optimizes the route thereafter could be replaced by an exact algorithm. In order to insert node i in route r, we could simply ask a constraint-based TSP solver to find the best Hamiltonian tour visiting i and all nodes previously covered by r. We already noticed in [3] that using such an exact CP solver could yield substantial improvements on ILO heuristics.
- Extending the algebra: more combinators could be available for building algorithmic terms. In particular, it would be interesting to use other large neighborhoods such as SMART [12], or to experiment tabu control schemes over the sequence of local moves such as LNS.
- Improving the learning procedure: for instance, it could detect interesting interactions between algorithmic components by recognizing sub-terms in algorithms. Moreover, the "learner" could be more informed and assess the value of an algorithm not only by the final result produced by the algorithm, but by the full improvement curve of solutions over time.
- Finally, we would like to apply this algorithmic factory to other generalized assignment problems, such as roster scheduling.

6. Conclusions

Many interesting contributions can be derived from the experiments presented in this paper. First, we have shown that LNS + ILO is a powerful combination. It is a significant improvement both on previous work on ILO [3] on LNS [16].

The second contribution is an algebra for representing hybrid algorithms that use push/pull meta-heuristics. Following the principles that were established with SALSA, it is possible to represent a large family of meta-heuristics with a small set of parameterized operators. This abstraction has many advantages, including:

- *Genericity*: the library can be reused for other task assignment problems,
- *Ease of Maintenance*: the abstraction provides a better capture of the design, as was noticed for SALSA,
- *Ease of tuning*: the parameters are more visible and the handling of new algorithms is made easier,
- *Opportunity of automatic discovery*.

Automatic discovery of meta-heuristic is probably the most important contribution of this approach. Obtaining yet another great set of numbers on Solomon benchmarks may be of little significance if the algorithm is not robust or difficult to scale. The fact that real-world problems are both bigger and more complex advocates for automatic tuning. Our hope is that this approach will make hybrid algorithms more practical.

We consider this project to be a first step towards a new paradigm for industrial applications where applications are decomposed into two separate pieces that can be combined independently. The first piece uses constraint programming to model the domain-dependent part of the problem, because CP is the best technology for representing side constraints. The second piece is a meta-heuristic package that is totally generic. There is a small price to be paid for genericity (no smart tricks to guide the meta-heuristics) but the result is much more maintainable and can be tested on a variety of problem-dependent insertion modules. The flexibility of this meta-heuristic package is achieved by the algebraic model and the automatic tuning algorithm.

References

1. Y. Caseau, F. Laburthe. *Introduction to the Claire Programming Language*. LIENS Report 96-15, Ecole Normale Supérieure, 1996.
2. Y. Caseau, F. Laburthe. *Solving small TSPs with Constraints*. Proc. of the 14th International Conference on Logic Programming, The MIT Press, 1997.
3. Y. Caseau, F. Laburthe, *Heuristics for Large Constrained Vehicle Routing Problems*, to appear in the Journal of Heuristics, 1998.
4. Y. Caseau, F. Laburthe, *SALSA : A Language for Search Algorithms*, Proc. of Constraint Programming'98, M.Maher, J.-F. Puget eds., Springer, LNCS 1520, p.310-324, 1998.
5. B. De Backer, V. Furnon, *Local Search in Constraint Programming : Experiments with Tabu Search on the Vehicle Routing Problem*, Meta Heuristics : Advances and Trends in Local Search Paradigms for Optimization, S. Voss. et al. eds. Kluwer, 1999.
6. M. Gendreau, A. Hertz, G. Laporte. *A Tabu Search Heuristic for the Vehicle Routing Problem*, Management Science, vol 40,p. 1276-1290, 1994.
7. W. Harvey, M. Ginsberg. *Limited Discrepancy Search*, Proceedings of the 14th IJCAI, p. 607-615, Morgan Kaufmann, 1995.
8. G. Kontoravdis, J. Bard. *A GRASP for the Vehicle Routing Problem with Time Windows*, ORSA Journal on Computing, Vol 7, N. 1, 1995.
9. G. Laporte. *The Vehicle Routing Problem: an overview of Exact and Approximate Algorithms*, European Journal of Operational Research 59, p. 345-358, 1992.
10. S. Minton, Configurable Solvers : *Tailoring General Methods to Specific Applications*, Proc. of Constraint Programming, G. Smolka ed., Springer, LNCS 1330, p.372-374, 1997.
11. C. Rego, C. Roucairol. *A Parallel Tabu Search Algorithm Using Ejection Chains for the Vehicle Routing Problem*, in *Meta-Heuristics: Theory and Applications*, Kluwer, 1996.
12. L.-M. Rousseau, M. Gendreau, G. Pesant, *Using Constraint-Based Operators with Variable Neighborhood Search to solve the Vehicle Routing Problem with Time Windows*, CP-AI-OR'99 workshop, Ferrara, February 1999.
13. R. Russell. *Hybrid Heuristics for the Vehicle Routing Problem with Time Windows*, Transportation Science, vol 29, n. 2, may 1995.
14. G. Silverstein, M. Pazzani. *Relational clichés: Constraining constructive induction during relational learning*, Machine Learning Proceedings of the Eighth International Workshop (ML91), p. 203-207, Morgan Kaufmann 1991.
15. M. Solomon. *Algorithms for the Vehicle Routing and Scheduling Problems with Time Window Constraints*, Operations Research vol 35, n. 2, 1987.
16. P. Shaw, *Using Constraint Programming and Local Search Methods to Solve Vehicle Routing Problems*, Principles and Practice of Constraint Programming, proceedings of CP'98, LNCS 1520, Springer, 1998.
17. E. Taillard, P. Badeau, M. Gendreau, F. Guertain, J.-Y. Rousseau *A New Neighborhood Structure for the Vehicle Routing Problem with Time Windows*, technical report CRT-95-66, Université de Montréal, 1995.

Closure Functions and Width 1 Problems

Víctor Dalmau[1] and Justin Pearson[2]

[1] Departament LSI, Universitat Politècnica de Catalunya,
Mòdul C5. Jordi Girona Salgado 1-3. Barcelona 08034, Spain,
dalmau@lsi.upc.es
[2] Department of Computer Systems, Uppsala University,
Box 325, S-751 05 Uppsala, Sweden
justin@DoCS.UU.SE

Abstract. Local Consistency has proven to be an important notion in the study of constraint satisfaction problems. We give an algebraic condition that characterizes all the constraint types for which generalized arc-consistency is sufficient to ensure the existence of a solution. We give some examples to illustrate the application of this result.

1 Introduction

The constraint satisfaction problem provides a framework in which it is possible to express, in a natural way, many combinatorial problems encountered in artificial intelligence and elsewhere. A constraint satisfaction problem is represented by a set of variables, a domain of values for each variable, and a set of constraints between variables. Generally, a constraint C is represented by two components: a *scope* S that expresses the set of variables constrained and a *relation* R which expresses the combination of values allowed for those variables. The aim of a constraint satisfaction problem is then to find an assignment of values to the variables that satisfies the constraints.

Since solving a general constraint satisfaction problem is known to be NP-complete [1, 20], a natural and important question is: what restrictions to the general problem are sufficient to ensure tractability. Such restrictions may either involve the scope in the constraints, i.e., which variables may be constrained with other variables [6, 11, 12, 21, 22], or they may involve the relation in the constraints, in other words, which combinations of values are allowed for values which are mutually constrained [3, 15, 18, 19, 21, 27, 28].

In this paper, we focus in the second approach. More precisely we are interested in characterizing the complexity of solving constraint satisfaction problems in which every constraint belongs to a fixed set called *basis*. Jeavons, Cohen and Gyssens in [15, 16] introduced a novel framework for studying this class of constraint satisfaction problems. The approach started in [15, 16] relies on the fact that the tractability of constraint satisfaction problems using certain relations depends on some algebraic condition (that of closure) of the set of relations used to build the problem. This approach has lead to the identification of several tractable classes [15–18, 14].

Local consistency methods [20, 9, 10, 14, 7, 2] have been intensively studied as a fundamental tool for solving constraint problems. Briefly, the underlying idea in local consistency methods is the following: when a constraint network is inconsistent, this is probably due to the existence of an inconsistent subnetwork of reduced size. It is sometimes possible to decide the existence of a solution of a constraint satisfaction problem by checking the consistency of all the subproblems up to a certain size. Since there exists problems which can not be solved by local consistency methods, there is a large body of work [11, 5, 7, 14] which derives conditions that guarantee that a problem can be solved by a certain local consistency method.

In this paper we consider a family of local consistency methods called (j, k)-consistency, derived from the concept of bounded width Datalog programs [8]. This notion of consistency is related to the notion of consistency defined in [11]. We refer to the class of problems solvable by enforcing (j, k)-consistency as width (j, k) problems. It is not know, in general, whether a constraint satisfaction problem has width (j, k).

In particular, we will be interested in $(1, k)$-consistency, which can be regarded as the natural generalization of arc-consistency [20] to non-binary problems. The class of problems that can be solved by enforcing $(1, k)$-consistency for some fixed k is called width 1. This class contains some previously known tractable families of problems including Horn, constant and ACI Problems [25, 17]. The main result of this paper is a characterization of width 1 problems in terms of closure functions. That is, we present an algebraic condition (in the sense of [17]) on the relations used to build constraint problems which ensure that any problem built using these relations can be solved in polynomial time by enforcing $(1, k)$-consistency for some k. Furthermore, we show that this condition is also necessary.

With this new characterization we revisit some already known tractable families, as constant and ACI problems [17], and we see that they fit into this common scheme, in other words, we prove that they are particular case of width 1 problems. Furthermore, we derive a new tractable class called CSCI (from Constant Semiprojection Commutative Idempotent) using purely algebraic arguments.

The motivation of these results is an alternative characterization of width 1 problems due to Feder and Vardi [8]. In [8] three main families of tractable problems, referred to as *subgroup*, *bounded strict width* and *width* 1 problems are identified using concepts from Database theory (Datalog programs) and group theory. These three classes include all previously known tractable problems. In [14], the family of strict width problems was characterized in terms of closure functions. An important subclass of subgroup problems called *affine* problems was introduced in [17] and was generalized to the whole class of subgroup problems in [4] studying the learnability of quantified formulas. The results in this paper characterize the remaining class, completing the research work started in [14].

2 Preliminaries and Definitions

2.1 Constraint Satisfaction Problems

A constraint satisfaction problem is a natural way to express simultaneous requirements for values of variables. More precisely,

Definition 1. An instance of a *constraint satisfaction problem* consists of:

- a finite set of variables, V. For simplicity we assume $V = \{x_1, x_2, \ldots x_n\}$;
- a finite domain of values, D;
- a finite set of constraints $\{C_1, \ldots, C_q\}$; each constraint C_i $(1 \leq i \leq q)$ is a pair (s_i, R_i) where:
  - s_i is a tuple of variables of length k_i, called the *constraint scope*; and
  - R_i is an k_i-ary relation over D, called the *constraint relation*.

For each constraint (s_i, R_i), the tuples in R_i indicate the allowed combinations of simultaneous values for the variables in s_i. The length of s_i, and of the tuples in R_i, is called the *arity* of the constraint.

A *solution* to a constraint satisfaction problem instance is a function from the variables to the domain such that the image of each constraint scope is an element of the corresponding constraint relation. Deciding whether or not a given problem instance has a solution is NP-complete in general, even when the constraints are restricted to binary constraints [20] or the domain of the problem has size 2 [1]. However, by imposing restrictions on the constraint interconnections (see [6, 11, 12, 21, 22]), or the form of the constraints (see [3, 15, 18, 19, 21, 27, 28]), it is possible to obtain restricted versions of the problem that are tractable. As we have said, the aim underlying this research is to determine all the possible restrictions on the form of the constraints that ensure tractability. The central object of study is the set of problems defined from some fixed set (or basis), and the associated complexity of the constraint problems in that set.

Definition 2. For any set of relations Γ, C_Γ is defined to be the class of decision problems with:

- Instance: A constraint satisfaction problem instance $\mathcal{P}$, in which all constraint relations are elements of Γ.
- Question: Does $\mathcal{P}$ have a solution?

2.2 Closure Functions

To our knowledge even though there exists a large collection of individual results about the complexity of C_Γ, there has only been two attempts to study the complexity of C_Γ in a uniform way. The first attempt, due to Feder and Vardi [8], uses an approach based in Datalog Programs and Group Theory and produced, among other important results, a classification of the known tractable classes in three families of basis, called *width 1*, *bounded strict width*, and *subgroup problems*. The second attempt was originally defined by Jeavons et al. [15, 16]

and focuses on the algebraic properties of constraints. We follow the second approach in this paper. In the rest of this section we will introduce the basic concepts of this approach (see [15–17, 14] for more information).

Any operation on the elements of a set D can be extended to an operation on tuples over D by applying the operation to the values in each coordinate position separately.

Definition 3. Let $f : D^k \to D$ be a k-ary operation on D. For any collection of n-ary tuples $t_1, t_2, \ldots, t_k \in D^n$, (not necessarily all distinct) define the tuple $f(t_1, t_2, \ldots, t_k)$ as follows:

$$f(t_1, \ldots, t_k) = f(t_1[1], \ldots, t_k[1]), f(t_1[2], \ldots, t_k[2]), \ldots, f(t_1[n], \ldots, t_k[n]) \rangle.$$

Using this definition, we now define the following closure property of relations.

Definition 4. Let R be a relation over a domain D, and let $f : D^k \to D$ be a k-ary operation on D. R is said to be *closed* under f (f preserves R, or f is a polymorphism of R) if, for all $t_1, t_2, \ldots, t_k \in R$ (not necessarily all distinct),

$$f(t_1, t_2, \ldots, t_k) \in R.$$

We say that an operation f preserves a basis Γ if f preserves every relation in Γ. The next lemma indicates that the property of being closed under some operation is preserved by some operations on relations.

Lemma 1. *Let R_1 be an n-ary relation over a domain D and let R_2 be a m-ary relation over a domain D. Both R_1 and R_2 are closed under some operation f. The following relations are also closed under f.*

- *The Cartesian Product, $R_1 \times R_2$ defined to be the $(n + m)$-ary relation*

$$R_1 \times R_2 = \{\langle t[1], t[2], \ldots, t[n + m] \rangle \mid \langle t[1], t[2], \ldots, t[n] \rangle \in R_1 \wedge \\ \langle t[n + 1], t[n + 2], \ldots, t[n + m] \rangle \in R_2\}$$

- *The equality selection $\sigma_{i=j}(R)$ $(1 \leq i, j \leq n)$ defined to be the n-ary relation*

$$\sigma_{i=j}(R) = \{t \in R | t[i] = t[j]\}$$

- *The projection $\pi_{i_1, \ldots, i_k}(R)$ where $(i_1, \ldots, i_k)$ is a list of indices chosen from $\{1, 2, \ldots, n\}$, defined to be the k-ary relation*

$$\pi_{i_1, \ldots, i_k}(R) = \{\langle t[i_1], \ldots, t[i_k] \rangle | t \in R\}$$

Proof. Follows directly from the definitions. ∎

The set of all relations that which can be obtained from a given set of relations Γ, using some sequence of Cartesian product, equality selection, and projection operations will be denoted Γ^+. Consequently every operation preserving Γ, preserves Γ^+ as well.

On the other hand, the property of being closed under some operation is preserved by some operations on functions.

163

Lemma 2. *Let $g : D^m \to D$ be a m-ary function and let $f_1, f_2, \ldots, f_m : D^n \to D$ be n-ary functions. If $g, f_1, f_2, \ldots, f_m$ preserve R, for some relation R, then the following functions preserve also R:*

- *The composition $g(f_1, f_2, \ldots, f_m)$ defined to be the n-ary operation*

$$g(f_1, f_2, \ldots, f_m)(x_1, \ldots, x_n) = g(f_1(x_1, \ldots, x_n), \ldots, f_m(x_1, \ldots, x_n))$$

- *For every $j \leq k$, the projection $\mathrm{proj}_{j,k}$ defined to be the k-ary operation*

$$\mathrm{proj}_{j,k}(x_1, x_2, \ldots, x_k) = x_j$$

Proof. Follows from the definitions. ∎

Any set of operations closed under composition and containing all the projection operations is called *Clone* (See [26] for example). In [13], it was established that the complexity of C_Γ is determined by the set of closure functions of Γ. We say that a closure function guarantees tractability if for every basis Γ closed under f, class C_Γ is tractable. Following this approach, some functions that guarantee tractability have been identified. Up to the present moment four families of tractable functions are know. They correspond to the near-unanimity operations [14], coset-generating operations [4], ACI operations [17], and constant operations [17].

2.3 Local Consistency

Local consistency methods are refutation methods, similar in aim to the resolution method for propositional formulas in conjunctive normal form. Different notions of local consistency have been defined [20, 9, 10, 14, 7] but all of them fit into this common scheme: A Local consistency method takes an instance $\mathcal{P}$ and adds all the constraints that appear implicitly in $\mathcal{P}$ (and therefore, eliminating no solution) up to a certain level. A constraint $\langle s, \emptyset \rangle$ with empty constraint relation is called *empty constraint*. If during the process of enforcing consistency, some empty constraint is added, then instance $\mathcal{P}$ has obviously no solution. Unfortunately, the reciprocal is not always true, i.e., the absence of the empty constraint does not imply in general the existence of a solution. So, it is an interesting topic of research to establish under which conditions over the set of constraint relations Γ, establishing a certain level of local consistency guarantees the existence of a solution.

Definition 5. Let $\mathcal{P}$ be a constraint satisfaction instance with set of variables V, domain D, and constraint set C. For any subset W of V the *restriction of $\mathcal{P}$ to W*, denoted $\mathcal{P}_W^*$ is the problem instance with set of variables W and domain D, where the constraints are obtained from the constraints of $\mathcal{P}$ eliminating all the constraints with constraint scope not completely contained in W. That is, the constraint (s, R) is in $\mathcal{P}_W^*$ if and only if (s, R) is in $\mathcal{P}$ and every element of the tuple s is in W.

We now define the notion of consistency used in this paper.

164

Definition 6. A constraint satisfaction problem instance $\mathcal{P}$ with set of variables V is said to be (j, k)-*consistent* $(0 \leq j \leq k)$ if for any sets of variables W, W', such that $W \subseteq W' \subseteq V$, containing at most j and k variables respectively, any solution to $\mathcal{P}_W^*$ can be extended to a solution to $\mathcal{P}_{W \cup W'}^*$.

Informally, a problem is (j, k)-consistent if every partial solution on any set of at most j variables can be extended to a partial solution on any superset containing at most k variables. This notion of consistency generalizes the notion of (i, j)-consistency in [11] to constraint problems with non-binary constraints.

Since the constraint literature contains few similar notions of consistency we believe that it is appropriate to enclose here a brief discussion of the more popular notions of consistency. Informally we can say that the different notions of consistency are characterized by the way in which they define a subproblem. Roughly, consistency notions can be divided in two main types: (1) *variable-based* consistency and (2) *relation-based* consistency.

In variable-based consistency a subproblem is specified as the subproblem containing all the restrictions "concerning" a set of variables. Variable-based consistency has received more attention (see [20, 9, 10] for example) than its relational counterpart. We have different consistency notions depending on how "concerning" is formalized. Very often, the subproblem "concerning" a set of variables W is defined as the subproblem containing all the constraints with scope strictly contained in W, as in the definitions in this paper. This approach is due to [20] and was generalized to sets of variables with arbitrary size in [9]. This notion of consistency in closely related to the notion defined here. More precisely, k-consistency in the sense of [9] coincides exactly with $(k-1, k)$-consistency, as defined in this paper. In some other cases, the problem "concerning" a set of variables W has been defined as the problem containing the projection of all the constraints over W (see [14], for example). In fact, both definitions are equivalent for the purposes of this paper (this will be shown in the forthcoming full version of this paper) We choosed this particular notion of consistency to simplify the proofs. Finally, in relation-based consistency (see [7] for example), a subproblem is specified by a set of restrictions rather than variables. It is important to note that for constraint satisfaction problems with only binary constraints many of the different possible notions of consistency coincide.

Given a CSP instance $\mathcal{P}$, there exists some instance $\mathcal{P}'$ such that (1) Every constraint in $\mathcal{P}$ is in $\mathcal{P}'$, (2) $\mathcal{P}'$ is (j, k)-consistent, and (3) instances $\mathcal{P}$ and $\mathcal{P}'$ have the same set of solutions. Instance $\mathcal{P}'$ is referred to as a (j, k)-consistent instance associated to $\mathcal{P}$. We say that $\mathcal{P}'$ is obtained from $\mathcal{P}$ by enforcing (j, k)-consistency. The CSP literature [21, 20, 9, 2] contains some efficient methods to enforce certain level of consistency. Here we present simple brute-force algorithm, called $\text{Cons}_{(j,k)}$ (j, k fixed), that enforces (j, k)-consistency.

Procedure $\text{Cons}_{(j,k)}$
Input: $\mathcal{P}$
$\mathcal{P}' = \mathcal{P}$

repeat
    for every subset W with $|W| \leq j$
        for every superset W' of W with $|W'| \leq k$
            for every tuple $s = \langle x_1, \ldots, x_i \rangle$ with variables in W
                let R be the projection of $\mathcal{P'}^*_{W'}$ over s, i.e.,
                  $R = \{\langle \mu(x_1), \ldots, \mu(x_i) \rangle : \mu \text{ solution of } \mathcal{P'}^*_{W'}\}$
                (R contains all the assignment over s that can be extended to
                a solution of $\mathcal{P'}^*_{W'}$)
                if $\langle s, R \rangle$ not in $\mathcal{P}'$ then add $\langle s, R \rangle$ to $\mathcal{P}'$.
until no constraint has been added.
return $\mathcal{P}'$.

Basically, the algorithm looks for subsets $W \subseteq W'$ of variables falsifying the (j, k)-consistency condition (Definition 6) and adds the correspondent constraint until the instance $\mathcal{P}'$ satisfies the (j, k)-consistency condition and no constraint has to be added. For fixed values of j, k, procedure $\mathrm{Cons}_{(j,k)}$ runs in time polynomial to the size of the input instance $\mathcal{P}$.

Notice that the constraints added by algorithm $\mathrm{Cons}_{(j,k)}$ are minimal in the sense that for every (j, k)-consistent instance $\mathcal{P}'$ associated to $\mathcal{P}$ and every variable x_i $(1 \leq i \leq n)$, every solution of $\mathcal{P'}^*_{\{x_i\}}$ is a solution of $(\mathrm{Cons}_{(j,k)}(\mathcal{P}))^*_{\{x_i\}}$.

Furthermore, for every constraint $\langle s, R \rangle$ added by the algorithm, its associated relation R is the projection of subproblem $\mathcal{P'}^*_{W'}$ over s. Since every relation associated to a problem (or equivalently subproblem) with constraint relations in Γ can be obtained by a sequence of of cartesian products and equality selections using relations in Γ. We have that if $\mathcal{P} \in C_\Gamma$, then $\mathcal{P}' \in C_{\Gamma^+}$.

Definition 7. A CSP instance $\mathcal{P}$ is said to have *width* (j, k) if $\mathcal{P}$ has a solution if and only if every (j, k)-consistent instance associated to $\mathcal{P}$ does not contain the empty constraint relation $\langle s, \emptyset \rangle$. Similarly, a set of relations Γ over D is said to have width (j, k) if every CSP instance $\mathcal{P}$ in C_Γ has width (j, k). Furthermore Γ is said to have width j if it has width (j, k) for some fixed k.

Hence, a set of relations Γ has width (j, k) if and only if every problem in C_Γ is solvable by enforcing (j, k)-consistency (using the previous algorithm for example). In consequence, any constraint instance in C_Γ is solvable in polynomial-time, since for fixed values j and k, it is possible to enforce (j, k)-consistency in time polynomial in the size of the problem.

Feder and Vardi [8] gave an alternative characterization of these concepts in terms of Datalog Programs. Datalog Programs are far beyond the scope of this paper. Nevertheless, we will only note here, that the notion of width defined above is exactly equivalent to the notion of width, as defined in [8].

166

3 Width 1 Problems

We are interested in the class of problems that can be solved by enforcing $(1,k)$-consistency for some fixed k, also called width 1 problems. The notion of $(1,k)$ consistency is the natural generalization of arc-consistency to non-binary problems.

In this section we prove that the family of basis of width 1 is absolutely characterized in terms of closure functions. In other words, we will see that for every basis Γ, C_Γ is solvable by enforcing $(1,k)$-consistency for some $k \geq 1$ if and only if some condition over the set of closure functions is satisfied. First we introduce the concept of set function.

A *set function* is any function $f : \mathcal{P}(D)/\emptyset \longrightarrow D$ where D is some set and $\mathcal{P}(D)$ is the set of subsets of D.

Associated to every set function f we have a *family of functions associated to f* $\{f_i : i = 1, \ldots, n\}$, where for every i, $f_i : D^i \longrightarrow D$ is given by

$$f_i(x_1, \ldots, x_i) = f(\{x_1, \ldots, x_i\}),$$

Let f be a set function over D and let R be any relation over D, we say that f preserves R, (or R is closed under f) if the family of functions associated to f preserves R (Definition 4).

Theorem 1. *Let Γ be a finite set of relations over D. Then the following conditions are equivalent:*

a.- The set Γ is width 1.
b.- Γ is closed under some set function.

The proof of the theorem uses the following result. Given any set of relations Γ, consider the constraint satisfaction problem $C(\Gamma)$ defined as follows:

The variables of $C(\Gamma)$ are the nonempty subsets A of D. For a relation R of arity k, impose $R(A_1, A_2 \ldots, A_k)$, the A_i not necessarily distinct, if for every $1 \leq i \leq k$ and every a_i in A_i there exist elements a_j in the remaining A_j such that $(a_1, a_2, \ldots, a_k) \in R$.

There is an alternative characterization of the constraints in $C(\Gamma)$: It is easy to verify that a constraint $R(A_1, \ldots, A_k)$ is in $C(\Gamma)$ iff there exists some assignments $t_1, \ldots, t_m$ in R such that $\{t_1[l], t_2[l], \ldots, t_m[l]\} = A_l$ for all $1 \leq l \leq k$.

Theorem 2. *[8] A set of relations Γ is width 1 then $C(\Gamma)$ has a solution.*

Proof of Theorem 1
$[(a) \rightarrow (b)]$. Let h be any solution of $C(\Gamma)$ (the existence of such solution is guaranteed by Theorem 2) and let f_h be the set function defined as:

$$f^h(A_i) = h(A_i).$$

We will prove that f^h preserves Γ: Let m be any integer $m > 1$, let R be any k-ary relation in Γ, and let $t_1, t_2, \ldots, t_m$ (not necessarily different) tuples in R. Let A_i $(1 \leq i \leq k)$ be subsets of D given by:

$$A_i = \{t_l[i] : 1 \leq l \leq m\}, \quad 1 \leq i \leq k$$

By, construction, $R(A_1, A_2, \ldots, A_k)$ appears in $\mathcal{C}(\Gamma)$ and therefore h satisfies it. Then we have

$$\langle h(A_1), h(A_2), \ldots, h(A_k) \rangle = \langle f^h(A_1), f^h(A_2), \ldots, f^h(A_k) \rangle = f^h_m(t_1, \ldots, t_m) \in R.$$

[(b) → (a)]. Let Γ be a set of relations over D closed under a set function f. Let k be the maximum arity of the relations in Γ. We will prove that enforcing $(1, k)$-consistency is enough to decide satisfiability. Let $\mathcal{P}$ be any problem in C_Γ and let $\mathcal{P}'$ be a problem obtained by enforcing $(1, k)$-consistency to $\mathcal{P}$. For every variable x, let D_x be the set of values that can be assigned to the variable x, i.e., the set of solutions of the problem $\mathcal{P}'$ restricted to x: $D_x = \mathcal{P}'^*_{\{x\}}$.

Consider the vector t, assigning to every variable x the value of the set function over D_x, that is,

$$t(x) = f(D_x)$$

We will see that t is a solution. Let $\langle (x_1, x_2 \ldots, x_m), R \rangle$ be any constraint in $\mathcal{P}$. Clearly, $D_{x_i} \subseteq \pi_i R$ $(1 \le i \le m)$. Consider now, the subset R' of R, obtained enforcing for every variable x appearing in the scope of the constraint to have a value in D_x. More formally,

$$R' = R \cap (D_{x_1} \times \cdots \times D_{x_m}).$$

Since, D_{x_i} $(1 \le i \le m)$ is obtained by enforcing $(1, k)$-consistency, we have $D_{x_i} = \pi_i R'$ $(1 \le i \le m)$. Let $t_1, t_2, \ldots, t_l$ be the tuples in R'. Since R is closed under f_l, we have:

$$f_l(t_1, t_2, \ldots, t_l) = \langle f(D_{x_1}), f(D_{x_2}), \ldots, f(D_{x_m}) \rangle \in R.$$

So t satisfies R. ∎

The characterization of width 1 problems in terms of closure functions is interesting theoretically but it is not absolutely satisfactory. First, if we want to use this characterization to check whether a given basis Γ is width 1 then we have to test the closure condition for an infinite family of operations.

Actually it is possible, for a given Γ, fix a bound in the arity of the operations that we have to consider.

Theorem 3. *Let Γ be a finite set of relations over D, let m be the maximum number of tuples of any relation in Γ, and let f be a set function over D. If f_m preserves Γ then f preserves Γ.*

Proof.

Most of the next proofs have a similar structure. We will be interested in proving that if some function h_1 (or set of functions) preserves a relation R then another function h_2 preserves also R. We will prove that by showing that function h_2 can be obtained by a sequence of compositions using h_1 and projection operations only. Then, since the set of closure functions of a relation contains projection operations and is closed under composition (Lemma 2), operation h_2 preserves any relation preserved by h_1. We will say that h_2 is contained in any clone containing h_1.

In the present proof, we will see that every clone containing f_m, contains f_k ($k > 0$), or in other words, f_k can be obtained by a composition using f_m and projections.

It is immediate to prove that, in general, for every set function f and every $k > 0$, f_k belongs to any clone containing f_{k+1}. Just consider the identity.

$$f_k(x_1, x_2, \ldots, x_k) = f_{k+1}(x_1, x_2, \ldots, x_k, x_k)$$

For the proof in the opposite direction, let R be any relation in Γ, let k be any integer greater than m, and let $t_1, t_2, \ldots, t_k$ tuples in R. Since $k > m$, some tuples are repeated. Consider a sublist with m tuples $t_{i_1}, t_{i_2}, \ldots, t_{i_m}$ in which we have deleted only repeated tuples, i.e., such that $\{t_j : 1 \leq j \leq k\} = \{t_{i_j} : 1 \leq j \leq m\}$. By the structure of the set functions we have:

$$f_k(t_1, t_2, \ldots, t_k) = f_m(t_{i_1}, t_{i_2}, \ldots, t_{i_m}) \in R$$

∎

It would be interesting to get rid of this dependence on the number of tuples, that is, to prove that it is possible to verify whether or not a basis is closed under a set function by checking only the closure property up to a fixed point. The previous assertion is true for the boolean case, since it is known that every clone in the boolean domain is finitely generated [24, 23] but it is false for higher domains. We present a counterexample.

Example 1. Let $D = \{0, 1, 2, \ldots, d\}$ be a domain with size $|D| > 2$. Consider the set function $f : \mathcal{P}(D)/\emptyset \longrightarrow D$ defined by:

$$f(S) = \begin{cases} 0 \text{ if } S = \{0, 1\} \\ 2 \text{ otherwise} \end{cases}$$

For every m, consider the m-ary relation R_m containing all the tuples such that either (1) exactly one of its components is 1 and the remaining $m - 1$ are 0, or (2) at least one of its components is 2. Clearly, f_k preserves R_m if and only if $k < m$. As a consequence, for any value of k there exists some basis given by $\Gamma_k = \{R_{k+1}\}$ such that f_k preserves Γ_k but f does not.

4 Applications of the closure conditions

Using the characterization of width 1 problems established in Theorem 1 it is possible reformulate some already known tractable classes and derive new ones. From now on, we will say that a function (or set of functions) *guarantees tractability* if for every basis Γ closed under it, C_Γ is tractable.

4.1 Constant operations

An unary function f_1 mapping every element to a fixed element $d \in D$ is called *constant function*. Every relation closed under f_1 contains the tuple $\langle d, d, \ldots, d \rangle$

and therefore operation f_1 guarantees tractability, i.e., for every Γ closed under f_1, C_Γ is tractable. Constant operations correspond for example with the families of 0-valid and 1-valid basis in Schaefer's dichotomy [25].

Constant operations are a particular case of width 1 problems. Since clones are closed under addition of inessential variables, for all $i > 0$, function $f_i :$ $D^i \longrightarrow D$ given by $f_i(x_1, \ldots, x_i) = f_1(x_1) = d$ belongs to any clone containing f_1. In consequence, any set of relations Γ closed under f_1 is closed under the set function $f : \mathcal{P}(D)/\emptyset \longrightarrow D$ given by $f(S) = d$.

4.2 ACI operations

A binary operation f is called ACI if it is associative, commutative and idempotent. The class of ACI operations was identified in [17]. Some known tractable families of problems containing for example horn basis [25] or the constraints allowed in the constraint language CHIP [28] can be explained in terms of ACI functions.

Let f be an ACI operation. It is not difficult to see that, as a consequence of the properties of ACI functions, the set function g, given by

$$g(\{x_1, x_2, \ldots, x_i\}) = f(x_1, f(x_2, \ldots f(x_{i-1}, x_i) \ldots))$$

is well defined. For every i, g_i can be built by a sequence of compositions using f. Thus, any basis closed under f is also closed under g.

4.3 Class CSCI (Constant Semiprojection and Commutative Idempotent)

In this section, we identify a new tractable family of set functions. This new class is obtained from the class ACI replacing the associativity condition by the closure under a particular kind of semiprojection. First we need the following definition:

Let D be a finite set. A *semiprojection* f is a function of rank $k \geq 3$ such that for some index $1 \leq i \leq k$, $f(x_1, \ldots, x_k) = x_i$ whenever $|\{x_1, \ldots, x_k\}| < k$. Furthermore, f is called *constant semiprojection* if $f(x_1, \ldots, x_k) = d$ for some fixed $d \in D$ when the semiprojection condition is not satisfied, i.e., $|\{x_1, \ldots, x_k\}| = k$.

Theorem 4. *Let Γ be a finite set of relations closed under some CI operation f and under some constant semiprojection g of arity 3. Then C_Γ is tractable.*

Proof. The proof has to main parts. First, we see that semiprojections can be extended to any arbitrary arity. Let g_k be a constant semiprojection of arity k where the variable projected is the first one and the constant is d. Then, for every $j > k$, the j-ary function g_j given by:

$$g_j(x_1, \ldots, x_j) = \begin{cases} x_1 & \text{if } |\{x_1, \ldots, x_j\}| < k \\ d & \text{otherwise} \end{cases}$$

belongs to any clone containing g_k. That is, we will see that for every $j > k$, g_j can be obtained as a sequence of compositions using only g_k and projections.

We proceed by induction. Assume that g_j with $j \geq k$ belongs to the clone. Operation g_{j+1} can be constructed from g_j in the following way:

$$g_{j+1}(x_1, \ldots, x_{j+1}) = g_j(g_j(\ldots g_j(g_j(x_1, x_2, \ldots, x_j), x_2, \ldots$$
$$\ldots, x_{j-1}, x_{j+1}), \ldots), x_3, \ldots, x_{j+1})$$

Now consider the set function h given by:

$$h(S) = \begin{cases} f(S) \text{ if } |S| \leq 2 \\ d \quad \text{otherwise} \end{cases}$$

For every $k > 3$, function h_k can be constructed by a sequence of compositions using f and g_k in the following way.

$$h_k(t_1, t_2 \ldots, t_k) = f(\ldots f(f(g_k(t_1, t_2, \ldots, t_k), g_k(t_2, t_3, \ldots, t_1)), \ldots,$$
$$\ldots, g_k(t_3, t_4, \ldots, t_2)), \ldots, g_k(t_k, t_1, \ldots, t_{k-1}))$$

∎

In consequence, every clone containing f and g contains h_k for all $k \geq 3$. For $k \leq 2$ we have the easy equivalences: $h_2(x_1, x_2) = f(x_1, x_2)$ and $h_1(x_1) = f(x_1, x_1)$. Then set function h preserves any relations closed under f and g.

The class of constant operations and ACI operations have been previously shown to be tractable by other means. The class CSCI has not been previously identified. It is important to know if the tractability of the class CSCI is simply a consequence of a previously known class of tractable relations, or if a new class of tractable problems has been found. We show that the class CSCI does include problems which can not be accounted for in the framework of closure functions as in [17] by producing a relation which gives rise to tractable constraint problems but does not belong to any of the previously identified classes. At present, tractable classes of constraint problems can be classified in for main families: (1) coset generating functions, (2) near-unanimity operations, and some set functions (as introduced in these pages). More precisely, the set functions already known are (3) constant operations and (4) ACI operations.

Thus, it is necessary to prove that there exists some CI function φ and some constant semiprojection ϕ of arity 3 and some relation $\mathcal{R}$, all of them over the same domain D, such that φ and ϕ preserve $\mathcal{R}$, but none of the other known tractable classes preserves $\mathcal{R}$.

Let $D = \{0, 1, 2\}$ be the domain. Let $\varphi : D^2 \to D$ the CI operation with the Cayley table

	0	1	2
0	0	0	2
1	0	1	1
2	2	1	2

Operation φ is a tournament; it is known as *the scissors-paper-stone algebra.*
Let $\mathcal{R}$ be the 3-ary relation with tuples

$$\{ \langle 0, 0, 1 \rangle \\ \langle 0, 2, 1 \rangle \\ \langle 0, 2, 2 \rangle \\ \langle 1, 0, 2 \rangle \}$$

It is immediate to verify that $\mathcal{R}$ is preserved by φ. Furthermore, since every
column contains only two different values, $\mathcal{R}$ is preserved by all the semiprojections (and, in particular, $\mathcal{R}$ is preserved by all the constant semiprojections of
arity 3).

The hard work is to prove that relation $\mathcal{R}$ is not closed under any other
known tractable operation. We do a case analysis.

Coset Generating Operations Coset generating operations [4] are a direct
generalization of affine functions [17] to non-abelian groups. For every coset
generating operations $f : D^3 \to D$ there exists some group $(D; \cdot, ^{-1})$ such that
$f(x, y, z) = x \cdot y^{-1} \cdot z$. In consequence [4], every n-ary relation R closed under
f is a right coset of a subgroup of the group $(D; \cdot, ^{-1})^n$. Thus, $\mathcal{R}$ is not closed
under any coset generating operation because, in finite groups, the cardinality
of every coset should divide the cardinality of the group.

Near-Unanimity operations An operation $f : D^k \to D$ $(k \geq 3)$, is called a
'near-unanimity (NU) operation' if for all $x, y \in D$,

$$f(x, y, y, \ldots, y) = \varphi(y, x, y, \ldots, y) = \cdots = \varphi(y, y, \ldots, y, x) = y.$$

In [14], it is proved that closure under a near-unanimity operation is condition sufficient to guarantee the tractability of a constraint satisfaction problem.
To prove that none of the near-unanimity functions preserves $\mathcal{R}$ requires some
detailed study. We study every arity k separately.

For $k = 3$ the analysis is simple. For every 3-ary near-unanimity operation
m (also called majority operation) we have

$$m(\langle 0, 0, 1 \rangle, \langle 0, 2, 2 \rangle, \langle 1, 0, 2 \rangle) = \langle 0, 0, 2 \rangle \notin \mathcal{R}.$$

Thus, operation m does not preserve $\mathcal{R}$.

Now, assume $k \geq 4$. Let m be an k-ary near-unanimity operation over the
domain D preserving $\mathcal{R}$. Since $m(0, 2, \ldots, 2) = 2$ and $m(0, 0, \ldots, 0, 2) = 0$ there
exists some integer $1 \leq n \leq k - 2$ such that one of the following conditions is
satisfied:

$$- \; m(\overbrace{0, \ldots, 0}^{n}, 2 \ldots, 2) = 1, \text{ or}$$

$$- \; m(\overbrace{0, \ldots, 0}^{n}, 2, \ldots, 2) = 2 \text{ and } m(\overbrace{0, \ldots, 0}^{n+1}, 2, \ldots, 2) = 0$$

In the first case, we get a contradiction with

$$m(\overbrace{\langle 1, 0, 2 \rangle, \ldots, \langle 1, 0, 2 \rangle}^{n}, \langle 0, 2, 2 \rangle, \ldots, \langle 0, 2, 2 \rangle) = \langle x, 1, 2 \rangle \in \mathcal{R}$$

(Impossible for any value for x).

In the second case we have,

$$m(\overbrace{\langle 1, 0, 2 \rangle, \ldots, \langle 1, 0, 2 \rangle}^{n}, \langle 0, 0, 1 \rangle, \langle 0, 2, 2 \rangle, \ldots, \langle 0, 2, 2 \rangle) = \langle x, 0, 2 \rangle \in \mathcal{R}$$

$$m(\overbrace{\langle 1, 0, 2 \rangle, \ldots, \langle 1, 0, 2 \rangle}^{n}, \langle 0, 2, 2 \rangle, \langle 0, 2, 2 \rangle, \ldots, \langle 0, 2, 2 \rangle) = \langle x, 2, 2 \rangle \in \mathcal{R}$$

Then, we get a contradiction since any value for x can satisfy both conditions.

Constant functions Immediate from the fact that $\mathcal{R}$ does not contain any tuple of the form (d, d, d).

ACI functions Let f be an affine function preserving $\mathcal{R}$. Since f is associative and commutative we have

$$f(\langle 0, 2, 1 \rangle, \langle 1, 0, 2 \rangle) = \langle 0, 0, 1 \rangle \text{ or } \langle 0, 2, 2 \rangle.$$

In the first case we get a contradiction considering $f(\langle 0, 2, 2 \rangle, \langle 1, 0, 2 \rangle) = \langle 0, 0, 2 \rangle \notin \mathcal{R}$. For the second case, take $f(\langle 0, 0, 1 \rangle, \langle 1, 0, 2 \rangle) = \langle 0, 0, 2 \rangle \notin \mathcal{R}$

References

1. S.A. Cook. The Complexity of Theorem-Proving Procedures. In *3rd Annual ACM Symposium on Theory of Computing STOC'71*, pages 151–158, 1971.
2. M.C. Cooper. An Optimal k-consistency Algorithm. *Artificial Intelligence*, 41:89–95, 1989.
3. M.C. Cooper, D.A. Cohen, and P.G. Jeavons. Characterizing Tractable Constraints. *Artificial Intelligence*, 65:347–361, 1994.
4. V. Dalmau and P. Jeavons. Learnability of Quantified Formulas. In *4th European Conference on Computational Learning Theory Eurocolt'99*, volume 1572 of *Lecture Notes in Artificial Intelligence*, pages 63–78, Berlin/New York, 1999. Springer-Verlag.
5. R. Dechter. From Local to Global Consistency. *Artificial Intelligence*, 55:87–107, 1992.
6. R. Dechter and J. Pearl. Network-based Heuristics for Constraint Satisfaction Problems. *Artificial Intelligence*, 34(1):1–38, 1988.
7. R. Dechter and P. van Beek. Local and Global Relational Consistency. *Theoretical Computer Science*, 173:283–308, 1997.
8. T. Feder and M.Y. Vardi. The Computational Structure of Monotone Monadic SNP and Contraint Satisfaction: A Study through Datalog and Group Theory. *SIAM J. Computing*, 28(1):57–104, 1998.

9. E.C. Freuder. Synthesizing Constraint Expressions. *Comm. ACM*, 21:958–966, 1978.

10. E.C. Freuder. A Sufficient Condition for Backtrack-free Search. *Journal of the ACM*, 29:24–32, 1982.

11. E.C. Freuder. A Sufficient Condition for Backtrack-bounded Search. *Journal of the ACM*, 32:755–761, 1985.

12. M. Gyssens, P. Jeavons, and D. Cohen. Decomposing Constraint Satisfaction Problems using Database Techniques. *Artificial Intelligence*, 66(1):57–89, 1994.

13. P. Jeavons. On the Algebraic Structure of Combinatorial Problems. *Theoretical Computer Science*, 200:185–204, 1998.

14. P. Jeavons, D. Cohen, and M.C. Cooper. Constraints, Consistency and Closure. *Artificial Intelligence*, 101:251–265, 1988.

15. P. Jeavons, D. Cohen, and M. Gyssens. A Unifying Framework for Tractable Constraints. In *1st International Conference on Principles and Practice of Constraint Programming, CP'95, Cassis (France), September 1995*, volume 976 of *Lecture Notes in Computer Science*, pages 276–291. Springer-Verlag, 1995.

16. P. Jeavons, D. Cohen, and M. Gyssens. A Test for Tractability. In *2nd International Conference on Principles and Practice of Constraint Programming CP'96*, volume 1118 of *Lecture Notes in Computer Science*, pages 267–281, Berlin/New York, August 1996. Springer-Verlag.

17. P. Jeavons, D. Cohen, and M. Gyssens. Closure Properties of Constraints. *Journal of the ACM*, 44(4):527–548, July 1997.

18. P. Jeavons and M. Cooper. Tractable Constraints on Ordered Domains. *Artificial Intelligence*, 79:327–339, 1996.

19. L. Kirousis. Fast Parallel Constraint Satisfaction. *Artificial Intelligence*, 64:147–160, 1993.

20. A. K. Mackworth. Consistency in networks of relations. *Artificial Intelligence*, 8:99–118, 1977.

21. U. Montanari. Networks of Constraints: Fundamental Properties and Applications to Picture Processing. *Information Sciences*, 7:95–132, 1974.

22. U. Montanari and F. Rossi. Constraint Relaxation may be Perfect. *Artificial Intelligence*, 48:143–170, 1991.

23. N. Pippenger. *Theories of Computability*. Cambridge University Press, 1997.

24. E.L. Post. *The Two-Valued Iterative Systems of Mathematical Logic*, volume 5 of *Annals of Mathematics Studies*. Princeton, N.J, 1941.

25. T.J. Schaefer. The Complexity of Satisfiability Problems. In *10th Annual ACM Symposium on Theory of Computing*, pages 216–226, 1978.

26. A. Szendrei. *Clones in Universal Algebra*, volume 99 of *Seminaires de Mathématiques Supéreiores*. University of Montreal, 1986.

27. P. van Beek and R. Dechter. On the Minimality and Decomposability of Row-convex Constraint Networks. *Journal of the ACM*, 42:543–561, 1995.

28. P. van Hentenryck, Y. Deville, and C-M. Teng. A Generic Arc-consistency Algorithm and its Specializations. *Artificial Intelligence*, 1992.

An Overview of HAL

Bart Demoen[1], Maria García de la Banda[2], Warwick Harvey[2], Kim Marriott[2], and Peter Stuckey[3]

[1] Dept. of Computer Science, K.U.Leuven, Belgium
[2] School of Computer Science & Software Engineering, Monash University, Australia
[3] Dept. of Computer Science & Software Engineering, University of Melbourne, Australia

Abstract. Experience using constraint programming to solve real-life problems has shown that finding an efficient solution to the problem often requires experimentation with different constraint solvers or even building a problem-specific constraint solver. HAL is a new constraint logic programming language expressly designed to facilitate this process. It provides a well-defined solver interface, mutable global variables for implementing a constraint store, and dynamic scheduling for combining, extending and writing new constraint solvers. Equally importantly, HAL supports semi-optional type, mode and determinism declarations. These allow natural constraint specification by means of type overloading, better compile-time error checking and generation of more efficient run-time code.

1 Introduction

Constraint logic programming (CLP) languages are evolving to support more flexible experimentation with constraint solvers. First generation CLP languages, such as CLP($\mathcal{R}$) [9], provided almost no support. They had a fixed underlying solver for each constraint domain which was viewed as a closed "black box." Second generation CLP languages, such as clp(fd) [3], provided more support by viewing the solver as a "glass box" which the programmer could extend to provide problem-specific complex constraints. However, CLP programmers want more than this: they want to be able to develop new problem-specific constraint solvers, for example by using "hybrid" methods that combine different constraint solving techniques (see e.g. [14]). For this reason, recent versions of the CLP languages ECLiPSe and SICStus support the addition and specification of new constraint solvers by providing features such as dynamic scheduling, constraint handling rules [4] and attributed variables [8]. Unfortunately, support for developing solvers in these languages is still less than satisfactory for the reasons detailed below.

We describe a new CLP language, HAL, which has been explicitly designed to support experimentation with different constraint solvers and development of new solvers. Our specific design objectives were four-fold:

- *Efficiency*: Current CLP languages are considerably slower than traditional imperative languages such as C. This efficiency overhead has limited the use of CLP languages, and becomes even more of an issue when constraint solvers are to be (partially) implemented in the language itself.
- *Integrability*: It should be easy to call procedures (in particular, solvers) written in other languages, e.g. C, with little overhead. Conversely, it should be possible for HAL code to be readily called from other languages, facilitating integration into larger applications. Although most CLP languages provide a foreign language interface, it is often complex and may require rewriting the foreign language code to use "safe" memory management routines.
- *Robustness*: Current CLP languages provide little compile-time checking. However, when developing complex multi-layered software such as constraint solvers and when calling foreign language procedures, additional compile-time checking can detect common programming errors and so improve program robustness.
- *Flexible choice of constraint solvers:* It should be easy to "plug and play" with different constraint solvers over the same domain. Furthermore, it should be straightforward to extend an existing solver, create a hybrid solver by combining solvers and to write a new constraint solver.

HAL has four interesting features which allow it to meet these objectives. The first is semi-optional type, mode and determinism declarations for predicates and functions. Information from the declarations allows the generation of efficient target code, improves robustness by using compile-time tests to check that solvers and other procedures are being used in the correct way, and facilitates efficient integration with foreign language procedures. Type information also means that predicate and function overloading can be resolved at compile-time, allowing a natural syntax for constraints even for user-defined constraint solvers.

The second feature is a well-defined interface for solvers. Solvers are modules which provide various fixed predicates and functions for initializing variables and adding constraints. Obviously, such an interface supports "plug and play" experimentation with different solvers.

The third feature is support for "propagators" by means of a specialized delay construct. HAL allows the programmer to annotate goals with a delay condition which tells the system that execution of that goal should be delayed until the condition is satisfied. By default, the delayed goal remains active and is reexecuted whenever the delay condition becomes true again. Such dynamic scheduling of goals is useful for writing simple constraint solvers, extending a solver and combining different solvers.

The fourth feature is a provision for "global variables." These behave a little like C's static variables and are only visible within a module. They are not intended for general use; rather they allow the constraint solver writer to efficiently implement a persistent constraint store.

A well-defined solver interface and global variables are, to the best of our knowledge, novel in the context of CLP. While declarations and dynamic scheduling are not new, incorporating them into a CLP language which also allows user-defined constraint solvers has proven challenging. In isolation, each feature is relatively well understood; it is their combination that is not. Major difficulties have been to provide (limited) automatic coercion between types, compile-time reordering of literals during mode-checking with appropriate automatic initialization of solver variables, and efficient, yet accurate mode and determinism checking in the presence of dynamic scheduling. Dynamic scheduling has also complicated the design of the solver interface since the choice and implementation of delay conditions is necessarily solver dependent. One interesting feature has been the need to provide an external and internal view of the type and mode of a solver variable.

Broadly speaking, HAL unifies two recent directions in constraint programming language research. The first direction is that of earlier CLP languages, including CLP($\mathcal{R}$), clp(fd), ECLiPSe and SICStus. The second direction is that of logic programming languages with declarations as exemplified by Mercury [13]. Earlier CLP languages provided constraints and constraint solvers for pre-defined constraint domains and many provided dynamic scheduling. However, they did not allow type, mode and determinism declarations. Providing such declarations has influenced the entire design of HAL, from the module system to delay constructs. Another important difference is explicit language support for extending or writing constraint solvers. Like HAL, the Mercury language also provides type, mode and determinism declarations. It is probably the most similar language to HAL, and we have leveraged greatly from its sophisticated compilation support by using it as an intermediate target language. The key difference is that Mercury is logic programming based and does not support constraints and constraint solvers. Indeed, it does not even fully support Herbrand constraints since it provides only a limited form of unification.

We know of only one other language that integrates declarations into a CLP language: CIAO [7]. The design of CIAO has proceeded concurrently with that of HAL. HAL has been concerned with providing a language for experimentation with constraint solvers. In contrast, CIAO has focused on exploring the design and use of more flexible declarations for program analysis, debugging, validation, and optimization, and on supporting parallelism and concurrency. Constraint solving in CIAO is inherited from the underlying &-Prolog/SICStus Prolog implementation: solvers are written using attributed variables. Thus, CIAO does not provide an explicit solver interface, does not provide a dual view of constraint variables, requires the programmer to explicitly insert initialization and coercion predicate calls, and, if more than one (non-Herbrand) constraint solver is used, the programmer must explicitly call the appropriate solver.

2 The HAL Language

In this section we provide an overview of the HAL language. The basic HAL syntax follows the standard CLP syntax, with variables, rules and predicates defined as usual (see, e.g., [11] for an introduction to CLP). Our philosophy has been to design a language which is as pure as possible, without unduly compromising efficiency. Thus, HAL does not provide many of the non-pure but standard logic programming built-ins. For instance, it does not provide database predicates; instead global variables can be used to provide most of this functionality.

The module system in HAL is similar to the Mercury module system. A module is defined in a file, it imports the modules it uses and has export annotations on the declarations for the objects that it wishes to be visible to those importing the module. Selective importation is also possible.

The base language supports integer, float, string, atom and term data types. However, the support is limited to assignment, testing for equality, and construction and deconstruction of ground terms. More sophisticated constraint solving on these types is provided by importing a constraint solver for the type.

As a simple example, the following program is a HAL version of the now classic CLP program mortgage for modelling the relationship between P the principal or amount owed, T the number of periods in the mortgage, I the interest rate of the mortgage, R the repayment due each period of the mortgage and B the balance owing at the end.

```
:- module mortgage.                                          (L1)
:- import simplex.                                           (L2)
:- export pred mortgage(cfloat,cfloat,cfloat,cfloat,cfloat). (L3)
:-         mode mortgage(in,in,in,in,out) is semidet.        (L4)
:-         mode mortgage(oo,oo,oo,oo,oo) is nondet.          (L5)
mortgage(P,0.0,I,R,P).                                       (R1)
mortgage(P,T,I,R,B) :- T >= 1.0, NP = P + P * I - R,         (R2)
                mortgage(NP,T-1.0,I,R,B).
```

The first line of the file ($L1$) states that this is the definition of the module mortgage. Line ($L2$) imports a previously defined module called simplex. This provides a simplex-based linear arithmetic constraint solver for constrained floats, called cfloats. Line ($L3$) declares that this module exports the predicate mortgage which takes five cfloats as arguments. This is the *type* declaration for mortgage. Lines ($L4$) and ($L5$) are examples of *mode of usage* declarations. Since there are two declarations, mortgage has two possible modes of usage. In the first, the first four arguments have an in mode meaning their values are fixed when the predicate is called, and the last has a mode out which means it is uninitialized when called, and fixed on the return from the call to mortgage. Line ($L5$) gives another mode for the mortgage where each argument has mode oo meaning that each argument takes a "constrained" variable and returns a "constrained" variable. This more flexible mode allows arbitrary uses of the mortgage predicate, but will be less efficient to execute. Line ($L4$) also states that for this mode mortgage is semidet, meaning that it either fails[1] or succeeds with exactly one answer.[2] For the second mode ($L5$) the determinism is nondet meaning that the query may return 0 or more answers. The rest of the file contains the standard two rules defining mortgage.

---

[1] For example mortgage(0.0,-1.0,0.0,0.0,B) fails

[2] HAL currently does not perform determinism analysis and Mercury is unable to confirm this determinism declaration.

2.1 Type, Mode and Determinism Declarations

As we can see from the above example, one of the key features of HAL is that programmers may annotate predicate definitions with type, mode and determinism declarations (modelled on those of Mercury). Information from the declarations allows the generation of efficient target code, compile-time tests to check that solvers and other predicates are being used in the correct way and facilitates integration with foreign language procedures.

By default, declarations are checked at compile-time, generating an error if they cannot be confirmed by the compiler. However, the programmer can also provide "trust me" declarations. These generate an error if the compiler can definitely prove they are wrong, but otherwise the compiler trusts the programmer and generates code according to the trusted declarations. A compile-time warning is issued if the declaration cannot be confirmed by the compiler's checker.

Type Declarations: These specify the representation format of a variable or argument. Thus, for example, the type system distinguishes between constrained floats (cfloat) and the standard numerical float (float) since these have a different representation.

Types are specified using type definition statements. They are (polymorphic) regular tree type statements. For instance,

```
:- typedef list(T) -> []; [T|list(T)].
```

Equivalence types are also allowed. For example,

```
:- typedef vector = list(float).
```

where the right-hand side must be a type.

Overloading of predicates is allowed, although the predicate definitions for different type signatures must be in different modules. Overloading is important since it allows the programmer to overload the standard arithmetic operators and relations (including equality) for different types, allowing a natural syntax in different constraint domains.

As an example, imagine that we wish to write a module for handling complex numbers. We can do this by leveraging from the simplex solver.

```
:- module complex.
:- import simplex.
:- export_abstract typedef complex -> c(cfloat,cfloat).
:- export pred cx(cfloat,cfloat,complex).       % access/creation
:-         mode cx(in,in,out) is det.
:-         mode cx(out,out,in) is det.
:-         mode cx(oo,oo,oo) is semidet.
cx(X,Y,c(X,Y)).
:- export func complex + complex --> complex.   % addition
:-         mode in + in --> out is det.
:-         mode oo + oo --> oo is semidet.
c(X1,Y1) + c(X2,Y2) --> c(X1+X2,Y1+Y2).
```

Note that the type definition for complex is exported abstractly, which means that the internal representation of a complex number is hidden within the module. This ensures that code cannot create or modify complex numbers outside of the `complex` module. Thus, this module also needs to export a predicate, `cx`, for accessing and creating a complex number. As this example demonstrates, the programmer can use functions. The symbol "`-->`" should be read as "returns."

Using this module the programmer can now use complex arithmetic as if it were built into the language itself. If both `simplex` and `complex` are imported, type inference will determine the type of the arguments of each call to + and appropriately qualify the call with the correct module.

One of the hardest issues we have faced in type checking and inference is the need to handle automatic coercion between types. For instance, in the definition of `mortgage` we have used the constraint `T >= 1.0`. The constraint `>=` expects to take two `cfloat`s whereas `1.0` is of type `float`. The compiler overcomes this typing problem by automatically inserting a call to a coercion function (defined in `simplex`) to coerce `1.0` to a `cfloat`. Such automatic coercion is important because it allows constraints and expressions to be written in a natural fashion. Currently, the type system for HAL only supports simple coercion, namely, a type can be involved in at most one coercion relationship. Even handling this restricted kind of coercion is difficult and is one of the most complex parts of the type checking and inference mechanism.

Mode Declarations: A mode is associated with an argument of a predicate. It has the form $Inst_1 \rightarrow Inst_2$ where $Inst_1$ describes the input instantiation state of the argument and $Inst_2$ describes the output instantiation state. The basic instantiation states for a solver variable are `new`, `old` and `ground`. Variable X is `new` if it has not been seen by the constraint solver, `old` if it has, and it is `ground` if X is constrained to take a fixed value.

For data structures, such as a list of solver variables, more complex instantiation states (lying between `old` and `ground`) may be used to describe the state of the data structure. Instantiation state definitions look something like type definitions. An example is

```
:- instdef fixed_length_list -> ([] ; [old | fixed_length_list]).
```

which is read as the variable is bound to either an empty list or a list with an `old` head and a tail with the same instantiation state.

Mode definitions have the following syntax:

```
:- modedef to_groundlist -> (fixed_length_list -> ground).
:- modedef same(I) -> (I -> I).
```

We have already seen examples of predicate mode declarations in the previous two programs. As another example, a mode declaration for an integer variable labelling predicate `labeling` would be

```
:- mode labeling(to_groundlist) is nondet.
```

Mode checking is a relatively complex operation involving reordering body literals in order to satisfy mode constraints, and inserting initialization predicates for solver variables. The compiler performs multi-variant specialization by generating different code for each declared mode for a predicate. The code corresponding to a mode is referred to as a "procedure" and calls to the original predicate are replaced by calls to the appropriate procedure.

Determinism Declarations: These detail how many answers a predicate may have. We use the Mercury hierarchy: nondet means any number of solutions; multidet at least one solution; semidet at most one solution; det exactly one solution; failure no solutions; and erroneous a runtime error.

2.2 Constraint Solvers

Constraint solvers are implemented as modules in HAL. Selective importation of modules supports "plug and play" experimentation with different solvers over the same domain. For instance, if we define two solvers intsolv1 and intsolv2 for finite domain integer constraints, then we can compile a HAL program using either solver by changing which solver module is imported.

A constraint solver is a module that defines some type for the constrained variable, and predicates to initialize and equate these variables. Typically, it will also define a coercion function and a function for returning the value of a ground variable.

Consider implementing a simple integer bounds propagation solver. The following declarations can be used:

```
:- module bounds.
:- export_abstract typedef cint = ... %% internal cint representation
:- export pred init(cint).
:-        mode init(no) is det.
:- export_only pred cint = cint.
:-        mode oo = oo is semidet.
:- coerce coerce_int_cint(int) --> cint.
:- export func coerce_int_cint(int) --> cint.
:-        mode coerce_int_cint(in) --> out is det.
```

The type cint is the type of bounds variables. It might be defined, for example, as an integer indexing into a HAL global variable tableau, as an integer representing a CPLEX variable number, or as a C pointer for a solver implemented in C. Usually, a constraint solver type is exported abstractly. As discussed earlier, this ensures other modules cannot modify cint variables without calling module bounds.

The init predicate is used to initialize a variable, its mode is no or new -> old. The compiler will automatically add appropriate calls to the initialization predicate in user code that makes use of the bounds solver.

The equality predicate is required for all constraint solvers. In the above code for cints it is annotated as export_only. This indicates that it should be visible to importing modules but not within this module. This is useful because inside the module bounds we manipulate the internal (rather than the external) representation of cints using equality. We can, however, access the equality predicate by using explicit module qualification.

A complete bounds module would also export declarations for (primitive constraint) predicates such as >=, <=, != as well as functions such as +, - and *.

As we have seen previously, it is useful to allow solver-dependent type coercion. In this case, we would like to be able to write integer constants as cint arguments of predicates and functions, for example as in X + 3*Y >= Z + 2.

Thus, we need to instruct the compiler to perform automatic coercion between an int and a cint. The coerce declaration does this, indicating that the coercion function is coerce_int_cint. Thus the constraint above (assuming X, Y and Z are old) is translated to

```
coerce_int_cint(3,T1), *(T1,Y,T2), +(X,T2,T3),
coerce_int_cint(2,T4), +(Z,T4,T5), =(T3,T4).
```

The above translation may appear very inefficient, since many new solver variables are introduced, and many constraints each of which will involve propagation to solve. This is not necessarily the case. The solver could be defined so that cints are structured terms, which are built by coerce_int_cint, + and *, and only the constraint relations build propagators. Thus, the + function would be defined as

```
:- export_abstract typedef cint -> (var(bvar) ; int(int)
                                    ; plus(cint,cint) ; times(cint,cint) ).
:- export func cint + cint --> cint.
:-         mode oo + oo --> no.
X + Y --> plus(X,Y).
```

Using this scheme, the goal above builds up a structure representing the terms of the constraint and then the equality predicate simplifies the structure and implements the appropriate propagation behaviour.

Herbrand Solvers: Most HAL types are structured data types defined in terms of constructors where elements of these data types correspond to terms in traditional CLP languages. For example, our earlier type definition defined the (polymorphic) list type in terms of the constructors [] (nil) and "." (cons). As indicated previously, the HAL base language only provides limited operations for dealing with such data structures. In essence, it provides an equality predicate that only supports modes for constructing a new term, deconstructing a bound term or comparing two bound terms. This corresponds to the operations that Mercury allows on its data structures.

If the programmer wishes to use more complex constraint solving for some type, then they must explicitly declare they want to use the Herbrand constraint solver for that type. Conceptually, the HAL run-time system provides a Herbrand constraint solver for each term type defined by the programmer. This solver provides full equality (unification without occurs check), supporting the use of Prolog-like variables for structured data types and allowing programming idioms like difference lists. In practice, the constraint solver is implemented by automatically generating code for each functor in the type definition, and replacing Herbrand constraints by calls to this code.

For example, if the programmer wishes to use difference lists then they need to include the declaration:

```
:- herbrand list/1.
```

However, we note that in most cases data structure manipulation, even if the data structures contain solver variables, does not require the use of a Herbrand constraint solver.

Inside and Outside View of the Solver: Solver modules are more complicated than other modules because they define solver variables which will be viewed in two different ways. For example, outside the solver module a solver variable might be seen as a `cint` with old instantiation state, which cannot be modified without calling the solver. Inside the module the solver variable might be a fixed integer index into a global variable tableau, and hence have type `int` and instantiation ground.

Abstract exportation of the type ensures that the different views of type are handled correctly, but there is also the issue of the different views of modes. In particular, the exported predicates need to be viewed as having instantiations which are old while internally they are something different. To handle this we allow a renaming instantiation declaration, for example

```
:- reinst_old cint_old = ground.
```

declares that the instantiation name `cint_old` is treated as ground within this module (the solver's internal view), but exported as old. Typically, where a dual view of modes is required, the declarations for exported predicates are similar to the following:

```
:- modedef cint_oo = (cint_old -> cint_old).
:- export pred cint >= cint.
:-          mode cint_oo >= cint_oo is semidet.
```

2.3 Dynamic Scheduling

HAL includes a form of "persistent" dynamic scheduling designed specifically to support constraint solving. HAL's delay construct is of the form

$$cond_1 \implies goal_1 \ || \ \cdots \ || \ cond_n \implies goal_n$$

where the goal $goal_i$ will be executed when delay condition $cond_i$ is satisfied. By default, the delayed goals remain active and are reexecuted whenever the delay condition becomes true again. This is useful, for example, if the delay condition is "the lower bound has changed." However, the delayed goals may contain calls to the special predicate `kill`. When this is executed, all delayed goals in the immediate surrounding delay construct are killed; that is, they will never be executed again.

For example, the following delay construct implements bounds propagation for the constraint $X \leq Y$. The delay conditions $lbc(V)$, $ubc(V)$ and $fixed(V)$ are respectively satisfied when the lower bound changes for variable V, the upper bound changes for V, and V is given a fixed value. The functions $lb(V)$, $ub(V)$ and $val(V)$ respectively return the current lower bound, upper bound and value for V, while the predicates upd_lb, upd_ub and upd_val update these.

```
lbc(X) ==> upd_lb(Y,lb(X)) || fixed(X) ==> upd_lb(Y,val(X)), kill ||
ubc(Y) ==> upd_ub(X,ub(Y)) || fixed(Y) ==> upd_ub(X,val(Y)), kill
```

One important issue is the interaction between dynamic scheduling and mode and determinism analysis. While it is possible to analyze programs with arbitrary dynamic scheduling, currently this is complex, time consuming and sometimes inaccurate. Instead, by judiciously restricting the kind of goals which can be delayed, we guarantee that standard mode and determinism analysis techniques will still be correct in the presence of delayed goals.

The first restriction is that the mode for non-local variables in a delayed goal must be either in (i.e. ground -> ground) or oo (i.e. old -> old). This means that execution of the delayed goal, regardless of when it occurs, will not change the instantiation of the current variables of interest.[3] (This also relies on the instantiations old and ground being "downward closed.")

The second restriction is that the delayed goal must either be det or semidet. This ensures that if the current goal wakes up a delayed goal, the delayed goal's determinism cannot change that of the current goal. This is correct because det goals cannot wake up delayed goals, since they are only allowed to change the instantiation states for new variables, and a new variable cannot have previously occurred in a delay construct.

Combining Constraint Solvers: HAL is designed to make it easy to combine constraint solvers to form new hybrid constraint solvers. Imagine combining an existing propagation solver (variable type cint in module bounds) and an integer linear programming solver (type ilpint in module cplex) to create a combined solver (type combint). Each variable in the combined solver is a pair of variables, one from each of the underlying solvers. Constraints in the combined solver cause the constraints to be sent to both underlying solvers. Communication between the solvers is managed by delayed goals created when a variable is initialized. A sketch of such a module (with communication only from the propagation solver to the ILP solver) is given below.

```
:- module combined.
:- import bounds.
:- import cplex.
:- export_abstract typedef combint -> p(cint,ilpint).
:- export pred combint >= combint.
:-        mode oo >= oo is semidet.
p(XB,XC) >= p(YB,YC) :- XB >= YB, XC >= YC.
:- export pred init(combint).
:- trust mode init(no) is det.
init(p(XB,XC)) :- init(XB), init(XC),
          (lbc(XB) ==> XC >= lb(XB) || ubc(XB) ==> ub(XB) >= XC ||
          fixed(XB) ==> XC = val(XB), kill).
```

Solver Support: Delayed goals in HAL execute when a delay condition is found to be true. Delay conditions are defined by a constraint solver, and it is the role of that constraint solver to determine when a delay condition has become true. Delay conditions are defined as a type attached to the solver. By exporting types for delay constructs to the user, the solver writer can build a "glass box" solver which the user can extend to new constraints. Similarly, delay constructs allow the implementation of features such as invariants [12].

As an example, the bounds propagation solver might support the delay conditions ubc(V), lbc(V) and fixed(V) which are true, respectively, when variable

---

[3] More generally we could allow any mode of the form i -> i.

V has an upper or lower bound change, or becomes fixed. In order to support delayed goals, the bounds module would need to include the following declarations:

```
:- export typedef dcon -> (ubc(cint) | lbc(cint) | fixed(cint)).
:- export delay dcon.
:- export_abstract typedef delay_id = ... % internal representation
:- export pred get_id(delay_id).
:-           mode get_id(out) is det.
:- export pred delay(list(dcon),delay_id,list(pred)).
:-           mode delay(in,in,same(list(pred is semidet))) is semidet.
:- export pred kill(delay_id).
:-           mode kill(in) is det.
```

The delay conditions are simply defined as an exported type. The **delay** declaration allows them to appear in the left hand side of the "==>" construct.

The predicate **get_id** returns a new delay ID for a newly encountered delay construct. The predicate **delay** is then called with the list of delay conditions, the delay ID of the construct, and the list of actions (closures) corresponding to each condition. A kill/0 predicate in the delay construct is replaced with a call to kill/1 whose argument is the delay ID. It is the solver's responsibility to ensure that the action is called when the appropriate delay condition fires, and to remove killed actions.

Delay constructs are automatically translated by the compiler to use these predicates. For example, the delay construct in module **combined** translates to

```
get_id(D), delay([lbc(XB),ubc(XB),fixed(XB)],D,
       [XC >= lb(XB), XC <= ub(XB), (XC = val(XB), kill(D))]).
```

2.4 Global Variables

When implementing constraint solvers or search strategies it is vital for efficiency to be able to destructively update a global data structure which might, for example, contain the current constraints in solved form.

To cater for this, HAL provides both statically scoped and dynamically scoped global variables. However, these variables are local to a module and cannot be accessed by name from outside the module, so the statically scoped version is more akin to C's **static** variables. Global variables behave as references. They can never be directly passed as an argument to a predicate; they are always de-referenced at this point. They come in two flavours: backtracking and non-backtracking. Non-backtracking global variables must be ground.

A major reason for designing HAL to be as pure as possible it that it simplifies the use of powerful compile-time optimizations such as unfolding, reordering and many low level optimizations. However, global variables break this purity, and so restrict the applicability of such optimizations. Typically a solver, though implemented using impure features, presents a "pure" interface to other modules that use it. To this end, HAL supports purity declarations which control the inheritance of an impurity from a predicate to the predicates that call it. By declaring exported primitive constraint predicates as pure, the code using them may still be pure, and hence amenable to more optimization.

3 Current System

The HAL compiler, system and libraries consists of some 24,000 lines (comments and blank lines excluded) of HAL code (which is also legitimate SICStus Prolog code). HAL programs may be compiled to either SICStus Prolog or Mercury. In the longer term only compilation to Mercury will be supported. Mercury compiles to C and makes use of the information in declarations to produce efficient code. However, better debugging facilities in SICStus Prolog and the ability to handle code without type and mode declarations have made compilation to SICStus Prolog extremely useful in the initial development of the compiler.

Currently, we require full type, mode and determinism declarations for exported predicates and functions. The HAL compiler performs type checking and inference. Partial type information may be expressed by using a '?' in place of an argument type. The type checking algorithm is based on a constraint view of types and is described in [2]. The HAL compiler currently does not perform mode inference, but does perform mode checking. Currently, determinism declarations are not checked by the HAL compiler but simply passed through to the Mercury compiler. They are ignored when compiling to SICStus Prolog.

Compilation into Mercury required extending and modifying the Mercury language and its runtime system in several ways. Some of these extensions have now been incorporated into the Mercury release. The first extension was to provide an "any" instantiation, corresponding loosely to HAL's old instantiation. The second extension was to add purity declarations, as well as "trust me" declarations indicating to the Mercury compiler that it should just trust the declarations provided by the user (in our case the HAL compiler). The third extension was to provide support for global variables. The backtracking version needs to be trailed, while for the non-backtracking version the data needs to be stored in memory which will not be reclaimed on backtracking. Another extension was to provide run-time support for different equality operations. In order to support polymorphic operations properly, Mercury needs to know how to equate two objects of a (compile-time unknown) type. Mercury provides support for comparing two ground terms, but we needed to add similar support for equating two non-ground terms, as well as overriding the default ground comparison code to do the right thing for solver types.

Currently the HAL system provides three standard solvers: one for integers, one for reals and a Herbrand solver for term equations. The Herbrand solver is more closely built into the HAL implementation than the other two solvers, with support at the compiler level to leverage from the built-in term equation solving provided by SICStus Prolog and Mercury. One complicating issue has been that, as discussed earlier, Mercury only provides restricted forms of equality constraints. Since we wished to support full equality constraints, this required implementing a true unification based solver which interacted gracefully with the Mercury run-time system. This integration is described more fully in [1].

The integer solver is the same as that described in [5]. It is a bounds propagation solver which keeps linear constraints in a tableau form, and simplifies them during execution to improve further propagation. It was originally embedded in

CLP($\mathcal{R}$)'s compiler and runtime system, yielding the language CLP($\mathcal{Z}$). It has since been interfaced to Mercury, and then to HAL via the Mercury interface. The real solver is the solver from CLP($\mathcal{R}$), interfaced in the same way.

3.1 Evaluation

We now give some feel for the performance of HAL programs using the current HAL compiler when compiling to Mercury. This is not intended to provide a comprehensive comparison with other CLP languages, but rather to act as a "sanity check" confirming that the implementation has adequate efficiency.

For each of the three solvers—Herbrand, integer and real—we have selected four to five standard benchmarks and compared them to another CLP system. For the Herbrand benchmarks we compare with SICStus Prolog 3.7.1 (compact code), while for the integer and real benchmarks we compare with CLP($\mathcal{Z}$) [5] and CLP($\mathcal{R}$) v1.02 respectively. Since CLP($\mathcal{Z}$) and CLP($\mathcal{R}$) use exactly the same underlying solvers as HAL, these comparisons are solver independent. The results are shown in Table 1.

The Herbrand benchmarks are executed both with and without garbage collection. HAL's garbage collection is provided by the (Mercury) conservative garbage collector. The integer and real benchmarks are executed without garbage collection since CLP($\mathcal{Z}$) and CLP($\mathcal{R}$) do not provide garbage collection. All timings are the best over 20 runs on a dual Pentium II-400MHz with 384M of RAM running under Linux RedHat 5.2 with kernel version 2.2, and are given in milliseconds. Note that while the Herbrand benchmarks deriv, hanoi and qsort are effectively equivalent to Mercury programs, all other benchmarks require constraint solving.

The Herbrand benchmarks are four standard Prolog benchmarks: deriv, serialize, hanoi and qsort. The last two are shown in two forms: using ground lists and append, and using difference lists. For each benchmark we give two SICStus Prolog versions: the original benchmark "SICStus (Orig.)" and a modified version "SICStus (Mod.)" in which built-ins not present in HAL (such as cut) have been replaced by their HAL equivalents (such as if-then-else). As expected the HAL system is significantly faster than SICStus because of the use of declarations. Difference lists are not such a big win for HAL; this is due to the immaturity of the Herbrand solver and the advantages of compiling append with declarations.

The integer benchmarks include two standard benchmarks crypta and eq10, a forward checking and (the more usual) generalized forward checking version of queens and a Hamiltonian path program from [5]. Even though the communication overhead to the $\mathcal{Z}$ solver is presently greater in HAL than in CLP($\mathcal{Z}$), the efficiency is comparable. The improvement in queens_fc arises because of repeated data structure manipulation within the search.

The real benchmarks are: mg_extend, an extended version of the mortgage program [10]; matmul, matrix multiplication used backwards to invert a matrix; fib, Fibonacci run backwards; and circ, a circuit design program from [6]. The CLP($\mathcal{R}$) system puts considerable effort into compiling arithmetic constraints

Benchmark	Preds	Lits	no garbage collection			garbage collection		
			SICStus (Orig.)	SICStus (Mod.)	HAL	SICStus (Orig.)	SICStus (Mod.)	HAL
deriv	1	27	1430	1710	309	5220	5270	510
serialize	5	19	1700	1770	389	6260	6180	560
hanoi	2	9	2130	1680	199	15000	7710	640
hanoi_difflist	2	8	1060	410	139	5090	1110	290
qsort	3	10	10210	6470	629	15710	11310	1510
qsort_difflist	3	10	10210	6400	689	15160	11220	1450

(a) Herbrand benchmarks

Benchmark	Pred	Lits	CLP($\mathcal{Z}$)	HAL
crypta	7	28	2990	2919
eq10	5	23	2610	2579
queens_fc	8	27	10840	8089
queens_gfc	9	28	6720	7669
hamil	13	29	223040	254549

(b) Integer benchmarks

Benchmark	Preds	Lits	CLP($\mathcal{R}$)	HAL
mg_extend	7	44	4900	5619
matmul	7	45	11833	4679
fib	1	10	3317	6229
circ	18	112	4050	1929

(c) Real benchmarks

Table 1. Empirical evaluation of HAL

efficiently, as opposed to the simple HAL interface. Hence, for fib where most time is spent adding constraints which are simple to solve, HAL is significantly slower. For the other benchmarks HAL is comparable, and it is faster when there is significant amounts of term manipulation (as in matmul and circ).

The preliminary results are very encouraging and augur well for the efficiency of new solvers implemented (perhaps partially) in HAL. Although the solver interfaces currently add significant overhead, much of this is due to the immaturity of HAL. We are confident that most of this overhead can be removed by relatively straightforward optimizations such as cross-module inlining.

4 Conclusion

We have introduced HAL, a new language which extends existing CLP languages by providing semi-optional declarations, a well-defined solver interface, dynamic scheduling and global variables. These combine synergistically to give a language which is potentially more efficient than existing CLP languages, allows ready integration of foreign language procedures, is more robust because of compile-time checking, and, most importantly, allows flexible choice of constraint solvers which may either be fully or partially written in HAL. An initial empirical evaluation of HAL is very encouraging.

Despite several programmer years of effort, much still remains to be done on the HAL implementation. Currently type checking and inference is supported but not mode inference or determinism analysis. One important extension is to provide support for type classes. These are a natural mechanism for defining a solver's capabilities, since a solver is (essentially) a module defining a certain set of predicates and functions. Another important extension is to provide mutable data structures. Currently, only global variables are mutable but we would also like non-global mutable variables. One way is to provide references; another is to provide **unique** and **dead** declarations as is done in Mercury. We will explore both. Finally, we wish to support solver dependent compile-time analysis and specialization of solver calls. This is important since it will remove most of the runtime overhead of constructing arguments for constraints.

Acknowledgements

Many people have helped in the development of HAL. They include Peter Schachte, and Fergus Henderson, David Jeffery and other members of the Mercury development team. We also thank members of the CIAO team for helpful discussions.

References

1. B. Demoen, M. García de la Banda, W. Harvey, K. Marriott, and P.J. Stuckey. Herbrand constraint solving in HAL. In *Procs. of ICLP99*, to appear.
2. B. Demoen, M. García de la Banda, and P.J. Stuckey. Type constraint solving for parametric and ad-hoc polymorphism. In *Procs. of the 22nd Australian Comp. Sci. Conf.*, pages 217–228, 1999.
3. D. Diaz and P. Codognet. A minimal extension of the WAM for clp(fd). In *Procs. of ICLP93*, pages 774–790, 1993.
4. T. Früwirth. Theory and practice of constraint handling rules. *Journal of Logic Programming*, 37:95–138, 1998.
5. W. Harvey and P.J. Stuckey. Constraint representation for propagation. In *Procs. of PPCP98*, pages 235–249, 1998.
6. N.C. Heintze, S. Michaylov, and P.J. Stuckey. CLP($\mathcal{R}$) and some electrical engineering problems. *Journal of Automated Reasoning*, 9:231–260, 1992.
7. M. Hermenegildo, F. Bueno, D. Cabeza, M. García de la Banda, P. López, and G. Puebla. The CIAO multi-dialect compiler and system. In *Parallelism and Implementation of Logic and Constraint Logic Programming*. Nova Science, 1999.
8. C. Holzbaur. Metastructures vs. attributed variables in the context of extensible unification. In *Procs. of the PLILP92*, pages 260–268, 1992.
9. J. Jaffar, S. Michaylov, P. Stuckey, and R. Yap. The CLP($\mathcal{R}$) language and system. *ACM Transactions on Programming Languages and Systems*, 4(3):339–395, 1992.
10. A. Kelly, A. Macdonald, K. Marriott, P.J. Stuckey, and R.H.C. Yap. Effectiveness of optimizing compilation of CLP($\mathcal{R}$). In *Procs. of JICSLP92*, pages 37–51, 1996.
11. K. Marriott and P.J. Stuckey. *Programming with Constraints: an Introduction*. MIT Press, 1998.
12. L. Michel and P. Van Hentenryck. Localizer: A modeling language for local search. In *Procs. of the PPCP97*, pages 237–251, 1997.
13. Z. Somogyi, F. Henderson, and T. Conway. The execution algorithm of Mercury: an efficient purely declarative logic programming language. *Journal of Logic Programming*, 29:17–64, 1996.
14. M. Wallace, editor. *CP98 Workshop on Large Scale Combinatorial Optimization and Constraints*, 1998. http://www.icparc.ic.ac.uk/~mgw/chic2_workshop.html.

Cost-Based Domain Filtering

F. Focacci[2], A. Lodi[1], M. Milano[2]

[1] DEIS, Univ. Bologna, Viale Risorgimento 2, 40136 Bologna, Italy
email: alodi@deis.unibo.it
[2] Dip. Ingegneria, Univ. Ferrara, Via Saragat, 41100 Ferrara, Italy
email: {ffocacci, mmilano}@deis.unibo.it

Abstract. Constraint propagation is aimed at removing from variable domains combinations of values which cannot appear in any consistent solution. Pruning derives from *feasibility reasoning*. When coping with optimization problems, pruning can be performed also on the basis of costs, i.e., *optimality reasoning*. Propagation can be aimed at removing combination of values which cannot lead to solutions whose cost is better then the best one found so far. For this purpose, we embed in global constraints optimization components representing suitable relaxations of the constraint itself. These components provide efficient Operations Research algorithms computing the optimal solution of the relaxed problem and a gradient function representing the estimated cost of each variable-value assignment. We exploit these pieces of information for pruning and for guiding the search. We have applied these techniques to a couple of ILOG Solver global constraints (a constraint of difference and a path constraint) and tested the approach on a variety of combinatorial optimization problems such as Timetabling, Travelling Salesman Problems and Scheduling Problems with setup. Comparisons with pure Constraint Programming approaches and related literature clearly show the benefits of the proposed approach. By using cost-based filtering in global constraints, we can optimally solve problems that are one order of magnitude greater than those solved by pure CP approaches, and we outperform other hybrid approaches integrating OR techniques in Constraint Programming.

1 Introduction

Finite Domain Constraint Programming (CP) has been recognized as a powerful tool for modelling and solving combinatorial optimization problems. CP tools provide *global constraints* offering concise and declarative modelling capabilities together with efficient and powerful *domain filtering* algorithms. These algorithms remove combinations of values which cannot appear in any consistent solution.

When coping with optimization problems, an objective function f is defined on problem variables. With no loss of generality, we restrict our discussion to minimization problems. CP systems usually implement a Branch and Bound algorithm to find an optimal solution. The idea is to solve a set of satisfiability problems (i.e., a feasible solution is found if it exists), leading to successively better solutions. In particular, each time a feasible solution s^* is found (whose cost is $f(s^*)$), a constraint $f(x) < f(s^*)$ is added to each subproblem in the remaining search tree. The purpose of the added constraint, called *upper bounding constraint*, is to remove portions of the search space which cannot lead to better solutions than the best one found so far. The problem with this approach is twofold: (i) only the upper bounding constraint is used to reduce the domain of the objective function; (ii) in general, the link between the variable representing the objective function and problem decision variables is quite poor and does not produce effective domain filtering.

As concerns the first point, previous works have been proposed that compute also lower bounds on the objective function by (possibly optimally) solving relaxed problems [2], [5], [21], [22].

Concerning the second point, two notable works by Caseau and Laburthe ([6] and [7]) embed in optimization constraints lower bounds from Operations Research and define a regret function used as heuristic information. Here we propose a further step in the integration of OR technology in CP, by using well known OR techniques, i.e., lower bound calculation and reduced cost fixing [15], for cost-based propagation. We embed in global constraints an *optimization* component, representing a proper relaxation of the constraint itself. This component provides three information: (i) the optimal solution of the relaxed problem, (ii) the optimal value of this solution representing a lower bound on the original problem objective function, and (iii) a *gradient function* $grad(V,v)$ which returns, for each possible couple variable-value (V,v), an optimistic evaluation of the additional cost to be paid if v is assigned to V. The *gradient function* extends and refines the notion of regret used in [6] and [7]. We exploit these pieces of information both for propagation purposes and for guiding the search.

We have implemented this approach on two global constraints in ILOG Solver [18]: a constraint of difference and a path constraint. The *optimization* component used in both constraints embeds the Hungarian Algorithm [4] for solving Assignment Problem (AP) which is a relaxation of the problem represented by the path constraint and exactly the same problem as the one modelled by the constraint of difference. The Hungarian Algorithm provides the optimal solution of the AP, its cost and the *gradient function* in terms of reduced costs matrix. Reduced costs provide a significant information allowing to perform cost-based domain filtering, and to guide the search as heuristics. In general however, any relaxation can be used, e.g., a LP relaxation or a spanning tree (spanning forest) for the path constraint, provided that it produces the information needed (i.e., the lower bound and reduced costs).

We have used the resulting constraints to solve Timetabling Problems, Travelling Salesman Problems and Scheduling Problems with setup times (where the path constraint has been interpreted and adapted to be a multi-resource transition time constraint). By using the cost-based domain filtering technique in global constraint, we achieve a significant computational speedup with respect to traditional CP approaches: in fact, we can optimally solve (and prove optimality for) problems which are one order of magnitude greater than those solved by pure CP approaches. Also, comparisons with related literature describing other OR-based hybrid techniques show that integrating cost-based reduction rules in global constraints gets unarguable advantages.

2 Motivations and Background

In this section, we present the main motivation of this paper. We start from the general framework, Branch & Infer, proposed by Bockmayr and Kasper [3], which unifies and subsumes Integer Linear Programming (ILP) and Constraint Programming (CP). In a constraint language, the authors recognize two kind of constraints: *primitive* and *non primitive* ones. Roughly speaking, primitive constraints are those which are easily handled by the constraint solver, while non primitive ones are those for which it does not exist a (complete) method for satisfiability, entailment and optimization running in polynomial time. Thus, the purpose of a computation in a constraint-based system is to infer primitive constraints p from non primitive ones c.

As mentioned, when solving optimization problems, CP systems usually perform the branch and bound method. In particular, each time a feasible solution s^* is found (whose cost is $f(s^*)$), a constraint $f(x) < f(s^*)$ is added to each subproblem in the remaining search tree. The purpose of the added *upper bounding constraint* is to remove portions of the search tree which cannot lead to better solution than the best one found so far. Two are the main limitations of this approach: (i) we do not have good information on the problem lower bound, and consequently, on the quality of the solutions found; (ii) the relation between the cost of the solution and the problem variables is in general not very tight, in the sense that is usually represented by a non primitive constraints.

Many works have been proposed in order to solve the first problem by computing a lower bound on the problem, thus obtaining in CP a behaviour similar to the OR branch and bound technique. In global constraints, for example, a lower bound is computed on the basis of variable bounds involved in the constraint itself, see for instance [22]. Alternatively, Linear Programming (LP) [8] can be used for this purpose as done for example in [2], [5], [21].

The second problem arises from the fact that in classical CP systems primitive constraints are the following:

$$Prim = \{X \leq u, X \geq b, X \neq v, X = Y, integral(X)\}$$

where X and Y are variables, u, v, b are constants. All other constraints are *non primitive*. The branch and bound a-la CP would be very effective if the *upper bounding constraint* would be a primitive constraint. Unfortunately, in general, while the term $f(s^*)$ is indeed a constant, the function $f(x)$ is in general not efficiently handled by the underlying solver.

For example, in scheduling problems, the objective function may be the *makespan* which is computed as the $max_{i \in Task}\{St_i + d_i\}$ where St_i is a variable representing the start time of Task i and d_i its duration. In matching, timetabling and travelling salesman problems, each variable assignment is associated with a cost (or a penalty), the objective function is the sum of the assignment costs. In these cases, the function f representing the objective function makes the upper bounding constraint a non primitive one.

The general idea we propose is to infer primitive constraints on the basis of information on costs. We use *optimization* components within global constraints representing a proper relaxation of the problem (or exactly the same problem) represented by the global constraint itself. The optimization component provides the optimal solution of the relaxed problem, its value and a gradient function computing the cost to be added to the optimal solution for each variable-value assignment. In this section, we provide an intuition on how this information is exploited. In section 3 we formally explain the proposed technique.

With no loss of generality, we consider here as optimization component a Linear Program (LP) representing a (continuous) linear relaxation of the constraint itself. The optimal solution of the relaxed problem can be used as heuristic information as explained in section 4. The optimal value of this solution improves the lower bound of the objective function and prunes portions of the search space whose lower bound is bigger than the best solution found so far. The reduced costs associated to linear variables is proportional to the cost to be added to the optimal solution of the relaxed problem if the corresponding linear variable becomes part of a solution. If this sum is greater than the best solution found so far, the linear variable can be fixed to 0, i.e., it is excluded from the solution. This technique is known in OR as variable fixing [15]. Given a mapping between LP and CP variables, we have the same information for CP variable domain values. Thus, we can infer primitive constraints of the kind $X \neq v$, and we prune the subproblem defined by the branching constraint $p = (X = v)$.

The advantage of this approach is twofold. First, we exploit cost-based information for domain filtering in global constraints. The advantage with respect to traditional OR variable fixing technique is that in our case domain filtering usually triggers propagation of other constraints thanks to shared variables. Second, we do not need to define each time a proper relaxation of the original problem, but we associate a proper relaxation to each global constraint which can be written once for all for optimization purposes. A complementary approach could instead generate a single linear program containing a linearization of the inequalities corresponding to the whole set of constraint representing the problem as done in [21]. This would allow to have one single global optimization constraint in the form of LP. However, it can be applied only if we consider as a relaxed problem a linear problem, while our approach is more general and we can apply more sophisticated techniques such as additive bounds [10].

3 Global optimization constraints

In this paper we apply our ideas on two global constraints of ILOG solver: a constraint of difference (IlcAllDiff) and a path constraint (IlcPath) which was extended in order to handle transition costs depending on the selected path.

The constraint IlcAllDiff [19] applied to an array of domain variables $Vars = (X_1, ..., X_n)$, ensures that all variables in $Vars$ have a different value.

The constraint IlcPath ensures that, given a set of nodes I, a maximum number of paths NbPath, a set of starting nodes S and a set of ending nodes E, there exists at most NbPath paths starting from nodes in S, visiting all nodes in I and ending at nodes in E. Each node will be visited only once, will have only one predecessor and only one successor. The constraint works on an array of domain variables $Next$, each representing the next node in the path ($Next[i] = j$ if and only if node i precedes j in the solution).

In both cases, as LP relaxation we use the Assignment Problem (AP) solved by the Hungarian algorithm described in [4]. We have chosen the AP solver as a Linear Component for two reasons: (i) it is a suitable relaxation for the IlcPath constraint and exactly the same problem represented by IlcAllDiff constraint; (ii) we have a specialized, polynomial and incremental algorithm (the Hungarian method) for solving it and computing the reduced costs[1]. Notice that the proposed approach is independent from the used relaxation. In fact, the algorithm providing lower bound values and reduced costs can be seen as a software component, and it can be easily substituted by other algorithms. For example, an algorithm which incrementally solves the Minimum Spanning Arborescence can be easily used instead of the Hungarian algorithm for computing the lower bound and the reduced costs for the path constraint as shown in [13].

Two important points that should be defined are (i) the mapping between variables appearing in the global constraint and variables appearing in the AP formulation; (ii) the cost based propagation.

In the next sections, we formally define the Assignment Problem, the mapping and the cost-based propagation.

3.1 The Assignment Problem as *optimization* component

The well known *Linear Assignment Problem* (AP) (see [9] for a survey) states as follows. Given a square cost matrix c_{ij} of order n, the problem is to assign to each row a different column, and vice versa in order to minimize the total sum of the row-column assignment costs.

This problem can be seen as the *Minimum Cost Perfect Matching* problem. Let $G = (V \cup T, A)$ be a bipartite graph where V and T are the vertex sets and $|V| = |T| = n$, $A = \{(i,j)|i \in V, j \in T\}$ the arc set, and c_{ij} is the cost of arc $(i,j) \in A$. The minimum cost perfect matching gives the solution to the AP. Vertex $i \in V$ corresponds to row i and vertex $j \in T$ to column j. A classic Integer Linear Programming (ILP) formulation for the AP is:

$$Z(AP) = \min \sum_{i \in V} \sum_{j \in T} c_{ij} x_{ij} \tag{1}$$

---

[1] Note that the AP can be formulated as an Integer Linear Program. However, being the cost matrix totally unimodular, the LP relaxation of the AP always provides an integer (thus optimal) solution.

194

$$\text{subject to} \sum_{i \in V} x_{ij} = 1, \quad j \in T \tag{2}$$

$$\sum_{j \in T} x_{ij} = 1, \quad i \in V \tag{3}$$

$$x_{ij} \text{ integer}, \ i \in V, j \in T \tag{4}$$

where $x_{ij} = 1$ if and only if arc (i,j) is in the optimal solution. Constraints (2) and (3) impose in-degree and out-degree of each vertex equal to one.

Alternatively, AP can also be defined on a digraph (of n vertices) as the graph theory problem of finding a set of *disjoint* sub-tours such that all the vertices in the digraph are visited and the sum of the costs of selected arcs is a minimum.

It is well-known that the AP optimal solution can be obtained through a *primal-dual* algorithm. We have used a C++ adaptation of the Hungarian algorithm described in [4]. The solution of the AP requires in the worst case $O(n^3)$, whereas each re-computation of the optimal AP solution, needed in the case of modification of one value in the cost matrix, can be efficiently computed in $O(n^2)$ time through a single augmenting path step.

The information provided by the Hungarian algorithm is the AP optimal solution and a reduced cost matrix $\bar{c}$. In particular, for each arc $(i,j) \in A$ the reduced cost value is defined as $\bar{c}_{ij} = c_{ij} - u_i - v_j$, where u_i and v_j are the optimal values of the Linear Programming dual variables associated with the i-th constraint of type (2) and the j-th constraint of type (3), respectively. The reduced cost values are obtained from the AP algorithm without extra computational effort during AP solution. Each $\bar{c}_{ij}$ is a lower bound on the cost to be added to the optimal AP solution if we force arc (i,j) in solution.

3.2 Mapping

In this section, we define the mapping between variables and constraints used in our optimization component and those used in the CP program. The mapping between the ILP formulation and the CP formulation is straightforward and has been previously suggested in [21]. In CP, we have global constraints involving variables $X_1, ..., X_n$ (in the path constraints they are called $Next_i$), ranging on domains $D_1, ..., D_n$, and cost c_{ij} of assigning value $j \in D_i$ to X_i. Obviously, the cost of each value not belonging to a variable domain is infinite. The problem we want to solve is to find an assignment of values to variables consistent with the global constraint, and whose total cost is minimal. If an ILP variable x_{ij} is equal to 1, the CP variable X_i is assigned to the value j, $x_{ij} = 1 \leftrightarrow X_i = j$. Constraints (2) and (3) correspond to a constraint of difference imposing that all CP variables assume different values. The ILP objective function corresponds to the CP objective function.

It is worth noting that the AP codes work on square matrices, while, in general, in the CP problem considered, it is not always true that the number of variables is equal to the number of values. Thus, the cost matrix of the original problem should be changed. Suppose we have n variables $X_1, ..., X_n$, and suppose that the union of their domains contains m different values. A necessary condition for the problem to be solvable is that $m \geq n$. The original cost matrix has n rows (corresponding to variables) and m columns (corresponding to values). Each matrix element c_{ij} represents a cost of assigning j to X_i if value j belongs to the domain of X_i. Otherwise, $c_{ij} = +INF$. In addition, we have to change the matrix so as to have a number of rows equal to the number of columns. Thus, we can add to the matrix $m - n$ rows where each value $c_{ij} = 0$ for all $i = n+1, \ldots, m$ and for all $j = 1, \ldots, m$, obtaining an $m \times m$ cost matrix. The addition of these $m - n$ rows brings the algorithm to a time complexity of $O(mn^2)$ (and not $O(m^3)$), whereas each re-computation of the optimal AP solution requires only $O(nm)$ time.

Note that the constraint of difference and the AP component have exactly the same semantics: they compute a solution where all variables are assigned to different values. Thus, each solution of the AP is feasible for the constraint of difference. In general, in a CP program the same variables appear in different constraints. Thus, the constraint of difference alone (and the AP component alone) can be seen as a relaxation of a more general problem. As a consequence, the AP optimal solution Z_{LB} is a lower bound on the optimal solution of the overall problem. On the contrary, when used within a path constraint, the AP component represents a relaxation of the constraint itself (where sub-tours may appear) and it is no longer true that the optimal solution of the AP is feasible for the path constraint. In this case, the AP optimal solution Z_{LB} is a lower bound of the sum of the arcs appearing in the path constraint.

As already mentioned, the AP provides a reduced cost matrix. Given the mapping between LP and CP variables, we know that the LP variable x_{ij} corresponds to the value j in the domain of the CP variable X_i. Thus, the reduced cost matrix $\bar{c}_{ij}$ provides information on CP variable domain values, $grad(X_i, j) = \bar{c}_{ij}$.

3.3 The Cost-Based Propagation

In this section we describe filtering techniques based on the information provided by the optimization component. We have a first (trivial) propagation based on the AP optimal value Z_{LB}. At each node of the search tree, we check the constraint $Z_{LB} < Z$ where Z is the variable representing the CP objective function. This kind of propagation generates a yes/no answer on the feasibility of the current node of the search tree; therefore it does not allow any real interaction with the other constraints of the problem.

More interesting is the second propagation from reduced costs $\bar{c}$ towards decision variables $X_1, \ldots, X_n$, referred to as RC-based propagation. This filtering algorithm directly prunes decision variables $X_1, \ldots, X_n$ domains on the basis of reduced costs $\bar{c}$. Suppose we have already found a solution whose cost is Z^*. For each domain value j of each variable X_i, $Z_{LB_{X_i=j}} = Z_{LB} + \bar{c}_{ij}$ is a lower bound value of the subproblem generated if value j is assigned to X_i. If $Z_{LB_{X_i=j}}$ is greater or equal to Z^*, j can be deleted from the domain of X_i. This filtering algorithm performs a real back-propagation from Z to X_i. Such domain filtering usually triggers other constraints imposed on shared variables, and it appears therefore particularly suited for CP. Indeed, the technique proposed represents a new way of inferring primitive constraints starting from non primitive ones. In particular, primitive constraints added (of the form $X_i \neq j$) do not derive, as in general happens, from reasoning on feasibility, but they derive from reasoning on optimality. Furthermore, note that the same constraints of the form $X_i \neq j$ are also inferred in standard OR frameworks (variable fixing). However, this fixing is usually not exploited to trigger other constraints, but only in the next lower bound computation, i.e., the next branching node.

When the AP is used as optimization component, an improvement on the use of the reduced costs can be exploited as follows: we want to evaluate if value j could be removed from the domain of variable X_i on the basis of its estimated cost. Let $X_i = k$ and $X_l = j$ in the optimal AP solution. In order to assign $X_i = j$, a minimum augmenting path, say PTH, from l to k has to be determined since l and k must be re-assigned. Thus, the cost of the optimal AP solution where $X_i = j$ is $Z_{LB} + \bar{c}_{ij} + cost(PTH)$, by indicating with $cost(PTH)$ the cost of the minimum augmenting path PTH. In [13], two bounds on this cost have been proposed, whose calculation does not increase the total time complexity of the filtering algorithm ($O(n^2)$). We will refer to this propagation as *improved reduced cost* propagation (*IRC-based* propagation).

3.4 Propagation Events

In this section, we describe the data structures which should be built and maintained by the global constraints, and the events triggering propagation.

When the constraint is stated for the first time, the cost matrix is built and the Hungarian Algorithm is used to compute the AP optimal solution and the reduced cost matrix in $O(n^3)$. Each time the AP optimal solution is computed, the lower bound of the variable representing the objective function is updated and the RC-based propagation is performed (or IRC-based if the corresponding flag is set). The constraint is triggered each time a change in a variable domain happens and each time the upper bound of the objective function is updated. Each time a value j is removed from the domain of variable X_i, the cost matrix is updated by imposing $c_{ij} = +\infty$, i.e., $x_{ij} = 0$. If value j belongs to the solution of the AP (and only in this case), the lower bound Z_{LB} is updated by incrementally re-computing the assignment problem solution in $O(n^2)$. The AP re-computation leads to a new reduced cost matrix. Thus, the RC-based propagation (or IRC-based) is triggered and some other values may be removed.

Note that since the re-computation of the AP solution is needed only if the value removed from the domain of a variable is part of the current AP solution, it is possible to write the optimization constraint in such a way that whenever a value is assigned to a variable only one incremental re-computation is needed. Each time the objective function upper bound is updated, the RC-based propagation (or IRC-based) is triggered.

4 Heuristics

The optimal solution of a relaxed problem, the lower bound value, and the set of reduced costs can be used for the heuristics during the search for a solution. Different examples of such use are described in the next section where three combinatorial problems are considered. In general, we can say that the gradient information (reduced costs) can be used to calculate a regret function (see for example [7] for the definition of regret) useful for the variable selection, whereas the optimal assignment in the relaxed problem can be used for the value selection, and finally the lower bound value can be used to select a working subproblem in a local improvement framework, as described in section 5.3.

5 Computational Results on Different Problems

In this section we present the empirical results on different problems for which the linear assignment problem turns out to be a relaxation. We report computing times (given in seconds on a Pentium II 200 MHz) and number of fails. We refer to different strategies: (*i*) a pure CP approach exploiting the Branch & Bound *a-la* CP; (*ii*) a strategy exploiting the *LB-based* propagation, referred to as **ST1**; (*iii*) a strategy exploiting both the *LB-based* and *RC-based* propagation, referred to as **ST2**; (*iv*) a strategy exploiting the *LB-based* and *IRC-based* propagation, referred to as **ST3**. Also comparisons with related approaches on the same applications (if any) are shown. The problems considered are: Travelling Salesman Problems instances taken from the TSP-lib and solved also in [6], Timetabling problems described in [7]. Scheduling Problems with setup times are finally considered and solved using a local improvement technique.

Travelling Salesman Problems have been chosen because standard CP techniques perform very poorly on these problems; we are able to solve problems which are one order of magnitude greater than those solved by a pure CP approach. Caseau and Laburthe in [7] have already shown the advantages of CP techniques in Timetabling problems w.r.t. pure OR approaches. Here we show that the tighter integration proposed outperforms their approach. Indeed, the modelling uses different constraints of difference embedding information on cost. These constraints represent different relaxations of the same problem on shared decision variables. Thus, they smoothly interact with each other and with the entire set of problem constraints allowing to efficiently solve the problem. Finally, preliminary results obtained on Scheduling Problems with setup times show the generality of the approach, and propose a new method for modelling and solving such problems. Implementation details, and more computational results on the TSP and Timetabling problems presented can be found respectively in [13] and [11].

5.1 TSPs

TSP concerns the task of finding a tour covering a set of nodes, once and only once, with a minimum cost. The problem is strongly NP-hard, and has been deeply investigated in the literature (see [14] for a survey). Although CP is far from obtaining better results than the ones obtained with state of the art OR technology, it is nevertheless very interesting to build an effective TSP constraint; in fact, many problems contain subproblems that can be described as TSPs, e.g., *Vehicle Routing Problem* (VRP), *Scheduling Problems*, and many variants of TSP are also interesting, e.g., TSP with *Time Windows* (TSPTW). In these cases the flexibility and the domain reduction mechanism of Constraint Programming languages can play an important role, and hybrid CP-OR systems could outperform pure OR approaches (as shown in [16] and [17]).

In this section, a set of symmetric TSP instances (up to 30 nodes, from TSP-lib [20]) is analyzed. The pure CP approach has not been reported because it is not able to prove optimality within 30 minutes on none of the instances considered. Our results have been compared with those achieved by Caseau and Laburthe [6] and reported in row CL97, Table 1. The computing times of this last row are given in seconds on a Sun Sparc 10.

Problem	gr17		gr21		gr24		fri26		bayg29		bays29	
	Time	Fails	Time	Fails	Time	Fails	Time	Fails	Time	Fails	Time	Fails
ST1	8.79	13k	0.11	96	1.7	1.5k	19.88	16.6k	89.4	79.8k	135.7	112.8k
ST2	0.71	758	0.05	31	0.28	145	3.68	1.8k	10.6	9.4k	15.4	10.8k
ST3	0.66	646	0.06	31	0.27	120	2.86	1.6k	11.09	7.8k	13.7	8.8k
CL97	3.10	5.8k	7.00	12.5k	6.90	6.6k	930.0	934k	4.4k	4.56M	1.2k	1.1M

Table 1: Results on small symmetric TSP instances.

The search strategy used exploits the information coming from the optimization component. It implements a sub-tour elimination branching rule often used in OR-based Branch and Bound algorithm for the TSP. In any stage of the search tree, we consider the solution of the AP, we choose a tour belonging to the optimal AP solution, and we branch by removing one arc of the tour in each branch. Note that the tour chosen, infeasible for the TSP, will not appear in any of the generated branches.

Results show that the use of the back propagation from the objective function to the decision variables (strategies ST2 and ST3) turns out to be very important for efficiently solve optimization problems.

As previously mentioned, one of the interests in solving TSP by Constraint Programming is the flexibility of CP that allow the immediate addition of further constraints to the original problem, e.g., Time Windows, by performing separate propagation on them. In [12] we have shown how to optimally solve TSP with Time Windows by using the path constraint embedding cost-based domain filtering together with well known CP propagation algorithms deriving from the field of scheduling. The resulting algorithm achieves the best known results on some instances, thus being competitive with pure OR approaches.

5.2 Timetabling Problems

The timetabling problems considered have been described in [7]. The problems consist in producing a weekly schedule with a set of lessons whose duration goes from 1 to 4 hours. Each week is divided in 4-hours time slots and each lesson should be assigned to one time slot. The problem involves disjunctive constraints on lessons imposing that two lessons cannot overlap and constraints stating that one lesson cannot spread on two time slots. The objective function to be minimized is the sum of weights taking into account penalties associated to pairs lesson-hour. We have modelled the problem by considering: (*i*) an array of domain variables Start representing the course starting times; (*ii*) an array of variables Slot representing the slot to which the course is assigned; (*iii*) an array of variables SingleHours representing the single hours of each course. Different variables are linked by the following constraints:

    Start[i] mod 4 = Slot[i]
    Start[i] = SingleHours[i][0]

Two different matching problems representing two relaxations of the timetabling problem have been modelled by two constraints of difference embedding an optimization component. The first one is the linear assignment relaxation arising when lessons are considered interruptible involving variables SingleHours. The cost of assigning each SingleHours[i] variable to a value H is the cost of assigning the corresponding course to the time slot H mod 4 divided by the duration of the course. The second relaxation considers variables Slot for courses lasting 3 and 4 hours. The corresponding problem is an AP since two 3 or 4 hours courses cannot be assigned to the same slot for limited capacity. The cost of assigning a course to a slot is defined by the problem. The interesting point here is that different problem relaxations coexist and easily interact through shared variables.

In Table 2 we report, in addition to the results of the four described approaches, the results obtained by the constraint *MinWeightAllDifferent* described by Caseau and Laburthe [7]. (In the last row of Table 2, we refer to row 4 of Table 6 of [7], and the corresponding computing times are given in seconds on a Pentium Pro 200 MHz.)

Problem	Problem 1		Problem 2		Problem 3	
	Time	Fails	Time	Fails	Time	Fails
Pure-CP	3.77	5.4k	5.50	8.5k	11.20	14.5k
ST1	0.70	213	0.15	58	7.60	2.5k
ST2	0.70	199	0.10	30	4.00	1.3k
ST3	0.90	182	0.16	28	6.10	1.2k
CL [7]	29.00	3.5k	2.60	234	120.00	17k

Table 2: Results on timetabling instances.

Table 2 shows that for these instances ST2 outperforms in terms of computing times other approaches, although ST3 has more powerful propagation (less number of fails). In this case, in fact, the reduction of the search space does not pay off in terms of computing time.

We have used the information provided by the AP solution also for guiding the search. Defining the regret of a variable as the difference between the cost of the best assignment and the cost of the second best, a good heuristic consists in selecting first variables with high regret. In [7] the regret has been heuristically evaluated directly on the cost matrix as the difference between the minimum cost and the second minimum of each row (despite of the fact that these two minimum could not be part of the first best and the second best solutions). Reduced cost provide a more accurate computation of the regret: for each variable, a lower bound on the regret is the minimum reduced cost excluding the reduced cost of the value in the AP solution. This regret is then combined in a weighted sum with the size of the domain (following the First-Fail principle), and such a weighted sum is used in the variable selection strategy. Concerning the value selection strategy for variable X_i, we have used the solution of the AP.

5.3 Scheduling with Set up times

We are given a set of n activities $A_1, ..., A_n$ and a set of m unary resources (resources with maximal capacity equal to one) $R_1, ..., R_m$. Each activity A_i has to be processed on a resource R_j for p_i time units. Resource R_j can be chosen within a given subset of the M resources. Activities may be linked together by precedence relations. Sequence dependent setup times exist among activities. Given a setup time matrix S^k (square matrix of dimension equal to n), s_{ij}^k represents the setup time between activities A_i and A_j if A_i and A_j are scheduled sequentially on the same resource R_k. In such a case, $start(A_j) \geq end(A_i) + s_{ij}^k$. Also a setup time su_j^k before the first activity A_j can start on resource R_k may exist. A teardown time td_i^k after the last activity A_i ends on resource R_k may exist.

Constraints of the problem are defined by the resource capacity, the temporal constraints, and the time bounds of the activities (release date, and due date). The goal is to minimize the sum of setup time, given a maximal makespan.

A multiple-TSP M-TSP can model a relaxation of the scheduling problem where each resource, and each activity are represented by nodes and arc costs are the setup times. The solution of the M-TSP provides both an assignment of activities to resources and their minimum cost sequencing. Again, the AP can be used to calculate a lower bound on the optimal M-TSP, thus to perform pruning on problem variables, and to guide the search.

In the following, we will give some preliminary results. The scheduling problem analyzed were solved in two phases: we first looked for a feasible solution, and then we iteratively select a small time window TW_i, we freeze the solution outside TW_i, and perform a Branch and Bound search within the selected window. The scheduling problem considered consists in 25 job of 6 activities each. The activities of each job are linked by temporal constraints and the last activity of each job is subject to a deadline. Each activity requires a set of alternative unary resources and a discrete resource with a given capacity profile.

	Makespan	Total Setup	CPU Time
First Sol.	2728	930	8
Pure-CP	2705	750	386
ST2	2695	600	249

Table 3: Results on a Scheduling Problem with setup times.

The first solution (first row of Table 3) produces a makespan equal to 2728 and a total setup time equal to 930. This first solution is used as starting point for the local improvement phase. The second row of Table 3 reports the improvement on the first solution obtained using a pure CP approach, while the third row reported the results obtained using the optimization constraint (LB-based and RC-based propagation). Both approaches used the same search strategy. The use of the optimization constraint played an important role in the local improvement phase. In fact for a given time window TW_i, the lower bound gives very good information on the local optimal solution because the scheduling constraints (relaxed on the M-TSP) are locally not tight. Indeed, in some cases the gap between the value of the lower bound calculated at the root node and the value of the local optimal solution found is zero.

In this application the optimization constraint is also very important for the selection of the time window TW_i. For each time window TW_i we calculate the gap between the current cost and the lower bound. Such a value is used to select the time window in which running the Branch and Bound optimization. In fact, the higher the gap is, the more chances we have to obtain a good improvement on the solution.

It is important to stress that in this case the optimization constraint interacts with all the scheduling constraints (time bounds, precedence relationship, capacity constraints) thought shared variables. The Edge Finder [1] constraint may, for example, deduce that a given activity A_i must precede a set of other activities, and this information is made available to the optimization constraint.

6 Conclusion and Future Work

In this paper, we have proposed the use of an optimization component such as a Linear Program in global constraints. For feasibility purposes, global constraints represent a suitable abstraction of general problems. For optimization purposes embedding OR methods in global constraints is a necessary condition for efficiently handle objective functions.

The advantages of the proposed integration are that we are able to infer primitive constraints starting from non primitive ones on the basis of lower bound and reduced costs information. This enhances operational behaviour of CP for optimization problems by maintaining its flexibility and its modelling capabilities.

Although most of the OR techniques used are fairly standard in the OR community we believe that their introduction in CP global constraints leads to significant new contributions. We greatly powered the CP constraints for optimization problems. We also powered the back-propagation from the objective function to the decision variables; such propagation is limited in a pure OR framework since pure OR branch and bound does not have a constraint store active on shared variables. This last point, in particular, allowed us to easily model and solve problems whose pure OR modelling would lead to very complex algorithms. Finally, the different prospective in which reduced cost fixing is used brought (and may bring) to new contributions such as the *improved reduced cost* propagation.

Future work concern further generalization of the method by integrating in global constraint a general LP solver providing information on lower bound and on reduced costs. Also, we are currently investigating the use of additive bounds [10] and other specialized cost-based methods in global constraints.

7 Acknowledgements

This work has been partially supported by ILOG S.A. (France). The authors are grateful to F. Laburthe, U. Junker, T. Kasper, W. Nuijten, J. Pommier, J.F. Puget, P. Toth and D. Vigo for fruitful discussions and suggestions. Thanks are also due to anonymous referees for useful comments on an earlier version of this paper.

References

1. P. Baptiste, C. Le Pape, and W. Nuijten. Efficient operations research algorithms in constraint-based scheduling. In *Proceedings of IJCAI'95*, 1995.
2. H. Beringer and B. De Backer. Combinatorial problem solving in Constraint Logic Programming with Cooperating Solvers. In C. Beierle and L.Plumer, editors, *Logic Programming: formal Methods and Practical Applications*. North Holland, 1995.
3. A. Bockmayr and T. Kasper. Branch-and-Infer: A unifying framework for Integer and Finite Domain Constraint Programming. *INFORMS J. Computing*, 10(3):287 – 300, 1998.
4. G. Carpaneto, S. Martello, and P. Toth. Algorithms and codes for the Assignment Problem. In B. Simeone et al., editor, *Fortran Codes for Network Optimization - Annals of Operations Research*, pages 193–223. 1988.
5. Y. Caseau and F. Laburthe. Improving Branch and Bound for Jobshop Scheduling with Constraint Propagation. In M. Deza, R. Euler, and Y. Manoussakis, editors, *Combinatorics and Computer Science*, LNCS 1120, pages 129–149. Springer Verlag, 1995.
6. Y. Caseau and F. Laburthe. Solving small TSPs with constraints. In *Proceedings of the Fourteenth International Conference on Logic Programming - ICLP'97*, pages 316–330, 1997.
7. Y. Caseau and F. Laburthe. Solving various weighted matching problems with constraints. In *Proceedings of CP'97*, 1997.
8. G.B. Dantzig. *Linear Programming and Extensions*. Princeton Univ. Press, 1963.
9. M. Dell'Amico and S. Martello. Linear assignment. In F. Maffioli M. Dell'Amico and S. Martello, editors, *Annotated Bibliographies in Combinatorial Optimization*, pages 355–371. Wiley, 1997.

10. M. Fischetti and P. Toth. An additive bounding procedure for the asymmetric travelling salesman problem. *Mathematical Programming*, 53:173–197, 1992.

11. F. Focacci, A. Lodi, and M. Milano. Integration of CP and OR methods for Matching Problems. In *CP-AI-OR'99 Workshop on Integration of AI and OR techniques in Constraint Programming for Combinatorial Optimization Problems*, 1999.

12. F. Focacci, A. Lodi, and M. Milano. Solving tsp with time windows with constraints. In *ICLP'99 International Conference on Logic Programming*, 1999.

13. F. Focacci, A. Lodi, M. Milano, and D. Vigo. Solving TSP through the integration of OR and CP techniques. *Proc. CP98 Workshop on Large Scale Combinatorial Optimisation and Constraints*, 1998.

14. M. Jünger, G. Reinelt, and G. Rinaldi. The Travelling Salesman Problem. In M. Dell'Amico, F. Maffioli, and S. Martello, editors, *Annotated Bibliographies in Combinatorial Optimization*. Wiley, 1997.

15. G.L. Nemhauser and L.A. Wolsey. *Integer and Combinatorial Optimization*. John Wiley and Sons, 1988.

16. G. Pesant, M. Gendreau, J.Y. Potvin, and J.M. Rousseau. An exact constraint logic programming algorithm for the travelling salesman problem with time windows. *Transportation Science*, 32(1):12–29, 1998.

17. G. Pesant, M. Gendreau, J.Y. Potvin, and J.M. Rousseau. On the flexibility of Constraint Programming models: From Single to Multiple Time Windows for the Travelling Salesman Problem. *European Journal of Operational Research*, 117(2):253–263, 1999.

18. J.F. Puget. A C++ implementation of CLP. Technical Report 94-01, ILOG Headquarters, 1994.

19. J.C. Régin. A filtering algorithm for constraints of difference in CSPs. In *Proceedings of AAAI'94*, 1994.

20. G. Reinelt. TSPLIB - a Travelling Salesman Problem Library. *ORSA Journal on Computing*, 3:376–384, 1991.

21. R. Rodosek, M. Wallace, and M.T.Hajian. A new approach to integrating Mixed Integer Programming and Constraint Logic Programming. *Annals of Operational Research*, 1997. Recent Advances in Combinatorial Optimization.

22. H. Simonis. Calculating lower bounds on a resource scheduling problem. Technical report, Cosytec, 1995.

Resource Allocation in Networks Using Abstraction and Constraint Satisfaction Techniques

Christian Frei[1] and Boi Faltings[1]

Artificial Intelligence Laboratory, Swiss Federal Institute of Technology (EPFL),
1015 Lausanne, Switzerland,
{Christian.Frei, Boi.Faltings}@epfl.ch

Abstract. Most work on constraint satisfaction problems (CSP) starts with a standard problem definition and focuses on algorithms for finding solutions. However, formulating a CSP so that it can be solved by such methods is often a difficult problem in itself. In this paper, we consider the problem of routing in networks, an important problem in communication networks. It is as an example of a problem where a CSP formulation would lead to unmanageable solution complexity. We show how an abstraction technique results in tractable formulations and makes the machinery of CSP applicable to this problem.

1 Introduction

Communication networks are expected to offer a wide range of services to an increasingly large number of users, with a diverse range of quality of service. This calls for efficient control and management of these networks. In this paper, we address the problem of quality-of-service routing. Shortest path routing is the traditional technique applied to this problem. However, this can lead to poor network utilization and even congestion, especially in highly loaded networks. From the routing point of view, the key resource to manage in networks is bandwidth. Therefore, in order to make better use of available network resources, there is a need for *planning the bandwidth allocation* to communication demands, in order to set up routing tables (or any other route selection criterion) more purposefully. This can be achieved by the use of *global information*, including not only the available link capacities but also the expected traffic profile. This traffic profile may be given, as when setting up virtual private networks in an ATM backbone of a provider, or estimated by objective traffic measurements (which almost every network operator carries out).

A communication network is composed of nodes interconnected with communication links. We model it as a connected *network graph* $\mathcal{G} = (\mathcal{N}, \mathcal{L})$ an undirected multi-graph without loops, i.e., edges whose endpoints are the same vertex, see Fig. 1 (d). The set of nodes $\mathcal{N}$ are processing units, switches, routers, etc., and the links $\mathcal{L}$ correspond to bidirectional communication media, such as optical fibers. Each link l is characterized by its *bandwidth capacity*, the (currently) *available bandwidth*. In Fig. 1.d, the weights on the links denote their available bandwidth. Our network must fulfill communication needs between pairs of nodes, or *demands*. A demand d_u is defined by a triple: $d_u = (x_u, y_u, \beta_u)$. where x_u and y_u are distinct nodes of the network graph $\mathcal{G}$ and define the nodes between which communication is required to take place: the demand's *endpoints*. Parameter β_u describes the demand's bandwidth requirement. A network $\mathcal{G}$ satisfies a set of demands by allocating a *connection* for each demand. A connection is a simple path in the network graph that satisfies the bandwidth requirement.

We define the problem of resource allocation in networks (RAIN) as follows:

Given a network composed of nodes and links, each link with a given resource capacity, and a set of demands to allocate,

Find one route for each demand so that the bandwidth requirements of the demands are simultaneously satisfied within the resource capacities of the links.

It is important to note that because of technological limitations (for ATM typically) and/or performance reasons, it is impossible to divide demands among multiple routes. However, there may be several demands between same endpoints. With this restriction, the RAIN problem is NP-hard in the number of demands. When demands are subject to multiple additive or multiplicative quality of service (QoS) criteria (such as delay and loss probability), then Wang and Crowcroft [1] have shown that the allocation of every single demand is NP-complete by itself. This creates a new situation for the networking community, as traditional routing algorithms such as shortest paths do not perform very well on this problem.

Constraint satisfaction [2] is a technique which has been shown to work well for solving certain NP-hard problems. Indeed, the RAIN problem is easily formulated as a CSP in the following way: variables are demands, the domain of each variable is the set of all routes between the endpoints of the demand, and constraints on each link must ensure that the resource capacity is not exceeded by the demands routed through it. A solution is a set of routes, one for each demand, respecting the capacities of the links.

However, this formulation presents severe complexity problems. It is too expensive to compute the domains of the variables, i.e., all the routes that join the endpoints of each demand. Suppose the network is simple but complete (note that this is not even the worst case, since a communication network is a multigraph: it allows multiple links between same endpoints) with n nodes. A route is a simple path, its length in number of links is therefore bounded by $n - 1$. Since a route of length j has $j - 1$ intermediate (and distinct) nodes, the number of routes of length j is $(n - 2)!/(n - j - 1)!$. The total number of routes between two nodes is therefore equal to $\sum_{i=1}^{n-1} (n - 2)!/(n - i - 1)!$. Storing all routes between a pair of nodes would require exponential space. For instance, in a complete graph with 10 nodes, there are 69'281 routes between any pair of nodes. Since methods such as forward checking or dynamic variable ordering require explicit representation of domains, they would be very inefficient on a problem of realistic size.

In this paper, we show how abstractions of the network, called Blocking Islands, create a compact representation of the problem which allows applying well-known CSP techniques such as forward checking, variable and value ordering to the RAIN problem, with manageable complexity. When a dead-end is reached during search, blocking island abstractions also allow to prove in some cases that the problem is infeasible by identifying global bottlenecks in the network, or to identify culprit assignments of routes to demands that prevent the allocation of another demand. The latter feature is used as a backjumping criteria for improved search.

2 Related Work

Surprisingly, there has been little published research on the RAIN problem. Currently, most network providers use some kind of best effort algorithm, without any backtracking due to the complexity of the problem: given an order of the demands, each demand is assigned the shortest possible route supporting it, or just skipped if there is no such route. There are some proprietary tools for this, about which nothing much is known.

To our knowledge, the closest published work to ours is the CANPC framework [3]. It is based on the successive allocations of shortest routes to the demands, without any backtracking when an assignment fails. They propose several heuristics to order the demands (such as bandwidth ordering) to provide better solutions, i.e., to route more demands. They are currently developing an optimization tool that takes the partial solution as input to try to allocate all demands. However, preliminary results show that the methods we propose clearly outperform theirs.

Mann and Smith [4] search for routing strategies that attempt to ensure that no link is over-utilized (hard constraint) and, if possible, that all links are evenly loaded (below a fixed target utilization), for the predicted traffic profile. Finally, the routing assignment attempts to minimize the communication costs. Genetic algorithms and simulated annealing approaches were used to develop such strategies. However, their methods do not apply well, if not at all, to highly loaded networks.

Abstraction and reformulation techniques have already been applied to permit more efficient solution of a CSP. [5] relate interchangeability to abstraction in the context of a decomposition heuristic for resource allocation. [6] cluster variables to build abstraction hierarchies for configuration problems viewed as CSPs, and then use interchangeability to merge values on each level of the hierarchy. [7] present abstraction and reformulation techniques based on interchangeability to improve solving CSPs. [8] is a recent collection of papers addressing abstraction, reformulation, and abstraction techniques in a variety of AI techniques.

3 The Blocking Island Paradigm

[9] introduce a clustering scheme based on Blocking Islands (BI), which can be used to represent bandwidth availability at different levels of abstraction, as a basis for resource allocation by intelligent agents. A β-blocking island (β-BI) for a node x is the set of all nodes of the network that can be reached from x using links with at least β available resources, including x. Figure 1 (d) shows all 64-BIs for a network. Note that some links inside a β-BI, i.e., the links that have both endpoints in the β-BI, may have less than β available resources. In such a case, it simply means that there is another route with β available resources between the link's endpoints. As a matter of fact, link (a, b) has both endpoints in 64-BI N_1 but has less than 64 available resources. However, there are at least 64 available resources along route $\{(a, c), (c, b)\}$.

β-BIs have some fundamental properties. Given any resource requirement, blocking islands partition the network into equivalence classes of nodes. The BIs are *unique*, and *identify global bottlenecks*, that is, inter-blocking island links. If inter-blocking island links are links with low remaining resources, as some links inside BIs may be, inter-blocking island links are links for which there is no alternative route with the desired resource requirement. Moreover, BIs highlight the *existence* and *location* of routes at a given bandwidth level:

Proposition 1 (route existence property). *There is at least one route satisfying the bandwidth requirement of an unallocated demand $d_u = (x, y, \beta_u)$ if and only if its endpoints x and y are in the same β_u-BI. Furthermore, all links that could form part of such a route lie inside this blocking island.*

Blocking islands are used to build the β-blocking island graph (β-BIG), a simple graph representing an *abstract* view of the available resources: each β-BI is clustered into a single node and there is an abstract link between two of these nodes if there is a link in the network joining them. Figure 1 (c) is the 64-BIG of the network of Fig. 1 (d). An abstract link between two BIs clusters all links that join the two BIs, and the abstract link's available resources is equal to the maximum of the available resources of the links it clusters (because a demand can only be allocated over one route). These abstract links denote the critical links, since their available bandwidth do not suffice to support a demand requiring β resources.

In order to identify bottlenecks for different βs, e.g., for typical possible bandwidth requirements, we build a recursive decomposition of BIGs in decreasing order of the requirements: $\beta_1 > \beta_2 > ... > \beta_b$. This layered structure of BIGs is a *Blocking Island Hierarchy* (BIH). The lowest level of the blocking island hierarchy is the β_1-BIG of the network graph. The second layer is then the β_2-BIG of the first level, i.e., β_1-BIG, the third layer the β_3-BIG of the second, and so on. On top of the hierarchy there is a 0-BIG abstracting the smallest resource requirement β_b. The abstract graph of this top layer is reduced to a single abstract node (the 0-BI), since the network graph is supposed connected. Figure 1 shows such a BIH for resource requirements $\{64, 56, 16\}$. The graphical representation

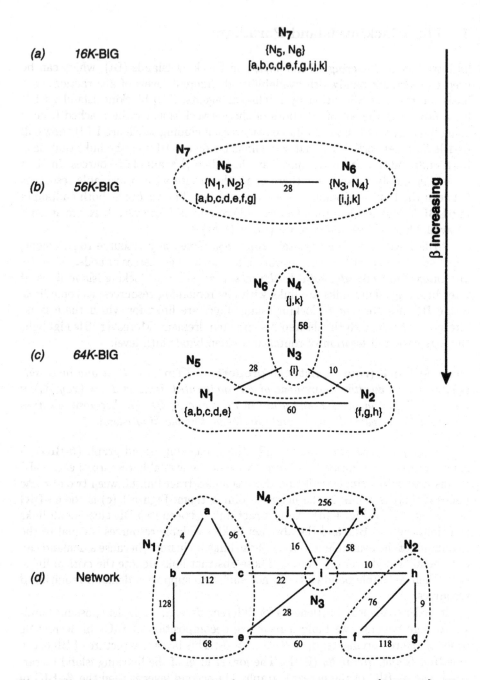

Fig. 1. The blocking island hierarchy for resource requirements {64, 56, 16}. The weights on the links are their available bandwidth. Abstract nodes' description include only their node children and network node children in brackets. Link children (of BIs and abstract links) are omitted for more clarity, and the 0-BI is not displayed since equal to N_7. (a) the 16-BIG. (b) the 56-BIG. (c) the 64-BIG. (d) the network.

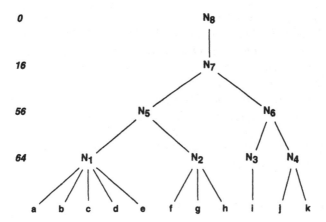

Fig. 2. The abstraction tree of the BIH of Fig. 1 (links are omitted for clarity).

shows that each BIG is an abstraction of the BIG at the level just below (the next biggest resource requirement), and therefore for all lower layers (all larger resource requirements).

A BIH can not only be viewed as a layered structure of β-BIGs, but also as an *abstraction tree* when considering the father-child relations. In the abstraction tree, the leaves are network elements (nodes and links), the intermediate vertices either abstract nodes or abstract links and the root vertex the 0-BI of the top level in the corresponding BIH. Figure 2 is the abstraction tree of Fig. 1.

The blocking island hierarchy summarizes the available bandwidth given the currently established connections at a time t. As connections are allocated or deallocated, available bandwidth changes on the communication links and the BIH may need to be modified to reflect this. The changes can be carried out incrementally, only affecting the blocking islands which participate in the demand which is being allocated or deallocated, as explained in [9]:

- When a new demand is allocated along a particular route, the bandwidth of each link decreases. If it falls below the bandwidth β of its blocking island, and no alternative route exists with capacity $\geq \beta$ within the BI, it causes a split of the BI. Furthermore, this split must be propagated to all BI in the hierarchy with a higher β.
- When a demand is deallocated, bandwidth across each link increases. If it thus becomes higher than the β of the next higher level in the hierarchy, it will cause two disjoint blocking islands to merge into a single one. This merge is propagated to all levels with a lower β.

The β-BI S for a given node x of a network graph can be obtained by a simple greedy algorithm, with a linear complexity of $O(m)$, where m is the number of links. The construction of a β-BIG is straightforward from its definition and is also linear in $O(m)$. A BIH for a set of constant resource requirements ordered decreasingly is easily obtained by recursive calls to the BIG computation algorithm. Its complexity is bound by $O(bm)$, where b is the number of different resource requirements. The adaptation of a BIH when demands are allocated or deallocated can be carried out by $O(bm)$ algorithms. Therefore, since the number of possible bandwidth requirements (b) is constant, all BI algorithms are linear in the number of links of the network.

A BIH contain at most $bn+1$ BIs, that is, one BI for each node at each bandwidth requirement level, plus the 0-BI. In that worst case, there are $\min\{m, n(n-1)/2\}$ links at each bandwidth level, since multiple links between same BIs are clustered into a single abstract link. Therefore, the memory storage requirement of a BIH is bound by $O(bn^2)$.

4 Routing from a BIH Perspective

Consider the problem of routing a single demand $d_u = (c, e, 16)$ in the network of Fig. 1 (d). Since c and e are clustered in the same 16-BI (N_7), we know that at least one route satisfying d_u exists. A classical choice would select the shortest route, that is the route r_S: $c \to i \to e$. However, allocating this route to d_u is here not a good idea, since it uses resources on two critical links, that is (c, i) and (i, e): these two links join 64-BIs N_1 and N_2 in the 64-BIG of Fig. 1 (c). After that allocation, no other demand requiring 16 (or more) between any of the nodes clustered by 56-BI N_5 and one of the nodes inside 56-BI N_6 can be allocated anymore. For instance, a demand $(c, i, 16)$ is then impossible to allocate. A better way to route d_u is r_L: $c \to b \to d \to e$, since r_L uses only links that are clustered at the lowest level in the BIH, that is in 64-BI N_1, and no critical links (that is inter-BI links). The only effect here on latter assignments is that no demand $(d, e, 64)$ can be allocated after that anymore, which is a less drastic restriction than before.

r_L is a route that satisfies the *lowest level* (LL) heuristic. Its principle is to route a demand along links clustered in the lowest BI clustering the endpoints of the demand, i.e., the BI for the highest bandwidth requirement containing the endpoints. This heuristic is based on the following observation: the lower a BI is in the BIH, the less critical are the links clustered in the BI. By assigning a route in a lower BI, a better *bandwidth connectivity* preservation effect is achieved, therefore reducing the risk of future allocation failures. Bandwidth connectivity can therefore be viewed as a kind of *overall load-balancing*.

Another way to see the criticalness of a route is to consider the *mapping* of the route onto the abstraction tree of Fig. 2: r_S is by far then the longest route, since its mapping traverses BIs N_1, N_5, N_7, N_6, N_3, and then back; r_L traverses only BI N_1. This observation (also) justifies the LL heuristic.

5 Solving a RAIN Problem

Solving a RAIN problem amounts to solving the CSP introduced in Sect. 1. This can be done using a *backtracking algorithm* with *forward checking* (FC) [2]. Its basic operation is to pick one variable (demand) at a time, assign it a value (route) of its domain that is compatible with the values of all instantiated variables so far, and propagate the effect of this assignment (using the constraints) to the future variables by removing any inconsistent values from their domain. If the domain of a future variable becomes empty, the current assignment is undone, the previous state of the domains is restored, and an alternative assignment, when available, is tried. If all possible instantiations fail, backtracking to the previous past variable occurs. FC proceeds in this fashion until a complete solution is found or all possible assignments have been tried unsuccessfully, in which case there is no solution to the problem.

The formulation of the CSP presents severe complexity problems (see Sect. 1). Nonetheless, blocking islands provide an abstraction of the domain of each demand, since any route satisfying a demand lies within the β-BI of its endpoints, where β is the resource requirement of the demand (Proposition 1). Therefore, if the endpoints of a demand are clustered in the same β-BI, there is at least one route satisfying the demand. We do not know what the domain of the variable is *explicitly*, i.e., we do not know the set of routes that can satisfy the demand; however we know it is non-empty. In fact, there is a mapping between each route that can be assigned to a demand and the BIH: a route can be seen as a path in the abstraction tree of the BIH. Thus, there is a route satisfying a demand if and only if there is a path in the abstraction tree that does not traverse BIs of a higher level than its resource requirement. For instance, from the abstraction tree of Fig. 2, it is easy to see that there is no route between a and f with 64 available resources, since any path in the tree must at least cross BIs at level 56.

This mapping of routes onto the BIH is used to formulate a forward checking criterion, as well as dynamic value ordering and dynamic variable ordering heuristics. Some of these were briefly introduced in [10]. (We note that a patent for the methods given below is pending.)

5.1 Forward Checking

Thanks to the route existence property, we know at any point in the search if it is still possible to allocate a demand, without having to compute a route: if the endpoints of the demand are clustered in the same β-BI, where β is the resource requirement of the demand, there is at least one, i.e., the domain of the variable (demand) is not empty, even if not explicitly known.

Therefore, after allocating a demand (for instance using the LL heuristic for computing a route – see Sect. 4), forward checking is performed first by updating the BIH, and then by checking that the route existence property holds for all uninstantiated demands in the updated BIH. If the latter property does not hold at least once, another route must be tried for the current demand. Domain pruning of open variables is therefore implicit while maintaining the BIH.

5.2 Value Ordering

A backtracking algorithm involves two types of choices: the next variable to assign (see Sect. 5.3), and the value to assign to it. As illustrated above, the domains of the demands are too big to be computed beforehand. Instead, we compute the routes as they are required. In order to reduce the search effort, routes should be generated in "most interesting" order, so to increase the efficiency of the search, that is: try to allocate the route that will less likely prevent the allocation of the remaining demands. A natural heuristic is to generate the routes in *shortest path* order (SP), since the shorter the route, the fewer resources will be used to satisfy a demand.

However, Sect. 4 shows how to do better using a kind of min-conflict heuristic, the lowest level heuristic. Applied to the RAIN problem, it amounts to considering first, in shortest order, the routes in the lowest blocking island (in the BIH). Apart from attempting to preserve bandwidth connectivity, the LL heuristic allows to achieve a computational gain: the lower a BI is, the smaller it is in terms of nodes and links, thereby reducing the search space to explore. Moreover, the LL heuristic is especially effective during the early stages of the search, since it allows to take better decisions and therefore has a greater pruning effect on the search tree, as shown by the results in Sect. 7. Generating one route with the LL heuristic can be done in linear time in the number of links (as long as QoS is limited to bandwidth).

5.3 Variable Ordering

The selection of the next variable to assign may have a strong effect on search efficiency, as shown by Haralick [11] and others. A widely used variable ordering technique is based on the "fail-first" principle: "To succeed, try first where you are most likely to fail". The idea is to minimize the size of the search tree and to ensure that any branch that does not lead to a solution is pruned as early as possible when choosing a variable.

There are some natural static variable ordering (SVO) techniques for the RAIN problem, such as first choose the demand that requires the most resources. Nonetheless, BIs allow dynamic (that is during search) approximation of the difficulty of allocating a demand in more subtle ways by using the abstraction tree of the BIH:

DVO-HL (Highest Level): first choose the demand whose lowest common father of its endpoints is the highest in the BIH (remember that high in the BIH means low in resources requirements). The intuition behind DVO-HL is that the higher the lowest common father of the demand's endpoints is, the more constrained (in terms of number of routes) the demand is. Moreover, the higher the lowest common father, the more allocating the demand may restrict the routing of the remaining demands (fail first principle), since it will use resources on more critical links.

DVO-NL (Number of Levels): first choose the demand for which the difference in number of levels (in the BIH) between the lowest common father of its endpoints and its resources requirements is lowest. The justification of DVO-NL is similar to DVO-HL.

There are numerous other *Dynamic Variable Ordering* (DVO) heuristics that can be derived from a BIH, and their presentation is left for a later paper.

6 Conflict Identification and Resolution

In a classical backtracking algorithm, when a dead-end is reached, the most recent assignment is undone and an alternate value for the current variable is tried. In case all values have been unsuccessfully assigned, backtracking occurs to the preceding allocation. However, if we have the means to identify a culprit assignment of a past variable, we are able to directly *backjump* [12] to it (the intermediate assignments are obviously undone), thereby possibly drastically speeding up the search process.

When approximating the RAIN problem with a network multi-flow problem, BIs provide means to identify culprit allocations and, better, allow in some cases to prove that the problem is in fact unsolvable, since they highlight global bottlenecks in the network. Flow theory says that the maximal value of a flow from a node s to a node t never exceeds the capacity of any cut[1] separating s and t.

Suppose a set of demands were allocated in the network and that the network's available resources is given by Fig. 1 (d), and that we are now to allocate a new demand $d_n = (c, h, 64)$. Since c and h are not clustered in the same 64-BI, it is impossible to satisfy d_n, and a dead-end is reached. We call *primary blocking islands* (PBI) of a demand that cannot be allocated the two BIs of its endpoints at its bandwidth requirement level. The PBIs for d_n are N_1 and N_2.

Given the latter definition and the result of flow theory, the following is easily established when a dead-end is reached during search:

- If for any of the two PBIs the sum of the bandwidth requirements of the demands that have one and only one endpoint inside the PBI is higher than the capacity of the links of the PBI's cocycle, then the problem is infeasible obviously. Search can then be aborted, thereby saving us much effort[2].
- In case infeasibility cannot be proven, analyzing the situation on the links of the PBIs cocycle indeed helps to identify a *culprit assignment*. There are two cases:
  1. The sum of the bandwidth requirements of all unallocated demands that have one and only one endpoint in the PBI is less than the sum of the available bandwidth on the links of the PBI's cocycle. This means that there is at least one already allocated demand that is routed over more than one link of the PBI's cocycle, thereby using up many critical resources. We therefore have to backjump to the point in the search where

---

[1] A *cut* separating two nodes s and t is a set of links $\omega(A)$ (the cocycle of A), where A is a subset of nodes such that $s \in A$ and $t \notin A$.

[2] Note that if a problem is infeasible, it does not mean that unsolvability can be always be proven that way, firstly because not all cuts are being examined, and secondly because the RAIN problem is not a network flow problem.

214

the total available bandwidth on the cocycle was enough to support all
unallocated demands that have one and only one endpoint in the PBI.

2. Otherwise, re-allocating some of the demands that are routed over the
PBI's cocycle over different routes may suffice to solve the problem.
Therefore, the most recent culprit assignment is the latest demand that
is routed over the PBI's cocycle.

7 Empirical Results

In practice, the RAIN problem poses itself in the following way: a service provider
receives a request from the customer to allocate a number of demands, and must
decide within a certain decision threshold (for example, 1 second), whether and
how the demands could be accepted. A meaningful analysis of the performance
of the heuristics we proposed would thus analyze the probability of finding a
solution within the given time limit, and compare this with the performance that
can be obtained using common methods of the networking world, in particular
shortest-path algorithms.

For comparing the efficiency of different constraint solving heuristics, it is
useful to plot their performance for problems of different tightness. In the RAIN
problem, tightness is the ratio of resources required for the best possible allocation (in terms of used bandwidth) divided by the total amount of resources
available in the network. This approximates the "constraint tightness" in the
CSP. Since it is very hard to compute the best possible allocation, we use an
approximation, the best allocation found among the methods being compared.

We generated 23'000 RAIN problems in total, each with at least one solution.
Each problem has a randomly generated network topology of 20 nodes and 38
links, and a random set of 80 demands, each demand characterized by two endpoints and a bandwidth constraint. The problems were solved with six different
strategies on a Sun Ultra 60: *basic-SP* performs a search using the shortest path
heuristic common in the networking world today, without any backtracking on
decisions; *BT-SP* incorporates backtracking to the previous in order to be able
to undo "bad" allocations. The next search methods make use of the information derived from the BIH: *BI-LL-HL* uses the LL heuristic for route generation
and DVO-HL for dynamic demand selection, whereas *BI-LL-NL* differs from the
latter in using DVO-NL for choosing the next demand to allocate. *BI-BJ-LL-HL*
and *BI-BJ-LL-NL* differ from the previous in the use of backjumping to culprit
decisions, as described in Sect. 6.

Figure 3 (a) gives the probability of finding a solution to a problem in less
than 1 second, given the tightness of the problems (as defined above). BI search
methods prove to perform much better than brute-force, even on these small
problems, where heuristic computation (and BIH maintenance) may proportion-
ally use up a lot of time. Backjumping methods show slightly better performance
over their purely backtracking counterparts. The benefits of backjumping seem
to be somewhat canceled by the computing overhead associated with calculating the culprit assignment, at least on these small problems. On problems of

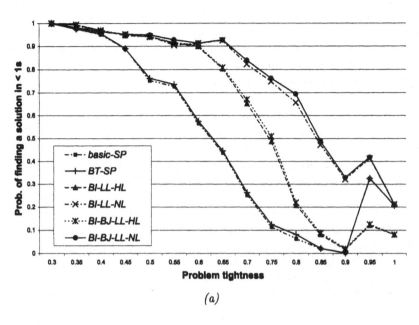

(a)

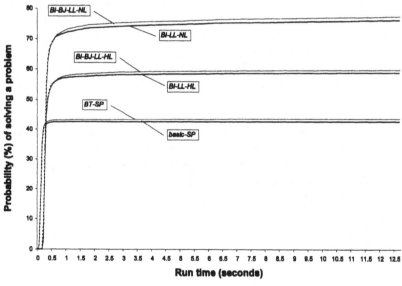

(b)

Fig. 3. Statistics on solving 23'000 randomly generated solvable problems with 20 nodes, 38 links, 80 demands each. (a) the probability of finding a solution within 1 second, given the tightness of the problems. (b) the probability of solving the problems according to run time.

much larger size, BJ algorithms do perform much better in average than their non-backjumping counterparts. Noteworthy, NL outperforms HL: NL is better at deciding which demand is the most difficult to assign, and therefore achieves a greater pruning effect. The shape of the curves are similar for larger time limits. Figure 3 (b) provides the probability of solving a problem according to run time. Two conclusions can be derived from the latter figure: first, BI methods curves continue to grow with time, albeit slowly, which is not the case for basic-SP and BT-SP; second, maintaining the BIH on these small problems does not affect the BI algorithms very much.

The quality of the solutions, in terms of network resource utilization, were about the same for all methods. However, when the solutions were different, bandwidth connectivity was generally better on those provided by BI methods.

Note that the experimental results allow quantifying the gain obtained by using our methods. If an operator wants to ensure high customer satisfaction, demands have to be accepted with high probability. This means that the network can be loaded up to the point where the allocation mechanism finds a solution with probability close to 1. From the curves in Fig. 3 (a), we can see that for the shortest-path methods, this is the case up to a load of about 40% with a probability > 0.9, whereas the NL heuristic allows a load of up to about 65%. Using this technique, an operator can thus reduce the capacity of the network by an expected 38% without a decrease in the quality of service provided to the customer!

According to phase transition theory [13], relative performance can be expected to scale in the same way to large networks. This is corroborated by first results on larger problems. We generated 800 different RAIN problems with 38 nodes, 107 links, and 1200 demands. The probability of solving such a problem according to run time is given in Fig. 4. Here, we see that the maintenance of the BIH has a larger effect on solving "easy" problems. However, after 20 seconds of run time the BI methods clearly are more efficient than the non-BI techniques. The facts noticed for the smaller problems (in Fig. 3) remain valid: NL outperforms HL, even if it requires slightly more run-time, and backjumping brings only a small advantage over their non-backjumping counterparts.

Further, as another result, BI-BJ-LL-NL solved a much larger RAIN problem (50 nodes, 171 links, and 3'000 demands) in 4.5 minutes. BT-SP was not able to solve it within 12 hours.

8   Conclusion

Much research in AI has focused on efficient algorithms to search for answers to problems posed in a particular way. However, intelligence not only involves answering questions, but also *asking* the right questions. It has long been observed that the complexity of finding a solution by search can depend heavily on how it is formulated. It is surprising how little attention has been paid to methods for putting search problems in a suitable form.

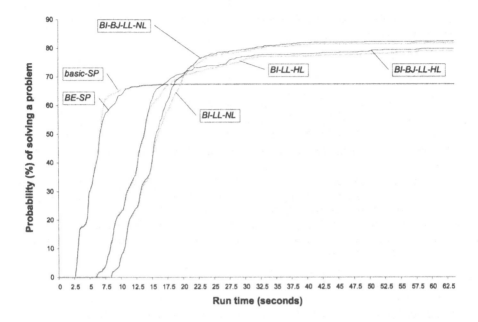

Fig. 4. The probability of solving a problem according to run time (800 problems, with 38 nodes, 107 links, 1200 demands).

In order to obtain general results in this direction, it is important to first consider techniques for *particular* difficult problems. In this paper, we have shown a dynamic abstraction technique for such a problem, resource allocation in networks (RAIN).

The next step will be to generalize this result to a larger class of problems with similar characteristics. For example, in techniques such as Graphplan [14], plans become paths in a graph. When many plans must be executed in parallel while sharing resources, for example in a factory, finding a suitable combination of plans again becomes a RAIN problem. Among other such problems are frequency allocation in radio networks, product configuration, and road traffic planning. We can hope to eventually develop quite general techniques for deciding when good abstractions are possible, and also for generating them.

Acknowledgments

This work is partly a result of the IMMuNe (Integrated Management for Multimedia Networks) Project, supported by the Swiss National Science Foundation (FNRS) under grant 5003-045311. The authors are grateful to Dean Allemang, Beat Liver, Steven Willmott, and Monique Calisti for their invaluable comments, suggestions, and encouragements during the last years. The authors also wish to thank George Melissargos and Pearl Pu for their work on the graphical interface of the developed tool. A special thank also to the reviewers for their help to improve this paper.

References

[1] Zheng Wang and Jon Crowcroft. Quality-of-Service Routing for Supporting Multimedia Applications. *IEEE Journal on Selected Areas in Communications*, 14(7):1228–1234, September 1996.

[2] Edward Tsang. *Foundations of Constraint Satisfaction*. Academic Press, London, UK, 1993.

[3] Bruno T. Messmer. A framework for the development of telecommunications network planning, design and optimization applications. Technical Report FE520.02078.00 F, Swisscom, Bern, Switzerland, 1997.

[4] Jason W. Mann and George D. Smith. A Comparison of Heuristics for Telecommunications Traffic Routing. In *Modern Heuristic Search Methods*, John Wiley & Sons Ltd, 235–254, 1996.

[5] Berthe Y. Choueiry and Boi Faltings. A Decomposition Heuristic for Resource Allocation. In *Proc. of the 11 th ECAI*, pages 585–589, Amsterdam, The Netherlands, 1994.

[6] Rainer Weigel and Boi V. Faltings. Structuring Techniques for Constraint Satisfaction Problems. In *Proceedings of the 15th International Joint Conference on Artificial Intelligence (IJCAI-97)*, pages 418–423, San Francisco, August 1997, Morgan Kaufmann Publishers.

[7] E.C. Freuder and D. Sabin. Interchangeability Supports Abstraction and Reformulation for Multi-Dimensional Constraint Satisfaction. In *Proc. of AAAI-97*, pages 191–196, Providence, Rhode Island, 1997.

[8] Symposium on Abstraction, Reformulation and Approximation (SARA-98). Supported in Part by AAAI, Asilomar Conference Center, Pacific Grove, California, May 1998.

[9] Christian Frei and Boi Faltings. A Dynamic Hierarchy of Intelligent Agents for Network Management. In *2nd Int. W. on Intelligent Agents for Telecommunications Applications, IATA '98*, pages 1–16, Paris, France, July 1998. Lecture Notes in Artificial Intelligence, Springer-Verlag.

[10] Christian Frei and Boi Faltings. Bandwidth allocation heuristics in communication networks. In *1ères Rencontres Francophones sur les Aspects Algorithmiques des Télécommunications, ALGOTEL'99*, pages 53–58, Roscoff, France, 1999.

[11] R. M. Haralick and G. L. Elliott. Increasing Tree Search Efficiency for Constraint Satisfaction Problems. *Artificial Intelligence*, 14:263–313, 1980.

[12] J. Gaschnig. Experimental case studies of Backtrack vs. Waltz-type new algorithms. In *Proceedings 2-nd Biennial Conf. Canadian Society for Computational Study of Intelligence*, Toronto, Ontario, July 1978.

[13] Peter Cheeseman and Bob Kanefsky and William M. Taylor. Where the Really Hard Problems Are. In *Proc. of the 12 th IJCAI*, pages 331–337, Sidney, Australia, 1991.

[14] Avrim Blum and Merrick Furst. Fast Planning Through Planning Graph Analysis. *Artificial Intelligence*, 90:281–300, 1997.

Optimal Distributed Arc-Consistency

Youssef Hamadi

LIRMM UMR 5506 CNRS-UMII
161, Rue Ada, 34392 Montpellier Cedex 5, France
hamadi@lirmm.fr

Abstract. This paper presents *DisAC-9*, the first optimal distributed algorithm performing the arc-consistency of a constraint network. Our method is optimal according to the number of message passing operations. This algorithm can firstly, give speedup over the fastest central arc-consistency algorithms. Secondly, achieve the fast processing of distributed constraint satisfaction problems (DCSP). Experimental results use classical benchmarks and large hard randoms problems. These results allow us to give the first characterization of the hardest instances of this distributed computation.

1 Introduction

The constraint satisfaction problem (CSP) is a powerful framework for general problem solving. It involves finding a solution to a constraint network, i.e., finding one of d values for n variables subject to constraints that are restrictions on which combinations of values are acceptable. It is widely used in artificial intelligence (AI), its applications ranging from machine vision to crew scheduling and many other fields (see [1] for a survey). Since it is an NP-complete task, many filtering techniques have been designed. These methods reduce the problem search space by pruning the set of possible values. Owing to their interesting complexities, arc-consistency algorithms which detect and eliminate inconsistencies involving all pairs of variables are widely used [2].

In the last years, the distributed constraint satisfaction (DCSP) paradigm emerges from the necessity of solving distributed AI problems. These distributed problems are more and more crucial because of the wide distribution of informations allowed by Internet facilities. So several authors tried to bring classical CSP procedures to the distributed framework [3,4].

More relevant works on distributed arc-filtering were brought by P. R. Cooper and M. J. Swain who proposed in [5] two massively parallel (nd processes) versions of AC-4 [6]. More recently, T. Nguyen and Y. Deville [7] distributed AC-4 in a more realistic framework since their granularity varies from 1 to n process(es).

Nevertheless all these works do not address the real difficulty of distributed systems which is the complexity of message passing operations. S. Kasif who has studied the complexity of parallel relaxation [8] concludes that discrete relaxation is inherently a sequential process. This means that due to dependencies between deletions, a distributed/parallel algorithm is likely to perform a lot of messages since it is likely to perform in a sequential fashion.

We have learned from all the previous works and focused our work on message passing reduction. Our DisAC-9 algorithm is optimal in the number of message passing operations. This major improvement over the previous works was possible by the exploitation of the bidirectionality property of constraint relations which allows agents to induce acquaintances deletions. Since bidirectionality is a general property of constraints, DisAC-9 is a general purpose algorithm. Worst time complexity is $O(n^2d^3)$ which allows us to reach optimality in message operations, nd. According to that, our method can achieve the fast processing of DCSPs and even give major speed-up in the processing of large CSPs.

The paper is organized as follows. We first give background about constraints, arc-consistency and message passing in section 2. Section 3 presents previous works. Then we present the centralized algorithm AC-6. Next we introduce our distributed algorithm, DisAC-9. Theoretical analysis follows in section 6. Before concluding, we present experimental results in section 7.

2 Definitions

2.1 Constraint and arc-consistency background

A *binary CSP*, $P = (\mathcal{X}, \mathcal{D}, \mathcal{C})$ involves, $\mathcal{X}$ a set of n variables $\{i, j, ...\}$, $\mathcal{D} = \{D_i, D_j, ...\}$ where each element is a variable's domain, $\mathcal{C}$ the set of binary constraints $\{C_{ij}, ...\}$ where C_{ij} is a constraint between i and j. $C_{ij}(a, b) = true$ means that the association value a for i and b for j is allowed. A *solution* to a constraint satisfaction problem is an instantiation of the variables in a way that all the constraints are satisfied. A constraint network (CN) $\mathcal{G} = (\mathcal{X}, \mathcal{C})$ can be associated to any binary CSP.

Each element of a domain represents a *value*. A *label* (i, a) is the instantiation of the value a to the variable i. It is supported by a value b along C_{ij} iff $C_{ij}(a, b) = true$, b is called a *support* for a along C_{ij}. The value a is also a support for b along C_{ji}. A value a from D_i is *viable* iff $\forall C_{ij}$, there exists a support b for a in D_j. The domain $\mathcal{D}$ of a constraint network is *arc-consistent* for this CN if for every variable i, all values in D_i are viable. The maximal arc-consistent domain $Dmax$-AC of a constraint network is defined as the union of all domains included in $\mathcal{D}$ and arc-consistent for this CN. This maximal domain is also *arc-consistent* and is computed by an arc-consistency algorithm.

2.2 Distributed constraint satisfaction background

A *binary distributed CSP*, $P = (\mathcal{X}, \mathcal{D}, \mathcal{C}, \mathcal{A})$ involves a binary CSP, $(\mathcal{X}, \mathcal{D}, \mathcal{C})$ partitioned among $\mathcal{A}$, a set of p autonomous agents $(1 \leq p \leq n)$. Each agent owns the domains/constraints on its variables. An agent that owns variable i owns D_i, and the binary constraints C_{ij}.

We assume the following communication model [3]. Agents communicate by sending messages. An agent can send messages to other agents *iff* he knows their addresses in the network. For the transmission between any pair of agents, messages are received in the order in which they were sent. The delay in delivering messages is finite.

For readers unfamiliar with exchanges in distributed systems, we present in table 1 the real data transmission costs for some nowadays parallel computers [9]. In common local area networks (LAN), these costs are orders of magnitudes largers. These values are computed in an empty communication network, this means that these are lower bounds values. In real systems, the more you send messages, the more it takes time to achieve transmissions.

Table 1. The real cost of message passing operations

	iPSC	nCUBE/10	iPSC/2	nCUBE/2	iPSC/860	CM-5
T_s [μs/msg]	4100	400	700	160	160	86
T_b [μs/byte]	2.8	2.6	0.36	0.45	0.36	0.12
T_{fp} [μs/flop]	25	8.3	3.4	0.50	0.033	0.33

The line T_s represents the *start-up* cost of a message, T_b is the per/byte cost. We give as a reference point, T_{fp} which is the cost of one floating point operation on the machines. Each message reception brings to a cost, generally this cost is similar to T_s. So the estimated cost for a message m is, $\geq 2 * T_s + |m| * T_b$.

3 Previous works

We emphasize previous works performing distributed arc-filtering here. We do not present works which use the PRAM machine model like [10] since this model is not representative of current computing facilities which all use the message passing paradigm. We also do not present works which are not based on optimal central method [11]. In table 2 we summarize the headlines of 3 methods. These methods propose a distributed implementation of the AC-4 sequential algorithm. The #ps column gives the granularities, *first step* gives the complexity of the first step of the methods since these are two step procedures like the central AC-4. Then, *complexity* gives the methods full complexities and #msg the number of message passing operations required by a worst case execution.

Informally a distributed algorithm is *local*, if its messages transmissions are limited i.e. its transmissions do not involve the whole processes. This definition of locality is sufficient for our use. For a comprehensive work on locality in distributed systems, see [12]. The column *local* specifies if a method is local.

AC Chip This algorithm presented in [5] defines a VLSI circuit. It uses a very fine granularity and it does not use explicit message passing operations. Both allows a pretty good complexity. Nevertheless it would need $O(n^2 d^2)$ initializing steps for loading the network in the digital chip.

Table 2. Distributed arc-consistency algorithms

Algo.	#ps	first step	complexity	#msg	local
AC Chip	nd	nd	$O(nd)$	-	-
ACP	nd	nd	$O(nd \log_2(nd))$	$n^2 d^2$	no
DisAC-4	$1 \leq p \leq n$	$(n^2 d^2)/p$	$O((n^2 d^2)/p)$	nd	no

ACP This is the software version of the previous algorithm [5]. It uses nd synchronous processes which communicate by messages operations. Each message is sent with $O(\log_2(nd))$ steps and is received by the whole processes (excepted the sender). The method is not local.

DisAC-4 This coarse grain method uses p processes [7] sharing an Ethernet network. This allows "efficient" broadcasting of messages between processes. Nevertheless, this brings to an underlying synchronism since "collision networks" cannot carry more than one message in a given time. If we consider a more realist framework for the method, each broadcast requires p messages which brings to $n^2 d$ messages.

4 The arc-consistency algorithm AC-6

We briefly describe here Bessière's AC-6 algorithm [13]. This method introduces a total ordering between values in each domain, it computes one support (the first one) for each label (i, a) on each constraint C_{ij}. That to make sure of the current viability of (i, a). When (j, b) is found as the smallest support of (i, a) on C_{ij}, (i, a) is added to S_{jb} the list of values currently having (j, b) as smallest support. Then, if (j, b) is deleted, AC-6 looks for a new support in D_j for all values in S_{jb}. During this search, the method only checks values greater than b. The algorithm incrementally computes support for each label on each constraint relation. On average cases, it performs less checks than AC-4 whose the initialization step globally computes and stores the whole support relations.

In the following, we adapt this incremental behavior to our distributed framework, moreover we drastically improve efficiency by reaching optimality in the messages transmissions.

5 The distributed arc-consistency algorithm DisAC-9

The key steps of this new distributed algorithm are the following. According to local knowledge, each agent that owns a set of variables starts computing inconsistent labels. After this computation, *selected labels* are transmitted. This means that only the deleted labels that induce new deletions are sent to an acquaintance. After this initializing step, each agent starts the processing of incoming messages. These messages will modify its local knowledge about related acquaintances. This will allow it to update support information for its labels. Naturally, this can lead to new deletions and maybe to new outcoming messages. Since communications occurs between acquaintances agents which are defined by agents that share binary constraints, DisAC-9 is local (see section 3).

5.1 Minimal message passing

Constraints bidirectionality allows agents to partially share acquaintances knowledge: since $C_{ij}(a,b) = C_{ji}(b,a)$, an agent owning i but not owning j knows any C_{ji} relations. This knowledge can be used to infere over acquaintances deletions.

More generally, *agent-1* currently deleting (i,a) computes for any acquaintance *agent-2*, labels (j,b) having (i,a) as support. If another local value (i,a') can support (j,b), it is useless to inform *agent-2* for (i,a) deletion. Otherwise, *agent-2* must delete (j,b) as an outcome of the deletion of (i,a). It must be informed of the local deletion.

5.2 A complete example

Figure 1 illustrates this on a particular DCSP, in this problem, two agents share a constraint C_{12}. The constraint relation is represented in the left part of the figure by the micro-structure graph. In this graph, allowed pairs of values are linked. In the right part, we represent the support relation computed by the two agents. An arrow goes from value a to value b if b supports a.

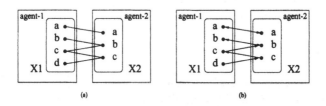

(a)   (b)

Fig. 1. Message minimizing in a DCSP

For *agent-1*, support lists are the following, $S_{2a} = \{(1,a)\}$, $S_{2b} = \{(1,b),(1,c)\}$ and $S_{2c} = \{(1,d)\}$. The second agent, *agent-2* computes $S_{1a} = \{(2,a)\}$, $S_{1b} = \{(2,b)\}$, $S_{1c} = \{(2,c)\}$ and $S_{1d} = \{\}$.

An extra data structure is used during the message minimization process. $first_j[i][a] = b$ tracks that according to C_{ij}, (j,b) is the first label supporting (i,a) in D_j. The *first* table of agent-1 contains the following values, $first_2[1][a] = a$, $first_2[1][b] = b$, $first_2[1][c] = b$, $first_2[1][d] = c$. For agent-2, $first_1[2][a] = a$, $first_1[2][b] = b$ and $first_1[2][c] = c$.

224

Assuming the loss of $(1, c)$ (according to some incoming event) let us consider the information of *agent-2* about this deletion. We can just consider in D_2 values greater or equal to $first_2[1][c]$, the first support for $(1, c)$. Among these values, we must check the ones possibly supported by $(1, c)$. We find $(2, b)$ and $(2, c)$. For $(2, b)$ we determine $(1, b)$ as possible support and for $(2, c)$ we find $(1, d)$. According to these local computations, *agent-1* states that any message about $(1, c)$ deletion is useless. Such a message could update *agent-2* knowledge but it cannot lead to new domain reductions.

Now assuming the loss of $(1, b)$, we detect that $(2, b)$ must be deleted by *agent-2* since there are no more supports in D_1. Hence, we must send deletion information to *agent-2*. But if we only inform for $(1, b)$ deletion, *agent-2* by considering S_{1b} will compute $(1, c)$ as new support for $(2, b)$ since it is always assuming $(1, c)$ as a viable value. One solution is to inform for all previous deletions. In this example, *agent-1* informs in the same message for deletion of $(1, b)$ and $(1, c)$. As a result *agent-2* will delete $(2, b)$ but it will not inform for this deletion *agent-1* since the agent knows that $(1, b)$ was deleted. It will remove $(2, c)$ from S_{1c} and add it to S_{1d}.

This example shows that by performing more local computations, an agent can avoid outcoming messages. This exchange between local work and message transmissions is quite interesting in a distributed environment (see table 1).

5.3 Algorithm

After this illustration, we present the related algorithm. Our distributed system contains $1 \le p \le n$ autonomous agents (cf. 2.2) (plus an extra agent performing termination detection see section 6).

The knowledge of agent k $(1 \le k \le p)$ is represented/handled by the following data structures/primitives.

Data structures

- *Acquaintances*, agents sharing constraints with k are referenced in this set
- *localVar*, this set stores the variables for k
- *localD_i* this set stores the current domain of i $(\forall i \in localVar)$
- *localM_i* boolean state vector, keeps tracks of deleted values from the initial domain D_i $(\forall i \in localVar)$
- *linkedVar*, this set stores the non local variables which are linked to local variables by a constraint relation
  $linkedVar=\{i \in \mathcal{X}, \text{tq } i \notin localVar \text{ and } \exists j \in localVar \text{ tq } C_{ij} \in \mathcal{C}\}$
- *linkedM_i* boolean state vector, keeps track of external variables deleted labels, $(\forall i \in linkedVar)$
- A set of lists, $S_{jb} = \{(i, a) | a \in D_i \text{ and } b \text{ is the smallest value in } D_j \text{ supporting } (i, a)\}$
- *first* an integer table, $first_j[i][a] = b$ tracks that according to C_{ij}, (j, b) is the first label supporting (i, a)

- *localList, extList*, these lists store the deleted labels, the second one is used for external propagation
- *sendSet*, vector of sets, stores outcoming deletions informations
- *inform*, boolean table, $inform_{acc}[i]$ means that *acc* has been selected for $localD_i$ transmission

Constant time primitives

- *affected(j)* returns the acquaintances that owns the variable j. *owns(A,i)* returns *true* if agent A owns the variable i
- *higher(D)* returns the last element of the domain D. if $D = \emptyset$ returns -1. *next(a,M)*, M is a state vector, returns the smallest indice *ind*, greater than a | M[ind]=true
- *get(S)* returns the first element from S. *addTo(S,a)* inserts a in S. *emptyP(S)* returns *true* if S is empty
- *localDUpdate(i,a)* this primitive realizes severals important updates. It removes the value a from $localD_i$ then it stores this deletion in $localM_i$ ($localM_i[a] \leftarrow false$). After performing these updates, the method checks the size of $localD_i$. If ($localD_i = \emptyset$), a *stop* message is broadcasted to the whole processes and termination occurs with the detection of problem inconsistency

Message passing primitives

- *getMsg()* blocking instruction, returns the first incoming message
- *broadcast(m, P)* the message m is broadcasted to processes in the set P, it uses $O(log_2(|P| + 1)$ operations

Each agent starts with a call to the *main* procedure (see algo. 1). This procedure has two steps. In the first one, agent's knowledge allows the filtering of local domains. For each local variable i, each value a in $localD_i$ is checked for viability. To achieve this test, agent looks for support for each related constraint C_{ij}. The *nextSupport* procedure (see algo. 3) looks for the first support according to C_{ij}. If this procedure returns with *emptySupport=false*, then b is the first support for (i, a) in D_j. We can add (i, a) to local support list S_{jb} and update *first* for later use (lines 9 and 10). Otherwise, (i, a) is non-viable. A call to *localDUpdate* (line 6) removes this label and test for domain wipe-out. Then the deletion is stored in both *localList* and *extList* (lines 7,8).

At the end of this initialization step, the *main* procedure processes deletions by calling *processLists* (see line 11). This procedure first, uses *localList* for the local propagation of deletions. This is done by calling the *deletionProcessing* procedure (see algo. 4) for each deleted label (j, e). This algorithm, removes labels (i, a) from S_{je}, then for each viable one ($a \in localD_i$), a call to *nextSupport* looks for a new support (j, c) greater than (j, e). If such a new support is found, (i, a) is added to S_{jc}. Otherwise, the procedure updates $localD_i$ and stores (i, a) in both *localList* and *extList* (lines 2,3,4).

Algorithm 1: DisAC-9 main

```
      begin
          localList ← ∅; extList ← ∅
          for each i ∈ localVar do
1             localD_i ← D_i
2             for each a ∈ D_i do localM_i[a] ← true; S_{ia} ← ∅
          for each j ∈ linkedVar do
3             for each a ∈ D_j do linkedM_j[a] ← true; S_{ja} ← ∅
4             for each i ∈ localVar do
                  for each a ∈ D_i do first_j[i][a] ← 0

          %
          % first step, init. supports
          for each arc (i,j) | i ∈ localVar do
              for each a ∈ localD_i do
                  b ← 0
5                 nextSupport(j,i,a,b,emptySupport)
                  if emptySupport then
6                     localDUpdate (i,a)
7                     addTo (localList, (i,a))
8                     addTo (extList, (i,a))
                  else
9                     addTo (S_{jb}, (i,a))
10                    if j ∈ linkedVar then first_j[i][a] ← b

          % internal and external propagations
11        processLists (localList, extList)
          %
          % second step, interactions
          termination ← false
          while !termination do
12            m ← getMsg()
              switch m do
13                case stop
                      termination ← true
14                case deletedLabels:set
                      while !emptyP(set) do
15                        (j, M_j) ← get(set)
                          for each a ∈ D_j do
16                            if linkedM_j[a] ≠ M_j[a] then
17                                linkedM_j[a] ← false
18                                addTo (localList, (j,a))

19                    processLists (localList, extList)

      end
```

After these local propagations, *processLists* considers each locally deleted label from *extList*. For each label (j, e), a call to *selectiveSend* allows the agent to find which acquaintances to inform.

The *selectiveSend* procedure implements the previously detailed minimizing. While considering the deleted label (i, a), it finds for each non local variable j such that C_{ij} exists, the acquaintance *acc* that owns j (see line 2). Then, if *acc* has not be previously selected for $localD_i$ transmission ($inform_{acc}[i] = false$), it considers labels (j, b) supported by (i, a). Otherwise it is useless to check $localD_i$ transmission to *acc*.

We start the exploration of these labels by checking the current support of (i, a) ($first_j[i][a]$) since it is useless to consider previous labels (line 4). Two

Algorithm 2: DisAC-9 processLists

Algorithm: processLists(in-out: *localList*, *extList*)

begin

1   for *each* $j \in Acquaintances$ do
      for *each* $i \in localVar \mid \exists k \in linkedVar$ and owns(j,k) and C_{ik} do
2         $inform_j[i] \leftarrow false$

3   while *!emptyP(localList)* do
      $(j, e) \leftarrow$ get(*localList*)
4   deletionProcessing (j,e)

   while *!emptyP(extList)* do
5      $(j, e) \leftarrow$ get(*extList*)
6   selectiveSend (*j, e, sendSet*)

7   for *each* $j \in Acquaintances$ do
      if $sendSet_j \neq \emptyset$ then broadcast (*j, deletedLabels : sendSet_j*)

end

Algorithm 3: DisAC-9 nextSupport

Algorithm: nextSupport(in: *j,i,a*; in-out: *b*; out: *emptySupport*)

begin

1   if $b \leq higher(D_j)$ then
2   if $j \in localVar$ then $stateVector \leftarrow localM_j$
      else $stateVector \leftarrow linkedM_j$
3   while *!stateVector[b]* do b++
      $emptySupport \leftarrow false$
4   while *!emptySupport* and $!C_{ij}(a,b)$ do
         if $b < higher(D_j)$ then $b \leftarrow next(b, stateVector)$
         else $emptySupport \leftarrow true$
   else $emptySupport \leftarrow true$

end

boolean are used, $endD_j$ is used to stop checking against j values, *selected* is set to stop checking against *acc*.

Among j values, we can restrict to viable ones ($linkedM_j[b]=true$) (line 6). Then if $C_{ij}(a,b)$ holds *true*, the procedure looks for another possible support (i,a'). If there is no (i,a') label such that $C_{ij}(a',b)$, *acc* is selected for message transmission (line 9). We add the pair $(i, localM_i)$ in $sendSet_{acc}$. This inclusion of the current domain of i allows the transmission of previously non informed labels deletions. Of course this can lead to long messages but the sizes of messages are not prohibitives comparing to their start-up costs (see table 1).

After these computations, *processLists* respectively addresses its *sendSet* set to each acquaintance (line 7).

The second step of the *main* procedure allows agents to revise their knowledge according to incoming messages (line 12). There are two kinds. The *stop* messages which stop the processing. These messages can result from both a domain wipe-out (see *localDUpdate* primitive) or can be addressed by an extra agent, called *System*. This agent is in charge of global termination detection. In our system, we use a global state detection algorithm [14]. So global termination occurs with a domain wipe-out or when the p agents are waiting for a message and when no message transits in the communication network.

Algorithm 4: DisAC-9 deletionProcessing

Algorithm: deletionProcessing(in: j,e; in-out: $localList, extList$)

```
begin
    while !emptyP(S_je) do
        (i, a) ← get(S_je)
1       if a ∈ localD_i then
            c ← e + 1
            nextSupport(j, i, a, c, emptySupport)
            if emptySupport then
2               localDUpdate (i, a)
3               addTo (localList, (i, a))
4               addTo (extList, (i, a))
            else
                addTo (S_jc, (i, a))
5               if j ∈ linkedVar then first_j[i][a] ← c
end
```

Algorithm 5: DisAC-9 selectiveSend

Algorithm: selectiveSend(in : (i, a); in-out : $sendSet$)

```
begin
1   for each arc (i, j) | j ∈ linkedVar do
2       acc ← affected(j)
3       if !inform_acc[i] then
4           b ← first_j[i][a]
            endD_j ← false
            selected ← false
5           while !selected and !endD_j and b ≤ higher(D_j) do
6               if linkedM_j[b] and C_ij(a, b) then
                    endD_i ← false
                    otherSupport ← false
                    a' ← 0
7                   while !otherSupport and !endD_i and a' ≤ higher(localD_i) do
8                       if localM_i[a'] and C_ij(a', b) then otherSupport ← true
                        else
                            if a' < higher(localD_i) then a' ← next(a', localD_i)
                            else endD_i ← true
9                   if !otherSupport then selected ← true
10              if b < higher(D_j) then b ← next(b, D_j)
                else endD_j ← true
11          if selected then
12              addTo (sendSet_acc, (i, localM_i))
13              inform_acc[i] ← true
end
```

The processing of incoming deletions messages (*deletedLabels:set*) starts with line 14. Remember that agents receive a set of pairs $(j, localD_j)$. They temporary store these pairs in (j, M_j). Then by comparing their local beliefs stored in $linkedM_j$ and the new reported situation they can detect new deletions (line 16). Agents store these new deletions and add them in their own *localList*. After considering the whole incoming *set*, a call to *processLists* allows the local propagation of externals deletions.

6 Analysis

6.1 Complexities

The worst time execution of a distributed algorithm occurs when it proceeds with a sequential behavior. With our DisAC-9, this occurs when only one value is deleted at a time. This leads to nd successive deletions between $p = n$ processes. In $O(nd^2)$ our *selectiveSend* procedure allows the detection of the unique outcome of each deletion. While receiving a deletion message each agent updates $linkedM[j]$ in $O(d)$, then *processLists* leads to one call to *deletionProcessing*. The S_{je} list contains exactly one label and *nextSupport* uses $O(d)$ steps in search of a new support. So each deletion conducts to $O(nd^2 + d)$ constant time operations. Since there are $O(nd)$ successive deletions, the overall time complexity is $O(n^2 d^3)$ with exactly nd point-to-point messages.

With n variables, each one using d values, each agent data structures use $O(nd)$ space. Since there are n agents in the worst case, the total amount of space is $O(n^2 d)$.

6.2 Termination

Termination is detected by the System agent, this agent performs a classical global detection state algorithm [14]. With our system it detects a situation where each agent is waiting for an incoming message and no message transit between agents. Domain wipe-out is another case of algorithm termination (see *localDUpdate*).

6.3 Correctness and message passing optimality

We present here the main steps of complete proofs (see [15] for proofs). For correctness we must ensure at the termination. (i) $\forall a \in localD_i, (i, a) \in Dmax$-$AC$, this can be achieved by considering the deletions made by the algorithm. (ii) $\forall (i, a) \in Dmax$-AC, $a \in localD_i$, suppose that a current deletion (j, b) is in $Dmax$-AC, then, an inductive proof which suppose that all the previous deletions are out of $Dmax$-AC, gives (j, b) out of $Dmax$-AC.

For optimality, we must show that
(i) each *deletedLabels* message induces at least a label deletion for the receiver. This is exactly what is checked by the *selectiveSend* procedure.
(ii) each label suppression made during the interactions step is the outcome of an incoming *deletedLabels* message. We must observe that during the second step, deletions are made by *deletionProcessing* which is called by *processLists* which is always called for the processing of a *deletedLabels* message.

230

7 Experimentations

We have made ours experiments on an *IBM sp2* supercomputer[1] (*C++* language and *MPI* message passing library). We have used two algorithms against DisAC-9. First the sequential AC-6 to assess distribution benefits. Then to strictly evaluate our message minimizing we have built a modified version of our algorithm called DisAC-6 which does not use our minimizing method:

- each deleted label (i, a) is selected for diffusion to *acc* if this agent owns a variable j such that C_{ij} exists
- *sendSet* are composed of (j, a) labels so reception of deletions messages is straight forward ($linkedM[j][a] \leftarrow false$ and *localList* inclusion).

This simplified implementation has a worst time complexity $O(nd(n + d))$ requiring $n^2 d$ messages. Since all deleted labels are transmitted to acquaintances, it also allows comparisons with previous works (see section 3). Nevertheless, this new method is local since transmissions occur with respect to the CN. According to that, we think that DisAC-6 should outperform previous works.

7.1 Hard random problems

We have generated randoms problems with 90 variables, domains sizes set to 20, and connectivity p_1 set to 0.2, 0.5 and 0.8. Tightness p_2 varies from 0.1 to 0.9. For the distributed methods we set *p=90* which is the finest granularity in our framework since each agent owns one variable and *p=15* (each agent owns 6 variables). For each connectivity/tightness pair we have used 100 randoms instances.

We detail results with $p_1 = 0.5$. Figure 2 presents median time in seconds for the three algorithms. These results show the efficiency of DisAC-9[2]. With 90 agents, our procedure complexity peak is 1.06 seconds, while DisAC-6 needs up to 22.23 seconds.

Figure 3, presents the amount of *deletedLabels* messages processed in the whole system. DisAC-9 process up to 2029 messages while the second method process up to 32493 messages. Interestingly we can observe that in DisAC-9 messages transmissions start at $p_2 = 0.5$. Of course this minimizing has a cost in constraint checks (see figure 3), but it is limited to 4.41 times.

AC-6 time peak is 0.6 second while DisAC-9 with 15 agents uses up to 0.17 second. For $p2 \in \{0.71, 0.72, 0.73\}$, DisAC-9 with 90 agents is faster than AC-6.

Figure 2 allows some surprising new results. The time peaks of the methods are not located at the same tightness value. For the sequential AC-6, it occurs for $p_2 = 0.71$, for the methods using 90 agents, the time peak is located at $p_2 = 0.69$ while with 15 agents, the peak occurs at $p_2 = 0.7$. Our data results show 0%,

[1] Message passing latency is $35\mu s$, bandwidth is *90Mo/s*, each CPU is a *PowerPC* 120Mhz.
[2] We can remark that experimentations on Ethernet networks give much larger speedup since communications are slower than on the sp2.

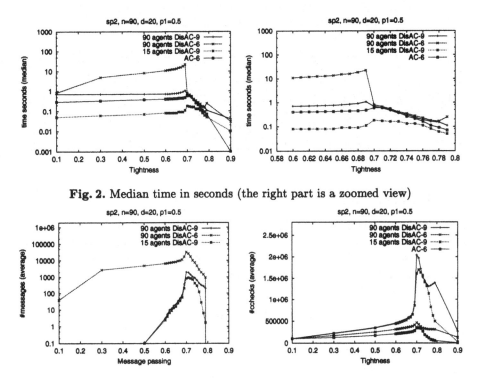

Fig. 2. Median time in seconds (the right part is a zoomed view)

Fig. 3. Message passing (left) and constraints checks (right)

11%, 88% and 100% of inconsistent instances respectively at $p_2 = 0.68$, 0.69, 0.7 and 0.71.

To give a general explanation of this phenomenon, let us consider AC-6. It checks the set of arcs in a sequential way. So if an instance is inconsistent according to the last arc (i, j), the detection is very expensive. While with our distributed methods using n agents, the two agents respectively owning i and j rapidly detect inconsistency and immediately broadcast the end of the processing. With intermediate granularities, the previous reasoning occurs. But since the methods owns severals variables and consider their arcs successively, they are less efficient in these detections. The previous explains why inconsistent instances are relatively easier for distributed methods (see [15] for a complete analysis).

Table 3 presents computational peaks results. The first table gives results with $p = 90$. The second table gives speed-up over central AC-6. For $p_1 = 0.8$, DisAC-6 exceeds sp2 message passing capacities[3] for $p_2 \geq 0.63$, so comparisons are not available with this connectivity parameter.

---

[3] Overflow in message buffering capacities.

Table 3. Random problems computational peaks results

P1	time			#msg			#ccks		
	0.2	0.5	0.8	0.2	0.5	0.8	0.2	0.5	0.8
DisAC-6 90 agents	10.52s	22.23s	-	13660.20	32493	-	206243	460272	-
DisAC-9 90 agents	0.79s	1.06s	1.50s	1663	2029	2431	761619	2.03e6	3.50e6
ratio	13.23	21	-	8.20	16	-	0.27	0.23	-
AC-6	0.28s	0.6s	0.91s	-	-	-	171370	344953	501970
DisAC-9 15 agents	0.09s	0.17s	0.25s	865.4	908.8	823.5	660964	1.69e6	2.60e6
ratio	3.06	3.53	3.64	-	-	-	0.26	0.20	0.19

7.2 The zebra problem

This classical benchmark uses 25 variables, 5 labels per variable ($n = 25, d = 5$) and 61 binary constraints. In our experimentations we have used $p \in \{2, 3, 4, 5, 10, 25\}$ which brings $11, 16, 27, 11, 43, 61$ inter-agents constraints. For each granularity we have used one hundred runs.

Table 4. The zebra problem

Algorithm	p =	1	2	3	4	5	10	25
AC-6	time	0.004s	-	-	-	-	-	-
	#msg	-	-	-	-	-	-	-
	#ccks	1161	-	-	-	-	-	-
DisAC-9	time	-	0.0052s	0.07s	0.0104s	0.0102s	0.0176s	0.0524s
	#msg	-	6	17	21.18	19.3	43.56	64.02
	#ccks	-	1463	1667.18	1815.58	1391.5	2444.58	3098.82
DisAC-6	time	-	0.008s	0.0092s	0.0096s	0.011s	0.0328s	0.1616s
	#msg	-	8	34	44.42	36.84	135.4	321
	#ccks	-	1248	1298.5	1290.06	1251.62	1347.24	1356

Table 4 gives executions results. According to the small size of this problem, distributed methods do not give any speed-up over the central algorithm. But speed-up is not our first goal since we also try to give efficient methods for distributed problems processing. As expected, DisAC-9 is faster than the other algorithm and particularly for finest granularities. We can also observe that the performance of the methods are strongly dependent of the number of inter-agents constraints.

8 Conclusion

We have provided DisAC-9, a coarsely grained distributed algorithm performing the arc-filtering of binary constraint networks. Our method is optimal in message passing operations which are critical in distributed systems[4]. DisAC-9 allows ef-

---

[4] In [15], we have extended our algorithm for achieving optimality in the number and in the size of the messages.

ficient processing of DCSP and with coarser granularity, give speed-up on the central AC-6. Surprisingly the experiments allow a characterization of computational peaks in distributed arc-consistency problems. Hard instances do not occur at the same tightness for CSP and for DCSP. Inconsistent problems are relatively easier for distributed procedures and the location of their time peaks depends of their granularities. This phenomenon requires a full theoretical study since it could allow efficient cost predictions in distributed frameworks.

As a practical extension of this work, we are combining it with a distributed search procedure. Since these kinds of combination have brought interesting results in the central framework [2], they should be studied with distributed CSPs. This will prune inconsistent parts of a distributed search space and by the way could save critical message passing operations.

References

1. Simonis, H.: A problem classification scheme for finite domain constraint solving. In: Proc. of the CP'96 workshop on Constraint Programming Applications: An Inventory and Taxonomy. (1996) 1–26
2. Sabin, D., Freuder, E.C.: Contradicting conventional wisdom in constraint satisfaction. In: ECAI. (1994) 125–129
3. Yokoo, M., Hirayama, K.: Distributed breakout algorithm for solving distributed constraint satisfaction problems. In: ICMAS. (1996) 401–408
4. Hamadi, Y., Bessière, C., Quinqueton, J.: Backtracking in distributed constraint networks. In: ECAI. (1998) 219–223
5. Cooper, P.R., Swain, M.J.: Arc consistency: Parallelism and domain dependence. AI **58** (1992) 207–235
6. Mohr, R., Henderson, T.C.: Arc and path consistency revisited. Artificial Intelligence **28** (1986) 225–233
7. Nguyen, T., Deville, Y.: A distributed arc-consistency algorithm. In: First Int. Workshop on concurrent Constraint Satisfaction. (1995)
8. Kasif, S.: On the parallel complexity of discrete relaxation in constraint satisfaction networks. AI **45** (1990) 275–286
9. Culler, D.E., Liu, L.T., Martin, R.P., Yoshikawa, C.: LogP performance assessment of fast network interfaces. IEEE Micro (1996)
10. Samal, A., Henderson, T.: Parallel consistent labeling algorithms. Int. J. Parallel Program. **16** (1987) 341–364
11. Prosser, P., Conway, C., Muller, C.: A distributed constraint maintenance system. In: Proc. of the 12th Int. Conf. on AI. (1992) 221–231
12. Naor, M., Stockmeyer, L.: What can be computed locally ? SIAM J. Comput. **24** (1995) 1259–1277
13. Bessière, C.: Arc-consistency and arc-consistency again. Artificial Intelligence **65** (1994) 179–190
14. Chandy, K.M., Lamport, L.: Distributed snapshots: Determining global states of distributed systems. TOCS **3** (1985) 63–75
15. Hamadi, Y.: Traitement des problèmes de satisfaction de contraintes distribués. PhD thesis, Université Montpellier II (1999) (in french).

The Goldilocks Problem*

Tudor Hulubei and Eugene C. Freuder

Department of Computer Science
University of New Hampshire
Durham, NH, 03824, USA
tudor,ecf@cs.unh.edu

Abstract. A lot of work in constraint satisfaction has been focused on finding solutions to difficult problems. Many real life problems however, while not extremely complicated, have a huge number of solutions, few of which are acceptable from a practical standpoint. In this paper we will present a value ordering heuristic that attempts to guide the search towards solutions that are acceptable. More specifically, by considering the weights assigned to values and pairs of values, the heuristic will guide the search towards solutions for which the total weight is within an acceptable interval.

1 Introduction

"So away upstairs she went to the bedroom, and there she saw three beds. There was a very big bed for Father bear, but it was far too high. The middle-sized bed for Mother bear was better, but too soft. She went to the teeny, weeny bed of Baby bear and it was just right." – Goldilocks and the Three Bears.

Many practical problems have search spaces so huge that searching them exhaustively is impossible in practice. We have a lot more options to consider than Goldilocks did, and since we don't know if any of them will be exactly right, we are willing to be somewhat flexible about our interpretation of "just right", and stop our testing when we find one that is "close enough". When solutions can be ranked along a certain dimension, we may want to look for solutions at a desired point along that scale. There may not be a solution at that exact point, or it may be too costly to search until we find an exact match, so we are willing to specify a tolerance range around that point in which to search. We will present an algorithm that is good at finding a solution within such a range.

Most search algorithms use heuristics to guide the search towards those regions of the search space that are believed to contain solutions. The most common types of heuristics are variable and value ordering heuristics. When solving a particular class of problem, in addition to relying on general purpose heuristics (like `min-domain`), class-specific heuristics can be used in order to take advantage of the structure of the class at hand. In this paper we will describe a value

---

* This material is based on work supported by Oracle Corporation and by the National Science Foundation under Grant No. IRI-9504316.

ordering heuristic that can be used for a particular class of binary constraint satisfaction problems where each value in the domain of a variable and each allowed pair of values in a constraint has an associated weight. An earlier version of this paper appeared as [4].

2 Example

The following example will give a short preview of the things that are going to be discussed in the next sections. Consider a small problem consisting of three variables and two constraints (Fig.1). Both the values in the domain of a variable, and the pairs of values in a constraint have an associated weight, because the goodness of a solution is usually influenced by both the quality of the components and the way they are interconnected.

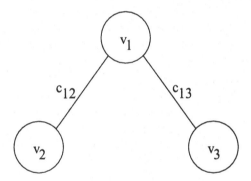

Fig. 1. Small example (weights are given in *italics*):
$v_1=\{0=0.2,1=0.8\}$, $v_2=\{1=0.1,2=0.7\}$, $v_3=\{-1=0.8,4=0.9\}$,
$c_{12}=\{(0,1)=0.1,(1,1)=0.7,(1,2)=0.9\}$, $c_{13}=\{(0,-1)=0.2,(0,4)=0.3,(1,-1)=0.5\}$

The weight of a solution to this problem is defined as the sum of the weights of all the values and pairs of values involved in the solution. We can easily see that $v_1=\{1\}$, $v_2=\{1\}$ and $v_3=\{-1\}$ is a solution to our problem, and its weight is $(0.8+0.1+0.8)+(0.7+0.5)=2.9$.

We can compute lower and upper bounds for the solution weight, by summing up the minimum and maximum weights in each variable and constraint. In our example, the lower bound is $MinSW=(0.2+0.1+0.8)+(0.1+0.2)=1.4$, and the upper bound is $MaxSW=(0.8+0.7+0.9)+(0.9+0.5)=3.8$. That is, no solution weight can be smaller than MinSW or greater than MaxSW. As we will see next, MinSW and MaxSW are theoretical limits, i.e. solutions with these weights might not exist.

3 Definitions

Let $P = \{V, C\}$ be a constraint satisfaction problem with a set of variables $V = \{v_i | v_i$ a variable involved in $P\}$, and a set of constraints $C = \{c_{ij} | c_{ij}$ a constraint between v_i and $v_j\}$. For each $v_i \in V$ we define $domain(v_i) = \{x_{ik} | x_{ik}$ is a value that can be assigned to v_i, with $1 \leq k \leq |domain(v_i)|\}$. Each value x_{ik} has an associated weight $w_{ik}^v \in [0, 1]$.

Each constraint c_{ij} defines a set of pairs of values that are allowed by the constraint. That is, $c_{ij} = \{(x_{im}, x_{jn}) | x_{im} \in domain(v_i), x_{jn} \in domain(v_j),$ and (x_{im}, x_{jn}) is allowed by the constraint$\}$. We associate a weight $w_{ij}^p(x_{im}, x_{jn}) \in [0, 1]$ with each pair of values $(x_{im}, x_{jn}) \in c_{ij}$ (exactly how the weights are selected is outside of the scope of this paper; see [6] for details). If a pair $(x_{im}, x_{jn}) \notin c_{ij}$ then that pair is not allowed by the constraint. Finally, if $c_{pq} \notin C$, then all the possible pairs of values from v_p and v_q are implicitly allowed, but their weights are undefined.

A *solution* to the problem P is a set of values $S = \{x_{1a_1}, x_{2a_2}, ..., x_{|V|a_{|V|}}\}$ s.t. $\forall c_{ij} \in C$ $(x_{ia_i}, x_{ja_j}) \in c_{ij}$. A partial solution consists of a set of values $\{x_{a_1b_1}, x_{a_2b_2}, .., x_{a_kb_k}\}$ s.t. $k < |V|$, and $\forall m, n \leq k \exists c_{a_m a_n} \in C \Rightarrow (x_{a_m b_m}, x_{a_n b_n}) \in c_{a_m b_n}$. We define the *weight of a solution* as the sum[1] (over all the variables and constraints) of the weights of all the values and pairs of values involved. Formally, $sw(S) = \sum_{v_i \in V} w_{ik}^v + \sum_{c_{ij} \in C} w_{ij}^p(x_{ia_i}, x_{ja_j})$ with $x_{ik}, x_{ia_i}, x_{ja_j} \in S$, and $(x_{ia_i}, x_{ja_j}) \in c_{ij}$. The weight of a partial solution is defined similarly, with the exception that only variables included in the partial solution and the constraints among them are taken into account.

For each variable v_i we can compute the *range* of possible weights by simply taking the minimum and maximum weights among all the values in the domain of that variable. For all k s.t. $1 \leq k \leq |domain(v_i)|$, and $x_{ik} \in domain(v_i)$:
$$MinVW(v_i) = min(w_{ik}^v)$$
$$MaxVW(v_i) = max(w_{ik}^v)$$
Similarly, for each constraint c_{ij} we can compute the *range* of possible weights by taking the minimum and maximum weights among all the pairs of values allowed by the constraint. For all a, b s.t. $1 \leq a \leq |domain(v_i)|, 1 \leq b \leq |domain(v_j)|$, and $(x_{ia}, x_{jb}) \in c_{ij}$:
$$MinCW(c_{ij}) = min(w_{ij}^p(x_{ia}, x_{jb}))$$
$$MaxCW(c_{ij}) = max(w_{ij}^p(x_{ia}, x_{jb})).$$
Lower and upper bounds for the weight of a solution to P are computed as:
$$MinSW(P) = \sum_{v_i \in V} MinVW(v_i) + \sum_{c_{ij} \in C} MinCW(c_{ij})$$
$$MaxSW(P) = \sum_{v_i \in V} MaxVW(v_i) + \sum_{c_{ij} \in C} MaxCW(c_{ij}).$$
Note that there might be no solutions with these weights, all we are saying here is that $\forall S, MinSW(P) \leq sw(S) \leq MaxSW(P)$. In order to compute the exact minimum and maximum solution weights we would have to look at all the solutions.

---

[1] See [1] for a discussion on egalitarianism versus utilitarianism.

4 The "acceptable-weight" Heuristic

One way of looking for solutions with weights in a given range is to simply use a general purpose search algorithm (like **MAC** [5]) and every time a solution is found check whether or not its weight is within the acceptable range. However, unaware of the importance of the solution weight, such an algorithm will look for *any* solution, leaving to chance the discovery of an acceptable one.

The `acceptable-weight` value ordering heuristic is an attempt to do better than that by guiding the search towards areas of the search space that are likely to contain solutions with acceptable weights.

Consider a constraint satisfaction problem P and two positive real numbers, $MinASW$ and $MaxASW$, representing the minimum and maximum *acceptable* solution weights, with

$$MinSW(P) \leq MinASW \leq MaxASW \leq MaxSW(P).$$

A solution S is *acceptable* if:

$$MinASW \leq sw(S) \leq MaxASW.$$

Given the range of acceptable solution weights $[MinASW, MaxASW]$, we consider the *ideal* solution weight ($IdealSW$) as being at the center of that range (actually, this can be viewed in two ways: either start with a $[MinASW, MaxASW]$ range and consider the midpoint as an useful point to head for, or start with a "target" weight and define a tolerance around it – the algorithm will work both ways).

During the search, a constraint that involves at least one variable that has not been instantiated (i.e. assigned a value) is considered *active*, while a constraint that involves only instantiated variables is considered *inactive*. This distinction is useful when computing the weight of a partial solution, since only *instantiated* variables and *inactive* constraints can be considered. For brevity, we define the *weight* of an instantiated variable as the weight of the value that has been assigned to it, and the *weight* of an inactive constraint as the weight of the pair of values assigned to the variables involved in that constraint.

The idea behind `acceptable-weight` is to keep track of the weight of the current partial solution S' and attempt to obtain a solution for the rest of the problem whose weight, combined with the first one, will bring the global solution weight as close to $IdealSW$ as possible. Based on p, the number of currently *uninstantiated* variables, and q, the number of currently *active* constraints in the problem, `acceptable-weight` computes the average of the individual weights (AIW) that these variables and constraints would contribute to the global solution weight $sw(S)$, should it equal $IdealSW$:

$$AIW = \frac{IdealSW - sw(S')}{p + q}.$$

When the heuristic attempts to suggest a value for the current variable v_c, it considers the subproblem $P'' = \{V'', C''\}$ with $V'' \subset V$ containing the current variable and the past variables with which it is connected by constraints, and $C'' \subset C$ containing all the constraints between the current variable and past variables. The ideal weight of a solution S'' to P'' would be:

$$IdealSW'' = \sum_{v_i \in V'' - \{v_c\}} w_{ik}^v + AIW + |C''| \cdot AIW,$$

with $x_{ik} \in domain(v_i)$ and $x_{ik} \in S'$.

The acceptable-weight heuristic will select the value that will minimize the absolute difference between $sw(S'')$ and $IdealSW''$. The following example will illustrate a typical situation.

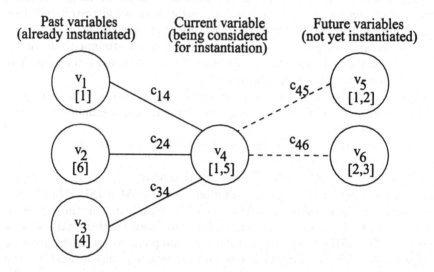

Fig. 2. The instantiation of the current variable:
$v_1=\{1=0.1\}$, $v_2=\{6=0.2\}$, $v_3=\{4=0.4\}$, $v_4=\{1=0.4, 5=0.8\}$,
$c_{14}=\{(1,1)=0.1, (1,5)=0.2\}$, $c_{24}=\{(6,1)=0.8, (6.5)=0.9\}$,
$c_{34}=\{(4,1)=0.6, (4,5)=0.7\}$

The values in the domain of each variable and the pairs of allowed values in each constraint are given between parenthesis. The number printed in *italics* represents the corresponding weight. Future variables are depicted, but not considered - this might be the subject of further improvements.

In this example the search is at the point of instantiating v_4. The possible values are 1 (whose weight is 0.4) and 5 (whose weight is 0.8), and the acceptable-weight heuristic is supposed to suggest one of them. Let us take a look at the implications of selecting each value, assuming that $AIW = 0.4$ at this point in the search.

In this example $V'' = \{v_1, v_2, v_3, v_4\}$, and $C'' = \{c_{14}, c_{24}, c_{34}\}$. If we choose to assign 1 to v_4, then $sw(S'') = (0.1+0.2+0.4)+0.4+(0.1+0.8+0.6) = 2.6$. If we choose 5, then $sw(S'') = (0.1+0.2+0.4)+0.8+(0.2+0.9+0.7) = 3.3$. After computing $IdealSW'' = (0.1 + 0.2 + 0.4) + AIW + 3 \cdot AIW = 2.3$, we see that selecting the value 1 will yield a better weight for S'' (closer to $IdealSW''$). After the assignment of v_4, acceptable-weight recomputes the AIW, to compensate for the amount we were off.

The strategy behind the heuristic described is two-fold. Locally, we try to make sure that each small subproblem centered around the current variable has a weight that is in line with the global *IdealSW*. Globally, by constantly adjusting the *AIW* we try to control the overall deviation of the solution weight. This strategy appears to work well in practice, as we will see in the next section.

5   Experimental Results

We have performed some experimental tests on problems that have been randomly generated (weights included) using a fixed parameter value model. The constraint satisfaction library used was developed at UNH and is freely available at *http://www.cs.unh.edu/~tudor/csp*.

Our tests compare the performance of MAC+`acceptable-weight` with that of MAC. In both cases we used AC-3 arc consistency and the dynamic minimal domain size variable ordering heuristic. The algorithms were used to find acceptable solutions to problems with 100 variables, each variable having 5 values in its domain. All the instances we tested exhibited a very similar behaviour, and we used one of them in the experiments presented here. The reason for using just one problem instance is that we were interested in studying the behaviour of MAC+`acceptable-weight` around the difficulty peak, which is different for each such randomly generated problem.

The constraint density (defined as the fraction of the possible constraints beyond the minimum n-1, that the problem has) and the constraint tightness (defined as the fraction of all possible pairs of values from the domains of two variables that are not allowed by the constraint) were used to vary the difficulty of the generated problems and study the changes in the behavior of `acceptable-weight`. In the following tests we will compare the time required by the two algorithms to find an acceptable solution. Both algorithms will look for solutions in ranges of a given size (0.05 and 0.1 in the examples below) centered around the solution weight on the **X** axis, which has been translated and scaled from $[MinSW(P), MaxSW(P)]$ to $[0,1]$. We arbitrarily set a timeout limit at 6 seconds.

Before going any further, we need to briefly explain the behavior of MAC. Without going into details, we will just say that, probabilistically speaking, there are many solutions with weights around 0.5 and very few solutions with extreme weights (close to 0 or 1). MAC does not take weights into account, and thus from its point of view the solutions are uniformly distributed throughout the search space. However, since most solutions have weights around 0.5, MAC will tend to find those pretty quickly.

The first test we did was with density=0 and tightness=0. Fig.3 shows the performance difference between the two algorithms. While MAC can only find solutions with weights in the 0.455-0.54 range, MAC+`acceptable-weight` is capable of finding solutions with weights in the 0.226-0.79 range. Moreover, in most of the cases the very first solution that MAC+`acceptable-weight` finds is within the acceptable range.

The interval in which MAC+`acceptable-weight` quickly finds acceptable solutions narrows as the density and/or tightness increase.

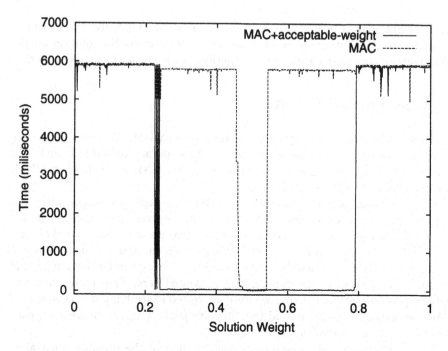

Fig. 3. Range=0.05, Density=0, Tightness=0

The test in Fig.4 was similar to the one in Fig.3 except that the constraint tightness has been increased to 0.25. As a result, the range in which MAC+acceptable-weight can find acceptable solutions decreases to 0.244-0.752. The range in which MAC finds acceptable solutions also changes a little: 0.469-0.560.

In terms of weights, the density of the solutions is given by a normal distribution. The reason for the performance degradation is that as density and/or tightness increase, the number of solutions decreases, and the areas affected the most are those at the sides of the normal distribution curve, which contain a very small number of solutions to begin with. Gradually, the range covered by MAC+acceptable-weight will shrink to a range comparable to that covered by MAC alone (Fig.6), because there will be virtually no solution outside a small range around 0.5 and MAC will be able to find those just as fast.

The first two results presented were performed with ranges of size 0.05. That is, any solution with a weight that differs in absolute value by at most 0.025 from the weight on the **X** axis was considered acceptable. As we widen the acceptable range, the interval in which both algorithms quickly find solutions widens. In the test pictured in Fig.5, MAC was capable of finding acceptable solutions with weights in the 0.444-0.584 range. MAC+acceptable-weight performed much better, covering the 0.216-0.798 range (also note that this compares better with the 0.244-0.752 range in Fig.4).

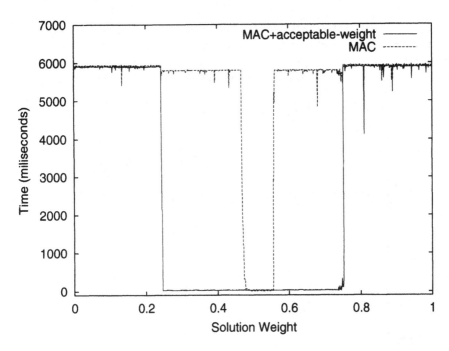

Fig. 4. Range=0.05, Density=0, Tightness=0.25

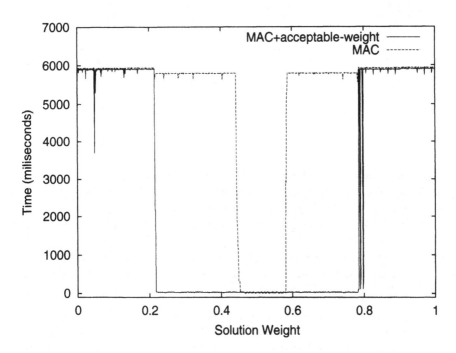

Fig. 5. Range=0.1, Density=0, Tightness=0.25

In our fourth test (Fig.6), MAC alone covered the 0.447-0.569 range while MAC+acceptable-weight covered 0.415-0.568 (the spike around 0.601 marks a small region where MAC+acceptable-weight found acceptable solutions - with a longer time limit it would have covered the 0.568-0.601 range as well).

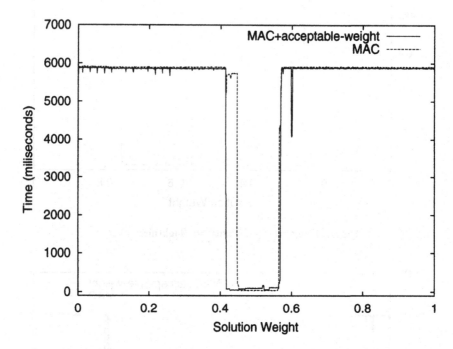

Fig. 6. Range=0.1, Density=0.055, Tightness=0.25

For the problem tested here (100 variables, domain size 5), the difficulty peak for tightness=0.25 is around density=0.0651 (Fig.8). As the problem gets harder and harder, the impact of acceptable-weight becomes less noticeable. Intuitively, as the problem gets harder, the number of solutions gets smaller, and if an acceptable one exists, chances are that MAC alone will find it pretty quickly by just looking for *any* solution, not necessarily an acceptable one. Finally, MAC+acceptable-weight compares well with MAC around the difficulty peak (Fig.7).

It should be noted however that we are not targeting hard problems with this heuristic. Configuration problems for instance are relatively easy - there are lots of solutions, the real challenge is to find one that is acceptable. For problems around the difficulty peak, a standard algorithm would have similar performance characteristics.

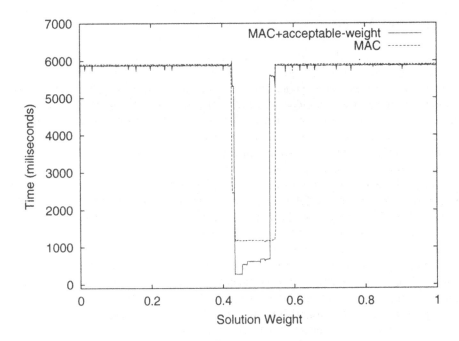

Fig. 7. Range=0.1, Density=0.0651, Tightness=0.25

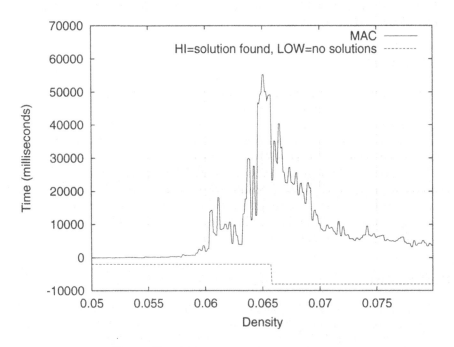

Fig. 8. The difficulty peak for tightness=0.25

6 Future Work

One way to improve the performance of the heuristic might be by trying to detect situations where the search gets stuck in a given range. There are situations where MAC+acceptable-weight obtains a partial solution, but there is no way of extending it to a complete solution with an acceptable weight. It is clear that in those situations the heuristic has made a few mistakes, and it might be interesting to see if the overall performance can be improved by refusing to listen to the heuristic's suggestions until the range of solution weights obtained changes. Somewhat related ideas can be found in [3].

Another idea would be to avoid searching in subtrees where there is no way of extending the current partial solution to a complete solution with an acceptable weight. Rough estimates of the potential contribution of the unsolved part of the problem can be obtained by computing its minimum and maximum solution weights ($MinSW$ and $MaxSW$).

Finally we plan to look at ways of obtaining better weight evaluations for the small subproblems centered around the current variable. Taking future variables into account is on top of our list of potential improvements.

Applications for this algorithm can range from suggesting upgrades and alternative solutions, to promoting particular configurations. The customer obtains an initial solution by a matchmaker [2] or deep-interview strategy, then the vendor suggests successive upgrades. The upgrades can be computed by looking for solutions with weights within a range that is close to (but not centered in[2]) the weight of the original solution.

7 Conclusions

Goldilocks learned a very important lesson. There are things in life that are not of the "right size" for everyone. It is often the case that there is a wide range of choices to pick from, and we have to determine which one is "too big", "too small", or "just right". Worst yet, sometimes we have to relax our notion of "just right", to get something that is "good enough".

The acceptable-weight heuristic presented here is designed to guide the search towards solutions with acceptable weights, when solutions can be ranked along a given dimension. Although we believe there are avenues for improvement, experiments with random problems showed that this heuristic, combined with MAC, can find acceptable solutions very quickly.

References

[1] S. Bistarelli, H. Fargier, U. Montanari, F. Rossi, T. Schiex, and G. Verfaillie. Semiring-based csps and valued csps: Basic properties and comparison. In M. Jampel, E. Freuder, and M. Maher, editors, *Over-Constrained Systems (LNCS 1106,*

---

[2] Remember that the acceptable-weight heuristic attempts to guide the search towards the center of the range.

Selected Papers from the Workshop on Over-Constrained Systems at CP '95.). Springer, 1996.

[2] E. Freuder and R. Wallace. Suggestion strategies for constraint-based matchmaker agents. In *Constraints and Agents, Papers from the 1997 AAAI Workshop.* AAAI Press, July 1997. TR WS-97-05.

[3] W. Harvey and M. Ginsberg. Limited discrepany search. In *Proceedings of the Fourteenth International Joint Conference on Artificial Intelligence,* Montreal, Canada, August 1995.

[4] T. Hulubei and E. Freuder. The goldilocks problem. In *Configuration, Papers from the 1999 AAAI Workshop,* Florida, USA, July 1999. AAAI Press. TR WS-99-05.

[5] D. Sabin and E. Freuder. Contradicting conventional wisdom in constraint satisfation. In *11th European Conference on Artificial Intelligence,* Amsterdam, The Netherlands, August 1994. John Wiley & Sons LTD.

[6] D. von Winterfeldt and W. Edwards. *Decision Analysis and Behavioral Research,* chapter 8, pages 259–313. Cambridge University Press, Cambridge, 1986.

Multistep Filtering Operators
for Ordinary Differential Equations

Micha Janssen, Yves Deville, and Pascal Van Hentenryck

UCL, Place Sainte-Barbe, 2, B-1348 Louvain-La-Neuve, Belgium

Abstract. Interval methods for ordinary differential equations (ODEs) provide guaranteed enclosures of the solutions and numerical proofs of existence and unicity of the solution. Unfortunately, they may result in large over-approximations of the solution because of the loss of precision in interval computations and the wrapping effect. The main open issue in this area is to find tighter enclosures of the solution, while not sacrificing efficiency too much. This paper takes a constraint satisfaction approach to this problem, whose basic idea is to iterate a forward step to produce an initial enclosure with a pruning step that tightens it. The paper focuses on the pruning step and proposes novel multistep filtering operators for ODEs. These operators are based on interval extensions of a multistep solution that are obtained by using (Lagrange and Hermite) interpolation polynomials and their error terms. The paper also shows how traditional techniques (such as mean-value forms and coordinate transformations) can be adapted to this new context. Preliminary experimental results illustrate the potential of the approach, especially on stiff problems, well-known to be very difficult to solve.

1 Introduction

Differential equations (DE) are important in many scientific applications in areas such as physics, chemistry, and mechanics to name only a few. In addition, computers play a fundamental role in obtaining solutions to these systems.

THE PROBLEM A (first-order) *ordinary differential equation* (ODE) system $\mathcal{O}$ is a system of the form u'(t) = f(t,u(t)) (in vector notations) or, more simply, $u' = f(t, u)$. Given an initial condition $u(t_{init}) = u_{init}$ and assuming existence and uniqueness of the solution, the solution of $\mathcal{O}$ is a function $s^* : \mathcal{R} \to \mathcal{R}^n$ satisfying $\mathcal{O}$ and the initial condition $s^*(t_{init}) = u_{init}$. Note that differential equations of order p (i.e. $f(t, u, u', u'', \ldots, u^p) = 0$) can always be transformed into an ODE by introduction of new variables.

Discrete variable methods aim to approximate the solution $s^*(t)$ of an ODE system at some points $t_0, t_1, \ldots, t_m$. They include *one-step methods* (where $s^*(t_j)$ is approximated from the approximation u_{j-1} of $s^*(t_{j-1})$) and *multistep methods* (where $s^*(t_j)$ is approximated from the approximation $u_{j-1}, \ldots, u_{j-p}$ of $s^*(t_{j-1}), \ldots, s^*(t_{j-p})$). In general, these methods do not guarantee the existence of a solution within a given bound and can only return approximations since they ignore error terms.

INTERVAL ANALYSIS IN ODE Interval techniques for ODE systems were introduced by Moore [Moo66]. These methods provide numerically reliable enclosures of the exact solution at points $t_0, t_1, \ldots, t_m$. They typically apply a one-step Taylor interval method and make extensive use of automatic differentiation to obtain the Taylor coefficients [Moo79,Ral80,Ral81,Cor88,Abe88]. The major problem of interval methods on ODE systems is the explosion of the size of resulting boxes at points $t_0, t_1, \ldots, t_m$ that is due to two reasons. On the one hand, step methods have a tendency to accumulate errors from point to point. On the other, the approximation of an arbitrary region by a box, called the **wrapping effect**, may introduce considerable imprecision after a number of steps. Much research has been devoted to address this problem. One of the best systems in this area is Lohner's AWA [Loh87,Sta96]. It uses the Picard iteration to prove existence and uniqueness and to find a rough enclosure of the solution. This rough enclosure is then used to compute correct enclosures using a mean value method and the Taylor expansion on a variational equation on global errors. It also applies coordinate transformations to reduce the wrapping effect.

A CONSTRAINT SATISFACTION APPROACH Our research takes a constraint satisfaction approach to the problem of producing tighter enclosures. The basic idea [DJVH98] is to view the solving of ODEs as the iteration of two steps: a forward process that produces an initial enclosure of the solution at a given time (given enclosures at previous times) and a pruning process that tightens this first enclosure. Our previous results, as most research in interval methods, mostly focused on the forward process. Our current research, in contrast, concentrates on the pruning step, where constraint satisfaction techniques seem particularly well adapted. It is important to mention that taking a constraint satisfaction approach gives a fundamentally new perspective on this problem. Instead of trying to adapt traditional numerical techniques to intervals, the constraint satisfaction approach looks at the problem in a more global way and makes it possible to exploit a wealth of mathematical results. In this context, the basic methodology consists of finding necessary conditions on the solution that can be used for pruning. This paper will also show experimentally that the forward and backward steps are in fact orthogonal, clearly showing the interest of the approach. We thus may hope that constraint satisfaction will be as fruitful for ODEs as for combinatorial optimization and nonlinear programming.

GOAL OF THE PAPER As mentioned, the main goal of this paper is to design filtering algorithms to produce tighter enclosures of the solution. The problem is difficult because, contrary to traditional discrete or continuous problems, the constraints cannot be used directly since they involve unknown functions (and their derivatives). The key idea of the paper is to show that effective multistep filtering operators can be obtained by using conservative approximations of these unknown functions. These approximations can be obtained by using polynomial interpolations and their error terms. Once these multistep filtering operators are available, traditional constraint satisfaction techniques (e.g., box(k)-consistency [VHLD97]) can be applied to prune the initial enclosure.

CONTRIBUTIONS This paper contains three main contributions. First, it proposes a generic filtering operator based on interval extensions of a multistep solution function and its derivatives. Second, it shows how these interval extensions can be obtained using Lagrange and Hermite interpolation polynomials. Third, it shows how the filtering operator can accommodate standard techniques such as mean-value forms and coordinate transformations to address the wrapping effect during the pruning step as well. The paper also contains some preliminary experimental evidence to show that the techniques are effective in tightening the initial enclosures.

The rest of this paper is organized as follows. Section 2 sets up the background and recall the constraint satisfaction approach from [DJVH98]. Sections 3 and 4 are the core of the paper: Section 3 contains the novel generic multistep pruning operator, while Section 4 shows how to build the interval approximations it needs using Lagrange and Hermite polynomials. Section 5 describes how to adapt the multistep filtering operator to the mean-value form. Section 6 discusses the implementation issues and contains the experimental results. The proof of all results, as well as a discussion on how to adapt the techniques to coordinate transformations, are in the technical report version of this paper.

2 Background and Definitions

The following conventions are adopted in this paper. (Sequences of) small letters denote real values, vectors and functions of real values. (Sequences of) capital letters denote real matrices, sets, intervals, vectors and functions of intervals. Capital letters between square brackets denote interval matrices. Bold face small letters denote sequences (delimited by "⟨" and "⟩") of real values. Bold face capital letters denote sequences (delimited by "⟨" and "⟩") of intervals. All these (sequences of) letters may be subscripted.

We use traditional conventions for abstracting floating-point numbers. If $\mathcal{F}$ is a floating-point system, the elements of $\mathcal{F}$ are called $\mathcal{F}$-numbers. If $a \in \mathcal{F}$, then a^+ denotes the smallest $\mathcal{F}$-number strictly greater than a and a^- the largest $\mathcal{F}$-number strictly smaller than a. $\mathcal{I}$ denotes the set of all *closed* intervals $\subseteq \mathcal{R}$ whose bounds are in $\mathcal{F}$. A vector of intervals $D \in \mathcal{I}^n$ is called a *box*. If $r \in \mathcal{R}$, then $\bar{r}$ denotes the smallest interval $I \in \mathcal{I}$ such that $r \in I$. If $r \in \mathcal{R}^n$, then $\bar{r} = (\bar{r_1}, ..., \bar{r_n})$. If $A \subseteq \mathcal{R}^n$, then $\blacksquare A$ denotes the smallest box $D \in \mathcal{I}^n$ such that $A \subseteq D$. We also assume that $t_0, \ldots, t_k$, t_e and t are reals, $u_0, \ldots, u_k$ are in $\mathcal{R}^n$, and $D_0, \ldots, D_k$ are in $\mathcal{I}^n$. Finally, we use $\mathbf{t}_k$ to denote $\langle t_0, ..., t_k \rangle$, $\mathbf{u}_k$ to denote $\langle u_0, ..., u_k \rangle$, $T_{\mathbf{t}_k}$ to denote the interval $[\min(t_0, ..., t_k), \max(t_0, ..., t_k)]$, $T_{\mathbf{t}_k, t}$ to denote the interval $[\min(t_0, ..., t_k, t), \max(t_0, ..., t_k, t)]$ and $\mathbf{D}_k$ to denote $\langle D_0, ..., D_k \rangle$. The following definitions are standard.

Definition 1. Let A, B be sets, $a \in A$, g a function and r a relation defined on A, and op $\in \{+, -, \cdot, /\}$. Then, $g(A) = \{g(x) \mid x \in A\}$, $r(A) = \bigvee_{x \in A} r(x)$, A op $B = \{x \text{ op } y \mid x \in A, y \in B\}$ and a op $A = \{a \text{ op } x \mid x \in A\}$.

We assume traditional definitions of interval extensions for functions and relations. In addition, if f (resp. c) is a function (resp. relation), then F (resp. C) denotes an interval extension of f (resp. C). We overload traditional real operators (e.g., $+$, $*$, $=$, ...) and use them for their interval extensions. Because the techniques proposed here use multistep solutions (which are partial functions), it is necessary to define interval extensions of partial functions and relations.

Definition 2 (Interval Extension of a Partial Function). The interval function $G : I^n \to I^m$ is *an interval extension* of the partial function $g : E \subseteq \mathcal{R}^n \to \mathcal{R}^m$ if $\forall D \in I^n : g(E \cap D) \subseteq G(D)$.

Definition 3 (Interval Extension of a Partial Relation). The interval relation $R \subseteq I^n$ is an *interval extension* of the partial relation $r \subseteq E \subseteq \mathcal{R}^n$ if $\forall D \in I^n : r(E \cap D) \Rightarrow R(D)$.

Notation 1 Let $g : (x,y) \mapsto g(x,y)$. Then, $g(a, \bullet)$ denotes the unary function $g(a, \bullet) : y \mapsto g(a,y)$. A similar definition holds for $g(\bullet, a)$. The generalization to n-ary functions is straightforward.

Definition 4 (Interval Extension wrt a Subset of the Variables). The function $G : I \times \mathcal{R} \to I$ is *an interval extension* of the function $g : \mathcal{R} \times \mathcal{R} \to \mathcal{R}$ *wrt the 1st variable* if the function $G(\bullet, a)$ is an interval extension of $g(\bullet, a)$ for all $a \in \mathcal{R}$. A similar definition holds for an interval extension wrt the 2nd variable. The generalization to $\mathcal{R}^n \to \mathcal{R}^m$ (partial) functions is straightforward.

The solution of an ODE system can be formalized mathematically as follows.

Definition 5 (Solution of an ODE System with Initial Value). The *solution* of an ODE system $\mathcal{O}$ with initial conditions $u(t_{init}) = u_{init}$ is the function $s^*(t) : \mathcal{R} \to \mathcal{R}^n$ satisfying $\mathcal{O}$ and the initial conditions $s^*(t_{init}) = u_{init}$.

In this paper, we restrict attention to ODE systems that have a unique solution for a given initial value. Techniques to verify this hypothesis numerically are well-known [Moo79,DJVH98]. Moreover, in practice, as mentioned, the objective is to produce (an approximation of) the values of the solution function s^* of the system $\mathcal{O}$ at different points $t_0, t_1, \ldots, t_m$. It is thus useful to adapt the definition of a solution to account for this practical motivation.

Definition 6 (Solution of an ODE System). The *solution* of an ODE system $\mathcal{O}$ is the function $s(t_0, u_0, t) : \mathcal{R} \times \mathcal{R}^n \times \mathcal{R} \to \mathcal{R}^n$ such that $s(t_0, u_0, t) = s^*(t)$, where s^* is the solution of $\mathcal{O}$ with initial conditions $u(t_0) = u_0$.

Definition 7 (Multistep solution of an ODE). *The multistep solution* of an ODE system $\mathcal{O}$ whose solution is s is the *partial* function $ms : A \subseteq (\mathcal{R}^{k+1} \times (\mathcal{R}^n)^{k+1} \times \mathcal{R}) \to \mathcal{R}^n$ defined by

$$ms(\mathbf{t}_k, \mathbf{u}_k, t) = s(t_0, u_0, t) \text{ if } u_i = s(t_0, u_0, t_i) \text{ for } 1 \leq i \leq k,$$
$$\text{undefined otherwise}$$

It is important to stress that the multistep function is a partial function. Hence, interval extensions of multistep functions may behave very differently outside the domain of definition of the functions. This fact is exploited by the novel filtering operators proposed in this paper. Finally, we generalize the concept of bounding boxes, a fundamental concept in interval methods for ODEs, to multistep methods. Intuitively, a bounding box encloses all solutions of an ODE going through certain boxes at given times.

Definition 8 (Bounding box). Let $\mathcal{O}$ be an ODE system, ms be the multistep solution of $\mathcal{O}$, and $\{t_0, ..., t_k\} \subseteq T \in \mathcal{I}$. A box B is a *bounding box* of ms over T wrt $\mathbf{D}_k$ and $\mathbf{t}_k$, if, for all $t \in T$, $ms(\mathbf{t}_k, \mathbf{D}_k, t) \subseteq B$.

The constraint satisfaction approach followed in this paper was first presented in [DJVH98]. It consists of a generic algorithm for ODEs that iterates two steps: (1) a *forward* step that computes an initial enclosure at a given time from enclosures at previous times and bounding boxes and (2) a *pruning* step that reduces the initial enclosures without removing solutions. The forward process also provides numerical proofs of existence and unicity of the solution. Various techniques were presented in [DJVH98] for the forward step and are not discussed here. In contrast, this paper focuses on the pruning step, the main novelty of the approach. The pruning step prunes the last box D_k at t_k produced by the forward step, using, say, the last k boxes $D_0, \ldots, D_{k-1}$ obtained at times $t_0, \ldots, t_{k-1}$.[1] To our knowledge, no research has been devoted to pruning techniques for ODEs, except for the proposal in [DJVH98] to use the forward step backwards. These techniques however are promising since they open new directions to tackle the traditional problems of interval methods for ODEs.

3 A Multistep Filtering Operator for ODEs

This section presents a multistep filtering operator for ODEs to tighten the initial enclosure of the solutions effectively. It starts with an informal presentation to convey the main ideas and intuitions before formalizing the concepts.

To understand the main contribution of this paper, it is useful to contrast the techniques proposed herein with interval techniques for nonlinear equations. In nonlinear programming, a constraint $c(x_1, \ldots, x_n)$ can be used almost directly for pruning the search space (i.e., the carthesian products of the intervals I_i associated with the variables x_i). It suffices to take an interval extension $C(X_1, \ldots, X_n)$ of the constraint. Now if $C(I'_1, \ldots, I'_n)$ does not hold, it follows, by definition of interval extensions, that no solution of c lies in $I'_1 \times \ldots \times I'_n$. This basic property can be seen as a filtering operator that can be used for pruning the search space in many ways, including box(k)-consistency as in Numerica [VHLD97,VH98b]. Recall that a constraint C is box(1)-consistent wrt $I_1, \ldots, I_n$ and x_i if the condition

$$C(I_1, \ldots, I_{i-1}, [l_i, l_i^+], I_{i+1}, \ldots, I_n) \wedge C(I_1, \ldots, I_{i-1}, [u_i^-, u_i], I_{i+1}, \ldots, I_n)$$

---

[1] Note that the time t_0 is not, in general, the time t_{init} of the initial condition.

holds where $I_i = [l_i, u_i]$. The filtering algorithm based on box(1)-consistency reduces the interval of the variables without removing any solution until the constraint is box(1)-consistent wrt the intervals and all variables. Stronger consistency notions, e.g., box(2)-consistency, are also useful for especially difficult problems [VH98a]. It is interesting here to distinguish the filter or pruning operator, i.e., the technique used to determine if a box cannot contain a solution, from the filtering algorithm that uses the pruning operator in a specific way to prune the search space.

The goal of the research described in this paper is to device similar techniques for ODEs. The main difficulty is that there is no obvious filter in this context. Indeed, the equation $u' = f(t, u)$ cannot be used directly since u and u' are unknown functions. We now discuss how to overcome this problem and, in a first step, restrict attention to one-dimensional problems for simplicity.

Assume first that we have at our disposal the multistep solution ms of the equation. In this case, the equation $u' = f(t, u)$ can be rewritten into

$$\frac{\partial ms}{\partial t}(\langle t_0, \dots, t_k \rangle, \langle v_0, \dots, v_k \rangle, t) = f(t, ms(\langle t_0, \dots, t_k \rangle, \langle v_0, \dots, v_k \rangle, t)).$$

Let us denote this equation $fl(\langle t_0, \dots, t_k \rangle, \langle v_0, \dots, v_k \rangle, t)$. At first sight, of course, this equation may not appear useful since ms is still an unknown function. However, as Section 4 shows, it is possible to obtain interval extensions of ms and $\frac{\partial ms}{\partial t}$ by using, say, polynomial interpolations together with their error terms. If MS and DMS are such interval extensions, then we obtain an interval equation

$$DMS(\langle t_0, \dots, t_k \rangle, \langle X_0, \dots, X_k \rangle, t) = F(\bar{t}, MS(\langle t_0, \dots, t_k \rangle, \langle X_0, \dots, X_k \rangle, t))$$

that can be used as a filtering operator. Let us denote this operator by

$$FL(\langle t_0, \dots, t_k \rangle, \langle X_0, \dots, X_k \rangle, t)$$

and illustrate how it can prune the search space. If the condition

$$FL(\langle t_0, \dots, t_k \rangle, \langle I_0, \dots, I_k \rangle, t)$$

does not hold, then it follows that no solution of $u' = f(t, u)$ can go through intervals $I_0, \dots, I_k$ at times $t_0, \dots, t_k$.

How can we use this filter to obtain tighter enclosures of the solution? A simple technique consists of pruning the last interval produced by the forward process. Assume that I_i is an interval enclosing the solution at time t_i ($0 \le i \le k$) and that we are interested in pruning the last interval I_k. A subinterval $I \subseteq I_k$ can be pruned away if the condition $FL(\langle t_0, \dots, t_k \rangle, \langle I_0, \dots, I_{k-1}, I \rangle, t_e)$ does not hold for some evaluation point t_e.

Let us explain briefly the geometric intuition behind this formula. Figure 1 is generated from an actual ordinary differential equation, considers only points instead of intervals, and ignores error terms for simplicity. It illustrates how this technique can prune away a value as a potential solution at a given time. In the figure, we consider the solution to the equation that evaluates to u_0 and u_1

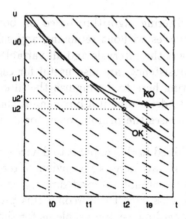

Fig. 1. Geometric Intuition of the Multistep Filtering Operator

at t_0 and t_1 respectively. Two possible points u_2 and u_2' are then considered as possible values at t_2. The curve marked KO describes an interpolation polynomial going through u_0, u_1, u_2' at times t_0, t_1, t_2. To determine if u_2' is the value of the solution at time t_2, the idea is to test if the equation is satisfied at times t_e. (We will say more about how to choose t_e later in this paper). As can be seen easily, the slope of the interpolation polynomial is different from the slope specified by f at time t_e and hence u_2' cannot be the value of the solution at t_2. The curve marked OK describes an interpolation polynomial going through u_0, u_1, u_2 at times t_0, t_1, t_2. In this case, the equation is satisfied at time t_e, which means that u_2 cannot be pruned away.

Of course, the filter proposed earlier generalizes this intuition to intervals. The interval function DMS is an interval extension of $\frac{\partial ms}{\partial t}$ obtained, say, by taking an interval extension of the derivative of an interpolation polynomial and a bound on its error term. The interval function MS is an interval extension of an interpolation polynomial and a bound on its error term. These interval functions are evaluated over intervals produced by the forward process. The filtering operator thus tests whether a solution can go through interval I by *testing* this interval equation at time t_e. If a solution goes through I, then the filter must hold because the left- and the righ-hand sides of the filter are both interval extensions of $\frac{\partial ms}{\partial t}$. If I does not contain a solution, by definition of partial interval extension (See Definition 3), no constraints are imposed on MS and DMS and there is no reason to believe that the filter will hold. It may hold because of a loss of precision in the computation or because we are unlucky but a careful choice of the interpolation polynomials will minimize these risks.

It is important to stress that traditional consistency techniques and filtering algorithms based on this filtering operator can now be applied. For instance, one may be interested in computing the set

$$I_k' = \blacksquare\{r \in I_k \mid FL(\langle t_0, \ldots, t_k \rangle, \langle I_0, \ldots, I_{k-1}, \overline{r} \rangle, t_e)\}.$$

For multi-dimensional problems, one may be interested in obtaining box(k)-approximations of the multi-dimensional sets defined in a similar fashion.

It is also important to mention that the filtering operator can be used in many different ways, even if only the last interval (or box) is considered for pruning. For instance, once an interval $I \subseteq I_k$ is selected, it is possible to prune the intervals $I_0, \ldots, I_{k-1}$ using, say, the forward process run backwards as already suggested in [DJVH98]. This makes it possible to obtain tighter enclosures of ms and $\frac{\partial ms}{\partial t}$, thus obtaining a more effective filtering algorithm for I.

Finally, it is useful to stress that the filtering operator suggested here shares some interesting connections with Gear's method, a traditional implicit multistep procedure that is particularly useful for stiff problems. We may thus hope that the filtering operator will be particularly well adapted for stiff problems as well (as our prelimininary results show). We will say more about these connections once some more technical details have been given.

We now formalize the intuition just given. A multistep filtering operator is defined as an interval extension of the original equation rewritten to make the multistep solution explicit.

Definition 9 (Multistep Filtering Operator). Let $\mathcal{O}$ be an ODE $u' = f(t, u)$ and let ms be the multistep solution of $\mathcal{O}$. A *multistep filtering* operator for $\mathcal{O}$ is an interval extension wrt the variables in $\mathbf{u}_k$ of the constraint

$$\frac{\partial ms}{\partial t}(\mathbf{t}_k, \mathbf{u}_k, t_e) = f(t_e, ms(\mathbf{t}_k, \mathbf{u}_k, t_e))$$

We show that a multistep filtering operator never prunes solutions away.

Proposition 1 (Soundness of the Multistep Filtering Operator). Let $\mathcal{O}$ be an ODE $u' = f(t, u)$, let FL be a multistep filtering operator for $\mathcal{O}$. If $FL(\mathbf{t}_k, \mathbf{D}_k, t_e)$ does not hold, then there exists no solution of $\mathcal{O}$ going through $\mathbf{D}_k$ at times $\mathbf{t}_k$.

The intuition given earlier was based on a natural multistep filtering operator.

Definition 10 (Natural Multistep Filtering Operator). Let $\mathcal{O}$ be an ODE $u' = f(t, u)$, let ms be the multistep solution of $\mathcal{O}$, let F be an interval extension of f, and let MS and DMS be interval extensions of ms and $\frac{\partial ms}{\partial t}$ wrt to their second argument. A *natural multistep filtering* operator for $\mathcal{O}$ is an interval equation

$$DMS(\langle t_0, \ldots, t_k \rangle, \langle X_0, \ldots, X_k \rangle, t_e) = F(\overline{t_e}, MS(\langle t_0, \ldots, t_k \rangle, \langle X_0, \ldots, X_k \rangle, t_e)).$$

There are other interesting multistep filtering operators, e.g., the mean-value form of the natural multistep filtering operator (see section 5). Different multistep filtering operators may be more appropriate when close or far from a solution as was already the case for nonlinear equations [VHLD97]. qIt remains to show how to obtain interval extensions of the qsolution function ms and its derivative $\frac{\partial ms}{\partial t}$.

4 Interval Extensions of the Solution Function

This section is devoted to interval extensions of the multistep solution function and its derivative. These extensions are, in general, based on decomposing the (unknown) multistep function into the summation of a computable approximation p and an (unknown) error term e, i.e., $ms(t_k, u_k, t) = p(t_k, u_k, t) + e(t_k, u_k, t)$. There exist standard techniques to build p and to bound e. In the rest of this section, two such approximations are presented. We also show how to bound the error term of the derivative of the multistep solution functions, since these are critical to obtain multistep filtering operators.

4.1 A Lagrange Polynomial Interval Extension

Our first interval extension is based on Lagrange polynomial interpolation.

Definition 11 (Lagrange Polynomial [KC96]). Let $t_0, ..., t_k$ be distinct points. The *Lagrange polynomial* that interpolates points $(t_0, u_0), ..., (t_k, u_k)$ is the *unique* polynomial $p_L : \mathcal{R} \to \mathcal{R}^n$ of degree $\leq k$ satisfying $p_L(t_i) = u_i$ $(0 \leq i \leq k)$. It is defined by $p_L(t) = \sum_{i=0}^{k} u_i \varphi_i(t)$, where $\varphi_i(t) = \frac{\prod_{j=0, j \neq i}^{k}(t-t_j)}{\prod_{j=0, j \neq i}^{k}(t_i-t_j)}$ $(0 \leq i \leq k)$.

We now bound the errors made by a Lagrange polynomial.

Theorem 1 (Lagrange Error Term). *Let* $a, b \in \mathcal{R}$, g *be a function in* $C^{k+1}([a, b], \mathcal{R}^n)$, *let* p_L *be the Lagrange polynomial of degree* $\leq k$ *that interpolates* g *at* $k + 1$ *distinct points* $t_0, ..., t_k$ *in the interval* $[a, b]$, *and* $t \in ([a, b] \setminus T_{t_k}) \cup \{t_0, ..., t_k\}$. *Then,*

1. $\exists \zeta_t \in \,]a, b[: g(t) - p_L(t) = \frac{1}{(k+1)!} g^{(k+1)}(\zeta_t) w(t);$
2. $\exists \xi_t \in \,]a, b[: g'(t) - p'_L(t) = \frac{1}{(k+1)!} g^{(k+1)}(\xi_t) w'(t).$

where $w(t) = \prod_{i=0}^{k}(t - t_i)$.

This result makes it possible to obtain interval extensions of ms and its derivative. Consider, for instance, function ms. The key idea to obtain an interval extension of ms consists of considering $f^{(k)}(\zeta_t, ms(t_k, u_k, \zeta_t))$ in the error term obtained from Theorem 1 and of

1. replacing the unknown time ζ_t by the interval $[a, b]$ in which it takes its value;
2. replacing the unknown function ms by one of its bounding boxes.

Together, these ideas gives conservative approximations of the error terms and thus interval extensions of the multistep solution function and of its derivative.

Definition 12 (Lagrange Interval Polynomial). Let $\mathcal{O}$ be an ODE $u' = f(t, u)$ and ms be the multistep solution of $\mathcal{O}$. A *Lagrange Interval Polynomial* and its derivative for $\mathcal{O}$ are the functions MS_L and DMS_L respectively defined by

$$
\begin{aligned}
MS_L(t_k, D_k, t) &= P_L(t_k, D_k, t) + E_L(t_k, D_k, t), \\
DMS_L(t_k, D_k, t) &= DP_L(t_k, D_k, t) + DE_L(t_k, D_k, t),
\end{aligned}
\tag{1}
$$

where

$$P_L(t_k, \mathbf{D}_k, t) = \sum_{i=0}^k D_i \varphi_i(t),$$
$$DP_L(t_k, \mathbf{D}_k, t) = \sum_{i=0}^k D_i \varphi_i'(t),$$
$$E_L(t_k, \mathbf{D}_k, t) = \frac{1}{(k+1)!} F^{(k)}(T_{t_k,t}, B_{t_k,t}) w(t), \qquad (2)$$
$$DE_L(t_k, \mathbf{D}_k, t) = \frac{1}{(k+1)!} F^{(k)}(T_{t_k,t}, B_{t_k,t}) w'(t),$$
$$w(t) = \prod_{i=0}^k (t - t_i).$$

and where F is an interval extension of f and $B_{t_k,t}$ is a bounding box of ms over $T_{t_k,t}$ wrt $\mathbf{D}_k$ and t_k.

We now show that, under certain restrictions on t, MS_L and DMS_L are interval extensions respectively of ms and $\frac{\partial ms}{\partial t}$ wrt the variables in $\mathbf{u}_k$.

Proposition 2 (Correctness of Lagrange Interval Polynomials). *Let $\mathcal{O}$ be an ODE $u' = f(t, u)$ whose solutions are in $C^{k+1}(T_{t_k,t}, \mathcal{R}^n)$, ms be the multistep solution of $\mathcal{O}$, and $\frac{\partial ms}{\partial t}$ be its derivative. Let MS_L and DMS_L be a Lagrange interval polynomial and its derivative for $\mathcal{O}$. Then, MS_L and DMS_L are interval extensions of ms and $\frac{\partial ms}{\partial t}$ wrt their second arguments forall $t \in (T_{t_k,t} \setminus T_{t_k}) \cup \{t_0, ..., t_k\}$.*

It is interesting at this point to make the connection between a natural multistep filtering operator based on Lagrange polynomials and Gear's method. Gear's method is a (traditional) implicit multistep method for solving ODEs that consists of solving (locally) a system of nonlinear equations based on Lagrange polynomial to find an (approximate) value at t_k given the (approximate) values at $t_0, \ldots, t_{k-1}$. The nonlinear equations in Gear's method specify implicitly the value of the solution at time t_k (i.e., there is no evaluation point t_e as in our case). The multistep filtering operator defined here uses Lagrange polynomials in a global way to prune the search space. As a consequence, at a very high level, the multistep filtering operator based on Lagrange polynomials is to Gear's method for ODEs what the interval Newton method is to Newton method for nonlinear equations.

4.2 An Hermite Polynomial Interval Extension

Lagrange polynomial interpolations are simple to compute but they only exploit a subset of the information available. For instance, they do not exploit the derivative information available at each evaluation point. This section presents an interpolation based on Hermite polynomials using this information. The intuition, depicted in Figure 2, is to constrain the polynomials to have acceptable slopes at the evaluation times. The figure, that uses the same differential equation as previously, shows that the interpolation polynomial must now have the correct slope at the various times. As can be seen, the slope at time t_e differs even much more from the solution than with Lagrange polynomials. As confirmed by our preliminary experimental results, the use of Hermite polynomials in the filtering operator should produce tighter enclosures of the multistep solution and its derivatives since the additional constraints tend to produce interpolation polynomials whose slopes are more similar (thus reducing the approximations due to interval computations).

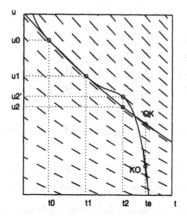

Fig. 2. Geometric Intuition for the Hermite Polynomials

Definition 13 (Hermite Polynomial [Atk88]). Let $u'_0, ..., u'_k \in \mathcal{R}^n$. Assume that $t_0, ..., t_k$ are distinct points. The *Hermite polynomial* that interpolates points $(t_0, u_0), ..., (t_k, u_k)$ and whose derivative interpolates points $(t_0, u'_0), ..., (t_k, u'_k)$ is the *unique* polynomial $p_H : \mathcal{R} \to \mathcal{R}^n$ of degree $\leq 2k + 1$ satisfying

$$p_H(t_i) = u_i, \quad 0 \leq i \leq k,$$
$$\frac{\partial p_H}{\partial t}(t_i) = u'_i, \quad 0 \leq i \leq k.$$

It is given by $p_H(t) = \sum_{i=0}^{k} u_i \varphi_i(t) + \sum_{i=0}^{k} u'_i \psi_i(t)$, where

$$l_i(t) = \frac{w(t)}{(t - t_i) w'(t_i)},$$
$$w(t) = \prod_{i=0}^{k} (t - t_i),$$
$$\psi_i(t) = (t - t_i)[l_i(t)]^2,$$
$$\varphi_i(t) = [1 - 2l'_i(t_i)(t - t_i)][l_i(t)]^2, \quad 0 \leq i \leq k.$$

We now bound the errors made by a Hermite polynomial.

Theorem 2 (Hermite Error Term). *Let $a, b \in \mathcal{R}$, g be a function in $C^{2k+2}([a, b], \mathcal{R}^n)$, p_H be the Hermite polynomial of degree $\leq 2k + 1$ that interpolates g at $k + 1$ distinct points $t_0, ..., t_k$ in the interval $[a, b]$ and whose derivative interpolates g' at $t_0, ..., t_k$, and $t \in [a, b] \setminus T_{t_k}$, Then,*

1. $\exists \zeta_t \in]a, b[: g(t) - p_H(t) = \frac{1}{(2k+2)!} g^{(2k+2)}(\zeta_t) w^2(t);$

2. $\exists \xi_t \in]a, b[: g'(t) - p'_H(t) = \frac{1}{(2k+2)!} g^{(2k+2)}(\xi_t)(w^2)'(t)$

It is now possible to obtain interval extensions of ms and its derivative.

Definition 14 (Hermite Interval Polynomial). Let $\mathcal{O}$ be an ODE $u' = f(t, u)$ and ms be the multistep solution of $\mathcal{O}$. An *Hermite interval polynomial* and its derivative for $\mathcal{O}$ are respectively the functions MS_H and DMS_H defined by

$$MS_H(\mathbf{t}_k, \mathbf{D}_k, t) = P_H(\mathbf{t}_k, \mathbf{D}_k, t) + E_H(\mathbf{t}_k, \mathbf{D}_k, t),$$
$$DMS_H(\mathbf{t}_k, \mathbf{D}_k, t) = DP_H(\mathbf{t}_k, \mathbf{D}_k, t) + DE_H(\mathbf{t}_k, \mathbf{D}_k, t), \tag{3}$$

where

$$P_H(\mathbf{t}_k, \mathbf{D}_k, t) = \sum_{i=0}^{k} D_i \varphi_i(t) + \sum_{i=0}^{k} F(t_i, D_i) \psi_i(t),$$
$$DP_H(\mathbf{t}_k, \mathbf{D}_k, t) = \sum_{i=0}^{k} D_i \varphi_i'(t) + \sum_{i=0}^{k} F(t_i, D_i) \psi_i'(t),$$
$$E_H(\mathbf{t}_k, \mathbf{D}_k, t) = \frac{1}{(2k+2)!} F^{(2k+1)}(T_{t_k,t}, B_{t_k,t}) w^2(t),$$
$$DE_H(\mathbf{t}_k, \mathbf{D}_k, t) = \frac{1}{(2k+2)!} F^{(2k+1)}(T_{t_k,t}, B_{t_k,t})(w^2)'(t),$$

(4)

and where F is an interval extension of f and $B_{t_k,t}$ is a bounding box of ms over $T_{t_k,t}$ wrt $\mathbf{D}_k$ and t_k.

We prove that MS_H and DMS_H are interval extensions respectively of ms and $\frac{\partial ms}{\partial t}$ wrt the variables in $\mathbf{u}_k$, under the conditions of Theorem 2.

Proposition 3 (Correctness of Hermite Interval Polynomials). *Let $\mathcal{O}$ be an ODE $u' = f(t, u)$ whose solutions are in $C^{2k+2}(T_{t_k,t}, \mathcal{R}^n)$, ms be the multistep solution of $\mathcal{O}$, and $\frac{\partial ms}{\partial t}$ be its derivative. Let MS_H and DMS_H be a Lagrange interval polynomial and its derivative for $\mathcal{O}$. Then, MS_H and DMS_H are interval extensions of ms and $\frac{\partial ms}{\partial t}$ wrt their second arguments forall $t \in (T_{t_k,t} \setminus T_{t_k})$.*

It is also important to discuss the choice of the evaluation point t_e in the filters using Hermite polynomials. On the one hand, because of the derivative constraints, choosing t_e too close from t_k produces too weak a constraint, since the filter is trivially satisfies at t_k. On the other hand, choosing it too far from t_k increases the sizes of the time intervals, of the bounding box, and, possibly, the polynomial evaluation itself. Hence, a reasonable choice of t_e should be a compromise between these two extremes. Of course, it is always possible to use several evaluation times.

5   A Mean-Value Multistep Filtering Operator

In solving nonlinear equations, it is often useful to use several interval extensions (e.g., the natural extension and the Taylor extension) since they complement each other well. The natural extension is in general more appropriate far from a solution, while the Taylor extension is better suited when the search is closer to a solution [VHLD97]. This idea has also been used in solving systems of differential equations [Loh87]. In this section, we present a mean-value form (MVF) of the multistep pruning operator.

To understand the main intuition, recall that the multistep filtering operator is a constraint of the form $\frac{\partial ms}{\partial t} - f(t_e, ms) = 0$ The idea is to replace the left-hand side of this equation by its mean-value form, while assuming that the multistep solution is of the form $ms = p + e$. Note that a direct application of the mean-value form would require to approximate a term of the form $\frac{\partial e}{\partial u}$, which is impossible since e is unknown. As a consequence, it is necessary to consider an interval extension E of function e that is independant from the variable u.

Definition 15 (Mean-Value Multistep Filtering Operator). Let $\mathcal{O}$ be an ODE $u' = f(t, u)$, let ms be the multistep solution of $\mathcal{O}$ expressed in the form $ms(t_k, u_k, t) = p(t_k, u_k, t) + e(t_k, u_k, t)$. A *mean-value multistep filtering* operator for $\mathcal{O}$ is an interval equation $K - [A]R^T = 0$ where $K \in \mathcal{I}^n$, $[A] \in \mathcal{I}^{n \times n(k+1)}$ and $R \in \mathcal{I}^{n(k+1)}$ are defined as

$$
\begin{aligned}
K &= DP(t_k, \overline{m_k}, t_e) + DE(t_k, \mathbf{D}_k, t_e) - F(\overline{t_e}, P(t_k, \overline{m_k}, t_e) + E(t_k, \mathbf{D}_k, t_e)), \\
[A] &= DF(\overline{t_e}, P(t_k, \mathbf{D}_k, t_e) + E(t_k, \mathbf{D}_k, t_e)) \cdot DUP(t_k, \mathbf{D}_k, t_e) \\
&\quad - DDP(t_k, \mathbf{D}_k, t_e), \\
R^T &= \begin{pmatrix} D_0^T - \overline{m_0}^T \\ \vdots \\ D_k^T - \overline{m_k}^T \end{pmatrix}
\end{aligned}
\tag{5}
$$

where P, DP, E, DE, DF, DUP, and DDP are interval extensions of $p, \frac{\partial p}{\partial t}, e, \frac{\partial e}{\partial t}, \frac{\partial f}{\partial u}$ (Jacobian of f), $\frac{\partial p}{\partial u_k}$ and $\frac{\partial}{\partial u_k}\frac{\partial p}{\partial t}$, wrt the variables in u_k and where $m_i \in D_i$ $(0 \le i \le k)$ and $\mathbf{m}_k = \langle m_0, \dots, m_k \rangle$.

Proposition 4 (Soundness of the Mean-Value Multistep Filtering Operator). *A mean-value multistep filtering operator is a pruning operator.*

6   Implementation Issues and Experimental Results

Let us briefly discuss implementation issues to indicate that the approach is reasonable from a computational standpoint. First, recall that any interval method should compute bounding boxes and Taylor coefficients over these boxes to produce the initial enclosures (forward step). As a consequence, the error terms in the interpolation polynomials can be computed during this forward step, without introducing any significant overhead. Second, observe that the polynomials themselves are trivial to construct and evaluate. The construction takes place only once and is about $O(k^2)$, where k is the number of evaluation times considered. An evaluation of the natural multistep filtering operator based on these polynomials takes $O(kn)$, where n is the dimension of the ODE system, which is close to optimality. As a consequence, the main complexity will be associated with the filtering algorithm itself. Finally, the mean-value and preconditioned operator can be constructed efficiently since they only require information (e.g. the Jacobian) that is needed in the forward step based on these techniques. An evaluation is slightly more costly but remains perfectly reasonable. Note also that the cost of the filter is substantially less than the backwards pruning technique proposed in [DJVH98] which involves computing the Taylor coefficients for each evaluation.

Let us now report some preliminary evidence that the filtering operator is an effective way to tighten the enclosures produced by the forward process. The results are only given for stiff problems although the filtering operator is also effective on simpler problems. The experimental results are obtained by applying box-consistency on the filtering operator based on Hermite polynomials of degree 5 (i.e. $k = 2$). Table 1 presents the results on a simple problem. It shows the

t	Taylor	With Natural Pruning	Ratio
0.0	[0.99900 , 1.00000]	[0.99900 , 1.00000]	1.0
0.1	[0.36248 , 0.37574]	[0.36347 , 0.37379]	1.3
...	...	...	...
0.5	[-0.23236 , 0.24592]	[-0.00021 , 0.01375]	34.2
...	...	...	...
1.0	[-35.38525 , 35.38534]	[-0.01066 , 0.01075]	3305.4
...	...	...	...
1.5	[-5236.05915 , 5236.05915]	[-0.01641 , 0.01641]	319077.3

Table 1. ODE $u'(t) = -10u(t)$

t	Piecewise Taylor	Taylor with Natural Pruning	Ratio
0.0	[0.00000 , 0.00000]	[0.00000 , 0.00000]	1.0
0.3	[-0.30291 , 0.89395]	[-0.07389 , 0.41865]	2.4
...	...	...	...
1.5	[-109.32716 , 111.32215]	[0.09149 , 1.95039]	118.7
...	...	...	...
3.0	[-50148.94757 , 50149.22981]	[-3.27441 , 3.96133]	13861.5

Table 2. ODE $u'(t) = -10(u(t) - \sin(t)) + \cos(t)$

substantial gain produced by the pruning step over a traditional interval Taylor method of order 4, using a natural filtering operator. Note that even with higher order interval Taylor series, the gain remains substantial (e.g. with a Taylor series of order 8, the gain is bigger than 10^5 at time 1.5). Table 3 considers a quadratic ODE and compares a Taylor MVF (mean-value form) method (of order 4) as in Lohner's method [Loh87] with a natural filtering operator and a mean-value filtering operator. The Taylor MVF method deteriorates quickly and explodes after time 3. The natural filtering operator does much better as can easily be seen. The mean-value filtering operator is even better and, in fact, converges towards the interval [0,0] when t grows. Table 2 considers another problem that leads to an explosion of the piecewise Taylor method (of order 4), i.e., the best forward method possible. The pruning step, using a natural filtering operator, substantially reduces the explosion in this case, although the step size is large (0.3). This clearly shows that the pruning step is orthogonal to the forward step (since it improves the best possible forward step) and is thus a promising research direction. Note also that a smaller step size (e.g., 0.2) would produce a tighter enclosure (e.g., [-0.14803,0.46879] at time 3) and smaller steps further improve the precision.

Acknowledgment This research is partially supported by the *Actions de recherche concertées (ARC/95/00-187)* of the Direction générale de la Recherche Scientifique – Communauté Franaise de Belgique and by an NSF NYI award.

260

t	Taylor MVF	With Natural Pruning	With Mean-Value Pruning
0.0	[0.99900 , 1.00000]	[0.99900 , 1.00000]	[0.99900 , 1.00000]
0.5	[0.46864 , 0.70655]	[0.55967 , 0.70655]	[0.55996 , 0.70655]
...	...	...	...
3.0	[-3.05917 , 2.54748]	[0.04613 , 0.29898]	[0.17931 , 0.21180]
...	...	...	...
5.0	...	[-0.07463 , 0.22312]	[0.11644 , 0.12998]

Table 3. ODE $u'(t) = -1.5u^2(t)$

References

[Abe88]   Oliver Aberth. *Precise Numerical Analysis*. William Brown, 1988.

[AH83]   G. Alefeld and J. Herzberger. *Introduction to Interval Computations*. Academic Press, New York, NY, 1983.

[Atk88]   K.E. Atkinson. *An Introduction to Numerical Analysis*. Wiley, 1988.

[BBCG96] Martin Berz, Christian Bischof, George Corliss, and Andreas Griewank, editors. *Computational Differentiation: Techniques, Applications, and Tools*. SIAM, Philadelphia, Penn., 1996.

[Cor88]   George F. Corliss. Applications of differentiation arithmetic. In R.E. Moore, editor, *Reliability in Computing*, pages 127–148. Academic Press, 1988.

[DJVH98] Y. Deville, M. Janssen, and P. Van Hentenryck. Consistency Techniques in Ordinary Differential Equations. In *International Conference on Principles and Practice on Constraint Programming, LNCS 1520*, pages 162–176, 1998.

[KC96]   D. Kincaid and W. Cheney. *Numerical Analysis*. Brooks/Cole, 1996.

[Loh87]   Rudolf J. Lohner. Enclosing the solutions of ordinary initial and boundary value problems. In Edgar W. Kaucher, Ulrich W. Kulisch, and Christian Ullrich, editors, *Computer Arithmetic: Scientific Computation and Programming Languages*, pages 255–286. Wiley, 1987.

[Moo66]   R.E. Moore. *Interval Analysis*. Prentice-Hall, Englewood Cliffs, NJ, 1966.

[Moo79]   R.E. Moore. *Methods and Applications of Interval Analysis*. SIAM, 1979.

[Neu90]   A. Neumaier. *Interval Methods for Systems of Equations*. PHI Series in Computer Science. Cambridge University Press, Cambridge, 1990.

[Ral80]   Louis B. Rall. Applications of software for automatic differentiation in numerical computation. In Götz Alefeld and R. D. Grigorieff, editors, *Fundamentals of Numerical Computation (Computer Oriented Numerical Analysis)*, Computing Supplement No. 2, pages 141–156. Springer-Verlag, 1980.

[Ral81]   Louis B. Rall. *Automatic Differentiation: Techniques and Applications*, volume 120 of *Lecture Notes in Computer Science*. Springer-Verlag, 1981.

[Sta96]   O. Stauning. Enclosing Solutions of Ordinary Differential Equations. Tech. Report IMM-REP-1996-18, Technical University Of Denmark, 1996.

[VH98a]   P. Van Hentenryck. A Constraint Satisfaction Approach to a Circuit Design Problem. *Journal of Global Optimization*, 13:75–93, 1998.

[VH98b]   P. Van Hentenryck. A Gentle Introduction to Numerica. *Artificial Intelligence*, 103(1-2):209–235, 1998.

[VHLD97] P. Van Hentenryck, M. Laurent, and Y. Deville. *Numerica, A Modeling Language for Global Optimization*. MIT Press, 1997.

A Framework for Constraint Programming Based Column Generation*

Ulrich Junker[1], Stefan E. Karisch[2], Niklas Kohl[2], Bo Vaaben[3], Torsten Fahle[4],
and Meinolf Sellmann[4]

[1] ILOG S.A., 1681, route des Dolines, F-06560 Valbonne, France,
junker@ilog.fr
[2] Carmen Systems AB, Odinsgatan 9, S-41103 Gothenburg, Sweden,
stefank@carmen.se and niklas@carmen.se
[3] Technical University of Denmark, Department of Mathematical Modelling,
Building 321, DK-2800 Lyngby, Denmark,
bo.vaaben@sas.dk
[4] University of Paderborn, Department of Mathematics and Computer Science,
Fürstenallee 11, D-33102 Paderborn, Germany,
tef@uni-paderborn.de and sello@uni-paderborn.de

Abstract. Column generation is a state-of-the-art method for optimally solving difficult large-scale optimization problems such as airline crew assignment. We show how to apply column generation even if those problems have complex constraints that are beyond the scope of pure OR methods. We achieve this by formulating the subproblem as a constraint satisfaction problem (CSP). We also show how to efficiently treat the special case of shortest path problems by introducing an efficient path constraint that exploits dual values from the master problem to exclude nodes that will not lead to paths with negative reduced costs. We demonstrate that this propagation significantly reduces the time needed to solve crew assignment problems.

Keywords: constraint satisfaction, column generation, path constraint, airline crew assignment, hybrid OR/CP methods

1 Introduction

The column generation method, also known as Dantzig-Wolfe decomposition, is a powerful method for solving large-scale linear and integer programming problems. Its origins date back to the works of Dantzig and Wolfe [6] and Gilmore and Gomory [9].

---

* The production of this paper was supported by the PARROT project, partially funded by the ESPRIT programme of the Commission of the European Union as project number 24 960. The partners in the project are ILOG (F), Lufthansa Systems (D), Carmen Systems (S), Olympic Airways (GR), University of Paderborn (D), University of Athens (GR). This paper reflects the opinions of the authors and not necessarily those of the consortium.

Column generation is a method to avoid considering all variables of a problem explicitly. Take as an example a linear program with an extremely large number of variables. We could solve this problem by only considering a small subset X' of the set of variables X. The resulting problem is usually denoted the *master problem*. Once it is solved, we pose the question: "Are there any variables in $X \backslash X'$ which can be used to improve the solution?". Duality theory provides a necessary condition that a variable with negative reduced cost is the right choice and the simplex algorithm tries to find such a variable by explicitly calculating the reduced cost of all variables. The column generation idea is to find the variables with negative reduced costs without explicitly enumerating all variables. In the case of a general linear program this is not possible, but for many kinds of problems it is possible, as we shall see. The search for variables with negative reduced costs is performed in the so called *subproblem*. Theoretically, this may still require the generation of all variables. However, in practice such behavior is rare.

In the discussion above the master problem was assumed to be a linear program. In many applications, including the one described in this work, the master problem is a mixed integer linear program (MIP). This is a complication because the linear programming duality theory is not valid for MIPs, and there is no easy way to characterize a variable which may improve the current solution. In practice one solves the continuous relaxation of the problem first, and then applies branch-and-bound to obtain an integer solution. We will not discuss this issue further and refer to [7] for a more detailed discussion. The subproblem consists of finding the variables which will have negative reduced costs in the current master problem. Usually the subproblem is not a linear program, but rather a specially structured integer program. However, this does not constitute a problem as it can be solved reasonably fast.

Column generation has been applied to a large number of problems. The first application consisted of specially structured linear programs. An other classical application is the so called "cutting stock problem" [9] where the subproblem is a knapsack problem. More recent applications include specially structured integer programs such as the generalized assignment problem and time constrained vehicle routing, crew pairing, crew assignment and related problems [7].

In this work we consider the integration of column generation and constraint programming (CP). The problem may be formulated as a linear integer program with an extremely large number of variables. Again, since one cannot consider all these explicitly, one wants to generate the variables as needed. Often, the subproblem contains a large number of non-linear constraints and it is therefore not so well suited for the traditional operations research (OR) algorithms. Instead, we propose to apply a CP approach to solve the subproblem. The column generation theory tells us, that a useful variable must have a negative reduced cost in the current master problem. This can obviously be used to introduce a negative reduced costs constraint in the CP model.

The main contribution of our work is the bridging of CP and OR by introducing a general framework for column generation based on CP. Moreover, we show how to efficiently implement an important special case of this framework, i.e. we establish the valid propagation rules and show how the propagation can be performed efficiently. The special case of the framework is then applied successfully to the airline crew assignment problem, a difficult large scale resource allocation problem with a huge number of complex constraints. The integration of OR and CP techniques applied to airline crew assignment is investigated in the ESPRIT project PARROT (Parallel Crew Rostering) [14] where also this work has been carried out.

The usefulness of column generation compared to a direct CP/LP approach has, for example, been demonstrated in the ESPRIT project CHIC II for a large-scale resource allocation problem with maintenance scheduling [12]. We go a step further and address problems where traditional column generation cannot be applied.

The organization of this paper is as follows. Section 2 presents the case study of airline crew assignment. The framework for CP based column generation is introduced in Sect. 3 and efficient propagation methods for an important special case of the framework are described in Sect. 4. In Sect. 5 the new generation approach is applied to the airline crew assignment problem and numerical results based on real data are presented which indicate the effectiveness of our approach.

2 Case study: airline crew assignment

Crew scheduling at airlines is usually divided into a crew pairing and a crew assignment (or rostering) phase. Firstly, anonymous pairings (or crew rotations) are formed out of the flight legs (flights without stopover) such that the crew needs on each flight are covered. Then in crew assignment, the pairings together with other activities such as ground duties, reserve duties and off-duty blocks are sequenced to rosters and assigned to individual crew members. In both problems, complex rules and regulations coming from legislation and contractual agreements have to be met by the solutions and some objective function has to be optimized. The airline crew assignment problem can be viewed as resource allocation problem where the activities to be assigned are fixed in time. In practice, around 100 complex rules and regulations have to be met by the created rosters, and additional constraints between rosters and/or crew members have to be taken into account. The problem is considered to be large scale, and in concrete applications, several thousand activities have to be assigned to up to 1000 crew members. In this paper, we apply our approach to real data of a major European airline.

The standard methods for solving crew assignment problems are based on the generate and optimize principle, i.e. on column generation. In the master problem, a set partitioning type problem is solved to select exactly one roster for each crew member such that the capacities of the activities are met, the solution satisfies constraints between several crew members, and the objective is optimized. Since it is not possible to have an explicit representation of all possible rosters, the master problem is always defined on a subset of all possible rosters.

In the subproblem, a large number of legal rosters is generated. This is either done by partial enumeration based on propagation and pruning techniques [13], or by solving a constrained shortest path problem where the constraints ensure that only legal rosters are generated, and where the objective function is equivalent to the reduced costs of the roster with respect to the solution of the continuous relaxation of the master problem defined on the previously generated rosters [8]. The latter approach is known as constrained shortest path column generation. In that approach the subproblem is solved optimally and one can prove that it is possible to obtain the optimal solution to the entire problem without explicit enumeration of all possible rosters. In either case one can iterate between the subproblem and the master problem.

Constrained shortest path column generation is a very powerful technique in terms of optimization potential, but efficient algorithms for the constrained shortest path problem do not permit arbitrary constraints. Therefore this approach is not compatible with all real-world rules and regulations. Using the framework presented below, we show how to overcome these limitations for the difficult problem of crew assignment. As a result, we maintain full expressiveness with respect to rules and regulations, and obtain the optimization benefits of the column generation approach.

3 A framework for CP based column generation

3.1 The general framework

In this section, we introduce a general framework for constraint programming based column generation where the master problem is a MIP. The novelty is that the subproblem can be an arbitrary CSP which has two major advantages. Firstly, it generalizes the class of subproblems and thus allows to use column generation even if the subproblem does not reduce to a MIP-problem. Secondly, it allows to exploit constraint satisfaction techniques to solve the subproblem. Constraint-based column generation is particularly well-suited for subproblems that can partially, but not entirely be solved by polynomial OR methods. In this case, some constraints do not fit and have to be treated separately. In the constraint satisfaction approach, the optimization algorithm, as well as the algorithms of the other constraints will be used in a uniform way, namely to reduce the domains of variables. We can also say that the CSP-approach allows different algorithms to communicate and to co-operate.

The basic idea of constraint programming based column generation is very simple. The master problem is a mixed integer problem which has a set of linear constraints and a linear cost function and the columns (or variables) of the master problem are not given explicitly. Without loss of generality, we assume that the objective is to be minimized. The subproblem is an arbitrary CSP. For each solution of the subproblem there exists a variable in the master problem. Of course, we have to know the coefficients of the variable in all linear constraints of the master problem and in its linear cost function. For each of these coefficients $a_{i,j}$, we introduce a corresponding variable y_i in the subproblem. Furthermore, we introduce a variable z for the coefficient c_j in the cost function. Given a solution v_j of the subproblem, the coefficient $a_{i,j}$ of the variable x_j in the i-th linear constraint is then obtained as the value of the variable y_i in the given solution.

Representing coefficients by variables of the subproblem also allows to ensure that solutions of the subproblem have negative reduced costs. Given a solution of a linear relaxation of the master problem, we consider the dual values λ_i of each constraint i. We then simply introduce a linear constraint in the subproblem which is formulated on z and the y_i-s and which uses the dual values as coefficients.

We now introduce these ideas more formally. A constraint satisfaction problem is defined as follows:

Definition 1. *Let $P := (\mathcal{X}, D, \mathcal{C})$ be a constraint satisfaction problem (CSP) where $\mathcal{X}$ is a set of variables, D is a set of values, and $\mathcal{C}$ is a set of constraints of the form $((x_1, \ldots, x_n), R)$ where $x_i \in \mathcal{X}$ and $R \subseteq D^n$ is a relation. A mapping $v : \mathcal{X} \rightarrow D$ of the variables to the values of the domain satisfies a constraint $((x_1, \ldots, x_n), R)$ of $\mathcal{C}$ iff $(v(x_1), \ldots, v(x_n))$ is an element of the relation R. A solution of P is a mapping $v : \mathcal{X} \rightarrow D$ that satisfies all constraints in $\mathcal{C}$.*

When defining a specific constraint with variables $(x_1, \ldots, x_n)$ then we define the relation of this constraint as the set of all tuples $(\bar{x}_1, \ldots, \bar{x}_n)$ satisfying a given condition $C(\bar{x}_1, \ldots, \bar{x}_n)$. Thus, $\bar{x}$ is used to denote the value of x in the considered tuple.

A subproblem can be represented by an arbitrary CSP. A constraint of the master problem is represented by a variable of this subproblem, a sign, and a right-hand-side.

Definition 2. *Let $SP := (\mathcal{X}, D, \mathcal{C})$ be a CSP. A master constraint for SP is a triple (y, s, b) where $y \in \mathcal{X}$, $s \in \{-1, 0, +1\}$ and b is arbitrary.*

The master problem is then specified by a subproblem, a set of m master constraints, and a variable representing the cost coefficient of a column.

Definition 3. *A master problem MP is specified by a triple $(SP, \mathcal{M}, z)$ where SP is a CSP $(\mathcal{X}, D, \mathcal{C})$, $\mathcal{M} = \{mc_1, \ldots mc_m\}$ is a set of master constraints for SP and $z \in \mathcal{X}$ is a variable of SP.*

Given a master problem and a set S of solutions of the subproblem, we define a mixed integer problem MIP representing MP as follows:

Definition 4. *Let MP be a master problem as in Def. 3 and S be a set of solutions of the subproblem SP of MP. The MIP representing MP and S is defined as follows:*

1. *For each solution $v \in S$ of SP there exists a variable x_v.*

2. *For each master constraint $mc_i = (y_i, s_i, b_i)$ there exists a linear constraint of the following form*

$$\sum_{v \in S} v(y_i) \cdot x_v \leq b_i \quad \sum_{v \in S} v(y_i) \cdot x_v = b_i \quad \sum_{v \in S} v(y_i) \cdot x_v \geq b_i \tag{1}$$
$$\text{for } s_i = -1 \qquad \text{for } s_i = 0 \qquad \text{for } s_i = 1$$

3. *The objective is to minimize $\sum_{v \in S} v(z) \cdot x_v$.*

(Again, without loss of generality we consider a minimization problem only.) An optimal solution of the linear relaxation of this MIP (plus optional branching decisions) produces dual values for the master constraint (y, s, b). We can use them to add a negative reduced cost constraint to the subproblem:

Definition 5. *Let λ_i be a dual value for the master constraint (y_i, s_i, b_i). Then the* negative reduced cost constraint *(NRC) for these dual values has the variables $(z, y_1, \ldots, y_n)$ and is defined by the following condition:*

$$\overline{z} - \sum_{i=1}^{n} \lambda_i \cdot \overline{y}_i \leq 0 \tag{2}$$

Although it is sufficient to generate arbitrary columns with negative reduced costs, columns with smaller reduced costs will lead to better solutions of the master problem. We therefore introduce a variable for the left-hand-side of (2) and we use it as objective for the subproblem.

Hence, we obtain a simple framework that defines constraint programming based column generations. A column of the master problem is represented by a solution of a subproblem. Furthermore, the coefficient of a column in a constraint is represented by a variable of the subproblem. Our framework is compatible with different methods for solving the master problem, e.g. the Branch-and-Price method where columns are generated in the search nodes of the master problem (cf. e.g. [1] for details).

3.2 Path optimization subproblems

In many applications of column generation, the subproblem reduces to a problem of finding a shortest path in a graph that satisfies additional constraints. We now show how to express this important special case in our framework.

For the sake of brevity, we limit our discussion to directed acyclic graphs. Let (V, E) be a directed acyclic graph where $V := \{0, \ldots, n+1\}$ is the set of nodes. Let $e := |E|$ be the number of edges. We suppose that $s := 0$ is a unique source node, that $t := n+1$ is a unique sink node, and that the graph is topologically ordered[1] (i.e. $(i, j) \in E$ implies $i < j$).

We now suppose that the subproblem consists of finding a path through this graph that respects additional constraints. Furthermore, we suppose that there

---

[1] Each directed acyclic graph can be transformed into a graph of this form in time $O(n + e)$.

are master constraints that count how often a node occurs in a path. Given a solution of the subproblem, the coefficient of the corresponding column in such a constraint has the value 1 iff the considered node occurs in the selected path. For each node $i \in \mathcal{N} := \{1, \ldots, n\}$, we therefore introduce a boolean variable y_i in the subproblem. This variable has the value 1 iff node i is contained in the selected path. Thus, the path is represented by an array of boolean variables. In some cases, it is also of advantage to represent it by a constrained set variable[2] Y. The value $v(Y)$ of this variable is a subset of $\mathcal{N}$. Given this set variable, we can define the boolean variables by the following constraint:

$$\overline{y}_i = 1 \text{ iff } i \in \overline{Y} \tag{3}$$

The cost coefficient of a variable in the master problem can often be expressed as costs of the selected path. We therefore suppose that edge costs $c_{i,j}$ are given for each edge $(i,j) \in E$. In order to determine the path costs, we need the next node of a given node $i \in \mathcal{N} \cup \{s\}$. For direct acyclic graphs, this next node is uniquely defined.[3]

$$next(i, Y) := min(\{j \in \overline{Y} \mid j > i\} \cup \{t\}) \tag{4}$$

We now suppose that the cost variable z of the subproblem is the sum between the path costs and a remainder z'.

$$\overline{z} = \overline{z}' + \sum_{i \in \overline{Y} \cup \{s\}} c_{i, next(i,Y)} \tag{5}$$

We can also express the negative reduced cost constraint in this form. In addition to the boolean variable y_i, we can have n' variables y_i' for other kinds of master constraints. Let λ_i be the dual values for y_i and λ_i' be the dual values for y_i'. The dual vales λ_i can immediately be subtracted from the original edge costs:

$$c_{i,j}' := \begin{cases} c_{i,j} & \text{if } i = s \\ c_{i,j} - \lambda_i & \text{otherwise} \end{cases} \tag{6}$$

The negative reduced cost constraint has then the form

$$\sum_{i \in \overline{Y} \cup \{s\}} c_{i, next(i,Y)}' + \left(\overline{z}' - \sum_{i=1}^{n'} \lambda_i' \cdot \overline{y}_i' \right) \leq 0 \tag{7}$$

The first part is the modified path costs. The second part treats the remaining costs and has the form of the usual negative reduced cost constraint. Below, we introduce a single constraint that ensures that Y represents a path and that also determines the cost of the path. It thus allows to encode the constraints above. This constraint needs only the set variable and a description of the graph. It avoids the introduction of additional variables for $next(i, Y)$ and $c_{i, next(i,Y)}$.

---

[2] Constrained set variables are supported by [11] and allow a compact representation of an array of boolean variables. Constraints on set variables such as sum-over-set constraints often allow a better and more efficient propagation than corresponding constraints on boolean variables.

[3] For cyclic graphs, we have to introduce constraint variables for the next node.

4 An efficient path constraint on set variables

4.1 Semantics and propagation

In this section, we introduce an efficient path constraint for directed acyclic graphs with edge costs (so-called networks). The constraint ensures that a given set variable represents a path through this graph. Furthermore, the constraint ensures that a given variable represents the cost of this path. We also show how bound consistency can be achieved by determining shortest and longest paths.

The path constraint is defined for a directed acyclic graph (V, E) (of the same form as introduced in Sect. 3.2), the edge costs $c_{i,j}$, a set variable Y and a variable z. The constraint has the variables Y and z and is defined by two conditions:

1. Y represents a path in the graph from source s to sink t, i.e. $\overline{Y} \subseteq \mathcal{N}$ and

$$\{(i, next(i, Y)) \mid i \in \overline{Y} \cup \{s\}\} \subseteq E \qquad (8)$$

2. z is the sum of the edge costs

$$\overline{z} = \sum_{i \in \overline{Y} \cup \{s\}} c_{i, next(i, Y)} \qquad (9)$$

Compared to the existing path constraint of ILOG SOLVER 4.3 [11], the new path constraint is formulated on a set variable and can thus add arbitrary nodes of $\mathcal{N}$ to a partially known path or remove them from it.

Next we discuss how to achieve bound consistency for the path constraint. We introduce lower and upper bounds for the variables z and Y. Let $min(z)$ be a lower bound for the value of z and $max(z)$ be an upper bound. Furthermore, let $req(Y)$ be a lower bound for the set variable Y. This set contains all the elements that must be contained in the path and is therefore called required set. Furthermore, let $pos(Y)$ be an upper bound for Y. This set is also called possible set since it contains the nodes that can possibly belong to the path.

We say that a path P is *admissible* (w.r.t. the given bounds) if it starts in the source s, terminates in the sink t, and $req(Y) \subseteq P \subseteq pos(Y)$. We say that a path P is *consistent* (w.r.t. the given bounds) if it is admissible and if the costs of the path are greater than $min(z)$ and smaller than $max(z)$. We say that the *bounds are consistent* if they satisfy the following conditions:

1. For each $i \in pos(Y)$ there exists a consistent path P through i and for each $i \notin req(Y)$ there exists a consistent path P that does not contain i.
2. There exist a consistent path with costs $max(z)$ and a consistent path with costs $min(z)$.

If the given bounds are not consistent then we can make them tighter using the following propagation rules.

1. If the bound $min(z)$ is smaller than the costs lb of the shortest admissible path (or $+\infty$ if there is no admissible path) then we replace it by lb. If the bound $max(z)$ is greater than the costs ub of the longest admissible path (or $-\infty$ if there is no admissible path) then we replace it by ub.
2. If the costs of the shortest admissible path through i for $i \in pos(Y)$ are strictly greater than the upper bound $max(z)$ then we can remove i from $pos(Y)$. If the costs of the longest admissible path through i for $i \in pos(Y)$ are strictly smaller than the lower bound $min(z)$ then we can remove i from $pos(Y)$.
3. If the costs of the shortest admissible path that does not contain i for $i \notin req(Y)$ are strictly greater than the upper bound $max(z)$ then we have to add i to $req(Y)$. If the costs of the longest admissible path that does not contain i for $i \notin req(Y)$ are strictly smaller than the lower bound $min(z)$ then we have to add i to $req(Y)$.

Repeated application of these propagation rules will establish consistent bounds (or lead to an empty domain, i.e. an inconsistency). The propagation rules themselves require the detection of shortest (and longest) admissible paths. Some of them require that these paths contain a given node i, others require that the paths do not contain a node i. In the next section, we show how shortest paths satisfying these conditions can be computed efficiently. Furthermore, we discuss how to maintain these paths when incremental updates occur. Longest paths can be determined similarly by applying the algorithms to the negated edge costs $-c_{i,j}$ and to the negated cost variable $-y$.

4.2 Initial and incremental propagation algorithms

In order to achieve bound consistency for the path constraint, we have to find shortest paths from the source to all the nodes. Since we deal with directed acyclic graphs we can use a variant of Dijkstra's shortest path algorithm that visits nodes in topological order and thus runs in linear time $O(n + e)$. Furthermore, it does not require that edge costs are positive (cf. e.g. [5] for details).

However, we have to ensure that the algorithm determines only nodes which are subsets of $pos(Y)$ and supersets of $req(Y)$. For this purpose, we consider only nodes in $pos(Y)$ and we ignore all edges (i, j) that go around a node of $req(Y)$. That means if there is a $k \in req(Y)$ s.t. $i < k < j$ then we do not consider (i, j). This can be done efficiently by determining the smallest element of $req(Y)$ that is strictly greater than i.

For propagation rule 2 we must determine the cost of a shortest admissible path going through node $i \in pos(Y)$. This cost is simply the sum of the costs y_i^s of the shortest path from the sink to node i and the costs y_i^t of the shortest path from i to the sink. The latter can be computed with the same algorithm by just inverting all the edges and by applying it to the sink. If $y_i^s + y_i^t$ is strictly greater than $max(z)$ we remove i from the possible set. Algorithm 1 shows the implementation of propagation rules 1 and 2.

For the sake of brevity, we omit the detailed algorithm for propagation rule 3 and outline only the idea. We remove all edges (i, j) if the costs of the shortest

---

Algorithm 1 Shortest Path with propagation rules 1 and 2

---

  for all $i \in V$ do
    $y_i^s := \infty;\ y_i^s := \infty;\ \pi_i := \text{NIL};\ \sigma_i := \text{NIL};\ /\!/\ Init$
    $y_s^s := 0;\ y_t^t := 0;\ k^s := 0;\ k^t := 0\ /\!/\ Init\ source\ and\ sink$
  $/\!/\ determining\ shortest\ path\ from\ source\ s\ to\ all\ nodes$
  for all $i \in V$ taken in increasing topological order do
    if $k^s \leq i$ then
      $k^s := min\{l \in req(Y) \mid l > i\};$
    for all $j \in pos(Y)$ s.t. $(i,j) \in E$ and $j \leq k^s$ do
    if $y_j^s > y_i^s + c_{i,j}$ then
      $y_j^s := y_i^s + c_{i,j};\ \pi_j := i;$
  $/\!/\ determining\ reverse\ shortest\ path\ from\ sink\ t\ to\ all\ nodes$
  for all $i \in V$ taken in decreasing topological order do
    if $k^t \geq i$ then
      $k^t := max\{l \in req(Y) \mid l < i\};$
    for all $j \in pos(Y)$ s.t. $(j,i) \in E$ and $j \geq k^t$ do
    if $y_j^t > y_i^t + c_{j,i}$ then
      $y_j^t := y_i^t + c_{j,i};\ \sigma_j := i$
  if $y_t^s > min(z)$ then
    $min(z) := y_t^s\ /\!/\ propagation\ rule\ 1$
  for all $i \in pos(Y)$ do
    if $y_i^s + y_i^t > max(z)$ then
      $pos(Y) := pos(Y) \setminus \{i\}\ /\!/\ propagation\ rule\ 2$

---

path through this edge are strictly greater than $max(z)$. We then determine the cut nodes of the resulting graph and add them to $req(Y)$. The edge removal and the cut point detection can be achieved in time $O(n+e)$ which allows us to state the following theorem.

Theorem 1. *Bound consistency for the path constraint on a directed acyclic graph can be computed in time $O(n + e)$.*

We are also interested in how to maintain bound consistency efficiently and we suppose that we can use the AC5-algorithm [10] as implemented in ILOG SOLVER as a framework for this. We thus obtain changes of the domains of z and Y (increase of $min(z)$; decrease of $max(z)$; elements added to $req(Y)$; elements removed from $pos(Y)$). We detail only the last event. Interestingly, the shortest path algorithm already provides a notion of current support that allows to implement an incremental algorithm in the style of AC6 [3]. Each node i has a current predecessor π_i and a current successor σ_i. We have to update the costs y_i^s if the the current predecessor π_i is removed from the possible set or the costs $y_{\pi_i}^s$ have been changed. In order to achieve this, we introduce a list of nodes that are currently supported by a given node. If k is removed from the possible set we visit all nodes i supported by k and update their costs. If the costs change then we apply propagation rule 2 to i. Furthermore, we repeat the procedure for the nodes supported by i. Further work is needed to elaborate the details of this procedure and to check whether propagation rule 3, as well as the other events can be treated similarly. Moreover, we will analyze the precise complexity of maintaining bound consistency.

5 Application to crew assignment

5.1 The subproblem of column generation

The constraints of the crew assignment problem are formulated in the PARROT roster library which provides a modeling layer on top of ILOG SOLVER. This layer facilitates the expression of complex crew regulations and translates them into constraints on set variables describing the activities of a crew member and on integer variables describing derived attributes of crew members and activities.

The roster library introduces new constraints on set variables such as a sum-over-set-constraint, a next- and a previous-constraint, and a gliding-sum constraint. The previous constraint can, for example, be used to define the rest time before an activity as the difference between its start time and the end time of the previous activity. The gliding-sum constraint ensures that the amount of flight time of a crew member in time windows of a given length does not exceed a maximal flight time. Those constraints ensure bound consistency for the set and integer variables.

When we generate rosters for a selected crew member we additionally set up a legality graph between the possible activities of this crew member and post the path constraint on his/her set variable. The graph describes the possible successions between activities as established by roster library propagation. An activity j can be a direct successor of an activity i if we do not get an inconsistency when assigning i and j to the crew member and when removing all activities between i and j from her/him.

The generation process is usually iterative, i.e. after generating a certain number of rosters, the master problem is solved. The duals are then used to generate new rosters, and so on. We point out, that in the application to crew assignment, we usually do not encounter a gap between the final continuous linear programming relaxation of the master problem, thus we can prove optimality in the present case. We also note that in most cases, the cost structure of crew assignment problems meets the assumption of Sect. 3.2.

5.2 Numerical results

In this section, we present computational results on real test data of a major European airline. The considered test cases consist of typical selections of the rules and regulations from the production system of the airline. These, together with crew information and the activities to be assigned, form the so called Large-Size-Airline-Case in PARROT. In the present paper, we use a simplified but representative objective function and we do not consider constraints concerning more than one roster which means that the master problem is a set partitioning problem. However, from our experience with the data we consider the obtained results as representative.

In the following we highlight some of the findings of the experiments. Thereby we characterize an instance by the number of crew members, the number of preassigned activities, and the number of activities to be assigned. For example, an instance of type 10-16-40 consists of 10 crew members, 16 preassignments, and 40 activities.

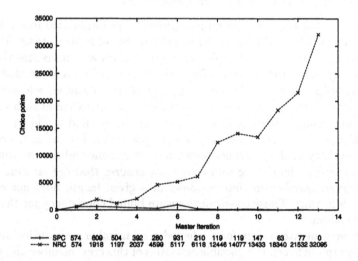

SPC	574	609	504	392	280	931	210	119	119	147	63	77	0
NRC	574	1918	1197	2037	4599	5117	6118	12446	14077	13433	18340	21532	32095

Fig. 1. Number of choice points for NRC and SPC for an instance of type 7-0-30.

Firstly, we compare the number of choice points considered when using the shortest path constraint (SPC) with the propagation as described in Sect. 4 and with the use of the "pure" NRC as defined in Def. 5. The result for a small instance of type 7-0-30, where one can still prove optimality using NRC only, is shown in Fig. 1. The pruning effect of SPC allows to prove optimality in iteration 13 without considering any choice points, while it becomes very expensive to prove optimality when using NRC only. Figure 2 presents the pruning behavior of SPC for instances of type 40-100-199 and 65-165-250 which is of the same type as for the smaller instance.

The reduction of choice points does not automatically yield a better computation time, as the time spent per choice point tends to be higher. However, Fig. 3 shows that the latter is not the case. The left plot shows a comparison of two program versions, one using SPC and one using NCR only, in a time versus quality diagram. Although the SPC version needs more time in the beginning (due to the more costly initial propagation), it catches up quickly and performs much better than the version not using it. In Fig. 3 we also compare the behavior of IP-costs and LP-costs in the right diagram. As mentioned above, the gap between IP and LP diminishes, i.e. it is possible to prove optimality. We also performed experiments on how well SPC scales. The results showed that the pruning effect of SPC gets better for growing input size.

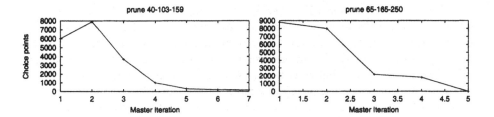

Fig. 2. Pruning for SPC for instances of type 40-100-199 and 65-165-250.

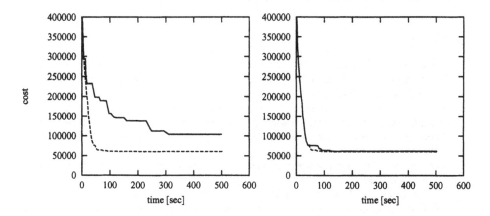

Fig. 3. The left picture shows time versus quality with and without SPC and the right picture the development of LP- and IP-costs with SPC on an instance of type 10-16-40.

To give two concrete examples for running times for solving problems to optimality using SPC: an instance of the type 40-103-199 took 1921 seconds and an instance of the type 65-165-250 took 3162 seconds of CPU time on a Sun Ultra Enterprise 450 with 300 MHz. These running times are encouraging, considering the early stage of the development of the different software components used to perform the computations.[4]

6 Conclusions

In this paper, we introduced and applied a framework for constraint programming based column generation, which is a new way for integrating constraint programming and linear programming. This allows to tackle large-scale optimization problems of a certain structure. Compared to traditional methods of column generation, we formulate the subproblem as a CSP and thus extend the modeling facilities of column generation. Compared to co-operative solvers (cf.

---

[4] In PARROT, these software components are currently further developed and significant performance improvements can be expected.

e.g. [2,4,15]), the CP and LP solver do not communicate only by reducing domains, but mainly by exchanging solutions and dual values. The use of the duals in the negative reduced cost constraint reduces the domains for the next solution. Optimization methods that are usually used for solving the subproblem can be encapsulated in a global constraint. We demonstrated this for shortest path problems and developed a path constraint on set variables for networks that achieves bound consistency in linear time. This new path constraint has been a key element for optimally solving difficult airline crew assignment problems. We have thus demonstrated that constraint programming can indeed increase the power of the column generation method.

References

1. C. Barnhart, E.L. Johnson, G.L. Nemhauser, M.W.P. Savelsbergh, and P.H. Vance. Branch-and-Price: Column Generation for Huge Integer Programs. In *Operations Research*, 46:316-329, 1998.
2. H. Beringer and B. De Backer. Combinatorial problem solving in constraint logic programming with cooperative solvers. In C. Beierle and L. Plumer, editors, *Logic Programming: Formal Methods and Practical Applications*, pages 245-272. Elsevier, 1995.
3. C. Bessière. Arc-consistency and arc-consistency again. *Artificial Intelligence*, 65:179-190, 1994.
4. A. Bockmayr and T. Kasper. Branch-and-Infer: A unifying framework for integer and finite domain constraint programming. *INFORMS Journal of Computing*, 10(3):287-300, 1998.
5. T.H. Cormen, C.E. Leierson, R.L. Riverste. *Introduction to Algorithms*, McGraw-Hill, 1990.
6. G.B. Dantzig and P. Wolfe. The decomposition algorithm for linear programs. *Econometrica*, 29(4):767-778, 1961.
7. J. Desrosiers, M.M. Solomon, and F. Soumis. Time constrained routing and scheduling. In *Handbooks of Operations Research and Management Science*, 8:35-139, 1993.
8. F. Gamache, F. Soumis, D. Villeneuve, J. Desrosiers, and E. Gélinas. The preferential bidding system at Air Canada. *Transportation Science*, 32(3):246-255, 1998.
9. P.C. Gilmore and R.E. Gomory. A linear programming approach to the cutting stock problem. *Operations Research*, 9:849-859, 1961.
10. P. Van Hentenryck, Y. Deville, and C.M. Teng. A generic arc-consistency algorithm and its specializations. *Artificial Intelligence*, 57:291-321, 1992.
11. ILOG. ILOG SOLVER. Reference manual and user manual. V4.3, ILOG, 1998.
12. E. Jacquet-Lagreze and M. Lebbar. Column generation for a scheduling problem with maintenance constraints. In *CP'98 Workshop on Large-Scale Combinatorial Optimization and Constraints*, Pisa, Italy, 1998.
13. N. Kohl and S.E. Karisch. Airline crew assignment: modeling and optimization. Carmen Report, 1999. In preparation.
14. PARROT. Executive Summary. ESPRIT 24960, 1997.
15. R. Rodosek, M. Wallace, and M.T. Haijan. A new approach to integrating mixed integer programming and constraint logic programming. *Annals of Operations Research*, 86:63-87, 1999.

Improving a Heuristic Repair Method for Large-Scale School Timetabling Problems

Kazuya Kaneko, Masazumi Yoshikawa, and Yoichiro Nakakuki

C&C Media Research Laboratories, NEC Corporation
Miyazaki 4-1-1, Miyamae-ku, Kawasaki, 216-8555, Japan
{neko, yosikawa, nakakuki}@ccm.cl.nec.co.jp

Abstract. Timetable construction is extremely difficult and time-consuming in large high-schools and universities. Even latest high-quality heuristic repair methods leave constraint violations to be fixed manually. This paper describes two improvements, initialization and repair. The improved initialization method applies a heuristic repair method whenever inconsistencies are found during the construction. The improved repair method escapes from local minima by moving two lectures at once in a way similar to the way billiard balls move. Evaluating these methods by using them on real high-school and university timetabling problems showed that they left between 30% and 97% fewer violations than a previous method left.

1 Introduction

Timetable construction is extremely difficult and time-consuming in large high-schools and universities because the scheduling problems there are large and tightly constrained. Kouchi Prefectural Okou High School, for example, used to spend 150 person-days making one timetable. Much effort has been focused on solving these timetabling problems ([1], [2], [3], [5], [6]). We developed a heuristic repair method that automatically constructs a high-quality timetable within a reasonable amount of time [7]. Using this heuristic repair method, which is significantly better than such well-known repair methods as min-conflicts hill-climbing and simulated annealing, we have developed an automatic scheduling system that reduces the cost of timetable development from 150 to 3 person-days [8]. Further improvements to this automatic scheduling system are required, however, because even this latest system leaves several crucial constraints in violation when the problems are tightly constrained. Teachers need to resolve these violations manually, but satisfying each remaining constraint is sometimes so hard that it takes a day or more.

This paper describes and evaluates two improvements to the latest heuristic repair method that reduce the manual work of teachers. The following sections describe the large-school timetabling problem, the heuristic repair method, and the improvements to the heuristic method. Section 5 then describes and discusses the evaluation. Section 6 discusses work related to these improvements, and Section 7 concludes by briefly summarizing this paper.

2 Timetabling Problem

This section describes two large-school timetabling problems: the high-school timetabling problem and the university timetabling problem.

2.1 High-school Timetabling Problem

High-school timetabling assigns to every lecture a weekly time-slot (period) in a way that minimizes the total penalty due to violated constraints. The timetable associates lectures with classes, subjects, teachers, and rooms, and the timetabling problem can be formalized as a constraint relaxation problem (CRP). A CRP consists of a set of variables and constraints. A variable has a domain that is the set of values applicable for the variable. A constraint is associated with a set of variables. It not only has a condition to be satisfied, but also a penalty point to be incurred by a violation. The goal is to minimize the total penalty due to inconsistent constraints. In a high-school timetabling problem, a variable is a lecture and its domain is the set of all time-slots during a week.

There are hard constraints, which must be satisfied if the timetable is to be practical, and soft constraints, which should be satisfied as far as is possible. The hard constraints are as follows:

- The schedules of a lecture's attributes (e.g., inconvenient days for part-time teachers, days on which extra rooms cannot be used).
- A set of lectures must be taken simultaneously or continuously.
- A teacher and a class can have no more than one lecture in a time-slot (no-collision constraint).
- No class has a free time-slot during any week.

The soft constraints are:

- On one day a class should have no more than one lecture on any one subject.
- Two-credit lectures should be attended two or more days apart.
- Each teacher has limits on the number of all lectures and continuous lectures that he or she can give in a day.

2.2 University Timetabling Problem

University timetabling also assigns to every lecture a weekly time-slot (period) during a week and a teaching place (lecture rooms, laboratories, playgrounds, and so on) in a way that tries to minimize the total penalty due to violated constraints. A lecture is associated with courses and teachers, but the university timetabling problems are more acute than those of the high school because there are two variables for each lecture: a time-variable whose domain is the set of all time-slots during a week, and a place-variable whose domain is the set of all places on the university.

In university problems the hard constraints are these:

- The schedules of a lecture's attributes (e.g., inconvenient days for part-time teachers, days on which extra rooms cannot be used).
- A set of lectures must be taken simultaneously or continuously.
- A teacher can have no more than one lecture in a time-slot (no-collision constraint).
- The number of students attending a lecture is less than the capacity of the assigned room.
- A course (faculty or department course) should have no more than one lecture of required subjects in any time-slot.

  The one soft constraint is:

- A course (faculty or department) should have no elective subject in a time-slot assigned to any required subject.

3 Previous method

This section describes our previous method in [7]. It combines the *Really-Full-Lookahead Greedy (RFLG)* algorithm and the min-conflicts hill-climbing (MCHC) algorithm ([4]). The RFLG algorithm is one of the highest quality initial assignment algorithms that eliminates in appropriate candidates by *arc-consistency* and assigns a value to each variable consistently. If a variable without a consistent candidate appears, the algorithm postpones that variable, goes on as far as possible with the consistent variables, and finally assigns an inconsistent value to the postponed variable using the greedy algorithm. The MCHC algorithm is a heuristic repair method that keeps changing the assigned value of one variable in a way to minimize the total penalty due to violated constraints.

There are two problems with this method. First, the MCHC algorithm frequently falls into a local optimum when the problem is a tightly constrained one. This is because once it changes an assignment it never changes it to a worse one. Second, the quality of the initial assignment generated by the RFLG algorithm. The RFLG algorithm postpones variables without a candidate by arc-consistency; however any postponed variable at an early stage of the RFLG is very important in the problem. Since some of the most important variables are suspended, it is impossible to refine the solution in the MCHC algorithm. Thus it is difficult to generate a high-quality timetable.

4 Improved Method

This section describes two improvements to the previous method. Each one address the two problems with the previous method.

4.1 Escaping from local minima

As noted in Section 3, the first problem with the previous method is that that the MCHC algorithm falls into a local optimum. We developed a method of escape from local optima based on the characteristics of school timetabling problems.

Figure 1 shows a local optimum typical of high-school timetabling problems. Class 1-1 has an empty slot, the fourth Monday, and two lectures X and Y in collision on the fourth Tuesday. The empty slot is unavailable to either of the lectures in collision because of other constraints. And because every other slot has a lecture, moving one of the lectures in the collision would cause another collision. At this local optimum, therefore, there is no one-step move to solve the problem. Moving two lectures at once, however, resolves the violation: move Lecture X (in collision) to the first Tuesday (another slot) while moving Lecture C (the lecture scheduled for the first Tuesday) to the fourth Monday (the empty slot). This movement of two lectures is similar to the movement of billiard balls: the first lecture knocks another into the hole. So we call this **billiard movement** algorithm. The billiard movement algorithm operates as follows:

STEP 1. Search for a lecture in collision and a free time-slot (hole). **STEP 2.** Try the billiard movement on the two lectures: select the movement that causes no serious violation and that results in the smallest total penalty due to violated constraints. **STEP 3.** Try moving one lecture to a hole: select the movement that causes no serious violation and that results in the smallest total penalty due to violated constraints.

The billiard movement algorithm can resolve constraint violations because it uses the following three ideas. **(a)** It tries to move two lectures together. **(b)** It allows the movement to be a change for the worse, as long as the movement causes no serious violation. **(c)** It tries movements based on two characteristics of high-school timetabling problems: no class can have two or more lectures at a time, and no class should have a free time-slot during a week. It tries to change the search space to another without serious violation.

Timetables of Classes

	1-1	1-2
Mon.1	Lecture.A1	Lecture.A1
Mon.2	Lecture.A2	Lecture.A2
Mon.3	Lecture.B	Lecture.E
Mon.4		Lecture.F
Tue.1	*Lecture.C*	Lecture.G
Tue.2	Lecture.D1	Lecture.H
Tue.3	Lecture.D2	Lecture.I
Tue.4	*Lecture.X* / Lecture.Y	Lecture.Y

Timetables of Teachers

	A	B	C	D
Mon.1	*absent*			
Mon.2	*absent*	Meeting	Meeting	
Mon.3	*absent*	Lecture.E		Lecture.B
Mon.4	*absent*			Meeting
Tue.1		*Lecture.C*	*Lecture.C*	
Tue.2	Meeting			
Tue.3		Lecture.I		
Tue.4	*Lecture.X*	Lecture.Y	*Lecture.X*	Lecture.Y

Fig. 1. Escape from local minima.

4.2 Step-by-step RFLG algorithm

As noted in Section 3, the second problem with the previous method is that the RFLG algorithm postpones several important variables with no candidate. This causes some constraint violations on more important variables that cannot be repaired by MCHC. We developed an improved initialization algorithm, step-by-step RFLG (S-RFLG) algorithm. The S-RFLG algorithm tries to resolve these inconsistencies at the time a variable without consistent candidate is found, before the other variables are assigned. The S-RFLG algorithm operates as follows:

STEP 1. Eliminate candidates by *arc-consistency*. **STEP 2.** Select a lecture by using the most-constrained variable first heuristic. **STEP 3.** Select a time-slot for the lecture with no violation. **STEP 4.** Assign the time-slot to the lecture and return to STEP 1. **STEP 5.** If in STEP 3 there are no time-slots with no violation, resolve the violations by using the MCHC algorithm and return to STEP 1. **STEP 6.** If the violations cannot be resolved, store the lecture in the set of failure lectures and return to STEP 1. **STEP 7.** After dealing with all the other variables, assign to each failure lecture a time-slot resulting in the smallest total penalty.

The S-RFLG algorithm changes the value of the variable that was already assigned by considering the constraint of the variable that is assigned next. Therefore it generates the timetable with the fewer violations of the constraints. The following section evaluates the two improvements.

5 Evaluation

This section describes and discusses the experimental evaluation of the improved methods in the preceding section. They were carried out on an EWS4800/360 programmed on general-purpose CRP solver, COASTOOL/C++([8]). Using COASTOOL/C++, each timetabling problems is described in the COASTOOL model, and each evaluated method is offered as the assignment library of COASTOOL/C++.

5.1 High-school Timetabling Problem

Problem. The improvements were evaluated in experiments with actual high-school timetabling problems: the 1992 timetabling problem for Saitama Prefectural Kuki-Hokuyou High School (Kuki 92), the 1994 timetabling problem for Daito Bunka University Dai-Ichi High School (Daito 94), and the 1994 timetabling problems for Okou High School (Okou 94E, Okou 94H): Okou 94E was a normally constrained problem, and Okou 94H was a tightly constrained problem. Kuki 92 had 30 classes, 60 teachers, 34 time-slots per week, and 806 lectures. Preparing its timetable manually required 100 person-days. Okou 94H had 34 classes, 82 teachers, 33 time-slots per week, and 930 lectures. Preparing its timetable manually required 150 person-days. Daito 94 had 25 classes, 70 teachers, 34 time-slots per week, and 647 lectures. Preparing its timetable with commercial timetabling software required more than twelve days.

Escaping from local minima.

Experiment 1. This experiment investigated the effectiveness of using the billiard movement to escape from local minima. The Kuki 92, Okou 94E, and Daito 94 problems were used to test the following three combinations of algorithm.

RFLG+MCHC (R/M)

This was our previous method [8].

RFLG+MCHC+Escape (R/M+E)

Escaping from local minima using the billiard movements of two lectures. It allows the movement to increase the penalty points.

RFLG+MCHC+Escape2 (R/M+E2)

Escaping from local minima using the billiard movements of two lectures. It does not allows the movement to increase the penalty points.

R/M+E and R/M+E2 started the escaping from local minima when 500 iterations of the MCHC resulted in no reduction of the total number of penalty points.

Figures 2 and 3 show the experimental results. Kuki 92 in Figure 2 shows that the initial assignment generated by RFLG, with 152 total penalty points, was refined by MCHC to ten penalty points, but fell into a local minimum. At this point, R/M+E tried to escape from the local minimum and resolved all constraint violations. R/M+E2, on the other hand, generated a solution with one penalty point. The plots of R/M+E in the figures show that the escaping phase caused the increase in the total penalty points and the MCHC phase refined the constraint violations.

The total penalty points due to violated constraints and the computation time required by the improvements are listed in Table 1.

Table 1. Results of Experiment 1.

Problem	Penalty point(reduction rate) Computation time [sec.]		
	R/M	R/M+E	R/M+E2
Kuki 92	9.2(0%)	0.5(95%)	1.8(80%)
	0	15.2	161.3
Okou 94E	131.9(0%)	58.4(56%)	108.3(18%)
	0	228.6	2198.9
Daito 94	180.0(0%)	91.7(49%)	135.5(25%)
	0	742.8	3308.9

Each value is the mean of ten experiments.
The reduction rate is the percentage reduction from the total penalty points after R/M.
The computation time is the time after the MCHC algorithm fell into a local minimum.

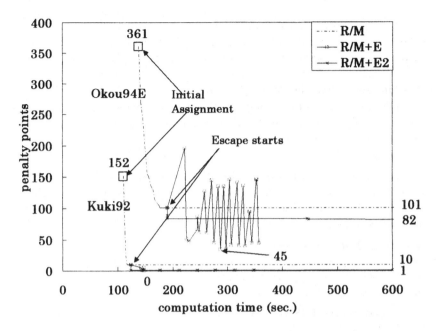

Fig. 2. Experiment 1 for Kuki 92 and Okou 94E.

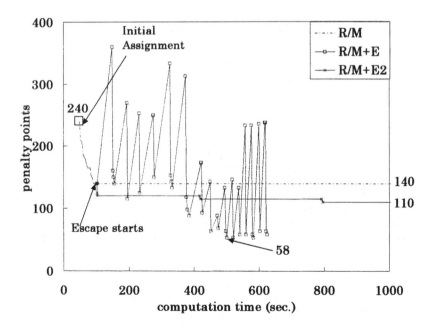

Fig. 3. Experiment 1 for Daito 94.

For Kuki 92, R/M+E reduced the timetable penalty from 9.2 points to 0.5 points. For Okou 94E, it reduced it from 132 points to 58 points. And for Daito 94, it reduced it from 180 points to 92 points. R/M+E2 also decreased the total number of penalty points, but it was less effective than R/M+E.

The results show that the improved escaping method, with the billiard movements, is effective for escaping from local minima in high-school timetabling problems. They also show that R/M+E, which allows a change for the worse, is better than R/M+E2, which does not.

Experiment 2. This experiment investigated variations of the billiard movement : the number of moved lectures and the selection heuristics. The Kuki 92, Okou 94E, and Daito 94 problems were used to test the following three combinations of algorithms.

RFLG+MCHC+Escape (R/M+E)
Billiard movement with two lectures and selection minimizing the total penalty.
RFLG+MCHC+Escape3 (R/M+E3)
Billiard movement with two lectures and random selection.
RFLG+MCHC+Escape4 (R/M+E4)
Billiard movement with three lectures.

The total penalty points and computation time are listed in Table 2.

Table 2. Results of Experiment 2.

Problem	Penalty points(reduction rate) Computation time[sec.]		
	R/M+E	R/M+E3	R/M+E4
Kuki 92	0.5(95%)	1.1(82%)	0.4(96%)
	15.2	81.9	509.2
Okou 94E	58.4(56%)	109.6(17%)	48.6(63%)
	228.6	829.1	4177.9
Daito 94	91.7(49%)	176.3(2%)	96.4(46%)
	742.8	792.2	16627.7

Each value is the mean of ten experiments.
The reduction rate is the percentage reduction from the total penalty points after R/M.
The computation time is the time after the MCHC algorithm fell into a local minimum.

The reduction rate after R/M+E3 was less than that after R/M+E, and the computation time was longer. The random selection is thus less effective than the selection minimizing the total number of penalty points.

On the other hand, the computation times for R/M+E4 with three lectures using the billiard movement were twenty or more times longer than the computation times for R/M+E, and the penalty points for R/M+E4 were the same as

R/M+E. So using the billiard movement with three or more lectures is not the best selection.

Consequently, the improvement in which the billiard movement of two lectures is used with a selection minimizing the total penalty is more effective than the combination random selection, and there is no advantage to the billiard movement of three or more lectures despite the vastly greater computation time it requires. So R/M+E is the best combination with regard both to penalty points and computation time.

Step-by-step RFLG algorithm.

Experiment 3. This experiment investigated the effectiveness of the improved initialization provided by the step-by-step RFLG. The Kuki 92, Okou 94E, and Daito 94 problems were used to test the following three combinations of algorithms.

RFLG+MCHC (R/M)
This was our previous method [8].
S-RFLG(MCHC)+MCHC (S(M)/M)
Step-by-step RFLG initialization method (S(M)) and MCHC.
S-RFLG(MCHC+Escape)+MCHC (S(M+E)/M)
Step-by-step RFLG initialization method with escaping from local minima (S(M+E)) and MCHC.

Figure 4 shows the experimental results for Kuki 92. It shows the total penalty points plotted against computation time. For the S(M)/M and S(M+E)/M, there are six plots with the different iterations of MCHC in S-RFLG initialization.

The percentages by which the number of penalty points were reduced from that obtained with R/M are listed in Table 3.

Table 3. Results of Experiment 3.(Percentage reduction of penalty points)

Problem	R/M	S(M)/M	S(M+E)/M
Kuki 92	0%	48%	91%
Okou 94H	0%	18%	19%
Daito 94	0%	29%	42%

As a result, S(M)/M was able to reduce 48% of the penalty points of the R/M solution for Kuki 92, 18% for Okou 94H, and 29% for Daito 94. S(M+E)/M was able to reduce 91% of the penalty points of the R/M solution for Kuki 92, 19% for Okou 94H, and 42% for Daito 94. The computation times for both the improved methods were from three to four times the computation time for R/M.

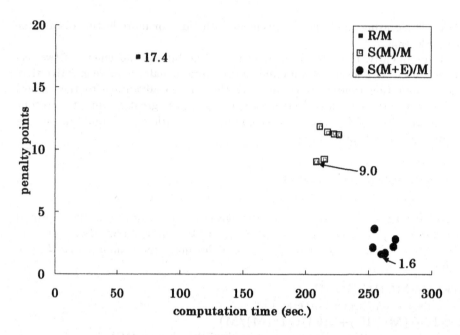

Fig. 4. Experiment 3 for Kuki 92. (Each plot is the mean of ten experimental results.)

The step-by-step RFLG initialization methods are therefore effective for high-school timetabling problems. Moreover, using the escaping from local minima for the refinement in step-by-step RFLG initialization (S(M+E)/M) is better than using only the MCHC for the refinement (S(M)/M).

Incorporating both kinds of improvements.

Experiment 4. This experiment looked at the combination of both improvements. The Kuki 92, Okou 94H, and Daito 94 problems were used to test the following three combinations of algorithms.

RFLG+MCHC (R/M)
    This was our previous method [8].
RFLG+MCHC+Escape (R/M+E)
    Escaping from local minima using the billiard movements of two lectures. It allows the movement to increase the penalty points.
S-RFLG(MCHC+Escape)+MCHC+Escape (S(M+E)/M+E)
    The method incorporating the two proposed algorithms.

The experimental results for Kuki 92 are shown in Figure 5, where total penalty points are plotted against computation time. For the S(M+E)/M+E, there are six plots with the different iterations of MCHC in S-RFLG initialization. R/M+E and S(M+E)/M+E start the escaping from local minima when 500 iterations of MCHC produce no reduction in the total penalty points.

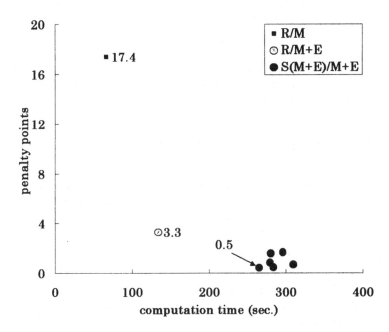

Fig. 5. Experiment 4 for Kuki 92. (Each plot is the mean of ten experimental results.)

The percentages by which the total number of penalty points obtained with S(M+E)/M, R/M+E, and S(M+E)/M+E were reduced from those obtained with R/M are listed in Table 4.

Table 4. Results of Experiment 4.(Percentage reduction of penalty points)

Problem	S(M+E)/M	R/M+E	S(M+E)/M+E
Kuki 92	91%	95%	97%
Okou 94H	19%	16%	30%
Daito 94	42%	49%	55%

As a result, S(M+E)/M+E was able to reduce 97% of the penalty points of the R/M solution for Kuki 92, 30% for Okou 94H, and 55% for Daito 94. Moreover, the computation times of the S(M+E)/M+E method are from four to nine times longer than the computation time of R/M.

As a result, each of the improved methods is effective for each of the normal tightly constrained problems. For the most tightly constrained problem, however, the method incorporating the two proposed algorithms is more effective than each improved method applied on its own.

5.2 University Timetabling Problem

Problem. The improved approaches were evaluated experimentally by using 14 timetabling problems at a real university. Each problem had from 290 to 1339 lectures, 700 places, 42 weekly time-slots, and from 287 to 687 teachers.

Incorporating both kinds of improvements.

Experiment 5. This experiment investigated the incorporation of both kinds of improvement. The following three combinations of algorithms were each tested on seven pairs of problems, one member of each pair having partial pre-assignments, and the other member having no pre-assignment.

RFLG+MCHC (R/M)
This was our previous method [8].
S-RFLG(MCHC+Escape)+MCHC+Escape (S(M+E)/M+E)
The method incorporating the two proposed algorithms.
Greedy+MCHC (G/M)
The greedy initialization algorithm and the MCHC refining algorithm.

Table 5 shows the total penalty points due to the violated constraints, the computation time, and the number of problems that generated the best solution in the three methods.

Table 5. Results of Experiment 5.

Problem	Method	penalty points	time (sec.)	#best
partial pre-assign-ments	G/M	399.2	193.7	0
	R/M	395.1	3349.2	0
	S(M+E)/M+E	0.9	704.0	7
no pre-assign-ment	G/M	96.9	178.1	0
	R/M	8.5	678.4	6
	S(M+E)/M+E	26.5	837.6	6

Each value is the mean of ten results.
#best is the number of problems for which the best solution (of the three methods) was obtained.

The results listed in Table 5 show that for the problems with partial pre-assignments, S(M+E)/(M+E) generated timetables with few violations, whereas R/M generated timetables accruing 395.1 total penalty points and G/M generated timetables accruing 399.2 total penalty points. The reason S(M+E)/(M+E) generated high-quality timetables is that it tries to refine constraint violations during the initial assignment phase. The R/M and G/M methods are less effective because they try to refine constraint violations during the MCHC phase. For these problems the computation time with S(M+E)/(M+E) was only 20% of that with R/M but was four times longer from that with G/M.

For the problems without a pre-assignment, S(M+E)/(M+E) generated a timetable with 26.5 total penalty points and generated the best solutions for six of the seven problems. The R/M method, however, also generated the best solutions for six of the seven problems and it generated a timetable with only 8.5 total penalty points. For the problems without a pre-assignment the computation time with S(M+E)/(M+E) was 1.2 times longer than the computation time with R/M and 4.7 times longer than the computation time with G/M.

The method incorporating both improvements thus generated the best solution for 13 of the 14 problems and is therefore effective for producing high-quality university timetables within a reasonable amount of time.

Furthermore, these evaluations show that the method incorporating both improvements is effective for the university timetabling problem in addition to the high-school timetabling problem.

6 Related Work

Schaerf applied the tabu search [5] to high-school timetabling problems. The tabu search repeats two processes, first exchanging the lectures of a teacher in two different time-slots (this is called an atomic move) and then carrying out a pair of the atomic moves, the second of which repairs the infeasibility created by the first one. Our improved repair method described in this paper tries to repair two lectures of a class at once in a similar way to the billiard ball movement that allows to increase the penalty points. It tries the billiard movement based on two characteristics of high-school timetabling problems: no class can have two or more lectures at a time, and no class has a free time-slot during a week. So it can escape from local minima and rapidly converge to produce high-quality timetables for high-school timetabling problems.

Schaerf also combined a backtracking-free constructive method and a local search method for timetabling problems [6]. This combination performs a local search on a partial solution whenever the construction reaches a dead-end. Our improved initialization method takes the same approach that implements the local search in the middle of the constructive method. In addition to this, our method uses arc-consistency to try to assign an order of importance to the variables and resolve any inconsistencies at the time they are found. Therefore it can generate a high-quality initial assignment.

7 Conclusion

This paper described two improvements to our previous method of high-school timetabling. The improved initialization method tries to construct a consistent assignment incrementally at every assignment using a repair algorithm if there is a violation. The improved repair method escapes from local minima by shifting classes in a way that is based on two characteristics of high-school timetabling problems: no class can have two or more lectures at the same time, and no class has a free time-slot during a week. This improved method tries to repair the violation by moving two lectures of a class at once in a way similar to the way billiard balls move: it moves a lecture that is in violation to another time-slot, where it "hits" the lecture there and pushes it into a "hole"(an empty time-slot). Testing these methods on real high-school timetabling problems showed that the use of both removed almost all the penalties when the problems were normal tightly constrained problems, and removed 30% of the penalties when the problem was the most tightly constrained problem. The improvements were shown to be effective for university timetabling as well as high-school timetabling.

References

1. Carter, M. W., "A survey of practical applications of examination timetabling algorithms," *Operations Research*, Vol. 34, No. 2, pp. 193-202 (1986).
2. Corne, D., Fang, H. L., and Mellish, C., "Solving the modular exam scheduling problem with GAs," *Proceedings of the 1993 International Conference on Industrial and Engineering Application of AI and ES*," (1993).
3. Feldman, R., and Golumbic, M. C., "Constraint satisfiability algorithms for interactive student scheduling," *Proceedings of the Eleventh International Joint Conference on Artificial Intelligence*, pp. 1010-1016, (1989).
4. Minton, S., Johnston, M. D., Philips, A. B., and Laird, P., "Minimizing conflicts: A heuristic repair method for constraint satisfaction and scheduling problems," *Artificial Intelligence*, Vol. 58, pp. 160-205 (1992).
5. Schaerf, A., "Tabu search techniques for large high-school timetabling problems," *AAAI-96*, pp. 363-368 (1996).
6. Schaerf, A., "Combining local search and look-ahead for scheduling and constraint satisfaction problems," *IJCAI-97*, pp. 1254-1259 (1997).
7. Yoshikawa, M., Kaneko, K., Nomura, Y. and Watanabe M., "A constraint-based approach to high-school timetabling problems: A case study," *AAAI-94*, pp. 1111-1116 (1994).
8. Yoshikawa, M., Kaneko, K., Yamanouchi, T. and Watanabe M., "A constraint-based high school scheduling system," *IEEE Expert*, Vol. 11, No. 1, pp. 63-72 (1996).

Applying Constraint Programming to Protein Structure Determination

Ludwig Krippahl and Pedro Barahona

Dep. de Informática, Universidade Nova de Lisboa, 2825 Monte de Caparica, Portugal
ludi@dq.fct.unl.pt, pb@di.fct.unl.pt

Abstract. In this paper, we propose a constraint-based approach to determining protein structures compatible with distance constraints obtained from Nuclear Magnetic Resonance (NMR) data. We compare the performance of our proposed algorithm with DYANA ("Dynamics algorithm for NMR applications" [1]) an existing commercial application based on simulated annealing. For our test case, computation time for DYANA was more than six hours, whereas the method we propose produced similar results in 8 minutes, so we show that the application of Constraint Programming (CP) technology can greatly reduce computation time. This is a major advantage because this NMR technique generally demands multiple runs of structural computation.

1   Introduction

Proteins play a wide role in metabolism control, and protein shape is an essential factor in controlling function and reactivity. A widely used analogy of the importance of shape for protein function is the lock and key model, that can be found on any biochemistry textbook. The knowledge of protein structure is thus of major importance in many fields of research, including biotechnology and medicine.

The great advances in genetics have made a large number of proteins easily available for study. At present approximately 100.000 protein sequences are known, but structures were only determined for about 10% of those. Structural determination is still a major limiting step in the study of protein function, but the demand for structure elucidation is very high due to the major market of pharmaceutical and biotechnology applications.

X-ray crystallography is the most used method for protein structure determination. NMR spectroscopy, however, is the only alternative method, and is growing in importance as technical means improve because it does not require crystallisation, an uncertain and demanding step essential for x-ray determination. Currently approximately 15% of all known protein structures were determined by NMR techniques.

NMR spectroscopy measures the absorption of radio frequency radiation by a sample when placed in a strong magnetic field (9-18T). Each NMR active nucleus in a sample (normally ^{1}H, ^{13}C or ^{15}N) will resonate at a certain frequency. This frequency depends on the local magnetic field that each nucleus feels. This local magnetic field is related to the chemical and structural environment (due to the magnetic fields generated by electrons and by other nuclei) of the nucleus. The frequency of resonance of each nucleus can therefore be used to obtain chemical and structural information about the sample under study.

The basis for the application of NMR to protein structure determination is the influence one resonating nucleus can have on nearby nuclei. This is called the Nuclear Overhauser Effect and can be measured by detecting a variation in the absorption at one resonance frequency when a different frequency is irradiated. This effect is proportional to the distance between nuclei, and so allows the distance between two Hydrogen (^{1}H, or proton) nuclei to be estimated. Since two different frequencies are used, a two-dimensional NMR spectrum is generated. The absorption variations detected show as cross-peaks on this two-dimensional chart, so called because they are located at the crossing point of two resonance frequencies.

A major difficulty at this stage is the identification of the ^{1}H nuclei generating each cross-peak. This is the assignment problem, and it can be very complex to solve for 2D NMR experiments.

The assignment generates a set of distance constraints that can be used to calculate the protein structure. However, the complexity of the assignment process makes errors very common, and requires that several candidate structures be calculated before a completely correct assignment can be made. This makes any improvement in the computation efficiency of the structural constraint solver a major advantage.

Other constraints (bond lengths, bond angles, etc.) are also available via the primary structure of the protein (sequence of amino acids) and the chemical structure of the amino acids (see below).

A protein consists of one or more strings of aminoacids chemically bonded by the reaction of the carboxyl acid group of one aminoacid with the amino group of the next aminoacid in the sequence. The sequence of aminoacids is called the protein sequence or primary structure. As all aminoacids have the same structure at the amino and carboxyl end groups, the protein chain will consist of a backbone structure that is independent of the actual aminoacid sequence. The sidechains, which are the chemical structures unique to each aminoacid type, are attached to the backbone (see Fig. 1).

The knowledge of the amino acid sequence provides a large amount of information regarding the structure of the protein, as the chemical bonds within and between amino acids are revealed. However, since the majority of these bonds can rotate freely, the protein chain has a large degree of freedom and so the constraints given by this information are not enough to satisfactorily determine the three dimensional folding of the protein (encompassing the usually referred to as the secondary, tertiary and quaternary structures). Thus additional constraints, as provided by NMR spectroscopy, are needed.

Our motivation for this work arose from the nature of the problem, which is clearly a constraint satisfaction problem. Therefore, right from the beginning, we were confident that the use of CP techniques would improve performance relative to the conventional approach of using only unconstrained optimisation algorithms (i.e. not using actively the constraints to narrow the search but rather including constraint violations in some objective function that should be minimised).

Constraint programming is proving to be a valuable tool for solving diverse biochemical problems, such as genome mapping [12] and protein structure prediction on a more theoretical basis [5]. On the particular field of protein NMR spectroscopy, CP has been applied to the problem of peak assignment as a feasibility study [6] or in the more amenable case of 3D and 4D NMR spectra [8] (the assignment of 2D NMR spectra is still beyond a reliable automation).

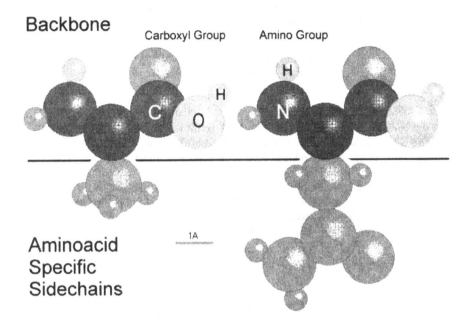

Fig. 1. Shown in this figure are two aminoacids: Alanine (left) and Aspargine (right). The Oxygen (O) and the two Hydrogen (H) atoms are lost (and form a water molecule) when two aminoacids bind. This peptide bond is formed between the Carbon atom (C) and the Nitrogen (N) atom of the other aminoacid, thus creating a continuous backbone along the protein chain. The aminoacid sidechains are shown below the backbone atoms. Each aminoacid type has a different sidechain structure. The scale bar is 1Å, 10^{-10}m.

In our work, we show that the application of CP to protein structure determination by NMR provides a significant improvement in performance relative to the commonly used techniques. We begin (section 2. Modelling the Problem) by describing how the variable domains and constraints are modelled, and how constraints are propagated. Our algorithm is then compared to DYANA, the program currently in use in our chemistry department for protein structural NMR (section 3. Desulforedoxin - A Test Case), in which we show that our approach can produce similar results in far less time. Finally, we present the work currently being done to overcome some shortcomings our implementation still has (4. Conclusion and Future Developments).

2   Modelling the Problem

We currently model the protein structures by the positions and restrictions between the non-Hydrogen atoms of the proteins. All the atoms mentioned in this discussion, unless otherwise stated, will refer to non-Hydrogen atoms. Although the information provided by NMR is mostly related to ^{1}H nuclei, Hydrogen atoms are closely bound to other atoms (e.g. Carbon, Nitrogen or Oxygen atoms). Furthermore, a Hydrogen atom can only bind to one atom, so it is a useful simplification to consider the restrictions as applying to the larger, more relevant to structure and less numerous atoms.

2.1 Constraints:

The NMR data provides constraints by showing that two atoms must be close enough for the Nuclear Overhauser Effect to be felt, so these are distance constraints.

The chemical information that is known from the protein sequence provides bond length and bond angle constraints. Bond length constraints are also distance constraints, and the bond angles can be modelled by sets of distance constraints. In fact, the structure and flexibility of an aminoacid can be modelled by a conjunction of pairwise distance constraints between all the atoms. We chose this approach, so we need only use distance constraints. There are two types of constraints, that we called *In* constraints (eq. 1) and *Out* constraints (eq. 2).

$$In \text{ constraint} \qquad \sqrt{(x_1 - x_2)^2 + (y_1 - y_2)^2 + (z_1 - z_2)^2} \leq k \qquad (1)$$

$$Out \text{ constraint} \qquad \sqrt{(x_1 - x_2)^2 + (y_1 - y_2)^2 + (z_1 - z_2)^2} \geq k \qquad (2)$$

These two constraint types are used to model all the chemical structural information, whether it is known beforehand or from the NMR spectroscopy experiments.

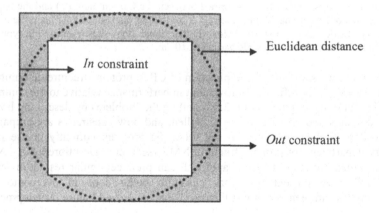

Fig. 2. This figure shows the difference between an Euclidean distance constraint and the simplified constraints of our model. An *In* constraint region contains the Euclidean distance region, whereas an *Out* constraint must be contained within the Euclidean distance region.

In practice, these Euclidean distance constraints are expensive to propagate, so we use an approximation (eqs. 3 and 4).

$$\textit{In constraint} \qquad \max(|x_1 - x_2| + |y_1 - y_2| + |z_1 - z_2|) \le k \qquad (3)$$

$$\textit{Out constraint} \qquad |x_1 - x_2| \ge \alpha k \vee |y_1 - y_2| \ge \alpha k \vee |z_1 - z_2| \ge \alpha k \qquad \alpha = \frac{1}{\sqrt{3}} \qquad (4)$$

The parameter α is needed to insure that the simplified *Out* constraint does not exclude regions allowed by the Euclidean distance constraint. This simplification is illustrated in figure 2.

Finally, there is an implicit constraint involving all atoms, which is that no two atoms can occupy the same volume. This is an additional *Out* constraint that is imposed on all atom pairs that are not already constrained by an *Out* constraint.

2.2 Variables and Domains:

The variables we wish to determine are the Cartesian (x, y and z) coordinates of each atom. However, treating these variables as independent is problematic, because the *Out* constraints are actually disjunctions of constraints on the coordinate variables.

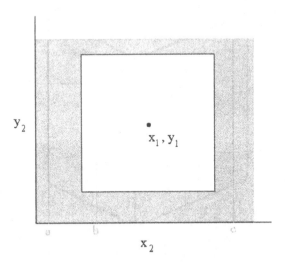

Fig. 3. In this figure we show an atom at x_1, y_1 which is excluding atom 2 from the region marked in white. The domains of variables x_2 and y_2, corresponding to atom 2, are represented in grey. We can see that for any value (a, b, c) that x_2 can take, there is always a possible value for y_2. If the variables x and y are considered independently, arc-propagation cannot reduce the domains.

294

Arc-consistency alone will not propagate these constraints, as can be seen of figure 3. This is because, in arc-consistency, we would guarantee that (to simplify, eq.5 and fig.3 illustrate for two dimensions):

$$\forall x_2 \in Dx_2 \exists y_2 \in Dy_2 : \left(\| x_1 - x_2 \| \geq k \vee | y_1 - y_2 | \geq k \right) \tag{5}$$

This is true for any x_2 so no domain reduction is possible using arc-consistency, as can be seen in fig. 3.

To account for this the actual variables defined are the positions of the geometric centres of the atoms, which we will refer to as the position of the atoms for brevity. In this way all three coordinate variables (x, y, z) of each atom are processed as a single variable with a three dimensional domain.

This domain is a set of cuboid regions. One cuboid defines the *Good* region, which is the volume that contains the possible positions for the atom. A set of non-overlapping cuboids contained in the *Good* region defines the *NoGoods* region, which contains the positions from which the atom must be excluded (see Fig. 4).

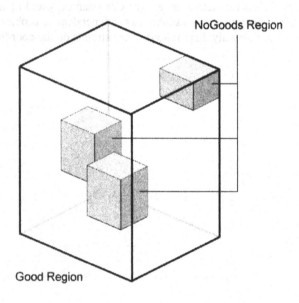

Fig. 4. The domain for the position of an atom is composed of two regions. The *Good* region is a cuboid that defines the positions for the atom that comply with the set of *In* constraints. The *NoGoods* region is a set of non-overlapping cuboids that define the volumes within the *Good* region from which the atom is excluded by the *Out* constraints.

Alternativa representations for spatial reasoning, such as octrees [13] could be applied in this case. However, we feel that the use of cuboid regions, and the associated constraint processing is quite adequate for this (and similar problems) and obviates the need for these more complex representations, making our simpler representation more efficient.

2.3 Constraint Propagation

We distinguished between the two types of distance constraints (*In* and *Out*) because of the way in which they are propagated (also see fig. 5).

- The *In* constraints are propagated simply by intersection operations. The *Good* region of atom A will be the intersection of the current *Good* region of A with the neighbourhood of the *Good* region of atom B. This neighbourhood is defined as the *Good* region of B augmented by the distance value of the *In* constraint between A and B. After this operation the *NoGoods* region of A is intersected with the *Good* region to guarantee that it is always contained in the latter. The intersection of two cuboid blocks simply requires Max and Min operations on the extremity coordinates, so propagation of *In* constraints is very efficient.
- For an *Out* constraint the propagation involves adding the exclusion region defined by the constraint to the *NoGoods* region of the affected atom. The most complex operation in this process is insuring that the *NoGoods* region consists of non-overlapping cuboids. This reduces propagation efficiency, but simplifies the task of determining the cases of failure when the *NoGoods* region becomes identical to the *Good* region.

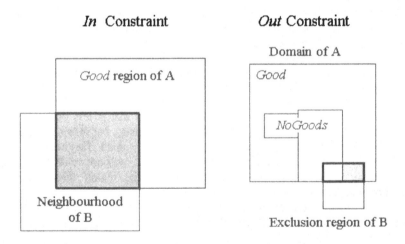

Fig. 5. This figure shows the propagation of both types of constraints. For *In* constraint propagation, the domain of atom A is reduced by intersecting the *Good* region of A with the neighbourhood of B. For *Out* constraint propagation a *NoGood* cuboid region is added. This *NoGood* region is obtained by intersecting the *Good* region of A with the exclusion region of B. Note that part of the new *NoGood* block in A (thick line rectangle) overlaps the original *NoGoods* region, so only the non-overlapping part is added (grey shaded area).

Arc-consistency is guaranteed by propagating the constraints on each atom that suffered a domain restriction until no domain changes. After complete propagation, one atom is selected for enumeration (see below), and the propagation step is repeated.

Unfortunately, arc consistency cannot guarantee consistency of this constraint system, making a global constraint algorithm (e.g. *diffn* [7]) highly desirable to account for the effects of the *Out* constraints. However, the high number of constraints (typically 5.000 to 10.000), variables (several hundred three-dimensional domain variables) and cardinality of the domains (approximately 3.000 in each coordinate axis) makes complete consistency very hard to guarantee. In this context, we opted to approximate such global consistency by imposing some redundant constraints over specific atom pairs [14]. Currently this is still done only in a limited fashion, as redundant constraints are used solely between atoms belonging to the same aminoacid.

Furthermore, it is quite common in real applications to have impossible constraint systems due to ambiguous assignment of the NMR spectrum cross-peaks. In this case, it is desirable to have a system that can proceed far enough to produce a partially consistent solution, which can indicate corrections on the peak assignments.

2.4 Enumeration

Enumeration follows a first fail approach on a round robin system. First, the atom with the smallest domain that was not selected in the current enumeration round is selected for enumeration. Exception is made if the coordinate domain is smaller than 2.0Å for all three coordinates, in which case the atom is considered sufficiently determined and no domain reduction is necessary.

The domain of this atom is then split into two similarly sized domains by 'cutting' across the longest coordinate axis (x, y or z) of the domain. The domain of the atom will be one of these two 'halves'.

An enumeration heuristic now comes into play. The first choice for the new domain after the split is the half of the original region that is less occupied by the domains of all other atoms. This is a very useful heuristic, because *Out* constraints can only be applied when the atom domain is sufficiently small. This heuristic gives a high probability that *Out* constraints, when later applied, will not result in failure, so essentially we are choosing at each enumeration the region with the highest probability of success of the most restricted domain.

Since the domain for the enumerated atom is reduced, constraints are then propagated (as discussed above), and then another atom is selected for enumeration (the atom with the smallest domain not selected yet).

This process of selection and domain reduction is repeated until all atoms were selected once, after which a new round of enumeration starts.

2.5 Backtracking

Since only arc consistency is maintained, it is often necessary to backtrack during the enumeration phase. Backtracking occurs whenever the domain of the coordinates for an atom is empty, and consists on recovering the domains assigned to all atoms before the last enumeration.

The last enumeration is then repeated, but choosing the region that was previously rejected (enumeration, as explained above, consists on splitting the domain in two, and choosing one of the resulting regions).

If both regions produced by the enumeration split result in failure, then backtracking proceeds to a previous enumeration.

This process is repeated until no more backtracking is possible (resulting in a failure) or all atoms have sufficiently small domains (less than 2.0Å for all coordinates, see above) to be considered satisfactorily determined (success).

2.6   Minimization

After complete enumeration, the atomic coordinates were generated by a quick minimization of the difference between the interatomic distances and the average values expected for those distances (using Powell's multi-dimension minimization method as described in [4]). This was necessary because enumeration terminates when all atomic coordinates have domains spanning less than 2.0A, but an actual value for each variable is necessary to produce a solution, and a purely random assignment could produce distorted structures.

This minimization procedure has some significant shortcomings, as it does not take into account the fact that many bond angles and distances are very rigid, which results in a lower accuracy. This algorithm is thus being replaced with an improved version (see Conclusion and Future Work below).

3   Desulforedoxin - A Test Case

The implementation of the method described was tested on a monomer of the dimeric protein Desulforedoxin. This is a conveniently small structure for testing, containing only 36 aminoacids. Furthermore, the structure of Desulforedoxin has been determined both by x-ray crystallography [2] and by NMR spectroscopy [3].

The knowledge of the structure was essential to test the algorithm, and because the present model cannot yet use all constraints deduced from NMR spectroscopy. Under real conditions some constraints cannot be unambiguously assigned (because the resonance frequencies of the different atoms are very similar). One solution used for this common problem is to consider an extra atom (called pseudo-atom because chemically it does not exist) between the atoms that are usually indistinguishable (see Conclusion and Future Work below). The constraint is then assigned to this pseudo-atom, which is considered bonded to the real atoms. At this stage this feature is not yet implemented, so we cannot yet compare the two programs if we use a set of constraints obtained experimentally. We can, however, easily create a set of constraints from the x-ray structure of the protein. This is done simply by determining which pairs of ^{1}H atoms are sufficiently close for the Nuclear Overhauser Effect to be observed. This way we created a set of constraints that could be used in both programs.

The eligible atom pairs for the constraints were the atoms with bound ^1H, and with interatomic distances inferior to 6Å (which is a practical upper limit for NMR).

The constraint set generated for this case contained 1273 distance constraints between atoms not belonging to the same aminoacid. This set of constraints was solved both by our method and by DYANA. DYANA [1] is a recent software package for structural NMR. It is widely used and its efficiency is representative of the software available for these problems. It is also the software used in our chemistry department, so we had access not only to the software but also to experienced users. This made it a very good choice for comparing the performance of our approach.

Our program used an additional set of 3677 distance constraints to model the bond structure of within each aminoacid, for a total of 4950 constraints over the 247 atoms (i.e. 3-D variables). These additional constraints are not required by DYANA, as this program assumes that each aminoacid is a rigid structure, in which all covalent bond distances and angles are fixed in the model.

Generally, in structural NMR studies, the set of constraints still allows for considerable conformational freedom. Because of this, it is useful to produce not one single solution, but a set of solutions, which can give a better idea of the freedom (and uncertainty) in different regions of the protein chain. This is why each program produced a set of 15 solutions (shown on figure 6).

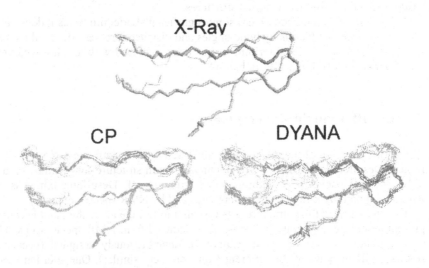

Fig. 6. This figure shows the comparison of the results obtained for the solution of the set of constraints defining the shape of one monomer of Desulforedoxin. This protein chain is 36 aminocids long. The topmost figure shows the structure as determined by x-ray crystallography. On the bottom left are shown 15 structures obtained by our program, and bottom left are 15 structures generated by DYANA. Only the backbone is shown to simplify the diagrams, and the 15 solutions for each algorithm (CP and DYANA) are shown as thin lines. The size of this protein is 25Å.

For our implementation, the 15 solutions to the constraint problem were produced by backtracking a random number of steps (between 40% and 70% of the total enumeration steps) after each solution was found.

The solutions presented for DYANA are the 15 solutions with a smaller number of constraint violations from a total set of 500 solutions generated. DYANA generates solutions by a simulated annealing algorithm that minimizes constraint violations starting from random folds. This requires that many solutions be generated, as a considerable proportion is trapped in local minima and never converges to a satisfactory solution. DYANA usually produces solutions with no constraint violations. The reason some constraints were violated in this case is that DYANA does not allow for bond distortions (only for dihedral angle rotation). In this test system some constraints could not be satisfied, possibly because a large number of constraints were used.

Both methods produce good solutions for the problem. A common measure of the similarity between two protein folds is the root mean square of the deviation (RMSD) of the atoms. It is generally accepted in this context that structures of an RMSD of 1Å are nearly identical. Therefore, for this test, a good solution should have an RMSD of about 1Å from the target x-ray solution. Both methods produce good solutions by this criterion (see Table 1).

	Root Mean Square Deviation (RMSD) in Å				
	From x-ray structure			Within solution set	
	Best	Average	Std. Deviation	Average	Std. Deviation
DYANA	0.8	1.04	0.16	0.86	0.30
CP	0.9	1.20	0.19	0.52	0.26

Table 1. Summary of the results obtained for the two algorithms. The best solution is the one with smallest RMSD relative to the x-ray structure. RMSDs within the solution sets are for all pairwise combinations of the 15 solutions in each set. All values are in Ångstrom, and refer to backbone atoms.

Solutions produced by DYANA are slightly better on average, although the difference is small. This is essentially due to the shortcomings of the simple minimization algorithm we are using.

Another difference in the results is the sampling of the universe of possible solutions. The set of solutions produced by DYANA has a larger variation, as can be seen by the larger average RMSD between solutions. This is a useful feature as it shows which segments of the protein are better defined (i.e. more constrained) and which have more freedom. In the results produced by our algorithm, this is less evident because the structures have a smaller variation. This is in part due to the minimization process, which tends to homogenize the solution set, and in part due to the method used to produce the different solutions. Both methods are being perfected (see Conclusion and Future Work below).

The final solutions generated by both methods contained some violations on the constraints derived from the x-ray structure. DYANA, due to the assumptions of rigidity in bond length and angle, violated 17% of these constraints, whereas our method only violated 8%. Our method produced a very small fraction (0,08%) of violations larger than 0,5Å, the maximum observed for DYANA (see Fig. 7).

Though there is a small difference in constraint violation patterns between the two methods, it is important to stress that these violations are largely irrelevant, as even the largest ones are smaller than an atomic radius (see fig. 1 for an idea of the scale).

Where our method really excelled was in speed and computation requirements. The 15 solutions obtained with DYANA took more than 6 hours running on an O2 workstation (R5000 CPU), which is the typical duration of a computation run. Our implementation took 8 minutes on a Pentium133 personal computer. Given that the quality of the results was nearly identical, this shows a remarkable improvement in performance.

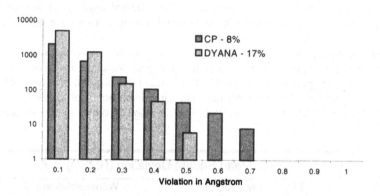

Fig. 7. This chart shows the number of constraints violated as a function of the violation magnitude. The constraints violated are a relatively small proportion of the total constraints (17% for DYANA, 8% for CP). The magnitude of the violations is also small (the diameter of a typical atom is around 2Å, nearly three times the largest violations observed). Please note the logarithmic scale.

Obviously, a single test case is not sufficient to assess potential scalability problems. Although a careful analysis of other protein structures was still not possible, we have preliminary results on three other, larger, proteins: two Trypsin Inhibitors [9,10] and Horse Cytochrome C [11] (Figure 8).

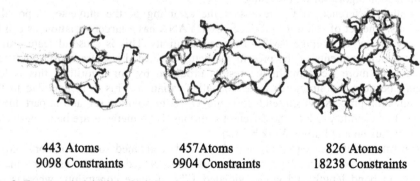

| 443 Atoms | 457 Atoms | 826 Atoms |
| 9098 Constraints | 9904 Constraints | 18238 Constraints |

Fig. 8. Two trypsin inhibitors [9,10] and Horse cytochrome C [11]. The thick black lines show the actual X-Ray structure. The gray thin lines show the 15 solutions calculated with our CP implementation. The number of atoms and constraints used is indicated for each case.

These proteins have from 50 to 100 aminoacids. The practical limit for NMR structural analysis is approximately twice this size, so these cases are representative of the structures that will be calculated by this method. The computation time ranged from 15 to 30 minutes, indicating a linear increase with protein size. No comparison with DYANA was done at the time this document was prepared, but we estimate a similar increase in computation time for DYANA

4. Conclusion and Future Developments

Although some work must still be done to produce a practical application for structural NMR studies, our results so far show that the use of CP techniques greatly increases the speed with which these problems can be solved. More tests are necessary for an accurate comparison, but we can estimate that CP techniques can provide approximately a hundredfold increase in computation speed relative to the currently available applications.

The main problem we have to tackle is the ambiguity in constraint assignment. In real NMR data, many distance constraints can be applied to more than one atom. As was mentioned above, this is often be solved by the use of pseudo-atoms, which occupy a position between the eligible atoms. We are currently implementing the necessary improvements on our model to account for this, which only involves slight changes on the way aminoacid structures are handled.

Some other improvements are also being made. One is a better minimization algorithm for the final refinement, which will take into account much more information on molecular structure than currently is being used. This will not only improve the quality of the final solutions, but also the sampling of the universe of possible solutions, as was discussed previously.

Another improvement that is being made is in the enumeration of the various solutions. This sampling in our current implementation was done simply by random backtracking, but we are developing an algorithm to differentiate highly constrained regions from regions with more freedom. This will serve to guide a more intelligent sampling.

Techniques for processing global constraints are being considered to improve the propagation of the *Out* constraints affecting all atom pairs due to the impossibility of two atoms occupying the same location. Arc-consistency cannot detect most of the cases where too many atoms are restricted to a volume that is too small to contain them all, so a specific solution to the propagation of these constraints is desirable. One option under consideration is a more general use of redundant constraints. This technique has been proven efficient in other domains [14].

As a future development, we are considering associating this constraint solving algorithm to an automated assignment system. The assignment of the experimental constraints is a time consuming process. This is not only due to the complexity of the task itself, but also because of the time required to test the assignments by calculating the corresponding structures. The creation of a system that could quickly generate likely assignments and test them would greatly facilitate structural protein NMR. We feel that the computational speed of our method will make this system practical.

Acknowledgements

We would like to thank Brian Goodfellow for his precious assistance. This work was partly supported by grant PRAXIS XXI BM 17904/98.

References

1. Güntert, P., Mumenthaler, C. & Wüthrich, K. (1997). Torsion angle dynamics for NMR structure calculation with the new program DYANA. J. Mol. Biol. 273, 283-298.
2. Archer M, Huber R, Tavares P, Moura I, Moura JJ, Carrondo MA, Sieker LC, LeGall J, Romao MJ (1995). Crystal structure of desulforedoxin from Desulfovibrio gigas determined at 1.8 A resolution: a novel non-heme iron protein structure. J Mol Biol 1995 Sep 1;251(5):690-702
3. Goodfellow B:J, Rusnak F., Moura I., Domke T., Moura J.J.G., NMR determination of the global structure of the 113Cd derivative of Desulforedoxin: Investigation of the Hydrogen bonding pattern at the metal center, Protein Sc.7, 928-937 (1998)
4. Press, Vetterling, Teukolsky, Flannery, Numerical Recipes in C 2nd ed, Cambrige Univ. Press 1994
5. Backofen, R, Constraint Techniques for Solving the Protein Structure Prediction Problem, CP98, Lecture Notes in Computer Science 1520, Springer-Verlag, 72-86
6. Leishman, S., Gray, PMD and Fothergill, JE, ASSASSIN: A Constraint Based Assignment System for Protein 2D Nuclear Magnetic Resonance, Applications and Innovations in Expert Systems II, (Proceedings of Expert Systems 94, Cambridge), ed. R.Milne and A.Montgomery, 263-280, December 1994
7. Beldiceanu, N., Contejean, E., Introducing Global Constraints in CHIP. Mathl. Comp. Modelling, Vol 20, No. 12, 97-123, 1994
8. Zimmerman, D.E., Kulikowski C.A., Montelione G.T., A constraint reasoning system for automating sequence-specific resonance assignments from multidimensional protein NMR spectra. Ismb 1993;1:447-55
9. Hecht, Szardenings, Collins, Shomburg, Three-dimensional structure of the complexes between bovine chymotrypsinogen *A and two recombinant variants of human pancreatic secretory trypsin inhibitor (*Kazal-Type), J. Mol. Biol., V.220, 711, 1991
10. Marquart, Walter, Deisenhofer, Bode, Huber, The geometry of the reactive site and of the peptide groups in trypsin, trypsinogen and its complexes with inhibitors, Acta Crystallogr., Sect. B, V.39, 480, 1983
11. Bushnell, G. W., Louie, G. V., Brayer, G. D.High-Resolution Three-Dimensional Structure of Horse Heart Cytochrome C. J.Mol.Biol. 214 pp. 585, 1990
12. Revesz, P., Refining Restriction Enzyme Genome Maps, Constraints, V. 2, 361, 1997
13. Sam-Haroud, D., Faltings, B., Consistency Techniques for Continuous Constraints, Constraints, V. 1, 85, 1996
14. Cheng, B., Choi, K., Lee, J., Wu, J., Increasing Constraint Propagation by Redundant Modeling: an Experience Report. Constraints, V. 4, 167, 1999

Partition-Based Lower Bound for Max-CSP [*]

Javier Larrosa[1] and Pedro Meseguer[2]

[1] Dep. Llenguatges i Sistemes Informàtics
Universitat Politècnica de Catalunya
Jordi Girona Salgado, 1-3, 08034 Barcelona, Spain
larrosa@lsi.upc.es
[2] Institut d'Investigació en Intel.ligència Artificial
Consejo Superior de Investigaciones Científicas
Campus UAB, 08193 Bellaterra, Spain.
pedro@iiia.csic.es

Abstract. The efficiency of branch and bound-based algorithms for Max-CSP depends largely on the quality of the available lower bound. An existing approach for lower bound computation aggregates individual contributions of unassigned variables. In this paper, we generalize this approach. Instead of aggregating individual contributions, we aggregate global contributions of disjoint subsets of unassigned variables, which requires a partition of the set of unassigned variables. Using this idea, we introduce the *partition*-based lower bound, which is superior to previous ones based on individual contributions. Interestingly, this lower bound includes elements already existing in the literature (IC and DAC). We present two algorithms, PFC-PRDAC and PFC-MPRDAC, which are the natural successors of PFC-RDAC and PFC-MRDAC using this new bound. We provide experimental evidence for the superiority of the new algorithms on random problems and real instances of weighted over-constrained problems.

1 Introduction

When solving a Constraint Satisfaction Problem (CSP), one has to assign values to variables satisfying a set of constraints. In real applications it often happens that problems are over-constrained and do not have any solution. In this situation, it is desirable to find the assignment that *best respects* the constraints under some preference criterion. Under this view, over-constrained CSPs are optimization problems for which *branch and bound* is a suitable solving strategy. The efficiency of branch and bound-based algorithms greatly depends on the lower bound used to detect deadends and to avoid the exploration of large regions in the search space. This lower bound should be both as large and as cheap to compute as possible.

An approach [3, 10, 4, 5] for lower bound computation aggregates two main elements: (i) the global contribution of assigned variables, and (ii) the addition

---

[*] This research is supported by the Spanish CICYT project TIC96-0721-C02-02.

of individual contributions of unassigned variables. Another approach [9] keeps (i) but substitutes (ii) by a global contribution of unassigned variables. In this paper we generalize the first approach in the following sense. Instead of aggregating individual contributions of unassigned variables, we aggregate global contributions of disjoint subsets of unassigned variables. This requires a partition of the set of unassigned variables (which gives the name of *partition*-based lower bound). The contribution of each subset is greater than or equal to the addition of the individual contributions of each variable in the subset. Because of that, the partition-based lower bound dominates any other lower bound of the first approach.

In this paper we restrict ourselves to Max-CSP where all constraints are considered equally important and the goal is to find the assignment that maximizes the number of satisfied constraints. However, the idea can be adapted to other frameworks such as probabilistic or hierarchical [8]. We present two algorithms based on our approach and experimentally show that they outperform state of the art competitors. Our experiments include random over-constrained CSPs and real instances of weighted CSPs.

This paper is structured as follows. In Section 2 we introduce notation and briefly review previous approaches to Max-CSP lower bound. In Section 3 we introduce our approach, illustrated with examples. In Section 4 we analyze its complexity and we present two new algorithms. Experimental results of these algorithms on two different domains appear in Section 5. Finally, Section 6 contains some conclusions and directions of further work.

2 Preliminaries

A discrete binary constraint satisfaction problem (CSP) is defined by a finite set of variables $X = \{1, \ldots, n\}$, a set of finite domains $\{D_i\}_{i=1}^n$ and a set of binary constraints $\{R_{ij}\}$. Each variable i takes values in its corresponding domain D_i. A constraint R_{ij} is a subset of $D_i \times D_j$ which only contains the allowed value pairs for variables i, j. An assignment of values to variables is complete if it includes every variable in X, otherwise it is incomplete. A *solution* for a CSP is a complete assignment satisfying every constraint. If the problem is over-constrained, such an assignment does not exist, and it may be of interest to find a complete assignment that best respects all constraints [1, 8]. We consider the Max-CSP problem, for which the solution of an over-constrained CSP is a complete assignment satisfying the maximum number of constraints. The number of variables is n, the maximum cardinality of domains is d and the number of constraints is e. Letters $i, j, k \ldots$ denote variables, $a, b, c \ldots$ denote values, and a pair (i, a) denotes the value a of variable i.

Most exact algorithms for solving Max-CSP follow a *branch and bound* schema. These algorithms perform a depth-first traversal on the search tree defined by the problem, where internal nodes represent incomplete assignments and leaf nodes stand for complete ones. Assigned variables are called *past* (P), while unassigned variables are called *future* (F). The *distance* of a node is the number of constraints violated by its assignment. At each node, branch and bound computes the *upper bound* (UB) as the distance of the best solution found so far, and the *lower bound* (LB) as an underestimation of the distance of any leaf node descendant from the current one. When $UB \leq LB$, we know that the current best solution cannot be improved below the current node. In that case, the algorithm prunes all its successors and performs backtracking.

In this paper, we focus on *partial forward checking* algorithm (PFC) [3], a branch and bound based algorithm which lower bound has been improved repeatedly, as summarized in the sequel. When a variable is assigned, PFC performs lookahead on future variables and its effects are recorded in *inconsistency counts* (IC). The inconsistency count of value a of a future variable i, ic_{ia}, is the number of past variables inconsistent with (i, a). PFC simplest lower bound is $distance(P) + \sum_{i \in F} \min_a(ic_{ia})$, where $distance(P)$ is the number of inconsistencies among past variables. This lower bound is improved including inconsistencies among future variables by the usage of *directed arc-inconsistency counts* (DAC) [10]. Given a static ordering in X, the directed arc-inconsistency count of value a of variable i, dac_{ia}, is the number of variables in X which are arc-inconsistent[1] with (i, a) and appear after i in the ordering. A new lower bound is $distance(P) + \sum_{i \in F} \min_a(ic_{ia}) + \sum_{i \in F} \min_a(dac_{ia})$ [10], provided variables are assigned following the static order. The second and third terms of this expression can be combined to form a better lower bound as $distance(P) + \sum_{i \in F} \min_a(ic_{ia} + dac_{ia})$ in the PFC-DAC algorithm [4].

A new approach uses *graph-based* DAC [5], relaxing the condition of a static ordering in X. Its only requirement is that constraints among future variables must be directed: if $i, j \in F$, R_{ij} is given a direction, for instance from j to i. Arc-inconsistencies of R_{ij} are recorded in the DAC of i. In this way, the same inconsistency cannot be recorded in the DAC of two different variables. Directed constraints among future variables induce a directed constraint graph G^F, where $\text{NODES}(G^F) = F$ and $\text{EDGES}(G^F) = \{(j, i) | i, j \in F, \text{direction of } R_{ij} \text{ from } j \text{ to } i\}$. Given a directed constraint graph G^F, the graph-based DAC of value a of variable i, $dac_{ia}(G^F)$, is the number of predecesors of i in G^F which are arc-inconsistent with (i, a). The minimum number of inconsistencies recorded in variable i, $MNI(i, G^F)$, is as follows,

$$MNI(i, G^F) = \min_a (ic_{ia} + dac_{ia}(G^F))$$

and the graph-based lower bound (based on the directed graph G^F) is,

$$LB(P, F, G^F) = distance(P) + \sum_{i \in F} MNI(i, G^F)$$

This approach is complemented with the dynamic selection of G^F. Given that any G^F is suitable for DAC computation, a local optimization process looks

---

[1] A variable j is arc-inconsistent with (i, a) when no value of j is compatible with (i, a).

for a good[2] G^F with respect to current IC values at each node. Since the only possible change in G^F is reversing the orientation of its edges (by reversing the direction of its constraints), this approach is called *reversible* DAC. These features are included in the PFC-MRDAC algorithm [5], where in addition, DAC are updated during search considering future value pruning. To allow for an efficient computation of $dac_{ia}(G^F)$, the data structure *GivesDac* is used. If $i, j \in X$, $a \in D_i$, *GivesDac* is defined as follows,

$$GivesDac(i, a, j) = \begin{cases} \text{true if } j \text{ is arc-inconsistent with } (i, a) \\ \text{false otherwise} \end{cases}$$

Regarding future value pruning, all previous PFC-based algorithms can compute the lower bound associated with value b of future variable j. This is done substituting in the lower bound the minimum contribution among the values of variable j by the contribution of value b. When this lower bound reaches UB, value b can be pruned from D_j because it cannot belong to a solution including the current assignment and better than the current best solution. For instance, with graph-based DAC, the lower bound associated with value b of future variable j, $LB(P, F, G^F)_{jb}$ is,

$$LB(P, F, G^F)_{jb} = distance(P) + ic_{jb} + dac_{jb}(G^F) + \sum_{i \in F,\ i \neq j} min_a(ic_{ia} + dac_{ia}(G^F))$$

In addition, the reversible DAC approach tries to increase $LB(P, F, G^F)_{jb}$ looking for a good G^F, by a local optimization process on each future value.

3   Partition-Based Lower Bound

Let us suppose the following situation,

1. $i, j \in F$ are two mutually constrained variables, $(i, j) \in \text{EDGES}(G^F)$,
2. (i, a) and (j, b) are the values with the minimum number of recorded inconsistencies in their respective domains (we assume a strict minimum, that is, any other value has a greater number of recorded inconsistencies),
3. (i, a) and (j, b) are incompatible, but i is not arc-inconsistent with (j, b).

The joint contribution of variables i, j to $LB(P, F, G^F)$ is,

$$ic_{ia} + dac_{ia}(G^F) + ic_{jb} + dac_{jb}(G^F)$$

that is, simply the sum of its individual contributions. $LB(P, F, G^F)$ does not consider inconsistencies among future variables which are not recorded in a DAC counter. However, the minimum number of inconsistencies provided by the subset $\{i, j\}$ as a whole is,

$$ic_{ia} + dac_{ia}(G^F) + ic_{jb} + dac_{jb}(G^F) + 1$$

---

[2] Finding the best subgraph is an NP-hard problem [7].

because the constraint R_{ij} is unsatisfied with values a and b. Since this inconsistency is not recorded in $dac_{ia}(G^F)$, it can be added. With other values different from a or b, R_{ij} may be satisfied, but since a and b are strict minima, any other value will increase the number of recorded inconsistencies in at least 1. Therefore, the above expression is the actual contribution of the subset $\{i,j\}$ to the lower bound. This is a simple example for the new lower bound approach presented in this paper: *to include inconsistencies among future variables that are not recorded in DAC counters and that will necessarily occur in the best (lowest cost) case.*

In the previous paragraph we grouped two variables. In general, this can be done with subsets of variables, which can be obtained from a partition among future variables. Let $\mathcal{P}(F) = \{\mathcal{F}_q\}$ be a partition of F ($\mathcal{F}_q \cap \mathcal{F}_{q'} = \emptyset$ if $q \neq q'$, $\bigcup_q \mathcal{F}_q = F$). The minimum number of inconsistencies provided by a subset $\mathcal{F}_q = \{i_1, \ldots, i_p\}$, $MNI(\mathcal{F}_q, G^F)^3$, is defined as follows,

$$MNI(\mathcal{F}_q, G^F) = min_{a_1 \ldots a_p}\{\sum_{j=1}^{p}[ic_{i_j a_j} + dac_{i_j a_j}(G^F)] + cost'((i_1, a_1), \ldots, (i_p, a_p))\}$$

where value a_j corresponds to variable i_j. The expression $cost'((i_1, a_1), \ldots, (i_p, a_p))$ accounts for the number of constraints among variables in $\{i_1, \ldots, i_p\}$, which are violated by the values $a_1, \ldots, a_p$ and this violation is not recorded as a directed arc-inconsistency. It is defined as follows,

$$cost'((i_1, a_1), \ldots, (i_p, a_p)) = \sum_{i_j, i_k \in \{i_1, \ldots, i_p\}} r'_{i_j i_k}(a_j, a_k)$$

where, if $(i_j, i_k) \in \text{EDGES}(G^F)$, $r'_{i_j i_k}(a_j, a_k)$ is,

$$r'_{i_j i_k}(a_j, a_k) = \begin{cases} 1 \text{ if } (a_j, a_k) \notin R_{i_j i_k} \text{ and } GivesDac(i_k, a_k, i_j) = false \\ 0 \text{ otherwise} \end{cases}$$

and 0 if $(i_j, i_k) \notin \text{EDGES}(G^F)$.
The new lower bound[4], called *partition-based lower bound* because it depends on the selected partition $\mathcal{P}(F)$, is defined as follows,

$$LB(P, \mathcal{P}(F), G^F) = distance(P) + \sum_{\mathcal{F}_q \in \mathcal{P}(F)} MNI(\mathcal{F}_q, G^F)$$

An example of this new lower bound appears in Figure 1. It is easy to check that $LB(P, \mathcal{P}(F), G^F)$ has the following properties

---

[3] Abusing notation, we use the same term MNI to express the minimum number of inconsistencies recorded in a single variable or in a subset of variables.

[4] We use the same term, LB, to denote the previous, graph-based, lower bound and this new, partition-based, lower bound. The second parameter makes the difference (F for the graph-based, $\mathcal{P}(F)$ for the partition-based).

$X = \{1, 2, 3, 4\}$ $D_1 = D_2 = D_3 = D_4 = \{a, b, c\}$

$R_{12} = \{(a,b), (b,a), (c,b)\}$ $R_{13} = \{(b,b), (c,c)\}$
$R_{14} = \{(a,b), (b,c), (c,a)\}$ $R_{23} = \{(a,b), (a,c), (c,b)\}$
$R_{24} = \{(a,b), (b,a), (b,c)\}$ $R_{34} = \{(b,a), (b,c)\}$

$P = \{(1,a)\}$, $F = \{2, 3, 4\}$

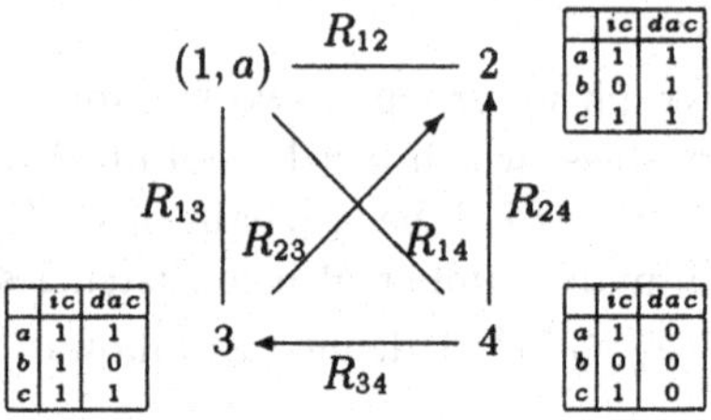

$MNI(2, G^F) = 1$, $MNI(3, G^F) = 1$, $MNI(4, G^F) = 0$;
$LB(P, F, G^F) = 0 + 1 + 1 + 0 = 2$

$\mathcal{P}_1(F) = \{\{2,3\}, \{4\}\}$, $MNI(\{2,3\}, G^F) = 2$;
$LB(P, \mathcal{P}_1(F), G^F) = 0 + 2 + 0 = 2$

$\mathcal{P}_2(F) = \{\{2\}, \{3,4\}\}$, $MNI(\{3,4\}, G^F) = 2$;
$LB(P, \mathcal{P}_2(F), G^F) = 0 + 1 + 2 = 3$

$\mathcal{P}_3(F) = \{\{2,3,4\}\}$, $MNI(\{2,3,4\}, G^F) = 3$;
$LB(P, \mathcal{P}_3(F), G^F) = 0 + 3 = 3$

Fig. 1. A simple problem and the computation of the $LB(P, F, G^F)$ and $LB(P, \mathcal{P}(F), G^F)$, the later using three different partitions. Constraints among future variables are oriented, each constraint pointing to the variable which records its inconsistencies. The ic and dac counts of each future variable are shown.

Property 1 $LB(P, \mathcal{P}(F), G^F)$ *is a lower bound.*

Proof. First, no inconsistency is recorded twice. ic_{ia} record inconsistencies between past and future variables, $dac_{ia}(G^F)$ and $cost'((i_1, a_1) \dots, (i_p, a_p))$ record inconsistencies among future variables, and those recorded in $cost'((i_1, a_1) \dots, (i_p, a_p))$ cannot be recoded in any $dac_{ia}(G^F)$. So these three quantities always record different inconsistencies and can be added. Second, the contribution $MNI(\mathcal{F}_q, G^F)$ of subset $\mathcal{F}_q$ is, by definition, the minimum number of inconsistencies that will occur in that subset, no matter which values are finally assigned. And third, no repeated inconsistency exists among different subsets. Therefore, $LB(P, \mathcal{P}(F), G^F)$ is a lower bound of the number of inconsistencies of any node descendant from the current node. □

Property 2 $LB(P, \mathcal{P}(F), G^F) \geq LB(P, F, G^F)$.

Proof. If every $cost'((i_1, a_1) \ldots, (i_p, a_p)) = 0$, then $LB(P, \mathcal{P}(F), G^F)$ is equal to $LB(P, F, G^F)$. If some $cost'((i_1, a_1) \ldots, (i_p, a_p)) > 0$, then $LB(P, \mathcal{P}(F), G^F)$ may be greater than or equal to $LB(P, F, G^F)$, but never lower. □

Property 3 $MNI(\mathcal{F}_q, G^F) - \sum_{i_j \in \mathcal{F}_q} MNI(\{i_j\}, G^F) \leq \frac{p(p-1)}{2}$

Proof. The maximum value of $cost'((i_1, a_1), \ldots, (i_p, a_p))$ is $\frac{p(p-1)}{2}$, when all variables in $\mathcal{F}_q$ are mutually constrained and every constraint contributes with one. It may happen that values achieving individual minima of $ic_{i_j a_j} + dac_{i_j a_j}(G^F)$ are the same that minimize the joint contribution of $\{i_1, \ldots, i_p\}$. □

Regarding future value pruning, one can compute the corresponding partition-based lower bound of a future value (j, b) by removing the future variable j from the partition element where it belongs and adding the contribution of (j, b). If $\mathcal{F}_{q'}$ is the subset containing j, it takes the following form,

$$LB(P, \mathcal{P}(F), G^F)_{jb} = distance(P) + MNI(\mathcal{F}_{q'} - \{j\}, G^F) + ic_{jb} + dac_{jb}(G^F) +$$

$$+ \sum_{\mathcal{F}_q \in \mathcal{P}(F), \ q \neq q'} MNI(\mathcal{F}_q, G^F)$$

4 Practical Usage of Partition-Based Lower Bound

4.1 Computing Partition-Based Lower Bounds

The number of steps required to compute $LB(P, F, G^F)$ is in $O(nd)$ (looking for the minimum among d values of a variable, times at most n future variables). The number of steps required to compute $LB(P, \mathcal{P}(F), G^F)$ is in $O(\sum_{\mathcal{F}_q \in \mathcal{P}(F)} d^{|\mathcal{F}_q|})$ (looking for the minimum among $d^{|\mathcal{F}_q|}$ values of subset $\mathcal{F}_q$, summed over all subsets in $\mathcal{P}(F)$). Then, the new lower bound is exponentially more expensive to compute than the old one, and the exponent depends on the size of the largest subset in $\mathcal{P}(F)$. Although large subsets may cause large increments in the old lower bound (up to quadratic in the size of the largest subset, Property 3), the conditions for each new contribution are so demanding that large increments rarely occur. Therefore, we prefer partitions with small subsets, in which the cost of computing the new lower bound is not prohibitive. In addition, if we restrict to partitions with subsets not greater than two elements, we simplify the computation of $LB(P, \mathcal{P}(F), G^F)$, because the following property.

Property 4 Let D_i^{min} and D_j^{min} be the values with the minimum number of recorded inconsistencies for variable i and j, respectively.

$$\forall a \in D_i^{min}, \ b \in D_j^{min}, \ r'_{ij}(a, b) = 1 \ if \ and \ only \ if$$

$$MNI(\{i, j\}, G^F) = MNI(\{i\}, G^F) + MNI(\{j\}, G^F) + 1$$

The proof of this property is the generalization to non strict minima in the introductory example of Section 3. This result has an obvious practical interest. Instead of computing $MNI(\{i, j\})$ by evaluating all combinations of values of i and j, only combinations of those values with minimum recorded inconsistencies have to be considered.

4.2 PFC-PRDAC and PFC-MPRDAC

In this subsection, we describe the PFC-PRDAC and PFC-MPRDAC algorithms. They are new versions of PFC-RDAC and PFC-MRDAC algorithms [5], in which the partition-based lower bound has been introduced. For the sake of simplicity, we only give a high level description. The interested reader will find the source code with every implementation detail at:

http://www.lsi.upc.es/~larrosa/PFC-MPRDAC.

In PFC-RDAC each node inherits the directed graph from its parent. After propagating the current assignment, the algorithm goes through a process in which some graph edges are reversed for LB improvement. If the new bound detects a deadend, the algorithm backtracks. Otherwise, search continues on the current node successors.

Algorithm 1: Builds a partition of future variables, $\mathcal{P}(F)$, and returns its associated lower bound $LB(P, \mathcal{P}(F), G^F)$.

PartitionBasedBound(P, F, G^F);
$NewLB \leftarrow LB(P, F, G^F)$
$\mathcal{P}(F) \leftarrow \bigcup_{i \in F} \{i\}$
foreach $i, j \in F, s.t.R_{ij}$ **do**
    if $\forall a_i \in D_i^{min}, \forall a_j \in D_j^{min}, r'_{ij}(a_i, a_j) = 1$ **then**
        $\mathcal{P}(F) \leftarrow \mathcal{P}(F) - \{i\} - \{j\} \cup \{i, j\}$
        $NewLB \leftarrow NewLB + 1$
    end
end
if $NewLB \leq UB$ **then**
    foreach $i \in F$ **do**
        foreach $a \in D_i$ **do**
            if $LB(P, \mathcal{P}(F), G^F)_{ia} \geq UB$ **then**
                prune(i, a)
            end
        end
    end
end
return $NewLB$

PFC-PRDAC takes over at this point. If LB with the optimised graph cannot produce a deadend by itself, PFC-PRDAC builds a partition on future variables aiming at further LB increment. This is done in the *PartitionBasedBound* function. This function constructs a partition $\mathcal{P}(F)$, computes its associated lower bound $LB(P, \mathcal{P}(F), G^F)$ and prunes future values accordingly. From a partition in which every future variable forms an independent element, it iterates over pairs of future connected variables. For each pair $(i,j) \in \text{EDGES}(G^F)$, it checks if every value with minimum IC+DAC of variable i is inconsistent with every value with minimum IC+DAC of variable j, and this inconsistency is not recorded in DAC of variable j. If this condition is satisfied, the two variables are merged into a single partition element and the current lower bound is increased by one (Property 4). After this process, if no deadend is detected, all future values go through the corresponding pruning process. It is worth noting that during the partition construction, when two variables are merged, they are not further considered. This ensures that $\mathcal{P}(F)$ is formed by singletons and pairs, only. It is also worth mentioning that pairs of variables are merged upon a greedy criterion (immediate LB increment). Thus, the algorithm does not guarantee that the best partition (*i.e.* the partition producing the highest lower bound) is generated. *PartitionBasedBound* has cost $O(ed^2)$.

PFC-MPRDAC is exactly like PFC-PRDAC except in the following aspect. If *PartitionBasedBound* does not produce a deadend, DAC counters are updated considering values pruned up to this point in the current node. The new recorded inconsistencies may cause lower bound increments, which may render new values unfeasible that must also be propagated.

5 Experimental Results

In this Section we evaluate the practical use of our approach on the benchmarks already used in [5]. In the first experiment, we have tested the performance of our algorithms on over-constrained binary random CSP. A binary random CSP class is characterized by $\langle n, d, p_1, p_2 \rangle$ where n is the number of variables, d the number of values per variable, p_1 the graph *connectivity* defined as the ratio of existing constraints, and p_2 the constraint *tightness* defined as the ratio of forbidden value pairs. The constrained variables and the forbidden value pairs are randomly selected [6]. Using this model, we have experimented on the following problem classes:

1. $\langle 10, 10, 1, p_2 \rangle$,   2. $\langle 15, 5, 1, p_2 \rangle$,
3. $\langle 15, 10, 50/105, p_2 \rangle$,   4. $\langle 20, 5, 100/190, p_2 \rangle$,
5. $\langle 25, 10, 37/300, p_2 \rangle$,   6. $\langle 40, 5, 55/780, p_2 \rangle$.

Observe that (1) and (2) are highly connected problems, (3) and (4) are problems with medium connectivity, and (5) and (6) are sparse problems. For each problem class and each parameter setting, we generated samples of 100 instances.

Each problem is solved by four algorithms: PFC-RDAC and PFC-MRDAC as described in [5], PFC-PRDAC and PFC-MPRDAC as described in Section 4. All four algorithms use *domain size* divided by *forward degree* as dynamic variable ordering. Values are always selected by increasing $ic + dac$. All algorithms share code and data structures whenever it is possible. Experiments were performed using a Sun Sparc 2 workstation.

312

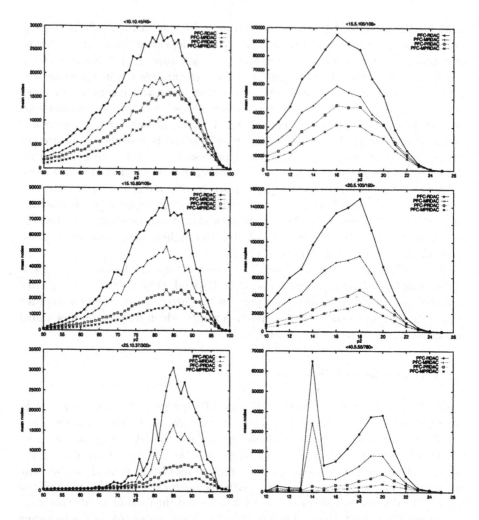

Fig. 2. Average visited nodes versus tightness for six classes of binary random problems.

Figure 2 reports the mean number of visited nodes required for solving the six problem classes. It can be seen that PFC-PRDAC and PFC-MPRDAC visit significantly less nodes than PFC-RDAC and PFC-MRDAC. It can be observed that the partition-based lower bound produces greater gains as problems become sparser. Improvement ratios for PFC-PRDAC versus PFC-RDAC range from 2 for the most dense problems to 7 for the most sparse problems, at the left of the peak. The highest average gain occurs at the $\langle 40, 5, 55/780, 14 \rangle$ class where PFC-PRDAC visits 22 times less nodes than PFC-RDAC. A closer look to this class shows that there is a particular problem instance that is very hard for PFC-RDAC and PFC-MRDAC, but it turns out to be easy when these algorithms are enhanced with our approach. Comparing PFC-MPRDAC with PFC-MRDAC,

313

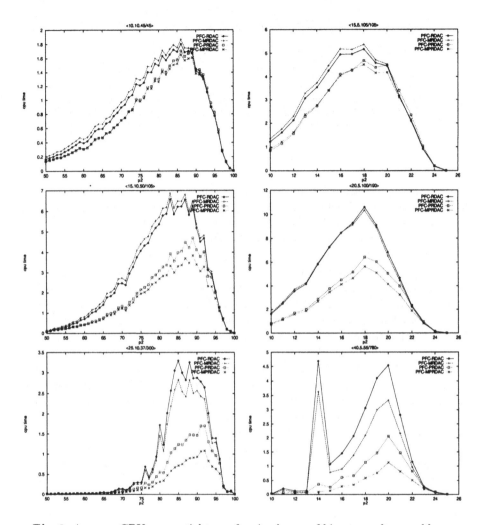

Fig. 3. Average CPU versus tightness for six classes of binary random problems.

a similar behaviour is observed although the dominance of PFC-MPRDAC is slightly smaller. Regarding PFC-PRDAC versus PFC-MPRDAC, it is clear that the latter dominates.

Figure 3 reports the mean cpu time required to solve the six problem classes. Cpu time results are in agreement with those of visited nodes. The same dominance behaviour with respect problem density is observed. In addition, it can be observed that the left-side of the complexity peak is the region where the new lower bound is most beneficial. Since computing the partition-based lower bound is time consuming, the dominance ratios are smaller. Typical improvement ratios for PFC-PRDAC versus PFC-RDAC range from 1.2 for dense problems to 3 for sparse problems. In the $\langle 40, 5, 55/780, 14 \rangle$ class PFC-PRDAC is 13 times faster than PFC-RDAC. Regarding PFC-PRDAC versus PFC-MPRDAC, the overhead

Table 1. Cost of solving subinstances 1 to 4 of the CELAR6 problem.

	PFC-RDAC		PFC-MRDAC		PFC-PRDAC		PFC-MPRDAC	
	nodes	cpu time	nodes	cpu time	nodes	cpu time	nodes	cpu time
SUB$_1$	$1.9\ 10^7$	$3.5\ 10^3$	$1.8\ 10^6$	$2.3\ 10^3$	$4.6\ 10^6$	$1.7\ 10^3$	$1.4\ 10^6$	$1.7\ 10^3$
SUB$_2$	$1.2\ 10^8$	$2.9\ 10^4$	$1.6\ 10^7$	$2.3\ 10^4$	$1.9\ 10^7$	$9.5\ 10^3$	$9.0\ 10^6$	$1.3\ 10^4$
SUB$_3$	$2.7\ 10^8$	$7.1\ 10^4$	$3.7\ 10^7$	$6.8\ 10^4$	$3.5\ 10^7$	$2.0\ 10^4$	$1.7\ 10^7$	$2.7\ 10^4$
SUB$_4$	$1.2\ 10^9$	$3.4\ 10^5$	$1.2\ 10^8$	$2.6\ 10^5$	$1.5\ 10^8$	$1.0\ 10^5$	$7.6\ 10^7$	$1.3\ 10^5$

of propagating deletions hardly pays off in dense problem classes, where PFC-MPRDAC is slightly faster than PFC-PRDAC. On medium and sparse classes, PFC-MPRDAC is up to 1.6 times faster than PFC-PRDAC.

Our second experiment considers the Radio Link Frequency Assignment Problem (RLFAP). It is a communication problem where the goal is to assign frequencies to a set of radio links in such a way that all the links may operate together without noticeable interference [2]. Some RLFAP instances can be naturally cast as *weighted* binary Max-CSP where each forbidden tuple has an associated penalty cost. We have extended the use of partition-based lower bound to this framework and tested them on four publicly available RLFAP subinstances called CELAR6-SUB$_i$ ($i = 1, \ldots, 4$) in [2]. Each CELAR6-SUB$_i$ is a sub-instance of CELAR6-SUB$_{i+1}$ and is therefore presumably easier to solve. As in the previous experiment, each instance is solved with the same four algorithms. They use the same variable ordering heuristic that was used in [5].

Table 1 shows the cost required to prove optimality (*i.e.* the upper bound is initialized with the optimum cost). We report both number of visited nodes and cpu-time in seconds. We can see that the partition-based lower bound is clearly beneficial in this domain as well. Regarding visited nodes, PFC-MPRDAC is the best algorithm. Comparing it with PFC-MRDAC, it visits nearly half the nodes in the hardest instances. However, the overhead of maintaining DAC updated does not pay off in performance. In terms of cpu time, PFC-PRDAC is the algorithm of choice. It clearly outperforms PFC-MRDAC, which was the best algorithm for this domain reported in [5]. In SUB$_4$, the hardest instance, our approach causes a cpu speed up of 2.6 with respect previous results. It is worth noting that there is a saving of 1.8 CPU days for a single problem instance.

6 Conclusions

The presented approach shows once more that branch and bound efficiency greatly depends on lower bound quality. Small increments in the lower bound may cause large gains in performance. The partition-based lower bound, developed in the Max-CSP context, can be successfully applied to other constraint satisfaction frameworks such as weighted CSPs. Although the proposed lower bound performs more work per node than previous approaches, it is clearly beneficial in terms of performance.

Regarding future work, local optimization of G^F for future value pruning using the partition-based lower bound requires more investigation. In addition, finding good partitions causing extra increments in the lower bound (partitions with subsets of more than two elements) deserves further research, to really assess all the potential of the proposed approach.

References

1. Bistarelli S., Montanari U., Rossi F. Constraint Solving over Semiring. In Proc. of the 14th IJCAI, Montreal, Canada, 1995.
2. Cabon B., de Givry S., Lobjois L., Schiex T., Warners J.P. Radio Link Frequency Assignment. Constraints (to appear).
3. Freuder E.C., Wallace R.J. Partial Constraint Satisfaction. Artificial Intelligence **58** (1992) 21–70.
4. Larrosa J., Meseguer P. Exploiting the use of DAC in Max-CSP. In Proc. of the 2nd. CP, Boston, USA, 1996.
5. Larrosa J., Meseguer P., Schiex T. Maintaining reversible DAC for Max-CSP. Artificial Intelligence **107** (1999) 149–163.
6. Prosser P. Binary Constraint Satisfaction Problems: Some are Harder than Others. In Proc. of the 11th. ECAI, Amsterdam, The Netherlands, 1994.
7. Schiex T. Maximizing the reversible DAC lower bound in Max-CSP is NP-hard. Technical Report 1998/02, INRA, 1998.
8. Schiex T., Fargier H., Verfaillie G. Valued Constraint Satisfaction Problems: hard and easy problems. In Proc. of the 14th IJCAI, Montreal, Canada, 1995.
9. Verfaillie G., Lemaitre M., Schiex T. Russian Doll Search. In Proc. of the 13th AAAI, Portland, USA, 1996.
10. Wallace R. Directed Arc Consistency Preprocessing. In M. Meyer, editor, Selected Papers from the ECAI94 Workshop on Constraint Processing, number 923 in LNCS, 121–137. Springer, 1995.

Constraint Diagram Reasoning

Bernd Meyer*

School of Computer Science and Software Engineering
Monash University, Australia
bernd.meyer@acm.org

Abstract. Diagrammatic human-computer interfaces are now becoming standard. In the near future, diagrammatic front-ends, such as those of UML-based CASE tools, will be required to offer a much more intelligent behavior than just editing. Yet there is very little formal support and there are almost no tools available for the construction of such environments. The present paper introduces a constraint-based formalism for the specification and implementation of complex diagrammatic environments. We start from grammar-based definitions of diagrammatic languages and show how a constraint solver for diagram recognition and interpretation can automatically be constructed from such grammars. In a second step, the capabilities of these solvers are extended by allowing to axiomatise formal diagrammatic systems, such as Venn Diagrams, so that they can be regarded as a new constraint domain. The ultimate aim of this schema is to establish a language of type CLP(Diagram) for diagrammatic reasoning applications.

1 Envisioning Intelligent Diagrammatic Environments

Graphical user interfaces have become an integral part of almost every modern application type. However, most existent GUIs are still relatively basic with interaction methods centered around such simple devices as icons, buttons, menus, etc. In non-computer-based work much more richly structured graphical notations dominate visual communication. Complex diagrammatic languages, such as circuit diagrams, are used in every technical discipline, software engineering is embracing all kinds of diagrammatic design methods and non-technical fields use their own notations, for example in choreography. Utilising such highly structured diagrammatic languages to their full extent in the human-computer interface would require the computer to "intelligently" interpret diagrammatic user input. Building the required domain-specific diagram interpretation components, however, is a labour-intensive and error-prone process, because very little formal support and even less tool support is available.

An approach that can promise to make the complexity of such "intelligent" diagrammatic environments manageable must comprise at least two components: (a) high-level specification formalisms for diagram languages and (b) tools that are able to automatically construct interactive environments from these specifications. In the following we will show how constraint-based techniques provide an ideal basis for such an approach.

---

* The research described here was undertaken while the author was working at University of Munich, Germany. It was supported by DFG grant Wi-841.

Ever since Sketchpad [25] constraint-based methods have been used for processing interactive graphics, as is highlighted by a recent special issue [6]. However, only little work has been dedicated to the constraint-based *interpretation* of graphical notations. Exceptions are [12, 15, 18] where constraint-based grammars and constraint-logic based formalisms, respectively, are used for diagram parsing and interpretation. The major new contribution of the approach presented here is that it introduces the notion of *diagrammatic systems as constraint domains* by showing how many aspects of a diagrammatic system can be axiomatised and how this axiomatisation can actually be implemented. We are not only interested in parsing and interpretation of a given diagram, but also in its logical aspects, such as its consistency and the consequences it entails. The approach presented thus extends the idea of diagrammatic parsing and aims to provide a basis for executable specifications in diagrammatic reasoning. At the same time it bridges the gap to managing the interactive nature of diagrammatic environments.

Section 2 begins by introducing Constraint Relational Grammars (CRGs, [19, 20]), a formalism for the syntactic specification and syntax-based interpretation of diagram languages. In Section 3 we show how "parsing as constraint solving" can be developed from the well-known concept of "parsing as deduction." For the formalisation and implementation of these ideas we will use rule-based solver definitions in the form of constraint handling rule programs (CHR [9]) into which CRG specifications can automatically be translated. Section 4 will generalise from diagram parsing to diagrammatic reasoning by extending these solvers with additional axiomatic definitions that operate on the level of diagrams. Because our schema is based on CHR solvers and because CHR is seamlessly integrated with constraint logic programming, we obtain a first approximation of CLP(Diagram) as a particular variant of the CLP(X)-schema [13]. In Section 5 we will discuss the problems arising from dynamic diagrams in interactive settings and sketch a solution based upon non-monotonic extensions of CHR. These extensions render the constructed diagram solvers capable of automatically handling dynamic interactive diagrams. Section 6 presents the generic diagram environment construction tool Recopla built upon the above ideas. A comparison with related work and conclusions are given in Section 7.

2   Specifying Diagrammatic Languages

Systems of diagrams, such as Venn diagrams or class diagrams, can be regarded as formal languages, but it is obvious that they differ from textual languages in some crucial ways. Most importantly, texts are sequential structures and the only operation needed to compose a sentence from tokens is sequential concatenation. In diagrams concatenation alone is not sufficient. Consider the example of circuit diagrams (Figure 1).

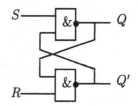

Fig. 1. Circuit Diagram

Obviously basic graphical elements like *line, point,* and *label* can be used as tokens, but the composition must also be made explicit, since several different spatial composition types like *inclusion, overlap* or *touching* may be used to compose a picture from tokens.

A widely used method for the grammatical definition of graphical languages is to model the picture by a set of tokens plus a set of spatial relations applied to these tokens. A multidimensional grammar for a graphical language can then be understood as a rewrite system operating on a set of graphical objects and a set of spatial relations simultaneously [17]. Such a grammar for a tiny subset of digital circuit diagrams can, for example, be formulated as in Figure 2.

$B : box \Rightarrow L_1, L_2, L_3, L_4 : line$
such that L_1 connects_to $L_2 \land L_2$ connects_to $L_3 \land$
L_3 connects_to $L_4 \land L_4$ connects_to L_1
and set $B.lines = \{L_1, L_2, L_3, L_4\}$.

$A : and\_gate \Rightarrow B : box, L : label$ such that L inside B
with $L.text = $ "&" and set $A.frame = B.lines$.

$N : nand\_gate \Rightarrow A : and\_gate, P : point$ such that P on $A.frame$
and set $N.frame = A.frame, N.out = P$.

$S : sr\_latch \Rightarrow N_1, N_2 : nand\_gate, L_1, L_2, L_3, L_4 : line, L_5, L_6 : polyline$
such that L_1 touches $N_1.frame \land L_2$ touches $N_2.frame$
$\land L_3$ touches $N_1.out \land L_4$ touches $N_2.out$
$\land L_5$ touches $L_3 \land L_5$ touches $N_2.frame$
$\land L_6$ touches $L_4 \land L_6$ touches $N_1.frame$
and set $S.set = L_1, S.reset = L_2, S.out_1 = L_3, S.out_2 = L_4$.

Fig. 2. Constraint Relational Grammar Rules

The syntactic structure of a diagram can therefore be given by a set O of graphical objects together with a set R of spatial relations between them. A diagrammatic language $\mathcal{L}$ is a tuple of such sets $< O, R >$. If $\mathcal{L}$ is finite, it can be specified by enumeration, otherwise it must be specified structurally, e.g. by a multidimensional grammar. Several such formalisms with subtle differences have been described in the literature and the interested reader is invited to refer to [17] for a survey and comparison. Here, we are presenting Constraint Relational Grammars (CRGs, [19, 20]), a formalism that inherits from Constraint Multiset Grammars (CMGs, [12, 15]) and Relational Grammars (RGs, [26]). RGs only use a relational representation for spatial relationships and CMGs solely rely on constraints over real-valued attributes to express spatial constraints. In contrast, CRGs use a dual representation: Symbolic relations are their primary representation for spatial arrangement of tokens, but these are not regarded as "passive" symbols. Rather they are considered as "active" constraints, which can be interpreted in some underlying constraint theory, for example linear real constraints for interpreting symbolic spatial constraints in terms of the underlying geometry. In [18] we have given a detailed account of why such a dual representation is crucial if complex diagram manipulations are intended, such as animation, interaction handling or arbitrary rewriting.

Like CMGs, CRGs allow context-sensitive productions. In addition to the specification of syntax, appearance and semantics (i.e. interpretation) of diagrammatic notations, Constraint Relational Grammars also provide mechanisms to specify interpretation-based modal interaction, but a detailed discussion of this aspect is beyond the scope of this paper. The rules in Figure 2 are examples of CRG productions. We will now give a first formalisation of CRGs, which does not yet take the dual representation into account, i.e. symbolic spatial relations are treated purely as passive symbols. Constraint interpretations will be added in Section 4.

Definition 1. *A* picture vocabulary *is a tuple* $V = < OT_{nt}, OT_t, RT >$ *of a set* OT_t *of terminal object types, a set* OT_{nt} *of non-terminal object types and a set* RT *of spatial relation types. A* diagram *over* V *is a tuple* $D = < O, R >$ *of a set* O *of objects and a set* R *of relations with types according to* V. *Arbitrary attributes can be attached to the objects in* O.

Definition 2. *A* Constraint Relational Grammar (CRG) *is a quadruple* $< V, P, S, CT >$ *of a picture vocabulary* $V = < OT_{nt}, OT_t, RT >$, *a set of CRG productions* P, *a distinguished start symbol* $S \in OT_{nt}$ *and a constraint theory* CT.

Definition 3. *A* CRG production *in a CRG* $G = < V, P, S, CT >$ *is a rule* $< N \Rightarrow o_1, \ldots o_k$ *where* $\text{exists}(o_{k+1}, \ldots, o_l)$ *such that* $r_1, \ldots, r_m$ *and* $r_{m+1}, \ldots, r_n$ *with* C *and set* $F >$ *where* N *is a typed variable over* OT_{nt}; $o_1, \ldots, o_l$ *are typed variables over* $OT_{nt} \cup OT_t$; $r_{m+1}, \ldots, r_n$ *are typed relations over* RT *involving only the object variables* $o_{k+1}, \ldots, o_l$ *and* $r_1, \ldots, r_m$ *are typed relations over* RT *involving the object variables* $o_1, \ldots, o_l$. C *is a constraint in* CT *on the attribute values of* $o_1, \ldots, o_l$ *and* F *is an assignment of the attributes of* N *given as a formula that involves only these objects' attribute values. Any part on the right-hand side may be omitted except for* $o_1, \ldots, o_k$. *Omission is defined as declaring the omitted part to be the empty set* $\emptyset$ *in the case of* $o_{k+1}, \ldots, o_l, r_1, \ldots, r_n$ *and as setting it to true in the case of* C.

Definition 4. *A CRG production is* context-sensitive *iff* $\{o_{k+1}, \ldots, o_l\} \neq \emptyset$, *it is* context-free *otherwise.*

CRGs actually also allow negative (universally quantified) contexts, but in the interest of brevity we will not discuss them here. A CRG-production of the form $< N \Rightarrow o_1, \ldots o_k$ where $\text{exists}(o_{k+1}, \ldots, o_l)$ such that $r_1, \ldots, r_m$ and $r_{m+1}, \ldots, r_n$ with C and set $F >$ in a production set P can be applied to a sentential form $< O, R >$ if there is a substitution θ of object variables $o_1, \ldots, o_l$ into O such that $\{o_1, \ldots o_l\}\theta \cup X = O \wedge \{r_1, \ldots, r_n\}\theta \cup Y = R \wedge CT \models C\theta$. It rewrites the current sentential form into $< O', R' >$ with $O' = O - \{o_1, \ldots, o_k\} \cup \{N\}$ and $R' = R - \{r_1, \ldots, r_m\}$ where the attributes of N are constrained or set according to $F\theta$. We write $< O, R > \Rightarrow_P < O', R' >$ and interpret $\Rightarrow_P^*$ as the transitive closure of $\Rightarrow_P$.

Definition 5. *A CRG* $G = < V, P, S, CT >$ *defines the language* $\mathcal{L}(G) = \{< O, R > | < O, R > \Rightarrow_P^* < S, R' >\}$.

Drawing on the ideas of "parsing as deduction" and on the operational semantics of constraint handling rules, we will next show how a parser for a diagrammatic language $\mathcal{L}(G)$ can automatically be derived from the corresponding CRG G.

3 Parsing as Constraint Solving

The interpretation of parsing as logical deduction has a long-standing tradition which is manifest in Definite Clause Grammars [23]. Some familiarity with these methods is assumed. We will extend these ideas and show how incremental bottom-up parsing of sequential and multidimensional languages can be regarded as constraint solving. It will prove beneficial to employ a declarative high-level definition language for constraint solvers as an intermediate level, namely we will use Constraint Handling Rules (CHR [9]). The advantages gained are threefold: (1) The transformation of CRGs into CHR is straightforward, still the resulting CHR programs are directly executable. (2) CHR is a declarative formalism so that a formal analysis of solver properties, such as confluence, is possible. (3) CHR is seamlessly integrated with CLP [9]. A CLP system with builtin CHR, such as Sicstus Prolog, can thus be used to instantiate the CLP(X) schema with new domains. Let us express this as $CHR(X) + CLP(CHR) = CLP(X)$. Casting our approach into these terms, we define a transformation function $\tau : CRG(D) \mapsto CHR(D)$ on diagrammatic grammars and arrive at

$$CRG(Diag) + CLP(CHR) = CHR(Diag) + CLP(CHR) = CLP(Diag)$$

CHR is essentially a committed-choice language with multi-headed guarded rules that transform constraints into simpler ones until they are solved. A *CHR constraint* is a first order term. A constraint is either *built-in* or *user-defined*. Built-in constraints are handled by a predefined black-box constraint solver, such as a Simplex solver. The primitives *true, false* and the syntactic equality $=$ are always required to be part of the built-in constraint theory. A CHR program consists of *simplification* and *propagation* rules operating on the user-defined constraints. Simplification rules, such as X≥Y∧Y≥X <=> X=Y, replace constraints by simpler constraints while preserving logical equivalence. They have the form *Rulename @ H ⇔ C | B* where *Rulename* is an optional rule identifier, the head H is a non-empty conjunction of user-defined constraints, the guard C is a conjunction of built-in constraints and the body B is a conjunction of built-in and user-defined constraints. Propagation rules have the form *Rulename @ H ⇒ C | B* and add new constraints which are logically redundant but may cause further simplification, e.g. X≥Y∧Y≥Z => X≥Z. Both types of rules can be combined into *simpagation* rules, which divide the rule head into two parts: The second part of the head constraints is removed when the rule fires, while the first part of the head constraints is left untouched. For example, X=Y\Y≥X <=> true removes redundant inequalities. A full explanation of CHR is far beyond the scope of this paper and the reader is referred to [9].

A *CHR program* is a finite set of rules which defines a transition system that operates on a global constraint store given as a triple $<G, C_U, C_B>$. Here G is a conjunction of user-defined and built-in constraints called *goal store*, C_U is a conjunction of user-defined constraints and C_B is a conjunction of built-in constraints. Each computation step is of one of the following types: (a) *Introduce* moves a constraint for further reduction from the goal store to the user-defined constraint store. (b) *Simplify* matches some constraint with the head of a rule.

If the guard holds, it deletes the head from the user-defined constraint store and adds the body to the goal store. (c) *Propagate* works analogously to simplification, but the head is not removed from the user-defined constraint store. (d) *Solve* activates the built-in solver. In this step a built-in constraint is removed from the goal store and transferred to the built-in constraint store which is then re-normalised by the built-in solver.

An *initial state* for a goal G is of the form $<G, \top, true>$ where $\top$ and *true* define the empty user-defined and built-in constraint store, respectively. The *final state* $<G, C_U, false>$ is called *failed* and the final state $<\top, C_U, C_B>$ with no computation step possible any more and C_B not *false* is called *successful*.

(a)
$$\frac{H \text{ is a user-defined constraint}}{<H \wedge G, C_U, C_B> \mapsto <G, H \wedge C_U, C_B>}$$

(b)
$$\frac{(R @ H \Leftrightarrow C \mid B) \text{ is a fresh variant of a rule in } P \text{ with the variables } \bar{x}}{CT \models C_B \to \exists \bar{x}(H = H' \wedge C)}$$
$$\frac{}{<G, H' \wedge C_U, C_B> \mapsto <G \wedge B, C_U, C \wedge H = H' \wedge C_B>}$$

(c)
$$\frac{(R @ H \Rightarrow C \mid B) \text{ is a fresh variant of a rule in } P \text{ with the variables } \bar{x}}{CT \models C_B \to \exists \bar{x}(H = H' \wedge C)}$$
$$\frac{}{<G, H' \wedge C_U, C_B> \mapsto <G \wedge B, H' \wedge C_U, C \wedge H = H' \wedge C_B>}$$

(d)
$$\frac{C \text{ is a built-in constraint}}{CT \models C_B \wedge C \leftrightarrow C'_B}$$
$$\frac{}{<C \wedge G, C_U, C_B> \mapsto <G, C_U, C'_B>}$$

Evidently there is an effective mapping from grammars to CHR rules. We will illustrate this mapping as well as the derivation process with a toy grammar for a fragment of English. A linguistic example rather than a diagrammatic example is chosen so that it can be related more easily to well-known concepts of formal languages. The example grammar has the production set $\{S \to NP\ VP,$ $NP \to D\ N,\ VP \to V\ NP,\ D \to the|a,\ N \to dog|cat,\ V \to bites\}$. Every token and every non-terminal can be represented by a constraint term (say, w/2 and p/3, respectively). Since the sequencing information is lost in this representation, we capture it explicitly by interpreting p(X,Y,T) as "a phrase of type T extends from position X to position Y" and—in analogy to spatial relations—we make concatenation explicit by using additional tokens of type $c/2$. A constraint $c(X,Y)$ is read as "index Y follows index X." The rules are translated such that the initial state is reduced to p(1,Y,s) iff the initial sentence is in the language. The corresponding CHR rule set is

```
w(X,cat)   <=>  p(X,X,n).      w(X,dog)  <=>  p(X,X,n).
w(X,the)   <=>  p(X,X,d).      w(X,a)    <=>  p(X,X,d).
w(X,bites) <=>  p(X,X,v).
p(X1,X2,v), p(X3,X4,np), c(X2,X3)  <=> p(X1,X4,vp).
p(X1,X2,d), p(X3,X4,n),  c(X2,X3)  <=> p(X1,X4,np).
p(X1,X2,np), p(X3,X4,vp), c(X2,X3) <=> p(X1,X4,s).
```

For the example sentence "The cat bites the dog" given by the constraint conjunction $w(1, the) \land w(2, cat) \land c(1, 2) \land w(3, bites) \land c(2, 3) \land w(4, the) \land c(3, 4) \land w(5, dog) \land c(4, 5)$ we obtain the following derivation structure:

$$< w(1, the) \land w(2, cat) \land c(1, 2) \land w(3, bites) \land \ldots, \top, true >$$
$$\mapsto^*_{\text{Introduce}} < \top, w(1, the) \land w(2, cat) \land c(1, 2) \land w(3, bites) \land \ldots, true >$$
$$\mapsto_{\text{Simplify}} < p(1, 1, d), w(2, cat) \land c(1, 2) \land w(3, bites) \land \ldots, true >$$
$$\mapsto^*_{\text{Simplify}} < p(1, 1, d) \land p(2, 2, n) \land p(3, 3, v) \land p(4, 4, d) \ldots, c(1, 2) \land \ldots, true >$$
$$\mapsto^*_{\text{Introduce}} < \top, p(1, 1, d) \land p(2, 2, n) \land c(1, 2) \land p(3, 3, v) \land p(4, 4, d) \ldots, true >$$
$$\mapsto_{\text{Simplify}} < p(1, 2, np), p(3, 3, v) \land p(4, 4, d) \ldots, true >$$
$$\ldots \qquad < \top, p(1, 2, np) \land c(2, 3) \land p(3, 5, vp), true >$$
$$\mapsto_{\text{Simplify}} < p(1, 5, s), \top, true >$$
$$\mapsto_{\text{Introduce}} < \top, p(1, 5, s), true >$$

In the above sequential parser we had to model concatenation explicitly, since the formalism is inherently order-free. We exploit this property and generalise the translation for CRGs such that instead of just concatenation arbitrary relations between tokens can be used. $\tau : CRG \to CHR$ defines the complete transformation of CRG productions into equivalent CHR rules.

Let $p = \; < N \Rightarrow o_1, \ldots o_k$ such that $r_1, \ldots, r_m$ with C and set $F >$ be a context-free production, then $p' = \tau(p) = \tau_o(o_1), \ldots, \tau_o(o_k), \tau_r(r_1), \ldots, \tau_r(r_m) \leftrightarrow \tau_c(C) \mid \tau_n(N), \tau_f(F)$. The functions τ_o and τ_r map CRG objects and relationships to their CHR representation. A naive transformation maps each object $o_i = X_i : type_i$ to $\tau_o(o_i) = type_i(X_i, A_i)$ and $\tau_n(N : type_0) = type_0(Id, A_0)$ where the A_js are lists of fresh variables that match the lists of the objects' attributes and Id is a unique new identifier. Each relationship $r_i = rel\_type_i(X_i, Y_i)$ is mapped to $\tau(r_i) = rel\_type_i(X_i, Y_i)$. The translations $\tau_f(F)$ and $\tau_c(C)$ are performed by replacing each attribute term $o_i.attr\_name$ in C and F with the corresponding variable in the attribute list of $\tau(o_i)$. A more sophisticated translation does not require explicit identifiers. It can instead use the unique constraint identifiers provided by CHR implementations. This modification improves the efficiency of the resulting rules, but it also renders the mapping more difficult to follow, since CHR's constraint identifiers can only be used in relatively restricted ways.

From the operational semantics of CHR rules outlined above, it follows that $\tau(p)$ defines a *simplify* step that removes the LHS constraints from the user-defined constraint store and inserts the RHS constraints $\tau_n(N), \tau_f(F)$ into the goal store. This step can immediately be followed by an *introduce* step for $\tau(N)$ and a *solve* step for $\tau(F)$. We abbreviate the conjunction of constraints that decides the applicability of $\tau(p)$ with C_p, i.e. $C_p \equiv (\tau(B) = \tau(B') \land \tau(C))$, and arrive at the following derivation relation:

$$\frac{(N \Rightarrow B \text{ with } C \text{ set } F) \text{ is a fresh variant of production } p \text{ in } G \text{ with variables } \bar{x}}{CT \models (C_B \to \exists \bar{x} \; C_p) \land (C_B \land C_p \land \tau(F) \leftrightarrow C'_B)}$$
$$<G, \tau(B') \land C_U, C_B> \mapsto <G, C_U \land \tau(N), C'_B>$$

We extend the translation schema to use simpagation for context-sensitive rules, since the constraints resulting from the context have to be kept in the store. The extension of the derivation relation is straightforward according to

$(H_1 \backslash H_2 \Leftrightarrow G \mid B)$ is a fresh variant of a rule in P with the variables $\bar{x}$

$$\frac{CT \models C_B \rightarrow \exists \bar{x}(H_1{=}H_1' \wedge H_2{=}H_2' \wedge G)}{<Gs, H_1' \wedge H_2' \wedge C_U, C_B> \mapsto <Gs \wedge B, H_1' \wedge C_U, G \wedge H_1{=}H_1' \wedge H_2{=}H_2' \wedge C_B>}$$

Let $p = \; < N \Rightarrow o_1, \ldots o_k$ where $exists(o_{k+1}, \ldots, o_l)$ such that $r_1, \ldots, r_m$ and $r_{m+1}, \ldots, r_n$ with C and set $F >$ be a context-sensitive production, then $\tau(p) =$

$$\tau(o_{k+1}, \ldots, o_l), \tau(r_{m+1}, \ldots, r_n) \backslash \tau(o_1, \ldots, o_k), \tau(r_1, \ldots, r_m) \Rightarrow \tau(C) \mid \tau(N), \tau(F)$$

Due to the one-to-one correspondence between derivation steps of CRG G and its corresponding CHR program $\tau(G)$ their operational semantics are equivalent:

Theorem 1. $D \in \mathcal{L}(G)$ iff $<\tau(D), \top, true> \mapsto^*_{\tau(G)} <\top, \tau(S) \wedge C_U, C_B>$ with $C_B \neq false$ and C_U contains no constraints corresponding to diagram object types in G.

Proof: (Sketch) From the above derivation relation and the definition of derivations steps for a CRG $G =< V, P, S, CT >$ it is immediate that $< O, R >\Rightarrow^*_P< S, R' >$ iff $<\tau(< O, R >), \top, true> \mapsto^*_{\tau(G)} <\top, \tau(S) \wedge \tau(R'), C_B>$ with C_B not false. $\tau(R')$ can only contain constraints corresponding to additional spatial relations. □

Such CHR parsers can only be used without limitations for confluent grammars, because no backtracking or search is involved, but for incremental parsing in interactive systems this does not present any serious limitation. Here backtracking is prohibitive anyway, since it would usually mean to revoke previously given feedback. Confluence analysis of CHR systems was investigated in [2] and a completion procedure was introduced in [1]. These results immediately carry over to our parsers, because they are defined as CHR systems.

4 From Diagram Recognition to Diagrammatic Reasoning

We have defined how to map a CRG G to a CHR program $\tau(G)$ that implements an incremental parser for $\mathcal{L}(G)$. By using the logical semantics of $\tau(G)$ we can give a logical reconstruction of G.

We only sketch the declarative semantics of CHR here; a full treatment is found in [9]. Basically, the logical interpretation of a simplification rule $H \leftrightarrow G \mid B$ is the equivalence $\forall \bar{x} \, ((\exists \bar{y} \; G) \rightarrow (H \leftrightarrow \exists \bar{z} \; B))$, the logical meaning of a propagation rule $H \Rightarrow G \mid B$ is the implication $\forall \bar{x} \, ((\exists \bar{y} \; G) \rightarrow (H \rightarrow \exists \bar{z} \; B))$ and that of a simpagation rule $H_1 \backslash H_2 \leftrightarrow G \mid B$ is $\forall \bar{x} \, ((\exists \bar{y} \; G) \rightarrow (H_1 \wedge H_2 \leftrightarrow \exists \bar{z} \; H_1 \wedge B))$ where $\bar{x}$ are the variables in H, $\bar{y}$ the variables in G and $\bar{z}$ those in B. Since we are translating each context-free CRG production $p_{cf} : \; < N \Rightarrow O$ such that R with C and set $F >$ into a CHR rule $\tau(O), \tau(R) \leftrightarrow \tau(C) \mid \tau(N), \tau(F)$ and each context-sensitive production $p_{cs} : \; < N \Rightarrow O$ where $exists(\overline{O})$ such that R and $\overline{R}$ with C and set $F >$ into a CHR rule $\tau(\overline{O}), \tau(\overline{R}) \backslash \tau(O), \tau(R) \leftrightarrow \tau(C) \mid \tau(N), \tau(F)$ it follows that the logical reading of p_{cf} is $\forall \bar{x} \, ((\exists \bar{y} \; \tau(C)) \rightarrow ((\tau(O) \wedge \tau(R)) \leftrightarrow \exists \bar{z} \; (\tau(N) \wedge \tau(F))))$ and that of p_{cs} is $\forall \bar{x} \, ((\exists \bar{y} \; \tau(C)) \rightarrow ((\tau(O, \overline{O}) \wedge \tau(R, \overline{R})) \leftrightarrow \exists \bar{z} \; (\tau(\overline{O}) \wedge \tau(\overline{R}) \wedge \tau(N) \wedge \tau(F))))$.

Therefore the parse tree of a diagram D according to G can also be read as a proof tree for $\tau(S)$ from $\tau(D)$ according to $\tau(G)$. The CRG G can thus be viewed as a constraint theory defining diagram structures. We are now set to move from diagram parsing to an initial concept of diagrammatic reasoning by making use of the integration of CHR and CLP as introduced in [9]. Essentially this gives us a CLP(X)-style language where X is given be the logical interpretation $\mathcal{P}$ of a CHR program P. Therefore, if $P = \tau(G)$, we obtain a language CLP($\mathcal{L}(G)$).

By treating the diagrammatic system as a constraint domain in CLP(X) we gain the possibility to realise three additional concepts that form the basis for implementing diagrammatic reasoning: (1) Axiomatisation of diagrammatic systems, (2) Integration of diagrammatic constraints with deductive reasoning, (3) Integration of diagrammatic structures with other constraint domains. We also gain the ability to implement programs that interpret and reason about partial diagram structures. This is crucial for building interactive diagrammatic environments and will be discussed separately in Section 5.

Axiomatisation of diagrammatic systems The structure of diagrammatic systems is often more complicated than can easily be described by a grammar, in particular if the correctness of a diagram depends on outside conditions like domain knowledge. Regarding a diagrammatic system as a constraint theory defined by a CHR rule system enables us to introduce additional axioms on its structure by extending $\tau(G)$ much more easily than we could do by extending the grammar G directly.

Consider a system working with a variant of object-oriented class diagrams where classes may be represented by multiple boxes in different places. If spatial intersection is part of the picture vocabulary we can, for example, use the following axioms to impose the rule that different classes must graphically be kept apart: `class(X), class(Y), intersects(X,Y) <=> X=/=Y | false`. Similar axioms could be used to enforce additionally desired properties like single inheritance, etc. It is important to note that constraint axioms which refine the diagram language can now be introduced in a much more modular fashion than could be done by extending the grammar.

Let us tackle a more complex case. Above we have used an axiom to restrict admissible diagram structure. A much more powerful form of diagrammatic axioms, in fact the basis of all diagrammatic reasoning, allows us to express conclusion relations between diagrams without interpreting them first

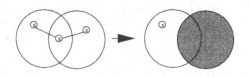

Fig. 3. Two Venn Diagrams

(!) so that we can make inferences directly on the level of diagrams. We will illustrate this with a hypothetical system for reasoning in the domain of sets which uses Shin's variant of Venn diagrams [24]. In these diagrams sets are represented by regions, shaded basic regions imply that the corresponding set is empty, and chains of Xs indicate that at least one of the set regions marked by an X in the chain must be non-empty.

As an example, the diagram on the left side of Figure 3 depicts three sets $s_1, s_2, s_3 = s_1 \cap s_2$ at least one of which is non-empty. This diagram could be represented by the constraint formula $region(r_1) \wedge region(r_2) \wedge region(r_3) \wedge x(x_1) \wedge x(x_2) \wedge x(x_3) \wedge line(l_1) \wedge line(l_2) \wedge inside(x_1, r_1) \wedge inside(x_2, r_2) \wedge inside(x_3, r_3) \wedge connected(x_1, l_1) \wedge connected(x_2, l_2) \wedge connected(x_3, l_1) \wedge connected(x_3, l_2) \wedge leftend(x_1) \wedge rightend(x_2) \wedge intersection(r_1, r_2, r_3)$.

To exemplify the case we will only introduce a single conclusion relation for Venn diagrams known as "Erasure of Links." Together with a number of other similar axioms, Venn diagrams can be extended into a self-contained, complete and sound system for reasoning about sets [24]. "Erasure of Links" formalises the idea that we can deduce $z \in Z_1 \vee \ldots \vee z \in Z_n$ from $z \in Z_1 \vee \ldots \vee z \in Z \vee \ldots \vee z \in Z_n$ if $Z = \emptyset$. In the diagram system this rule is restated as "an X in a shaded region may be dropped from an X-chain provided the chain is kept connected." This can be expressed by the following set of CHR axioms: (V1) expresses the diagrammatic deduction rule that the X terminating a chain can be removed if the chain ends in a shaded (empty) region and if X is not the only element of the chain. (Obviously dual rules are needed for the left end and inner elements of a chain). (V2) expresses the fact that a chain shrinks to an isolated element when the last-but-one element is removed. (V3) states that an isolated element in some region implies that the corresponding set is non-empty. (V4) expresses that an empty set cannot contain an element and finally (V5) propagates shading (and thus emptiness) to subsets.

```
v1 @ region(A), shaded(A), x(C) \ x(B), inside(B,A), rightend(B),
        line(D), connected(B,D), connected(C,D) <=> rightend(C).
v2 @ x(A) \ leftend(A), rightend(A) <=> isolated(A).
v3 @ x(A), region(B), inside(A,B), isolated(A) => nonempty(B).
v4 @ region(A), shaded(A), nonempty(A) <=> false.
v5 @ region(A), intersection(A,B,C), shaded(A) => shaded(C).
```

The integration of diagrammatic axioms and parsing requires parsing to be split into two distinct stages. In a first phase the primitive graphical entities (terminals) are lifted to the level on which the axioms are expressed. The second stage, which completes the parsing process and ultimately reduces the entire expression to the start symbol, is used to check the correctness of the expression and can only be applied after reasoning is finished.

Integration with Deduction With a parser, we can only make *observations* from a diagram, but we could not *introduce* new constraints into it. Our integrative schema makes exactly this possible. Let us extend our hypothetical system such that it reasons using Venn Diagrams and classical logic sentential assertions simultaneously. A natural way to implement the sentential inference component is as a logic program. This program will infer additional facts about the sets from sentential knowledge not represented in the diagram. Still, the diagram and the sentential knowledge must be kept consistent and it would be desirable to also represent additional new knowledge in the diagram. Our schema facilitates such a bidirectional coupling by virtue of the CLP(X) schema.

Let us show how an inference in the sentential deduction mechanism of our set reasoning system can trigger additional inferences in the diagrammatic component (and vice versa). We have already prepared the ground for this in the previous paragraphs by showing how diagrammatic conclusion relations can be implemented with CHR axioms. Suppose we have the diagram given on the left side of Figure 3 and the sentential component deduces the additional fact that the set s_2 corresponding to region r_2 is empty by non-diagrammatic reasoning. Since the diagrammatic constraints are available to the logic programming component as first order terms, it can assert the constraint shaded(r2). This will in turn trigger the following diagrammatic inference: shaded(r2) will propagate by v5 to shaded(r3). Rule v1 will then cause all elements from the chain to be removed except for the X in the region r_1. The solver will further simplify the diagram maintaining logical equivalence until it is deduced by v2 and by v3 that the set corresponding to r_1 is non-empty. The diagrammatic reasoning component has thus inferred the non-emptiness of the set s_1 corresponding to r_1 from the emptiness of s_2 and the diagram. The logic programming component can now use the entailment of this fact for further inferences. On the diagrammatic side, v4 will prevent further shading of r_1, because this would make the diagram inconsistent.

Integration with other constraint domains Finally we can use the built-in constraint theory in CHR as a hook to integrate the domain of diagrams with other additional domains. In particular there are two uses: We may want to have a constraint theory modelling the application domain depicted in the diagram, for example *boolean* when working with circuit diagrams, or we may want to use an arithmetic domain to give symbolic spatial relationships a concrete interpretation. Let us illustrate the latter case by showing how a spatial constraint like *leftof* operating on axis-parallel rectangular boxes can be equipped with an arithmetic semantics. This is done by using rules that propagate the symbolic constraint to arithmetic constraints on the geometric attributes of the diagrammatic symbols involved (and vice versa). Assuming that attributes are modelled as in Section 3, this can be done by the following two rules:

```
box(B1, [Xmin1,Ymin1,Xmax1,Ymax1]),
box(B2, [Xmin2,Ymin2,Xmax2,Ymax2])
   => ground(Xmax1), ground(Xmin2), Xmax1 < Xmin2 | leftof(B1,B2).
box(B1, [Xmin1,Ymin1,Xmax1,Ymax1]),
box(B2, [Xmin2,Ymin2,Xmax2,Ymax2]), leftof(B1,B2)
   =>  Xmax1 < Xmin2.
```

The first rule detects *leftof* for two given boxes with fixed coordinates. Conversely, the second rule gives an arithmetic interpretation to the symbolic constraint. Assuming that the underlying constraint theory handles linear inequalities, the constraint Xmax1 < Xmin2 will be transferred to the built-in constraint store in a *solve* step where it will be handled by the underlying solver.

This tight integration of diagrammatic and sentential reasoning with concrete domains as well as the direct support for diagrammatic conclusions make the CLP(Diag) schema a much more powerful basis for reasoning with diagrams than a loosely coupled combination of a diagram recogniser with an inference component could provide.

5   Interactive Diagrams

We have argued that one of the reasons to introduce the CLP(Diag) schema is declarative support for interactive visual environments in which diagrammatic input is processed incrementally. Fortunately the CLP(X) schema is built around incremental constraint solving and solvers implemented with CHR are automatically incremental. Therefore our schema is naturally incremental.

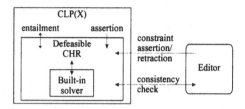

Fig. 4. Overall System Architecture

What needs to be done is to couple a diagram editor with the deductive system in such a way that it adds new constraints to the constraint store whenever the user adds graphical elements to the diagram or whenever a new spatial relationship between diagram objects is detected. It must also reject all editing actions that cause the solver to detect an inconsistency (Figure 4). The state of the store will then always correctly model the interpretation of the diagram in its current state. Graphical elements added will trigger further constraint propagation until eventually the entire diagram can be analysed: This is the constraint-based variant of incremental parsing.

However, standard constraint solving assumes that constraints are only added, i.e. the solver behaves monotonic. In our setting this is prohibitive, since constraints represent the state of the interactive input. If they could only be added, no editing operation could ever be undone: Basically no corrections could be applied to the diagram except for by chronological undo. No graphical element, once added, could ever be deleted again and no spatial relationship, once observed, could ever become invalid again. Therefore support for non-monotonic adaptation of the constraint store under constraint deletion is mandatory.

Our approach to this is to use source-level transformation on the CHR meta-level. We provide a generic transformation function that produces a non-monotonic solver from the definition of a monotonic solver. This function converts a confluent rule set P written in core CHR into a CHR program P' that exploits meta-features of full CHR to react adequately to constraint addition and deletion. Thus it turns a given CHR solver into a defeasible solver for the same domain. The basic idea of this transformation is inspired by Truth Maintenance Systems (TMS, [8]).

Informally, a TMS is a system which maintains a database of propositions and justifications for them. A proposition considered true is called a "belief" and such beliefs can either be added from the outside as premises ("observations") or by inference. Since the inference rules are usually given by clauses of a non-monotonic logic, such as auto-epistemic logic [22], the logical interpretation of a TMS is obviously non-monotonic. The TMS is concerned with maintaining a consistent state of beliefs under arbitrary changes of premises and it does so by utilising a dependency network of propositions and justifications, i.e. it records which propositions were used to derive new beliefs. The connections between TMS and constraint relaxation are well known and have been discussed in [7, 14]. Viewing constraints corresponding to diagram elements as premises and viewing interpretations as beliefs enables us to use TMS techniques for maintaining a consistent diagram interpretation under arbitrary changes.

The basic idea is to let the transformed CHR program P' performs the same functionality as P, but to let it additionally keep a trace of the dependencies in the derivation. This is done by using two types of meta-constraints: $\rightsquigarrow (Id_1, Id_2)$ is used to tag the constraint Id_1 as dependent on the constraint Id_2, because Id_1 was created by a propagation rule triggered by Id_2. $\not\rightsquigarrow (Id_1, Id_2)$ is used to tag the constraint Id_1 as negatively dependent on the constraint Id_2, because Id_1 was removed from the store by a simplification rule that was triggered by Id_2. Simpagation rules accordingly create both types of dependencies. Using these recorded dependencies a few simple meta-rules can be given which are triggered by constraint deletions and traverse the dependency network to delete dependent constraints (and re-instantiate negatively dependent constraints, respectively). A full exposition of this transformation cannot be given here due to space restrictions.

6 Recopla

In previous work we have presented a system for the automatic construction of diagrammatic environments from declarative high-level specifications [20]. This meta-environment consists of a syntax-based high-level interpretation component [19] on top of the generic graphic editor-builder Recopla [10]. It uses a CRG G as a specification to generate a specialised diagram editor for $\mathcal{L}(G)$ that can interpret a given diagram and check its correctness. Attributed CRGs are used to define the translation of $\mathcal{L}(G)$ into representations suitable for processing by back-end applications. The front-ends constructed by Recopla are Java applications that can flexibly communicate with such back-end applications via dedicated bidirectional Internet channels. Since a vast number of diagrammatic notations used in practice essentially have graphs as their underlying backbone structure, the system is designed to offer special support for the definition of and interaction with graph structures. Recopla has already successfully been used to build editors for a number of standard notations, among them animated Petri nets, object-oriented class diagrams, timing diagrams, digital circuit diagrams, extended flow charts and even interactive board games.

Recopla's interpretation component is based on CRGs and already accommodates non-monotonic change, but it does not fully implement the schema discussed in Section 5. As yet, it implements a predecessor in which CRGs are compiled into Prolog-programs that handle non-monotonic change via side-effects. Since CHR is already integrated with the Prolog system that we are using for Recopla's interpretation component, it will be easy to fully switch to the CHR-based schema in the future.

329

7 Conclusions and Related Work

We have presented a schema for constraint-based specification and implementation of diagrammatic environments. While the basic schema is operational, this is only a start. Experiments with prototypes have shown that their performance under constraint deletion is not yet satisfactory. A possible way to improve this is to move the functionality provided by the CHR source-level transformation directly into the CHR kernel. Another important issue is the inter-operability of defeasible diagrammatic solvers with the remaining components. A smoother integration of defeasible CHR solvers with the underlying black-box solvers for built-in domains would be desirable. With the current framework, a constraint that has been transferred to the built-in constraint store can not be deleted again, because the underlying black-box solvers, for example Simplex solvers, do not allow constraint deletion. We are currently experimenting with the integration of CHR and novel arithmetic solvers that allow constraint deletion [3].

The grammatical aspects of our work obviously draw on some ideas developed for Constraint Multiset Grammars [15] and their predecessors [12]. They are also related to relational grammars [26]. In a sense, CRGs can be viewed as a generalisation of CMGs and RGs. In principle, there are two possible approaches to model geometric properties of diagrammatic objects: They can be handled as arithmetic constraints on geometric attributes, such as positions, or as abstract symbolic relations. CMGs have taken the first approach, RGs the second one. In [18] we have argued why a mixed representation is required to support more complex forms of automatic diagram manipulation and diagrammatic reasoning: Such a dual representation is present in CRGs.

Only few other construction toolkits for diagram environments exist that support declarative high-level specifications: Penguins [4] uses CMGs, DiaGen [21] uses hypergraph grammars and GenEd [11] is based on description logic. A comparison with these systems was given in [20]. All the approaches mentioned here have limited themselves to diagram recognition and syntax-based translation. While this is also our starting point, we pursue an open-ended integrative approach that allows to implement axiomatic diagrammatic systems as a new constraint domain and offers a basis for diagrammatic reasoning. We intend to demonstrate the viability of this new schema by building tutor systems for visual mathematical notations such as Venn diagrams or visual lambda calculus [5].

Acknowledgments We owe thanks to Martin Wirsing and Thom Frühwirth for discussions on this subject.

References

1. S. Abdennadher and T. Frühwirth. On completion of constraint handling rules. In *CP98: Int. Conf. on Principles and Practice of Constraint Programming*, 1998.
2. S. Abdennadher, T. Frühwirth, and H. Meuss. On confluence of constraint handling rules. In *CP96: Int. Conf. on Principles and Practice of Constraint Programming*, August 1996.
3. A. Borning, K. Marriott, P. Stuckey, and Y. Xiao. Solving linear arithmetic constraints for user interface applications. In *UIST'97: ACM Symp. on User Interface Software and Technology*, October 1997.

4. S.S. Chok and K. Marriott. Constructing user interfaces for pen-based computers. In *FRVDR'98: AAAI Symp. on Formalizing Reasoning with Visual and Diagrammatic Representations*, Orlando, October 1998.

5. W. Citrin, R. Hall, and B. Zorn. Programming with visual expressions. In *VL95: IEEE WS on Visual Languages*, Darmstadt, 1995.

6. Isabel Cruz, Kim Marriott, and Pascal van Hentenryck (Eds.). Special issue on constraints, graphics and visualization. *Constraints*, 3(1), April 1998.

7. J. de Kleer. A comparison of assumption-based truth maintenance and constraint satisfaction. In *Proc. Int. Joint Conf. on Artificial Intelligence*, 1989.

8. J. Doyle. A truth maintenance system. In B. Webber and N. Nilsson, editors, *Readings in Artificial Intelligence*. Tioga, Palo Alto, 1981.

9. Th. Frühwirth. Theory and practice of constraint handling rules. *Journal of Logic Programming*, 37:95–138, 1998.

10. Z. Gassmann. A graphic meta-editor for the generation of syntax-oriented graph editors. Diplomarbeit, University of Munich, 1998.

11. V. Haarslev. A fully formalized theory for describing visual notations. In [16].

12. R. Helm and K. Marriott. A declarative specification and semantics for visual languages. *Journal of Visual Languages and Computing*, 2:311–331, 1991.

13. J. Jaffar and J.-L. Lassez. Constraint logic programming: A survey. *Journal of Logic Programming*, 19/20:503–582, 1994.

14. N. Jussien and P. Boizumault. Implementing constraint relaxation over finite domains using assumption-based truth maintenance systems. In M. Jampel, E. Freuder, and M. Maher, editors, *Over-Constrained Systems*. Springer, 1996.

15. K. Marriott. Constraint multiset grammars. In *VL94: IEEE Symp. on Visual Languages*, 1994.

16. K. Marriott and B. Meyer, editors. *Visual Language Theory*. Springer-Verlag, New York, 1998.

17. K. Marriott, B. Meyer, and K. Wittenburg. A survey of visual language specification and recognition. In [16].

18. B. Meyer. Formalization of visual mathematical notations. In *DR-II: AAAI Symp. on Diagrammatic Reasoning*, Boston/MA, November 1997.

19. B. Meyer and H. Zweckstetter. Interpretation of visual notations in the Recopla editor generator. In *FRVDR'98: AAAI Symp. on Formalizing Reasoning with Visual and Diagrammatic Representations*, Orlando, October 1998.

20. B. Meyer, H. Zweckstetter, L. Mandel, and Z. Gassmann. Automatic construction of intelligent diagramming environments. In *HCI'99: Int. Conf. on Human-Computer Interaction*, Munich, Germany, August 1999.

21. M. Minas. DiaGen: A generator for diagram editors providing direct manipulation and execution of diagrams. In *VL95: IEEE WS on Visual Languages*, Darmstadt, 1995.

22. R.C. Moore. Semantical considerations of non-monotonic logic. *Artificial Intelligence*, 25(1):75–94, 1995.

23. F.C.N. Pereira and D.H.D. Warren. Parsing as deduction. In *21st Annual Meeting of the Association for Computational Linguistic*, Cambridge, MA, 1983.

24. S.-J. Shin. *The Logical Status of Diagrams*. Cambridge University Press, Cambridge, 1995.

25. I. Sutherland. Sketchpad: A man-machine graphical communication system. In *Proceedings of the Spring Joint Computer Conference*, pages 329–346, 1963. IFIPS.

26. K. Wittenburg. Predictive parsing for unordered relational languages. In H. Bunt and M. Tomita, editors, *Recent Advances in Parsing Technology*. Kluwer, 1996.

Automatic Generation of Music Programs

François Pachet[1] and Pierre Roy[2]

[1]SONY CSL-Paris, 6, rue Amyot, 75005 Paris, France
pachet@csl.sony.fr
[2]INRIA, Domaine de Voluceau, Rocquencourt, France
CREATE, Dept. of Music, UCSB, California, USA
pierre@create.ucsb.edu

Abstract. Advances in networking and transmission of digital multimedia data bring huge catalogues of multimedia items to users. In the case of music, accessing these catalogues raises a problem for users and content providers, which we define as the music selection problem. From the user point of view, the goals are to match preferences, as well as provide them with new music. From the content provider viewpoint, the goal is to exploit the catalogue in an optimal fashion. We propose a novel approach to music selection, based on computing coherent sequences of music titles, and show that this amounts to solving a combinatorial pattern generation problem. We propose a language to specify these sequences and a solving technique based on global constraints.

1 Music Delivery and Music Selection

Electronic music delivery - transportation of music in a digital format to users - is now becoming a reality. On the one hand, progress in networking transmission, compression of audio, and protection of digital data (Memon and Wong, 1998) will allow in the near future to deliver quickly and safely music to users in a digital format through networks or digital broadcasting. On the other hand, digitalization of data makes it possible to transport not only data itself, but also information on content (see e.g. Mpeg-7, 1998). Together, these techniques give users access at home to huge catalogues of annotated multimedia data, music in particular.

A typical database of music titles contains about 500.000 titles (see, e.g. the MusicBoulevard or Amazon databases). A database containing all published music recordings would probably reach 10 millions titles. Every month, about 4000 CDs are created in western countries. These technological advances raise a new problem for the user as well as for the content provider: how to choose among these catalogues?

1.1 The User's Viewpoint

How to choose items is a general problem in western societies, in which there is an ever increasing number of available products. For entertainment and especially music, the choosing problem is specific, because the underlying goals - personal enjoyment and excitement - do not fall in the usual scheme of rational decision making. Although understanding a user's goals in listening to music is complex in full generality, we can summarize the problem to two basic and contradictory ingredients: desire of *repetition*, and desire of *surprise*.

The desire of repetition is well known in music cognition and experimental psychology. At the melodic or rhythmic levels of music "repetition breeds content." Music theorists have tried to capture this phenomenon by proposing theories of musical perception based on expectation mechanisms (Meyer, 1956), for instance for modeling the perception of melodies (Narmour, 92). At the global level of music selection, this desire of repetition tends to have people wanting to listen to music that they know already (and like) or music that is similar to music they already know. For instance, a Beatles fan will probably be interested in listening to the latest Beatles bootleg containing hitherto unreleased versions of his favorite hits.

On the other hand, the desire for surprise is a key to understanding music, at all levels of perception. The theories that emphasize the role of expectation in music also show that listeners do not favor expectations that are always fulfilled, and enjoy surprises and untypical musical progressions (Smith and Melara, 1990). At a larger level, listeners want from time to time to discover new music, new titles, new bands, or new musical styles.

These two desires are contradictory, and the issue in music selection is precisely to find the right compromise between these two desires: provide users with items they already know, and also with items they do not know, but will probably like.

1.2 The Content Provider's Viewpoint

From the viewpoint of record companies, one goal of music delivery is to achieve a better exploitation of the catalogue than achieved by standard distribution schemes. The analysis of music sales shows clearly decreases in the sales of albums, and that short-term policies based on selling lots of copies of a limited number of *hits* are no longer profitable. Additionally, the general-purpose "samplers" (e.g. "Best of Love Songs") appear to be no longer appealing, because users have already the hits in their own discotheque, and do not want to buy samplers in which they like only a fraction of the titles. Exploiting more fully the catalogues has become a necessity for record companies. Instead of proposing a small number of hits to a large audience, a natural solution is to increase diversity, by proposing more customized albums to users.

We will now examine the main approaches to music selection according to these three goals: repetition, surprise, and exploitation of catalogues, and show that these approaches only achieve the goals partially. We then propose a novel approach to music selection based on building music *programs*, and discuss its advantages and applications for music delivery services.

2 Approaches to Music Selection

Current approaches in music selection can be split up in two categories: database systems and recommendation systems. Both approaches provide sets of items to the user, which he/she has still to choose from.

2.1 The Database Approach

Database approaches to music selection address the issues of storing and representing musical data, with an access through explicit queries. Various kinds of queries can be issued by users, either very specific (e.g. the title of the Beatles song which contains the word "pepper"), or largely under specified, e.g. "Jazz" titles. More sophisticated query systems were proposed for music experts, in which *semantic* queries can be made. For instance, in the Humdrum system (Huron, 1994), the user can issue queries such as "all Mozart sonatas which modulate 3 times." In all cases the database approach, however sophisticated, satisfies the goal of repetition, since it provides users with exactly what they ask for. It addresses the goal of surprise in a restricted way only because the properties of the resulting items have to be explicitly specified.

2.2 Collaborative Filtering Approaches

Collaborative filtering approaches (Shardanand, and Maes, 1995) aim at achieving the "surprise" goal, i.e. issue recommendations of novel titles to users, with the hope that the user will like them. Recommendation systems based on collaborative filtering techniques have had some success in many domains such as books (Amazon), or personalized news (Resnick et al., 1994). Typical collaborative filtering systems for music are the Firefly system (Firefly, 1998), MyLaunch (MyLaunch, 1998), Amazon (Amazon, 1998), or the similarity engine (Infoglide, 1998).

Collaborative filtering is based on the idea that there are *patterns* in tastes: tastes are not distributed uniformly. This idea can be exploited simply by managing a *profile* for each user connected to the service. The profile is typically a set of associations of items to grades. For instance, in the *MyLaunch* system, grades vary from 0 (*I hate it*) to 5 (*this is my preferred item*). In the recommendation phase, the system looks for all the users having a *similar* profile. This similarity can be computed by a distance measure on profiles, such as a Hamming or Pearson distance. Finally, the system recommends items liked by these similar users.

Experimental results achieved so far on real systems show that such systems produce interesting recommendations for naïve profiles (Shardanand, and Maes, 1995). However, there are limitations to this approach. These limitations appear by quantitative studies of collaborative filtering systems, using simulations techniques inspired from works on the dissemination of cultural tastes (Epstein, 1996; Cavalli-Sforza and Feldman, 1981).

The first one is the inclination to "cluster formation," which is induced by the very dynamics of the system. Recommendation systems get stuck when profiles get bigger (about 120 items): eclectic profiles are somehow disadvantaged. Another problem, shown experimentally, is that the dynamics inherently favors the creation of hits, i.e. items which are liked by a huge fraction of the population. These hits limit the probability of other items to "survive" in a world dominated by weight sums, and hence bias the exploitation of the catalogue.

Collaborative filtering is a means of building similarity relations between items, based on statistical properties of groups of agents. As such, it addresses the goal of surprise in a restricted way, by proposing users items which are similar to already known ones. Cluster formation and uneven distribution of chances to items are the main drawbacks of the approach, both from the user viewpoint (clusters from which it is difficult to escape), and the content provider viewpoint (no systematic exploitation of the catalogue).

3   On-the-Fly Music Programs

We propose a different approach to music selection, by shifting the focus of attention: instead of proposing sets of individual titles, we build fully-fledged music programs, i.e. sequences of titles, satisfying particular properties.

There are several motivations for producing music programs, rather than unordered collections of titles. One is based on the recognition that music titles are rarely listened to in isolation: CD, radio programs, concerts are all made up of temporal, ordered sequences of pieces.

The second motivation is that properties of sequences play an important role in the perception of music: for instance, several music titles in a similar style convey a particular atmosphere, and create expectations for the next coming titles. This order is most of the time significant, and the whole craft of music program selection is precisely to build coherent sequences, rather than simply select individual titles. An individual title may not be particularly enjoyed by a listener *per se*, but may be the *right piece at the right time* within a sequence.

3.1   General Idea

Our proposal is the following. First, we build a database of titles, with content information for each title. Then we specify the properties of the program as a whole. Our main contribution is a language to specify these properties. Before describing this language, we will give an example of a typical music program, designed with the three goals of music selection in mind.

3.2   Working Example

Here is a "liner-note" description of a typical music program, seen as a set of partial properties of the program. These properties are of different nature and may be grouped in three categories: 1) user preferences, 2) global properties on the coherence of sequences, and 3) constraints on the exploitation of the catalogue. The following example describes a music program called "Driving a Car," ideally suited for listening to music in a car:

User preferences
- No slow tempos
- At least 30% female-type voice
- At least 30% purely instrumental pieces
- At least 40% brass
- At most 20% "Country Pop" style
- One song by "Harry Connick Jr."

Properties on the coherence of the sequence
- Styles of titles should be close to their successor and predecessor. This is to ensure some sort of continuity in the sequence, style-wise.
- To ensure variety on the authors, we impose to have at least 10 different authors in the program.

Properties on the exploitation of the catalogue
- The total duration is less than 74 minuntes, to fit on a typical CD format.
- The program should contain at least 5 titles from the label "Epic/Sony Music." This is a bias to exploit the catalogue in a particular region.

4 Database of Music Titles

The database contains all the content information required to specify the properties of music programs.

4.1 Format of the Database

Each item is described by a set of attributes, which take their value in predefined taxonomies. The attributes are of two sorts: technical attributes and content attributes.

Technical attributes include the *title* (e.g. "Learn to love you"), the *author* (e.g. "Connick Harry Jr."), the *duration* (e.g. "279 s"), and the *label* (e.g. "Epic/Sony Music").

Content attributes describe musical properties of individual titles. The attributes are the following: *style* (e.g. "Jazz Crooner"), *type of voice* (e.g. "muffled"), *music setup* (e.g. "instrumental"), *type of instruments* (e.g. "brass"), *tempo* (e.g. "slow-fast"), and other optional attributes such as the *type of melody* (e.g. "consonant"), or the main *theme* of the lyrics (e.g. "love").

4.2 Taxonomies

An important aspect of the database is that the values of content attributes are linked to each other by *similarity* relations. These relations are used for specifying properties of continuity in the sequence, and therefore establish links of partial similarity between items, according to a specific dimension of musical content. For instance, the working example specifies continuity on styles.

Some of these relations are simple ordering relations, e.g. tempos and durations. Other attributes such as *style*, take their value in full-fledged taxonomies.

The taxonomy of styles is particularly worth mentioning, because it embodies expert knowledge on music catalogues. Music retailers, such as Amazon (1998) or MusicBoulevard (1998), have designed several taxonomies of musical styles. These classifications are usually hierarchies oriented toward query-based search. Figure 1 shows such a classification with a relation of "generalization-specialization" between styles: "Blues" is more general than "Chicago-Blues." The classification is well suited for finding under-specified items. However, it does not represent similarities between styles, for instance styles having common origins, like, say, "Soul-Blues" and "Jazz-Crooner".

- All Styles
  - Blues
    - Acoustic Blues
    - Chicago Blues
    - ...
  - Country ...
  - Jazz ...

Fig. 1. Excerpts of the taxonomy of styles of the Amazon web site (a tree of depth three). Here, a focus on the "Blues" node

Conversely, we designed a taxonomy representing explicitly relations of similarity between styles. Our taxonomy is a non-directed graph in which vertices are styles and edges express similarity. It currently includes 120 styles, covering most of western music (see Figure 2).

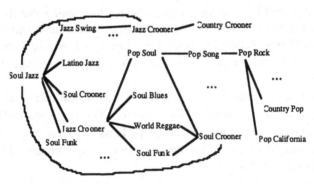

Fig. 2. A part of our taxonomy of musical styles. Links indicate a similarity relation between styles. For instance, the relation *similar ("Soul-Blues", "Jazz-Crooner")* holds

5 Constraints for Music Sequences

The properties of music programs that are sought hold on sequences as a whole, and not on individual items. In this respect, building music programs may be formulated as a combinatorial pattern generation problem.

Constraint satisfaction programming (CSP) is a paradigm for solving combinatorial problems, particularly in the finite domain (Mackworth, 1977). In CSP, problems are represented by variables, having a finite set of values, and constraints, which represent properties of the solutions. The most widely used CSP algorithms are based on the notion of constraint filtering: each constraint is taken individually to reduce the search space; and filtering depends heavily on the constraint (Roy et al., 1999). An important trend in CSP is to propose *global constraints* (Beldiceanu and Contejean, 1994), i.e. general-purpose constraints that can be used to specify particular classes of problems, with efficient filtering procedures.

In the following section we propose a small set of global constraints that can be used to specify most of music programs, together with efficient filtering procedures. The resulting system, *RecitalComposer* consists of a solver, a database, and taxonomies of attribute values.

5.1 Sequence Constraints

A music program can be seen as a solution of a constraint satisfaction problem, where the sequence is composed of successive items represented as variables $v_1, v_2, \ldots v_n$. Each v_i represents the ith item in the sequence. The domain of each v_i is the - finite - catalogue to look from. Properties of the sequence can be expressed as constraints holding on the variables v_i, and their attributes v_i^j (see 4.1). This formulation yields a hard combinatorial problem. For instance, finding a sequence of 20 items, with 100,000 values for each item (about the size of a catalogue of a major label) represents a search space of 10^{100}. Therefore, efficient filtering procedures have to be designed to find solutions in a reasonable time.

Constraints on sequences have been studied in the community of constraint satisfaction. The *Sequence Constraint* of CHIP (Beldiceanu and Contejean, 1994) enables the expression of complex regulation rules. This constraint is used to control the occurrences of patterns in a sequence. This constraint is typically used for timetable problems to specify regulation rules (e.g. any employee has at least a two-day rest twice a month (Chan et al., 1998)). The *Global Sequencing Constraint* (Régin and Puget, 1997) of IlogSolver (Puget and Leconte, 1995) is used to specify the number of successive items having their values in a given set. This constraint is a generalization of the global cardinality constraint (Régin, 1996) and is filtered by the same method. This constraint was successfully applied, for instance, to schedule the production of cars on an assembly line.

Our problem is different because we need to constrain not only the value of each item, but also the value of item's attributes (e.g. *style*, *tempo*, etc). For instance, we want to have five Jazz titles and 3 slow titles in a raw. These requirements cannot be expressed neither in terms of the Sequence Constraint of CHIP nor of the Global Sequencing Constraint. We state these requirements by a set of global constraints whose description follows.

5.2 Global Constraints

Most of the properties needed to specify music programs (user preferences, constraints on program coherence, and constraints on the exploitation of the catalogue) can be expressed using the following global constraints: similarity, difference, and cardinality.

5.2.1 Similarity Constraints

This constraint states that within a given range, items are successively "similar" to each other. The similarity is defined by a binary predicate, holding on one given attribute j. The general formulation is:

$$S(a, b, j, similar(,))$$

meaning that:

$$\text{For every item } v_i, i \in [a, b-1], similar(v_i^j, v_{i+1}^j).$$

where a and b are integers representing indices, j is an attribute, and $similar(,)$ is a binary predicate. Each variable of the predicate denotes an item's j^{th} attribute. For instance, this constraint allows to state that the 10 first pieces should have "close" styles, in the sense of the similarity relation of the classification of styles.

This constraint is decomposed into a series of binary constraints holding on each pair of successive items v_i and v_{i+1}, so no specific filtering procedure is needed.

5.2.2 Difference Constraints

This constraint enforces differences of attributes on a set of items. Its general formulation is:

$$D(I, j)$$

meaning that: all items v_i, $i \in I$, have pairwise different values for attribute j.

Here, I is a set of item indices, j is an attribute. This constraint allows to state that, e.g. the 10 first pieces should have different authors, or different styles. This constraint is an extension of the all-different constraint, for which an efficient filtering procedure was proposed in (Régin, 1994).

5.2.3 Cardinality Constraints (CC)

Cardinality constraints (CC in short) impose properties on *sets of items*. They are the most difficult from a combinatorial point of view because they state properties on the whole sequence. In our context, we identified two such CCs: cardinality on items and cardinality on attributes.

Cardinality on Items

This constraint states that the number of items whose attribute j belongs to a given set E is within [a, b]. The general formulation is:

$$CI(I, j, a, b, E)$$

meaning that:

$$Card \{i \in I; v_i^j \in E \} \in [a, b]$$

where I is a set of item indices, j is an attribute, a and b are integers and E is a subset of the possible values for attribute j. For instance, this constraint can be used to state that there should be between 4 and 6 pieces within a given range (e.g. the first 10), whose style is "Rock."

Cardinality on Attribute Values

This constraint states that the number of different values for attribute j of a number of items is within [a, b]. The general formulation is:

$$CA(I, j, a, b)$$

meaning that:

$$Card \{v_i^j ; i \in I\} \in [a, b]$$

where I is a set of item indices, j is an attribute index, a and b are integers. This constraint can be used for instance to state that among a sequence, there should be pieces from at least three different labels.

Filtering CCs

The filtering procedures for CCs are more sophisticated than for previous constraints. For reasons of space limitation, we describe only the filtering procedures for CCs on items.

One can implement CCs in two different ways: as single global constraints, with a specific filtering method, or as a logically equivalent set of elementary standard constraints. The first approach is used for the Cardinality constraint implemented in Ilog Solver (Puget and Leconte, 1995), while the second one is used in the clp(FD) system (Codognet and Diaz, 1996). Both implementations are efficient, as shown by benchmarks using these systems (Fernandez and Hill, 1998). We have followed the second approach to implement our CCs. The detailed implementation follows: we define CC on items by a set of Boolean variables linked by elementary constraints

- $CI(I, j, a, b, E)$

- $\forall\, i \in I$, let B_i be a Boolean variable (0/1)
- $\forall\, i \in I$, state constraint $B_i = 1$ iff $v_i^j \in E$
- State linear constraints: $a \leq \Sigma_{i \in I} B_i \leq b$

A CC holding on n variables is defined by n additional Boolean variables, n constraints of type $x \in E$ and two linear inequalities. In this implementation, there is no specific filtering procedure for the CC constraints, because the $x \in E$ constraints and the linear inequality constraints are efficiently filtered during the resolution.

When several CCs are stated on a common sequence of items, the problem can become very hard. For example, consider a 12-title sequence and the 2 following CCs:

(C1) At least 7 titles with author = "Sinatra"
(C2) At least 7 titles with style = "Hard Rock"

The problem has obviously no solution because Sinatra has never recorded any Hard-Rock title. However, this implicit relation between Sinatra and Hard Rock is not represented explicitly. Therefore, the resolution is extremely hard for any consistency-based CSP algorithms. This is because constraints are considered (filtered) individually during resolution of the problem. Note that this is independent of the underlying implementation of the CCs.

To address this issue, we propose to add redundant CCs, which will represent a link between two different attributes (here, author and style). To do so, we use formal reasoning. The method has two steps:

1) We introduce a CC (C1') that holds on the type attribute and that is deduced from (C1). In our example, (C1') would be the following constraint:

(C1') At least 7 songs have their voice style attribute in {Pop Song, Love Song, Crooner Song}.

2) We combine (C1') with (C2). This results in detecting that we need 7 hard rock titles and 7 non-Hard Rock titles, which leads to an inconsistency right away, without backtracking.

Note that this problem cannot be handled directly using the Global Cardinality Constraint (Régin, 1996). In effect, the initial constraints do not involve the same variables, and after rewriting one of the constraints (C1 in the example above), the two constraints involve the same attribute variables, but not the same set of indices.

Therefore, we use a specific strategy to combine the CCs. The general formula for two CCs on the same attribute i is the following:

Let $CI(I, i, a, b, E)$ and $CI(J, i, a', b', F)$ be two CC on items, holding on the same attribute i.
Let $n := card(E \cap F)$

341

We state the two following redundant CCs:

$$CI\,(I \cup J,\, i,\, a + a' - n,\, b + b',\, E \cup F)$$
$$CI\,(I \cap J,\, i,\, a + a' - n - |I| - |J| + 2.|I \cap J|,\, b + b',\, E \cup F)$$

where $|I|$ denotes the number of elements of set I. The constraints are stated only if they are not trivially satisfied, i.e. if $a + a' - n > a$ and $a + a' - n > a'$

In practice, redundant constraints improve drastically the resolution of problems with several CCs. **Table 1** shows the number of backtracks needed to find solutions in several variations around the working example.

Table 1. Number of backtracks needed to compute solutions of four problems, with and without redundant constraints. #1 is the working example, #2 is #1 with a general difference constraint on authors, #3 is #2 with at least 20% Country-Pop songs, #4 is #3 with one song by Harry Connick Jr. Since the resolution time here is proportional to the number of backtracks, this shows the interest of redundant constraints to speed up the resolution

	No Redundant Constraint	With Redundant Constraints
#1	393 backtracks	358 backtracks
#2	898 backtracks	898 backtracks
#3	364 backtracks	73 backtracks
#4	2,531 backtracks	921 backtracks

5.3 Example

We can now express the example given in Section 3.2 as a constraint satisfaction problem on sequences, by instantiating the global constraints defined above.

- No slow tempos: unary constraints on each variable.
- At least 30% female voice: CC on "voice-type"
- At least 30% instrumental pieces: CC on "music setup"
- At least 40% brass: CC on "instrument"
- At most 20% "Country Pop" style: CC on "style"
- One song by "Harry Connick Jr": CC on "author"
- Styles of titles are close to their successor and predecessor: similarity constraint on attribute "style"
- At least 10 authors are different: cardinality on item constraint with attribute "author"
- Different pieces: standard all-different constraint
- At least 5 titles from label "Epic/Sony Music": CC on "label"

Figure 3 shows a solution of this problem, computed within a few seconds by our Java constraint solver (Roy et al., 1999), extended with sequence constraints, and applied to a 200-title sample catalogue.

```
 1. Sunrise (Atkins Chet, Jazz Calif, 250s, slow fast, instr,
    instr, jazz guitar, strings)
 2. Surrounded (Kreviazuk Chant, Pop-Calif, 238s, slow fast
    powerful Woman piano strings
 3. Still is still moving to (Nelson Willie, Country Calif, 210s,
    fast, nasal, Man, calif guitar, calif guitar)
 4. Not a moment too soon (Mac Graw Tim, Country Calif, 222s, slow
    fast, hoarse, Man, calif guitar, piano)
 5. Lovin' all night (Crowell Rodney, Country Pop, 227s, fast,
    normal, Man, calif guitar, brass)
 6. Hard way (the) (Carpenter Mary, Country Pop, 262s, slow fast,
    normal, Woman, calif guitar, piano)
 7. Point of rescue (the) (Ketchum Hal, Country Calif, 265s, fast,
    normal, Man, calif guitar, calif guitar)
 8. At seventeen (Ian Janis, Pop Folk, 281s, slow fast, soft,
    Woman, acoustic guitar, brass)
 9. Dream on (Labounty Bill, Pop Calif, 298s, slow fast, broken,
    Man, keyboard, brass)
10. Another time another place (Steely Dan, Jazz Calif, 245s, fast
    slow, instrumental, Instrumental, piano, keyboard)
11. Learn to love you (Connick Harry Jr, Jazz Crooner, 279s, slow
    fast, muffled, Man, brass, strings)
12. Heart of my heart (Elgart Les, Jazz Swing, 151s, slow fast,
    instrumental, Instrumental, double bass, brass)
```

Fig. 3. A solution of the program defined in Section 5.3

6 Evaluation

The comparison of *RecitalComposer* with other systems is difficult, since we do not know any other attempt at generating sequences of music titles. We give here indications about the scale-up to large catalogues, and the quality of results.

6.1 The Constraint Approach

The current prototype was used on a sample database of 200 titles. Solutions are computed within a few seconds. We did experiments on a dummy database of 10,000 items consisting of the initial database duplicated 50 times. These experiments show that resolution times grow linearly with the database size.

Experiments on databases larger by an order of magnitude are in progress and not reported here. We claim that such an increase in size do not pose any problem for at least two reasons. First, the database may be split up in smaller domains of interest for the solver, using simple heuristics. This permits to use only a small part of the actual database during the search. Second, the increase of the number of items is not related to the number of backtracks. More precisely, the only relevant parameter is the *density of solutions* in the search space, which, in our case, increases directly with the size of the catalogue, thus leading to easier problems.

6.2 Resulting Sequences

The solutions found by *RecitalComposer* satisfy trivially two goals of music selection: user preferences (repetition) are satisfied by definition, and exploitation of the catalogue is as systematic as can be; no clustering or bias is introduced, so the system searches the entire database for solutions. Moreover, as illustrated in the working example, specific constraints can be added to force the system to exploit particular regions of the catalogue.

Assessing the surprise goal is of course more difficult. The basic idea is that unknown titles may be inserted in music programs with a high probability of being accepted, because of the underlying properties of continuity in the sequence. Experiments are currently conducted, which consist in comparing programs produced by *RecitalComposer*, and programs produced by human experts (Sony Music) on the same sample database. Preliminary results show that the solutions found by the program are good, and yield unexpected items that experts would not have thought about.

7 Music Delivery Services

The simplest application of *RecitalComposer* is a system targeted at music professionals for building music program from a given database. In this system, the user has to express explicitly all the properties of the desired programs.

Other applications are dedicated to average users and allow them to express only their preferences, using automatic profiling systems, and contain predefined, fixed constraints sets for the coherence properties and catalogue exploitation, according to predetermined "ambiences" or configurations. Typical configurations are 1) "Progressive programs", in which the user only specifies the stylistic structure of the program (e.g. the styles of the beginning, middle and end), 2) "Path across different titles", in which the user specifies only a starting title and an ending title. The system contains hidden constraints on continuity of styles, and tempos, and builds a "morphing" path between the two titles 3) Applications for particular music domains, like Baroque Music, for which specific stylistic constraints are already predefined. Other applications for set-top-boxes and digital broadcasting are not detailed here for reasons of space.

8 Conclusion

RecitalComposer is a constraint system for building music delivery services. The system is based on the idea of creating explicit sequences of items, specified by their global properties, rather than computing sets of items satisfying explicit queries. Its main advantage over database or collaborative filtering approaches is that it produces ready to use ordered sequences of items, which satisfy the three goals of music selection, i.e. repetition, surprise, and exploitation of catalogues.

In the current state of our project, music experts create the database and related taxonomies by hand. Current work focuses on the semi-automatic creation and maintenance of large databases of titles. Indeed, some of the attributes can be extracted automatically from input signals (e.g. the tempo, see (Scheirer, 1998)). Finally, relations such as similarity relations between styles could be extracted using collaborative filtering techniques.

References

Amazon Music web site, www.amazon.com, 1998

Beldiceanu, N. Contejean, E. Introducing Global Constraints in CHIP, *Journal of Mathematical and Computer Modeling*, Vol. 20 (12), pp. 97-123, 1994

Cavalli-Sforza, L. and Feldman, M. Cultural Transmission and Evolution: a Quantitative Approach, Princeton University Press, 1981

Chan, P. Heus, K. Weil, G. Nurse scheduling with global constraints in CHIP: GYMNASTE, 4th International Conference on the Practical Application of Constraint Technology, London (UK), pp. 157-169, 1998

Codognet, Ph. And Diaz, D. Compiling Constraints in clp(FD), *The Journal of Logic Programming*, 27, pp. 1-199, 1996

Epstein, J. M. Growing Artificial Societies: Social Science from the Bottom Up, MIT Press, 1996

Fernandez, A. and Hill, P. A Comparative Study of Eight Constraint Programming Languages over the Boolean and Finite Domains, University of Leeds, School of Computer Studies, Technical Report #98.19.

Firefly web site, http://www.firefly.com, 1998

Huron, D. The Humdrum Toolkit Reference Manual, Center for Computer Assisted Research in the Humanities, Menlo Park, 1994

Infoglide web site, www.infoglide.com, 1998

Mackworth, A. Consistency on networks of relations, *Artificial Intelligence*, (8) pp. 99-118, 1977

Memon, N, Wong, P. W. Protecting Digital Media Content, CACM, July 1998, pp. 34-43, 1998

Meyer, L. Emotions and meaning in Music, University of Chicago Press, 1956

Mpeg-7, Context and objectives, International Organization for Standardization, report ISO/IEC JTC1/SC29/WG11, October 1998

MusicBoulevard web site, www.musicblvd.com, 1998

MyLaunch web site: www.mylaunch.com, 1998

Narmour, E. The analysis and cognition of meldic complexity, University of Chicago Press, 1992

Puget, J.-F. and Leconte, M. Beyond the Glass Box: Constraints as Objects, ILPS'95, Portland, Oregon, 1995

Régin, J.-C. A Filtering Algorithm for Constraints of Difference in CSPs AAAI'94, Seattle, pp. 362-367, 1994

Régin, J.-C. and Puget J-F. A filtering algorithm for global sequencing constraints, 3rd Int. Conference on Principles and Practice of Constraint Programming, pp 32-46, 1997

Régin, J.-C. Generalized Arc Consistency for Global Cardinality Constraints AAAI' 96, Seattle, WA, 1996

Resnick, P. Iacovou, N. Sushak, M. Bergstrom, P. Riedl, J. GroupLens: An Open Architecture for Collaborative Filtering of Netnews, CSCW conference, October 1994

Roy, P. Liret, A. Pachet, F. A Framework for Constraint Satisfaction, Object-Oriented Application Frameworks, Vol. 2, Fayad, M. Eds, Wiley, 1999

Scheirer, E. D. Tempo and beat analysis of acoustic musical signals, *Journal of the Acoustical Society of America* 103(1): 588-601, 1998

Shardanand, U. and Maes, P. Social Information Filtering: Algorithms for Automating "Word of Mouth", Proceedings of the 1995 ACM Conference on Human Factors in Computing Systems, pp. 210-217, 1995

Smith, D. Melara, R. Aesthetic preference and syntactic prototypicality in music: 'Tis the gift to be simple, Cognition, 34, pp. 279-298, 1990

Search Procedures and Parallelism in Constraint Programming

Laurent Perron*

ILOG SA
9, rue de Verdun, BP85, 94253 Gentilly Cedex, France
perron@ilog.fr

Abstract. In this paper, we present a major improvement in the search procedures in constraint programming. First, we integrate various search procedures from AI and OR. Second, we parallelize the search on shared-memory computers. Third, we add an object-oriented extensible control language to implement complex complete and incomplete search procedures. The result is a powerful set of tools which offers both brute force search using simple search procedures and parallelism, and finely tuned search procedures using that expressive control language. With this, we were able both to solve difficult and open problems using complete search procedures, and to quickly produce good results using incomplete search procedures.

1 Introduction

Combinatorial Optimization and Combinatorial Problem Solving is an interesting application for Constraint Programming (CP). It has grown out of the research world into the industrial world as demonstrated by the success of different products (ILOG optimization suite, CHIP).

However, when looking at real applications, it appears that Depth-First Search, which is a standard way of searching for solutions is often an obstacle to optimization. DFS, which is directly linked to the Constraint Logic Programming and the SLD resolution of Prolog, needs exponential time to break out of subtrees if initial choices have been incorrect. Searching for solutions using Depth-First Search usually goes against reactivity and robustness. Therefore, real applications, to be successful, have to override this limitation by using tailored search techniques. Over the years, many different approaches have been proposed: A simple approach using some *greedy heuristics*, coupled with some look-ahead can be interesting in scheduling [5]. Another traditional approach which has often proved successful is to change the *order of evaluation of nodes* [8, 20, 12] in the search tree. These approaches usually give good results, but they are difficult to implement in a generic way on any application of Constraint Programming. Usually, only a specific search procedure is implemented, or only on a limited subset of problems. Another promising family of techniques is based on *Local-Moves* and *Local-Search* methods. The first technique consists in applying local moves to a particular

---

* This research is partially funded by the Commission of the European Union contract ESPRIT 24960. The author is solely responsible for the content of the document.

solution of the problem until a improvement is found [3, 14, 13, 18]. The second one consists in freezing part of a problem and applying a tree-search based optimization process on the non-frozen part [2, 15]. Statistical methods have also been proposed: *Genetic Algorithm* [1, 6], *Simulated Annealing* [1]. All these techniques are appealing as they provide good results. They also have drawbacks: (1) Their implementations are linked to the problem they attack. Genericity is rare as it implies a uniform API to represent different problems and different optimization those implementations rely on. For instance, Simulated Annealing is based on a notion of temperature that may prove difficult to exhibit on different classes of problems. (2) They usually not extensible. Few efforts have been made to propose paradigm which offers genericity and versatility. (3) Recently, some very interesting ideas have been proposed [10, 19], but they lack usability as they provide (in our opinion) an API at too low a level, which ruins the expressiveness of their proposal.

Our work is a bottom-up approach which aims at improving the search performance of our constraint system. The starting point is tree search. We then distinguish between two orthogonal notions: *Search Heuristics* which are linked to the definition of the search tree and *Search Procedures* which are linked to the exploration of this search tree. This article deals only with search procedures. We try to improve the exploration of a search tree using (1) an expressive extensible object-oriented language to describe search procedures, and (2) parallelism to give more computing power.

We provide an efficient implementation of those search procedures – which leads to significant reductions in running time – and parallelism based on a multi-threaded architecture covering the full functionality of the sequential constraint solver. The combination of the search procedures and parallelism is a necessary element for solving large combinatorial problems such as crew rostering, large jobshop scheduling problems, and others.

Experimental results included in the paper show impressive speedups on jobshop problems, and demonstrate the benefits of both parallelism and the new search procedures.

The rest of the paper is organized as follows: Section 2 defines a few concepts on search trees. These concepts are the basis of the search procedures we introduce in section 3. Then, section 4 presents some examples of the use of the search procedures, while section 5 gives an overview of the experiments we have conducted.

2 Open Nodes and Search Procedures

In order to implement user-defined search procedures, we need to be able to get access to individual parts of the search tree. These parts are called *open nodes*. Once open nodes are defined, we can present how one search process can explore a given search tree arbitrarily. These are the fundamental building blocks needed to implement generic search procedures.

2.1 Open Nodes and Node Expansion

To model search, the search tree is partitioned into three sets: the set of *open nodes* or *the search frontier*, the set of *closed nodes* and the set of *unexplored nodes*. These sets evolves during the search through an operation called *node expansion*. Throughout this paper, we will make the assumption the search tree is a binary search tree. This is true in our implementation.

Open Nodes and Search Frontier At any point during the search, the set of nodes of the search tree is divided into three independent subsets: the set of *open nodes*; the set of *closed nodes*; the set of *unexplored nodes*.

These subsets have the following properties:

- All the ancestors of an open node are closed nodes.
- Each unexplored node has exactly one open node as its ancestor.
- No closed node has an open node as its ancestor.

The set of open nodes is called the *search frontier*. The following figure illustrates this idea.

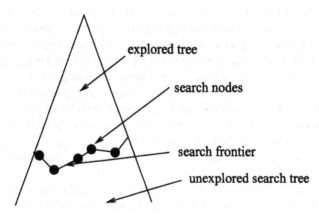

Node Expansion The search frontier evolves simply through a process known as *node expansion*. (Node expansion corresponds to the *branch* operation in a branch & bound algorithm.) It removes an open node from the frontier, transforms the removed node into a closed node, and adds the two unexplored children of that node to the frontier. This move is the only operation that happens during the search.

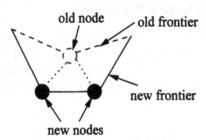

We shall later use the method to show how basic search procedures such as LDS[8] can be described as different selections of the next open node to expand.

2.2 Active Path and Jumps in the Search Tree

Expanding one node after another may require changing the state (the domains of the variables of the problem) of the search process from the first node to the second. However, from a memory consumption point of view, it is unrealistic to maintain in memory the state associated with every open nodes of the search tree. Therefore, the search process exploring the search tree must reconstruct each state it visits. This is done using an *active path* and a *jumping* operation.

Active Path in a Search Tree When going down in the search tree, our search process builds an *active path*. An active path is the list of ancestors of the current open node, as illustrated in the following figure.

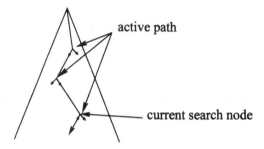

Jumping in the Search Tree When our search engine moves from one search node to another, it must jump in the search tree. To make the jump, it computes the maximum common path between the current position (1) and the destination. Then it backtracks to the corresponding choice point (the lowest node in the maximum common path). Next, it recomputes every move until it gets to (2). Recomputation does not change the search frontier as there is no node expansion during that operation.

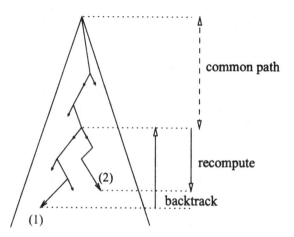

2.3 Discussion of the implementation of the Branch & Bound Paradigm

Other methods exist to implement the Branch & Bound paradigm. As the problem is closely related to the implementation of or-parallelism in Prolog, a comparison with available implementations can be enlightening. In [17], a complete presentation of the different techniques developed for parallel Prolog was made: many proposals have been made. These proposal were primarily motivated by hardware considerations. There are basically two kinds of parallel computers: *shared* memory and *non-shared* memory computers. From these two categories of computer come two categories of parallel implementation.

As we may deal with large problems, we cannot save the problem at each node. Thus our implementation must use recomputation. Furthermore, managing multiple binding to the same variable leads to quadratic behavior. Therefore, we decided that each search process would have its own copy of the problem. Thus, faced with the constraint of robustness, extensibility and memory consumption, it appeared early in our search design that the only practical choice was an implementation of the Delphi Model [4] on shared-memory computers. In our implementation, each search process share the same search tree with nodes being represented as binary paths in this tree.

3 A Object-Oriented Language for Search Procedures

Search heuristics and search trees are defined using goals. There are different goals: predefined goals and user-defined goals. Two important predefined goals are the And goal and the Or goal. They are the most fundamental blocks used when writing search heuristics.

Our approach relies on these goals. A search procedure will be defined as a constructor that will be build with search goals and special objects. Basically, each atomic search procedure, itself a goal, will be written as: Function (goal, object). We will present three different functions: Apply to change the order of evaluation of nodes, SelectSearch to select some leaves out of a search tree, and Limit-Search to limit the exploration of a search tree. These functions will be applied onto goals using objects. We will present predefined objects for each function and also a quick overview of how user-defined objects can be created.

3.1 Changing the Order of Evaluation of Nodes

Many references demonstrate the usefulness of changing the order of evaluation of nodes in a search tree [16, 8]. We perform these changes using the Apply function and instances of the NodeEvaluator class.

Node Evaluators for the Apply function A node evaluator is an object which has two purposes: evaluate a node and decide whether the search engine should jump from one node to another. This leads to an implementation of the B&B scheme where (1) the default behavior is chronological backtracking, and (2) nodes are stored in a priority queue, ordered by their evaluation.

Thus, the term `Apply(Goal g, NodeEvaluator e)` returns a goal which applies the evaluator e to the search tree defined by the goal g. This changes the order of evaluation of the open nodes of the search tree defined by g according to e.

Some Common Node Evaluators We implemented several important search procedures. **Depth First Search:** This is the standard search procedure. **Best First Search:** We have implemented a variation of Best First Search Strategy with a parameter ϵ. When selecting an open node, we determine the set of open nodes the cost of which is at most ϵ (this is a difference and not a factor) worse than the best open node. If a child of the current node is in the set, we go to this child. If not, we choose the best open node. **Limited Discrepancy Search:** Limited discrepancy search was first defined in [8]. We did not implement the original scheme but a variation name *Discrepancy Bounded Depth First Search*. This variation will be presented more fully in a future paper. The *discrepancy* of a search node is defined as its right depth, that is, the number of times the search engine has chosen the right branch of a choice point to go from the root of the search tree to the current node. Given a parameter k, the discrepancy search procedure is one that will first explore nodes with a discrepancy less than k. After this exploration is complete, it will explore nodes with a discrepancy between k and $2k$, and so on. This search procedure cuts the search tree into *strips*. **Depth Bounded Discrepancy Search:** This search procedure was introduced in [20]. It is a variation of LDS which makes the assumption that mistakes are more likely near the top of the search tree than further down. For this reason, not the number of discrepancies but the depth of the last one is used to evaluate the node. We do not implement Walsh's schema exactly, but a version we found more robust. Rather than the depth of the deepest discrepancy, we consider the depth of the wth deepest discrepancy, where w is a parameter of the search. This parameter is in fact an allowed width after the depth limit of the last discrepancy as described in the original DDS design. **Interleaved Depth First Search:** This search procedure was introduced by [12]. It tries to mimic the behavior of an infinite number of threads exploring the search tree. We use a variation which limits the depth limit of this interleaving behavior.

Defining a New Node Evaluator A node evaluator is linked to the life cycle of an open node. When a node is created, the method `evaluate` is called to give the node its evaluation. This method returns a real value which will be used when the node is stored. When the manager has to decide whether it should jump to another node, the method `subsume` is called. This function is called with the evaluations of the current open node and of the best open node. A return value of **true** indicates that the search engine should jump from the current open node to the best one.

For instance, we could implement the Best-First Search evaluator this way in a C++ syntax:

```
IntBFSEvaluator::IntBFSEvaluator(IntVar var, IlcInt epsilon) {
  _epsilon = epsilon;
  _var = var;
}
```

```
Float IntBFSEvaluator::evaluate(const SearchNode) const {
  return _var->getMin();
}

Bool IntBFSEvaluator::subsume(Float val1, Float val2) const {
  return  (val1 + _epsilon <= val2);
}
```

This node evaluator is constructed with a variable and an epsilon. The evaluation of a node is the minimum of the variable. The function subsume will return **true** if the minimum of the variable for the best node is lower than the current minimum value of the variable minus epsilon.

3.2   Selecting Leaves of a Search Tree

In a minimizing process, or in a incomplete search, it may be interesting to focus on some promising leaves of a search tree and to forget the other leaves. This is done using the `SelectSearch` function and instances of the `SearchSelector` class

A Goal to Select Leaves A search selector is used to select (or filters) leaves of a search tree. It has three purposes: to store leaves of the search tree and to re-activate them once the search tree is completely explored, to implement a minimization process, and to perform a simple feasibility check on nodes.

Thus, the term `SelectSearch(Goal g, SearchSelector s)` is a goal which applies the selector s to the search tree defined by g. A selector then executes the complete search tree and selects leaves of this search tree.

Some Search Selectors Some simple search selectors are already implemented. **Minimization:** The selector `Minimize(IntVar v)` implements a minimization process on the integer variable v and selects a leaf which minimizes this variable. **FirstSolution:** The selector `FirstSolution(int n)` simply selects the first n solutions of a search tree.

Defining a New Search Selector Defining a new search selector is more complex than defining a new node evaluator. There are three types of methods to implement:

Minimization Management: To implement a minimization process, the search selector must check whether a known upper bound on the objective is better than the current upper bound of the objective. In this case, the constraint stating that the objective is strictly less than this known bound is imposed. This information is stored so that it can be used during recomputation to re-post the same constraint. **Feasibility Test:** A feasibility test is implemented using an evaluation function which returns a real value and a test which decides whether the evaluation attached to a node corresponds to an infeasible node. When a node is declared infeasible, it is simply postponed and not

353

evaluated. **Leaf Management:** When the search engine arrives at a leaf of the search tree, it can decide to store it, to delete an old leaf, or to forget it. When the search tree is completely explored, another method is called to re-activate stored leaves.

3.3 Search Limits

In real application, one cannot afford to see its search for solution lost in a uninteresting sub-search tree. Therefore is needed some way to limit the time spent by a search process in any part of the search tree. This is done using the `LimitSearch` function and instances of the `SearchLimit` class.

A Goal to Limit Search A search limit is a function which implements a periodic test to decide whether a particular limit has been reached. When this limit arrives, the set of open nodes covered by this limit are discarded. Thus, a call to `LimitSearch(Goal g, SearchLimit l)` returns a goal which limits the exploration of the search tree defined by g with the limit l. Once a limit is crossed, all nodes explored afterwards are discarded.

Pre-defined Limits Two simple limits are offered. **Time limit:** The limit `Time-Limit(double time)` creates a search limit. With this limit, the search engine explores the search tree for only `time` seconds. Afterwards, all remaining open nodes are discarded. **Failure limit:** The limit `FailLimit(int numOfFails)` creates a search limit. With this limit, the search engine explores the search tree until `numOf-Fails` failures have been encountered. Afterwards, all unexplored open nodes in the search tree are discarded.

Defining a New Search Limit A limit is used to prune part of the search tree. Its main method is a check method which indicates whether the limit has been reached.

3.4 Parallelism

In parallel search, different instances of the search engine (called workers) run on different processes and explore the same search tree. The workers communicate and coordinate their work via a virtual communication layer.

A virtual communication layer must fulfill three tasks: **Starvation Balancing:** The layer must propagate the work and insure that no worker is starving while there is work available; this means moving nodes from one worker to another. **Load Balancing:** The layer can periodically balance good open nodes such that every worker can work on a promising part of the search tree. **Termination Detection:** The layer must also have a mechanism to detect termination (every worker is starving). In this case, it must terminate the search cleanly.

In our design(figure 1), the storage of open nodes is distributed over the different workers, the same open node cannot be expanded by two different workers. This choice reduces the synchronization cost between workers and minimizes the differences between the sequential code and the parallel code.

virtual communication

search engines   layer   node storages

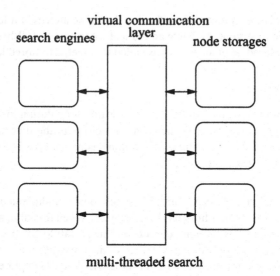

multi-threaded search

Fig. 1. Parallel Solver Architecture

3.5 Comparison with related work

All our work is greatly inspired from Salsa [10]. There are three main improvements over F. Laburthe's original design:

1. Salsa is based on choice points whereas our work is based on search goals and their corresponding search tree. Thus, basic search procedures like LDS are natural in our design. They are not so natural in Salsa because these basic search procedures are difficult to implement on a choice point level.
2. Furthermore, as we are dealing with goals, we do not need the two channels we find in Salsa (the leaf channel and the solution channel).
3. Our design is completely extensible. We can define easily new limits, new evaluators and new selectors. This is not the case in Salsa.

4 Using the Object-Oriented Language for Search Procedures

4.1 Some Small-Scale Examples to Illustrate Search Procedures

Given a goal g, we can write different search goals using our Search Language. We suppose we have a function `solve` which takes a goal as parameter and returns the first solution of this goal. Therefore,

- `solve(g)` will search for the first solution of the search tree defined by g.
- `solve(Apply(g, LDSEvaluator(3)))` will search in LDS with strips of width 3 for the first solution of the search tree defined by g.

- `solve(SelectSearch(g, Minimize(var)))` will minimize the variable var in the search tree defined by g. When `solve( )` returns, the solver is in the state of the best solution.
- `solve(SelectSearch(LimitSearch(g, TimeLimit(5.0)), Minimize(var)))` will return the best solution (according to var) found in a 5-second time frame in the search tree generated by g.

4.2 Using Search Procedures to Implement a Complex Incomplete Search

Using Limited-Discrepancy Search to solve a problem is already an improvement over standard Depth-First Search. But our language for search procedures can be used in a more ambitious way. We will present an example where we search for solutions by composing two goals, inner1 and inner2. We will change the search procedures such that the search (a) uses limits to keep the process from being stuck in a subtree; and (b) implements a two-phase decomposition of the problem to have a better overview of the complete search tree than with the limited one.

The original goal is equivalent to :

`LimitSearch(And(inner1, inner2), TimeLimit(t))` where t is a parameter of the search. Later, we will adjust t such that exactly the same time will be spent searching with the original goal and our complex goal. This will allows us to compare their behavior in the same time frame.

The First Phase This phase will try to solve the first part of the problem using a Depth-Bounded Discrepancy Search, along with a fail limit. We will restrain ourselves to the first five leaves of the search tree. The corresponding goal is:

```
Goal apply1 = Apply(inner1, DDSEvaluator(2, 2));
Goal limit1 = LimitSearch(apply1, FailLimit(15));
Goal restrict1 = SelectSearch(limit1, FirstSolution(5));
```

The goal limit1 will explore the search tree associated with the goal inner1 only until 15 failures happen. This search tree will be explored by increments of 2, with 2 remaining discrepancies after the depth limit. Afterward, this goal will simply fail. Thus the effect of the LimitSearch function is to prune part of the search tree. The goal restrict1 will keep the first 5 solutions of the goal limit1.

The Second Phase This second phase will solve the second part of the problem using a Limited-Discrepancy Search. We will limit the maximum number of discrepancies during the search to 1 in order to have a simple limit on the time spent. The code is the following: `Goal apply2 = Apply(inner2, LDSEvaluator(1, 1));`

The Complete Goal The complete goal is the composition of the two previous goals (limit1 and apply2) embedded in a minimization process. The complete goal along with the search for solution results in the following code:

```
Goal comp1 = And(restrict1, apply2);
SearchSelector minim = Minimize(totalCost);
Goal minimizeGoal = SelectSearch(comp1, minim);
```

The Explored Search Tree Simple graphs can illustrate the explored part of the search tree in our case (figure 2) and in the original case (figure 3). The complex search is quite different than the simple limited one we could have obtained with a time limit. With this complex search procedure, we have a better overview of the complete search tree using our complex goal instead of the original one, we claim that our complex goal is more robust. This will be verified experimentally in section 5.2.

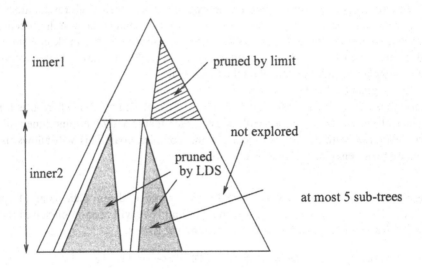

Fig. 2. Complex Search

5 Results

In this section, we will present some results to illustrate the benefits of the search procedures and parallelism. In these examples, the standard behavior is defined by a depth first search procedure and a single processor search.

All the times are given in seconds. The computer used was a 4 processors Pentium Pro 200Mz computer running Linux. The compiler used was egcs 1.1.1.

This was implemented on top of ILOG SOLVER and ILOG SCHEDULER.

5.1 Complete Search on Jobshops Problems

We will try complete search procedures on different jobshops in order to see how they find good solutions and how they prove them

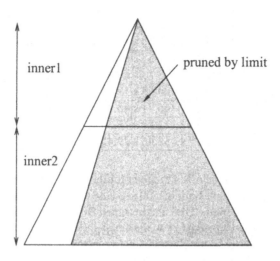

Fig. 3. Limited Simple Search

Two Jobshop Examples These two jobshops come from [7]. The search heuristic is a simple one based on ranking of activities. The edge finder algorithm is used at each stage. The time to find the best solution and the total time (best solution + proof) is given.

Problem	Strategy	1 worker	4 workers
MT10	DFS	434.79 s / 654.80 s	
MT10	LDS	83.12 s / 536.97 s	34.57 s / 177.87 s
MT20	DFS	not found	not found
MT20	LDS	111.50 s / 144.97 s	10.85 s / 11.95s

These examples demonstrate clearly the benefit of both parallelism and changing the order of evaluation of search nodes. The most interesting part is that LDS changes a problem too difficult to solve in a reasonable time into an easy one.

A Small Example : Abz5 Abz5 is a small jobshop (10×10) from [9]. It has been solved using various strategies. In the table below, the first figure represents the time (in seconds) to get the optimal solution; the second figure represents the total running time (best solution + proof of optimality). We can deduce that on a small problem, parallelism, as it gives more breadth during the exploration of the search tree, leverages the differences between different search procedures. However, when it comes to proving optimal solution, the best method is DFS as it implies no recomputation as opposed to other methods. This is visible with one processor when comparing LDS and DFS on a problem where the proof is difficult like this one. LDS finds the optimal solution much faster than DFS, but the total time is greater.

Strategy	1 worker	2 workers	4 workers
DFS	89.15 s / 98.98 s	52.90 s / 60.27 s	14.87 s / 22.11 s
BFS	92.91 s / 125.55 s	62.18 s / 78.41 s	10.67 s / 20.02 s
BFS with tuning	131.95 s / 133.85 s	65.39 s / 66.01 s	9.14 s / 28.8 s
LDS with k=4	35.04 s / 104.68 s	19.04 s / 52.06 s	3.86 s / 18.49 s
LDS with k=2	51.12 s / 116.71 s	40.24 s / 72.12 s	11.29 s / 32.47 s
DDS	63.98 s / 112.88 s	16.34 s / 36.72 s	2.21 s / 21.4 s
IDFS	51.77 s / 58.46 s	29.45 s / 32.07 s	12.37 s / 13.95 s

A Bigger Example : la36 la36 is a medium jobshop (15×15) from [11]. For solving these problems, a global time limit of 500 seconds was set on the resolution of these problems. With this time limit, IDFS and un-tuned BFS are not able to find a solution, even with 4 processors. The table below illustrates the fact that when the problem gets more difficult, the difference in robustness between search procedures becomes more evident. Which a medium problem and a good search heuristic, LDS and DDS appear more robust.

Strategy	1 worker	2 workers	4 workers
DFS	>500 s / >500 s	>500 s / >500 s	231.07 s / 246.71 s
BFS with tuning	>500 s / >500 s	>500 s / >500 s	100.37 s / 210.79 s
LDS with k=4	297.35 s / 361.12 s	241.69 s / 282.36 s	93.2 s / 141.4 s
LDS with k=2	402.35 s / 464.06 s	211.82 s / 252.57 s	131.23 s / 163.37 s
DDS	411.79 s / 479.90 s	269.87 s / 362.79 s	47.75 s / 83.60 s

An Open Problem: swv01 Using LDS, 4 processors and a good ranking goal and shaving, we were able to solve completely an open scheduling problem: SWV01 (20×10)

Strategy	No of Workers	Time for Best solution	Total time
LDS	4	451385 s	461929 s

Thus, five and a half days were necessary on a Quadri Pentium Pro computer to break this difficult problem and prove the optimal solution to be **1407**.

5.2 Incomplete Search on Some Jobshops

We have adapted the two goals of the section 4.2 on jobshop problems. The goal inner1 correspond to the complete ordering of two resources. The goal inner2 corresponds to the ranking of all remaining activities.

We fixed some parameters of the complex goal. We keep the 10 first solutions of the goal limit1. The goal limit1 has a failure limit of 50. The width of the LDS part of goal inner2 is respectively 1 in case A and 2 in case B. To compare with the original goal, we ran the original goal with a time limit equal to the total running time of the complex goal. When doing this, we can compare the objective value found. Here are the results on 4 different jobshops : ABZ5, FT10, LA19 and LA21. One cell display the running time for the modified goal, the bound found and the bouind found in the same time by the original goal.

Problem	Abz5(1165)	FT10 (930)	LA19 (842)	LA21 (1046)
Case A	2.87s : 1272/1256	2.18s : 1029/1044	2.27s : 884/900	15.08s : 1126/1135
Case B	5.62s : 1272/1256	2.86s : 1013/1044	5.19s : 867/867	35.09s : 1098/1127

We can see that except on easy problems where good solution are found fast using the original goal (Abz5), the complex goal give consistently better results than the original goal.

6 Conclusion

In this paper, we have stressed the importance of overriding the Depth-First Search limitation in constraint programming. We believe we have proposed an elegant language for both brute force search and finely tuned complex search procedures. We have shown that (a) this language is expressive and useful, (b) search procedures and parallelism greatly improves greatly the performance of our search engine, namely ILOG SOLVER and (c) this whole design can be implemented efficiently: the overhead between parallel DFS with 1 processor and the original ILOG SOLVER DFS is as low as 2-3% for the jobshop examples we have solved in this paper.

We think there are many perspectives for this work. The most important one being (a) using this control language to implement special search procedures like adaptative search for real time optimization problem; (b) implementing parallelism and distributed-memory architecture using PVM or MPI; and (c) extending the language itself with other `functions` implementing other useful behaviors.

Finally, in the long run, we would like to integrate other search techniques not based on tree search into this framework: for example local moves, statistical methods, genetic algorithms. This would allow us to prove our driving assumption which is that by improving the expressivity of search procedures, we increase radically the set of problems we can solve effectively.

Acknowledgement

First, I would like to thank the referee for their insightful comments on my article.

Then, I would like to thank everybody who helped me in my work, especially Paul Shaw for doing much more than a complete proofread of this article and Jean-François Puget for helping me getting out of design and implementation problems, and François Laburthe, for his work on Salsa, which was a wonderful start for my own work.

References

1. E.H.L. Aarts, P.J.M. van Laarhoven, J.K. Lenstra, and N.J.L. Ulder. A computational study of local search algorithms for job shop scheduling. 6:113–125, 1994.
2. D. Applegate and W. Cook. A computational study of the job-shop scheduling problem. *ORSA Journal on Computing*, 3(2):149–156, 1991.
3. J.W. Barnes and J.B. Chambers. Solving the job shop scheduling problem using tabu search. *IEE Transactions*, 27/2:257–263, 1994.

4. W. Clocksin. Principles of the DelPhi parallel inference machine. *Computer Journal*, 30(5):386–392, 1987.
5. M. Dell'Amico and M. Trubian. Appplying tabu-search to the job-shop scheduling problem. *Annals of Operational Research*, 41:231–252, 1993.
6. U. Dorndorf and E. Pesch. Evolution based learning in a job shop scheduling environment. *Computers and Operations Research*, 22:25–40, 1995.
7. G.L. Thompson H. Fisher. Probabilistic learning combinations of local job-shop scheduling rules. In G.L. Thompson J.F. Muth, editor, *Industrial Scheduling*, pages 225–251. Prentice Hall, Englewood Cliffs, New Jersey, 1963.
8. William D. Harvey and Matthew L. Ginsberg. Limited discrepancy search. In *Proceeding of IJCAI*, volume 1, pages 607–613, August 1995.
9. E. Balas J. Adams and D. Zawack. The shifting bottleneck procedure for job shop scheduling. *Management Science*, 34:391–401, 1988.
10. François Laburthe and Yves Caseau. Salsa: A language for search algorithms. In *Principles and Practice of Constraint Programming*, number 1520 in LNCS, pages 310–325, 1998.
11. S Lawrence. *Resource constrained project scheduling: an experimental investigation of heuristic scheduling techniques*. Carnegie-Mellon University, Pennsylvania, 1984. supplement.
12. Pedro Meseguer. Interleaved depth-first search. In *International Joint Conference on Artificial Intelligence*, volume 2, pages 1382–1387, August 1997.
13. L. Michel and P. Van Hentenryck. Localizer: A modelling language for local search. In *CP'97*, number 1330 in LNCS. Springer, 1997.
14. E. Nowicki and C. Smutnicki. A fast taboo search algorithm for the job shop problem. *Management Science*, 42(6):797–813, 1996.
15. W. Nuijten and C. Le Pape. Constraint-based job shop scheduling with ILOG SCHEDULER. *Journal of Heuristics*, 3:271–286, 1998.
16. Judea Pearl. *Heuristics: Intelligent Search Strategies for Computer Problem Solving*. Addison-Wesley, 1984.
17. Laurent Perron. An implementation of or-parallelism based on direct access to the MMU. In *Proc. of Compulog-Net worshop on parallelism and implementation technology, JICSLP'96*, 1996.
18. G. Pesant and M. Gendreau. A view of local search in constraint programming. In *CP'96*, number 1118 in LNCS, pages 353–366. Springer, 1996.
19. Christian Schulte. Oz Explorer: A visual constraint programming tool. In Lee Naish, editor, *Proceedings of the Fourteenth International Conference on Logic Programming*, pages 286–300, Leuven, Belgium, July 1997. The MIT Press.
20. Toby Walsh. Depth-bounded discrepancy search. In *International Joint Conference on Artificial Intelligence*, volume 2, pages 1388–1393, August 1997.

Ensuring a Relevant Visiting Order of the Leaf Nodes during a Tree Search

Nicolas Prcovic and Bertrand Neveu

CERMICS
BP 93, 06902 Sophia-Antipolis
France
email : Bertrand.Neveu@sophia.inria.fr

Abstract. We define a model for heuristic tree search which assumes that the quality of the heuristic used for ordering the successors of a node improves as depth increases. We show that a usual value ordering heuristic for solving constraint satisfaction problems fits to this model. Our model defines a partial order on the leaf nodes of the search tree, according to their probability to be a solution. We check which search strategies among interleaved depth-first search (IDFS), limited discrepancy search (LDS) and depth-bounded discrepancy search (DDS) visit the leaf nodes while respecting the partial order. Our study leads to conclude that, among these strategies, only Pure IDFS and a slight modification of improved LDS respect it.

1 Introduction

Some new kinds of depth-first searches have recently appeared: Limited discrepancy search (LDS) [HG95], Interleaved depth-first search (IDFS) [Mes97] and Depth-bounded discrepancy search (DDS) [Wal97]. They intend to be efficient alternatives to the traditional depth-first search (DFS) for which making an early mistake can be very costly to undo. These methods expand the search tree by trying to first reach the leaf nodes the most likely to be solutions, thanks to the knowledge of their *discrepancies*, i.e. the branching points where the heuristic decision is not respected. This improvement in the order for visiting the leaf nodes has a cost: internal nodes may be visited several times.

The purpose of this paper is to study how relevant are the visiting orders of the leaf nodes given by these search strategies. We define a model for heuristic tree search which induces a partial order on the leaf nodes and we check for every search algorithm whether it respects or not this partial order.

2 Background

In this section, we give an overview of some recent tree search algorithms. A heuristic guides the search towards promising leaf nodes. By convention, we state that left branches follow the heuristic while the other branches are discrepancies.

LDS is based on the following assumption: the leaf nodes the most likely to be solutions are the ones that have accumulated the fewest discrepancies before to be reached. LDS performs successive DFS iterations. Each iteration prunes the branches leading to leaves with a number of discrepancies higher than k. k starts from 0 and is incremented after each iteration. ILDS [Kor96] is an improved version that assumes knowing the maximum depth of the tree and then avoids redundant generation of leaf nodes. On the kth iteration, only the leaf nodes with exactly k discrepancies at the maximum depth may be reached. However, redundant visit of internal nodes remains.

DDS and IDFS assume that the quality of the heuristic increases with depth. This has been experimented in practice and can be explained by the usual lack of information used by the heuristic at the top of the tree compared to greater depths.

As ILDS, DDS performs several iterations, but, instead of fixing the total number of discrepancies allowed, it limits the depth below which discrepancies are forbidden. On the kth iteration, the depth limit is fixed to $k - 1$ so discrepancies are only allowed until depth $k - 1$.

IDFS also takes the increasing quality of the heuristic into account. Its behavior can be opposed to DFS behavior as, when meeting a dead end, DFS undoes the *last* choices first whereas IDFS undoes the *first* choices first. The justification is the following: the shallowest choices are the least trustworthy so the deepest choices are more to be preserved. Two versions of IDFS have been proposed. Pure IDFS exactly applies this behavior. The tree is expanded in such a way that, for every depth, every subtree will never be visited again before all other subtrees at the same depth will be visited too. Limited IDFS restrains this interleaving to a fixed depth for a limited number of subtrees. It simulates the exploration of the tree by a parallel search. The interleaving depth and the number of active subtrees correspond to the distribution depth and the number of processes.

DFS, ILDS, IDFS and DDS have been experimentally compared in [MW98] on various problem types. The authors concluded that interleaved and discrepancy based search strategies outperform DFS on large and lightly constrained problems. They also report that the depth where a discrepancy occurs is worth considering. Even if these methods increase the redundancy in internal node generation, they decrease the number of explored branches.

3 Pure IDFS Using Linear Space

While the Pure IDFS algorithm presented in [Mes97] needs exponential memory space, it is possible to achieve a Pure IDFS by modifying it so that it only requires linear space. However, saving space implies increasing redundancy in node generation. This has been mentioned in [MW98] but no algorithm was described. For the need of our study, we present the Pure IDFS algorithm using linear space [Prc98] in details.

Proposition 1. *Consider a complete tree with depth n and constant branching factor b. Let $C = \{c_1, ...c_n\}$ be a branch, beginning from the root and leading to a leaf node (of depth n), resulting from n choices $c_k \in \{0, ...b-1\}$. Let $num(C)$ be the branch number corresponding to the examination of C by Pure IDFS. Then, $num(C) = \sum_{k=1}^{k=n} c_k b^{k-1}$.*

This is easy to prove. c_k is incremented every b^{k-1} branch examinations (c_1 is always incremented, c_2 is incremented once all possible values of c_1 have been reviewed, that is, after b times, c_3 is incremented once all possible values of c_2 have been reviewed, that is, after b^2 times, etc). As the search begins by branch $\{0, ..., 0\}$, b^{n-1} iterations are performed before the branch $\{0, ..., 0, 1\}$ is examined, and $c_n b^{n-1}$ iterations are done before the branch $\{0, ..., 0, c_n\}$ is examined. Then, $c_{n-1} b^{n-2}$ more iterations are needed to reach the branch $\{0, ..., 0, c_{n-1}, c_n\}$, etc, leading to a total of $num(C) = \sum_{k=1}^{k=n} c_k b^{k-1}$ iterations to reach C.

Thus, we can deduce the set of heuristic choices from the number of a branch to examine, thanks to this formula: $c_k = E(\frac{num(C)}{b^{k-1}})$ modulo b. This can avoid memorizing the branches previously generated in order to know the next node to visit. Incrementing a simple counter after each branch examination is enough (see the algorithm in Figure 1) [1].

```
IDFS_lin(root):
1    I := 0; Stop := FALSE
2    REPEAT
3        node := root; h := 1
4        WHILE h ≤ n AND Stop = FALSE
                      AND node ≠ nil
5        IF node is a solution THEN Stop := TRUE
6        IF h ≠ n THEN
7            node := successor(node, (I mod bʰ)/bʰ⁻¹)
8        h := h + 1
9    I := I + 1
10   UNTIL Stop = TRUE OR I = bⁿ
11   return node
```

Fig. 1. Pure IDFS using linear memory space

In comparison with Pure IDFS originally defined by Meseguer, the required memory is linear but the internal nodes are redundantly generated. If no solution is found after a complete exploration of the tree, b^n leaf nodes have been visited, by generating n nodes in each branch. So the total number of generated nodes has been $n.b^n$. In the rest of the paper, when we will refer to Pure IDFS, it will implicitly be the linear memory space version.

---

[1] This algorithm can be easily extended to trees with a branching factor b_k depending on the depth k, by using n counters.

4 Model of Heuristic Search

Interleaved and discrepancy based searches have been theoretically compared using the Harvey and Ginsberg's abstract model of heuristic search in [HG95]. In this model of complete binary tree of depth n, a random choice of the successor has a constant probability m to be a mistake (i.e. a subtree not containing any solution is chosen whereas the other subtree contains at least one solution). With a heuristic, the first successor of a node has a heuristic probability p to have a solution in its subtree, with $p > 1 - m$. It was experimentally found that m can be considered constant [Har95]. But the heuristic probability p was also assumed to be constant, which is often not the case in practice and contradicts the assumption justifying IDFS and DDS that the heuristic quality increases with depth.

4.1 Definition of the proposed heuristic model

Definition 1. *Heuristic probabilities*
We define α_i as the probability for the heuristic to make a right choice at the depth i , i.e. to choose a subtree containing a solution, knowing that at least one of the two subtrees contains a solution.
β_i is the probability to make a right choice when violating the heuristic, i.e having a discrepancy at depth i, knowing that at least one of the two subtrees contains a solution.

The probability P that a given leaf node L is a solution is the probability that all the choices along the path leading to L are right choices. So, we have :
$P = Probability(choice_1 \text{ is } right \text{ and } choice_2 \text{ is } right \text{ ... and } choice_n \text{ is } right)$
$P = \prod_{i=1}^{i=n} Probability(choice_i \text{ is } right | \forall j < i, choice_j \text{ is } right)$
$P = \prod_{i=1}^{i=n} p_i$, where $p_i = \alpha_i$ if the choice of the heuristic was respected at depth i and $p_i = \beta_i$ in the opposite case.
We assume that our heuristic model has two properties:

- $\forall i\ \alpha_i \geq \beta_i$. It means that the heuristic is at least as good as tossing a coin at every depth. A heuristic model with this property will be called *h-consistent*.
- $\forall i < j, \alpha_i \beta_j \leq \alpha_j \beta_i$. It means that it is preferable to have a discrepancy high than low in the tree. A heuristic model with this property will be called *h-improving*.

4.2 An example : the promises value ordering heuristic

We think that a lot of problems solved by a dynamic value-ordering heuristic fit to a heuristic model which is h-consistent and h-improving.
An example of such a heuristic with increasing probabilities is the "promises" value ordering heuristic [Gee92] for a constraint satisfaction problem (CSP) when this heuristic is dynamically used with the forward-checking algorithm.

The promises heuristic orders the values in the domain of the current variable to assign, such as the values with largest remaining search space are tried first. One can compute the promises for the value v as the product of the sizes of the domains of the future variables, after having eliminated the values incompatible with v. Since forward-checking filters the domains of future variables by gradually eliminating values as more and more variables are instantiated, the heuristic becomes more accurate as depth increases because it avoids taking discarded values into account.

(p_1, p_2)	α_1/β_1	α_2/β_2	α_3/β_3	α_4/β_4	α_5/β_5	α_6/β_6	α_7/β_7	α_8/β_8	α_9/β_9
(0.1,0.5)	99/71	99/71	99/71	99/72	100/66	100/67	100/67	100/66	100/67
(0.1,0.7)	99/66	99/69	99/69	99/67	100/68	100/68	100/67	100/67	100/70
(0.1,0.8)	100/70	100/71	100/71	100/72	100/72	100/70	100/71	100/75	100/73
(0.1,0.9)	100/77	100/78	100/81	100/78	100/78	100/82	100/87	100/84	100/85
(0.5,0.2)	92/56	96/43	97/38	99/35	98/33	100/31	100/32	100/26	100/27
(1,0.2)	85/23	92/13	97/10	99/10	99/9	99/8	100/6	100/4	100/9
(1,0.15)	86/36	94/25	97/21	98/19	99/18	100/17	100/14	100/16	100/15
(1,0.1)	91/52	94/44	96/38	98/33	99/31	100/28	100/27	100/27	100/24
(1,0.05)	99/87	99/77	99/70	99/64	99/59	100/54	100/52	100/48	100/48

Table 1. α_i and β_i estimates in percentage for $< 10, 2, p_1, p_2 >$ random binary CSPs solved with the promises value ordering heuristic

Table 1 gives the α_i and β_i estimates for random binary CSPs solved by the forward-checking algorithm with the promises value ordering heuristic. We use the four parameters $< n, m, p_1, p_2 >$ model A defined in [MPSW98], where n is the number of variables, m the common cardinality of the domains, p_1 the probability of a constraint between two variables and p_2 the probability for a pair of values to be incompatible. For $n = 10$ and $m = 2$ and for each parameter set (p_1, p_2) in table 1, we have kept only the problems with solutions : there were between 200 and 2000 problems for each parameter set. We have with these experiments partially covered the zone of solvable problems. Indeed, the numbers of solutions vary between one solution to several hundreds of solutions.

We have computed α_i and β_i as follows. For each depth i, let N_i be the number of nodes with a solution in their subtrees, Nl_i and Nr_i be the numbers of left and right sons of these N_i nodes that still have a solution in their respective subtrees. We can then estimate the heuristic probabilities α_i and β_i as :

$$\alpha_i = \frac{\sum Nl_i}{\sum N_i} \text{ and } \beta_i = \frac{\sum Nr_i}{\sum N_i}.$$

We can see in Table 1 that α_i increases and β_i decreases as the depth i increases. These values fit exactly to the *h-consistent* and *h-improving* properties of our heuristic search model.

4.3 A partial order

If we knew the α_i and β_i values, we could design a search algorithm which would visit the leaf nodes in an increasing probability order. However, when a heuristic model is h-consistent and h-improving, even if we do not know the α_i and β_i values, we can compare some probabilities to be a solution for different leaf nodes. For example, if leaf node L1 has the probability $P_1 = \alpha_1\beta_2\alpha_3$ to be a solution and leaf node L2 has the probability $P_2 = \alpha_1\alpha_2\beta_3$ to be a solution, then we know that $P_1 \geq P_2$ because $\beta_2\alpha_3 \geq \alpha_2\beta_3$. However, if $P_1 = \alpha_1\alpha_2\beta_3$ and $P_2 = \beta_1\beta_2\alpha_3$ then we cannot neither establish that $P_1 \leq P_2$ nor that $P_1 \geq P_2$.

Definition 2. *P-consistency*
A search algorithm A is P-consistent if and only if for every consecutive leaf nodes L_k and L_{k+1} it visits, there exist h-consistent and h-improving α_i and β_i values such that $P_k > P_{k+1}$, P_k and P_{k+1} being the probabilities of the leaves L_k and L_{k+1} to be a solution.

To ensure that a search algorithm is P-consistent is a way to guaranty a visiting order of the leaf nodes compatible with the *h-consistent* and *h-improving* properties of the heuristic when we ignore the actual α_i and β_i values. But, this definition of P-consistency cannot easily be directly used for proving that a search algorithm is P-consistent. Therefore, we define a partial order on the leaf nodes which allows to compare them on a more operational way.

Definition 3. *Branch tail*
A branch tail of length l is the sequence of the l last choices of a branch going from the root to a leaf node.

Definition 4. *Partial order $\prec$*
Let C and C' be two branches going from the root of a search tree to their respective leaf nodes L and L'. $L \prec L'$ if and only if, for every length l, the tail of C with length l contains a number of discrepancies lower or equal than the tail of C' with the same length.

The relation $\prec$ is a partial order : it is trivially reflexive and transitive. It is also antisymmetric : if $L \prec L'$ and $L' \prec L$, then we can recursively prove, examining the tails of the branches leading to L and L' in increasing order of their size, that they are made of the same choices and conclude that $L = L'$.

We call this partial order *PO*. It is defined over the leaf nodes of any complete binary search tree. The following theorem will make a link between this partial order and the heuristic model.

Theorem 1. *Let C and C' be two branches going from the root of a search tree to their respective leaf nodes L and L' with probabilities P and P' to be a solution in a h-consistent and h-improving heuristic model.*
(1) ($\forall\{(\alpha_i, \beta_i), i = 1..n\}$ h-consistent and h-improving $P \geq P'$) $\Leftrightarrow$ (2) $L \prec L'$.

Proof.

$(2) \Rightarrow (1)$. Let P and P' be the probabilities of the leaf nodes L and L' to be a solution. $P = \prod_{i=1}^{i=n} p_i$ and $P' = \prod_{i=1}^{i=n} p'_i$, where p_i and p'_i can independently be α_i or β_i. $\frac{P}{P'} = \prod_{i=1}^{i=n} \frac{p_i}{p'_i}$. There are three possible expressions for the ratio $\frac{p_i}{p'_i}$:

1. $p_i = p'_i$, then $\frac{p_i}{p'_i} = 1$.
2. $\frac{p_i}{p'_i} = \frac{\alpha_i}{\beta_i}$, then $\frac{p_i}{p'_i} \geq 1$.
3. $\frac{p_i}{p'_i} = \frac{\beta_i}{\alpha_i}$, then $\frac{p_i}{p'_i} \leq 1$.

So $\frac{P}{P'}$ is a product of terms of types $\frac{\alpha_i}{\beta_i}$ and $\frac{\beta_i}{\alpha_i}$. One way to establish that $\frac{P}{P'} \geq 1$ is to split the product into terms all greater than 1. To perform that it is sufficient to associate every $\frac{\beta_i}{\alpha_i}$ element with a $\frac{\alpha_j}{\beta_j}$ element such that $j > i$ and that the latter is not already associated with another $\frac{\beta_k}{\alpha_k}$ element.

Suppose that $L \prec L'$. Then we can do this association in the decreasing order of the depth i of the term $\frac{\beta_i}{\alpha_i}$. Indeed, we can start with the term $\frac{\beta_{im}}{\alpha_{im}}$ with the greatest depth i_m. Such a term corresponds to a discrepancy in C and a respect of the heuristics in C'. As $L \prec L'$, if we consider the tail beginning at depth i_m, there exists a depth $j_m > i_m$ corresponding to a discrepancy in C' and a respect of the heuristic in C. We can associate our term with this term. Then, for each term $\frac{\beta_i}{\alpha_i}$, we can associate it with a term $\frac{\alpha_j}{\beta_j}$, by considering the tail beginning at depth i. As $L \prec L'$, there exists a discrepancy in the tail of C' that is not yet associated with a discrepancy in C, and we can associate it with the current term $\frac{\beta_i}{\alpha_i}$. So, we have proven $P \geq P'$, without using the actual values α_i and β_i, i.e. $P \geq P'$ for all possible α_i and β_i respecting the heuristic properties.□

$(1) \Rightarrow (2)$. We will actually prove $not(2) \Rightarrow not(1)$, i.e. *if $not(L \prec L')$, then* $\exists \alpha_i, \beta_i$ *such that* $P < P'$.

Let us consider that it exists at least one tail T of C containing more discrepancies than the tail T' of C' with the same length. Let l be the length of T and T'. Let P (respectively P') be the probability that C (respectively C') leads to a solution. We can express P as $P = P_0.P_T$ and P' as $P' = P'_0.P_{T'}$, where P_T and P'_T are products of l terms of types α_i and β_i, corresponding to the heuristic choices in T and T'. If $\forall i \leq n - l, \alpha_i = \beta_i = 0.5$ and $\forall i > n - l, \alpha_i = 0.6$ and $\beta_i = 0.4$, which is compatible with the assumptions of our heuristic search model, then $P_0 = P'_0 = 0.5^{n-l}$ and $P'_T \geq \frac{0.6}{0.4} P_T$ because T' has at least one more discrepancy than T. Then it is possible to give values to the α_i and β_i such that $P' > P$.□

We can now give a operational way to check the P-consistency of an algorithm.

Definition 5. *Respect of the partial order PO*
A tree search algorithm respects the partial order PO, if and only if every two consecutive branches C_k and C_{k+1} leading to the leaves L_k and L_{k+1} are such that $L_{k+1} \prec L_k$ is false, i.e. at least one tail of C_{k+1} has more discrepancies than the tail of C_k with the same length. We will say that an algorithm breaks PO if and only if it does not respect it.

Theorem 2. *A tree search algorithm is P-consistent if and only if it respects the partial order PO.*

Proof.
If an algorithm respects PO, then for every consecutive leaves L_k and L_{k+1} it examines, $L_{k+1} \prec L_k$ is false. Then, according to theorem 1, there exist α_i and β_i values for which $P_{k+1} > P_k$. Then, we cannot have $P_k \leq P_{k+1}$ for all h-consistent and h-improving α_i and β_i values. We can conclude, according to Definition 2 that the algorithm is P-consistent.

Conversely, if an algorithm breaks the partial order PO, then there exist two consecutive leaves L_k and L_{k+1} such that $L_{k+1} \prec L_k$. According to Theorem 1, for all h-consistent and h-improving α_i and β_i values $P_{k+1} \geq P_k$, and we can conclude that the search algorithm is not P-consistent.□

5 Non P-consistent Searches

We will show in this section through the example of a complete binary tree of depth 5, that neither DFS, nor ILDS, nor DDS are P-consistent because they do not respect the partial order PO.

$p_{i,j}$ refers to the probability to be a solution for the jth leaf node which has i discrepancies in the order defined by DFS. (see Figure 2).

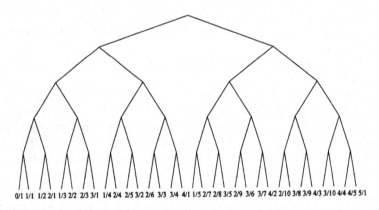

0/1 1/1 1/2 2/1 1/3 2/2 2/3 3/1 1/4 2/4 2/5 3/2 2/6 3/3 3/4 4/1 1/5 2/7 2/8 3/5 2/9 3/6 3/7 4/2 2/10 3/8 3/9 4/3 3/10 4/4 4/5 5/1

Fig. 2. Numbering of the leaf nodes of a complete binary tree of depth 5 expanded by DFS. i/j represents the jth leaf node with i discrepancies.

The partial order on the leaf nodes PO is presented in Figure 3 for the binary search tree of depth 5. According to Theorem 1, an arrow indicates a decrease of their probability to be a solution in our heuristic model.

The partial order is represented as a two dimensional table. We can remark that in each line the number of discrepancies is the same. This presentation highlights two particular ways for visiting the leaf nodes while respecting the partial order:

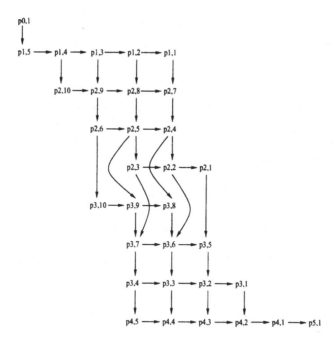

Fig. 3. Partial order PO on the leaf nodes of a complete binary tree of depth 5

- examination of the nodes line after line from top to bottom, each line being examined from the left to the right. This order corresponds with following the number of discrepancies.
- examination of the nodes column after column, from left to right, each column being examined from the top to the bottom. This order corresponds with the order followed by Pure IDFS.

Of course, many other more complex total orders can be built from PO.

number	DFS	p. IDFS	ILDS	DDS
1	0/1	0/1	0/1	0/1
2	1/1	1/5	1/1	1/5
3	1/2	1/4	1/2	1/4
4	2/1	2/10	1/3	2/10
5	1/3	1/3	1/4	1/3
6	2/2	2/9	1/5	2/6
7	2/3	2/6	2/1	2/9
8	3/1	3/10	2/2	3/10
9	1/4	1/2	2/3	1/2
10	2/4	2/8	2/4	2/3
11	2/5	2/5	2/5	2/5
12	3/2	3/9	2/6	3/4
13	2/6	2/3	2/7	2/8
14	3/3	3/7	2/8	3/7

The table above shows the visiting order of the first fourteen leaf nodes by each search method.

This example leads to the following conclusions:

- DFS does not respect the partial order at all.
- ILDS partially respects the partial order. Every set of leaf nodes with a given number of discrepancies is totally visited before leaf nodes containing more discrepancies. However, the partial order is broken inside these sets. Still, we can see that if the leaf nodes were visited in a reverse order within each iteration, the partial order would be respected.
- DDS breaks the partial order by making several "vertical" permutations. Ex: permutation in positions 6 and 7, then from position 10.
- Pure IDFS totally respects the partial order on this example.

On this example, Pure IDFS is the only algorithm, among the algorithms we studied, that respects the partial order. We can remark that ILDS could respect it if it was slightly modified. We call *Reverse ILDS* (RLDS) a variant of ILDS where the leaf nodes are visited in the reverse order within each iteration[2].

```
RLDS-iteration(node, k, depth):
1    IF node is a solution THEN return node
2    s := Successors(node)
3    IF s = ∅ THEN return NIL
4    result := NIL
5    IF k > 0 THEN result := RLDS-iteration(right-son(S),k − 1,depth − 1)
6    IF result = NIL AND depth > k
7        THEN result := RLDS-iteration(left-son(S),k,depth − 1)
8    return result
```

```
RLDS(node, max-depth)
1    FOR x from 0 to max-depth
2        result := RLDS-iteration(node, x, max-depth)
3        IF result ≠ NIL THEN return result
4    return NIL
```

Fig. 4. RLDS

In the next section, we will prove these results on binary trees of any size.

---

[2] Note that LDS also makes the choice of the right subtree first but for a different reason. LDS and ILDS are based on the assumption that the heuristic quality is constant over any depth, so there is no priority between leaf nodes with the same number of discrepancies. The right-to-left order followed by LDS pushes the already visited leaf nodes to the end of the iteration. ILDS, having suppressed the leaf nodes redundancy, has recovered a usual visiting order of the leaf nodes.

6 P-consistent Searches

We will use theorem 2 to prove that a tree search algorithm is P-consistent.

6.1 Pure IDFS

To prove that Pure IDFS is P-consistent, we use Proposition 1 with $b = 2$. The number $num(C)$ of a branch $C = \{c_1, ... c_n\}$ ($c_k \in \{0, 1\}$) is : $num(C) = \sum_{k=1}^{k=n} c_k 2^{k-1}$. We state that $c_k = 0$ stands for a respect of the heuristic choice and $c_k = 1$ for a discrepancy. The principle of IDFS is to undo the latest choices last in order to keep these choices respecting the heuristic as long as possible. The earliest choice is systematically changed, the second one every second time, the third one every fourth time, etc.

Lemma 1. *Let $C_i = \{c_{1,i}, ... c_{n,i}\}$ and $C_{i+1} = \{c_{1,i+1}, ... c_{n,i+1}\}$ be two consecutive branches explored by Pure IDFS. Let T be the common tail of C_i and C_{i+1} Let C'_i and C'_{i+1} be the sub-branches of C_i and C_{i+1} truncated by T. C'_i is a sequence of discrepancies ending by a respect of the heuristic choice while C'_{i+1} is a sequence of respects of the heuristic choice ending by a discrepancy.*

Proof.
Let t be the length of the common tail of C_i and C_{i+1} and let $num(T)$ be the common value for the number of the tail.
$num(T) = \sum_{k=n-t+1}^{k=n} c_{k,i} 2^{k-1} = \sum_{k=n-t+1}^{k=n} c_{k,i+1} 2^{k-1}$
We have
$num(C_i) = num(T) + c_{n-t,i} \times 2^{n-t-1} + \sum_{k=1}^{k=n-t-1} c_{k,i} 2^{k-1}$ and
$num(C_{i+1}) = num(T) + c_{n-t,i+1} \times 2^{n-t-1} + \sum_{k=1}^{k=n-t-1} c_{k,i+1} 2^{k-1}$
As $num(C'_i) < num(C'_{i+1})$, we have then
$c_{n-t,i} < c_{n-t,i+1}$, i.e $c_{n-t,i} = 0$ and $c_{n-t,i+1} = 1$
As $num(C_{i+1}) = num(C_i) + 1$, the only possible values for all the $c_{k,i}$ and $c_{k,i+1}$ such that
$2^{n-t} + \sum_{k=1}^{k=n-t-1} c_{k,i+1} 2^{k-1} = \sum_{k=1}^{k=n-t-1} c_{k,i} 2^{k-1} + 1$ are
$\forall k < n - t, c_{k,i+1} = 0$ and $c_{k,i} = 1$ $\square$

Theorem 3. *Pure IDFS is P-consistent.*

Proof.
Let d be the depth of the beginning of the common tail of C_i and C_{i+1}. According to Lemma 1, C_{i+1} contains one discrepancy at depth $d - 1$, while C_i respects the heuristic at the same depth. As C_i and C_{i+1} have a common tail beginning at depth d, the tail at depth $d - 1$ of C_{i+1} has one more discrepancy than the corresponding tail of C_i, so Pure IDFS respects the partial order PO and Theorem 2 states that Pure IDFS is P-consistent. $\square$

6.2 Reverse ILDS

Reverse ILDS (RLDS) chooses to visit the leaf nodes in the order corresponding to the line after line traversal of Table 3. The leaf nodes with fewer discrepancies are visited first and, in case of equality in the number of discrepancies, the rightmost leaf node is visited first. Let C_i and C_{i+1} be two consecutive branches explored by RLDS. There are two possibilities:

- C_{i+1} has one discrepancy more than C_i.
- C_i and C_{i+1} have the same number of discrepancies. C_i and C_{i+1} start from the root and make the same choices until depth d where they split up. C_{i+1} respects the heuristic choice at depth d whereas C_i does not. Thus, the tails of C_i and C_{i+1} beginning at depth d have the same number of discrepancies whereas the tail of C_{i+1} beginning at depth $d+1$ has one more discrepancy than the one of C_i.

In both cases there exists one tail of C_{i+1} containing one more discrepancy than the tail of C_i with the same length. So, Theorem 2 lets us conclude that RLDS is P-consistent.□

7 Discussion

ILDS, IDFS and DDS are search strategies that try to guide the search towards the most promising leaf nodes first. We have seen that they have not the same ability to achieve this goal within the framework of our heuristic search model because some are P-consistent while others are not. However, that criterion is not sufficient to declare that one search strategy is better than another one. Indeed, they all examine internal nodes several times and this redundancy restrains their efficiency. So, to compare these search methods more accurately, the redundancy criterion has also to be taken into account. Here is a table summarizing these two characteristics (respect of the partial order and maximum number of explored nodes) for the search methods we studied:

Algorithms	Respect of PO	max # of nodes
DFS	very poorly	2^{n+1}
Pure IDFS	totally	$n.2^n$
Lim. IDFS	partially	2^{n+1}
ILDS	partially	2.2^{n+1}
RLDS	totally	2.2^{n+1}
DDS	partially	2.2^{n+1}

The table shows that it is not possible to build a hierarchy of the search methods based on a theoretical analysis of their efficiency, by taking both P-consistency and redundancy criteria into account.

If there was no redundancy at all, Pure IDFS would be better than DDS because Pure IDFS visits the leaf nodes in a more accurate order. They are very much alike but Pure IDFS is more extremist in the sense it totally respects the idea of the predominance of the latter choices even if it produces a lot of redundant search. DDS accepts to partially contradict this idea in order to limit the amount of redundantly generated nodes.

In general, the better the partial order is respected, the more redundant is the search. However, there are two exceptions. First, Limited IDFS has no redundancy but examines the leaf nodes in a better order than DFS because the order of Limited IDFS is closer to the order of Pure IDFS, which is known to respect PO. Secondly, RLDS has the same redundancy as ILDS but RLDS respects PO. If we make the approximation that every i^{th} leaf node is met at the same time for all the search methods, then we can conclude that Limited IDFS is better than DFS and that RLDS is better than ILDS.

8 Conclusion and Perspectives

The purpose of interleaved and discrepancy based searches is to lead as quickly as possible to the most promising leaf nodes, being guided by a heuristic. We have therefore defined a model of heuristic search assuming the improvement of the heuristic quality with depth. We have shown that on random CSP with binary variables, the promises value ordering heuristic used with the forward-checking algorithm follows that model. We have proven that Pure IDFS and RLDS, which is a slight modification of ILDS, are the only search methods, among those we studied, which examine the leaf nodes in an order totally compatible with the assumptions of our model. However, they cannot pretend to be superior to the other ones because the redundancy in the generation of internal nodes and the time at which each leaf node is visited have also to be taken into account. Still, Limited IDFS, which eliminates redundancy while visiting the leaf nodes in a better order than DFS, will theoretically outperform DFS. A limited version of RLDS, suppressing the redundancy by partially degrading the visiting order of the leaf nodes, could also achieve the same goal.

To go further in this research area, it would be interesting to include some more specific information about the heuristic itself. A way would be to estimate the α_i values for a specific problem and then use these values to aid choosing the search algorithm to use. We could then estimate the success rate of each algorithm during the first leaves they reach with a calculus analogous to [HG95] replacing the p constant heuristic probability by α_i. Another point to study is to extend this model to n-ary search trees, as the search trees developed by algorithms solving CSPs, when the domains of the variables have a size greater than 2.

Acknowledgements

Thanks to Marie-Catherine Vilarem for useful discussions on this topic and to Gilles Trombettoni and anonymous reviewers for comments on an earlier draft of this paper.

References

[Gee92]   P. A. Geelen. Dual viewpoint heuristics for binary constraint satisfaction problems. In *Proceedings of the 10th European Conference on Artificial Intelligence*, 1992.

[Har95]   W. Harvey. *Nonsystematic Backtracking Search*. PhD thesis, Stanford University, 1995.

[HG95]   W. D. Harvey and M. L. Ginsberg. Limited discrepancy search. In *Proceedings of 14th International Joint Conference on Artificial Intelligence*, 1995.

[Kor96]   R. Korf. Improved limited discrepancy search. In *Proceedings of the 13th AAAI Conference*, 1996.

[Mes97]   P. Meseguer. Interleaved Depth-First Search. In *Proceedings of the 15th International Joint Conference on Artificial Intelligence*, pages 1382–1387, 1997.

[MPSW98]   E. MacIntyre, P. Prosser, B. Smith, and T. Walsh. Random constraint satisfaction : Theory meeet practice. In *Principles and Practice of Constraint Programming CP'98*, number 1520 in LNCS, pages 325–339. Springer, 1998.

[MW98]   P. Meseguer and T. Walsh. Interleaved and Discrepancy Based Search. In *Proceedings of the 13th European Conference on Artificial Intelligence*, 1998.

[Prc98]   Nicolas Prcovic. *Recherche arborescente parallèle et séquentielle pour les problèmes de satisfaction de contraintes*. PhD thesis, Ecole Nationale des Ponts et Chaussées, November 1998. in French.

[Wal97]   T. Walsh. Depth-bounded discrepancy search. In *Proceedings of the 15th International Joint Conference on Artificial Intelligence*, 1997.

Tight Cooperation and Its Application in Piecewise Linear Optimization

Philippe Refalo

ILOG, Les Taissounieres, 1681, route des Dolines,
06560 Sophia Antipolis, France
refalo@ilog.fr

Abstract. Many cooperative systems merge a linear constraint solver and a domain reduction solver over finite domains or intervals. The latter handles a high level formulation of the problem and passes domain variable information. The former handles a linear formulation of the problem and computes a relaxed optimal solution. This paper proposes an extension to this framework called *tight cooperation* where the linear formulation of a high level constraint is restated in a way, as domains are reduced. This approach is illustrated on piecewise linear optimization. Experimental results are given. These show that tight cooperation can give better results than classical cooperation and mixed-integer programming techniques.

1 Introduction

Early cooperative systems such as ICE [5], Prolog IV [8] and ECLIPSE [18] merge a linear constraint solver and a domain reduction solver over finite domains or intervals in constraint programming. The main motivation for combining two methods that are individually effective for solving combinatorial optimization problems is to solve them more efficiently or to tackle harder ones. The gain in merging two different solvers comes from the exchange of information that is valid for the problem, but not necessarily for the solver that receives them. Cooperative solvers have been shown to be effective in solving some combinatorial optimization and non linear problems (see [2], [13], [18], [7]). They are also competitive compared with pure domain reduction solving and linear optimization techniques.

The classical framework for cooperation states a (high-level) formulation of the problem to the domain reduction solver and a linear relaxation of the problem, or part of it, to the linear solver. The latter passes domain variable information (namely bounds) while the former determines fixed variables [5]. Both solvers pass failure detections.

This paper proposes an extension to this framework called *tight cooperation* where the linear formulation of a high level constraint is dynamicaly restated in a way, as variables domains are reduced, which in the classical framework it is not. Practically, the linearization is tightened by reducing bounds on variables of the linearization and generating locally valid inequalities (which are removed when backtracking).

For example consider a constraint over variables x and y whose admissible elements are $(1,1)$ and $(3,1)$. A possible linear relaxation of this problem is the smallest polyhedron including these solutions (the convex hull) that is defined as the convex combination of the two elements:

$$S = \{x = 1\lambda_1 + 3\lambda_2,\ y = 1\lambda_1 + 1\lambda_2,\ \lambda_1 + \lambda_2 = 1,\ \lambda_1 \geq 0,\ \lambda_2 \geq 0\}$$

Assume that, during the search, the constraint $x \geq 2$ is added. The first solution is then no longer an admissible element. In classical cooperation, the set S is updated to $S' = S \cup \{x \geq 2\}$ while in the tight cooperation the linear formulation becomes that of the convex hull of the new solution set, that is $S'' = \{x = 3,\ y = 1\}$. Note that a set equivalent to S'' can be obtained from S by fixing λ_1 to zero. It is easy to observe that the solutions of S'' are included in that of S'. In particular $x = 2 \wedge y = 1$ is a solution of S' but not of S''.

This framework is described in detail below. It is integrated in the commercial library ILOG Planner [16] which merges the linear optimization algorithms of ILOG CPLEX [1] with the domain reduction techniques of ILOG Solver [20].

As an illustration, we detail tight cooperation on piecewise linear optimization. Piecewise linear functions are frequent in transportation and planning problems [12] and can be used to express some non linear problems [3]. For each constraint $y = f(x)$ where f is piecewise linear, a linear relaxation is handled by the linear optimizer and arc-consistency on bounds [14] is maintained by the domain reduction solver. Results of practical experiments on optimization problems are described. They show that tight cooperation can give better results than classical cooperation and can outperform approaches using mixed-integer programming techniques.

The rest of the article is organized as follows. Section 2 recalls basic ideas about cooperative solvers. Section 3 recalls classical cooperation and details tight cooperation. Section 4 is devoted to piecewise linear optimization problems, their linearization and their solving. Section 5 gives some practical results and Section 6 concludes the article.

2 Cooperative Solvers

In this section we give our view of solver cooperation and detail the advantages and drawbacks of each solver.

2.1 Merging Linear Optimization and Domain Reduction

Our view of cooperative solvers is restricted to the merger in constraint programming of:

- a solver based on domain reduction over finite domains or intervals (using for instance arc-consistency over finite domains or bound consistency over floating-point intervals), and
- a linear optimizer based on linear programming techniques [6].

The problems tackled are combinatorial optimization problems of the form

$$P : \min f \text{ subject to } C$$

where f is a term to be minimized and C is a set of constraints containing global and logical constraints. This model can usually be handled directly by the domain reduction solver.

A linear optimizer handles a linear relaxation of the original problem or part of it. The linear relaxation of this problem is a *linear program* :

$$Q : \min \mathcal{L}(f) \text{ subject to } \mathcal{L}(C) \qquad (1)$$

where $\mathcal{L}(f)$ is a linear term and $\mathcal{L}(C)$ is a set of linear constraints whose solution set contains that of C.

The effectiveness of using a linear optimizer to solve problem P strongly depends upon the tightness of the relaxation $\mathcal{L}(C)$. In our approach, the emphasis is made on constraints, so we provide to the linear optimizer a formulation of the smallest polyhedron containing the solutions of constraints (the convex hull). However, in some cases this formulation is too large or computationally expensive to obtain, so an approximation may be preferred. For the sake of simplicity, we assume in the following that the convex hull is used.

Both solvers cooperate by exchanging constraints that are valid for the problem but not necessarily for the solver receiving them, in order to reduce domains, tighten the linear relaxation, and detect failures earlier.

2.2 Domain Reduction Solver

Solvers based on domain reduction make inferences about variable domains [21, 14]. We define a *domain* as a set of real values. Each variable x has a domain noted D_x which is is subset of $\mathcal{R}$ in our case. We note by $\min(D_x)$ and $\max(D_x)$, respectively, the smallest and the largest element of D_x. This domain definition includes the finite domains and floating-point intervals that are commonly used.

Domain reduction consists of removing inconsistent values w.r.t a constraint from the variable domains. So it mainly achieves a local consistency.

These solvers have been successfully applied to a variety of problems and some of their advantages are :

- the logical structure of the problem is used to reduce variable domains; consequently, during a branch & bound search the number of possible choices is reduced and thus the search tree;
- efficient search heuristics based on the structure of the problem or of the domains can be developed.

However, these solvers also have some drawbacks:

- they maintain local consistency and lack a global view of the problem;
- they do not really consider the objective function for domain reduction and solution search;

– all variables must be instantiated to ensure that a solution is found.

Some of these drawbacks are compensated for by the advantages of a linear optimizer.

2.3 Linear Optimizer

Unlike domain reduction solvers, a linear optimizer solves the linear relaxation Q and computes a *relaxed optimal solution*. This solution is maintained incrementally when new constraints are added with the dual simplex [6]. Among the advantages of this solver are the following:

– global consistency is achieved on Q, leading to an earlier failure detection;
– some domain reduction can be done: variables fixed to a single value are detected using reduced cost [24] and/or detection of implicit equalities [17];
– the search effort can be reduced since some variables may have the value required by their type in the relaxed solution;
– the objective function is considered in computing the relaxed solution, so search strategies can be developed to find optimal or near optimal solutions quickly (when the relaxation is tight, the relaxed optimal solution suggests where the solution of the original problem could be.)

However the main drawbacks are :

– the problem considered is different from the original and is destructured by the linear formulation; so search strategies may not be as effective as when they are applied to the high-level formulation;
– when the linear relaxation is not tight (that is the solution set of the linear relaxation is far from the convex hull of the problem solutions), the relaxed optimal solution is meaningless.

It appears clearly, that many of the drawbacks of one type of solver can be compensated for by the advantages of the other one. The results obtained in ICE, Planner and ECLIPSE illustrate some of these points on integer programming problems.

3 Schemes for Cooperative Solvers

To describe in a clear and concise manner the way cooperation is done and the restrictions we impose, we give the set of properties that are guaranteed by the cooperation algorithm.

Let us denote P, the problem handled by the domain reduction solver, and Q, the linear relaxation of P. Among the properties we have are those over (Q, σ) that maintain σ as the optimal solution of Q, those over (P, D) that maintain domains D reduced and finally those over (Q, σ, P, D) that achieve cooperation. Only these last properties are detailed here. We start first by giving the properties for classical cooperation and then those for tight cooperation.

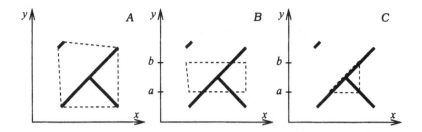

Fig. 1. Comparison Between Classical Cooperation and Tight Cooperation

3.1 Classical Cooperation

Classical cooperation is the scheme described in [5, 19, 4] and used in ICE, Prolog IV, and earlier versions of ILOG Planner. When applied to our case, it consists of exchanging information about bounds on variables that are shared by the two solvers.

Let X be the set of variables shared by P and Q. The following properties are sufficient to enforce classical cooperation as described in section 2:

$$
\begin{aligned}
&\forall x \in X,\ (x = \alpha) \in Q\ \rightarrow\ D_x = \{\alpha\} \\
&\forall x \in X,\ \min(D_x) \neq -\infty\ \rightarrow\ (x \geq \min(D_x)) \in Q \\
&\forall x \in X,\ \max(D_x) \neq \infty\ \rightarrow\ (x \leq \max(D_x)) \in Q \qquad (2)\\
&\exists x \in X,\ D_x = \emptyset\ \rightarrow\ \textit{fail} \\
&Q \text{ is unsolvable} \rightarrow\ \textit{fail}
\end{aligned}
$$

Let us see the effect of this scheme on the linear relaxation. Let $S(c)$ be the set of solutions of constraint c. The solution set T of the linear relaxation is the intersection of all convex hulls of $S(c)$ with the variables bounds; that is

$$
T = \text{convex\_hull}(D^X) \cap \bigcap_{c \in P} \text{convex\_hull}(S(c))
$$

where D^X denotes the Carthesian product of domains of variables in X.

The effect of this framework is illustrated on one constraint in the example shown in Figure 1. Graphic A represents the set of solutions of the constraints (in bold lines) and the convex hull of this set (in dashed lines). Graphic B represents the linear relaxation with classical cooperation (in dashed lines), when the domain of y is reduced to $[a, b]$ by the domain reduction solver.

3.2 Tight Cooperation

Tight cooperation features a more aggressive use of domain reduction to tighten the linearization more than classical cooperation. The set of solutions T' in the linear optimizer is the intersection the convex hulls of the new solution set of each constraint according to the domains D, that is:

$$T' = \bigcap_{c \in P} (\text{convex\_hull}(D^X \cap S(c)))$$

Thus the convex hull is not computed only once, but is reconsidered as domains are reduced. It is important to note that $T' \subset T$.

Denote $L(D, c)$ a linear formulation of $D^X \cap S(c)$. The properties that must be maintained for tight cooperation are simply:

$$\forall c \in P, \ L(D, c) \in Q$$

The consequences of this modification are illustrated in the example shown in Figure 1. Graphic C represents the set of solutions of the linear relaxation with tight cooperation, when the domain of y is reduced to $[a, b]$. It is strictly included in the one obtained with classical cooperation.

The goal of dynamically tightening the linear formulation is to strengthen the linear formulation in order to find infeasibilities earlier and to improve the relevance of the relaxed optimal solution. It is important to emphasize the relations between tight cooperation and domain reduction:

- as in domain reduction, the linear relaxation is tightened as constraints are added to the problem; during a search, this tightening occurs when going down the search tree;
- as global constraints that have a specific algorithm for maintaining consistency, there is a set of properties for achieving cooperation for each high-level constraint depending on its structure and linearization.

An important issue is the update of the linear formulation. A naive approach would be to introduce the new formulation in place of the previous one. However, it is more efficient to choose a linear formulation that can be updated incrementally. This update can, for instance, reduce bounds on variables of the linearization or add valid inequalities. This is detailed for piecewise linear optimization in the next section.

4 Piecewise Linear Optimization

Piecewise linear optimization deals with problems involving linear constraints and constraints $y = f(x)$ where f is piecewise linear. There is a large literature in mathematical programming about methods for solving these problems. Approaches commonly used are specialized simplex on convex cases [11], mixed-integer programming [3, 15] and descend methods [9] for approximated optimal solutions.

We first define piecewise linear functions and give a linear formulation of the convex hull of a constraint $y = f(x)$. Domain reduction on this constraint is briefly presented. Finally, properties for maintaining tight cooperation are given and illustrated.

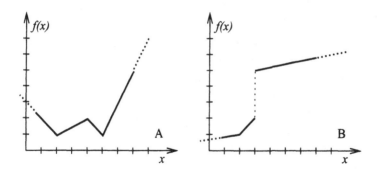

Fig. 2. Instances of Piecewise Linear Functions

4.1 Piecewise Linear Functions

Only unary functions are considered here. A unary piecewise linear function is a function that is linear over some intervals of its arguments. Graphic A in Figure 2 represents a piecewise linear function that has 4 *segments* and 3 *breakpoints* (points where the *slope* of the function changes). Discontinuous functions are also handled. Graphic B represents a discontinuous piecewise linear function that has 3 segments and a *step* between segment 2 and 3.

A piecewise linear function is defined by its breakpoints, its first and last slope and a set of forbidden segments. It is denoted

$$f_{X,Y,s_f,s_l,F} \tag{3}$$

where X is an ordered set of n real numbers, Y is a set of n real numbers, s_f and s_l are respectively the slope of first and last segment, and F is a list of forbidden segments.

The segment i is the set of points along a line that links points (X_i, Y_i) and (X_{i+1}, Y_{i+1}) (the last point is excluded). If $i \in F$, the function is not defined over the interval $[X_i, X_{i+1})$. For instance the function in graphic A of Figure 2 is defined as $f_{\{2,4,5\},\{1,2,1\},-1,2,\emptyset}$. The function in graphic B of figure 2 is defined as $f_{\{2,3,3\},\{1,2,5\},0.2,0.2,\{2\}}$.

4.2 Linear Relaxation

There exist several linear representations of the convex hull of a constraint $y = f(x)$ (see [10]). The one given here has the advantage of being able to be tightened when the domains of x and y are reduced.

Roughly, since the function is linear between each breakpoint, a point of the convex hull is a convex combination of these breakpoints. So assume f is defined as in (3) and introduce $n + 2$ new variables denoted $\lambda_0, \lambda_1, \ldots, \lambda_{n+1}$. A linear representation of the convex hull is

$$\begin{cases} x = X_1\lambda_1 + X_2\lambda_2 + \cdots + X_n\lambda_n - \lambda_0 + \lambda_{n+1} \\ y = Y_1\lambda_1 + Y_2\lambda_2 + \cdots + Y_n\lambda_n - s_f\lambda_0 + s_l\lambda_{n+1} \\ 1 = \lambda_1 + \lambda_2 + \cdots + \lambda_n \\ \lambda_i \geq 0, \ i \in \{0, \ldots, n+1\} \end{cases}$$

In the following, $\mathrm{var}(f, i)$ denotes the ith variable introduced in the linearization of f.

4.3 Domain Reduction

The constraint $y = f(x)$, where f is piecewise linear, is given as such to the domain reduction solver. Our implementation of domain reduction achieves arc-B-consistency [14]. That is, the domains D_x and D_y are such that there exist values α and β from D_x such that $\min(D_y) = f(\alpha)$ and $\max(D_y) = f(\beta)$ and values γ and η from D_y such that $\gamma = f(\min(D_y))$ and $\eta = f(\max(D_y))$.

It is not the purpose of this paper to describe the incremental algorithms that maintain bound consistency. However, this can be achieved with constructive disjunction [23] when $y = f(x)$ is formulated in disjunctive form. That is, with a disjunction of relations $X_i \leq x < X_{i+1} \wedge f(x) = \alpha x + \beta$ where $y = \alpha x + \beta$ is the line that represents the solution set when x lies between X_i and X_{i+1}. A dedicated and more efficient algorithm was developed for this constraint.

4.4 Tight Cooperation

Tight cooperation on piecewise linear functions can be implemented simply by replacing the linear formulation of a constraint $y = f(x)$ by that of $y = f'(x)$ where f' is the function whose breakpoints have been modified according to the new domains of x and y. This gives the convex hull of the new solution set.

This approach is not incremental, and we present below two approaches that are incremental, but maintain an approximation of the convex hull. The first updates the linear formulation by fixing the λ_i variables from the linearization. The second adds a fixed number of facets of the convex hull. In practice this approximation is tight and represents the exact convex hull in several cases.

Variable Fixing From domain reduction we can infer that some segments of the function are excluded from the set of solutions of the constraint $y = f(x)$. When two consecutive segments are excluded, the convex hull can no longer be defined as a convex combination of the breakpoint that relies on the two segments. Thus the λ_i variable corresponding to this breakpoint can be fixed to zero.

More formally we define the function $\mathrm{excluded}(i, f, D_x, D_y)$ where f is defined as in (3). It returns **true** if the ith segment is excluded from the set of solutions of the constraint $y = f(x)$ according to domains D_x and D_y and **false** otherwise.

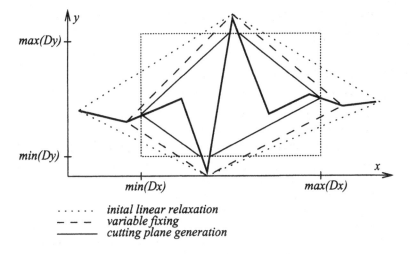

min(Dx)   max(Dx)

· · · · · ·   *inital linear relaxation*
− − −   *variable fixing*
─────   *cutting plane generation*

Fig. 3. Linear Relaxations on a Piecewise Linear Function

In addition to the properties 2, three properties are needed to maintain this approximation:

$$
\begin{aligned}
&\forall(y = f(x)) \in P, \ \text{excluded}(0, f, D_x, D_y) \ \rightarrow \ (var(f, 0) = 0) \in Q \\
&\forall(y = f(x)) \in P, \ \text{excluded}(n, f, D_x, D_y) \ \rightarrow \ (var(f, n+1) = 0) \in Q \\
&\forall(y = f(x)) \in P, \\
&\left(\begin{array}{l} \text{excluded}(i, f, D_x, D_y) \ \wedge \\ \text{excluded}(i+1, f, D_x, D_y) \end{array}\right) \ \rightarrow \ (var(f, i) = 0) \in Q, \ i \in \{1, \ldots, n\}
\end{aligned}
\tag{4}
$$

Bounds on variables of the linearization are added systematically to the problem Q because they do not increase the memory consumption of the linear optimizer. The effect of this tightening is illustrated in Figure 3. The initial convex hull is represented with dotted lines while the approximation of the new convex hull is represented with dashed lines.

Cutting Planes Generation In addition to variable fixing, we can generate some facets of the convex hull. Indeed at most 8 inequalities are generated.

The first inequality defines the facet that links the left most possible point $(\min(D_x), f(\min(D_x)))$ and a possible point $(u, f(u))$ such that $u \in D_x$, $f(u) \in D_y$ and the slope $s_1 = \frac{f(u) - f(\min(D_x))}{u - \min(D_x)}$ is *maximal*. The valid inequality is then

$$y \le s_1 x - (f(\min(D_x)) - \min(D_x)) \times s_1)$$

The other inequality defines the facet that links the same point and a possible point $(u, f(u))$ such that the slope s_2 is *minimal*. Two others are defined the same way from the right most point $(\max(D_x), f(\max(D_x)))$ to a possible point of the function such that the slopes s_3 and s_4 are respectively maximal and minimal. The properties maintained are then:

$$\forall(y = f(x)) \in P, \ (y \leq s_i x - (f(\min(D_x)) - \min(D_x)) \times s_i) \in Q, \ i \in \{1,4\}$$
$$\forall(y = f(x)) \in P, \ (y \geq s_i x - (f(\min(D_x)) - \min(D_x)) \times s_i) \in Q, \ i \in \{2,3\}$$

Similar reasoning can be done for $\min(D_y)$ and $\max(D_y)$ to find the four other valid inequalities.

These valid inequalities are represented in Figure 3. The valid inequalities are represented by thin lines. In this example, generating these valid inequalities provides the convex hull of the solution set.

These valid inequalities are generated from a reasoning on the high level formulation of the constraint $y = f(x)$. This would be much harder to do from the linear formulation. As a consequence, the valid inequalities are sparse and the set of inequalities subsumes a set obtained with larger domains for x and y. Removing the inequalities introduced at a previous step ensures that at most 8 valid inequalities for each piecewise linear function are simultaneously in the linear relaxation.

To avoid an excessive increase in size of the linear relaxation, these valid inequalities are added as cutting planes, that is, only when they are violated by the relaxed optimal solution. Once cutting planes have been generated for each constraint, a dual simplex optimization is performed. New inequalities may then be violated, so the process is repeated until all inequalities are satisfied.

4.5 Search Strategy

Our strategy for exploring the search tree is based on a depth-first branch & bound [21]. This is the strategy used in most constraint programming systems. It is well suited when generating constraints local to a node of the search tree.

The heuristic we have developed exploits the original formulation of piecewise linear functions and not the linear formulation. For a variable x its value in the relaxed optimal solution is noted x^*. If for every constraint $y = f(x)$, we have $y^* = f(x^*)$, then the optimal relaxed solution is an optimal solution of the (sub)problem considered. On the contrary, if we have $y^* \neq f(x^*)$ for some constraints, one of them is chosen and possible choices are enumerated. To choose, the *first fail principle* (in constraint programming terminology) also called the *maximum infeasibility rule* (in mathematical programming terminology) is applied. This principle (or rule) tries the most difficult part of the search tree first. Our criterion is to select first the constraint that is apparently the least satisfied, that is, that maximizes the value $|y^* - f(x^*)|$.

Once the function is chosen, we select the segment i of the function f from which the value x^* is the closest. The domain of x is then split by creating the choice point:
$$x < X_i \ \vee \ x \geq X_i$$
where X_i is the x-coordinate of the starting point of the segment i. The two sub problems are then considered alternatively by the branch & bound procedure.

5 Experimental Results

The tight cooperation scheme presented above for piecewise linear optimization is integrated in the C++ library **ILOG Planner 3.2**. This tool merges the linear programming algorithms of **ILOG CPLEX 6.5.2** and the domain reduction techniques and search programming of **ILOG Solver 4.4**.

The experimental results presented in this section compare several cooperative schemes and a MIP solver over 3 types of problems. For each of them we describe the piecewise linear model and give some explanations about the results obtained.

5.1 The Systems

The systems we compare are

- Planner without cooperation (constraints are added to the linear optimizer only, no domain reduction is done), denoted **LinOpt**;
- Planner with classical cooperation, denoted **Classical**;
- Planner with tight cooperation using variable fixing only, denoted **Tight Fix**;
- Planner with tight cooperation using variable fixing and cutting planes generation, denoted **Tight Cut**;
- CPLEX MIP solver which uses a mixed integer programming (MIP) formulation of piecewise linear functions, best-estimation-first search, and a combination of several linear optimization techniques; with parameters set to default, denoted **CPLEX**.

The MIP formulation make use of the convex hull and adds the requirement that at most two consecutive λ_i variables can be non-zero [15]. It uses a special structure called a *special ordered set* (SOS), that is considered only during the search process [3]. This approach is widely used for solving piecewise linear optimization problems.

In these tests, Planner uses the dual simplex of CPLEX for maintaining the relaxed optimal solution. All tests were made on a PC with a Pentium Pro 200 and 100 Mb of memory under Windows NT. All times are given in seconds (**Time**). The search space size is given in number of choice points for Planner and number of nodes for CPLEX (**Size**).

5.2 Transportation Problem

The transportation problem consists of delivering goods from suppliers to customers [12]. Suppliers have a maximum capacity and customers have a miminal demand to satisfy. The cost of delivering to a customer from a supplier is a piecewise linear function of the quantity shipped. This function is

$$f_{\{200,400\},\{24000,40000\},120,50,\emptyset}$$

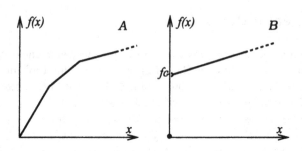

Fig. 4. Piecewise linear functions used in test problems

and is represented in figure 4. Observe that for this kind of piecewise linear function, tight cooperation with cuts maintains the convex hull of the solution set.

Two problems are solved: one with 3 suppliers and 4 customers and one with 6 suppliers and 10 customers. Although small, the second instance is difficult to solve.

The results are shown in Figure 5. On the first problem, they clearly show the superiority of tight cooperation with cutting planes over all other approaches. It is the only approach that can solve the second problem in reasonable time. Note that for this problem, the number of nodes opened by CPLEX is so large that it runs out of memory. Classical and tight cooperation with variable fixing provide the same reduction of the search space on both problems because the number of segments of the function is small and thus they provide the same tightening. Note also that the linear optimizer alone (LinOpt) using the previously described high-level search strategy, gives better performances than CPLEX MIP. This is due to search startegies that are less relevant when applied to a destructured problem.

5.3   Fixed Charge Problem

The other set of problems considered are small fixed charge problems from the instances maintained by J Gottlieb[1]. The objective function contains several different fixed cost functions. For instance the problem **gr4x6** has $4 \times 6 = 24$ different piecewise linear functions. When the quantity x is 0, the cost $f(x)$ is zero. When $x > 0$, the cost is greater to a fixed value and also depends on the quantity (see graphic B of figure 4). Here again, tight cooperation with cuts maintains the convex hull of the solution set on this kind of function.

The results are also shown in Figure 5. Again, tight cooperation with cutting planes generation is clearly superior to other approaches at least for the two biggest problems. For the first instance, the search space reduction does not compensate for the cost of reducing it. The line CPLEX (2) gives the results

---

[1] Problems are at http://www.in.tu-clausthal.de/gottlieb/benchmarks/fctp/

Problem	Transp. 3 × 4		Transp. 6 × 10		FC bk4x3		FCgr4x6		FC bal8x12	
Solver	Size	Time	Size	Time	Size	Time	Size	Time	Size	Time
CPLEX	161300	214.6	> 2.10^5 *	> 1500	48	0.2	1671	3.6	> 10^5 *	> 4.10^3
CPLEX(2)	-	-	-	-	1	0.2	3	0.2	8	0.6
LinOpt	15474	58.8	> 4.10^6	> 4.10^4	42	0.5	4196	40.1	> 4.10^4	> 4.10^4
Classical	7800	37.8	> 4.10^6	> 4.10^4	15	6.4	1291	12.5	19856	215.7
Tight Fix	7800	38.8	> 4.10^6	> 4.10^4	15	6.5	1291	13.4	19852	227.8
Tight Cut	87	1.2	4441	1685.2	5	2.1	17	1.1	79	12.4

* the system runs out of memory.

Fig. 5. Results on Transportation and Fixed-Charge Problems

obtained by using a linear formulation specific to fixed charge problems that uses a 0-1 variable for each piecewise linear function [24]. On this formulation which has more structural information, CPLEX MIP is very effective thanks to flow cover cut generation (see [24]). However on the classical formulation it runs out of memory on the larger instance.

5.4 Non-Linear Separable Programming Problems

A non linear separable programming problem is a problem composed of linear constraints and constraints of the form $y = g(x)$ where g is a non linear function [3]. Such functions can be approximated by a piecewise linear function with small intervals on x. This has been used for decades for solving some non-linear problems. We solved two optimization problems taken from [22] that can be transformed into separable form. Consecutive breakpoints are separated by 0.01 on the x axis.

	LinOpt		Classical		Tight Fix		Tight Cut		CPLEX	
Problem	Size	Time	Size	Time	Size	Time	Size	Time	Size	Time
Ineq1	211	51.2	107	19.2	17	7.3	16	8.1	212	12.7
H100	615	24.7	412	18.6	53	11.2	53	12.5	724	21.1

Fig. 6. Results on Non-Linear Separable Problems

The results are shown in Figure 6. CPLEX MIP behaves well on these problems but tight cooperation gives better results that other approaches. Note that the cutting plane generation is almost without effect. This is due to the step used for piecewise linear functions: fixing λ_i variables is sufficient to have nearly the convex hull of each constraint.

6 Conclusion

We have presented a cooperative framework that merges a domain reduction solver and a linear optimizer. The linear formulation of the problem is dynamically tightened around the new solution set of each constraint as domains are reduced. This tightening is done by bounding variables of the linear relaxation and by generating locally valid cutting planes. Compared to cutting plane generation in integer programming techniques, our approach is rather different. The goal in integer programming is to generate facets of the original problem. Tight cooperation is more related to domain reduction on a linear relaxation. The goal is to tighten the linear relaxation of each constraint in order to improve the relaxed optimal solution and to detect failures earlier.

The application to piecewise linear optimization problems demonstrates the effectiveness of this approach. In particular, reasoning at a high level permits tightening the linearization smartly by adding cutting planes while removing irrelevant ones. It also permits the development of branching strategies using relaxed optimal solutions while ignoring the linear formulation. Practical results demonstrate the effectiveness of the method. The search space is reduced; optimal solutions are found earlier; classical cooperation and mixed integer optimizers are outperformed on some examples.

Acknowledgments

The author is grateful to Jean-Francois Puget and Michel Rueher for benficial remarks on an earlier version of this paper.

References

1. ILOG CPLEX 6.5. *User Manual.* ILOG, S.A., Gentilly, France, June 1999.
2. B. De Backer and H. Beringer. Cooperative solvers and global constraints: The case of linear arithmetic constraints. In *Proceedings of the Post Conference Workshop on Constraint, Databases and Logic Programming, ILPS'95*, 1995.
3. E. Beale and J. Forrest. Global optimization using special ordered sets. *Mathematical Programming*, 10:52–69, 1976.
4. F. Benhamou. Heterogeneous Constraint Solving. In *Proceedings of the fifth International Conference on Algebraic and Logic Programming (ALP'96), LNCS 1139*, pages 62–76, Aachen, Germany, 1996. Springer-Verlag.
5. H. Beringer and B. de Backer. Combinatorial problem solving in constraint logic programming with cooperating solvers. In *Logic Programming : Formal Methods and Practical Applications*. Elsevier Science Publishers, 1994.
6. D. Bertsimas and J. N. Tsitsiklis. *Introduction to Linear Optimization*. Athena Scientific, Belmont, Massachusetts, 1997.
7. A. Bockmayer and T. Kasper. Branch and infer: A unifying framework for integer and finite domain constraint programming. *INFORMS Journal on Computing*, 10(3):287–300, 1998.

8. A. Colmerauer. Spécifications de Prolog IV. Technical report, Laboratoire d'Informatique de Marseille, 1996.
9. A. Conn and M. Mongeau. Discontinuous piecewise linear optimization. *Mathematical Programming*, 80:315–380, 1998.
10. R. Fourer. A simplex algorithm for piecewise-linear programing iii: Computational analysis and applications. *Mathematical Programming*, 53:213–235, 1992.
11. R. Fourer. Solving piecewise-linear programs: Experiments with a simplex approach. *ORSA Journal on Computing*, 4:16–31, 1992.
12. Robert Fourer, David M. Gay, and Brian W. Kernighan. *AMPL - A Modelling Langage for Mathematical Programming*. The Scientific Press, 1993.
13. J. N. Hooker and M. A. Osorio. Mixed logical / linear programming. *Discrete Applied Mathematics*, 1996. to appear.
14. O. Lhomme. Consistency techniques for numeric CSPs. In *Proceedings of IJCAI'93*, pages 232–238, 1993.
15. G. Nemhauser and L. Wolsey. *Integer and Combinatorial Optimization*. John Wiley and Sons, New York, 1988.
16. ILOG Planner 3.2. *User Manual*. ILOG, S.A., Gentilly, France, June 1999.
17. P. Refalo. Approaches to the incremental detection of implicit equalities with the revised simplex method. In *Proceedings of 10th International Symposium PLILP 98, LNCS 1490*, pages 481–496, Pise, Italy, September 1998. Springer-Verlag.
18. R. Rodosek and M. Wallace. A generic model and hybrid algorithm for hoist scheduling problems. In *Proceedings of the 4th International Conference on Principles and Practice of Constraint Programming - CP'98*, pages 385 – 399, Pisa, Italy, 1998. Also in LNCS 1520.
19. M. Rueher and C. Solnon. Concurrent cooperating solvers over the reals. *Reliable Computing*, 3(3):325–333, 1997.
20. ILOG Solver 4.4. *User Manual*. ILOG, S.A., Gentilly, France, June 1999.
21. P. van Hentenryck. *Constraint Satisfaction in Logic Programming*. MIT Press, Cambridge, Mass., 1989.
22. P. van Hentenryck, L. Michel, and Y. Deville. *Numerica: A Modelling Langage for Global Optimization*. MIT Press, Cambridge, Mass., 1997.
23. P. van Hentenryck, V. Saraswat, and Y. Deville. Constraint processing in cc(FD). Technical report, CS Departement, Brown University, 1992.
24. L.A. Wolsey. *Integer Programming*. Wiley, 1998.

Arc Consistency
for Global Cardinality Constraints with Costs

Jean-Charles Régin

ILOG
1681, route des Dolines
06560 Valbonne, France
e-mail : regin@ilog.fr

Abstract. A global cardinality constraint (gcc) is specified in terms of a set of variables $X = \{x_1, ..., x_p\}$ which take their values in a subset of $V = \{v_1, ..., v_d\}$. It constrains the number of times each value $v_i \in V$ is assigned to a variable in X to be in an interval $[l_i, u_i]$. A gcc with costs (costgcc) is a generalization of a gcc in which a cost is associated with each value of each variable. Then, each solution of the underlying gcc is associated with a global cost equal to the sum of the costs associated with the assigned values of the solution. A costgcc constrains the global cost to be less than a given value. Cardinality constraints with costs have proved very useful in many real-life problems, such as traveling salesman problems, scheduling, rostering, or resource allocation. For instance, they are useful for expressing preferences or for defining constraints such as a constraint on the sum of all different variables. In this paper, we present an efficient way of implementing arc consistency for a costgcc. We also study the incremental behavior of the proposed algorithm.

1 Introduction

Constraint satisfaction problems (CSPs) form a simple formal frame to represent and solve certain problems in artificial intelligence. They involve finding values for problem variables subject to constraints on which combinations are acceptable. The problem of the existence of solutions to the CSP is NP-complete. Therefore, methods have been developed to simplify the CSP before or during the search for solutions. The use of filtering algorithms associated with constraints is one of the most promising methods. A filtering algorithm associated with one constraint aims to remove values that are not consistent with the constraint. When all the values that are inconsistent with the constraint are deleted by the filtering algorithm we say that it achieves the arc consistency.

The design of specific filtering algorithms for some constraints is necessary to solve some CSPs. For instance, [Van Hentenryck et al., 1992] have studied monotonic and functional binary constraints. Furthermore, it is also necessary to deal with global constraints. This has been clearly shown by the great interest in solving some real-world problems using the constraints: diff-n, alldiff

[Régin, 1994], cumulative [Beldiceanu and Contejean, 1994], global cardinality constraint [Régin, 1996].

A global constraint can be seen as the conjunction of a set of constraints. For instance an alldiff constraint involving the variables x, y and z, gathers together all the binary $\neq$ constraints between variables x, y and z. The advantage of dealing with global constraints is that the globality of the constraint can be taken into account. This means that, generally, the filtering algorithm associated with a global constraint is more powerful than the conjunction of the filtering algorithms associated with each underlying constraint if we take them separately. A gcc is specified in terms of a set of variables $X = \{x_1, ..., x_p\}$ which take their

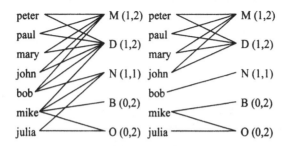

Fig. 1. An example of global constraint of cardinality.

values in a subset of $V = \{v_1, ..., v_d\}$. It constrains the number of times a value $v_i \in V$ is assigned variables in X to be in an interval $[l_i, u_i]$. Gccs arise in many real-life problems. For instance, consider the example derived from a real problem and given in [Caseau et al., 1993]. The task is to schedule managers for a directory-assistance center, with 5 activities (set A), 7 persons (set P) over 7 days (set W). Let us study only one part of this problem: Each day, a person has to perform an activity from the set A and we may have a minimum and maximum number of times that this activity can be performed. This constraint can be exactly formulated as gcc. It can be represented by a bipartite graph called a value graph (left graph in Figure 1). The left set corresponds to the person set, the right set to the activity set. There exists an edge between a person and an activity when the person can perform the activity. For each activity, the numbers in parentheses express the minimum and the maximum number of times the activity has to be assigned. A gcc can be efficiently handled by designing specific algorithms for this constraint [Régin, 1996]. For the example we considered, the achievement of arc consistency for the gcc leads to the right graph in Figure 1. Such a result can be obtained only by taking into account the globality of the constraint. In this paper we propose to add costs to a gcc.

The addition of costs to an alldiff constraint, which is a particular case of gcc, has been studied by Caseau and Laburthe [Caseau and Laburthe, 1997]. How-

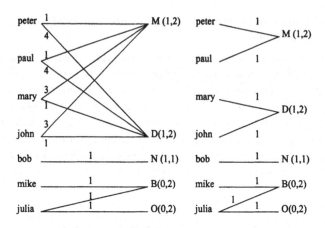

Fig. 2. An example of global cardinality with costs. The sum of the assignments must be strictly less than 12.

ever, they do not propose any filtering algorithm. They only show the interest of computing the consistency of such a constraint.

Consider again the previous example and suppose that each persons expresses some preferences on the activities that they can perform. These preferences can be represented by an integer. A small number indicates that the activity is preferred, while a large number corresponds to a penalty. Suppose also that there is for each day a constraint stating that the sum of the preferences must be less than a given number. For instance, consider Peter, Paul, Mary, and John. Peter has a preference 1 for the activity M and 4 for the activity D; Paul has a preference 1 for the activity M and 4 for the activity D; Mary and John a preference of 1 for the activity D and 3 for the activity M. For all the other persons preferences are 1 for all the activities. Preferences can be represented by costs in the value graph. (See Figure 2.) A preference p between a person and an activity corresponds to the cost p on the edge between the person and the activity. Thus, we can associate with each person a variable whose domain is defined by the preferences of the person. When an activity is assigned to a person, the variable associated with this person is instantiated to the preference of the person for this activity. We will denote by CPeter, CPaul, CMary, CJohn, CBob, CMike, CJulia these variables. CPeter can take the values 1 or 4; CPaul 1 or 4; CMary 1 or 3; CJohn 1 or 3; CBob, CMike, CJulia are instantiated to 1. The minimal solution has a cost 7 (each person is assigned to his preferred activity). Suppose that a solution with a global cost greater than 11 is not acceptable. This constraint on preferences corresponds to a sum constraint involving the variables associated with every person. More precisely, it is defined by CPeter + CPaul + CMary + CJohn + CBob + CMike + CJulia $<= 11$. If we consider this sum constraint independently from the gcc, nothing will be deduced because the greatest value of cost variables is consistent with the sum constraint: $4+1+1+1+1+1+1 = 10 <= 11$, so no value is removed. However, we can prove, for instance, that it is impossible to have the value 4 for CPeter. This means that the assignment (Peter,D) is incompatible w.r.t. the gcc in conjunction with the sum constraint. Suppose that Peter is assigned to D, then D can also be assigned to Mary or John for a cost 1, but together they cannot be assigned to D, because D can be assigned at the most twice. Thus Mary or John must be assigned to M for a cost 3. The minimum cost if Peter is assigned to D is: $4+1+1+3 = 9$. For the other persons their contribution is 3. The minimum global cost is 12 and so violates the acceptability constraint. The right graph of Figure 2 shows the result of the achievement of arc consistency for the costgcc.

In this paper we present an efficient way of implementing generalized arc consistency for the costgcc. The filtering algorithm is based on the minimum cost flow algorithm.

First, we give some preliminaries on graphs, constraint satisfaction problems and flows, because our results are based on flow theory. Then, we present an algorithm checking the consistency of a costgcc. Afterwards, we propose a simple algorithm for achieving generalized arc consistency, which is based on a new proposition in the flow theory. Finally, we conclude.

2 Preliminaries

2.1 Graph

The following definitions are due to [Tarjan, 1983].

A *directed graph* or *digraph* $G = (X, U)$ consists of a *vertex set* X and an *arc set* U, where every arc (u, v) is an ordered pair of distinct vertices. We will denote by $X(G)$ the vertex set of G and by $U(G)$ the arc set of G. The *cost* of an arc is a value associated with the arc.

A *path* from node v_1 to node v_k in G is a list of nodes $[v_1, ..., v_k]$ such that (v_i, v_{i+1}) is an arc for $i \in [1..k-1]$. The path *contains* node v_i for $i \in [1..k]$ and arc (v_i, v_{i+1}) for $i \in [1..k-1]$. The path is *simple* if all its nodes are distinct. The path is a *cycle* if $k > 1$ and $v_1 = v_k$. The *length* of a path p, denoted by $length(p)$, is the sum of the costs of the arcs contained in p. A *shortest path* from a node s to a node t is a path from s to t whose length is minimum. A cycle of negative length is called a *negative cyle*. Let s and t be nodes, there is a shortest path from s to t if and only if there exists a path from s to t and no path from s to t contains a negative cycle. If there is a shortest path from s to t, there is one that is simple. $S(m, n, \gamma)$ denotes the complexity of the search for shortest paths from a node to every node in a graph with m arcs, n nodes, a maximal capacity γ and with nonnegative arcs costs.

2.2 Flows

Let G be a graph for which each arc (i, j) is associated with three integers l_{ij}, u_{ij}, and c_{ij}, respectively called the *lower bound capacity*, the *upper bound capacity* and the *cost* of the arc.

A *flow* in G is a function x satisfying the following two conditions:

• For any arc (i, j), x_{ij} represents the amount of some commodity that can "flow" through the arc. Such a flow is permitted only in the indicated direction of the arc, i.e., from i to j.

• A *conservation law* is observed at each of the nodes[1]: $\forall j \in X(G) : \sum_i x_{ij} = \sum_k x_{jk}$.

The *cost* of a flow x is $cost(x) = \sum_{(i,j) \in U(G)} x_{ij} c_{ij}$.

We will consider three problems of flow theory:

• *the feasible flow problem*: Does there exist a flow in G that satisfies the *capacity constraint*, that is: $\forall (i, j) \in U(G) : l_{ij} \leq x_{ij} \leq u_{ij}$?

• *the problem of the maximum flow for an arc (i, j)*: Find a feasible flow in G for which the value of x_{ij} is maximum.

• *the minimum cost flow problem*: If there exists a feasible flow, find a feasible flow x such that $cost(x)$ is minimum.

Without loss of generality, and to overcome notational difficulties, we will consider that:[2]

• if (i, j) is an arc of G then (j, i) is not an arc of G.

• all boundaries of capacities are nonnegative integers.

The following well known theorem shows the interest of integral bound for the capacities:

Theorem 1 *If all the upper bounds and all the lower bounds are integers and if there exists a feasible flow, then for any arc (i, j) there exists a maximum flow from j to i which is integral on every arc in G.*

2.3 CSP

A finite *constraint network* $\mathcal{N}$ is defined as a set of n *variables* $X = \{x_1, \ldots, x_n\}$, a set of current *domains* $\mathcal{D} = \{D(x_1), \ldots, D(x_n)\}$ where $D(x_i)$ is the finite set of possible *values* for variable x_i, and a set $\mathcal{C}$ of *constraints* between variables. We introduce the particular notation $\mathcal{D}_0 = \{D_0(x_1), \ldots, D_0(x_n)\}$ to represent the set of initial domains of $\mathcal{N}$. Indeed, we consider that any constraint network $\mathcal{N}$ can be associated with an initial domain $\mathcal{D}_0$ (containing $\mathcal{D}$), on which constraint definitions were stated.

A *constraint* C on the ordered set of variables $X(C) = (x_{i_1}, \ldots, x_{i_r})$ is a subset $T(C)$ of the Cartesian product $D_0(x_{i_1}) \times \cdots \times D_0(x_{i_r})$ that specifies the *allowed* combinations of values for the variables $x_{i_1} \times \ldots \times x_{i_r}$. An element of $D_0(x_{i_1}) \times \cdots \times D_0(x_{i_r})$ is called a *tuple* on $X(C)$. $|X(C)|$ is the *arity* of C.

A value a for a variable x is often denoted by (x, a). $\mathbf{var}(C, i)$ represents the ith variable of $X(C)$, while $\mathbf{index}(C, x)$ is the position of variable x in $X(C)$. $\tau[k]$ denotes the kth value of the tuple τ. $D(X)$ denotes the union of domains of variables of X (i.e. $D(X) = \cup_{x_i \in X} D_{x_i}$). $\#(a, \tau)$ is the number of occurrences of the value a in the tuple τ.

---

[1] For convenience, we assume $x_{ij} = 0$ if $(i, j) \notin U(G)$.

[2] This is not a limitation see p.45 and p.297 in [Ahuja et al., 1993].

Let C be a constraint. A tuple τ on $X(C)$ is *valid* if $\forall(x, a) \in \tau, a \in D(x)$. C is *consistent* iff there exists a tuple τ of $T(C)$ which is valid. A value $a \in D(x)$ is *consistent with* C iff $x \notin X(C)$ or there exists a valid tuple τ of $T(C)$ with $a = \tau[\text{index}(C, x)]$. A constraint is *arc consistent* iff $\forall x_i \in X(C), D(x_i) \neq \emptyset$ and $\forall a \in D(x_i)$, a is consistent with C.

The *value graph* [Laurière, 1978] of an non-binary constraint C is the bipartite graph $GV(C) = (X(C), D(X(C)), E)$ where $(x, a) \in E$ iff $a \in D_x$.

2.4 Global Cardinality Constraints with costs

Throughout this paper, we are interested in global cardinality constraints with costs (costgcc). They introduce cost in global cardinality constraints that are defined by the minimal and the maximal number of times each value of $D(X(C))$ must appear in each tuple of the constraints. The minimal and the maximal number of occurrences of each value can be different from the others. More formally we have:

Definition 1 *A* **global cardinality constraint** *is a constraint C in which each value $a_i \in D(X(C))$ is associated with two positive integers l_i and u_i and*
$$T(C) = \{\, \tau \text{ such that } \tau \text{ is a tuple of } X(C)$$
$$\text{and } \forall a_i \in D(X(C)) : l_i \leq \#(a_i, \tau) \leq u_i\}$$
It is denoted by $gcc(X, l, u)$.

Definition 2 *A* **cost function** *on a variable set X is a function which associates with each value (x, a), $x \in X$ and $a \in D(x)$ an integer denoted by $cost(x, a)$.*

A costgcc is the conjunction of a gcc constraint and a sum constraint:

Definition 3 *A* **global cardinality constraint with costs** *is a constraint C associated with* **cost** *a cost function on $X(C)$, an integer H and in which each value $a_i \in D(X(C))$ is associated with two positive integers l_i and u_i*
$$T(C) = \{\, \tau \text{ such that } \tau \text{ is a tuple of } X(C)$$
$$\text{and } \forall a_i \in D(X(C)) : l_i \leq \#(a_i, \tau) \leq u_i$$
$$\text{and } \Sigma_{i=1}^{|X(C)|} cost(\text{var}(C, i), \tau[i]) \leq H \,\}$$
It is denoted by $costgcc(X, l, u, cost, H)$.

There is no assumption made on the sign of the costs.

3 Consistency for a costgcc

A gcc C is consistent iff there is a special flow in an oriented graph $N(C)$ called the value network of C [Régin, 1996]:

Definition 4 *Given $C = gcc(X, l, u)$ be a gcc; the* **value network** *of C is the oriented graph $N(C)$ with lower bound capacity and upper bound capacity on each arc. $N(C)$ is obtained from the value graph $GV(C)$, by:*

• *orienting each edge of $GV(C)$ from values to variables. For such an arc* (u, v): $l_{uv} = 0$ *and* $u_{uv} = 1$.

    • *adding a vertex s and an arc from s to each value. For such an arc* (s, a_i): $l_{sa_i} = l_i$, $u_{sa_i} = u_i$.

    • *adding a vertex t and an arc from each variable to t. For such an arc* (x, t): $l_{xt} = 1$, $u_{xt} = 1$.

    • *adding an arc (t, s) with* $l_{ts} = u_{ts} = |X(C)|$.

Proposition 1 *Let C be a gcc and $N(C)$ be the value network of C; the following two properties are equivalent:*

    • *C is consistent;*

    • *there is a feasible flow in $N(C)$.*

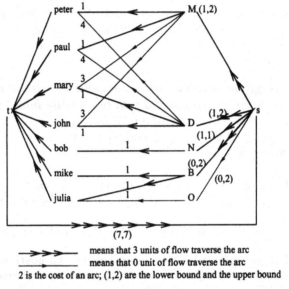

    →→→ means that 3 units of flow traverse the arc
    —— means that 0 unit of flow traverse the arc
    2 is the cost of an arc; (1,2) are the lower bound and the upper bound

Fig. 3. An example of the value network associated with a costgcc. An optimal solution is indicated by the bold edges.

Similarly, we can define the value network associated with a costgcc. (See Figure 3.)

Definition 5 *Given $C = costgcc(X, l, u, cost, H)$; the **value network** of C is the value network $N(C')$ of the underlying gcc $C' = gcc(X, l, u)$ of C, in which each arc has a cost defined as follows:*

    • $\forall a \in D(X(C)) : c_{sa} = 0$

    • $\forall x \in X(C) : c_{xt} = 0$

    • $c_{ts} = 0$

    • $\forall x \in X(C) : \forall a \in D(x) : c_{ax} = cost(x, a)$.

Note that this network is independent of H.

    For convenience, let $m = |U(N(C))|$ (i.e. the number of arcs in $N(C)$), $n = |X(C)|$ (i.e. the number of variables involved in $N(C)$) and $d = |D(X(C))|$

(i.e. the number of values involved in $N(C)$) and γ be the greatest cost involved in $N(C)$.

We can present the original proposition:

Proposition 2 *Given $C = costgcc(X, l, u, cost, H)$ and $N(C)$ the value network of C; the following two properties are equivalent:*
- *C is consistent;*
- *there is a minimum cost flow in $N(C)$ with a cost less than or equal to H.*

proof: Let C' be the gcc invoked in C. By proposition 1, C' is consistent if and only if there is a feasible flow in $N(C)$. Thus, from each feasible flow in $N(C)$ a tuple of $T(C')$ can be built and from each element of $T(C')$ a feasible flow in $N(C)$ can be defined. Every feasible flow has a cost. If this cost is less than or equal to H then a tuple of $T(C')$ is a tuple of $T(C)$. Moreover, a tuple of $T(C)$ is a tuple of $T(C')$ which corresponds to a feasible flow of cost less than H. $\odot$

There is no need to use sophisticated algorithms for computing the consistency of a costgcc, because the structure of $N(C)$ is particular. (See Theorem 12.2 p473 in [Ahuja et al., 1993]) The successive shortest path algorithm is easy to implement (see [Ahuja et al., 1993] p320) and achieves the consistency of a costgcc in $O(nS(m, n + d, \gamma))$[3]. Moreover, often in constraint programming, the consistency of the constraints are systematically checked during the search for solutions. In this case, we can use an incremental minimum cost flow algorithm, like the out-of-kilter (see in [Ahuja et al., 1993] p326). This means that if k values are deleted from the previous call of the consistency algorithm, then the consistency can be computed in $O(kS(m, n + d, \gamma))$.

4 Arc consistency for a costgcc

In order to present the new algorithm we propose, we need further definitions of flow theory.

Definition 6 *The* residual graph *for a given flow x in $N(C)$, denoted by $R(x)$, is the digraph with the same node set as $N(C)$. The arc set of $R(x)$ is defined as follows:*
$\forall(i, j) \in U(N(C))$:
- *If $x_{ij} < u_{ij}$, then $(i, j) \in U(R(x))$ and has cost $rc_{ij} = c_{ij}$ and upper bound capacity $r_{ij} = u_{ij} - x_{ij}$.*
- *If $x_{ij} > l_{ij}$ then $(j, i) \in U(R(x))$ and has cost $rc_{ji} = -c_{ij}$ and upper bound capacity $r_{ji} = x_{ij} - l_{ij}$.*
The upper bound capacities are called residual capacities.
All the lower bound capacities are equal to 0.

We have proved the following proposition [Régin, 1996].

---

[3] $S(m, n + d, \gamma)$ is defined in section 2.

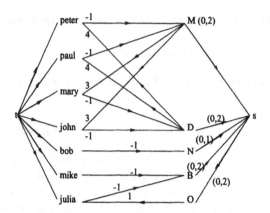

2 is the residual cost of an arc; (1,2) are the lower bound and the upper bound

Fig. 4. The residual graph of the optimal solution given in Figure 3.

Proposition 3 *Let C be a consistent gcc and f be a feasible flow in $N(C)$. A value a of a variable x is not consistent with C if and only if $f_{ax} = 0$ and a and x do not belong to the same strongly connected component in $R(f)$.*

The advantage of this proposition is that all the values not consistent with the gcc can be determined by only one identification of the strongly connected components in $R(f)$. The search for strongly connected components of a graph can be done in $O(m+n)$ [Tarjan, 1983], thus a remarkable complexity for computing arc consistency for a gcc is obtained.

Corollary 1 *Let C be a consistent gcc and f be a feasible flow in $N(C)$. Arc consistency for C can be achieved in $O(m)$.[4]*

In order to avoid any problem of the existence of a path from a node to another node, we will consider that the arc consistency algorithm of the underlying gcc has been applied, and that we consider successively each strongly connected component.

Nevertheless, with a costgcc the problem is more complex than with a gcc, because with a gcc we need only to know whether there is a cycle containing a given arc or not. With a costgcc we need to identify whether there is a particular cycle containing a given arc, that is, a cycle with a length greater than a given value, because there are costs on arcs and the global bound must be satisfied.

Definition 7
- A potential *function is a function π which associates with each node $i \in X(N(C))$ a number $\pi(i)$, which is referred as the* potential *of that node.*
- *With respect to the node potentials, the* reduced cost c_{ij}^{π} *of an arc (i,j) in $R(x)$ is defined by:*

$$c_{ij}^{\pi} = rc_{ij} - \pi(i) + \pi(j)$$

---

[4] In our case, $m \geq n + d$.

399

Theorem 2 *A feasible solution $\hat{x}$ is an optimal solution of the minimum cost flow problem if and only if some set of node potentials π satisfies* reduced cost optimality conditions: $c_{ij}^\pi \geq 0$ *for every arc* (i,j) *in* $R(x)$.

proof: see [Ahuja et al., 1993]. ⊙

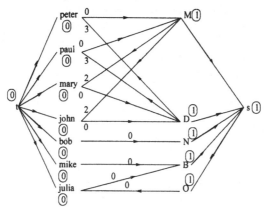

2 is the reduced cost of an arc; ① is the potential of the node

Fig. 5. A potential function and the reduced costs of residual graph given in Figure 4. The path [julia,B,s,O] has a cost 0 and $c_{Ojulia}^\pi = 0$, thus $(julia, O)$ is consistent with the constraint. The shortest path from john to M has a cost 3 and $c_{Mjohn}^\pi = 2$, thus $7 + 3 + 2 > 11$ and $(john, M)$ is not consistent with the constraint.

Given x^o a minimum cost flow in $N(C)$. The potential function $\pi^o(i) = d_t^{x^o}(i)$, where $d_t^{x^o}(i)$ represents the shortest paths distance in $R(x^o)$ from node t to every node in i, is an example of potential function that satisfies the reduced cost optimality conditions.

For convenience we will consider that:
- $C = costgcc(X, l, u, cost, H)$ is a consistent costgcc;
- x^o is a given optimal solution of the minimum cost flow problem in $N(C)$;
- π^o is a given potential function that satisfies the reduced cost optimality conditions;
- $d_i^{x^o,\pi^o}(k)$ is the shortest path distance from node i to every node k in $R(x^o)$ with $c_{uv}^{\pi^o}$ as the length of an arc (u, v);
- $d_{i,j}^{x^o,\pi^o}(k)$ is the shortest path distance from node i to every node k in the residual graph $R(x^o) - \{(i,j)\}$ with $c_{uv}^{\pi^o}$ as the length of an arc (u, v).

We can define an original correspondence between the consistency of a value with a costgcc and a particular path in the value network. (See figure 5.)

Proposition 4 *A value a of a variable y is not consistent with C if and only if the two following properties hold:*
(i) $x_{ay}^o = 0$
(ii) $d_{y,a}^{x^o,\pi^o}(a) > H - cost(x^o) - c_{ay}^{\pi^o}$

sketch of proof: See in [Régin, 1999] for a full proof. Consider an arc (a, y) for which $x^o_{ay} = 0$. The value a of y is consistent with C if the minimum cost flow in $N(C)$ in which the flow value of the arc (a, y) must be equal to 1 has a cost less than H. Imposing that the flow value of (a, y) must be equal to 1, is equivalent to setting $l_{ay} = u_{ay} = 1$. It is proven in flow theory that such a new feasible flow exists if and only if there is a path from y to a in $R(x^o) - \{(y, a)\}$. Then, this new feasible can be computed from x^o by sending one unit of flow along such a path. Moreover, it is proven that if this path is a shortest path in $R(x^o) - \{(a, y)\}$ with c^π_{uv} as the length of an arc (u, v), then the new flow is an optimal solution of the minimum cost flow in $N(C)$ in which $l_{ay} = 1$. (See Lemma 9.12 p321 in [Ahuja et al., 1993].) Furthermore, we can prove the cost of this new flow is equal to $cost(x^o) + d^{x^o, \pi^o}_{y,a}(a) + c^{\pi^o}_{ay}$. Therefore, if this value is greater than H, then the value a of y is not consistent with C. $\odot$

From this proposition we can define a simple algorithm for computing the arc consistency of a consistent costgcc:

> for every arc $\{a, y\}$: if the proposition does not hold then remove the arc from $N(C)$ and a from $D(y)$.

All the reduced costs are positive due to Theorem 2. Thus, the complexity of this algorithm is $O(mS(m, n + d, \gamma))$.

At first glance, it does not seem easy to improve this algorithm because for each value a of y the distance are computed in $R(x^o) - \{(y, a)\}$. However, in our case, when we search for a path from y to a, the arc (y, a) does not belong to $R(x^o)$ since $x^o_{ay} = 0 = l_{ay}$. Thus $R(x^o) - \{(y, a)\} = R(x^o)$.

Corollary 2 *The value a of y is not consistent with C if and only if*
$$x^o_{ay} = 0 \text{ and } d^{x^o, \pi^o}_y(a) > H - cost(x^o) - c^{\pi^o}_{ay}.$$

Thus, if for each variable y we compute the shortest path distance from y to every node in $R(x^o)$, we will be able to compute the arc consistency of a consistent costgcc. The complexity of this algorithm is $O(nS(m, n+d, \gamma))$ which is better than the previous one.

We can further use the particular structure of $R(x^o)$.

Corollary 3 *Let y be any variable such that $x^o_{by} = 1$. Then, the value a of y is not consistent with C if and only if*
$$x^o_{ay} = 0 \text{ and } d^{x^o, \pi^o}_b(a) > H - cost(x^o) - c^{\pi^o}_{ay} - c^{\pi^o}_{yb}.$$

proof: By definition of the value network and since C is consistent, (y, b) is the only one arc outgoing y in $R(x^o)$. Thus, $d^{x^o, \pi^o}_y(a) = d^{x^o, \pi^o}_y(b) + d^{x^o, \pi^o}_b(a) = c^{\pi^o}_{yb} + d^{x^o, \pi^o}_b(b)$, Hence by corollary 2 we have the corollary. $\odot$

Let Δ be the set of values b such that $x^o_{sb} > 0$. Consider such a value b, we will denote by $\delta(b)$ be the set of values defined by $\delta(b) = \{a \in D(X(C)) \text{ s.t. } a \neq b \text{ and } a \in D(y) \text{ and } x^o_{by} = 1\}$. Thus, arc consistency can be achieved by searching for each value b of Δ the shortest path distance from b to every node in $\delta(b)$. Algorithm 1 is a possible implementation of this algorithm. Function

ARCCONSISTENCY$(C, N(C), x^\circ, \pi^\circ)$
// x°, π° is an optimal solution of the minimum cost flow in $N(C)$
$\Delta \leftarrow \varnothing$
for *each value a* **do if** $x^\circ_{sa} > 0$ **then** $\Delta \leftarrow \Delta \cup \{a\}$
for *each value* $b \in \Delta$ **do**
$\quad$ $\delta(b) \leftarrow \varnothing$
$\quad$ **for** *each arc* $(b, y) \in N(C)$ **do**
$\quad\quad$ **if** $x^\circ_{by} = 1$ **then**
$\quad\quad\quad$ **for** *each* $a \in D(y)$ **do** $\delta(b) \leftarrow \delta(b) \cup \{a\}$

$\quad$ remove b from $\delta(b)$
$\quad$ COMPUTESHORTESTPATHS$(b, \delta(b), R(x^\circ))$
$\quad$ **for** *each arc* $(b, y) \in N(C)$ **do**
$\quad\quad$ **if** $x^\circ_{by} = 1$ **then**
$\quad\quad\quad$ **for** *each* $a \in D(y)$ **do**
$\quad\quad\quad\quad$ **if** $d^{x^\circ, \pi^\circ}_b(a) > H - cost(x^\circ) - c^{\pi^\circ}_{ay} - c^{\pi^\circ}_{yb}$ **then** remove a from $D(y)$

Algorithm 1: Arc consistency algorithm for a costgcc.

COMPUTESHORTESTPATHS$(b, \delta(b), R(x^\circ))$ computes the shortest path in $R(x^\circ)$ from a node b to every node in $\delta(b)$.

Since we have $|\Delta| \leq min(n, d)$, the previous complexity is improved.

Property 1 *Let C be a consistent costgcc, x° be a minimum cost flow in $N(C)$ and π° be a potential function that satisfies the reduced cost optimality conditions. Arc consistency for C can be achieved in $O(|\Delta|S(m, n + d, \gamma))$.*

Note that since all the costs are nonnegative then we can use a Dijkstra's algorithm for computing the shortest paths.

Practical improvements

We can propose some heuristics for improving the behavior of the arc consistency algorithm in practice .

Let (a, y) be any arc with $x^\circ_{ay} = 0$ and b be the value with $x^\circ_{by} = 1$. First, if $c^{\pi^\circ}_{ay} > H - cost(x^\circ) - c^{\pi^\circ}_{yb}$ then we can immediately remove the value a from $D(y)$, since any shortest path distance is nonnegative. Using for each arc (b, y) with $x^\circ_{by} = 1$, $m(b) = min(\{c^{\pi^\circ}_{zb} + c^{\pi^\circ}_{zc}$ with $z \neq y$ and $c \in D(z)\})$ can refine this idea. Let $M = H - cost(x^\circ)$, then, (y, a) is not consistent with C if one of the following conditions holds:

- $x_{sa} < u_{sa}$ and $x_{sb} > l_{sb}$ and $c^{\pi^\circ}_{ay} > M - c^{\pi^\circ}_{yb}$
- $x_{sa} < u_{sa}$ and $x_{sb} = l_{sb}$ and $c^{\pi^\circ}_{ay} + m(b) > M$
- $x_{sa} = u_{sa}$ and $x_{sb} > l_{sb}$ and $c^{\pi^\circ}_{ay} + m(a) > M - c^{\pi^\circ}_{yb}$
- $x_{sa} = u_{sa}$ and $x_{sb} = l_{sb}$ and $c^{\pi^\circ}_{ay} + m(a) + m(b) > M$

Furthermore, it is not necessary to search for the shortest path distances from a value b in Δ to every node in $\delta(b)$. When all the current distances from b to nodes in $\delta(b)$ do not satisfy the inequality of corollary 3 we can stop the algorithm, because all the values of δ are consistent with the constraint. Moreover, if the current scanned node of the Disjkstra's algorithm is greater than $H - cost(x^o)$ then we can also stop the algorithm, because the shortest path distances of the nodes that have not been scanned will not be less than the $H - cost(x^o)$[5]. And since all the reduced costs are nonnegative, all the values that have not been scanned will satisfy corollary 3.

There are several possible ways for implementing the priority queue needed by the Dijkstra's algorithm [Cherkassky et al., 1996]. We can implement the Dijkstra's algorithm in $O(m + H)$ with a simple bucket data structure or in $O(m + n \log \gamma)$ with a radix heap data structure. We can also use a Fibonacci heap in order to obtain a strongly polynomial algorithm $O(m + n \log(n))$.

5 Discussion

5.1 Removal of negative costs

Consider $C = costgcc(X, l, u, cost, H)$ and suppose that some costs are negative. This constraint can be transformed into an equivalent one in which there are only nonnegative costs [Puget, 1999]. Let K be the minimum value of costs. If this value is added to all costs then all the obtained costs are nonnegative. In general this method does not work, because the problem is transformed. Indeed, two paths with a different number of arcs and the same length in the initial problem will have different length in the new problem. However, in our case, each variable will be instantiated to exactly one value, thus by adding K to each cost, the cost of the minimum cost flow will be increased by $|X|K$. This means that the constraint $costgcc(X, l, u, cost + K, H + |X|K)$, where $(cost + K)(e) = cost(e) + K$, is equivalent to the constraint $costgcc(X, l, u, cost, H)$, and contains only nonnegative costs.

5.2 Constraint on the sum of all different variables

An interesting example of costgcc is the constraint on the sum of all different variables. Some real-world problems involve this constraint. More precisely, for a given set of variable X, this constraint is the conjunction of the constraint $\sum_{x_i \in X} x_i \leq H$ and alldiff(X).

Let us define the boundaries and cost function as follows:
- For each value $a_i \in D(X)$ we define $l_i = 0$ and $u_i = 1$
- For each variable $x \in X$ and for each value $a \in D(x)$, $cost(x, a) = a$

Then, it is easy to prove that the costgcc constraint $costgcc(X, l, u, cost, H)$ represents the conjunction of the constraint $\sum_{x_i \in X} x_i \leq H$ and alldiff(X).

Thus, with the algorithm we propose, we are able for the first time to achieve arc consistency for this constraint.

---

[5] This point can be improved by studying each arc independently in order to take into account the residual costs.

Moreover, note that the constraint which is the conjunction of the constraint $\sum_{x_i \in X} \alpha_i x_i \leq H$ and alldiff(X), can also be represented by a costgcc, by defining in the previous model $cost(x_i, a) = \alpha_i a$.

5.3 Constraint on the minimum value of the sum

Suppose that instead of constraining the maximum value of the sum of an instantiation of any solution of a gcc, we would like to constraint the minimum value of this sum. More precisely for each tuple τ of a given gcc $C = gcc(X, l, u)$, we impose that $\sum_{i=1}^{|X(C)|} cost(\text{var}(C, i), \tau[i]) \geq L$.

In this case we have to solve a maximum cost flow problem instead of a minimum cost flow problem. This problem can be solved by replacing all costs by their opposite value. Therefore this constraint can be represented by the costgcc defined by $costgcc(X, l, u, -cost, L)$.

However, it is not easy, to take into account at the same time a constraint on the minimum value of the sum and on the maximum value. We can prove that there is a tuple which satisfies the lower bound condition on the sum, we can also proves that there is a tuple which satisfies the upper bound condition on the sum, but, unfortunately, we have absolutely no guarantee on the existence of a tuple that satisfies both these two conditions. For instance, consider the problem involving three variables x_1, x_2 and x_3 with $D(x_1) = \{a, b\}$, $D(x_2) = \{b, c\}$ and $D(x_3) = \{a, c\}$. Each value has to be taken at most 1. A cost function is defined as follows: $cost(x_1, a) = cost(x_2, b) = cost(x_3, c) = 1$ and $cost(x_1, b) = cost(x_2, c) = cost(x_3, a) = 3$. The sum of any instantiation of all the variables must be greater than 4 and less than 8. Clearly, there are only two possible ways for satisfying the gcc: $((x_1, a), (x_2, b), (x_3, c))$ and $((x_1, b), (x_2, c), (x_3, a))$. The cost of the first solution is 3 and satisfies $3 \leq 8$, the cost of the second one is 9 and satisfies $9 \geq 4$. However, this problem has no solution. We do not know any general algorithm for obtaining such a result.

5.4 Interest of shortest path distances as heuristic

We can use the information given by the shortest path distance for guiding the search for solutions, and in particular, for choosing the next variable to instantiate.

In many optimization problems, the *max-regret* heuristic is considered as one of the best heuristics. For each variable the regret can be defined as the difference between the cost of the best assignment and the cost of the second best. Then, the variable with the regret of maximal value is chosen. Intuitively, the idea is that if we do not choose this variable and if this variable is instantiated with a value different from the one leading to the best assignment, we will have to pay at least the value of the regret.

Usually, the regret is not exactly computed and an approximation of the regret is considered. For instance, the regret is often defined for every variable as the difference between the minimum cost involving this variable and the second minimum. With our approach it becomes possible to exactly compute the value of the regret, and so to improve the search for solution.

6 Conclusion

In this paper we have proposed an efficient way of implementing generalized arc-consistency for the global cardinality constraint with costs. We have shown that costgcc constraints are powerful constraints for modelling several conjunctions of constraints often arising in practice. We have also explained how the algorithms we propose can help in the definition of an interesting heuristic.

References

[Ahuja et al., 1993] Ahuja, R., Magnanti, T., and Orlin, J. (1993). *Network Flows*. Prentice Hall.

[Beldiceanu and Contejean, 1994] Beldiceanu, N. and Contejean, E. (1994). Introducing global constraints in chip. *Journal of Mathematical and Computer Modelling*, 20(12):97–123.

[Caseau et al., 1993] Caseau, Y., Guillo, P.-Y., and Levenez, E. (1993). A deductive and object-oriented approach to a complex scheduling problem. In *Proceedings of DOOD'93*.

[Caseau and Laburthe, 1997] Caseau, Y. and Laburthe, F. (1997). Solving various weighted matching problems with constraints. In *Proceedings CP97*, pages 17–31, Austria.

[Cherkassky et al., 1996] Cherkassky, B., Goldberg, A., and Radzik, T. (1996). Shortest paths algorithms: Theory and experimental evaluation. *Mathematical Programming*, 73:129–174.

[Laurière, 1978] Laurière, J.-L. (1978). A language and a program for stating and solving combinatorial problems. *Artificial Intelligence*, 10:29–127.

[Puget, 1999] Puget, J.-F. (1999). Personal communication.

[Régin, 1994] Régin, J.-C. (1994). A filtering algorithm for constraints of difference in CSPs. In *Proceedings AAAI-94*, pages 362–367, Seattle, Washington.

[Régin, 1996] Régin, J.-C. (1996). Generalized arc consistency for global cardinality constraint. In *Proceedings AAAI-96*, pages 209–215, Portland, Oregon.

[Régin, 1999] Régin, J.-C. (1999). Arc consistency for global cardinality constraints with costs. Technical report, ILOG Optimization Internal Report OIR-1999-2.

[Tarjan, 1983] Tarjan, R. (1983). *Data Structures and Network Algorithms*. CBMS-NSF Regional Conference Series in Applied Mathematics.

[Van Hentenryck et al., 1992] Van Hentenryck, P., Deville, Y., and Teng, C. (1992). A generic arc-consistency algorithm and its specializations. *Artificial Intelligence*, 57:291–321.

The Brélaz Heuristic and Optimal Static Orderings

Barbara M. Smith

The APES Research Group, School of Computer Studies,
University of Leeds, Leeds LS2 9JT, U.K.

Abstract. The order in which the variables are assigned can have an enormous impact on the time taken by a backtracking search algorithm to solve a constraint satisfaction problem (CSP). The Brélaz heuristic is a dynamic variable ordering heuristic which has been shown to give good results for some classes of binary CSPs when the constraint graph is not complete. Its advantage over the simpler smallest-domain heuristic is that it uses information about the constraint graph. This paper uses theoretical work by Nudel to assess the performance of the Brélaz heuristic. Nudel's work gives the expected number of nodes at each level of the search tree when using the forward checking algorithm to find all solutions to a CSP, given a specified order of the variables. From this, optimal static orderings are found for a sample of small binary CSPs. The optimal orderings are used to learn rules for a static ordering heuristic, which are converted into modifications to the Brélaz heuristic. The improved heuristic is shown to halve the mean search cost of solving sparse random binary CSPs with 50 variables, at the phase transition. However, our modifications, and the Brélaz heuristic itself, are mainly in the form of improved tie-breakers for the smallest-domain heuristic, which the results suggest is still the basis of good heuristics for this class of problem.

1 Introduction

It is well known that the order in which variables are instantiated greatly affects the time taken to solve a constraint satisfaction problem (CSP) using a backtracking search algorithm. Although there are variable ordering heuristics available, which often give much better results than a random ordering of the variables, we currently have no way of judging their quality in any absolute sense. Are the heuristics that we currently have the best possible, or could there be others, not yet discovered, which would do much better? In this paper, we go some way towards answering this question.

The search algorithms currently in common use, including those incorporated into constraint programming tools, use some form of look-ahead to determine the effect of each assignment on the future variables, i.e. those not yet assigned, and their domains. These algorithms allow the choice of next variable to be made dynamically, i.e. the choice can take into account the available information about the effects of the assignments already made. Potentially, a different ordering could be used along each branch of the search tree. The alternative is a static ordering: the order of the variables is determined before search starts. We might expect a dynamic ordering heuristic to be better than a static one, since it can make use of current information, and in many cases this is true.

In this paper we re-visit some theoretical work by Nudel [7] which allows us to find, for some classes of CSP, the optimal static ordering of the variables. We show that we can to some degree convert between static and dynamic ordering heuristics and hence can compare the static version of a dynamic heuristic with the optimal ordering. This gives an indication of whether or not the dynamic heuristic is close to the best that can be achieved, or not. If the comparison indicates that the dynamic heuristic might not be optimal, we can use the optimal orderings to yield improvements.

This work is based on one search algorithm (the forward checking algorithm) and one class of problem (random binary CSPs). However, we believe that the study of optimal static orderings in this special case can give an insight into what variable ordering heuristics need to achieve in general, and so has wider application.

2 Existing Dynamic Ordering Heuristics

Perhaps the best known dynamic variable ordering heuristic is to choose next the variable with smallest remaining domain. This was described by Haralick and Elliott [6] and has often been called the fail-first heuristic, because of the justification which they gave for it. However, recent work [10] has shown that this explanation is suspect, and it will be referred to below as the smallest domain or SD heuristic.

The Brélaz heuristic [2], which was originally developed for graph colouring problems and has since been applied to CSPs, is a variant of SD. It chooses a variable with smallest remaining domain, but in case of a tie, chooses from these the variable with largest future degree, that is the one which constrains the largest number of unassigned variables. The Brélaz heuristic addresses a flaw of the SD heuristic, that it takes no account of the constraint graph. Another heuristic which addresses the same difficulty is dom/deg, introduced by Bessière and Régin [1], which chooses the variable minimizing the ratio of current domain size to (original) degree.

A number of dynamic variable ordering heuristics were introduced in [5], based on the principle of minimizing the constrainedness of the subproblem consisting of the future variables and their remaining values. These heuristics were compared with the Brélaz heuristic: the Brélaz heuristic was found to be the best of those studied on uniform binary problems with low constraint density, that is problems with uniform domain sizes and constraint tightnesses, of the kind described below in section 3. Two of the heuristics proposed in [5], however, have lower search costs than the Brélaz heuristic when the constraint graph is complete.

3 The Random CSP Model

Nudel's theory (outlined below) allows us to calculate the expected number of nodes visited in solving certain kinds of CSP. In order to apply the theory, we need a suitable class of CSP. Hence, we generate ensembles of random binary CSPs, using the parameters n, the number of variables; m, the number of values in each variable's domain; p_1, the proportion of pairs of variables which have a constraint between them; and p_2, the proportion of pairs of values which are not allowed by a constraint. In our experiments, p_2 is a fixed proportion, constant for all constraints and all instances in an ensemble, to reduce the variability in the generated instances. However, to simplify the analysis, we shall sometimes treat p_2 as a probability applying independently to each pair of values of a constrained pair of variables. p_1 on the other hand will be treated as a proportion in both the analysis and the experiments: we shall base the prediction of the expected number of nodes visited in solving an instance on the precise shape of its constraint graph, and we shall want to derive heuristics based on the constraint graph. We ensure that only connected constraint graphs are generated.

4 Expected Nodes Visited for Static Orderings

The following is based on Nudel's paper [7], with some changes of notation to make clearer the correspondence with the random binary CSP model already described. Suppose we have a binary CSP with n variables, and variable i has m_i values in its domain. Let q_{ij} be the probability that a value for variable i is consistent with a value for variable j. Then $q_{ij} = 1 - c_{ij}p_2$, where $c_{ij} = 1$ if there is a constraint between these two variables, and 0 otherwise, and p_2 is the constraint tightness, defined above. (In fact, it is not necessary for the analysis that p_2 should be constant; this is stipulated here to fit the random generation model.) We use the forward checking algorithm to find all solutions to the CSP.

The variables are to be instantiated in the order $1, 2, ..., n$: a different ordering will be accommodated by re-numbering the variables. Suppose we have currently assigned values to variables $1, 2, ... , k$ and have just completed forward checking, so that any value in the domain of a future variable which is inconsistent with these k instantiations has been deleted. A_k denotes the set of past variables, $\{1, 2, ..., k\}$, i.e. those already assigned, and F_k denotes the set of future variables, $\{k + 1, ..., n\}$.

Let m_k^f be the expected number of values for variable f ($f > k$) after forward checking the variable at level k, given that at least one value is left.

$$m_k^f = \frac{m_f \prod_{j \in A_k} q_{jf}}{S_f^{(k)}}$$

where $S_f^{(k)}$ is the probability that f has at least one of its m_f possible values consistent with the k past instantiations.

Let N_k be the expected number of nodes in the search tree at level k. Then Nudel shows that N_k can be expressed as:

$$N_0 = 1$$

$$N_k = \left(\prod_{i \in A_k} m_i \right) \left(\prod_{i < j \in A_k} q_{ij} \right) \left(\prod_{f \in F_k} S_f^{(k-1)} \right)$$

So, for instance, since $S_f^{(0)} = 1$, $N_1 = m_1$, and since $F_n = \emptyset$, $N_n = \prod_{1 \leq i \leq n} m_i \prod_{1 \leq i < j \leq n} q_{ij}$, which is the expected number of solutions.

For other values of k, the value of N_k can be calculated, provided that we know how to calculate $S_f^{(k-1)}$. For the random binary CSP model described above, given a fixed ordering of the variables,

$$S_f^{(k-1)} = 1 - \left(1 - \prod_{1 \leq i < k} (1 - c_{if} p_2) \right)^{m_f}$$

with $m_i = m$, for $1 \leq i \leq n$, for that model.

5 Minimizing the Expected Nodes Visited

Since the number of nodes visited in the search tree is a good measure of the cost of solving a CSP, we should like to be able to choose the instantiation order which minimizes the expected number of nodes visited. We could in theory find a static ordering of the variables which would minimize $N_1 + N_2 + N_3 + \ldots + N_n$ for a given constraint graph. We should have to minimize the sum over all $n!$ orderings of the variables. To find the best dynamic ordering of the variables would be much worse: we should have to find the best static ordering, assign a value to the first variable in this ordering, and then re-evaluate the subproblem consisting of the other $n - 1$ variables and their remaining domains. We should have to find the best static ordering for this new subproblem, assign a value to the first variable again, and repeat for every level of the tree in turn. Furthermore, since the optimal choice of next variable depends on the value assigned to the previous variables, and not just on which variables they are, this would have to be done at every node in the tree.

Even so, Nudel suggested that the formulae for the expected nodes visited could be used as the basis for dynamic variable ordering heuristics. At each node in the tree, we could choose the next variable so as to minimize N_1 in the subtree below this node; in case of a tie, $N_1 + N_2$ could be minimized, and so on. Since $N_1 = m_1$ and, if we are applying this after a number of previous instantiations, m_1 will be the *current* domain size of the next variable assigned, minimizing N_1 gives the familiar smallest-domain heuristic.

Using N_2 as a tie-breaker is considerably more complicated, since

$$N_2 = m_1 m_2 (1 - c_{12} p_2) \prod_{3 \leq f \leq n} (1 - c_{1f} p_2^{m_f})$$

Nudel points out further that instead of the original constraint tightness p_2, the current tightness of each constraint could be used, measured by the proportion of the remaining pairs of values which are inconsistent. For each variable with the current minimum domain size, we need to calculate N_2 for every other future variable which might follow it, and presumably choose the variable for which N_2 is minimized for some choice of following variable. This heuristic would be expensive to apply, even without recalculating the current constraint tightness after every assignment, and does not seem to have been generally adopted.

However, if all variable domains are equal in size, as is the case initially with $\langle n, m, p_1, p_2 \rangle$ problems, the second variable chosen by the SD heuristic will be one which is constrained by the first variable assigned (and whose domain will therefore have been reduced). In that case, $N_2 = m^2(1 - p_2)(1 - p_2^m)^d$ where d is the degree of the first variable. Hence, to minimize N_2 we should maximize d by starting with the variable with largest degree. This is a common variant of the SD heuristic [4, 10].

6 Optimal Orderings and Dynamic Heuristics

The approach taken in this paper is to return to the idea that in principle we can find the optimal static ordering of the variables which will minimize the expected nodes visited in finding all solutions to a $\langle n, m, p_1, p_2 \rangle$ problem using the forward checking algorithm. This is practicable if n is small enough. From the optimal ordering for each of a sample of constraint graphs, we plan to learn some easily applied heuristics which will give good static variable orderings, and translate these into good dynamic ordering heuristics.

The initial aim will be to assess the performance of the Brélaz heuristic and to improve on it if possible, at least for random binary problems generated by the model described earlier. We also hope to achieve new insights into why some heuristics are better than others, which could be transferred to other problem domains.

A correspondence between a static heuristic and a dynamic heuristic has previously been noted by Dechter and Meiri [3]. They point out that the maximum cardinality ordering, which selects the first variable arbitrarily and thereafter chooses a variable connected to the largest number of past variables, can be thought of (for this problem class) as a static version of SD. For $\langle n, m, p_1, p_2 \rangle$ problems, all the variables initially have the same domain size and all constraints have the same constraint tightness. Hence, at any point during search, the variable constrained by the largest number of past variables, which is therefore the variable whose domain has been reduced most often by the previous instantiations, is the variable whose expected domain size is least.

We can similarly extend the maximum cardinality heuristic to a static version of the Brélaz heuristic. When all variables initially have the same domain size, the Brélaz heuristic starts with the variable with largest degree. Thereafter it chooses a variable with smallest remaining domain and breaks ties by choosing the variable which constrains the largest number of future variables. We can add the choice of first variable and the tie-breaker to the maximum cardinality heuristic.

Hence, we choose the Brélaz heuristic as the basis of the investigation, partly because it is one of the best general heuristics currently available, especially for problems with sparse constraints from the class described earlier, but also because there is a straightforward translation between a static and a dynamic version of the heuristic.

In converting a static ordering heuristic to a dynamic one, the smallest remaining domain will be substituted for maximum past degree, and any reference to the future degree of a variable will be kept as it is.

There are a number of other obstacles to deriving new dynamic ordering heuristics from optimal static orderings, apart from the conversion of static to dynamic heuristics:

- we will normally want to find just one solution to a CSP, whereas Nudel's method gives the expected number of nodes to find all solutions. However, the instances which are on average hardest to solve, and for which improved heuristics potentially offer the greatest savings, are those in the phase transition region. There, about half the instances have no solution, so that proving that there is no solution requires the same amount of effort whether we want to find all solutions or just one. Those instances that do have a solution in the phase transition require, on average, a great deal of search before the first solution is found. Hence a heuristic which is based on finding all solutions will do well in this region of the parameter space, as well as in the insoluble region. If we can improve on the performance of existing heuristics in the phase transition region and the insoluble region, this will be worthwhile, even if we find that we cannot do better than the existing heuristics in the easy-soluble region.

- the optimal static ordering may change if the constraint tightness and the size of the domains change, even with the uniform $\langle n, m, p_1, p_2 \rangle$ model. In practice, m and p_2 can vary quite considerably without there being any change to the optimal ordering. We shall in any case ignore any potential dependence on these factors, and concentrate on making better use of the constraint graph to guide the search: however, to mitigate the effect of ignoring p_2, the new heuristics will be based on instances at the crossover point, i.e. the value of p_2 for which the probability of a solution is 0.5, so that the heuristics will be designed to deal best with the instances which are on average most difficult.

- Nudel's method is based only on the forward checking algorithm and so may not give good guidance when other search algorithms such as MAC [9] or CBJ [8] are used. However, existing heuristics which work well with FC also work well with other lookahead algorithms such as MAC or FC-CBJ, and there seems no reason to suppose that new heuristics would not do so too. Furthermore, if we can develop an understanding of how improved heuristics should be designed, we may be able to adapt the new heuristics to different algorithms. In section 8.1 below, we discuss how one proposed improvement might be adapted for use with MAC.

7 Rules from Optimal Static Orderings

A sample of 50 instances taken from the problem class $\langle 12, 10, 0.333, 0.68 \rangle$ was studied. These are small enough that the optimal ordering can be found quickly. In fact, it is not necessary to evaluate all $n!$ possible orderings in order to find the best. To find the expected number of nodes at level k in the search tree, it is only necessary to know the order of variables up to that point. Hence, if a reasonably good ordering is initially available, based for instance on the static Brélaz ordering, many partial orderings specifying the first k variables can be abandoned because the expected number of nodes up to level k is already greater than the best so far. Even so, it is too time-consuming to find the best orderings for problems with, say, 20 variables. A problem class with low constraint density was selected so that the effect of the constraint graph topology on the optimal ordering could be studied.

Figure 1 shows two of the sample instances, with the variables re-numbered to show an optimal ordering. The example in Figure 1(a) illustrates that the static

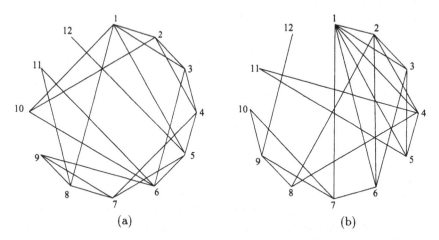

(a)   (b)

Fig. 1. Constraint graphs with optimal orderings for two $\langle 12, 10, 0.333, 0.68 \rangle$ instances.

Brélaz ordering can be much worse than the optimal ordering. The expected number of nodes visited with the optimal ordering is 154.2; with the static Brélaz ordering $(1 - 5 - 6 - 3 - 2 - 4 - 10 - 7 - 8 - 9 - 11 - 12)$ it is 283.3. The difference is mainly due to the fact that the choice of second variable allows the optimal ordering to choose next a variable which is constrained by both previous variables. On the other hand the Brélaz heuristic chooses second one of the variables which is connected to the first variable (2, 3, 5 or 8) and of these chooses the one with highest degree, i.e. variable 5. There is then no variable which is connected to both of the first two variables, and hence the expected number of nodes at level 3 is far higher than with the optimal ordering (88.2 compared with 20.3).

This example shows that the static Brélaz ordering is not always optimal, and suggests that it might therefore be possible to improve on the dynamic Brélaz heuristic as well.

The first step is to try to develop some simple rules for good static orderings from the optimal orderings for the sample instances. These may then give an indication of how to improve the Brélaz heuristic. The following rules have been derived informally from the sample instances. These rules are followed almost invariably, but with some exceptions: in some cases there was not enough evidence to be certain what the rules should be.

1. Choose the first *pair* of variables. They should constrain each other and the number of variables which are constrained by both of them should be maximized, i.e. choose a pair of variables involved in the largest number of constraint triangles. The variable with larger degree should be instantiated first: if they both have the same degree the order is immaterial. If there is more than one candidate pair, the one with largest total degree is chosen. In Figure1(a), the pair 1-2 constrain each other and two other variables (3, 10). The pair 2-3 also occurs in two triangles, but has smaller total degree. The third variable is then almost always one of those constrained by both of the first two variables, but subject to the following rules.

2. Apart from the first two variables, which are selected according to rule 1, the next variable chosen is usually one with largest past degree. If there is a tie, the choice is determined by each candidate variable's future neighbours, i.e. the variables which are constrained by the candidate variable and have not yet been assigned. The selected variable is the one with maximum past degree amongst its future neighbours. Further ties are broken by considering the next largest past degree amongst the future neighbours and so on; eventually, the variable with most future neighbours, i.e. the one with largest future degree, will win.

   An example of this is shown in Figure 1(b). Variable 3 is preferred to variable 4, because it is connected to a future variable with past degree 2 (variable 6) whereas the maximum past degree amongst variable 4's future neighbours is 1. The static Brélaz ordering would prefer variable 4 because it has larger future degree.

3. No variable whose future degree is zero should be chosen, unless there is no other choice. When only variables with 0 future degree are left, they should be instantiated in descending order of degree (although this part of the rule is only relevant if all solutions are required).

   In the example shown in Figure 1(a), this rule explains why variables 9 to 12 are instantiated last and in that order. The static Brélaz ordering, on the other hand, chooses variable 10, which constrains no future variables, in preference to variables 7 and 8, which do. Delaying instantiating variable 10 until no other variable with future degree > 0 remains would reduce the expected nodes visited from 283.3 to 276.0.

As a corollary of rule 2, if two variables have the same past degree and the same future degree, and the past degrees of their future neighbours are equal, they can be interchanged in the ordering without making any difference to the expected number of nodes. In Figure 1(b), variables 5 and 6 can be interchanged in the ordering: they both have past degree 3 and future degree 1, and their future neighbours (variables 11 and 7 respectively) have each been constrained by exactly one of the past variables. It makes no difference that variables 7 and 11 have different degrees, and that variable 11 now has future degree 0 and so will be left until the end, whereas variable 7 comes next in the ordering.

Sometimes, a variable is chosen which does not have the largest past degree amongst the remaining variables. This is illustrated in Figure 1(b), where variable 4, with past degree 2, is preferred to variable 6, with past degree 3. Choosing a variable with smaller past degree leads to a larger expected number of nodes at the current level, because the variable is expected to have more values left, but variable 4 compensates for this by leading to fewer nodes at the next level of the tree, since it is more likely than variable 6 to lead to a domain wipeout of one of its future neighbours (variable 5). However, in this example, re-ordering variables 4, 5 and 6 amongst themselves makes little difference to the expected nodes visited.

Overall, choosing next a variable with maximum past degree gives reasonably good results compared with the optimal ordering. When there is a large difference between the expected nodes visited for the optimal and the static Brélaz orderings, it is usually because they make different choices of the first two variables.

8 Modifications to the Brélaz Heuristic

Based on the rules derived from the sample of optimal static orderings, a number of potential improvements to the dynamic Brélaz heuristic have been investigated. These modifications are described below. Each was empirically evaluated on $\langle 20, 10, 0.2 \rangle$ problems, using the forward checking algorithm to find the first solution or prove that there is no solution. Figure 2 compares the results for the original Brélaz heuristic (BZ) and three modified heuristics, described below. At each value of p_2, 1000 instances were generated. The cost of solving these instances is measured by the number of consistency checks required to find the first solution or prove that there is no solution. Figure 2 shows the median cost using each heuristic, together with two of the higher percentiles to give an indication of the range of costs incurred.

8.1 Variables with Zero Future Degree

Rule 3 (do not assign a variable with future degree zero, unless there is no other choice) is easy to add to the (dynamic) Brélaz heuristic, and on reflection

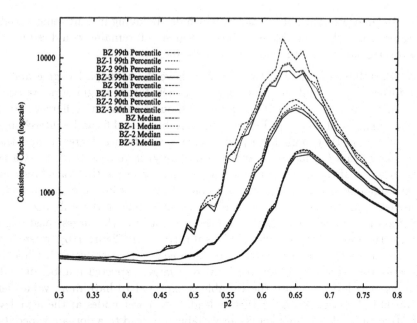

Fig. 2. Cost percentiles for $\langle 20, 10, 0.2 \rangle$ problems solved using forward checking with the Brélaz heuristic and variants

is clearly beneficial with forward checking. If a variable constrains no future variables, any remaining values in its domain, which have already been checked against the past assignments, will be consistent with any consistent assignment to the other variables. Hence, there is no sense in assigning such a variable before any of the variables which do constrain future variables and so have a possibility of failing. Assigning a variable with zero future degree can only impede chronological backtracking if a failure occurs later.

Although this rule seems an obvious improvement to any heuristic used with the forward checking algorithm, it does not appear to have been mentioned hitherto. The SD and Brélaz heuristics could easily choose a variable with zero future degree at any point in the search, if it has smallest domain. The variant of the dom/deg heuristic which uses the future degree of each variable would not, however, choose such a variable until last.

The main difficulty caused by variables with zero future degree is that if the algorithm backtracks to this variable, all alternative possible values for it will be tried in turn, without having any effect on the failure, thus potentially causing a great deal of unnecessary work. Hence, they would not be so detrimental in an algorithm such as FC-CBJ [8] which combines forward checking with an informed backtracker, conflict-directed backjumping. CBJ would simply ignore variables with zero future degree when backtracking, since they can never be responsible for any subsequent failure.

Rule 3 could be extended for the MAC algorithm [9], which re-establishes arc consistency after every instantiation. If two future variables constrain each other, but no other future variables, MAC will ensure that they have at least one mutually compatible pair of values, each of which is also consistent with all the past instantiations. Hence, these two variables should be left until last.

Rule 3 is cheap to implement, since the Brélaz heuristic is already calculating the future degree of any variable with smallest remaining domain. In Figure 2, BZ-1 is the Brélaz heuristic with the addition of this rule.

8.2 Second Tie-breaker

If the largest future degree amongst the variables with smallest remaining domain is shared by more than one of these variables, the Brélaz heuristic provides no further tie-breaker. From the rules given earlier, if more than one variable has largest past degree (corresponding to smallest remaining domain), the optimal static ordering chooses from these the variable which has a future neighbour with largest past degree. We can turn this into a second tie-breaker for the dynamic Brélaz heuristic: if more than one variable has smallest current domain size and largest future degree, choose the one for which the minimum domain size amongst its future neighbours is least.

This was combined with the previous rule (don't choose a variable with zero future degree) to give a second variant of the Brélaz heuristic, BZ-2. Examining each variable's future neighbours could be a relatively expensive addition to the heuristic, depending on how it is implemented. However, since this is only required as a second tie-breaker, it need not be done very often.

An alternative, which is in fact closer to the rules derived from the optimal static orderings, reverses the second and third tie-breakers. The heuristic then becomes: choose the variable with smallest remaining domain; break ties by choosing the variable which has smallest remaining domain amongst its future neighbours; break remaining ties by choosing the variable with largest future degree. This further reduces the mean consistency checks by about 2% in the phase transition region, but its implementation costs are higher.

8.3 Starting Variable

Rule 1 for optimal static orderings shows how to select the first *pair* of variables; thereafter the other rules are applied. With dynamic ordering, committing in advance to a fixed choice of second variable, irrespective of the results of the first assignment, is not a good strategy. However, we can modify the idea of considering triangles of constraints and choose the first variable accordingly. This has been implemented as a tie-breaker in selecting the first variable in the Brélaz heuristic. In $\langle n, m, p_1, p_2 \rangle$ problems, since all domains are initially the same size, the first variable chosen is one with largest degree. In many instances, there will be more than one such variable. The new tie-breaker chooses from these the one involved in the largest number of constraint triangles. This increases the likelihood that after the second variable has been assigned, there will be at least one variable constrained by both the variables assigned so far. Such a variable is likely to have a smaller domain than one constrained by only one of the first two variables, and hence the expected number of nodes at level 3 in the search tree is reduced.

Although finding triangles of constraints is not something that the Brélaz heuristic normally does, the extra work involved is small, and since it is only done once at the start of each search it does not contribute significantly to the overall cost.

In combination with the two previous modifications, this produces a third variant of the Brélaz heuristic, shown as BZ-3 in Figure 2.

9 Overall Results

Each successive modification to the Brélaz heuristic reduces the average cost of solving the experimental problems in the phase transition, as shown in Figure 2. The three modifications together reduce the mean consistency checks required to solve $\langle 20, 10, 0.2 \rangle$ problems by about 16-17% in the phase transition region. Elsewhere, the savings made are much less, although the average cost never increases. The reduction in the median cost in the phase transition is also much less, about 8-10%, indicating that BZ-3 helps to avoid the most expensive searches. These savings are significant, although not spectacular.

However, problems with 20 variables are relatively small and offer limited scope for going seriously wrong. BZ and BZ-3 were applied also to larger problems, with $n = 30$, 40 and 50, and $m = 10$. In each case, a sample of 1000 instances was generated at the crossover point. The average degree was kept constant: this ensures that the topology of the constraint graphs is unchanged at a local level, as n increases, and that the crossover point does not change very much with n, at least over the range 20 to 50. As far as possible, therefore, only the number of variables is being changed.

Figure 3 shows the means and medians of cost for the two heuristics. The increasing divergence between BZ and BZ-3 in both the means and the medians shows that BZ-3 reduces the average cost by an increasing proportion as the problems get larger. For instance, when $n = 50$, the mean cost using BZ is nearly twice that using BZ-3. The increasing divergence between the mean and the median for each heuristic as n increases also indicates the increasing influence of the tail of the cost distribution on the mean.

10 Conclusions

By analyzing the optimal static orderings for a sample of binary CSPs, we have derived rules constituting a good static ordering heuristic for this class of problem. We have also used the rules, and a correspondence between static and dynamic ordering heuristics, to yield improvements to the Brélaz heuristic. These improvements together reduce the search costs for our experimental problems by up to a half. Our comparison of the static Brélaz heuristic with the optimal ordering shows that in fact choosing the variable with largest past degree, which is equivalent for this problem class to choosing the variable with smallest domain

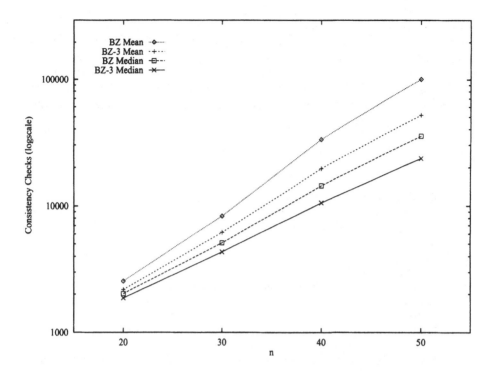

Fig. 3. Average cost of solving instances at the crossover point using forward checking with the Brélaz heuristic and an improved heuristic for samples of 1000 instances with a range of problem sizes, $m = 10$, average degree 3.8

in a dynamic heuristic, is often the right thing to do. Where the static Brélaz heuristic gives an ordering much worse than optimal, it is usually because it has made a wrong choice of the first one or two variables, which then leads to wrong choices later as well.

Hence, within the restrictions of the random binary problem class, our results show that the static Brélaz heuristic, with the improvements given by the rules of section 7, will often give an ordering not far from the optimal static ordering. Our results also suggest that for these problems, dynamic heuristics which choose the variable with smallest current domain are unlikely to be beaten by some unknown, radically different, heuristic. However, as is already known, the way in which ties are broken, if there is more than one variable with smallest domain, does have a great effect on performance of smallest-domain heuristics.

In general, we can see that a good variable ordering heuristic has two effects on the search tree. First, it gives a small number of nodes at the current level of the tree, by choosing a variable with a small domain. Secondly, it ensures that the variables chosen at future levels of the tree will have small domains; this is done by choosing a variable now whose assignment will lead to the removal of many values from the domains of future variables. So far, our improvements to the Brélaz heuristic still give priority to the first, considering future levels of the search tree only if a tie-breaker is required. However, it is possible to imagine cases where priority should be given to reducing the domains of future variables instead. For instance, this may be so if some constraints are much tighter than others. Viewing the role of variable ordering heuristics in this light may lead to the design of better heuristics for cases where the smallest domain heuristic and its variants do not give good results, as for instance is often the case when the constraints are non-binary.

References

1. C. Bessière and J.-C. Régin. MAC and Combined Heuristics: Two Reasons to Forsake FC (and CBJ?) on Hard Problems. In E. C. Freuder, editor, *Principles and Practice of Constraint Programming - CP96*, LNCS 1118, pages 61–75. Springer, 1996.
2. D. Brélaz. New Methods to Color the Vertices of a Graph. *Communications of the ACM*, 22:251–256, 1979.
3. R. Dechter and I. Meiri. Experimental evaluation of preprocessing techniques in constraint satisfaction problems. In *Proceedings IJCAI-89*, volume 1, pages 271–277, 1989.
4. D. Frost and R. Dechter. In search of the best constraint satisfaction search. In *Proceedings AAAI'94*, pages 301–306, 1994.
5. I. Gent, E. MacIntyre, P. Prosser, B. Smith, and T. Walsh. An empirical study of dynamic variable ordering heuristics for the constraint satisfaction problem. In E. C. Freuder, editor, *Principles and Practice of Constraint Programming - CP96*, LNCS 1118, pages 179–193. Springer-Verlag, 1996.
6. R. Haralick and G. Elliott. Increasing tree search efficiency for constraint satisfaction problems. *Artificial Intelligence*, 14:263–313, 1980.
7. B. Nudel. Consistent-labelling problems and their algorithms: Expected-complexities and theory-based heuristics. *Artificial Intelligence*, 21:135–178, 1983.
8. P. Prosser. Hybrid Algorithms for the Constraint Satisfaction Problem. *Computational Intelligence*, 9(3):268–299, 1993.
9. D. Sabin and E. Freuder. Contradicting Conventional Wisdom in Constraint Satisfaction. In A. Cohn, editor, *Proceedings ECAI94*, pages 125–129, 1994.
10. B. M. Smith and S. A. Grant. Trying Harder to Fail First. In H. Prade, editor, *Proceedings ECAI'98*, pages 249–253. Wiley, Aug. 1998.

A Fixpoint Definition of Dynamic Constraint Satisfaction

Timo Soininen[1], Esther Gelle[2], and Ilkka Niemelä[3]

[1] Helsinki University of Technology, TAI Research Center,
P.O.Box 9555, FIN-02015 HUT, Finland
Timo.Soininen@hut.fi
[2] ABB Corporate Research Ltd,
CHCRC.C2 Segelhof, CH-5405 Baden, Switzerland
Esther.Gelle@ch.abb.com
[3] Helsinki University of Technology, Dept. of Computer Science and Eng.,
Laboratory for Theoretical Computer Science,
P.O.Box 5400, FIN-02015 HUT, Finland
Ilkka.Niemela@hut.fi

Abstract. Many combinatorial problems can be represented naturally as constraint satisfaction problems (CSP). However, in some domains the set of variables in a solution should change dynamically on the basis of assignments of values to variables. In this paper we argue that such *dynamic constraint satisfaction problems (DCSP)*, introduced by Mittal and Falkenhainer, are more expressive than CSP in a knowledge representation sense. We then study the problem of generalizing the original DCSP with *disjunctive activity constraints* and *default negation* which are useful in, e.g., product configuration problems. The generalization is based on a novel definition of a solution to DCSP. It uses a fixpoint condition instead of the subset minimality condition in the original formulation. Our approach coincides with the original definition when disjunctions and default negations are not allowed. However, it leads to lower computational complexity than if the original definition were generalized similarly. In fact we show that the generalized DCSP is **NP**-complete. As a proof of concept, we briefly describe two novel implementations of the original DCSP and give test results for them.

1 Introduction

Constraint satisfaction problems (CSP) provide a convenient framework for representing combinatorial tasks. Powerful search algorithms have also been developed for solving CSPs [13] by integrating filtering (consistency algorithms) into a search algorithm. A CSP consists of a set of variables with domains on which allowed value combinations are specified as constraints. However, e.g. product configuration [8] problems exhibit dynamic aspects in the generation of problem spaces, i.e., the set of variables in a solution changes dynamically on the basis of assignments of values to variables. When configuring a mixer, for example, a condenser is a typical optional component which does not have to be present in every solution. It is only necessary if the vessel volume is large and chemical reactions occur during the mixing process.

Such dynamic aspects are difficult to capture in a standard CSP in which all variables are assigned values in every solution. One way to deal with an optional component is to add a special NULL value to the domain of the variable representing the component [3]. In addition, each constraint that refers to the variable needs to be modified to function properly in the presence of NULL. More seriously, an additional constraint is needed to prevent other values than NULL for the variable if there is no reason for including the optional component in the solution. Such constraints may have a very large arity and cardinality, as many variables may affect the value of the variable representing the optional component. Much effort has therefore been put to include dynamic aspects in CSPs [5, 7, 12, 3]. One of these is the framework of *dynamic constraint satisfaction problems (DCSP)* [5] which adds *activity constraints* to CSP. The activity constraints govern which variables are given values, i.e. are *active*, in a solution.

In this paper we provide evidence that there is a significant difference in the expressivity of DCSP and CSP in a knowledge representation sense using a concept of modularity [10]. Modularity of representation means that a small change of knowledge results in a small change in its representation. It is shown that a DCSP cannot be modularly represented as a CSP. Despite this increased expressiveness, the activity constraints of DCSP are relatively limited for product configuration problems. It is, e.g., difficult to encode, as an activity constraint, that for chemical dispersion either a condenser or a cooler should be included in the configuration of a mixer. Representing this type of knowledge conveniently requires *disjunctive activity constraints* [5]. However, already Mittal and Falkenhainer [5] note that finding solutions to DCSPs with disjunctive activity constraints seems to be computationally very expensive. We confirm this observation by showing that extending the original definition results easily in $\Sigma_2 P$-hard decision problems. This is due to a subset minimality condition on solutions in the original definition.

In order to keep the computational complexity of the decision problems for DCSP in **NP**, we present a new definition in which the minimality condition is replaced with a fixpoint condition. The definition allows more expressive activity constraints generalized to include disjunctions and *default negation* on constraints and their activity. The default negation is handled similarly as in the stable model semantics of normal logic programs [2]. Our definition of DCSP coincides with the original one when disjunctive activity constraints and default negations are not allowed. It does not guarantee subset minimality of solutions when disjunctions are permitted but ensures that active variables are justified in a weaker and computationally much more feasible sense. We feel that subset minimality is in fact a specific optimality criterion which is not very relevant in many applications where measuring, e.g., cost and resource consumption are more important. Our idea is that such optimality criteria can be added on top of our definition whose role is to provide the solutions satisfying the constraints.

Our generalization does not increase the complexity of the relevant decision tasks, which are shown to be **NP**-complete. This also provides a complexity result for the original DCSP class. As DCSP and CSP are computationally equally complex and DCSP is more expressive than CSP, DCSP seems to be a more feasible framework than CSP for domains with dynamic aspects.

We briefly discuss two novel implementations of the original DCSP to give a proof of concept. The first is based on an extension of a basic CSP algorithm, while the other is based on translating a DCSP to a set of rules in a logic program-like language [10]. The implementations exhibit acceptable running times for several problems from the configuration domain. We finally present some conclusions and topics for future work.

2 The DCSP Formalism

We first recall the original definition of a dynamic constraint satisfaction problem. An instance $\mathcal{P}$ of DCSP is of the form $\langle \mathcal{V}, \mathcal{D}, \mathcal{V}_I, \mathcal{C}_C, \mathcal{C}_A \rangle$, where $\mathcal{V} = \{v_1, \ldots, v_n\}$ is the set of *variables* and $\mathcal{D} = \{D_1, \ldots, D_n\}$ is the set of *domains* of the variables providing a set $D_i = \{d_{i1}, \ldots, d_{ij}\}$ of *values* for each variable v_i. The set of *initial* variables of $\mathcal{P}$ is denoted by $\mathcal{V}_I$, $\mathcal{V}_I \subseteq \mathcal{V}$, the set of *compatibility constraints* by $\mathcal{C}_C$ and the set of *activity constraints* by $\mathcal{C}_A$. We assume that all these sets are finite. Next, we define a *legal assignment* to a set of variables.

Definition 1. *An assignment of a value d_{ij} to a variable v_i is of the form $v_i = d_{ij}$, where $d_{ij} \in D_i$. A legal assignment $\mathcal{A}$ to a DCSP $\langle \mathcal{V}, \mathcal{D}, \mathcal{V}_I, \mathcal{C}_C, \mathcal{C}_A \rangle$ is a set of assignments with at most one assignment for each variable.*

In contrast to CSP, a variable can be in one of two states. A variable is *active* iff it is assigned a value in an assignment, otherwise it is *not active*.

A compatibility constraint c with arity j specifies the set of allowed combinations of values for a set of variables $v_1, \ldots, v_j$ as a subset of the Cartesian product of the domains of the variables. We denote the subset by $c(v_1, \ldots, v_j)$, i.e. $c(v_1, \ldots, v_j) \subseteq D_1 \times \ldots \times D_j$. A compatibility constraint is *active* iff all the variables it constrains are active. An activity constraint that activates variable v is of form $c \overset{ACT}{\to} v$, where c is defined equivalently to a compatibility constraint. Here we generalize the original definition slightly in that we do not require that the activated variable is distinct from the variables that the constraint on the left hand side refers to. We use the notation $v_i = d_{ij} \overset{ACT}{\to} v_k$ for activity constraints whose left hand side consists of one constraint with one tuple, and sometimes enclose the entire activity constraint in parentheses for clarity. *Always require*, *require not* and *always require not* activity constraints [5] are treated as shorthand notation for simplicity.[1]

---

[1] For example, an always require constraint of the form $v_1, \ldots, v_i \overset{ACT}{\to} v_j$ is defined as $c \overset{ACT}{\to} v_j$ where c allows all value combinations on the variables $v_1, \ldots, v_i$, i.e $c = D_1 \times \ldots \times D_i$.

A solution to a DCSP is a subset minimal legal assignment that satisfies all compatibility and activity constraints and has assignments for the initial variables. The subset minimality condition in effect excludes assignments with active variables whose activity is not *justified* by the variables being in the set of initial variables or by at least one activity constraint.

Definition 2. *A legal assignment A for a DCSP $P = \langle V, D, V_I, C_C, C_A \rangle$ satisfies the constraints in P iff the following conditions hold:*

1. *A satisfies each compatibility constraint $c \in C_C$, i.e., if c is active in A then the variables constrained by c are assigned values allowed by c.*
2. *A satisfies each activity constraint $(c \stackrel{ACT}{\to} v_k) \in C_{A,}$, i.e., if c is active in and satisfied by A then v_k is active in A.*

Definition 3. *A legal assignment A is a solution to a DCSP iff A*

1. *satisfies the constraints,*
2. *contains assignments of values to initial variables,*
3. *is subset minimal, i.e. there is no assignment A_1 satisfying 1. and 2. such that $A_1 \subset A$.*

Example 1. We use the simplified configuration task of an industrial mixer [14] to illustrate a DCSP. A *product configuration task* takes as input a *configuration model* and a set of *requirements*. The configuration model describes all the components that can be included in a product and all the dependencies that define how components can be combined. The requirements specify additional constraints on the product individual to be configured. The output of the configuration task is a *legal configuration* that satisfies the requirements. A *legal configuration* is a configuration that is allowed by the configuration model, i.e., that contains only components defined by the model and that satisfies the dependencies in it. In the framework of DCSP, the configuration model is described as a DCSP the solutions to which correspond to the set of legal configurations. The requirements are represented as a set of activity and compatibility constraints.

An industrial mixer can be used for different mixing processes, e.g. chemical reactions, mixing of side products etc. It consists of a set of standard components, such as a vessel containing the products to be mixed, the mixer itself with impellers and an engine, etc. Depending on the chemical properties of the products to be mixed, heat is produced which requires the use of a cooler or a condenser. To represent the configuration model of a mixer as a DCSP, the components and their properties, for example the volume, are represented as variables. The mixing process is represented by a variable for the mixing task. The components can be of different types, e.g. the mixer can be a reactor, storage tank, or simple mixer. These as well as the different types of mixing tasks are represented as discrete domains of the variables.[2] As a cooler and a condenser

---

[2] To designate variables and values in the problem, we use the first letters of their names.

are not needed in every solution, they are not included in the set of initial variables but are introduced by activity constraints. The configuration model for the mixer configuration task consists of the variables in Table 1 and the activity constraints $C_A = \{a_1, a_2\}$ and compatibility constraints $C_C = \{c_1, c_2\}$ given as follows:

$$a_1 = (Mi = r \overset{ACT}{\rightarrow} Coo)$$
$$a_2 = (Mt = d \overset{ACT}{\rightarrow} Con)$$
$$c_1(Con, Vol) = \{(con1, l), (con2, l), (con2, s)\}$$
$$c_2(Mi, Vol) = \{(r, s), (m, s), (m, l), (t, s), (t, l)\}$$

Table 1. Variables of the mixer configuration model.

Variable	Description	Domain
$Mt \in \mathcal{V}_I$	Mixing task	$\{d(dispersion), s(suspension), b(blending)\}$
$Mi \in \mathcal{V}_I$	Mixer	$\{m(mixer), r(reactor), t(tank)\}$
Coo	Cooler	$\{cool(cooler1)\}$
Con	Condenser	$\{con1(condenser1), con2(condenser2)\}$
$Vol \in \mathcal{V}_I$	Volume	$\{l(large), s(small)\}$

Given the above mixer DCSP, the assignment $\mathcal{A}_1 = \{Mi = m, Mt = b, Vol = l\}$ is a solution, i.e. a legal configuration, since it satisfies the constraints, contains assignments for the initial variables and there is no other solution $\mathcal{A}$ such that $\mathcal{A} \subset \mathcal{A}_1$. The assignment $\mathcal{A}_2 = \{Mi = r, Mt = b, Vol = s, Coo = cool\}$ is another solution with a different set of active variables. However, $\mathcal{A}_3 = \{Mi = r, Mt = b, Vol = s, Coo = cool, Con = con2\}$ is not a solution since the assignment $Con = con2$ is not justified by Con being in the set of initial variables or by being activated by an activity constraint, and thus $\mathcal{A}_2 \subset \mathcal{A}_3$.

The basic task in the DCSP framework is to find a solution to a given DCSP. However, for the configuration domain the relevant task is to find a solution that satisfies a set of requirements, which may also refer to the activity of variables. This is important when customer requirements concerning some functionality lead to conditions on the activity of the corresponding variables. We therefore analyze in subsequent sections the computational complexity of the decision versions of these tasks, defined as follows:

Definition 4. *DCSP(D): Given a DCSP $\mathcal{P}$, is there a solution for $\mathcal{P}$?*
$DCSP_R(D)$: Given a DCSP $\mathcal{P}$ and a set of requirements R, is there a solution S for $\mathcal{P}$ such that S satisfies R?

Note that the requirements of the configuration task cannot be handled by simply adding constraints or initial variables to a DCSP representing the configuration model, as this can change the configuration model to allow configurations which were not originally intended. For example, consider the following subset of the mixer problem:

Example 2. The configuration model is defined as follows: $\mathcal{V} = \{Mi, Coo\}$, the variables have the same domains as previously, $\mathcal{V}_I = \{Mi\}$, $\mathcal{C}_C = \emptyset$, and $\mathcal{C}_A = \{(Mi = r \overset{ACT}{\rightarrow} Coo)\}$. The set of legal configurations is now $\{\{Mi = r, Coo = cool\}, \{Mi = t\}, \{Mi = m\}\}$. Consider the set of requirements $\{(\overset{ACT}{\rightarrow} Coo), c(Mi) = \{(m)\}\}$, i.e., that cooler is active and $Mi = m$. There is no legal configuration with respect to the configuration model which would satisfy these requirements. However, adding them to the configuration model would change the set of legal configurations to $\{\{Mi = m, Coo = cool\}\}$, permitting a configuration that satisfies the requirements but is not allowed by the original configuration model.

3 Expressivity of DCSP vs. CSP

In this section we show that DCSP is more expressive than CSP in a knowledge representation sense. We use the concept of *modularity* [10] to establish this. Intuitively, a modular representation of knowledge is such that a small change in the knowledge leads to a small change in its representation. This property is important for maintaining and updating the knowledge. For example, if a DCSP could be represented as a CSP in a modular fashion, a simple update like adding a variable to the set of initial variables should result in a local change to the corresponding CSP. It seems that there is no modular representation of a DCSP as a CSP even under very weak notions of modularity. Here we demonstrate this in the case of updating the set of initial variables. This result can be extended to involve more complex changes to DCSP, such as additions and removals of compatibility and activity constraints and their allowed value tuples.

More precisely, we say that DCSP is *modularly representable* by CSP iff there is a mapping for each DCSP $\mathcal{P}$ to a CSP $T(\mathcal{P})$ such that the solutions to $\mathcal{P}$ *agree* with the solutions to $T(\mathcal{P})$ and the effect of changing the set of initial variables in $\mathcal{P}$ can be accomplished by a *simple update* to $T(\mathcal{P})$. The solutions are defined to agree iff each active variable in the solution to $\mathcal{P}$ is assigned the same value in the solution to $T(\mathcal{P})$ as in the solution to $\mathcal{P}$, and all other variables of $\mathcal{P}$ are assigned the value NULL. A simple update consists of an arbitrary number of either i) additions of constraints, removals of allowed tuples from constraints, removals of values from domains, and removals of variables with their domains, or ii) removals of constraints, additions of allowed tuples to constraints, additions of values to domains and additions of variables with their domains. In other words, a simple update cannot combine changes of the first and second type. In the case of removing variables, the constraints and assignments are projected to the remaining variables appropriately.

Theorem 1. *DCSP is not modularly representable by CSP.*

Proof. (Sketch) Consider the DCSP $\mathcal{P} = \langle \mathcal{V}, \mathcal{D}, \mathcal{V}_I, \mathcal{C}_C, \mathcal{C}_A \rangle$ with $\mathcal{V} = \{v_1, v_2\}$, $\mathcal{V}_I = \{v_1\}, D_1 = \{a\}, D_2 = \{b\}, \mathcal{C}_C = \mathcal{C}_A = \emptyset$, and assume it can be modularly represented by a CSP. Hence, there is a CSP $T(\mathcal{P})$ such that in all the solutions of $T(\mathcal{P})$ $v_1 = a$ and $v_2 = NULL$, as that is the only solution to $\mathcal{P}$. Consider now adding v_2 to $\mathcal{V}_I$. The resulting DCSP has only one solution where $v_1 = a$ and $v_2 = b$. This means that $T(\mathcal{P})$ updated with v_2 must not have a solution in which $v_1 = a$ and $v_2 = NULL$. In addition, $T(\mathcal{P})$ updated with v_2 must have at least one solution in which $v_1 = a$ and $v_2 = b$. It can be shown that simple updates cannot both add solutions and remove them, which is a contradiction and hence the assumption is false.

This result is caused by the condition that activity constraints or initial variables have to justify the activity of a variable in a solution. We note that there is a modular mapping from a CSP to DCSP, since CSP is a special case of DCSP. Thus, DCSP is strictly more expressive than CSP.

4 Generalized Definition of DCSP

In this section we give a new, generalized definition of DCSP. The activity constraints of the original DCSP are extended with disjunctive activity constraints and default negation. It is shown that a straightforward extension of the original definition by, e.g., disjunctive activity constraints would lead to significantly higher complexity. The new definition of a solution to DCSP utilizes a fixpoint condition instead of the minimality condition on the solutions. This allows a straightforward analysis and generalization of DCSP.

As noted in the introduction, the activity constraints of DCSP are not particularly expressive. For instance, in some configuration tasks a functional requirement can be satisfied by any of a given set of components, which would require disjunctive activity constraints [5]. Another case that cannot be represented in a straightforward manner is that a variable is active under the condition that some variables are not active or not given particular values in an assignment, i.e., under a condition referring to the complement of activity or constraints. The complement of activity can also be used to represent expressive requirements on the activity of variables in the desired solutions. Both these extensions can be included without increasing computational complexity (see Section 5).

We would thus like to extend DCSP to allow *generalized activity constraints* of the following form:

$$c_1, \ldots, c_j, not(c_{j+1}), \ldots, not(c_k) \overset{ACT}{\rightarrow} m\{v_1 \mid \ldots \mid v_l\}n \qquad (1)$$

where $0 \leq m \leq n$. Intuitively, this activity constraint states that if constraints $c_1, \ldots, c_j$ are active in and satisfied by an assignment and the constraints $c_{j+1}, \ldots, c_k$ are not satisfied or not active in the assignment, then for the subset of the variables $v_1, \ldots, v_l$ active in the assignment, the cardinality of the subset is between m and n. If $m = 1$ and $n = l$, this becomes an inclusive disjunction of the variables. On the other hand, if $m = n = 1$, the right hand side becomes an exclusive disjunction. We also allow rules with $m = 0$ for representing *optional* variables, i.e., variables that may be active or inactive. Always require activity constraints are again treated as short hand notation.

The original definition does not seem to provide a promising basis for generalizing DCSP with such activity constraints. It employs a minimality condition that makes it hard to extend basic DCSP without a substantial increase in computational complexity. For example, disjunctive always requires activity constraints of the form

$$v_1,\ldots,v_m \overset{ACT}{\to} 1\{v_{m+1} \mid \ldots \mid v_{m+n}\}n \tag{2}$$

already lead to $\Sigma_2\mathbf{P}$-hardness of $DCSP_R(D)$.

Theorem 2. *$DCSP_R(D)$ is $\Sigma_2\mathbf{P}$-hard for disjunctive activity constraints of the form (2). This holds even in the case where all variables have unary domains, there are no other constraints, and the requirements consist of only one compatibility constraint.*

Proof. (Sketch) This result can be established by a reduction from the problem of deciding whether a positive disjunctive database has a minimal model containing a given atomic formula, known to be $\Sigma_2\mathbf{P}$-complete [1]. The reduction is based on the following observation. If we map every rule $a_1 \vee \cdots \vee a_m \leftarrow a_{m+1},\ldots,a_n$ of a database to an activity constraint $a_{m+1},\ldots,a_n \overset{ACT}{\to} 1\{a_1 \mid \ldots \mid a_m\}m$ where each a_i is taken as a DCSP variable with a unary domain, then minimal models of the database coincide with minimal solutions of the corresponding DCSP.

In order to extend the basic DCSP formalism without increasing the complexity we employ a definition based on a fixpoint equation of an operator on the lattice formed by the set of assignments and their subset relation. However, we first define when an assignment satisfies a generalized activity constraint. The definition of when an assignment satisfies compatibility constraints remains the same as previously.

Definition 5. *A legal assignment A for a DCSP $P = \langle V, D, V_I, C_C, C_A \rangle$ satisfies the activity constraints in P iff for each activity constraint in C_A of the form (1) the following holds: if $c_1 \ldots c_j$ are active and satisfied, and $c_{j+1},\ldots,c_k$ are not satisfied by or not active in A, then for the set $V \subseteq \{v_1,\ldots,v_l\}$ active in A, $m \leq\mid V \mid\leq n$ holds.*

The fixpoint condition in the new definition is another way of ensuring that active variables are justified by initial variables and activity constraints. To capture this, we first define a reduction of a set of generalized activity constraints and the initial variables with respect to an assignment. The intuition behind the reduction is that, given an activity constraint, if a variable on the right hand side of it is active in a solution and the negated activity constraints are either not satisfied or not active, then the reduct includes a simpler *instantiated activity constraint* that can justify the activity of the variable. If a variable in the head of an activity constraint is not active, then there is no need for its activity to be justified and consequently no corresponding instantiated activity constraints are included.

More precisely, the reduct of each activity constraint contains one instantiated activity constraint for every active variable that occurs on its right hand side, if all the constraints with default negation on the left hand side are either not satisfied or not active in the assignment. The left hand side of the instantiated activity constraint is otherwise the same as that of the activity constraint, except that the constraints with default negation are removed. This treatment of default negation is similar to the stable model semantics of logic programs [2]. Further, the variables on the right hand side of the instantiated activity constraints are replaced by their assignments. Initial variables are also given a special activity constraint form, the left hand side of which is satisfied by every assignment.

Definition 6. *We define the reduct $(C_A, V_I)^A$ of a set of generalized activity constraints C_A and a set of initial variables V_I w.r.t. an assignment A as follows:*

$$(C_A, V_I)^A = \{ c_1, \ldots, c_i \overset{ACT}{\to} v_j = d_{jp} \mid$$

$$(c_1, \ldots, c_i, not(c_{i+1}), \ldots, not(c_k) \overset{ACT}{\to} m\{v_1 \mid \ldots \mid v_l\}n) \in C_A,$$
$$(v_j = d_{jp}) \in A \text{ for some } j \text{ where } 1 \leq j \leq l,$$
$$c_{i+1}, \ldots, c_k \text{ are not satisfied by or active in } A\}$$
$$\cup \{ \overset{ACT}{\to} v_j = d_{jk} \mid v_j \in V_I, (v_j = d_{jk}) \in A \} .$$

We denote the set of instantiated activity constraints resulting from the reduct $(C_A, V_I)^A$ by the shorthand notation C_I for brevity. We now define an operator on the lattice formed by the set of all possible assignments and the subset relation on these. The operator intuitively captures how the instantiated activity constraints introduce new active variables to an assignment when their left hand side constraints are active and satisfied.

Definition 7. *Given a set of instantiated activity constraints C_I, the operator $T_{C_I}(\cdot)$ on an assignment A is defined as follows:*

$$T_{C_I}(A) = \{ v = d \mid (c_1, \ldots, c_k \overset{ACT}{\to} v = d) \in C_I,$$
$$c_i \text{ is active in and satisfied by } A, 1 \leq i \leq k\}$$

Intuitively, a solution is a legal assignment that satisfies the constraints in the DCSP and contains all and only the active variables that are justified by the set of initial variables and activity constraints. Since active variables may be justified recursively, a solution to a DCSP is defined as a fixpoint of the above operator for a given reduct. A *fixpoint q* of an operator $\tau(\cdot)$ is such that $\tau(q) = q$. This ensures that every variable with a justification is active in the solution.

The operator T_{C_I} is monotonic, i.e., for assignments A_i and A_j, $A_i \subseteq A_j$ implies $T_{C_I}(A_i) \subseteq T_{C_I}(A_j)$. This can be seen by noting that if the left hand side of an instantiated activity constraint is satisfied by an assignment, it is satisfied by all its supersets as well. A monotonic operator has a unique *least fixpoint* that can be computed by iteratively applying the operator, starting from the empty set [4]. As a solution must not contain unjustified active variables, it should be such a least fixpoint, denoted by lfp(T_{C_I}). This ensures that all the assignments in a solution are justified by the instantiated activity constraints.

Definition 8. *Given a DCSP* $P = \langle V, D, V_I, C_C, C_A \rangle$ *a legal assignment* $\mathcal{A}$ *is a solution to* P *iff i)* $\mathcal{A}$ *satisfies the constraints in* P, *ii) the initial variables are active in* $\mathcal{A}$, *iii)* $\mathcal{A} = \mathrm{lfp}(T_{(C_A, V_I)^{\mathcal{A}}})$.

Example 3. Consider again the mixer DCSP of Example 1. The assignment $\mathcal{A}_2 = \{Mi = r, Mt = b, Vol = s, Coo = cool\}$ is still a solution according to the Definition 8 since it satisfies the constraints, the initial variables are active in it, and it is the least fixpoint of the operator. The last property can be established as follows. First, the reduct of the activity constraints is computed with respect to $\mathcal{A}_2$:

$$C_I = (C_A, V_I)^{\mathcal{A}_2} =$$
$$\{(\overset{ACT}{\to} Mi = r), (\overset{ACT}{\to} Mt = b), (\overset{ACT}{\to} Vol = s), (Mi = r \overset{ACT}{\to} Coo = cool)\} .$$

Then, the operator is applied iteratively starting from the empty set:

$$T_{C_I}(\emptyset) = \{Mi = r, Mt = b, Vol = s\} = \mathcal{A}_{21}$$
$$T_{C_I}(\mathcal{A}_{21}) = T_{C_I}(T_{C_I}(\emptyset)) = \{Mi = r, Mt = b, Vol = s, Coo = cool\} = \mathcal{A}_{22}$$
$$T_{C_I}(\mathcal{A}_{22}) = T_{C_I}(T_{C_I}(T_{C_I}(\emptyset))) = \{Mi = r, Mt = b, Vol = s, Coo = cool\}$$

Thus, $\mathcal{A}_{22}$ is the least fixpoint and $\mathrm{lfp}(T_{C_I}) = \mathcal{A}_2$.

On the other hand, the assignment $\mathcal{A}_3 = \{Mi = r, Mt = b, Vol = s, Coo = cool, Con = con2\}$ is not a solution. It does satisfy the constraints, but $C_I = (C_A, V_I)^{\mathcal{A}_3} = \{(\overset{ACT}{\to} Mi = r), (\overset{ACT}{\to} Mt = b), (\overset{ACT}{\to} Vol = l), (Mi = r \overset{ACT}{\to} Coo = cool), (Mt = d \overset{ACT}{\to} Con = con2)\}$. The least fixpoint can again be constructed similarly as above, and $\mathrm{lfp}(T_{C_I}) = \{Mi = r, Mt = b, Vol = s, Coo = cool\} \neq \mathcal{A}_3$.

Example 4. In Example 1, the configuration $\{Mi = r, Mt = d, Vol = s, Coo = cool, Con = con2\}$ with a condenser and a cooler is a legal configuration. In order to avoid having both condenser and cooler active, we consider the following DCSP obtained by replacing the activity constraint a_1 by an "exclusively disjunctive" activity constraint a_3:

$$a_2 = (Mt = d \overset{ACT}{\to} Con)$$
$$a_3 = ((c_4 \overset{ACT}{\to} 1\{Coo \mid Con\}1)$$
$$c_1(Con, Vol) = \{(con1, l), (con2, l), (con2, s)\}$$
$$c_2(Mi, Vol) = \{(r, s), (m, s), (m, l), (t, s), (t, l)\}$$

where $c_4(Mi, Mt) = \{(r, d)\}$. An assignment $\mathcal{A}_1 = \{Mi = r, Mt = d, Vol = s, Con = con2\}$ is a solution since it clearly satisfies the constraints, the initial variables are active in it, and for the reduct $(C_A, V_I)^{\mathcal{A}_1} = \{(\overset{ACT}{\to} Mi = r), (\overset{ACT}{\to} Mt = d), (\overset{ACT}{\to} Vol = s), (Mt = d \overset{ACT}{\to} Con = con2), (c_4 \overset{ACT}{\to} Con = con2)\}$, $\mathrm{lfp}(T_{(C_A, V_I)^{\mathcal{A}_1}}) = \mathcal{A}_1$. On the other hand, $\mathcal{A}_2 = \{Mi = r, Mt = d, Vol = s, Con = con2, Coo = cool\}$ is not a solution since it does not satisfy the activity constraint a_3 that only one of the variables Coo and Con should be active. If the activity constraint $a_4 = (not(Coo = cool) \overset{ACT}{\to} 1\{Con\}1)$ with default negation were further added to the example, the reduct with respect to $\mathcal{A}_1$ would be as follows: $\{(\overset{ACT}{\to} Mi = r), (\overset{ACT}{\to} Mt = d), (\overset{ACT}{\to} Vol = s), (Mt = d \overset{ACT}{\to} Con = con2), (c_4 \overset{ACT}{\to} Con = con2), (\overset{ACT}{\to} Con = con2)\}$. The last instantiated activity constraint is the reduct of a_4. Thus the assignment $\mathcal{A}_1$ would still remain a solution. This latter type of activity constraint can be seen as a default rule stating that, all things being equal, one should choose a condenser over cooler, if possible.

Example 5. Consider now the DCSP which is obtained by replacing the activity constraint a_1 in Example 1 by an "inclusively disjunctive" activity constraint $a'_3 = (c_4 \overset{ACT}{\to} 1\{Coo \mid Con\}2)$ with c_4 a constraint $\{(r, d)\}$ defined on Mi and Mt. Now, the assignment $\mathcal{A}_2 = \{Mi = r, Mt = d, Vol = s, Con = con2, Coo = cool\}$ is a solution, since it satisfies the constraints, the initial variables are active in it, and the reduct $(C_A, \mathcal{V}_I)^{\mathcal{A}_2} = \{(\overset{ACT}{\to} Mi = r), (\overset{ACT}{\to} Mt = d), (\overset{ACT}{\to} Vol = s), (Mt = d \overset{ACT}{\to} Con = con2), (c_4 \overset{ACT}{\to} Con = con2), (c_4 \overset{ACT}{\to} Coo = cool)\}$. The last two instantiated activity constraints are the reduct of a'_3, since both cooler and condenser are active in the assignment. Now $\text{lfp}(T_{(C_A, \mathcal{V}_I)^{\mathcal{A}_2}}) = \mathcal{A}_2$. Also the assignment $\mathcal{A}_1$ in the previous example remains a solution.

In our definition, we in fact relax the minimality requirement. Each active variable in a solution is justified by the activity constraints or initial variables, but a disjunctive activity constraint may justify more variables than a subset minimal solution would contain, as demonstrated by Example 5.

5 Computational Complexity of DCSP

In this section we analyze the complexity of the relevant decision problems for our generalization of DCSP. This also provides a complexity result for the original definition. We first show that our generalization is equivalent to the original definition for the activity constraints handled by it.

Theorem 3. *Definition 8 of a solution to a DCSP is equivalent to Definition 3 for problems without disjunctive activity constraints and default negation, and with only one constraint on the left hand side of every activity constraint.*

Proof. (Sketch) The difference between the two definitions is that the minimality condition of the original definition is replaced by the fixpoint condition in Definition 8. In order to prove the equivalence it remains to show that the fixpoint condition is equivalent to subset minimality when original activity constraints are allowed. This can be done using the following observations. A solution according to Definition 3 is a minimal set satisfying the constraints and making the initial variables active. Hence, it is contained in a solution according to Definition 8 which also satisfies the constraints and makes the initial variables active.

On the other hand, a solution according to Definition 8 is contained in a solution according to Definition 3 as it can be constructed iteratively by starting from the empty solution and by applying the operator T. It can be shown inductively that the result of this iteration is contained in a solution according to Definition 3.

Using the fixpoint definition of a solution it is straightforward to establish that both $DCSP(D)$ and $DCSP_R(D)$ remain **NP**-complete for the generalized DCSP. This is in contrast to the complexity of $DCSP_R(D)$ for the straightforward extension sketched in the beginning of Section 4.

Theorem 4. $DCSP(D)$ and $DCSP_R(D)$ are **NP**-complete for the generalized DCSP.

Proof. (Sketch) First, we note that $DCSP(D)$ is a special case of $DCSP_R(D)$ with an empty set of requirements. Then, we argue that both $DCSP(D)$ and $DCSP_R(D)$ are **NP**-hard since CSP, which is known to be **NP**-complete, is a special case of DCSP with $V_I = V$ and no activity constraints. Further, $DCSP_R(D)$ (and thus also $DCSP(D)$) is **NP**-complete because it is in **NP**. The containment in **NP** is due to the fact that whether an assignment is a solution and satisfies a set of requirements can be checked in polynomial time. This result can be shown by noting that whether an assignment satisfies a set of activity and compatibility constraints and whether it is the least fixpoint of the operator on the instantiated activity constraints can be both decided in polynomial time. The latter property holds since the reduct can obviously be computed in polynomial time, by processing one rule at a time, and the least fixpoint of the operator can be computed in polynomial time.

By Theorem 3 the original DCSP is a special case of the generalized DCSP and we obtain similarly the following corollary.

Corollary 1. $DCSP(D)$ and $DCSP_R(D)$ are **NP**-complete for the original DCSP, i.e. without disjunctive activity constraints and default negation.

6   Implementation

In this section, we briefly discuss two novel solution methods for the original DCSP. The first is similar to the original algorithm described in [5] whereas the second is based on mapping a DCSP to a type of propositional logic programs [10]. To test the performance of both algorithms, we use a set of examples from the configuration domain, CAR [5], CARx2 [10], a simplified form of a hospital monitor problem [11] and a simplified form of the mixer problem [14]. These problems are characterized in Table 2 by the number of variables, number of compatibility constraints and their maximum arity, number of activity constraints and the maximum arity of their left hand side constraints, maximum domain size, number of solutions, and size of the initial search space calculated by multiplying the domain sizes of the variables.

Table 2. Characteristics of the examples.

Problem	$\|\mathcal{V}\|$	$\|\mathcal{C}_C\|$ / max. arity	$\|\mathcal{C}_A\|$ / max. arity	$max(\|\mathcal{D}_i\|)$	$\|$ solutions $\|$	search space
CAR	8	7 / 3	8 / 1	3	198	1296
CARx2	8	7 / 3	8 / 1	6	44456	331776
Monitor	24	9 / 3	19 / 3	4	1320	196608
Mixer	8	4 / 2	6 / 1	4	88	1152

The first implementation differs from the one described in [5] in that it does not use an ATMS. The algorithm is based on a simple backtracking algorithm used to solve standard CSPs. As long as all variables are not yet assigned a value the algorithm chooses the next variable and a value to assign to that variable such that the value is still consistent with the compatibility constraints. Then the algorithm checks if some activity constraint has become relevant, i.e., if the left hand side of an activity constraint is activated and satisfied by the already assigned values. In that case, new variables are activated and added to the list of not yet assigned variables. If all values of a variable have been considered, the algorithm backtracks to the last variable that still has values left. Variables that have been activated by an activity constraint based on the value of a variable deassigned in the backtracking step have to be deactivated as well. The algorithm continues until no more activity constraints can be activated and all currently active variables have been assigned a value. In the current implementation, no consistency algorithms are applied. The implementation was written in Java (Sun's JDK) and run on a Pentium II, 266 MHz, with 96MB of memory, Windows NT operating system. The implementation and the test problems are available at www.cs.hut.fi/~pdmg/CP99/.

The second implementation is based on first translating the DCSP to a set of rules in Configuration Rule Language, a type of propositional logic programs [10], for which the solutions are found using an efficient C++ implementation of the stable model semantics of normal logic programs [6]. The translation results in a set of rules whose size is linear in the size of the DCSP, in fact roughly the same. Solutions are found using backtracking search through a binary search tree where nodes are Boolean valued variables modelling assignments of values to DCSP variables. The search space is extensively pruned using rule propagation. The tests were run on a Pentium II 266 MHz with 128MB of memory, Linux 2.2.3 operating system, smodels version 2.22 and lparse version 0.99.22. Further details can be found in [10], the implementation at www.tcs.hut.fi/pub/smodels and the test problems at www.tcs.hut.fi/pub/smodels/tests/cp99.tar.gz.

The time to find the first and all solutions are given in Table 3. We note that for the first implementation, the problem inputs and outputs are handled in main memory, whereas the results for the second implementation include the time for reading the input from a file and parsing it. However, the execution time for the second implementation does not include the time for translating the DCSP to **CRL** form, which was done manually. Since it is fairly difficult to compare the execution time of algorithms written in different languages, executed on different operating systems and based on different problem formulations, we provide as an additional characterization the number of non-deterministic guesses G for finding the first, respectively all, solutions in Table 3. In a non-deterministic guess of the backtracking algorithm, one variable is assigned a value and it is checked if the resulting (partial) assignment (together with the set of already assigned variables) remains consistent. In the **CRL**-based implementation, a non-deterministic guess chooses a Boolean valued variable corresponding to a particular value assignment of a DCSP variable.

Table 3. Results for the examples.

Implementation	first solution	all solutions	G^{first}	G^{all}
CAR backtrack-based	0.04 s	0.07 s	47	624
CAR **CRL**-based	0.05 s	0.06 s	5	197
CARx2 backtrack-based	0.01 s	11.8 s	217	71230
CARx2 **CRL**-based	0.05 s	3.2 s	6	44455
Monitor backtrack-based	< 1 ms	0.08 s	21	15060
Monitor **CRL**-based	0.06 s	0.31 s	9	1319
Mixer backtrack-based	< 1 ms	0.01 s	15	484
Mixer **CRL**-based	0.04 s	0.05 s	4	87

7 Conclusions and Future Work

Dynamic constraint satisfaction problems were introduced to capture dynamic aspects in generating problem spaces to combinatorial problems such as product configuration [5]. We argue that DCSP is indeed a more expressive representation than CSP for such problems. However, the activity constraints of DCSP are relatively restricted. We present a generalized definition of DCSP which allows disjunctions and default negation in activity constraints. We then show that the relevant decision problems remain **NP**-complete for the generalization, which employs a fixpoint condition instead of a minimality condition used in the original definition. Thus DCSP seems to be a more feasible framework for dynamic problems than CSP. We also show that a straightforward generalization of the original definition would increase the complexity significantly. As further work, the expressivity and computational complexity of combining the different elements of our generalization, minimality and further forms of optimization criteria should be analyzed.

There are few reports on implementations of algorithms for the original DCSP. We sketch two implementations, one based on a modified backtracking algorithm for CSP, the other based on mapping DCSP to a type of propositional logic program rules. The test results for both on a set of simple configuration problems are acceptable and indicate that they should be further pursued. Both implementations should be extended with the generalizations and empirically tested on larger problems. The logic program based implementation employs rule propagation at each point in search space which seems to reduce considerably the number of non-deterministic guesses needed for finding solutions. Hence, the backtrack implementation of DCSP can probably be enhanced similarly by integrating to it various consistency algorithms similar to standard CSP search algorithms.

Acknowledgements. The work of the first author has been supported by the Helsinki Graduate School in Computer Science and Engineering and the Technology Development Centre Finland, and that of the third author by the Academy of Finland (Project 43963). The work of the second author is a continuation of that done at the AI-Lab, EPFL. She would like to thank its director, Professor B. Faltings, and the colleagues there who contributed to the work.

References

1. T. Eiter and G. Gottlob. Complexity aspects of various semantics for disjunctive databases. In *Proc. of the 12th Symposium on Principles of Database Systems*, pages 158–167, 1993.
2. M. Gelfond and V. Lifschitz. The stable model semantics for logic programming. In *Proc. of the 5th Intern. Conf. on Logic Programming*, pages 1070–1080, 1988.
3. E. M. Gelle. *On the generation of locally consistent solution spaces.* Ph.D. Thesis, Ecole Polytechnique Fédérale de Lausanne, Switzerland, 1998.
4. J. Lloyd. *Foundations of Logic Programming.* Springer-Verlag, 2nd edition, 1987.
5. S. Mittal and B. Falkenhainer. Dynamic constraint satisfaction problems. In *Proc. of the 8th National Conf. on Artificial Intelligence*, pages 25–32, 1990.
6. I. Niemelä and P. Simons. Smodels – an implementation of the stable model and well-founded semantics for normal logic programs. In *Proc. of the 4th International Conf. on Logic Programming and Non-Monotonic Reasoning*, pages 420–429, 1997.
7. D. Sabin and E. C. Freuder. Configuration as composite constraint satisfaction. In *Configuration - Papers from the 1996 Fall Symposium. AAAI Technical Report FS-96-03*, 1996.
8. D. Sabin and R. Weigel. Product configuration frameworks – a survey. *IEEE Intelligent Systems & Their Applications*, pages 42–49, July/August 1998.
9. T. Soininen and E. M. Gelle. Dynamic constraint satisfaction in configuration. In *AAAI'99 Workshop on Configuration. To appear as AAAI Technical Report*, 1999.
10. T. Soininen and I. Niemelä. Developing a declarative rule language for applications in product configuration. In *Practical Aspects of Declarative Languages (PADL99), LNCS 1551.* Springer-Verlag, 1999.
11. T. Soininen, J. Tiihonen, T. Männistö, and R. Sulonen. Towards a general ontology of configuration. *AI EDAM*, 12:357–372, 1998.
12. M. Stumptner, G. Friedrich, and A. Haselböck. Generative constraint-based configuration of large technical systems. *AI EDAM*, 12:307–320, 1998.
13. E. Tsang. *Foundations of Constraint Satisfaction.* Academic Press, London, 1993.
14. M. van Velzen. A Piece of CAKE, Computer Aided Knowledge Engineering on KADSified Configuration Tasks. Master's thesis, University of Amsterdam, Social Science Informatics, 1993.

Solving Satisfiability Problems on FPGAs Using Experimental Unit Propagation

Takayuki Suyama, Makoto Yokoo, and Akira Nagoya

NTT Communication Science Laboratories
2-4 Hikaridai, Seika-cho
Soraku-gun, Kyoto 619-0237 Japan
e-mail: suyama/yokoo/nagoya@cslab.kecl.ntt.co.jp

Abstract. This paper presents new results on an innovative approach for solving satisfiability problems (SAT), that is, creating a logic circuit that is specialized to solve each problem instance on Field Programmable Gate Arrays (FPGAs). This approach has become feasible due to recent advances in Reconfigurable Computing, and has opened up an exciting new research field in algorithm design.

We have developed an algorithm that is suitable for a logic circuit implementation. This algorithm is basically equivalent to the Davis-Putnam procedure with Experimental Unit Propagation. The algorithm requires fewer hardware resources than previous approaches. Simulation results show that this method can solve a hard random 3-SAT problem with 400 variables within 1.6 minutes at a clock rate of 10MHz. Faster speeds can be obtained by increasing the clock rate. Furthermore, we have actually implemented a 128-variable, 256-clause problem instance on FPGAs.

1 Introduction

Recently, due to advances in Field Programmable Gate Array (FPGA) technologies [3], users can create original logic circuits and electronically reconfigure them. Furthermore, users are able to describe their designs in a Hardware Description Language (HDL) and obtain logic circuits by using current high level logic synthesis technologies [4, 12]. These recent hardware technologies enable users to rapidly create logic circuits specialized to solve each problem instance. We have chosen satisfiability problems to examine of the effectiveness of this approach.

A constraint satisfaction problem (CSP) is a general framework that can formalize various problems, and many theoretical and experimental studies have been performed on these problems [10]. In particular, a satisfiability problem for propositional formulas in conjunctive normal form (SAT) is an important subclass of CSP. This problem was the first computational task shown to be NP-hard.

In [17], we presented an initial report on innovative approach for solving satisfiability problems. In this approach, a logic circuit that is specialized to solve each problem instance is created on FPGAs. After this pioneer work, various researches following this line have been carried out [1, 8, 13, 16, 18]. As such, solving SAT using FPGAs is becoming a very vital research area.

The performance of the method described in [17] is equivalent to the basic Davis-Putnam procedure [5], and the performance is not very efficient since the variable ordering is static. In [16], we introduced dynamic variable ordering with Maximum Occurrences in clauses of Minimum Size (Mom's) heuristic [6, 7]. However, we were not able to implement large-scale problems since implementing Mom's heuristic on FPGAs require too many hardware resources. In this paper, we present a new method for implementing a more efficient algorithm that requires less hardware resources. This algorithm is basically equivalent to the Davis-Putnam procedure with Experimental Unit Propagation [9].

In the remainder of the paper, we describe Reconfigurable Computing approach (Section 2), and briefly describe the problem definition (Section 3). Then, we present in detail the developed algorithm, which is suitable for implementation on a logic circuit (Section 4). We show an implementation of this algorithm on FPGAs (Section 5). Finally, we show evaluation results obtained with the software simulation and actual implementation (Section 6).

2 Reconfigurable Computing Approach

In this section, we describe our Reconfigurable Computing (RC) approach. RC systems are hardware systems with logical configurations that can be changed to solve some problem or to quickly carry out some application. These systems are realized with FPGAs and logic synthesis systems. Ordinary RC systems are reconfigured to a target application. On the other hand, our RC system features reconfiguration for an instance of the application problem.

One might argue that it is natural to increase a system's speed by implementing an algorithm on hardware, and there is no significant reason for research on such an approach. This argument is not correct, since the operations that can be directly performed by hardware are rather limited. If we perform a complicated operation by iterating a number of simple operations, the performance is similar to that of general-purpose computers.

To obtain reasonable speed increases utilizing hardware, we need new and quite different methodologies for designing/implementing algorithms. For example, when implementing an efficient search algorithm using general-purpose computers, we often need to avoid duplicated computations by using a carefully designed data structure to represent a state. More specifically, we can maintain an integer vector for clauses (the initial value of each vector element is 3), when solving a 3-SAT problem. In determining a variable value, we subtract one from the element where the clause is reduced by this operation. With such a data structure, radically changing a state is not desirable, because its book-keeping would be too costly.

On the other hand, if we have enough hardware resources, all clauses can be checked in one clock cycle without using such a data structure. Since some kinds of computations can be performed very quickly using hardware, we can get more freedom in the design of algorithms. We believe that this approach brings a very exciting new dimension to algorithm design.

A logic circuit that solves a specific SAT problem is synthesized by the following procedure. First, a text file that describes a SAT problem is analyzed by an SFL generator written in the C language. This program generates a behavioral description specific to the given problem with an HDL called SFL. Then, a CAD system analyzes the description and synthesizes a netlist, which describes the logic circuit structure. Finally, the FPGA Mapper of the FPGA system generates FPGA mapping data from the netlist. We use a system called PARTHENON [12] developed at NTT. PARTHENON is a highly practical system that integrates a description language SFL, simulator, and logic synthesizer. Furthermore, the FPGA Mapper generates FPGA mapping data from the netlist. Only the SFL generator is newly developed for this research. Other parts are commercial software.

3 Problem Definition

A satisfiability problem for propositional formulas in conjunctive normal form (SAT) can be defined as follows. A boolean *variable* x_i is a variable that takes a true or false value (represented as 1 or 0, respectively). We call the value assignment of one variable a *literal*. A *clause* is a disjunction of literals, e.g., $(x_1 + \overline{x_2} + x_3)$. Given a set of clauses $C_1, C_2, \ldots, C_m$ and variables $x_1, x_2, \ldots, x_n$, the satisfiability problem is to determine if the formula $C_1 \cdot C_2 \cdot \ldots \cdot C_m$ is satisfiable, that is, to determine whether an assignment of values to the variables exists so that the above formula is true.

In this paper, if the formula is satisfiable, we assume that we need to find all or a fixed number of solutions, i.e., the combinations of variable values that satisfy the formula. Most of the existing algorithms for solving SAT problems aim to find only one solution. Although this setting corresponds to the original problem definition, some application problems, such as visual interpretation tasks [15] and diagnosis tasks [14] require finding all or multiple solutions. Furthermore, since finding all or multiple solutions is usually much more difficult than finding only one solution, it is worthwhile to solve the problem with special-purpose hardware.

For simplicity, we restrict our attention to 3-SAT problems, i.e., the number of literals in each clause is 3. Relaxing this assumption is rather straightforward.

4 Algorithm

4.1 Basic Algorithm

The algorithm used in this paper is basically equivalent to the Davis-Putnam procedure that introduces a dynamic variable ordering with *Experimental Unit Propagation* (EUP) [9]. The outline of the algorithm can be described as follows.

Let I be the input SAT problem instance, and L be the working list containing problem instances, where L is initialized as $\{I\}$. A problem instance is represented as a pair of a set of value assignments and a set of clauses that are not yet satisfied.

1. If L is empty, then I is unsatisfiable, so stop the algorithm. Otherwise, select the first element S from L and remove S from L.
2. If S contains an empty clause, then S is unsatisfiable, go to 1.
3. If all clauses in S are satisfied, print the value assignments of S as one solution, go to 1.
4. If S contains a unit clause (a clause with only one variable), then set this variable to the value which satisfies the clause, simplify the clauses of S and go to 2.
5. **Branching:** To select a variable to be assigned at the next step, we experimentally set each unassigned variable's value to 0 and 1. This procedure is called Experimental Unit Propagation. If some clause becomes unsatisfiable by setting a variable to 0, set it to 1, and vice versa, then go to 2. Otherwise, we select the variable x that causes the maximum number of unit propagation[1]. Add to the top of L the simplified instance S' obtained by setting x to 1. Set x to 0 and simplify S. Go to 2.

4.2 Differences between the Previous Approach

In [16], we developed a method for implementing a backtracking tree search algorithm without using a stack. In this approach, the overhead of sequential accesses to a large memory is avoided by using separate registers assigned for each variable. More specifically, there exists a register for each variable, which records the depth of the search tree where the variable value is determined. This information is used for backtracking.

We follow our previous method to implement backtracking tree search procedures, but use a different branching heuristic. In [16], Maximum Occurrences in the clauses of the Minimum Size (Mom's) heuristic [6, 7] is used for branching. However, we need a logic circuit that counts the number of occurrences of all variables in binary clauses to implement MOM's heuristic. This logic circuit tends to be very large, so it is very difficult to implement large-scale problems using currently available hardware resources. Actually, only a very small-scale problem with 30 variables was implemented in [16].

In this paper, we introduce another branching heuristic called Experimental Unit Propagation, which was shown to be at least as efficient as MOM's heuristic [9]. One advantage of using this heuristic is that the logic circuit for implementing this heuristic is very similar to the logic circuit for the main tree search procedures; thus, we can share the hardware resources between these routines.

---

[1] The detail of the branching rule is described later.

4.3 Details of the Algorithm

In this section, we are going to describe the detail of the algorithm. First, we are going to define concepts and terms used in the algorithm. We represent the fact that x_i is true as $(x_i, 1)$.

- Each variable x_i is associated with the value $depth(x_i)$, which represents the depth of the search tree where the variable value is determined.
- Each variable x_i is associated with the value $determined(x_i)$.
  If $determined(x_i) = 1$, this means that x_i's value is determined.
  If $determined(x_i) = 0$, x_i's value is not yet determined. The initial value of $determined(x_i)$ is 0.
- Each variable x_i is associated with the value $branch(x_i)$. If $branch(x_i) = 0$, this means that x_i's value is determined by unit resolutions. If $branch(x_i) = 1$, this means that x_i's value is determined by branching.
- A global variable $current\_depth$ is defined with an initial value of 1.
- For each clause $(x_i, v_i) \vee (x_j, v_j) \vee (x_k, v_k)$, we classify the condition of the clause into one of the following five cases.
  not-satisfied: for each variable x_i, x_j, x_k, the variable value is determined, and the value is not equal to v_i, v_j, v_k, respectively.
  satisfied: at least one of the following conditions is satisfied; 1) $determined(x_i) = 1$ and x_i's value is v_i, 2) $determined(x_j) = 1$ and x_j's value is v_j, 3) $determined(x_k) = 1$ and x_k's value is v_k.
  unit: for any two of x_i, x_j, x_k, the variable value is determined, and the value of the remaining one variable is not determined. The value is not equal to v_i, v_j, v_k, respectively, for the variable whose value is determined.
  other: the other condition above.
- If multiple unit clauses exist, and these unit clauses assign different values to the same variable, we call these unit clauses *inconsistent*.

Here, we show the details of the algorithm. The algorithm consists of "Main Procedure" and "Experimental Unit Propagation Procedure". The Experimental Unit Propagation Procedure is used in the **Branching** state for searching a variable that should be assigned at the next step. In the initial state, $current\_depth$ is 1, and for each variable x_i, $determined(x_i)$ and $branch(x_i)$ are 0.

Main Procedure

1. **Not Satisfied:** If a *not-satisfied* clause or inconsistent *unit* clauses exists, go to 5.
2. **Satisfied:** If all clauses are *satisfied*, print the current value assignments as a solution. Go to 5.
3. **Unit:** If *unit* clauses exist and are not inconsistent, for all unit clauses, for each variable x_i where $determinead(x_i)$ is 0, set the value to v_i, which is specified by the clause. Set $determined(x_i)$ to 1, $branch(x_i)$ to 0, and $depth(x_i)$ to $current\_depth$. Go to 1.

4. **Branching:** Otherwise, set max_eval_sum to 0, and max_eval_min to 0, and apply the conditions below for each variable x_i where $determined(x_i)$ is 0

   (a) Set $eval\_0$ to the return value of Experimental Unit Propagation$(x_i, 0)$ procedure. If $eval\_0$ is *not-satisfied*, set $determined(x_i)$ to 1, x_i to 1, $branch(x_i)$ to 0 and $depth(x_i)$ to $current\_depth$. Abort procedures for the other variables. Go to 1.

   (b) Set $eval\_1$ to the return value of Experimental Unit Propagation$(x_i, 1)$ procedure. If $eval\_0$ is *not-satisfied*, set $determined(x_i)$ to 1, x_i to 0, $branch(x_i)$ to 0 and $depth(x_i)$ to $current\_depth$. Abort procedures for the other variables. Go to 1.

   (c) If $max\_eval\_min < min(eval\_0, eval\_1)$, or $max\_eval\_min = min(eval\_0, eval\_1)$ and $max\_eval\_sum < eval\_0 + eval\_1$, set $best\_pos$ to x_i, max_eval_min to $min(eval\_0, eval\_1)$ and max_eval_sum to $eval\_0 + eval\_1$.

   Branching end: Set x_i that is specified by $best\_pos$ to 0, $determined(x_i)$ to 1, $branch(x_i)$ to 1 and $depth(x_i)$ to $current\_depth + 1$. Set $current\_depth$ to $current\_depth + 1$. Go to 1.

5. **Backtracking:**

   5.1 If $current\_depth$ is 1, stop the algorithm.

   5.2 Otherwise, for each variable x_i,
   If $depth(x_i) = current\_depth$ and $branch(x_i) = 0$, set $determined(x_i)$ to 0, and set $depth(x_i)$ to 0.
   If $depth(x_i) = current\_depth$ and $branch(x_i) = 1$, set x_i to 1, $branch(x_i)$ to 0, and set $depth(x_i)$ to $current\_depth - 1$.

   5.3 set $current\_depth$ to $current\_depth - 1$, go to 1.

Experimental Unit Propagation$(x_i, value)$ Procedure

Set $count = 0$, $x_i = value$, $branch(x_i) = 1$, $determined(x_i) = 1$, $depth(x_i) = current\_depth + 1$ and $current\_depth = current\_depth + 1$.

1. **Not Satisfied:** If a *not-satisfied* clause or inconsistent *unit* clauses exist, set $result$ to *not-satisfied*. Go to 5.
2. **Satisfied:** If all clauses are *satisfied*, set $result$ to n (the number of variables). Go to 5.
3. **Unit:** If *unit* clauses exists and are not inconsistent, for all unit clauses, for each variable x_i where $determinead(x_i)$ is 0, set the value to v_i, which is specified by the clause. Set $determined(x_i)$ to 1, $branch(x_i)$ to 0, $depth(x_i)$ to $current\_depth$, and $count$ to $count + 1$. Go to 1.
4. **Branching:** Otherwise, set $result$ to $count$. Go to 5.
5. **Backtracking:** For each variable x_i, if $depth(x_i) = current\_depth$, set $determined(x_i)$ to 0, $branch(x_i)$ to 0 and $depth(x_i)$ to 0. Set $depth(x_i)$ to $current\_depth - 1$. Return $result$.

5 Implementation

The algorithm described in Section 4 can be straightforwardly represented as a finite state machine.

Since there are many similarities between the Main Procedure and the Experimental Unit Propagation Procedure, hardware can be shared between them, that is, at some time the hardware works in the Main Procedure mode, while at other times, it works in the Experimental Unit Propagation Procedure mode. In order to distinguish these two modes, a flag called *eup* is set up. If *eup* is 0, the algorithm is in the Main Procedure, and if *eup* is 1, the algorithm is in the Experimental Unit Propagation Procedure mode. The *evaluation*, *unit* and *backtrack* states are used both in the Main Procedure mode and in the Experimental Unit Propagation Procedure mode. However, the behavior of these states is slightly different according to the value of *eup*.

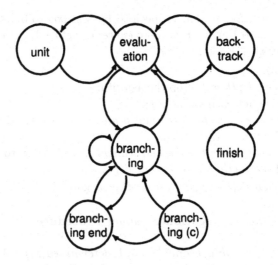

Fig. 1. Finite state machine transitions

The conditions of clauses are calculated and integrated in the *evaluation* state and the next state is determined. The condition of each clause can be calculated in parallel with other clauses. For example, we create a logic circuit that is equivalent to the following logic formula to check whether a clause is *not-satisfied*.

$$(determined(x_i) \cdot determined(x_j) \cdot determined(x_k)) \cdot$$
$$((x_i \oplus v_i) \cdot (x_j \oplus v_j) \cdot (x_k \oplus v_k))$$
$$\text{where } \oplus \text{ is Exclusive-OR.}$$

In the *backtracking* state, for each variable x_i, $depth(x_i)$ and *current_depth* are compared, and variable values, *determined*, *depth*, etc. are changed. These procedures can be done in parallel for each variable. If *current_depth* $= 1$, the algorithm is terminated. These procedures require one clock cycle.

In the *unit* state, several variable values are determined by unit clauses. These procedures are simple and can be executed within the same clock cycle of the *evaluation* state.

When the current state moves from the *evaluation* state to the *branching* state, *eup* is set to 1, and *eup* is 1 until it goes back to the Main Procedure mode. In the *branching (c)* state and *branching end* state, **Branching (c)** and **Branching end** in the Main Procedure are carried out, respectively.

The high-level hardware description language SFL can handle the finite state machine representation, and the LSI CAD system PARTHENON can automatically generate a RT-level hardware description. The state transitions of the finite state machine are shown in Figure 1.

6 Evaluation

6.1 Simulation

We first evaluate the efficiency of the developed algorithm with software simulation. We use hard random 3-SAT problems for evaluation. Each clause is generated by randomly selecting three variables, and each of the variables is given the value 0 or 1 (false or true) with a 50% probability. The number of clauses divided by the number of variables is called *clause density*, and the value 4.3 has been identified as a critical value that produces particularly difficult problem instances [11], which are called problems in *phase transition* region.

In Figure 2, we show the log-scale plot of the average required time of over 100 phase-transition problems, assuming the clock rate is 10MHz. Since a randomly generated 3-SAT problem tends to have a very large number of solutions when it is solvable, we terminate each execution after the first 100 solutions are found to finish the simulation within a reasonable amount of time.

Figure 2 shows that the new method (EUP) can solve a hard random 3-SAT problem with 400 variables within 1.6 minutes at a clock rate of 10MHz. In addition, we can see that the search tree growing at the rate of the EUP is $O(2^{n/20.0})$, where n is the number of variables, whereas the search tree of MOM's[16] grows at the rate of $O(2^{n/17.3})$. This result shows that the new method is more efficient with a larger number of variables.

Furthermore, we show the results for AIM benchmark problems[2] with 128 variables and 256 clauses on FPGAs. These problem instances are unsolvable, and are known to be very difficult. Table 1 shows the required number of states and the time to solve these problems when the clock rate is 10.0MHz. For comparison, we also show the cpu time of POSIT [7], a very sophisticated SAT solver that utilizes the MOM heuristic. We should have shown the result obtained by a software implementation that utilizes Experimental Unit Propagation, such as

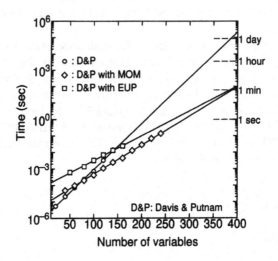

Fig. 2. Required time at 10MHz on hard random 3-SAT problems

Table 1. The required state and time for "aim-128-2_0-no-*.cnf"

problem	# of states	time (sec) @ 10MHz	cpu time of POSIT (sec)	speed-up ratio
aim-128-2_0-no-0	1,973,080,127	197.3	884.1	4.48
aim-128-2_0-no-1	1,662,111,245	166.2	931.6	5.61
aim-128-2_0-no-2	44,321,403	4.43	230.8	52.1
aim-128-2_0-no-3	3,651,710,074	365.2	2138.1	5.85
aim-128-2_0-no-4	2,726,316,935	272.6	2749.3	10.08
aim-128-2_0-no-5	839,166,228	83.9	471.6	5.62
average	1,816,117,668	181.6	1234.2	6.80

Satz [9]. Since we don't have a well-optimized code for this method at hand, we refrain from reporting the performance of this method. These programs run on a Sun Ultra 30 Model 300 (UltraSPARC-II 296MHz). We can see that the running time of EUP on FPGAs is faster than these programs.

Of course, this comparison is not very fair as we do not consider the time required to generate the logic circuit. Currently, generating a logic circuit from a problem description takes an hour. However, these routines can be highly optimized for SAT problems since many parts in a logic circuit are common in all problem instances. Therefore, the time required to generate a logic circuit would be negligible for larger-scale problems if we implement a logic circuit generator that is specialized for SAT problems.

6.2 Current Implementation Status

We use an ALTERA FLEX10K250 FPGA chip to implement the algorithm. FLEX10K250 has 12,160 Logic Cells (LCs) and its typical usable gates are from 149k to 310k. This system is connected to an IBM-PC via parallel port. The total system including mapping software costs around $16,000.

We have actually implemented a 3-SAT problem, "aim-128-2_0-no-*.cnf" as previously described. 11,042 LCs is used for implementing this problem. The utilized rate of LCs is 90%. We were able to run this circuit at a clock rate of 10.0MHz. In addition, we have successfully mapped "aim-200-1_6-yes1-1.cnf" with 200 variables and 320 clauses. The circuit is divided into 21 FLEX10K chips, and the total usability rate of LCs is low (13%). When a logic circuit cannot be fit into one chip, the circuit is divided into multiple chips. However, since the wiring resources among multiple chips (i.e., the number of interface pins of a chip) are very scarce compared with the wiring resources within one chip, we can implement only a small portion of the logic circuit on one chip.

Figure 3 shows the number of gates required for "aim-{50,100,200}-1_6-yes1-1.cnf". The figure shows the number of gates when the circuit is organized by primitive gates. Note that these circuits are the initial ones synthesized from HDL descriptions. If these circuits are optimized, the number of gates can be reduced further with keeping the same trend. EUP's required gates of are approximately 30% less than that of MOM. This is because almost all the circuits of Experimental Unit Propagation can be shared with the Main Procedure. On the other hand, the MOM algorithm requires additional circuits for branching.

7 Conclusions

This paper presented new results on solving SAT using FPGAs. In this approach, a logic circuit specific to each problem instance is created on FPGAs. We developed an algorithm that is suitable for implementation on a logic circuit. This algorithm is basically equivalent to the Davis-Putnam procedure, which introduces Experimental Unit Propagation.

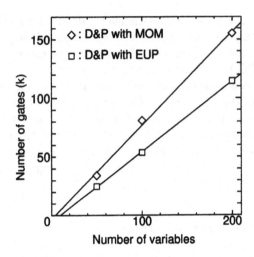

Fig. 3. Required gates for "aim-<#variables>-1_6-yes1-1.cnf"

The number of gates required to implement the proposed method is 30% less than that of MOM. In addition, the order of the proposed method is also better than that of MOM. We have actually implemented a benchmark problem with 128 variables that can run at 10MHz.

We are now refining the implementation of the algorithm on FPGAs, and planning to perform various evaluations on implemented logic circuits.

Acknowledgments

The authors would like to thank Yuichi Asahiro and Kazuo Iwama for providing AIM benchmark problems.

References

[1] Abramovici, M. and Saab, D.: Satisfiablilty on Reconfigurable Hardware, *International Workshop on Field Programmable Logic and Applications* (1997) 448–456

[2] Asahiro, Y., Iwama, K., and Miyano, E.: Random generation of test instances with controlled attributes, *Proceedings of the DIMACS Challenge II Workshop* (1993)

[3] Brown, S. D., Francis, R. J., Rose, J., and Vranesic, Z. G.: *Field-Programmable Gate Arrays*, Kluwer Academic Publishers (1992)

[4] Camposano, R. and Wolf, W.: *High-level VLSI synthesis*, Kluwer Academic (1991)

[5] Davis, M. and Putnam, H.: A computing procedure for quantification theory, *Journal of the ACM*, Vol. 7, (1960) 201–215

[6] Dubois, O., Andre, P., Boufkhad, Y., and Carlier, J.: Can a very simple algorithm be efficient for solving the SAT problem?, *Proc. of the DIMACS Challenge II Workshop* (1993)

[7] Freeman, J. W.: *Improvements to propositional satisfiability search algorithms*, PhD thesis, the University of Pennsylvania (1995)

[8] Hamadi, Y. and Merceron, D.: Reconfigurable Architectures: A New Vision for Optimizing Problem, *Proc. of Third International Conference on Principles and Practice on Constraint Programming (CP'97)* (1997) 209–221

[9] Li, C. M. and Anbulagan, : Heuristics Based on Unit propagation for Satisfiability Problems, *Proc. of 15th International Joint Conference on Artificial Intelligence* (1997) 366–371

[10] Mackworth, A. K.: *Encyclopedia of Artificial Intelligence*, Wiley-Interscience Publication (1992)

[11] Mitchell, D., Selman, B., and Levesque, H.: Hard and easy distributions of SAT problem, *Proc. of the Tenth National Conference on Artificial Intelligence* (1992) 459–465

[12] Nakamura, Y., Oguri, K., Nagoya, A., Yukishita, M., and Nomura, R.: High-level synthesis design at NTT systems labs., *IEICE Trans. Inf & Syst.*, Vol. E76-D, No. 9, (1993) 1047–1054

[13] Rashid, A., Leonard, J., and Mangione-Smith, W. H.: Dynamic Circuit Generation for Solving Specific Problem Instances of Boolean Satisfiability, *Proc. of IEEE Symposium on Field-Programmable Custom Computing Machines* (1998) 196–204

[14] Reiter, R.: A theory of diagnosis from first principles, *Artificial Intelligence 32(1):* (1987) 57–95

[15] Reiter, R. and Mackworth, A.: A logical framework for depiction and image interpretation, *Artificial Intelligence 41(2):* (1989) 125–155

[16] Suyama, T., Yokoo, M., and Sawada, H.: Solving Satisfiability Problems Using Logic Synthesis and Reconfigurable Hardware, *Proc. of the 31st Annual Hawaii International Conference on System Sciences Vol. VII* (1998) 179–186

[17] Yokoo, M., Suyama, T., and Sawada, H.: Solving satisfiability problems using field programmable gate arrays: First results, *Proc. of the Second International Conference on Principles and Practice of Constraint Programming*, Springer-Verlag (1996) 497–509

[18] Zhong, P., Martonosi, M., Ashar, P., and Malik, S.: Accelerating Boolean Satisfiability with Configurable Hardware, *Proc. of Symposium on Field-Programmable Custom Computing Machines* (1998) 186–195

On the Behavior and Application of Constraint Weighting

John Thornton[1] and Abdul Sattar[2]

[1] School of Information Technology, Griffith University Gold Coast,
Parklands Drive, Southport, Qld, 4215, Australia
j.thornton@gu.edu.au
[2] School of Computing and Information Technology, Griffith University,
Kessels Road, Nathan, Qld, 4111, Australia
sattar@cit.gu.edu.au

Abstract. In this paper we compare the performance of three constraint weighting schemes with one of the latest and fastest WSAT heuristics: rnovelty. We extend previous results from satisfiability testing by looking at the broader domain of constraint satisfaction and test for differences in performance using randomly generated problems and problems based on realistic situations and assumptions. We find constraint weighting produces fairly consistent behaviour within problem domains, and is more influenced by the number and interconnectedness of constraints than the realism or randomness of a problem. We conclude that constraint weighting is better suited to smaller structured problems, where it is can clearly distinguish between different constraint groups.

1 Introduction

The intensive research into satisfiability testing during the 1990s has produced a set of powerful new local search heuristics. Starting from GSAT [11], the latest WSAT techniques have raised the ceiling on solving hard 3-SAT problems from several hundred to several thousand variables [13]. At the same time, a new class of clause or constraint weighting algorithms have been developed [9, 12]. These algorithms have proved highly competitive with GSAT (at least on smaller problems with few solutions [1]), and have stimulated the successful application of related techniques in several other domains [14, 2, 15]. However, since the initial development of constraint weighting, WSAT has evolved new and more powerful heuristics to meet the challenges posed by planning problems (such as novelty and rnovelty [8]). The improved performance of these heuristics brings the usefulness of constraint weighting into question. This paper re-examines constraint weighting in the light of the latest WSAT developments. We take the basic heuristics of both techniques and apply them to a series of different problem domains. In the process we examine the following questions:

- Are there particular problem domains for which constraint weighting is preferred?
- Does constraint weighting do better on more realistic, structured problems?
- Is there one weighting scheme that is superior on all the domains considered?

The main aim of the study is to provide practical guidance as to the relevance and applicability of constraint weighting to the broader domain of constraint satisfaction. Research has already looked at applying WSAT to integer optimization problems [16], and applying constraint weighting to over-constrained problems (CSPs) [15]. However, outside the satisfiability domain, there has been little direct comparison between techniques. The research addresses this by applying both WSAT and constraint weighting to three CSP formulations: university timetabling, nurse scheduling and random binary constraint satisfaction. In addition we explore the behavior of constraint weighting on several classes of satisfiability problem, and look at the performance of a hybrid WSAT + constraint weighting algorithm.

The next section introduces the algorithms used in the study, and then the results for each problem domain are presented. From an analysis of these results we draw general conclusions about the applicability and typical behavior of constraint weighting.

2 CSPs and Local Search

The constraint satisfaction paradigm models the world in terms of variables with domains of values, and constraints that define allowable combinations of these values [7]. One of the aims of constraint satisfaction is to provide a uniform way of representing a range of problems that can then be solved using standard CSP techniques. Local search becomes relevant to constraint satisfaction when problems become too large or complex to solve using a systematic technique such as backtracking [6]. Instead of building up a solution by instantiating variables one at a time, local search starts with a complete instantiation of all variables and searches for improving 'local' moves. Generally this means trying domain values for each variable and accepting the value that most reduces the overall cost. Repeatedly making improving moves will either lead to a solution (all constraints satisfied) or to a local minimum (some constraints violated, but no more improving moves available). The basic issue for all non-trivial local search techniques is how to escape local minima and carry on the search.

2.1 Constraint Weighting

Constraint weighting schemes solve the problem of local minima by adding weights to the cost of violated constraints. These weights permanently increase

448

the cost of violating a constraint, changing the shape of the cost surface so that minima can be avoided or exceeded [9].

procedure ConstraintWeighting
begin
    CurrentState ← *set variables to initial assignments*
    BestCost ← *cost of CurrentState*
    while *BestCost* > 0 *and* iterations < MaxIterations **do**
        if MOVE **or** *CurrentState is not a local minimum* **then**
            Dlist ← Empty
            select a variable v_i involved in a constraint violation
            for each *domain value d_j of v_i | d_j ≠ current value of v_i* **do**
                TestCost ← *cost of accepting d_j*
                if *TestCost* ≤ *BestCost* **then**
                    if *TestCost* < *BestCost* **then**
                        Dlist ← Empty, *BestCost* ← *TestCost*
                    end if
                    Dlist ← *Dlist + d_j*
                end if
            end for
            if *Dlist not* Empty **then**
                CurrentState ← *randomly accept move from Dlist*
            else if MOVE **then**
                increment the weight of all violated constraints containing v_i
                BestCost ← *new cost of CurrentState*
            end if
        else if MIN **then**
            increment the weight of all violated constraints
            BestCost ← *new cost of CurrentState*
        else if *UTIL* **then**
            increment the weight of all violated constraints with the smallest weight
            BestCost ← *new cost of CurrentState*
        end if
        end while
end

Fig. 1. The Constraint Weighting Algorithm

Several weighting schemes have been proposed. In Morris's [9] formulation, constraint weights are initialised to one and violated constraint weights are incremented by one each time a local minimum is encountered. Frank [3, 4] adjusts weights after each move and experiments with different initial weights and weight increment functions and with allowing weights to decay over time. Further work has applied constraint weighting to over-constrained problems using dynamic weight adjustment [14] and utility functions [15].

In the current study we are interested in *when* and *what* to weight. Therefore we keep to Morris's original incrementing scheme and explore variations of three of the published weighting strategies:

1. MIN: Incrementing weights at each local minimum (based on [9]).
2. MOVE: Incrementing weights when no local cost improving move exists (based on [3], although Frank increments after all moves).
3. UTIL: Incrementing weights at each local minimum according to a utility function (based on [15]).

Voudouris and Tsang's [15] utility function is part of a more sophisticated algorithm (Guided Local Search or GLS) that handles constraints with different absolute violation costs. They penalise features in a local minimum that have the highest utility according to the following function:

$$utility_i(s^*) = I_i(s^*) \times (c_i / (1 + p_i))$$

where s^* is the current solution, i identifies a feature, c_i is the cost of feature i, p_i is the penalty (or weight) currently applied to feature i and $I_i(s^*)$ is a function that returns one if feature i is exhibited in solution s^* (zero otherwise). In the current study we assume each feature is a constraint with a cost of one. In this case the utility function will only select for weighting the violated constraint(s) in a local minimum that have the smallest current weight. Our aim is to test the utility function as a weighting strategy in isolation from the GLS algorithm, to see if it is useful in a more general weighting approach.

The three weighting strategies are tested within the same basic algorithm which randomly selects variables involved in constraint violations and accepts the best non-cost increasing move from the variable's domain (see Fig. 1). This algorithm was adjusted for SAT problems to randomly select violated *clauses* (rather than variables) and then accept the best non-cost increasing move from the combined domains of all variables involved in the clause (following the WSAT approach of Fig. 2). In addition, the MOVE heuristic was adapted for SAT to increment the weight of a selected clause if no improving move exists for that clause. These strategies were chosen due to the special structure of SAT problems in that all variables have two domain values (true or false), which would otherwise cause the original Fig. 1 algorithm to only consider a single move in each iteration.

2.2 WSAT

WSAT avoids local minima by allowing cost *increasing* moves. The algorithm proceeds by selecting violated constraints and then choosing a move which will improve or satisfy the constraint, even when this results in an overall cost increase. The various WSAT schemes differ according to the move selection heuristic employed. The rnovelty heuristic [8] considers both the overall cost of a move and when the move was *last* used. If the best cost move is also the most recently used move then (according to a probability threshold) the second best cost move may be accepted (as shown in figure 2). In using a least recently used comparison, rnovelty combines a stochastic search with a memory strategy similar to that proposed for HSAT [5]. It is the extra leverage obtained by considering the age of a move that distinguishes rnovelty from the earlier WSAT heuristics.

```
procedure rnovelty
begin
    CurrentState ← set variables to initial assignments
    while Cost(CurrentState) > 0 and iterations < MaxIters do
        if iterations modulus 100 = 0 then
            CurrentState ← CurrentState + random move
        end if
        select a violated constraint c
        Best ← n, SecondBest ← n | Cost(n) = LargeValue
        LastChange ← last iteration variable in c was changed
        for each variable vᵢ involved in c do
            for each domain value dⱼ of vᵢ | dⱼ ≠ current value of vᵢ do
                if Cost(dⱼ) < Cost(Best) or (Cost(dⱼ) = Cost(Best)
                and LastUsed(dⱼ) < LastUsed(Best)) then
                    SecondBest ← Best, Best ← dⱼ
                else if Cost(dⱼ) < Cost(SecondBest) or
                (Cost(dⱼ) = Cost(SecondBest) and
                LastUsed(dⱼ) < LastUsed(SecondBest)) then
                    SecondBest ← dⱼ
                end if
            end for
            if LastUsed(Best) = LastChanged and
            (Cost(Best) - Cost(SecondBest) < MinDiff or
            random value < NoiseParameter) then
                Best ← SecondBest
            end if
            CurrentState ← CurrentState + Best
        end for
    end while
end
```

Fig. 2. The rnovelty heuristic

3 Experimental Results

3.1 Satisfiability Results

Research has already demonstrated the superiority of constraint weighting over GSAT and early versions of WalkSAT for smaller randomly generated 3-SAT problems (up to 400 variables) and for single solution AIM generated problems [1]. To see if these earlier results still hold, we updated Cha and Iwama's study by comparing our constraint weighting algorithms with McAllester et al.'s WSAT implementation of rnovelty [8]. For our problem set we randomly generated 100, 200 and 400 variable 3-SAT problems with a clause/variable ratio of 4.3 and selected ten satisfiable problems for each problem size (shown as r100, r200 and r400 in table 1). At each problem size we calculated the average of 100 runs. We also used the 4 AIM generated single solution 100 variable problems available from the DIMACS benchmark set (see ftp://dimacs.rutgers.-

edu/pub/challenge/sat/benchmarks/cnf). Each problem was solved 100 times and the average for all 4 problems reported. Table 1 shows the results for these problems[1] and confirms constraint weighting's superiority for small AIM formula, but indicates rnovelty has better random 3-SAT performance. The results also show there is a growing difference between constraint weighting and rnovelty as the problem size increases. For the r400 problems rnovelty is still solving 98% of instances within 1,000,000 flips where the success rate for the best weighting strategy (MOVE) has dropped to 84%. Of the weighting strategies, MOVE outperforms MIN on most problem sizes (except r100), while MIN does somewhat better than UTIL (although the gap closes for the larger problems). In table 1, Max-Flips is the number of flips at which unsuccessful runs were terminated, average flips is the average number of flips for *successful* runs, time is the average time for *successful* runs and success is the percentage of problems solved at Max-Flips.

Table 1. Results for small 3-SAT problems

Problem	Max Flips	Constraints	Method	Average Flips	Time (secs)	Success
r100	250000	432	rnovelty	1165	0.03	100%
			MIN	2221	0.04	100%
			MOVE	2162	0.06	100%
			UTIL	11285	0.22	98%
r200	500000	864	rnovelty	5319	0.11	100%
			MOVE	42043	1.27	91%
			MIN	45799	0.90	74%
			UTIL	42512	0.79	64%
r400	1000000	1728	rnovelty	69223	1.42	98%
			MOVE	180168	3.23	84%
			MIN	128243	2.67	34%
			UTIL	114408	2.20	31%
AIM 100	100000	200	MOVE	3800	0.06	100%
			MIN	6767	0.09	100%
			UTIL	42457	0.48	81%
			rnovelty	-	-	0%

To investigate the gap between constraint weighting and rnovelty for larger problems, we looked at the relative performance of the two algorithms for the DIMACS benchmark large 3-SAT problems (800 to 6400 variables). The graph in figure 3 shows the best result obtained for each algorithm (after 10 runs of 4 million flips on each problem) and confirms that constraint weighting performance starts to degrade as problem size increases. However, an interesting effect is that the relative performance of UTIL starts to improve as the problem size grows until it significantly dominates the other weighting methods.

To test whether the random 3-SAT results are reproduced in more structured domains we looked at a selection of conjunctive normal form (CNF) encodings

---

[1]All problems were solved on a Sun Creator 3D-2000

of large realistic problems (again from the DIMACS benchmark). We found rnovelty to dominate the large and hard graph coloring problems (g) where as constraint weighting performed better on the smaller circuit fault analysis (ssa), parity function learning and inductive inference problems (ii32). Representative results averaging 100 runs on selected problems are given in table 2:

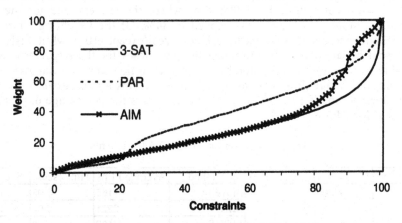

Fig. 3. Result plot for large DIMACS 3-SAT problems

Table 2. Results for large structured DIMACS problems

Problems	Max-Flips	Constraints	Method	Average Flips	Time(secs)	Success
g125.18	1000000	152064	rnovelty	5679	1.54	100%
g250.15			UTIL	160094	18.75	100%
Graph			MIN	218078	26.63	90%
Colouring			MOVE	222658	38.27	90%
ssa038-160	500000	3032	MOVE	2911	0.05	100%
Circuit			MIN	3182	0.08	100%
Fault			UTIL	17501	0.26	100%
Diagnosis			rnovelty	41897	0.97	100%
par8-2/4-c	250000	268	MOVE	1972	0.04	100%
Parity			rnovelty	2844	0.05	100%
Function			MIN	3981	0.06	100%
Learning			UTIL	12698	0.19	98%
ii32b3—e3	500000	8376	MIN	1125	0.25	100%
Inductive			UTIL	1241	0.27	100%
Inference			MOVE	2734	0.86	100%
			rnovelty	16097	3.30	100%

The overall DIMACS problem results show that constraint weighting does perform better on smaller, realistic (possibly structured) problems in comparison to rnovelty. The relative performance between weighting strategies is similar to the 3-SAT results, in that UTIL performs better on the larger problems (g), with MOVE dominating the majority of other problems (excepting ii32). However, rnovelty's superiority on the graph problems again suggests weighting performs less well in longer term searches, as in all domains where constraint weighting dominates, (AIM, par, ii32 and ssa) solutions are found relatively quickly. In the large *and* difficult problems (e.g. 3-SAT and graph coloring) the constraint weighting heuristics do not seem to provide effective long term guidance.

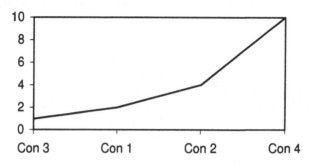

Fig. 4. An example constraint weight curve

Examining Constraint Weight Behavior. To further investigate the behavior of constraint weighting, we looked at the way constraint weights are built up during a search. To do this we developed *constraint weight curves* which plot the constraint weights on the y-axis and order the constraints on the x-axis according to their ascending weight values. For example, if at the solution point of a problem containing 4 constraints, constraint 1 has a weight of 2, constraint 2 has a weight of 4, constraint 3 has a weight of 1 and constraint 4 has a weight of 10, we would produce the graph in figure 4. In this way a picture is generated of the distribution of weights across the constraints.

Figure 5 shows the average weight curves for each 3-SAT problem size using the MOVE heuristic (normalized on axes from 0 to 100). We plotted additional curves for the larger 3-SAT problems and found that after an initial predictable adjustment period, curves very similar to those in figure 5 are produced. The other weighting strategies also produce consistent and similar curves, showing that in the longer term, the weighting process mainly serves to smooth the curves to an underlying distribution (for 3-SAT, curves of the form $y = a - b\log_n(c - x)$ provide a close fit).

To further explore this phenomenon we looked at curves for problems which constraint weighting found relatively easy to solve. Figure 6 shows the averaged MOVE curves for the DIMACS par and AIM problems and figure 7 shows the curves for the ii32, graph and ssa problems. In both figures an averaged 3-SAT curve is provided for comparison. The first feature observed from these graphs is that there is a high degree of consistency for the same problems but noticeable differences between domains. The graphs also show two distinct types of constraint weight curve: the figure 7 curves are similar (or uniform) in that after an initial steeper start all the curves have a steadily increasing gradient. These curves differ mainly in the steepness of their ascent and in the point at which the curve reaches the constraint axis. The curves in figure 6 show different behaviour, in that each curve deviates from the steadily increasing gradients of the other problems and exhibits some irregularity. For instance, the par problems

show a 'step' between 22 and 28 on the constraint axis and the AIM problems
show a similar step between 80 and 95.

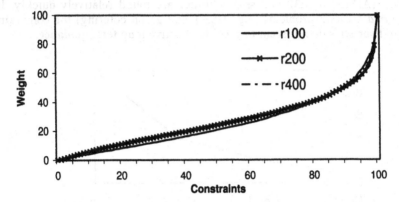

Fig. 5. Constraint weight curves for various 3-SAT problems

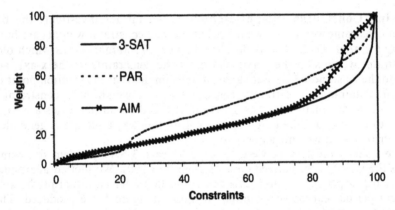

Fig. 6. Constraint weight curves for the DIMACS par and AIM problems

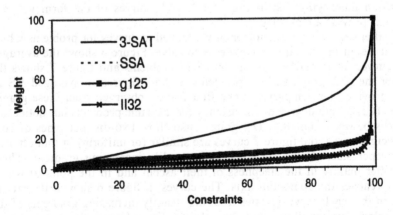

Fig. 7. Constraint weight curves for the DIMACS graph, ssa and ii32 problems

455

Adding Weights to rnovelty. Given that no one technique proved better on all the satisfiability problems, we decided to explore a hybrid rnovelty algorithm with constraint weighting guidance added in. The rnovelty heuristic was changed by weighting each selected constraint iff the selected move for the constraint causes an overall (weighted) cost increase. Move evaluation is then based on the weighted cost. The new algorithm improved rnovelty's performance on all problems where constraint weighting previously dominated (AIM, par, ssa and ii32) but was unable to reach constraint weighting's original performance levels. For those problems where rnovelty dominated (3-SAT and graph coloring), the hybrid algorithm was still superior to constraint weighting, but not as good as pure rnovelty. In no instance was the average performance of the hybrid superior to both of the original techniques. For this reason, further exploration of the algorithm was rejected. An alternative technique which added an rnovelty value selection heuristic into constraint weighting was also implemented. This proved slightly inferior to the rnovelty hybrid and was also rejected.

3.2 CSP Results

Satisfiability is a subset of the broader domain of constraint satisfaction. Although CNF formulations can model multiple problem domains, they all share the same constraint type (i.e. clauses of disjunct literals). For many CSPs there are more natural and efficient ways of modeling constraints and variables. It is therefore significant to explore the performance of constraint weighting and rnovelty on a broader range of problems (also, to our knowledge, this is the first time rnovelty has been applied to CSPs). To this end, we look at two CSP formulations of real-world problems (university timetabling and nurse scheduling), both involving complex non-binary constraints and large non-standard variable domains. In addition we run tests on the well-studied problem of random binary constraint satisfaction [10].

For the purpose of the research, a university timetable problem generator was developed. The generator can be tuned to produce a wide range of realistic problems, while also having a mode that creates relatively unstructured, randomised problems. We were interested in building identical sized problem pairs, one reflecting the structure of a realistic timetabling problem (i.e. students doing degrees, following predictable lines of study, etc.) and the other using purely random allocations. The motivation was to test if a realistic problem structure influences the relative performance of the two algorithms.

The nurse scheduling experiments were run on a set of benchmark problems, taken from a real hospital situation. Each schedule involves up to 30 nurses, over a 14 day period, with non-trivial constraints defining the actual conditions operating in the hospital (for more details, see [14]).

Finally two sets of hard random binary CSPs were generated, each with 30 variables of domain size 10, and constraint density (p1) and tightness (p2) values that placed them in the accepted phase transition area [10]. This made the problems large and difficult enough to challenge the standard backtracking techniques.

Table 3 shows the results of running each class of problem against our four algorithms (all results are averages of 10 runs on 10 different problems). We also report results for the binary CSPs using Van Beek's backtracking algorithm (see ftp://ftp.cs.ualberta.ca/pub/vanbeek/software). The table 3 results put rnovelty firmly ahead for the binary CSPs and slightly ahead for both classes of timetable problem, but strongly favor constraint weighting for the nurse scheduling problems. Adding structure to the timetabling problems does slow performance, but does not favor a particular method. As before, we are interested in the constraint weighting behavior, so figure 9 shows the average constraint weight curves for each class of CSP.

Table 3. Results for the CSP problems
(tt-struct = structured timetabling, tt-rand = random timetabling,
n-sched = nurse scheduling, binary = binary CSP)

Problem	Cut-off(secs)	Constraints	Method	Av. Iterations	Time (secs)	Success
tt-struct	500	500	rnovelty	306546	98.9	78%
			MIN	287874	101.3	74%
			MOVE	348327	164.9	70%
			UTIL	439288	177.4	62%
tt-rand	500	500	rnovelty	106357	28.7	95%
			MIN	111957	30.2	95%
			MOVE	113427	34.0	97%
			UTIL	187339	40.5	95%
n_sched	180	500	MIN	134303	57.7	94%
			MOVE	236142	103.3	81%
			UTIL	249317	108.6	81%
			rnovelty	1010629	99.4	77%
binary	350	200	rnovelty	103155	1.2	100%
n=30		200	MOVE	469329	5.2	93%
m=10		200	MIN	270339	3.3	79%
p1=80		200	UTIL	268949	3.4	75%
p2=17		1000	Backtrack	2.4×10^9	408.6	80%
binary	175	200	rnovelty	198833	1.4	100%
n=30		200	MOVE	239287	1.5	81%
m=10		200	MIN	254531	1.7	55%
p1=40		200	UTIL	226520	1.6	57%
p2=32		1000	Backtrack	33923486	16.4	100%

4 Analysis

The only direct way in which one constraint can influence another is by sharing variables. Hence we would expect problems with a high degree of interconnectedness between constraints to also form large difficult constraint groups. Random hard problem generators (as in 3-SAT and binary CSP) adjust the degree of connectedness to the critical level where the expected number of problem solutions approaches 1 [10]. Consequently, we expect such problems to exhibit an upper bound on the *average* degree of connectedness for which problem solutions are possible. The 3-SAT and binary CSP constraint curves in figures 5 and 9 show that on these hard problems, constraint weights become spread across nearly all the problem constraints. The curves are also very similar in shape, exhibiting (after an initially steeper start) a constantly increasing gradient. Combining this information suggests that nearly *all* the constraints in these hard random problems belong to a single difficult constraint group. Although some constraints consistently accrue more weight than others, there is no *separation point* where a weighting algorithm can recognise that one constraint group is significantly different from another. This lack of distinction between constraint groups could explain constraint weighting's poorer performance on the 3-SAT and binary CSP random problems.

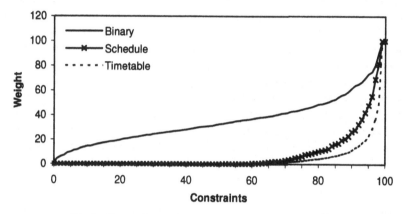

Fig.9. Constraint weight curves for the CSP problems

AIM and par curves. The constraint weight curves for the AIM and par problems in figure 6 diverge from the monotonically increasing curves of the other problems. These irregular curves indicate the weighting algorithm has found some difference between constraint groups. A closer inspection of the AIM problem structure supports this reasoning, as nearly all AIM variables appear in exactly 6 clauses. This tends to create tightly connected constraint groups that are relatively disconnected from the rest of the problem. Weighting can exploit this situation by ensuring the constraints in a harder group are kept true (by frequently placing weights on them) and then exploring the search space by violating constraints in the easier constraint groups. In doing this, constraint weighting will fix potential bottlenecks early in the search and quickly move to potential solution areas (in much the same way as a human problem solver). In contrast, non-weighting methods do not distinguish moves that violate difficult constraint groups and so are more likely to move into constraint violations that are harder to repair.

The parity learning function (par) curve in figure 6 also has an irregular shape, with a bulge appearing in the early part of the graph. This bulge indicates a group of relatively easy constraints that accrue less weight during the search, and offers an explanation of constraint weighting's relatively good performance on these problems. An examination of the par clauses also shows a structure of many small groups of tightly connected constraints (both the AIM and par problems were artificially constructed to have a guaranteed solution). In combination, the 3-SAT, AIM and par results suggest that a non-uniform constraint graph (i.e. one that deviates from a 3-SAT type curve) can be an indication of an 'engineered' problem, i.e. one that exhibits a certain degree of regularity or structure. If this structure causes a significantly greater or lesser degree of interconnectedness amongst constraint sub-groups then we also expect that a constraint weighting algorithm will exploit this situation and gain a certain amount of leverage of other non-weighting techniques.

Graph colouring, ssa and ii32 curves. Figure 7 shows the constraint weight curves for the larger DIMACS problems: circuit fault diagnosis (ssa), inductive inference (ii32) and graph colouring. In comparison to 3-SAT, these curves show a similar monotonic increase but start with a shallower gradient and then have a distinct turning point where the gradient becomes noticeably steeper. If we consider the performance of constraint weighting on these problems, we find that a shallower initial gradient correlates with relatively better constraint weight performance. This can be explained by the lower curves indicating a greater weight distinction between the easy and hard constraints in the problem. Following our earlier reasoning, constraint weighting can exploit this difference by tending to avoid moves that violate heavily weighted constraints, and exploring violations of relatively easier constraints. The poorer performance of constraint weighting on the graph colouring problems can be further explained by the larger size of these problems and consequent scaling effects discussed later.

CSP curves. In looking at constraint weight curves for the more realistic CSP problems (nurse scheduling and timetabling), familiar smoothly increasing gradients are observed (see figure 9). However, for both problem types, approximately 60% of constraints accrue virtually zero weight. This contrasts with the similar curves in figure 7 where at least some weight has accrued on nearly all the constraints. Zero weight constraints are unlikely to provide leverage to a constraint weighting algorithm, because such constraints are *hard to violate*. Consequently, weighting and non-weighting algorithms will both tend to search in the space where these constraints are satisfied. Following this line of reasoning, we would not expect constraint weighting to have an advantage on the timetabling or nurse scheduling problems, whereas, in practice, MIN significantly outperforms the other techniques on the nurse scheduling problems. To investigate this further we looked at the *individual* constraint weight curves for each timetabling and nurse scheduling problem (figure 9 shows the *average* curves for 10 different problems). An initial inspection showed the nurse scheduling curves exhibited more irregularity of shape than the timetabling curves. To quantify this, we took the standard deviation of the weight value for each curve at each of the 100 points on the constraint axis and calculated the sum of these values for each problem type. This produced a summed deviation of 190.8 for the timetabling curves and 358.7 for the nurse scheduling curves (confirming the visual inspection). In addition, the shapes of the nurse scheduling curves indicated that, in many cases, the constraint weighting algorithm was able to distinguish between constraint groups. Combining this information suggests that, although the constraint weight curves for timetabling and nurse scheduling were similar, the underlying behaviour of constraint weighting on the two problems was different and that constraint weighting was able to exploit irregularities in the nurse scheduling problems.

Scaling Effects. Given that constraint weighting does better when it finds distinctions between groups of constraints, we would expect the probability of randomly generating highly interconnected constraint groups to decline (causing the performance of constraint weighting to also decline) as problem size increases. For example, the number of constraints in a random 3-SAT problem grows at the rate of $4.32n$ (where n is the number of variables) whereas the number of *possible* constraints grows at a faster rate of $2n(n-1)(n-2)$. In addition there may be a *granularity* effect in constraint weighting, i.e. as the number of problem constraints increase, the effect of weighting a single constraint necessarily decreases, and constraints start to become weighted and violated in larger and larger groups. In this way the weight guidance becomes more general and less detailed, which could then cause promising search areas to be ignored. This is further backed up by the relative improvement in the performance of UTIL for longer searches: as UTIL increments weights less frequently than the other methods we would expect it's performance to deteriorate more slowly. This result ties in with Frank's work [4] on causing weights to decay during the search, and it may prove useful to investigate a combination of these strategies for larger problems.

5 Conclusions

The main conclusion of the paper is that constraint weighting is best suited to problems where the weighting process is able to distinguish sub-groups of constraints that have a distinctly different weight profile from the remaining problem constraints. We term such problems as having a structure which can be recognised either through an analysis of constraint weight curves or through a direct analysis of the interconnections of variables and constraints. Constraint weighting performance is therefore most influenced by the number and degree of interconnectedness of constraints rather than the degree of realism used in the problem generation. In addition, we found constraint weighting performance starts to degrade as problem size grows, due to a combination of larger problems tending to have less structure and a postulated weighting granularity effect. Additional experiments with hybrid constraint weight and rnovelty algorithms did not yield promising results, so further work in this area was rejected. Of the different weight heuristics, MOVE performed well on the binary CSP and satisfiability problems, while MIN did better on structured CSPs. UTIL was the best weighting strategy for larger problems, but was unable to match the performance of rnovelty. The paper also introduces constraint weight curves as a method for analysing and predicting the behaviour of constraint weight algorithms. In our ongoing work, an extended version of this paper will present a larger sample of results and explore and compare the behavior of several competing constraint weight, WSAT and tabu search heuristics.

References

1. B. Cha and K. Iwama. Performance test of local search algorithms using new types of random CNF formulas. *Proceedings of IJCAI-95*, pages 304-310, 1995.
2. A. Davenport, E. Tsang, C. Wang and K. Zhu. GENET: A connectionist architecture for solving constraint satisfaction problems by iterative improvement. *Proceedings of AAAI-94*, pages 325-330, 1994.
3. J. Frank. Weighting for Godot: Learning heuristics for GSAT. *Proceedings of AAAI-96*, pages 338-343, 1996.
4. J. Frank. Learning short-term weights for GSAT. *Proceedings of IJCAI-97*, pages 384-389, 1997.
5. I. Gent and T. Walsh. Towards an Understanding of Hill-climbing Procedures for SAT. *Proceedings of AAAI-93*, pages 28-33, 1993.
6. V. Kumar. Algorithms for constraint satisfaction problems: a survey. *AI Magazine*, 32-43, Spring 1992.
7. A. Mackworth. Consistency in networks of relations. *Artificial Intelligence*, 8(1):99-118, 1977.
8. D. McAllester, B. Selman and H. Kautz. Evidence for invariants in local search. *Proceedings of AAAI-97*, pages 321-326, 1997.
9. P. Morris. The Breakout method for escaping from local minima. *Proceedings of AAAI-93*, pages 40-45, 1993.
10. P. Prosser. An empirical study of phase transitions in binary constraint satisfaction problems. *Artificial Intelligence*, 81(1-2):81-111, March 1996.
11. B. Selman, H. Levesque and D. McAllester. A new method for solving hard satisfiability problems. *Proceedings of AAAI-92*, pages 440-446, 1992.
12. B. Selman and H. Kautz. Domain-independent extensions to GSAT: solving large structured satisfiability problems. *Proceedings of IJCAI-93*, pages 290-295, 1993.
13. B. Selman, H. Kautz and D. McAllester. Ten challenges in propositional reasoning and search. *Proceedings of IJCAI-97*, pages 50-54, 1997.
14. J. Thornton and A. Sattar. Dynamic Constraint Weighting for Over-Constrained Problems. *Proceedings of PRICAI-98*, pages 377-388, 1998.
15. C. Voudouris and E. Tsang. Partial Constraint Satisfaction Problems and Guided Local Search. *Proceedings of Practical Application of Constraint Technology (PACT'96)*, pages 337-356, 1996.
16. J. Walser, R. Iyer and N. Venkatasubramanyan. An integer local search method with application to capacitated production planning. *Proceedings of AAAI-98*, pages 373-379, 1998.

Simulated Annealing with Asymptotic Convergence for Nonlinear Constrained Global Optimization*

Benjamin W. Wah and Tao Wang

Department of Electrical and Computer Engineering
and the Coordinated Science Laboratory
University of Illinois, Urbana-Champaign
Urbana, IL 61801, USA
{wah, wangtao}@manip.crhc.uiuc.edu
http://www.manip.crhc.uiuc.edu

Abstract. In this paper, we present *constrained simulated annealing* (CSA), a global minimization algorithm that converges to constrained global minima with probability one, for solving nonlinear discrete non-convex constrained minimization problems. The algorithm is based on the necessary and sufficient condition for constrained local minima in the theory of discrete Lagrange multipliers we developed earlier. The condition states that the set of discrete saddle points is the same as the set of constrained local minima when all constraint functions are non-negative. To find the discrete saddle point with the minimum objective value, we model the search by a finite inhomogeneous Markov chain that carries out (in an annealing fashion) both probabilistic descents of the discrete Lagrangian function in the original-variable space and probabilistic ascents in the Lagrange-multiplier space. We then prove the asymptotic convergence of the algorithm to constrained global minima with probability one. Finally, we extend CSA to solve nonlinear constrained problems with continuous variables and those with mixed (both discrete and continuous) variables. Our results on a set of nonlinear benchmarks are much better than those reported by others. By achieving asymptotic convergence, CSA is one of the major developments in nonlinear constrained global optimization today.

1 Problem Definition

A general *discrete constrained minimization problem* is formulated as follows:

$$\begin{aligned}
minimize_x \quad & f(x) \\
subject\ to \quad & g(x) \leq 0; \qquad x = (x_1, \ldots, x_n) \\
& h(x) = 0
\end{aligned} \tag{1}$$

* Research supported by National Science Foundation Grant NSF MIP 96-32316.

where $f(x)$ is a lower-bounded objective function, $g(x) = [g_1(x), \cdots, g_k(x)]^T$ is a set of k inequality constraints, $h(x) = [h_1(x), \cdots, h_m(x)]^T$ is a set of m equality constraints, and all the discrete variables x_i are finite. The functions $f(x)$, $g(x)$, and $h(x)$ can be either convex or non-convex, linear or nonlinear, continuous or discontinuous, and analytic (*i.e.* in closed-form formulae) or procedural. The search space X is the finite Cartesian product of discrete variables x_i, $i = 1, \cdots, n$.

Without loss of generality, we discuss our results with respect to minimization problems, knowing that maximization problems can be converted to minimization ones by negating their objectives. We first define the following basic terms.

Definition 1. $\mathcal{N}(x)$, the neighborhood *of point x in space X, is a user-defined set of points $\{x' \in X\}$ such that $x \notin \mathcal{N}(x)$ and that $x' \in \mathcal{N}(x) \iff x \in \mathcal{N}(x')$. Neighborhoods must be defined such that any point in the finite search space is reachable from any other point through traversals of neighboring points.*

Definition 2. *A point $x \in X$ is a* feasible point *if $h(x) = 0$ and $g(x) \leq 0$.*

Given $\mathcal{N}(x)$ to be the neighborhood of point $x \in X$ in search space X, we define local and global minima for (1) as follows:

Definition 3. *Point $x \in X$ is called a* constrained local minimum *iff a) x is a feasible point, and b) for every feasible point $x' \in \mathcal{N}(x)$, $f(x') \geq f(x)$.*

Note that point x may be a local minimum to one definition of $\mathcal{N}(x)$ but may not be for another definition of $\mathcal{N}'(x)$. The choice of neighborhood, however, does not affect the validity of a search as long as one definition is used consistently throughout. Normally, one may choose $\mathcal{N}(x)$ to include the nearest discrete points to x so that neighborhood carries its original meaning. The search will still be correct even if the neighborhood is chosen to include "far away" points.

Definition 4. *Point $x \in X$ is called a* constrained global minimum *iff a) x is a feasible point, and b) for every feasible point $x' \in X$, $f(x') \geq f(x)$. The set of all constrained global minima is X_{opt}.*

Finding constrained global minima of (1) is challenging as well as difficult. First, $f(x)$, $g(x)$, and $h(x)$ may be non-convex and highly nonlinear, making it difficult to even find a feasible point or a feasible region. Moreover, it is not useful to keep a search within a feasible region, as feasible regions may be disjoint and the search may need to visit multiple feasible regions before finding the global minimum. Second, $f(x)$, $g(x)$, and $h(x)$ may be discontinuous or may not have derivatives, rendering it impossible to apply existing theories and methods in continuous space. Third, there may be a large number of constrained local minima, trapping trajectories that only utilize local information.

As nonlinear constrained problems do not have closed-form solutions and cannot be solved analytically except in some trivial cases, they are generally solved by some iterative procedure ψ. In general, let Ω be a search space. Given starting point $\omega(k = 0) \in \Omega$, ψ generates iteratively a sequence of points, $\omega(k = 1), \omega(k = 2), \cdots, \omega(k), \cdots$ in Ω, until some stopping conditions hold. Here we are interested in *global optimization*, and let Ω_s be the set of all global minima.

Definition 5. *Procedure ψ is said to have* <u>asymptotic convergence to global</u> <u>minimum</u>, *or simply* asymptotic convergence *[2], if ψ converges with probability one to an element in Ω_s; that is, $\lim_{k \to \infty} P(\omega(k) \in \Omega_s) = 1$, independent of starting point $\omega(k = 0)$.*

Definition 6. *Procedure ψ is said to have* <u>reachability of global minimum</u> *[2] if probability $\lim_{k \to \infty} P(\omega(l) \in \Omega_s, \exists\, l,\, 0 \le l \le k) = 1$.*

Reachability is much weaker than asymptotic convergence as it only requires $\omega(k)$ to hit a global solution sometime during the search. In practice, reachability can be achieved by keeping track of the best solution in the course of ψ, as done in a pure random search. Hence, reachability is also called *convergence in the best solution to the global minimum*. In contrast, asymptotic convergence requires ψ to converge to a global solution in Ω_s with probability one. Consequently, the probability of hitting a global solution increases as the search progresses, making it more likely to find the global solution than an algorithm with reachability alone if the search were stopped before it converges.

In this paper, we present a new global minimization algorithm, called *constrained simulated annealing* (CSA), for finding constrained global minima with asymptotic convergence. To achieve asymptotic convergence, we have built CSA based on simulated annealing (SA) because SA is the general algorithm that can guarantee asymptotic convergence in unconstrained optimization.

The paper has six sections. Section 2.2 reviews the theory of discrete Lagrange multipliers [8, 11, 12], that states that finding a discrete saddle point with the minimum objective value is necessary and sufficient for global minimization. Hence, CSA described in Section 3 aims to find such a saddle point by performing probabilistic descents of the Lagrangian function in the original-variable space and probabilistic ascents in the Lagrange-multiplier space. To prove its asymptotic convergence, we model the search by a strongly ergodic Markov chain, and show that CSA minimizes an implicit virtual energy at any constrained global minimum with probability one [10]. Section 4 sketches the proof and illustrates the search behavior. Finally, Section 5 shows improvements in applying CSA to solve some discrete, continuous, and mixed nonlinear optimization problems.

2　Previous Work

There are two approaches to solve (1): direct solution or transformation into an unconstrained problem before solving it. Examples of direct methods include reject/discard methods, repair methods, feasible-direction methods, and interval methods. These methods may be unable to cope with nonlinear constraints, or very problem-specific, or computationally expensive. Hence, the majority of methods are based on transformations and are discussed in this section.

2.1　Penalty Formulations

This approach first transforms (1) into an unconstrained optimization problem or a sequence of unconstrained problems, and then solves it by using existing unconstrained minimization methods. Many heuristics developed to handle constraints [7] are normally problem-dependent, have difficulties in finding feasible regions or in maintaining feasibility, and get stuck easily in local minima.

Static-penalty formulations [3,6] transform (1) into an unconstrained problem,

$$min_x \ L_\rho(x,\gamma) = f(x) + \sum_{i=1}^{m} \gamma_i |h_i(x)|^\rho + \sum_{j=1}^{k} \gamma_{m+j} max^\rho(0, g_j(x)) \qquad (2)$$

where $\rho > 0$, and penalty $\gamma = \{\gamma_1, \gamma_2, \cdots, \gamma_{m+k}\}$ is *fixed* and chosen to be large enough so that

$$L_\rho(x^*, \gamma) < L_\rho(x, \gamma) \quad \forall x \in X - X_{opt} \text{ and } x^* \in X_{opt}. \qquad (3)$$

Based on (3), an unconstrained global minimum of (2) over x is a constrained global minimum to (1), and thus it is sufficient to minimize (2). Because both $f(x)$ and $|h_i(x)|$ are lower bounded and because x takes finite discrete values, γ always exists and is finite. This ensures the correctness of the approach. Note that other forms of penalty formulations are also available in the literature.

The major problem of static-penalty methods is the ruggedness of $L_\rho(x, \gamma)$ and the depth of its unconstrained local minima due to the large γ used. Unless starting points are close to one of the unconstrained global minima, it becomes very unlikely to traverse the search space X and find the global solution. Selecting a suitable γ also proves to be difficult. If it is much larger than necessary, the terrain will become too rugged to be searched. If it is too small, the solution to (2) may be a constrained local minimum or even not be a feasible solution.

Dynamic-penalty formulations address these difficulties by increasing penalties gradually. They transform (1) into a sequence of unconstrained problems:

$$min_x \ L_\rho(x, \lambda(\kappa)) = f(x) + \sum_{i=1}^{m} \lambda_i(\kappa) |h_i(x)|^\rho + \sum_{j=1}^{k} \lambda_{m+j}(\kappa) max^\rho(0, g_j(x)) \ (4)$$

for an increasing sequence $\lambda(\kappa), \kappa = 1, 2, \cdots, \mathcal{K}$, where $0 < \lambda(\kappa) < \lambda(\kappa + 1)$, and $\lambda(\mathcal{K}) = \gamma$. Here $\lambda \geq \lambda'$ iff $\lambda_i \geq \lambda'_i$ for every $i = 1, 2, \cdots, m$, and $\lambda > \lambda'$ iff $\lambda \geq \lambda'$ and there exists at least one i such that $\lambda_i > \lambda'_i$.

Dynamic-penalty methods are asymptotically convergent if, for every $\lambda(\kappa)$, (4) is solved optimally [3,6]. The requirement of obtaining an unconstrained global minimum of (4) in every stage is, however, difficult to achieve in practice, given only finite amount of time in each stage. If the result in one stage is not a global minimum, then the process cannot be guaranteed to find a constrained global minimum. Approximations to the process that sacrifice global optimality of solutions have been developed, such as two-phase evolutionary programming and two-phase neural networks.

2.2 Lagrangian Formulations

Lagrangian methods are based on the theory of Lagrange multipliers that augment the original search space X by a Lagrange-multiplier space Λ, and gradually resolve constraints through iterative updates. We summarize our extensions and relevant theory of Lagrangian formulations that work in discrete space [8, 11, 12]. Let us first consider a discrete equality-constrained minimization problem,

$$minimize_x \quad f(x)$$
$$subject\ to \quad h(x) = 0; \qquad x = (x_1, \ldots, x_n) \qquad (5)$$

where x is a vector of finite discrete variables. A *generalized discrete Lagrangian function* [8] of (5) is defined to be:

$$L_d(x, \lambda) = f(x) + \lambda^T H(h(x)). \qquad (6)$$

where H is a continuous function, and $\lambda = \{\lambda_1, \cdots, \lambda_m\}$, is a set of Lagrange multipliers. Based on (6), we define point (x^*, λ^*) to be a *saddle point* if:

$$L_d(x^*, \lambda) \leq L_d(x^*, \lambda^*) \leq L_d(x, \lambda^*), \qquad (7)$$

for all $x \in \mathcal{N}(x^*)$ and all possible λ. The first inequality in (7) only holds when all the constraints are satisfied, which implies that it must be true for all λ. The following theorem [11, 12] states the first-oder necessary and sufficient conditions for all constrained local minima.

Theorem 1 (Necessary & Sufficient Condition for Discrete Constrained Local Minima). *In discrete space, if function H is a non-negative (or non-positive) continuous function satisfying $H(x) = 0$ iff $x = 0$, then the set of constrained local minima is the same as the set of discrete saddle points.*

The condition in Theorem 1 is stronger than its continuous counterpart. In continuous space, points that satisfy the first-order necessary and second-order sufficient conditions [6] are a *subset* of all the constrained local minima. Hence, the global minima of points satisfying these conditions are not necessarily the constrained global minima of the original problem. Further, these conditions require the existence of derivatives of the objective and constraint functions, and are not applicable when any one of these functions is discontinuous. In contrast, finding saddle points in discrete space always leads to a constrained local minimum. Further, if one can find the saddle point with the minimum objective value, then it is the constrained global minimum (according to Theorem 1). This observation provides the basis for the global minimization procedure studied here.

Theorem 1 also provides a way to handle inequality constraints. We first transform inequality constraint $g_j(x) \leq 0$ into an equivalent equality constraint $\tilde{g}_j(x) = max(0, g_j(x)) = 0$, resulting in an optimization problem with equality constraints only. We then use the absolute function H and define the Lagrangian function of (1) as:

$$L(x, \lambda) = f(x) + \sum_{i=1}^{m} \lambda_i |h_i(x)| + \sum_{j=1}^{k} \lambda_{m+j} \tilde{g}_j(x) \quad \text{where } \lambda = [\lambda_1, \cdots, \lambda_{m+k}]. (8)$$

```
1.  procedure CSA
2.      set starting point x = (x, λ);
3.      set starting temperature T = T⁰ and cooling rate 0 < α < 1;
4.      set N_T (number of trials per temperature);
5.      while stopping condition is not satisfied do
6.          for k ← 1 to N_T do
7.              generate a trial point x' from N(x) using G(x, x');
8.              accept x' with probability A_T(x, x')
9.          end_for
10.         reduce temperature by T ⟵ α × T;
11.     end_while
12. end_procedure
```

Fig. 1. CSA: the constrained simulated annealing algorithm (see text for the initial values of parameters).

3   Constrained Simulated Annealing (CSA)

Figure 1 presents our global minimization algorithm called CSA for solving (1) using Lagrangian function (8). The algorithm is based on SA that normally does probabilistic descents in one space, with probabilities of acceptance governed by a temperature that is reduced in an exponentially decreasing fashion. CSA, in contrast, does probabilistic ascents in the Lagrange-multiplier space and probabilistic descents in the original-variable space. Due to space limitation, we do not present the basic steps of SA, but only discuss the steps of CSA here.

Line 2 sets a starting point $\mathbf{x} = (x, \lambda)$, where x can be either user-provided or randomly generated (*e.g.* based on a fixed seed 123 in our experiments), and λ is initialized to be zero.

Line 3 initializes control parameter T, called *temperature*, to be large enough in order to allow almost all trial points $\mathbf{x}'$ to be accepted. In our experiments, we generate the initial temperature by first randomly generating 100 points of x and their corresponding neighboring points x' where each component $|x'_i - x_i| \leq 0.001$, and then setting $T = max_{x,x',i}\{|L(x', 1) - L(x, 1)|, |h_i(x)|\}$. Our rationale is based on the initial amount of violations observed in a problem. We also set α (to be discussed later) to be 0.8 in our experiments.

Line 4 sets the number of iterations at each temperature. In our experiments, we set $N_T = \zeta(20n + m)$ where $\zeta = 10(n + m)$, n is the number of variables, and m is the number of equality constraints. This setting is based on the heuristic rule in [4] using $n + m$ instead of n.

Line 5 stops CSA when the current point $\mathbf{x}$ is not changed, *i.e.*, no other new point $\mathbf{x}'$ is accepted, for a couple of successive temperatures, or the current temperature T is small enough (*e.g.* $T < 10^{-6}$).

Line 7 generates a random trial point $\mathbf{x}'$ in neighborhood $N(\mathbf{x})$ of current point $\mathbf{x} = (x, \lambda)$ in search space $S = X \times \Lambda$ using generation probability $G(\mathbf{x}, \mathbf{x}')$, where $N(\mathbf{x})$ and $N_2(\lambda)$, neighborhood of λ at $\mathbf{x}$, are defined as follows:

$$N(\mathbf{x}) = \{(x', \lambda) \in S \text{ where } x' \in N_1(x)\} \cup \{(x, \lambda') \in S \text{ where } \lambda' \in N_2(\lambda)\} (9)$$

$$\mathcal{N}_2(\lambda) = \{\mu \in \Lambda \mid \mu < \lambda \text{ and } \mu_i = \lambda_i \text{ if } h_i(x) = 0\}$$
$$\bigcup \{\mu \in \Lambda \mid \mu > \lambda \text{ and } \mu_i = \lambda_i \text{ if } h_i(x) = 0\} \tag{10}$$

where relation "$<$" on two vectors has been defined earlier. Neighborhood $\mathcal{N}_2(\lambda)$ prevents λ_i from being changed when the corresponding constraint is satisfied, i.e., $h_i(x) = 0$. An example of $\mathcal{N}_2(\lambda)$ is that μ differs from λ in one variable (e.g. $\mu_i \neq \lambda_i$, and $\mu_j = \lambda_j$ for $j \neq i$), and $\{\mu_i \mid i \neq j\}$ is a set of values, some of which are larger than λ_i and some are smaller. In short, a trial point (x', λ) is a neighboring point to (x, λ) if x' is a neighboring point to x in variable space X, and (x, λ') is a neighboring point to (x, λ) if λ' is a neighboring point to λ in Lagrange multiplier space Λ and $h(x) \neq 0$.

$G(\mathbf{x}, \mathbf{x}')$, the *generation probability* from $\mathbf{x}$ to $\mathbf{x}' \in \mathcal{N}(\mathbf{x})$ satisfies:

$$G(\mathbf{x}, \mathbf{x}') > 0 \quad \text{and} \quad \sum_{\mathbf{x}' \in \mathcal{N}(\mathbf{x})} G(\mathbf{x}, \mathbf{x}') = 1 \tag{11}$$

The choice of $G(\mathbf{x}, \mathbf{x}')$ is arbitrary as long as it satisfies (11). In our illustrative example, we use a uniform probability over $\mathcal{N}(\mathbf{x})$, independent of T.

$$G(\mathbf{x}, \mathbf{x}') = 1/|\mathcal{N}(\mathbf{x})| \tag{12}$$

Line 8 accepts $\mathbf{x}'$ with acceptance probability $A_T(\mathbf{x}, \mathbf{x}')$ that consists of two components, depending on whether x or λ is changed in $\mathbf{x}'$.

$$A_T(\mathbf{x}, \mathbf{x}') = \begin{cases} exp\left(-\dfrac{(L(\mathbf{x}')-L(\mathbf{x}))^+}{T}\right) & \text{if } \mathbf{x}' = (x', \lambda) \\[2mm] exp\left(-\dfrac{(L(\mathbf{x})-L(\mathbf{x}'))^+}{T}\right) & \text{if } \mathbf{x}' = (x, \lambda') \end{cases} \tag{13}$$

where $(a)^+ = a$ if $a > 0$, and $(a)^+ = 0$ otherwise for all $a \in R$.

The acceptance probabilities in (13) differ from the acceptance probabilities used in conventional SA, which only has the first part of (13) and whose goal is to look for global minima in the x space. Without the λ space, only probabilistic descents in the x space need to be done.

Our goal here is to look for saddle points in the joint space $X \times \Lambda$ of x and λ, which exist at local minima in x space and at local maxima in λ space. To this end, the first part of (13) carries out *probabilistic descents* of $L(x, \lambda)$ with respect to x for fixed λ. That is, when we generate a new point x' while λ is fixed, we accept it with probability one when $\delta_x = L(x', \lambda) - L(x, \lambda)$ is negative; otherwise we accept it with probability $e^{-\delta_x/T}$. This is performing exactly descents while allowing occasional ascents in x space as done in conventional SA.

However, descents in x space alone only lead to local/global minima of the Lagrangian function without satisfying the constraints. To this end, the second part of (13) carries out *probabilistic ascents* of $L(x, \lambda)$ with respect to λ for fixed x in order to increase the penalties of violated constraints and to force them into satisfaction. Hence, when we generate a new point λ' while x is fixed, we accept it with probability one when $\delta_\lambda = L(x, \lambda') - L(x, \lambda)$ is positive; otherwise we accept it with probability $e^{-\delta_\lambda/T}$. This is performing exactly ascents in λ space while allowing occasional descents (and reducing the ruggedness of the terrains and deepening the local minima) as done in conventional SA. Note that when a constraint is satisfied, the corresponding Lagrange multiplier will not be changed according to (10).

Although our algorithm only changes one variable in x or λ at a time, it is possible to derive $A_T(\mathbf{x}, \mathbf{x}')$ that allows multiple variables in x and λ to be changed together. In that case, we can decompose the aggregate change into a sequence of one-variable changes.

Finally, Line 10 reduces T using the following *cooling schedule* after looping N_T times at a given T:

$$T \longleftarrow \alpha \times T \qquad (14)$$

where α is a constant smaller than 1 (typically between 0.8 and 0.99). Theoretically, if T is reduced slow enough, then CSA will converge to a constrained global minimum of (1) with probability one as T approaches 0.

Note that (13) enables any trial point to be accepted with high probabilities at high T, allowing the search to traverse a large space and overcome infeasible regions. As T is gradually reduced, the acceptance probability decreases, and at very low temperatures the algorithm behaves like a local search.

4 Asymptotic Convergence of CSA

In this section, we prove the asymptotic convergence of CSA to constrained global minima by modeling the process by an inhomogeneous Markov chain, showing that the Markov chain is strongly ergodic, proving that the Markov chain minimizes an implicit virtual energy based on the framework of generalized SA (GSA) [10], and showing that the virtual energy is at its minimum at any constrained global minimum. Due to space limitations, we only sketch the proofs and illustrate the results by an example.

CSA can be modeled by an inhomogeneous Markov chain consisting of a sequence of homogeneous Markov chains of finite length, each at a specific temperature in a given temperature schedule. According to the generation and acceptance probabilities, $G(\mathbf{x}, \mathbf{x}')$ and $A_T(\mathbf{x}, \mathbf{x}')$, the *one-step transition probability* of the Markov chain is:

$$P_T(\mathbf{x}, \mathbf{x}') = \begin{cases} G(\mathbf{x}, \mathbf{x}') A_T(\mathbf{x}, \mathbf{x}') & \text{if } \mathbf{x}' \in \mathcal{N}(\mathbf{x}) \\ 1 - \sum_{\mathbf{y} \in \mathcal{N}(\mathbf{x})} P_T(\mathbf{x}, \mathbf{y}) & \text{if } \mathbf{x}' = \mathbf{x} \\ 0 & \text{otherwise} \end{cases} \qquad (15)$$

and the corresponding *transition matrix* is $P_T = [P_T(\mathbf{x}, \mathbf{x}')]$.

Example 1. The following simple example illustrates the Markov chain for a problem that minimizes a quadratic objective with one quadratic constraint.

$$minimize \quad f(x) = -x^2 \qquad (16)$$
$$subject\ to \quad h(x) = |(x - 0.6)(x - 1.0)| = 0$$

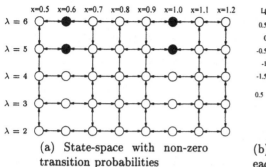
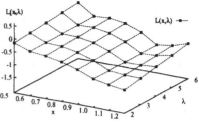

(a) State-space with non-zero transition probabilities

(b) Lagrangian function value at each state

Fig. 2. The Markov chain modeling the Lagrangian space of (16) and the corresponding Lagrangian function value. The four saddle points are shaded in (a).

where $x \in X = \{0.5, 0.6, \cdots, 1.2\}$ and $\lambda \in \Lambda = \{2, 3, 4, 5, 6\}$ are both discrete, and γ, the maximum Lagrange multiplier, is 6. The state space is, therefore, $S = \{(x, \lambda) | \ x \in X, \lambda \in \Lambda\}$, and the total number of states is $|S| = 8 \times 5 = 40$.

In the Markov chain, we define the neighborhoods for x and λ as follows:

$$\mathcal{N}_1(x) = \{x - 1, x + 1 | \ 0.6 \le x \le 1.1\} \cup \{x + 1 | \ x = 0.5\} \cup \{x - 1 | \ x = 1.2\}$$
$$\mathcal{N}_2(x) = \{\lambda - 1, \lambda + 1 | \ 3 \le \lambda \le 5, x \ne 0.6, \text{ and } x \ne 1.0\} \cup \{\lambda - 1 | \ \lambda = 6,$$
$$x \ne 0.6, \text{ and } x \ne 1.0\} \cup \{\lambda + 1 | \ \lambda = 2, x \ne 0.6, \text{ and } x \ne 1.0\} \quad (17)$$

Given $\mathcal{N}_1(x)$ and $\mathcal{N}_2(\lambda)$, $\mathcal{N}(\mathbf{x})$ is defined as in (9).

Figure 2 shows the Markov chain constructed. In the chain, a node $\mathbf{x} = (x, \lambda)$ represents a point in S, and an arrow from $\mathbf{x}$ to $\mathbf{x}' \in \mathcal{N}(\mathbf{x})$ (where $\mathbf{x}' = (x', \lambda)$ or (x, λ')) means that there is a one-step transition from $\mathbf{x}$ to $\mathbf{x}'$ with $P_T(\mathbf{x}, \mathbf{x}') > 0$. For $x = 0.6$ and $x = 1.0$, there is no transition among the λ's because the constraints are satisfied at these points (according to (10)).

There are two saddle points in this Markov chain at $(0.6, 5)$ and $(0.6, 6)$, corresponding to the local minima $x = 0.6$, and two saddle points at $(1.0, 5)$ and $(1.0, 6)$, corresponding to the local minima $x = 1.0$. Since $h(x)$ is non-negative, each saddle point has an associated constrained local minimum (according to Theorem 1). Hence, the solution space is the set of four saddle points or the set of two local minima. CSA is designed to locate the saddle points corresponding to the constrained global minimum $x^* = 1.0$ and $\lambda = \gamma$ at $(1.0, 6)$. ∎

Let $\mathbf{x}_{opt} = \{(x^*, \gamma) | \ x^* \in X_{opt}\}$, and N_L be the maximum of the minimum number of transitions required to reach $\mathbf{x}_{opt}$ from all $\mathbf{x} \in S$. By properly constructing $\mathcal{N}(\mathbf{x})$, we state without proof that P_T is irreducible, and that N_L can always be found. This property is illustrated in Figure 2 in which any two nodes can reach each other.

Consider the sequence of temperatures $\{T_k, k = 0, 1, 2, \cdots\}$, where $T_k > T_{k+1}$ and $\lim_{k \to \infty} T_k = 0$, and set N_T, the number of trials per temperature, to be N_L. The following theorem proves the strong ergodicity of the Markov chain.

Theorem 2. *The inhomogeneous Markov chain is strongly ergodic if the sequence of temperatures $\{T_k\}$ satisfies:*

$$T_k \geq \frac{N_L \Delta_L}{log_e(k+1)} \tag{18}$$

where $\Delta_L = 2 \max_{\mathbf{x}} \{|L(\mathbf{x}') - L(\mathbf{x})|, \mathbf{x}' \in \mathcal{N}(\mathbf{x})\}$.

This theorem can be proved by following the steps used to show weak ergodicity of SA [1] and by using the strong ergodicity conclusions [2]. Strongly ergodicity implies that the Markov chain has a unique stationary distribution π_T, where $\pi_T(\mathbf{x})$ is the probability of hitting point $\mathbf{x}$ during the search of CSA. The Markov chain in Figure 2 is strongly ergodic.

Our Markov chain also fits into the framework of generalized simulated annealing (GSA) [10] if we define an irreducible Markov kernel $P_T(\mathbf{x}, \mathbf{x}')$ and its associated communication cost $V(\mathbf{x}, \mathbf{x}')$:

$$V(\mathbf{x}, \mathbf{x}') = \begin{cases} (L(\mathbf{x}') - L(\mathbf{x}))^+ & \text{if } \mathbf{x}' = (x', \lambda) \\ (L(\mathbf{x}) - L(\mathbf{x}'))^+ & \text{if } \mathbf{x}' = (x, \lambda') \end{cases} \tag{19}$$

Obviously $V(\mathbf{x}, \mathbf{x}') \geq 0$ and function $V \colon S \times S \to [0, +\infty]$.

Note that CSA does not minimize $L(x, \lambda)$ due to its probabilistic descents in x space and probabilistic ascents in λ space. This property is illustrated in Figure 2b in which the four saddle points are not at the global minimum in the Lagrangian space. It is quite different from SA for unconstrained problems, whose explicit objective is to minimize a single objective by performing probabilistic descents. In fact, CSA aims at minimizing an implicit virtual energy $W(\mathbf{x})$ according to GSA [10], and converges to the global minimum of $W(\mathbf{x})$ with probability one. Here, the virtual energy $W(\mathbf{x})$ is the cost of the minimum spanning tree rooted at point $\mathbf{x}$ of the digraph governed by $\mathcal{N}(\mathbf{x})$. Hence, to prove that our Markov chain converges asymptotically to the constrained global minimum of the original problem (1), we need to show that $W(\mathbf{x})$ is minimized at (x^*, γ) for $x^* \in X_{opt}$, and for all $x \in X - X_{opt}$ and $\lambda \in \Lambda$, $W((x^*, \gamma)) < W((x, \lambda))$. This is stated in the following theorem.

Theorem 3. *The Markov chain modeling CSA converges to the constrained global minimum $x^* \in X_{opt}$ with probability one.*

We sketch the proof of the theorem that consists of two steps. First, we show that for a given x, the virtual energy satisfies $W((x, \lambda')) \leq W((x, \lambda))$ for any $\lambda' > \lambda$. Hence, $W((0.6, 4)) \leq W((0.6, 3))$ and $W((0.8, 6)) \leq W((0.8, 2))$ in Figure 2. Second, we show that $W((x^*, \gamma)) < W((x, \gamma))$, where $x^* \in X_{opt}$ and $x \in X - X_{opt}$ at the maximum value γ of the Lagrange multipliers. Hence, $W((1.0, 6)) < W((0.6, 6))$ and $W((1.0, 6)) < W((0.8, 6))$ in Figure 2. Finally, we show that $W(\mathbf{x})$ of $\mathbf{x} = (x, \lambda)$ is minimized at (x^*, γ), and the Markov chain converges to the constrained global minimum $x^* \in X_{opt}$ with probability one.

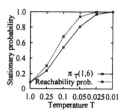
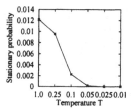
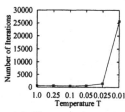

(a) Prob. of finding global sol'n   (b) $\pi_T((x = 1.2, \lambda = 2))$ (c) K_T to arrive at π_T

Fig. 3. Example showing the convergence probabilities of two states and the number of iterations to arrive at convergence. Part (a) also shows the reachability probability of reaching the global solution if the search were stopped.

Example 1 (cont'd). Since multiple runs of CSA do not illustrate the asymptotic convergence to the global minimum, we evaluate the stationary probabilities π_T numerically at a given T by first computing acceptance probability $A_T(\mathbf{x}, \mathbf{x}')$ using (13) and the one-step transition probability $P_T(\mathbf{x}, \mathbf{x}')$ using (15). The stationary distribution π_T of the Markov chain with transition matrix P_T is:

$$p(k + 1) = p(k)P_T \qquad \text{for any given initial vector } p(k = 0) \qquad (20)$$

until $\|p(k+1)-p(k)\| \le \varepsilon$. Here we select $\varepsilon = 10^{-16}$ as the convergence precision, and denote the number of iterations by K_T. As $\pi_T = \lim_{k \to \infty} p(k)$, independent of starting vector $p(k = 0)$, we set $p_i(k = 0) = 1/|S|$ for all $i = 1, 2, \cdots, |S|$.

In this simple example, the virtual energy $W(\mathbf{x})$ is minimal at $\mathbf{x}^* = (1.0, 6)$. Figure 3a shows the stationary probability $\pi_T(\mathbf{x}^*)$ at this point, which increases monotonically as T is reduced, and approaches one as T is small ($T = 0.01$). Thus the Markov chain converges asymptotically to the constrained global solution. The figure also shows the reachability probability at each temperature, which is the probability of hitting the constrained global minimum in any of the previous iterations. The stationary probabilities $\pi_T(\mathbf{x})$ for other states $\mathbf{x} \ne \mathbf{x}^*$ decrease monotonically to zero as T is reduced. Figure 3b illustrates this property at $\tilde{\mathbf{x}} = (1.2, 2)$. Note that the process does not minimize $L(x, \lambda)$, whose minimum exists at $\tilde{\mathbf{x}}$; instead, it minimizes virtual energy $W(\mathbf{x})$ implicitly defined over communication cost $V(\mathbf{x}, \mathbf{x}')$ in (19). Finally, Figure 3c shows K_T required to reach stationary distribution π_T with precision ε. The process arrives at π_T quickly at high T, but needs a large number of iterations at low T. The reason is that at low T, the probability of escaping from a local minimum is small, and hence it takes a long time to arrive at the global solution.

5 Experimental Results on Constrained Problems

In this section, we apply CSA to solve general discrete, continuous, and mixed nonlinear constrained problems. Due to a lack of discrete/mixed benchmarks, we derive them from some existing continuous benchmarks [7, 5] as follows. In generating a mixed problem, we assume that variables with odd indices are continuous and those with even indices are discrete. In discretizing continuous variable x_i in the range $[a_i, b_i]$, if $b_i - a_i < 1$, we force the variable to take values from the set $A_i = \{a_i + \frac{b_i - a_i}{s}j\}, j = 0, 1, \cdots, s$; otherwise, we force it to take values from the set $A_i = \{a_i + \frac{1}{s}j\}, j = 0, 1, \cdots, (b_i - a_i)s$. Here, $s = 10^4$ if the number of variables n is less than 5, and $s = 10^5$ otherwise. The discrete/mixed search space produced is, therefore, very huge. We also shift every discretized variable x_i by a very small constant value in such a way that the set A_i contains the value of the best solution.

5.1 Implementation Details

In theory, any neighborhood $\mathcal{N}_1(x)$ and $\mathcal{N}_2(\lambda)$ that satisfy Condition (10) and Definition 1 will guarantee asymptotic convergence. In practice, however, it is important to choose appropriate neighborhoods and generate proper trial points in x and λ in order to solve constrained problems efficiently.

In our implementation, we choose a simple neighborhood $\mathcal{N}_1(x)$ as the set of points x' that differ from x in one variable x_i. We characterize $\mathcal{N}_1(x)$ by vector σ, where σ_i is the scale parameter in the Cauchy distribution along x_i. Similarly, we choose $\lambda' \in \mathcal{N}_2(\lambda)$ to differ from λ in one variable and characterize $\mathcal{N}_2(\lambda)$ by vector ϕ, where ϕ_i is the maximum possible perturbation along λ_i.

In generating trial point $\mathbf{x}' = (x', \lambda)$ from $\mathbf{x} = (x, \lambda)$, we consider two cases. To generate a continuous trial point, we set:

$$x' = x + r_0\, \theta_i\, \mathbf{e}_i \tag{21}$$

where r_0 is a random variable uniformly generated in the range $[-1, +1]$, $\mathbf{e}_i$ is a vector with its ith component being 1 and the other components being 0, θ_i is generated from Cauchy distribution of density $f_d(x) = \frac{1}{\pi} \frac{\sigma_i}{\sigma_i^2 + x^2}$, and i is randomly generated from $\{1, 2, \cdots, n\}$. To generate a discrete trial point, we obtain x' by rounding the point generated by (21) to its closest discrete grid point. If it happens that $x' = x$, then we set $x' = x + s \times j$, where j has equal probability to take value $+1$ or -1.

In generating a trial point $\mathbf{x}' = (x, \lambda')$ from $\mathbf{x} = (x, \lambda)$, we apply the following:

$$\lambda' = \lambda + r_1\, \phi_j\, \mathbf{e}_j \tag{22}$$

where r_1 is randomly generated from $[-1, +1]$, and j is uniformly generated from $\{1, 2, \cdots, m\}$.

The trial point $\mathbf{x}' = (x', \lambda)$ or $\mathbf{x}' = (x, \lambda')$ generated is accepted according to probability (13). We set the ratio of generating (x', λ) and (x, λ') from the current point (x, λ) to be $20n$ to m, meaning that x is updated more frequently than λ.

During the course of CSA, we dynamically adjust the neighborhood $\mathcal{N}_1(x)$ by updating scale vector σ for x using a modified $1:1$ rate rule [4] in order to balance the ratio between accepted and rejected configurations.

$$\sigma_i = \begin{cases} \sigma_i\left[1 + \beta_0(p_i - p_u)/(1 - p_u)\right] & \text{if } p_i > p_u \\ \sigma_i/\left[1 + \beta_1(p_v - p_i)/p_v\right] & \text{if } p_i < p_v \end{cases} \tag{23}$$

where p_i is the ratio of accepting x' in which x_i' differs from x_i. We chose the parameters experimentally: $\beta_0 = 7$, $\beta_1 = 2$, $p_u = 0.3$, and $p_v = 0.2$. If p_i is low, then too many trials of (x', λ) are rejected, and σ_i is reduced. In contrast, if p_i is high, then trial points (x', λ) are too close to (x, λ), and σ_i is increased.

We adjust ϕ according to the degree of constraint violations, where

$$\phi = w \otimes h(x) = [w_1 h_1(x), w_2 h_2(x), \cdots, w_m h_m(x)] \tag{24}$$

and $\otimes$ represents vector product. When $h_i(x)$ is satisfied, λ_i does not need to be updated; hence, $\phi_i = 0$. In contrast, when a constraint is not satisfied, we adjust ϕ_i by modifying w_i according to how fast $h_i(x)$ is changing:

$$w_i = \begin{cases} \eta_0 \, w_i & \text{if } h_i(x) > \tau_0 T \\ \eta_1 \, w_i & \text{if } h_i(x) < \tau_1 T \end{cases} \tag{25}$$

where $\eta_0 = 1.25$, $\eta_1 = 0.8$, $\tau_0 = 1.0$, and $\tau_1 = 0.01$ were chosen experimentally. When $h_i(x)$ is reduced too quickly (i.e., $h_i(x) < \tau_1 T$), $h_i(x)$ is over-weighted, leading to possibly poor objective values or difficulty in satisfying other under-weighted constraints. Hence, we reduce λ_i's neighborhood. In contrast, if $h_i(x)$ is reduced too slowly (i.e., $h_i(x) > \tau_0 T$), we enlarge λ_i's neighborhood in order to improve its chance of satisfaction. Note that w_i is adjusted using T as a reference because constraint violations are expected to decrease when T decreases.

5.2 Evaluation Results

In this section, we show the results of applying CSA on 10 constrained optimization problems G1-G10 [7,5] with objective functions of various types (linear, quadratic, cubic, polynomial, and nonlinear) and constraints of linear inequalities, nonlinear equalities, and nonlinear inequalities. The number of variables is up to 20, and that of constraints, including simple bounds, is up to 42.

These problems were originally invented to be solved by evolutionary algorithms (EAs) using well-tuned constraint handling techniques for each problem in order to get good results. Examples of these techniques include keeping the search within feasible regions with some specific genetic operators, and dynamic and adaptive penalty methods.

We also solved the continuous problems using DONLP2 [9], a popular sequential quadratic programming (SQP) package that uses derivatives. SQP is an efficient local-search method widely used for solving constrained optimization problems, whose quality depends heavily on starting points. To be fair, we ran DONLP2 from multiple starting points using the same amount of average CPU time as one run of CSA for continuous problems.

Table 1 shows the comparison results for continuous problems. The first two columns show the problem identifiers and the constrained global minima (or maxima), if known. The third and fourth columns show the best solutions obtained by EAs and the specific constraint handling techniques used to generate the solutions. The fifth thru sixth columns show the best solutions of SQP, and

Table 1. Comparison results of DONLP2, GA, and CSA for 10 continuous problems. (S.T. stands for strategic oscillation, H.M. for homomorphous mappings, and D.P. for dynamic penalty. All runs were done on a Sun SparcStation Ultra 60 computer. Numbers in bold represent the best solution.)

Problem ID	Global Solution	EAs		SQP: DONLP2		CSA (average of 20 runs)		
		best sol'n	specific method	best sol'n	% with best sol'n	best sol'n	% with best sol'n	time (sec.) per run
G1 (min)	-15	**-15**	Genocop	**-15**	14.8%	**-15**	100%	17.04
G2 (max)	unknown	0.803553	S.T.	0.640329	0.4%	**0.803619**	100%	94.03
G3 (max)	1.0	0.999866	S.T.	**1.0**	93.1%	**1.0**	100%	69.62
G4 (min)	-30665.5	-30664.5	H.M.	**-30665.5**	61.4%	**-30665.5**	100%	2.70
G5 (min)	unknown	5126.498	D.P.	**4221.956**	94.0%	**4221.956**	100%	3.81
G6 (min)	-6961.81	**-6961.81**	Genocop	**-6961.81**	87.2%	**-6961.81**	100%	0.978
G7 (min)	24.3062	24.62	H.M.	**24.3062**	99.3%	**24.3062**	100%	14.71
G8 (max)	unknown	**0.095825**	H.M.	**0.095825**	44.9%	**0.095825**	100%	1.22
G9 (min)	680.63	680.64	Genocop	**680.63**	99.7%	**680.63**	100%	5.61
G10 (min)	7049.33	7147.9	H.M.	**7049.33**	29.1%	**7049.33**	100%	10.81

Table 2. CSA results on 10 derived discrete and mixed problems with 20 runs per problem. (All runs are done on a Sun SparcStation Ultra 60 computer.)

Problem ID	CSA for Discrete Problems			CSA for Mixed Problems		
	best sol'n	% with best sol'n	time (sec.) per run	best sol'n	% with best sol'n	time (sec.) per run
G1 (min)	**-15**	100%	17.97	**-15**	100%	21.56
G2 (max)	**0.803619**	90%	99.03	**0.803619**	100%	100.62
G3 (max)	**1.0**	100%	70.15	**1.0**	100%	74.78
G4 (min)	**-30665.5**	100%	2.43	**-30665.5**	100%	3.04
G5 (min)	**4221.956**	90%	3.32	**4221.956**	100%	4.16
G6 (min)	**-6961.81**	90%	0.962	**-6961.81**	100%	1.00
G7 (min)	**24.3062**	100%	17.48	**24.3062**	95%	17.39
G8 (max)	**0.095825**	100%	1.37	**0.095825**	100%	1.33
G9 (min)	**680.63**	100%	6.83	**680.63**	100%	6.76
G10 (min)	**7049.33**	100%	13.31	**7049.33**	100%	12.57

the percentage of runs reaching these solutions. The last three columns give the results of CSA and the average CPU time per run.

The results show that CSA is the best in terms of both solution quality and chance of reaching the best solutions. For problems with known global optima, CSA always found these optima, independent of starting points. For problems with unknown global optima, CSA always found the best solutions in every run. DONLP2, in contrast, worked well for problems with a small number of local optima if enough starting points were used. For these problems, DONLP2 was generally very fast and was able to complete within one second in many runs. However, DONLP2 has difficulty with G2, a maximization problem with a huge number of local maxima. In 243 runs of DONLP2, only one was able to find the best solution of 0.640329, which is much worse than those obtained by EAs (0.803553) and CSA (0.803619). Even with 10,000 runs, DONLP2 was only able to find the best solution of 0.736554. Finally, EA was only able to find the best solutions in three of the ten problems despite extensive tuning.

Table 2 shows the results of applying CSA to solve derived discrete and mixed problems. It shows that CSA can find the best solutions with high success ratios (larger than or equal to 90% for every problem). Overall, the experimental results indicate the robustness and wide applicability of CSA to solve discrete, continuous, and mixed nonlinear constrained problems.

6 Conclusions

We have reported in this paper a new algorithm called constrained simulated annealing that can achieve asymptotic convergence for solving nonlinear discrete constrained optimization problems.

1 It is based on a strong mathematical foundation of the theory of discrete Lagrange multipliers. By looking for saddle points in the discrete Lagrangian space, it can find the saddle point with the best objective value with asymptotic convergence. This amounts to finding the constrained global optimum.
2 It does not require derivatives of the objective and constraint functions, and can be applied to solve discrete, continuous, and mixed problems. To our knowledge, this is the first algorithm that can solve efficiently discrete, mixed, and continuous constrained optimization problems.
3 Even though CSA requires exponential time to have asymptotic convergence, it has higher reachability probability than algorithms using random restarts because its probability of hitting the global optimum increases with time rather than constant.

References

1. E. Aarts and J. Korst. *Simulated Annealing and Boltzmann Machines*. J. Wiley and Sons, 1989.
2. S. Anily and A Federgruen. Simulated annealing methods with general acceptance probabilities. *Journal of Appl. Prob.*, 24:657–667, 1987.
3. D. P. Bertsekas. *Constrained Optimization and Lagrange Multiplier Methods*. Academic Press, 1982.
4. A. Corana, M. Marchesi, C. Martini, and S. Ridella. Minimizing multimodal functions of continuous variables with the simulated annealing algorithm. *ACM Trans. on Mathematical Software*, 13(3):262–280, 1987.
5. S. Koziel and Z. Michalewicz. Evolutionary algorithms, homomorphous mappings, and constrained parameter optimization. *Evolutionary Computation*, 7(1):19–44, 1999.
6. D. G. Luenberger. *Linear and Nonlinear Programming*. Addison-Wesley Publishing Company, 1984.
7. Z. Michalewicz and M. Schoenauer. Evolutionary algorithms for constrained parameter optimization problems. *Evolutionary Computation*, 4(1):1–32, 1996.
8. Y. Shang and B. W. Wah. A discrete Lagrangian based global search method for solving satisfiability problems. *J. Global Optimization*, 12(1):61–99, January 1998.
9. P. Spellucci. An SQP method for general nonlinear programs using only equality constrained subproblems. *Mathematical Programming*, 82:413–448, 1998.
10. A. Trouve. Cycle decomposition and simulated annealing. *SIAM Journal on Control and Optimization*, 34(3):966–986, 1996.
11. B. W. Wah and Z. Wu. The theory of discrete lagrange multipliers for nonlinear discrete optimization. *Principles and Practice of Constraint Programming*, (accepted to appear) October 1999.
12. Zhe Wu. *Discrete Lagrangian Methods for Solving Nonlinear Discrete Constrained Optimization Problems*. M.Sc. Thesis, Dept. of Computer Science, Univ. of Illinois, Urbana, IL, May 1998.

On SAT01 Problem

Stanislav Busygin

busygin@a-teleport.com
http://www.busygin.dp.ua/npc.html

Abstract. We introduce a new NP-complete problem, which is denoted *SAT01*. It turns out that many other NP problems can be reduced to SAT01 easily and the new introduced SAT01 variables have natural meanings at that. We develop a propagation method for SAT01 that gives an opportunity to perform its reduction and to recognize hidden binary relations among variables. Besides, since the problem is formulated as a system of linear equations and inequalities for binary variables we are able to use heuristics based on solving of the real relaxation of its constraints. Due to all these properties we have solved many hard instances of different NP problems with good performance.

1 Definition of SAT01 Problem

SAT01 can be formulated in two ways. The first formulation is

$$\sum_{j=1}^{n} a_{ij} x_j = 1, \qquad i = 1, \ldots, m \tag{1}$$

$$\sum_{j=1}^{n} b_{ij} x_j \leq 1, \qquad i = 1, \ldots, m_1 \tag{2}$$

where $\{a_{ij}\}$ and $\{b_{ij}\}$ are given binary matrices and $x = (x_1, x_2, \ldots, x_n)$ is an unknown binary vector to be determined. SAT01 is NP-complete since it is a generalization of set partitioning problem known to be NP-complete [1]. To introduce the second formulation of SAT01 we consider a graph on the set of the variables. Thus, this graph has n vertices and $i^{\underline{th}}$ and $j^{\underline{th}}$ vertices are joined by an edge in it iff there is an equation of (1) or an inequality of (2) where these two variables appear simultaneously. We name this graph *the graph of contradictions*. Clearly, any solution of the problem must be an independent set of vertices of the graph as any its clique may contain not more than one true variable. Now we may omit (2) and consider SAT01 to be a problem to find a solution of (1) corresponding to an independent set of vertices of the graph of contradictions. This is the second formulation of the problem. To obtain the first formulation from it one can easily introduce such inequalities that each corresponds to a clique of the graph and each joined pair of variables, not included in an equation, has a common inequality. It can be done, for example, by the set of inequalities $x_j + x_k \leq 1$, where x_j and x_k are joined in the graph but do not have a common equation. Another way is to find some clique cover of the graph and to represent each clique of it as an inequality.

We say that a pair of variables is *contradictory a priori* iff it is joined in the graph of contradictions. We say that a pair of variables is *contradictory* iff there is no solution of the problem where these two variables are true simultaneously. All contradictory but not a priori pairs we name *implicitly contradictory*.

2 SAT01 Propagation

Apart from the usual unit propagation we have one particular reduction rule for SAT01. If there is an equation E_i and a variable x_j, which contradicts a priori to each variable of E_i, then $x_j = 0$. We name this *the main reduction rule*.

When we are able to prove somehow that some two variables not contradictory a priori cannot be true simultaneously we may add a new edge between these variables to the graph of contradictions. In that way we obtain a new SAT01 instance, which has the same set of solutions but a new pair contradictory a priori. This may give us a new opportunity to use the main reduction rule. The basic method to recognize an implicitly contradictory pair is to find an equation, whose each variable contradicts a priori to at least one variable of the pair.

3 Reduction of SAT to SAT01

Consider a clause of SAT and try to make a SAT01 equation from it. In order to do this we must successively separate simple cases when the clause is true and the current case has contradictions with all previous ones. This can be easily done by the following separation: the first case is when the first literal is true, the second case is when the first literal is false but the second is true, the third case is when the first and the second literals are false but the third is true, and so forth. So, clause

$$\ell_1 \vee \ell_2 \vee \ldots \vee \ell_k$$

should be converted to

$$\ell_1 + \overline{\ell_1}\&\ell_2 + \ldots + \overline{\ell_1}\&\overline{\ell_2}\& \ldots \&\ell_k = 1$$

So, we introduce all conjunctions of literals appearing in the obtained equations as SAT01 variables. To determine a priori contradictions among them we look for pairs containing a common variable of the original SAT problem. If the variable is negated in one conjunction of the pair but not negated in the other, then the pair is contradictory a priori.

References

1. Balas, E., Padberg, W. M.: Set Partitioning: a survey. In: SIAM Review, Vol. 18 (1976) 810–861

An Interval Constraint Approach to Handle Parametric Ordinary Differential Equations for Decision Support

Jorge Cruz and Pedro Barahona
{jc,pb}@di.fct.unl.pt
Dep. de Informática, Universidade Nova de Lisboa, 2825-114 Caparica, Portugal

Model-based decision support systems rely on an explicit representation of some system whose dynamics is often qualitatively described by specifying the rates at which the system variables change. Such models are naturally represented as a set of ordinary differential equations (ODEs) which are parametric (they include parameters whose value is not known exactly). If safe decisions are to be made based on the values of these parameters, it is important to know them with sufficient precision.

An example is the well-known model proposed by Ackerman and al [1] for the blood glucose regulatory system (g and h are deviations of the glucose and insulin blood concentrations from their fasting levels; p_1, p_2, p_3, p_4 are positive parameters):

$$\frac{dg}{dt} = -p_1g - p_2h \qquad\qquad \frac{dh}{dt} = -p_3h + p_4g \qquad\qquad (1)$$

After the ingestion of a large dose of glucose, the glucose and insulin levels oscillate (eventually converging to their fasting level concentrations), with period T:

$$T = \frac{2\pi}{\sqrt{p_1p_2 + p_3p_4}} \qquad\qquad (2)$$

This is commonly used for the diagnosis of diabetes mellitus ($T>240$ min for diabetic patients). In practice, for a particular patient, several trajectory points are observed (through blood tests over time) to narrow the range of possible values of the parameters p_i and reach a safe diagnosis (whether $T>240$ min). Table I shows an example for two patients whose parameters are assumed to range between +/- 50% of the typical normal values ($p_1=0.0044, p_2=0.04, p_3=0.0044, p_4=0.03$).

Table 1. Glucose and insulin blood concentration measurements in two patients.

	Initial	1 hour later	2 hours later	3 hours later
Patient 1	$g=80; h=0$	$g=-29.7; h=46.4$	$g=-24.8; h=-34.5$	$g=35.8; h=-1.5$
Patient 2	$g=80; h=0$	$g=18.1; h=41.4$	$g=-38.8; h=18.6$	$g=-28.0; h=-15.9$

In principle, this is an adequate field to model parameters with interval domains and use constraint propagation to obtain safe bounds for them. Despite its complexity, handling ODEs with interval constraints is receiving increasing interest [2], and was proposed for the representation of deep models of biomedical systems [3].

The main difficulty with parametric ODEs is the parameter uncertainty that can be quickly propagated and increased along the whole trajectory. This is a fundamental property of parametric ODEs, not due to any trajectory approximation technique. Moreover, the usual consistency maintenance techniques for interval domains (local hull-consistency and box-consistency [4]) are often unable to narrow the parameter ranges (in the example above the initial parameter domains would remain the same) so that a decision can be safely made. The worsening of the locality problem due to constraint decomposition and the magnification effect on the uncertainty of the parameters are the main reasons for the failure of these approaches.

To achieve a good narrowing of the domains of ODE parameters we propose global hull-consistency (which guarantees hull-consistency on the parametric ODE regarded as a single global constraint) and developed an algorithm to enforce it.

This algorithm searches the left- and rightmost values of each parameter domain that belong to some solution. To do so, it firstly finds an initial solution; secondly it recursively searches the sub-domain to the left (right) of the already found solutions; finally, it stops when the left (right) sub-domain is proved to be inconsistent. To find a particular solution the search space is recursively investigated by splitting the largest variable domain and considering each resulting box, till either the midpoint of the box is a solution or the box is proved to be inconsistent.

The above algorithm requires, in general, a very large number of consistency checks. This is a problem with current constraint approaches for ODEs, which are mainly focussed on the precision of the trajectories, and would spend useless effort in finding trajectories with more precision than necessary to detect inconsistency.

Hence, we developed an alternative approach where the interval approximation of the whole trajectory is done incrementally. Firstly the initial point of the trajectory is linked with the final point to obtain a first, and perhaps very imprecise, interval approximation of the true trajectory. If such approximation is not precise enough to check consistency, new intermediate points are considered. This will eventually narrow, through propagation, the bounds of the trajectory allowing the algorithm to stop whenever a consistency check is either solved or there is a reason to believe that it can never be solved due to the uncertainty of the parameters.

We believe that our stronger consistency criterion is required to handle parametric ODEs in the context of decision support. In particular, it resulted in sufficient pruning of the parameter domains to allow a correct diagnosis of our example (see Table 2).

Table 2. A safe decision can be made after considering the first two observed trajectory values.

	Initial	1 hour later	2 hours later
Patient 1	T=[131..295]→ ?	T=[138..233]→ Normal ?	T=[152..217]→ Normal !
Patient 2	T=[131..295]→ ?	T=[240..330]→ Diabetic ?	T=[256..308]→Diabetic !

References

1. Ackerman, E., Gatewood, L., Rosevar, J., and Molnar, G.: Blood Glucose Regulation and Diabetes. In: Concepts and Models of Biomathematics, Chapter 4, F. Heinmets, ed., Marcel Dekker, (1969) 131-156.
2. Deville, Y., Janssen, M. and Van Hentenryck, P.: Consistency Techniques in Ordinary Differential Equations. In: Procs. of CP'98, LNCS, vol. 1520, Springer (1998) 162-176.
3. Cruz, J., Barahona, P. and Benhamou, F.: Integrating Deep Biomedical Models into Medical Decision Support Systems: An Interval Constraints Approach. In: Procs. of AIMDM'99, LNAI, vol. 1620, Springer, (1999) 185-194.
4. Benhamou, F., McAllester, D. and Van Hentenryck, P.: CLP(intervals) revisited. In: Proceedings of the International Logic Programming Symposium. MIT Press, (1994).

CSPLIB:
A Benchmark Library for Constraints *

Ian P. Gent and Toby Walsh

Department of Computer Science, University of Strathclyde, Glasgow, United
Kingdom. Email ipg@dcs.st-and.ac.uk, tw@cs.strath.ac.uk

Constraint satisfaction algorithms are often benchmarked on hard, random problems. There are, however, many reasons for wanting a larger class of problems in our benchmark suites. For example, we may wish to benchmark algorithms on more realistic problems, to run competitions, or to study the impact on modelling and problem reformulation. Whilst there are many other constructive benefits of a benchmark library, there are also several potential pitfalls. For example, if the library is small, we run the risk of over-fitting our algorithms. Even if the library is large, certain problem features may be rare or absent. A model benchmark library should be easy to find and easy to use. It should contain as diverse and large a set of problems as possible. It should be easy to extend, and as comprehensive and up to date as possible. It should also be independent of any particular constraint solver, and contain neither just hard (nor just easy) problems.

There is one major and very significant problem in construction a benchmark library for constraint. Our ability to solve a constraint satisfaction problem often hinges upon exactly how we decide to represent it. A benchmark library for constraints cannot therefore be prescriptive about the representation of the problems in it. At the 1998 DIMACS Workshop on Constraint Programming and Large Scale Discrete Optimization, we discussed this problem and suggested that problems should be presented in natural language[2]. Any other representation may make assumptions about representation that are unwanted.

To be successful, the research community must become active users of the library and contributors to it. This is in fact the most important desideratum of all: if CSPLIB is not used and contributed to, the time spent in setting it up will have been wasted. However it is one aspect of the library beyond the control of the maintainers. We hope that researchers in constraints will come to view CSPLIB as a one stop shop for finding constraints benchmarks, and disseminating new benchmarks. Our experience is that writing an entry takes less than an hour, and the service to the community is invaluable.

---

* Supported by EPSRC award GR/K/65706. The authors are members of the the APES research group, http://apes.cs.strath.ac.uk/, and thank the other members at Leeds and Strathclyde. We wish to thank the many colleagues we have discussed CSPLib with, and especially those who have already helped in its construction. An extended version of this paper is available from http://apes.cs.strath.ac.uk/apesreports.html as report APES-09-1999.

[2] We first suggested English, but the non-native speakers of English quickly and correctly pointed out the bias in such a choice.

We intend to be liberal in the variety of problems in CSPLIB. There is no requirement that you present a solution to a benchmark problem. Test instances you have *failed* to solve will be just as valuable as those that you can. There is also no requirement that constraint programming is currently the best technique for solving the benchmark. We encourage such problems because they may suggest new techniques in constraint solving, or simply aid our understanding of its limits. There is no requirement that an encoding be given for a particular constraint solver. Beyond this, there is not even a requirement that an encoding be given for *any* constraint solver. The only requirement is a natural language specification. There is no requirement that specific test instances be given. Where possible, we hope that contributors will submit benchmark instances, but there will sometimes be good grounds for not doing so. For example, where random benchmark instances are used, a generating program may be more useful to the community than particular instances. In other cases detailed data may be confidential, but the community would still benefit from a description of the problem.

To help users submit benchmark problems to CSPLIB, we have prepared some simple guidelines. We repeat these in full:

> "We welcome submission of all your constraint problems. We hope that the library will thereby grow to become a valued resource within the constraints community.
>
> A key factor in solving many constraints problems is the modelling of the constraints. We therefore specify all problems in CSPLIB using natural language. We also provide hints about modelling these problems.
>
> As we want to help people benchmark their algorithms on problems in CSPLIB with minimum effort, we encourage users of the library to send us any tools that might be useful to others (e.g. C parsers for data files, AMPL specification of problems, ILOG Solver code, ...). All such code is placed in the library through the generosity of the authors, and comes with all the usual disclaimers.
>
> To make comparison with previous work easier, we provide links to papers that use these benchmarks. If you use a problem in CSPLIB, please send us the URL to your paper so we can add it to the references section.
>
> Finally, to make it easy to compare your results with others, we will provide a record of results. Please help us keep these records up-to-date by sending in your results promptly."

CSPLIB was first released on March 4th, 1999. The release version contained fourteen problems, divided into five, overlapping subject areas: scheduling and related problems, bin packing and related problems, frequency assignment and related problems, combinatorial mathematics, and games and puzzles. The total size of the library is just over 1 MByte. In its first month of operation, the library has received more than 100 visitors each week. A low-volume mailing list is maintained to make announcements about significant changes to the library. In addition, users can email csplib@cs.strath.ac.uk to propose new entries, or to extend or correct existing ones. The site is located at http://csplib.cs.strath.ac.uk and is mirrored at http://www.cs.cornell.edu/home/selman/csplib.

Validated Constraint Compilation

Timothy J. Hickey and David K. Wittenberg

Computer Science Department, Brandeis University
{tim|dkw}@cs.brandeis.edu

Inaccurate scientific computation is useless at best and dangerous at worst. We address several major sources of inaccuracy. Roundoff error is well known and there is a great deal of work on minimizing it [Act96,Tay97]. By using interval constraints, we don't eliminate roundoff error, but we make it explicit, so each answer comes with a clear indication of its accuracy. Another source of error arises from misapplying an algorithm (e.g. starting the Newton method with a poor initial choice, or using a method in a case where it does not perform well). We propose a method for reducing the chance of numerical errors in scientific programming by casting the problem as the design of an appropriate constraint solving algorithm and then separating the algorithm design process into two steps.

- First, the automatic construction of a set of validated constraint contractors which can be applied to the initial intervals in any order without affecting the correctness of the algorithm, and
- Second, the specification of the algorithm which determines which contractors are applied in which order. The specification of which operators are applied in what order determines the speed of convergence of the algorithm, but has no effect on correctness, which depends only on the correctness of the constraint contractors.

The chief advantage of our method is that it results in a procedure which returns an interval which is guaranteed[1] to contain the correct solution. We provide a comparison of the classical method with our proposed method for creating a procedure to invert $f(x) = x \sin(x)$ on a subset of its domain.

Standard Methods: We consider the following simple numerical problem ([Act96], pp. 77-80, pp. 223-224): Solve the validated constraint contraction problem for the following constraint:

$$h = x \sin(x), \ \ 0 \le x \le a_1,$$

where h is the input variable and x is the output variable. The method of first choice in numerical analysis is the Newton method, which works will except near the endpoints of the interval. Acton suggests two different approaches near these dangerous points. Near zero, he uses what he calls the pseudoconstant gambit, which converges rapidly for h near zero, but is slow for other h. Near the right endpoint $b_1 \approx 1.8197$, he uses what he calls the Quadratic method, which converges rapidly only near b_1. The end result of this standard numerical approach is

---

[1] Throughout this paper, we assume that hardware and compilers correctly meet their specifications.

to write a procedure which uses some number of iterations of the pseudoconstant gambit for h near zero, some number of iterations of the quadratic method for h near the upper bound b_1, and some number of iterations of the Newton method for the remaining cases. This method of constructing and analyzing numerical routines is highly heuristic and does not provide any guarantee that the stated precision bounds will be achieved. Either an interval arithmetic approach or a detailed line-by-line numerical analysis will be required if one wants a provably correct estimate of the error.

The key idea behind interval arithmetic constraints [BO97] is to view numeric computing problems as constraint systems that relate a set of real (or complex) variables or functions. The variables whose values are to be computed are initially unbounded in this model (i.e., they have the value $[-\infty, \infty]$). The goal of the computation is to shrink the intervals of the variables in such a way that no solution to the original system is removed. The shrinking is done by iteratively applying various contraction operators which are automatically generated from the constraint set.

In the full version of this paper [HW99] we present the **The Constraint Contractor Method**. The basic idea is to define a general family of validated contractors, based on arithmetic constraints[BO97] and to experiment with various combinations of these contractors. When a reasonably good sequence of contractions is found, one can then generate a procedure to implement these contractors and to signal an exception if the width of the computed intervals exceeds the required error bounds. This approach has three key benefits:

- First, the contractors can be generated automatically from the constraints using various parameters specified by the user (thereby eliminating a potential source of programming errors).
- Second, if the particular sequence of contractors does not sufficiently narrow the result intervals, then this can be detected at runtime and an exception can be thrown.
- Third, the contractors can be applied in any order without affecting the correctness of the algorithm. The only possible danger is that for some inputs, the particular sequence of contractors does not narrow the result interval sufficiently, which as noted above can be detected and handled at runtime.

References

[Act96] Forman S. Acton. *Real computing made real: Preventing Errors in Scientific and Engineering calculations.* Princeton University Press, Princeton, New Jersey, 1996.

[BO97] Frédéric Benhamou and William J. Older. Applying interval arithmetic to real, integer, and Boolean constraints. *Journal of Logic Programming*, 32, 1997.

[HW99] Timothy J. Hickey and David K. Wittenberg. Validated constraint compilation. Technical Report CS-99-201, Computer Science Department, Brandeis University, April 1999. URL: www.cs.brandeis.edu/~tim/Papers/cs99201.ps.gz.

[Tay97] John R. Taylor. *An introduction to Error Analysis: The Study of Uncertainties in Physical Measurements.* University Science Books, second edition, 1997.

Automated Theorem Proving with Disjunctive Constraints

Ortrun Ibens

Institut für Informatik, TU München, Germany
ibens@informatik.tu-muenchen.de

1 Introduction

Automated theorem proving (ATP) is an important research area in artificial intelligence. The objective of an ATP system is to find out whether or not a *query* (or *goal*) is a logical consequence of a set of *axioms* (the query and the axioms have to be formally specified, for example in first-order clause logic). For this purpose, system-specific *inference rules* are applied systematically. A sequence of inference rule applications which shows that a given query is a logical consequence of a given set of axioms is called a *proof*.

The main strength of ATP systems is that they allow a purely *declarative* description of knowledge. However, the ability to handle declarative specifications introduces the aspect of *search* into the deduction process. The set of all objects which can be derived from an input problem by means of the inference rules forms the *search space*. In general, a tremendous search space has to be explored during the search for a proof. A large amount of the research performed in the field of ATP, therefore, focuses on search space reduction. In the following text we are going to introduce a constraint approach to search space reduction in first-order ATP.

2 Connection Tableau Calculi with Constraints

In this paper we focus on the *connection tableau calculi* [2] which are successfully employed in ATP. The input problem has to be expressed by a set of first-order clauses. During the search for a proof so-called *connection tableaux* are generated from the input clauses. If all input clauses are Horn clauses, the search for a proof is similar to the interpretation of a PROLOG program, and the generated connection tableaux equal PROLOG computation trees (see Figure 1).

Structurally similar input clauses in general lead to structurally similar connection tableaux. For example, in the clause set S from Figure 1 the clauses in the sub-set $\{p(f(a_1)), \ldots, p(f(a_n))\}$ only differ from each other in certain sub-terms. Given the connection tableau T for S (see Figure 1), the possible inference rule applications to $\neg p(X)$ result in the connection tableaux $T_1, \ldots, T_n$ given in Figure 1. $T_1, \ldots, T_n$ only differ from each other in certain sub-terms occurring in the literals.

We can compress the structurally similar clauses $p(f(a_1)), \ldots, p(f(a_n))$ in S if we replace them by the new clause $p(f(X))$ with the constraint $X = a_1 \vee \cdots \vee X =$

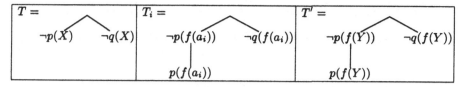

Fig. 1. T and T_i $(1 \leq i \leq n)$ are connection tableaux for the set $S = \{\neg p(X) \vee \neg q(X),$ $p(f(a_1)), \ldots, p(f(a_n)), q(g(b_1)), \ldots, q(g(b_m))\}$, $n \geq 1$, $m \geq 1$. T' and the constraint $Y = a_1 \vee \cdots \vee Y = a_n$ encode $T_1, \ldots, T_n$.

a_n. The new clause expresses the common information of the structurally similar clauses, and the constraint encodes their differences. The constraint defines the allowed instances of the clause $p(f(X))$. When given the connection tableau T and the changed input set, only one inference rule application is possible to $\neg p(X)$; it results in the connection tableau T' (see Figure 1) with the constraint $Y = a_1 \vee \cdots \vee Y = a_n$. The connection tableau T' has inherited the constraint from the attached clause. The constraint represents the allowed assignments to the variables occurring in the literals of T'. T' together with its constraint can therefore be viewed as encoding the ordinary connection tableaux $T_1, \ldots, T_n$.

Recapitulating, we have compressed the above connection tableaux $T_1, \ldots, T_n$ into a single connection tableau T' with an additional constraint. Since inference rule applications are neither possible to the tableaux $T_1, \ldots, T_n$ nor to the tableau T', we have achieved a reduction of the search space. The number of inference rule applications which may be tried can be reduced furthermore if also the structurally similar input clauses $q(g(b_1)), \ldots, q(g(b_m))$ are compressed into a single clause $q(g(X))$ with the constraint $X = b_1 \vee \cdots \vee X = b_m$.

Our approach (for details see [1]) can be outlined as follows. Each set S of structurally similar clauses is compressed by obtaining a *most specific generalization* G of it. For each clause C in S, a substitution σ_C is obtained such that $\sigma_C(G)$ equals C. Then, a constraint which expresses all the substitutions σ_C (for each $C \in S$) is associated with G. We use constraints with the following syntax. Firstly, if t and t' are terms, then $t = t'$ is a constraint. Secondly, if $c_1, \ldots, c_k$, $k \geq 0$, are constraints, then $c_1 \wedge \cdots \wedge c_k$ and $c_1 \vee \cdots \vee c_k$ are constraints. We have extended the connection tableau inference rules in order to allow the handling of constraints. Furthermore, we have developed efficient algorithms for the generation, simplification, and satisfiability testing of constraints and for the use of these algorithms during the proof search (see [1]). Our approach has been integrated into the connection tableau prover SETHEO [2]. Experiments which have been performed using problems from the benchmark library TPTP [3] show the performance increase achieved by our approach.

References

1. O. Ibens. Automated theorem proving with disjunctive constraints. Technical report AR-99-03, Institut für Informatik, TU München, 1999.
2. R. Letz, K. Mayr, and C. Goller. Controlled Integration of the Cut Rule into Connection Tableau Calculi. *Journal of Automated Reasoning*, 13:297–337, 1994.
3. G. Sutcliffe, C. B. Suttner, and T. Yemenis. The TPTP problem library. In Alan Bundy, editor, *Automated Deduction — CADE-12*, volume 814 of *LNAI*, pages 778–782. Springer, 1994.

Rewriting Numeric Constraint Satisfaction Problems for Consistency Algorithms

Claudio Lottaz

AI-Laboratory, Computer-Science Department,
Swiss Federal Institute of Technology, CH-1015 Lausanne (Switzerland)
Claudio.Lottaz@epfl.ch

Several constraint satisfaction algorithms focus on numeric constraint satisfaction problems (CSPs). A numeric CSP is defined by a set of variables, their domains, intervals in $\Re$, and the set of constraints, expressed as mathematical relations, which must be satisfied for any solution. Such CSPs can model many engineering and design problems from domains such as mechanical, electrical and civil engineering.

One major concept in constraint satisfaction is consistency. Consistency algorithms eliminate parts from the search space where no solution can be expected due to local inconsistencies. Thus they approximate the solution space of a CSP and improve efficiency of search for single solutions. In certain cases, consistency algorithms can achieve global consistency, i.e. compute the solution space of a numeric CSP exactly.

The arity of a constraint is the number of variables it involves. The arity of a CSP is equal to the arity of the highest-arity constraint. Reformulation of numeric CSPs in lower arity before computing consistency is a common procedure because CSPs of lower arity are considerably simpler to treat. Therefore, certain consistency algorithms such as 2-consistency as described in [1] or 2B- and 3B-consistency [2] only accept ternary constraints. The complexity of other consistency algorithms such as $(r, r-1)$-relational consistency [3] is exponential in the arity of the given CSP and therefore low-arity CSPs are treated much more efficiently.

Theoretical considerations about complexity of reaching global consistency through $(r, r-1)$-relational consistency algorithms for r-ary numeric CSPs show that reformulation of such CSPs in terms of ternary constraints is very promising. In fact, the complexity $O(n^{2r-1})$ for the computation on the original CSP compares to $O((n+m)^5)$ for the computation on the ternary CSP, where n is the number of variables and m is the number of binary operators in the CSP. It can be expected that in practical problems m is substantially less than would be needed to reverse the gain in complexity. Nevertheless, very few algorithms to perform the task of reformulating numeric CSPs in ternary form automatically have been suggested so far, in fact the rewriting is often done by hand.

It has been shown that rewriting numeric CSPs in terms of ternary constraints is possible as long as only unary and binary operators occur in the constraints. It is intuitively clear that any mathematical expression built using unary and binary operators can be rewritten in ternary form by introducing an auxiliary variable for each intermediary result generated by a binary operator. This method, however, on many examples generates far too many auxiliary variables. Since the performance of all above mentioned consistency algorithms also strongly depends on the number of variables involved in the given CSP, reformulation algorithms which introduce few auxiliary variables are needed.

Our algorithm improves existing suggestions by allowing complex definitions of auxiliary variables and by provoking the reuse of these auxiliaries, i.e., by choosing expressions, which reoccur in the CSP, to define auxiliary variables. Our tests show that the automatic rewriting introduces up to 40% fewer auxiliary variables than the straight forward manner in running times of few minutes for CSPs involving up to 100 variables.

Given the need of reformulation using few variables, opportunities to eliminate unnecessary variables from the original CSP are also of interest. When formalizing problems, engineers and designers often use intermediary variables and constants, which make the CSP more readable and reusable. However, in the context of computing consistency the elimination of such variables may be beneficial.

The method we suggest to eliminate constants and unnecessary intermediary variables automatically accelerates subsequent computing of consistency. Our method is adapted to the context of subsequent ternarization and does not remove intermediary variables which contribute to lower the arity of the CSP. It has been observed that in practical examples unnecessary variables are frequent and their elimination often renders large problems tractable.

Certain aspects of the reformulation still need further investigation, namely the interference between the reformulation and the convexity properties needed for global consistency, as well as the impact of reformulation on refinement when global consistency cannot be reached.

Acknowledgments

This work was performed within a project funded by the Swiss Priority Programme in Computer Science (SPP-IF). The author would also like to thank Djamila Sam-Haroud, Steven Willmott, Boi Faltings, Christian Bliek and Marc Torrens for encouragement and helpful discussions.

References

1. B. V. Faltings and E. M. Gelle. Local consistency for ternary numeric constraints. In *Internation Joint Conference on Artificial Intelligence (IJCAI)*, volume 1, pages 392–397, 1997.
2. O. Lhomme. Consistency techniques for numerical CSPs. In *Internation Joint Conference on Artificial Intelligence (IJCAI)*, volume 1, pages 232–238, 1993.
3. D. Sam-Haroud. *Constraint Consistency Techniques for Continuous Domains*. Phd-thesis no. 1826, Swiss Federal Institute of Technology in Lausanne, Switzerland, 1995.

Intelligent Domain Splitting for CSPs with Ordered Domains

Marius-Călin Silaghi, Djamila Sam-Haroud, and Boi Faltings

Swiss Federal Institute of Technology, Artificial Intelligence Lab, DI-LIA,
CH-1015 Lausanne, Switzerland
{silaghi, haroud, faltings}@lia.di.epfl.ch

This paper presents intelligent domain splitting, an approach for searching in CSPs with ordered domains. The technique has a particular strength for finding all solutions. It represents the search space by aggregations obtained through the cooperation of two known clustering concepts, namely intervals and cross-products. Intelligent domain splitting searches for solutions by iteratively breaking up the space into smaller subspaces in a meaningful way. The proposed backtracking technique benefits from the strengths of Hull-consistency (i.e. 2B-consistency [4]) and of the Cartesian product representation [2]. The algorithm can be applied to general systems of constraints with explicit representations. Even though designed for generating all solutions, it also proves useful for finding the first solution of hard problems, as shown by preliminary experiments.

Albeit the technique we present is general, we mainly focus on the applications where the order of the domains is given and induces a natural grouping of the feasible tuples within the explicit constraint representations (the legal entries tend to be consecutive in the matrix representation of the constraints). This is typical in integer programming and discrete numerical applications.

Informally, the idea is then to cover each constraint by entirely feasible boxes, this means that each box contains only legal tuples. The boxes are represented concisely as sets of intervals and are used as meta-values during search. In ordered domains, the simplest way to construct the covering is by hierarchical binary splitting, as usually done for numerical continuous applications. The domains are recursively cut in the middle until completely feasible/infeasible boxes (sub-matrices) are found. Figure 1 illustrates the aforementioned notions: a) an integer numerical CSP with two linear constraint (dashed lines), the shadowed regions represent legal entries, b) the box covering obtained by binary split.

Although this procedure constructs entirely feasible boxes, the aggregation mechanism provided remains uninformed since it does not take into account the characteristics of the constraints. This mechanism has therefore great chance to split just in the middle of contiguous feasible regions, requiring further additional splits to take place. In this work, we propose an intelligent splitting mechanism that tries to reduce the search space by choosing more appropriate splitting points (discontinuities/limits of the constraint space), see Figure 1.c).

The search space is generated as Cartesian products of intervals. From this hybrid continuous/discrete representation stems the idea of interleaving search with Hull-consistency(HC), a powerful local consistency technique commonly used for numerical constraints. Although weaker than AC in general, HC brings

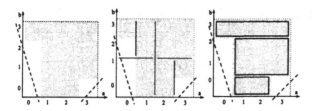

Fig. 1. *a) the constraints between a and b are $b \geq 3 - 3a \wedge b > a - 3$; b) binary split;
c) intelligent split*

similar pruning when the feasible entries tend to be consecutive. The space
needed reduces however from $O(nd^2)$ for AC to $O(n)$ for HC, where n is the
number of variables and d the size of domains.

A central difference with the previous works on Cartesian products representations is that we decide the dynamical aggregation and domain splitting
after each future variable is pruned. At each step, we apply incremental MHC
(Maintaining HC). This technique leads to earlier detection of domain wipe-out.

The backtracking algorithm implementing intelligent splitting is called DCPR
and its enhancement with hull-consistency, MHC-DCPR. Preliminary experiments were run to compare MHC-DCPR and DCPR against MHC and conventional backtracking on 400'000 instances of hard 3- and 4-coloring problems. Exponential improvements of the speed, as function of the number of variables, was
noticed for both obtaining the first solution and all solutions with MHC-DCPR.
Similar results were obtained for the compression of the spatial representation
when all the solutions were generated.

As to related work, an idea similar to our box-covering was presented in [1]
for the general case. However, the decomposition proposed was static, being done
as a preprocessing. Our algorithm performs dynamic covering, similarly to what
is done in [2] with a worst case complexity of $O(ad^a)$, where a is the maximal
arity (vs. $O(d^a)$ for [1]). It is however completely depth first with less structure
management, promising better average costs for ordered domains. An idea close
to our intelligent splitting was introduced in [3]. In that work, partitioning involves only future variables and instantiation is performed value by value during
search.

References

1. A. Haselböck. Exploiting interchangeabilities in constraint satisfaction problems.
   In *Proceedings of IJCAI'93*, pages 282–287, 93.
2. P. D. Hubbe and E. C. Freuder. An efficient cross product representation of the
   constraint satisfaction problem search space. In *AAAI-92, Proceedings*, pages 421–
   427. AAAI, July 92.
3. J. Larrosa. Merging constraint satisfaction subproblems to avoid redundant search.
   In *Proceedings of IJCAI'97*, pages 424–429, 97.
4. O. Lhomme. Consistency techniques for numeric CSPs. In *Proceedings of IJCAI'93*,
   pages 232–238, 93.

Frequency Assignment for Cellular Mobile Systems Using Constraint Satisfaction Techniques

Makoto Yokoo[1] and Katsutoshi Hirayama[2]

[1] NTT Communication Science Laboratories
2-4 Hikaridai, Seika-cho
Soraku-gun, Kyoto 619-0237 Japan
e-mail: yokoo@cslab.kecl.ntt.co.jp
[2] Kobe University of Mercantile Marine
5-1-1 Fukae-minami-machi,
Higashinada-ku, Kobe 658-0022, Japan
e-mail: hirayama@ti.kshosen.ac.jp

1 Introduction

The studies of a frequency assignment problem (also called a channel assignment problem) in cellular mobile systems have a long history [4], and various AI techniques have been applied to this problem [1, 3]. A frequency assignment problem is formalized as follows[1]. Frequencies are represented by positive integers $1, 2, 3, \ldots$.

Given: N: the number of cells
d_i, $1 \leq i \leq N$: the number of requested calls (demands) in cell i
c_{ij}, $1 \leq i, j \leq N$: the frequency separation required between a call in cell i
and a call in cell j
Find: f_{ik}, $1 \leq i \leq N$, $1 \leq k \leq d_i$: the frequency assigned to the kth call in
cell i.
such that,
subject to the separation constraints,
$| f_{ik} - f_{jl} | \geq c_{ij}$, for all i, j, k, l except for $i = j$ and $k = l$,
minimize
$max f_{ik}$ for all i, k.

2 Algorithm

The most straightforward way for solving such problems using constraint satisfaction techniques would be to represent each call as a variable (whose domain is available frequencies), then to solve the problem as a generalized graph-coloring problem. However, solving real-life, large-scale problems using this simple formulation seems rather difficult without avoiding the symmetries between calls

---

[1] We follow the formalization used in [4].

within one cell. The characteristics of the algorithm developed in this paper are as follows:

- instead of representing each call in a cell as a variable, we represent a cell (which has multiple calls) as a variable that has a very large domain, and determine a variable value step by step,
- a powerful cell-ordering heuristic is introduced,
- a branch-and-bound search that incorporates forward-checking is performed,
- the limited discrepancy search [2] is introduced to improve the chance of finding a solution in a limited amount of search.

3 Evaluations

We show the evaluation results for the benchmark problems presented in [1, 3]. There are 7×7 symmetrically placed cells (49 cells in all) in these problems. Table 1 shows the results obtained with our constraint satisfaction method (CS) for three instances (K1, K2, and K3). Furthermore, we show the best results obtained with a set of heuristic sequential methods (SE) reported in [4], and the results obtained with neural networks (NN) reported in [1]. Our method obtains much better solutions than those of NN for K2 and K3. These results show that state-of-the-art constraint satisfaction/optimization techniques are capable of solving realistic application problems when equipped with an appropriate problem representation and heuristics.

Table 1. Comparison of Solution Quality (Kim's Benchmark Problems)

Instance	CS	NN	SE
K1	168	168	178
K2	422	435	473
K3	619	630	673

References

[1] Funabiki, N., Okutani, N., and Nishikawa, S.: A Three-stage Heuristic Combined Neural Network Algorithm for Channel Assignment in Cellular Mobile Systems, *IEEE Transactions on Vehicular Technology* (1999): (to appear)

[2] Harvey, W. D. and Ginsberg, M. L.: Limited discrepancy search, *Proceedings of the Fourteenth International Joint Conference on Artificial Intelligence* (1995) 607–613

[3] Kim, S. and Kim, S. L.: A Two-Phase Algorithm for Frequency Assignment in Cellular Mobile Systems, *IEEE Transactions on Vehicular Technology*, Vol. 43, No. 3, (1994) 542–548

[4] Sivarajan, K. N., McEliece, R. J., and Ketchum, J. W.: Channel Assignment in Cellular Radio, *Proceedings of 39th IEEE Vehicular Technology Society Conference* (1989) 846–850

Author Index

Lecture Notes in Computer Science

For information about Vols. 1–1632
please contact your bookseller or Springer-Verlag